H.D.

The Life and Work
of an American Poet

Janice S. Robinson

Houghton Mifflin Company
Boston   1982

Library of Congress Cataloging in Publication Data

Robinson, Janice S. (Janice Stevenson)
    H.D., the life and work of an American poet.

    Bibliography: p.
    Includes index.
    1. H.D. (Hilda Doolittle), 1886–1961. 2. Poets,
American—20th century—Biography. I. Title. II. Title:
HD, the life and work of an American poet.
PS 3507.076Z85   811'.52 [B]   81-6900
ISBN 0-395-31855-6   AACR2

Printed in the United States of America

V 10 9 8 7 6 5 4 3 2 1

The Collection of American Literature, The Beinecke Rare Book and Manuscript Library, Yale University for permission to quote from unpublished letters and manuscripts of Richard Aldington, Hilda Doolittle, Sigmund Freud, Norman Holmes Pearson, and Ezra Pound.

The Morris Library, Southern Illinois University, Carbondale for permission to quote from H.D.'s letters to Richard Aldington from the Richard Aldington Papers, Special Collections, Morris Library.

The Houghton Library of Harvard University for permission to quote from H.D.'s letters to Amy Lowell.

Viking Penguin Inc. for permission to reprint selections from: *The Complete Poems of D. H. Lawrence* — Copyright © 1964 by Angelo Ravagli and C. M. Weekley, Executors of the Estate of Frieda Lawrence Ravagli; reprinted by permission of Viking Penguin Inc. Excerpts from *John Thomas and Lady Jane* by D. H. Lawrence — Copyright © 1972 by Angelo Ravagli and C. M. Weekley, Executors of the Estate of Frieda Lawrence Ravagli. Excerpts from *The Collected Letters of D. H. Lawrence,* edited by Harry T. Moore — Copyright © 1962 by Angelo Ravagli and C. M. Weekley, Executors of the Estate of the late Mrs. Frieda Lawrence Ravagli; reprinted by permission of Viking Penguin Inc.

Alfred A. Knopf, Inc. for permission to reprint excerpts from *St. Mawr* and *The Man Who Died,* by D. H. Lawrence. Copyright 1928 by Alfred A. Knopf, Inc.

Laurence Pollinger Ltd. and the Estate of the late Mrs. Frieda Lawrence Ravagli for permission to reprint excerpts from *The First Lady Chatterley,* by D. H. Lawrence, first published in the U.S.A. 1944, and first published in Great Britain 1972.

The Black Sparrow Press for permission to reprint excerpts from *The Escaped Cock* by D. H. Lawrence — Copyright © 1973 by the Estate of D. H. Lawrence and published by Black Sparrow Press.

David R. Godine, Publisher, Inc. for permission to reprint excerpts from *Tribute to Freud* by H.D. Copyright © 1974 by Norman Holmes Pearson.

Houghton Mifflin Company for permission to reprint excerpts from *Amy Lowell: A Chronicle* by S. Foster Damon. Copyright © renewed 1963 by S. Foster Damon.

Sigmund Freud Copyrights Ltd. for permission to quote from previously unpublished letters from Sigmund Freud to H.D.

Catherine Guillaume-Aldington and Alister Kershaw, Executor for the Literary Estate of Richard Aldington, for permission to quote from Richard Aldington's unpublished letters to H.D.

Rosica Colin Ltd. and Cassell Ltd. for permission to reprint excerpts from *Life for Life's Sake,* by Richard Aldington. Copyright 1941 by Richard Aldington; copyright © 1968 by Madame Catherine Guillaume.

The D. H. Lawrence Review and James C. Cowan, editor, and Professor Emile Delavenay for permission to reprint excerpts from "Making Another Lawrence: Frieda and the Lawrence Legend." Copyright © 1975 by the *D. H. Lawrence Review*.

Grove Press, Inc., for permission to reprint excerpts from *Lady Chatterley's Lover,* by D. H. Lawrence. Copyright © 1959 by Grove Press, Inc.

 # Acknowledgments

I ACKNOWLEDGE with gratitude the help I have had over the years that I have been engaged with this study. With deep gratitude I thank Perdita Schaffner, H.D.'s daughter, for her patience and candor in answering my questions about H.D. and for granting me access to thousands of previously unexamined letters and the entire collection of H.D.'s unpublished writings. I am much indebted to Donald Gallup and the staff of the Beinecke Rare Book and Manuscript Library of Yale University for useful assistance in my research. I owe special thanks to the staff of the McHenry Library of the University of Santa Cruz. I am also very indebted to Priscilla Shaw, who read and offered comment on two drafts of the manuscript and assisted me with research at the Houghton Library of Harvard University and the Lockwood Memorial Library of the State University of New York at Buffalo. Michael Cowan, Norman O. Brown, Bert Kaplan, Robert Duncan, Jonathan Galassi, John Brockman, John Russell, and the late Norman Holmes Pearson offered helpful advice and criticism as my study developed. Helene Moglen and Alfred Satterthwaite aided me in valuable ways. I shall be forever grateful to Barbara Wright and Ellen Borger for help with the preparation of the text.

Contents

ix

Illustrations

Unless otherwise credited, photographs are from the Collection of American Literature, Beinecke Rare Book and Manuscript Library, Yale University.

Bryher and Perdita, London, 1925
Courtesy of Perdita Schaffner

H.D. and Perdita, Switzerland, 1923
Courtesy of Perdita Schaffner

Great-Aunt Laura and Grandmother Doolittle with Perdita, Switzerland, 1923
Courtesy of Perdita Schaffner

H.D. and Perdita, London, 1925
Courtesy of Perdita Schaffner

D. H. Lawrence, c. 1925
Photograph by Edward Weston © 1981, center for Creative Photography, University of Arizona; used by permission

Painting by D. H. Lawrence for the frontispiece of *The Escaped Cock,* 1929
Reprinted by permission of Laurence Pollinger Ltd. and the Estate of the late Mrs. Frieda Lawrence Ravagli

D. H. Lawrence's painting of Dorothy "Arabella" Yorke

Freud in his study in Vienna

Sir John Ellerman and young Winifred (Bryher) in London
The Beinecke Rare Book and Manuscript Library, Yale University

Bryher in Switzerland, 1954
The Beinecke Rare Book and Manuscript Library, Yale University

Ezra Pound in 1958, on his release from St. Elizabeth's Hospital
Wide World Photos

Letter from H.D. to Pound, dated 4/6/38, with Dryad signature

H.D. in 1956

H.D. bookplate

Preface

H.D. IS WELL KNOWN in literary company as an early Imagist. The Imagist movement is now recognized to be a major turning point in modern poetry, and H.D. was at the center of the Imagist circle as poet and muse. Certainly her emergence as an Imagist brought early attention to her gift as a poet. And like Ezra Pound, with whom she was in touch throughout her life, H.D. went on to write extraordinarily beautiful long poems. She also wrote a good deal of prose, much of it in the precise lyric style of her verse. When "people learn how to read her," Norman Holmes Pearson wrote, H.D. will be "in the very center of the modern poetic movement."[1] She is "of the same order for me as Ezra Pound or William Carlos Williams," wrote Robert Duncan.[2]

In the last few years H.D. has begun to receive the critical attention that one would expect of a poet whose stature is of the level suggested by Pearson and Duncan. The recent publication of her expanded memoir of Freud and of her memoir of Pound gives fascinating glimpses into the life and thought of a complex writer, but the publicly available record of H.D.'s work and life has been incomplete, and her critical reputation has suffered as a result. Many important prose manuscripts are yet to be published. We are only just beginning to know H.D.

This study brings forth for the first time a substantial body of previously unpublished work and presents H.D. in the literary context in which she wrote — hence its emphasis upon the work of Ezra Pound, D. H. Lawrence, and Sigmund Freud as well as Richard Aldington and Bryher (Winifred Ellerman). The perspective of this study is informed by the Freudian orientation that influenced H.D.'s own work after her sessions with Freud. In an attempt to be true to the poet's life and work as she conceived it,

xiii

I have focused upon the works that H.D. proclaimed in her memoirs, notes on her writing, and letters to be most significant to her life as an artist. H.D.'s special use of language, grammar, and punctuation has been allowed to stand so as not to distort her meaning.

Early in her career H.D. learned that her own experience translated into the medium of art by her creative process influenced her fellow writers. As her art developed, the very act of writing became a form of concealed speech. If we have the keys, we can read a poem as a message to a friend as well as an "objective" statement. While H.D. did not begin her career as a writer with this radical perspective on the relation of art to experience, her involvement with Imagism led over the course of her life to a realization that her art was inseparable from her experience. Thus she said of her novel *Bid Me to Live* not "the Julia character is based upon myself" but rather "I am Julia." When asked by Lionel Durand if *Bid Me to Live* was autobiographical, she told him that it was completely so, "word for word."[3] In her memoirs and letters she freely interchanged the names of her friends and associates with the names she gave them in her poetry and prose. Following H.D.'s lead on this matter, I have read her autobiographical novels autobiographically and have attempted as well to illuminate this aspect of her poetry.

Since H.D. wrote novels and poems about many significant periods in her life, we can construct a kind of literary biographical narrative if we read her works in the chronological sequence of the actual historical events they concern. We will thus be looking at H.D.'s work and the work of her associates from her point of view. It should be stated in advance that her perceptions are sometimes at variance with recently established literary and critical canon.

H.D. was not only an extraordinarily autobiographical writer, but an acutely accurate recorder of detail. Since the cast of characters of the Imagist group were such prolific writers, we can learn much about the history of the period if we read their literature in relation to one another; it makes sense to read it this way because it was written this way. Few literary circles have given us such a remarkable amount of biographical detail in their work; few have developed such a complex and intelligent means of communication. If we understand the work of H.D., we understand more about that of Ezra Pound and the late work of D. H. Lawrence.

When we read H.D. and her poetic colleagues within the context in which they wrote, we get a surprisingly new sense of the communicative power of H.D.'s poetry as well as new insight into the meaning of Imagism. It becomes possible to envision a life in poetry, a life in which images become so actual that they create their own reality.

Chronology

1886   Hilda Doolittle is born September 10 in Bethlehem, Pennsylvania, to Helen Eugenia Wolle Doolittle and Professor Charles Leander Doolittle.

1895   Doolittle family moves to Philadelphia; father leaves Lehigh University and joins the faculty of the University of Pennsylvania.

1896   Father is appointed Flower Professor of Astronomy and founding director of the Flower Observatory at the University of Pennsylvania.

1901   Hilda Doolittle meets Ezra Pound at a Halloween party. Pound is a student at the University of Pennsylvania.

1903   Pound attends Hamilton College, Clinton, New York.

1904   Hilda Doolittle enters Bryn Mawr College.

1905   Pound completes undergraduate studies at Hamilton College (Ph.B., 1905) and returns to Philadelphia for graduate studies at the University of Pennsylvania. Hilda Doolittle and Ezra Pound become engaged to be married.

1906   Hilda Doolittle withdraws from Bryn Mawr College because of poor health. She remains at home, studying, until 1910. Pound graduates from the University of Pennsylvania (A.M., 1906).

1907   Pound becomes instructor at Wabash College, Crawfordsville, Indiana; is dismissed after four months following the discovery by college officials of a woman in his rooms. He presents H.D. with *Hilda's Book*.

1908	Pound travels to Venice in February; publishes *A Lume Spento;* moves to London in the autumn.
1909	Pound publishes *Personae;* lectures on Romance literature at the Regents Street Polytechnic and meets Yeats, Ford Madox Hueffner (Ford), T. E. Hulme, F. S. Flint, and other literary figures; meets Olivia and Dorothy Shakespear.
1910	Hilda Doolittle meets Pound in New York; Pound convinces her to come to London; engagement is "equivocally renewed."
1911	Hilda Doolittle travels to Europe, settles in London, and through Pound meets Richard Aldington, F. S. Flint, Brigit Patmore, T. E. Hulme, and other literary figures.
1912	Hilda Doolittle travels and studies with Aldington and Pound in the spring and summer; composes first Imagist poems. Pound appointed foreign correspondent for *Poetry* magazine; publishes *Ripostes.*
1913	H.D.'s first Imagist poems published; travels with Pound and Aldington in Italy; marries Aldington in October.
1914	Pound edits *Des Imagistes: An Anthology;* marries Dorothy Shakespear. Richard Aldington becomes assistant editor of the *Egoist.* H.D. and Aldington meet Amy Lowell; H.D. meets D. H. Lawrence. World War I begins.
1915	The Aldingtons move to Hampstead; H.D. loses her first child. Lawrence publishes *The Rainbow,* which is suppressed as obscene; the Lawrences move to Hampstead near the Aldingtons. Pound publishes *Cathay.* Aldington publishes *Images.* An anthology, *Some Imagist Poets,* is published.
1916	The Lawrences move to Cornwall; the Aldingtons move to Devon. Richard Aldington enlists in the army. H.D. takes over as assistant editor (literary editor) of the *Egoist;* publishes *Sea Garden* and *Choruses from the Iphigeneia in Aulis.* Pound publishes *Lustra.* Lawrence publishes *Amores.* The second volume of *Some Imagist Poets* is published.
1917	Richard Aldington is in training to be an army officer. H.D. lives in London and Corfe Castle near Aldington's army base; continues as assistant editor of the *Egoist* until June, when T. S. Eliot succeeds her. Law-

rence publishes *Look! We Have Come Through*. Pound publishes "Three Cantos" in *Poetry* magazine. The Lawrences are expelled from Cornwall in November and return to London to live in H.D.'s flat. Richard Aldington begins affair with Dorothy ("Arabella") Yorke. A third volume of *Some Imagist Poets* is published.

1918   Richard Aldington is sent to France. H.D. spends spring and early summer in Cornwall; meets Bryher (Winifred Ellerman). H.D.'s brother Gilbert is killed in France. Lawrence publishes *New Poems*. World War I ends.

1919   H.D.'s daughter, Perdita, is born; her father dies. H.D. separates from Aldington and seeks assistance from Bryher. H.D. publishes *Choruses from the Iphigeneia in Aulis and the Hippolytus*, a translation of Euripides. Lawrence publishes *Bay;* leaves England. Pound publishes "The Fourth Canto" and *Homage to Sextus Propertius*. Aldington publishes *Images of War, Images of Desire*, and *War and Love*. H.D. writes "Notes on Thought and Vision" in Scilly Isles with Bryher.

1920   H.D. travels to Greece in the spring and to America in the fall with Bryher. Bryher publishes *Development*. Lawrence publishes *Women in Love*. Pound publishes *Hugh Selwyn Mauberley* and leaves London for Paris.

1921   H.D. writes "Paint It Today" and publishes *Hymen*. Bryher marries Robert McAlmon. Lawrence publishes *Psychoanalysis and the Unconscious*.

1922   H.D. writes "Asphodel"; takes up residence in Switzerland; travels to America with Bryher; travels to Greece. Lawrence publishes *Aaron's Rod*.

1923   H.D. travels to Egypt with her mother, Perdita, and Bryher. Lawrence publishes *Kangaroo* and *Birds, Beasts and Flowers*. Bryher publishes *Two Selves*.

1924   H.D. begins "Pilate's Wife"; publishes *Heliodora and Other Poems*.

1925   H.D. publishes *Collected Poems of H.D.* and a selection from *Hedylus;* writes *The Hedgehog* and *Hedylus*. Pound takes up residence in Rapallo, Italy; publishes *A Draft of XVI Cantos*. Lawrence returns to England for brief visit.

1926   H.D. publishes *Palimpsest*. Lawrence publishes *The Plumed Serpent;* returns to England for brief visit; takes

	up residence near Florence, Italy, and writes first draft of *Lady Chatterley's Lover*. Pound publishes his collected shorter poems, *Personae*.
1927	H.D. publishes *Hippolytus Temporizes* and writes "Her." Bryher divorces Robert McAlmon; marries Kenneth Macpherson; meets Freud. Lawrence writes a second version of *Lady Chatterley's Lover* (*John Thomas and Lady Jane*) and *The Escaped Cock;* begins third version of *Lady Chatterley's Lover*. H.D.'s mother dies.
1928	H.D. publishes *Hedylus* and "Narthex." Lawrence publishes *Lady Chatterley's Lover, Collected Poems of D. H. Lawrence,* and part I of *The Escaped Cock*.
1929	Lawrence publishes *Pansies* and *The Escaped Cock* (*The Man Who Died*) in Paris. H.D. revises "Pilate's Wife." Aldington publishes *Death of a Hero*.
1930	Lawrence dies in Vence, France, of tuberculosis. H.D. makes film *Borderline* with Kenneth Macpherson and Bryher. Pound publishes *A Draft of XXX Cantos*.
1931	H.D. publishes *Red Roses for Bronze*. Lawrence's *The Man Who Died* (*The Escaped Cock*) is published in England and America.
1932	H.D. travels to Greece and visits Delphi with Perdita. Aldous Huxley's edition of *The Letters of D. H. Lawrence* is published.
1933	H.D. begins analysis with Freud. Sir John Ellerman, Bryher's father, dies.
1934	H.D. completes analysis with Freud; finishes "Pilate's Wife." H.D.'s *Usual Star, Two Americans, Kora and Ka,* and *Mira-Mare* are published.
1936	H.D. publishes *The Hedgehog*. D. H. Lawrence's essays are published as *Phoenix*.
1937	H.D. publishes her translation and commentary, *Euripides' Ion*.
1938	H.D. receives the Helen Haire Levinson Prize of *Poetry* magazine. H.D. and Richard Aldington are divorced.
1939	H.D. completes first draft of "Madrigal" (*Bid Me to Live*) and returns to London. Freud dies in England. World War II begins.
1940–44	Pound broadcasts speeches in support of fascism and Mussolini over Rome Radio.
1941	H.D. writes "The Gift." Aldington publishes his autobiography, *Life for Life's Sake*.
1942	H.D. writes *The Walls Do Not Fall*.
1943–44	H.D. writes "Magic Ring."

1944	H.D. writes *Writing on the Wall (Tribute to Freud)*, *Tribute to the Angels*, and *The Flowering of the Rod*, and publishes *The Walls Do Not Fall*. Lawrence's *The First Lady Chatterley* is published.
1945	H.D. publishes *Tribute to the Angels*; begins *By Avon River*. Pound confined in the Army Detention Training Center near Pisa, Italy, because of his wartime broadcasting; begins his Pisan Cantos. World War II ends.
1946	H.D. publishes *The Flowering of the Rod*, completes *By Avon River*, and returns to Switzerland; begins "The Sword Went Out to Sea." Pound committed to St. Elizabeth's Hospital for the Criminally Insane in Washington, D.C., after being declared medically unfit to stand trial for treason.
1947	H.D. completes "The Sword Went Out to Sea."
1948	H.D. writes "The White Rose and the Red" and *Advent (Tribute to Freud)*. Pound publishes the *Pisan Cantos*.
1949	H.D. completes "Madrigal" (*Bid Me to Live*) and begins "The Mystery." *By Avon River* is published.
1950	Aldington publishes his biography of D. H. Lawrence, *Portrait of a Genius, But . . .*
1951	H.D. completes "The Mystery."
1951	H.D. begins *Helen in Egypt*.
1954	H.D. completes *Helen in Egypt*.
1955	H.D. writes "Compassionate Friendship."
1956	H.D. publishes *Tribute to Freud*.
1957	H.D. writes "Magic Mirror" and "Vale Ave"; publishes *Selected Poems of H.D.*
1958	H.D. writes *End to Torment*. Pound released from St. Elizabeth's Hospital.
1959	H.D. writes "Winter Love"; receives the Brandeis University Creative Arts Award for Poetry.
1960	*Bid Me to Live* is published. H.D. becomes the first woman to receive the Award of Merit Medal for Poetry of the American Academy of Arts and Letters; writes "Thorn Thicket" and *Hermetic Definition*.
1961	*Helen in Egypt* published. H.D. dies September 28, near Zurich, Switzerland.
1962	Richard Aldington dies in Sury-en-Vaux, France. Bryher publishes her autobiography, *The Heart to Artemis*.
1972	H.D.'s *Hermetic Definition* published. Pound dies in Venice. Lawrence's *John Thomas and Lady Jane* published.
1973	H.D.'s *Trilogy* published in America, including *The*

Walls Do Not Fall, Tribute to the Angels, and *The Flow-ering of the Rod.*

1974   H.D.'s *Tribute to Freud* published, including *Writing on the Wall* and *Advent.*

1979   H.D.'s *End to Torment* and Pound's *Hilda's Book* are published in a single volume.

I

THE TEA ROOM

I

A Moravian Childhood in Bethlehem

"MY NAME WAS Hilda. Papa found the name in the dictionary . . ."[1]

On September 10, 1886, the poet who would be known to the world as H.D. was born in Bethlehem, Pennsylvania, to Helen Eugenia Wolle Doolittle, a member of a prominent family in the mystical Moravian brotherhood, and Charles Leander Doolittle, professor of mathematics and astronomy at Lehigh University.

Hilda's father was born in Indiana in 1843; his family had moved to the Midwest from New England, and H.D. thought of her father as a Puritan. "He comes from those Puritan fathers who wear high peaked hats in the Thanksgiving number of magazines. They fought with Indians and burned witches," she later wrote.[2] Both Charles and his older brother, Alvan, had fought in the American Civil War on the Yankee side, and Alvan had died in that war when Charles was seventeen. H.D. felt that the death of his brother had had a deep effect on her father; he became, she tells us, a "detached and impartial" man, "a scholar, or *savant.*"[3]

As a child Hilda had a deep respect for her father's intelligence and learning. Dr. Charles Doolittle wrote "Monographs on the Results of Observations with the Zenith Telescope" and *Practical Astronomy as Applied to Geodesy and Navigation* (1885). In 1896 he became Flower Professor of Astronomy and director of the Flower Observatory at the University of Pennsylvania. The family moved to the Philadelphia suburb of Upper Darby in 1895, the year he left the faculty at Lehigh and joined the faculty at Pennsylvania. "Everything revolved around him," writes H.D.[4]

Hilda had five brothers. Two of them were half-brothers, as her father's first wife had died, leaving Charles Doolittle with sons

3

Alfred and Eric. (Eric followed in his father's footsteps, becoming a professor of astronomy and succeeding Professor Doolittle as director of the observatory.) Another child of her father's first marriage, Alice, died in infancy. Hilda's father was forty-three when she was born; her mother was at least a decade younger. Helen Doolittle gave birth to five children: a little girl, Edith, who also died in infancy; Gilbert, H.D.'s older brother; Hilda; Harold, her younger brother (these three children were born within four years, from 1885 to 1888); and the baby brother, Charles, who was born just before the Doolittles moved from Bethlehem to Upper Darby.

Throughout the formative first eight years of her childhood, H.D. lived in Bethlehem as a member of a large family and thriving religious community. The Doolittles lived on Church Street, where Hilda's maternal grandparents were neighbors; the two families shared a garden. Hilda was so close to these grandparents, "Mamalie" and "Papalie," that she thought of them as her "other" father and mother. Her little cousins, Tootie, Dick, and Laddie (all boys), lived with her Uncle Hartley and Aunt Belle in the house next door; other relatives lived nearby.

Before her marriage Helen Wolle had taught music and painting at the nearby Moravian seminary. In "The Gift," a memoir of her childhood, H.D. writes, "Papa is not a Moravian, he does not go to church, he met Mama at a German class at the old Seminary when Papalie was principal there."[5]

Hilda's mother's disposition and inclinations were artistic and musical; her father's, mathematical and scientific. The marriage, which took place in 1882, proved to be a fortunate one, and H.D. enjoyed a happy childhood. In the opening section of *Advent,* the notes she kept during her psychoanalysis with Freud in 1933, H.D. recalls her mother's paintings: "The old plates of the saw-mills, the Lehigh River, summer-house with trellis, deer-park of the Seminary where her father was principal for many years . . ."[6] As an imaginative artist, H.D. identified her artistic efforts with her mother's. Her mother's name, Helen, was to become H.D.'s name for herself and for the Helen situation in all women, in all ages. "The mother is the Muse, the creator, and in my case especially, as my mother's name was Helen."[7]

H.D. led the sheltered life that was typical of a strict religious upbringing of the late nineteenth century, and was close to both her parents. The ties in her home followed a recognizable familial pattern. "My older brother was my mother's favorite; I my father's," writes H.D.[8] But there was a special burden. Hilda's father had lost his first and second daughters: "There were the two or twin graves."[9] Thus Hilda was the only daughter in her family. Papalie and Mamalie had lost a daughter, too; her name had been Frances. In "The Gift" H.D. writes of all these lost daughters and realizes that "I was the inheritor."[10] She inherited a special love and also an unusual sense of responsibility. Of her father H.D. remembers, "He said, his one girl was worth all his five boys put together. He should not say that. It made a terrible responsibility, it made one five times as much as one should be."[11] Hilda was acutely aware of the special love she enjoyed as her parents' only girl child; she was the survivor.

The Moravians, too, were survivors. Mamalie and Papalie filled Hilda's young mind with Moravian history and lore about the "hidden church," which some called the Invisible Church. The church was "hidden" because its members had been persecuted for centuries. "We were driven underground by the Inquisition," writes H.D. "Protestant intolerance, no less than Papal intolerance," had compelled "a sublime blending of the faiths."[12]

The Wolles, H.D.'s mother's family, were direct descendants of the Unitas Fratrum, the Bohemian brotherhood that had left Germany for England and America in the 1730s and 1740s, seeking religious toleration. The first Moravian community in America was founded in Bethlehem, Pennsylvania, by seekers of religious freedom from Bohemia, Moravia, and Germany who were loyal to Count Ludwig von Zinzendorf of Saxony, the patron of the mystical brotherhood. After a long history of persecution these fugitives had been welcomed to the estate of Zinzendorf, where the Moravian community of Herrnhut was established. Zinzendorf's doctrine of "free redemption, justification, and salvation through the Blood of Christ" found acceptance, and he became the leader and spokesman of the Moravian brotherhood.[13]

The colony in Bethlehem had been founded on Christmas Eve, 1741, with Zinzendorf and his daughter Benigna present to dedicate the first log house. The colony was originally communal and theocratic in its organization, although as time passed it underwent a series of reorganizations. At the time of H.D's birth, Bethlehem was a religion-oriented nineteenth-century town with a large Moravian population. Religious and social life centered on the church and the seminary.

In a sense Hilda lived as a child as a member of this mystical Moravian community, if only because her mother's side of the family was so deeply involved in the leadership of the church. Papalie, H.D.'s Moravian grandfather, was known to the community as the Reverend Francis Wolle, head of the Moravian seminary in Bethlehem. He was also a naturalist and the author of

Desmids of the United States (1884), *Freshwater Algae of the United States* (1887), and *Diatomaecae of North America* (1890). H.D.'s favorite uncle, J. Fred Wolle, had studied organ and counterpoint in Munich; he was the organist of the Moravian church and the organizer of the Moravian Bach festivals, which are still conducted in Bethlehem each spring.

Later in her life H.D. devoted many years to the study of Moravian history and doctrine and wrote a good deal on the subject. She observed Moravian customs throughout her life; at Christmastime, a central Moravian holiday, close friends could expect to receive Hilda's traditional gift of beeswax candles. In 1956, when H.D. returned to America to participate in an exhibition of her work at the Sterling Memorial Library at Yale University, Norman Holmes Pearson, her longtime friend and literary executor, took her to Bethlehem.

> She stood in the aisle of the Central Church, remembering the love feasts and the Unitas Fratrum. She was fascinated by Zinzendorf and his re-establishment of "a branch of the dispersed or 'lost' Church of Provence, the Church of Love that we touch on in *By Avon River.*" It was not casual when, as we left the Church, she signed the Register and added "Baptized Moravian."[14]

Bethlehem, Pennsylvania, is sometimes called the Christmas City. On the Christmas Eve of the founding of the Moravian settlement, the worshipers likened their experience in the wilderness to that of Mary and Joseph. The Christmas tree, which is so central to Moravian tradition, was originally the *ceppo* or pyramid tree, a triangular wooden form decorated with apples, candles, and verses of Scripture. The large, many-pointed Advent star hangs in halls and over porches to herald the season. The tradition of building the *putz,* a nativity scene, to depict the Christmas story goes back to the Middle Ages, when carved figures were displayed to give the unlettered a better sense of the story. The Christmas vigil, celebrated on Christmas Eve with a candlelight service, is one of the most important festivities of the church. The service is often combined with a love feast, a tradition that originated with the early Christians.

At the Doolittles' home at Christmastime uncles and aunts and cousins helped with preparations. Papalie made sheep for the *putz* under the tree. Even the gathering of the moss for the *putz* was a ceremonious occasion: "The aunts and uncles might hire a sleigh and go off together and come back, screaming and laughing, with bunches of mountain-laurel."[15]

According to Moravian practice, Mrs. Doolittle called her

6 § THE TEA ROOM

daughter Sister. "It was this special moment when Mama said, 'see if you can find the end of an old candle, Sister, among the paper cornucopias,' that the 'thing' began. The 'thing' could not begin if there were not an old end or several almost burnt-out stumps of last year's beeswax candles."[16] In Christmas Eve services of the Moravian church both the boys and the girls carry the candles to symbolize the spiritual equality of the sexes.

The children helped create Christmas. "The 'thing' was that we were creating. We were 'making' a field under the tree, for the sheep. We were 'making' a forest for the elk, out of small sprays of a broken pine-branch." Preparing for Christmas, H.D. was her mother's helper. "Maybe, you'll find the top of this ball among the papers, Sister, if not, you can fasten a lump of wax to stick the hook in, you know how to do it."[17]

§ § §

In "The Gift" H.D. discusses her family's move from Bethlehem to Philadelphia. "Last year just after Christmas, they moved from the old-town and the old-house, to this new big house that was built with the new Transit House and the new Observatory that wasn't yet finished, for Papa, when they asked him to come to the University in Philadelphia."[18] Things were different in Philadelphia. In Bethlehem life had centered on the Moravian church and seminary; in Philadelphia life centered on the university. "What did the Philadelphia ladies whisper about?" asks H.D.[19]

Some of the university ladies did not know about the Moravians. "They were not all German really, Mama would explain to the University ladies, they came from Moravia and Bohemia and England though they had Germans and Danes in the brotherhood that came to America, from Herrnhut, where they went from Moravia when Count Zinzendorf helped them to get to America."[20]

Moravianism was different; is that what the university ladies whispered about? Certainly H.D.'s mother and father were different. Her mother belonged to the house. Her father had a house outside, the Transit House. "He had a broom in the corner of his Transit House which was really a little house with windows and shutters that opened the whole roof. Snow blew in and he kept a broom to sweep out the snow from inside his house."[21]

The university ladies said he was brilliant. "They said, 'it's funny the children aren't gifted, with such a brilliant father.'" H.D. was told, "Your father is doing very important work." As a child she was troubled that her father was not a Moravian. "He never had a Christmas-tree when he was a child . . . he was not happy on Sunday and he had not had a Christmas tree."[22]

In her unpublished autobiographical novel "Paint It Today" (1921), H.D. describes her heroine's lineage as being "Polish or Lithuanian German" on her Moravian mother's side and "Norse English" on her Puritan father's side.[23]

William Carlos Williams was impressed by H.D.'s father.

> The old man who wore a flowing beard was tall and somewhat stooped; he was engaged in a project or upon a thesis to measure the oscillation, the seasonal oscillation, of the earth on its axis . . . On January nights, toward dawn, the doctor's wife, she told us, would go out with a kettle of boiling water to thaw the hairs of his whiskers that during his night-long vigil had become frozen to the eyepiece of the machine.[24]

H.D.'s mother was domestic and matriarchal; she was in complete charge of the household. Her father was stern, patriarchal, and hard-working: "[William Carlos] Williams recalls that the house dominated by the spirit of scientific research was ruled, though not oppressively, by the mother's authority."[25]

In "Afterword: The House of the Father's Science and the Mother's Art," Emily Wallace recognizes the extent to which H.D.'s mother influenced her life and her art. Wallace writes: " 'The household was free,' as Williams perceived, and the life of the imagination flourished in that freedom. The mother helped the children to create Christmas decorations and Halloween games, to learn the songs and stories she sang or read to them in her beautiful voice, to appreciate paintings and flowers, to enjoy visiting and visitors."[26]

William Carlos Williams was one of the visitors. According to his autobiography, Williams met H.D. in 1905 at Bryn Mawr College, where H.D. was a student. He called at the Doolittle home, usually with Ezra Pound but sometimes alone. He took Hilda to a dance, which incurred "some dirty looks from Ezra," so he apologized to Pound: "I'm not in love with Hilda nor she with me. She's your girl and I know it." Williams writes of standing around an upright piano with Ezra Pound, Hilda, and others, trying to sing together to the accompaniment of Mrs. Pound. He writes of how Hilda sat in the middle of a field when a thunderstorm struck, saying, "Come, beautiful rain."[27] Later Williams apologized for the distorted portrait he painted of H.D. (and others, including Pound) in his autobiography. H.D. was incomprehensible to him.

A keen wit, a strong will, a capacity for perseverance and hard work, creative ability, an inclination toward the mystical, a stern sense of order, a love of nature, an independent spirit — so many of the qualities that emerge in H.D.'s poetry are present in the view of her parents that has been given to us by those who knew them. In a letter to Norman Holmes Pearson of July 11, 1955, Williams presents a truer picture of H.D.'s ambience than he had painted in his autobiography:

> The spirit of [of?] a life of scientific research dominated the household. The older boy [Gilbert], a college undergraduate in engineering, was killed later in the first World War. The household was free, but there was nothing arty about it and no talk of art unless it was brought there by friends of the older daughter, Hilda, through her romantic friends who made a haunt of the premises, drawn on by Hilda's loose limbed beauty . . .
>
> In early spring there was frequently a crowd of young bucks led by Ezra of a Saturday afternoon or a Sunday for a walk across the beautiful countryside, rolling grassy hills crowded with violets, I remember especially the grape hyacinths that were to be found everywhere. Hilda was always at the head of the procession — I don't remember any other girls . . .
>
> I realized that Ezra was in love with the girl — or thought he was. Certainly he was paying her marked attention and she knew it. But there were others and she also knew it. Hilda was a careless dresser, her hair like as not would be flying about her head in the wind in abandon . . .
>
> I remember also a poem I wrote her, an acrostic on her birthday, the 13th of January, 1905.* It had cost me much sweat, laboring over the lines . . . She only laughed at me. You say you slaved over it! It should have burst from your lips as a song!
>
> The picture of Professor Doolittle at the pier on the departure of his daughter for England! to meet Ezra Pound (as he well knew) impressed me deeply. He was alone with her, aside from myself. He was sitting on a trunk, completely silent. No word to me or to anyone.[28]

*H.D.'s birthday was September 10.

2

Hilda and Ezra in Pennsylvania

HILDA DOOLITTLE met Ezra Pound at a Halloween party given by a friend in 1901. "Hilda, tall, blond, and with a long jaw and gay blue eyes," had just turned fifteen;[1] Pound was only a year older and created a sensation at the party by wearing a bright green robe that "set off not only his green eyes but his gold-red hair."[2] From the start the relationship between Pound and H.D. was powerful, both emotionally and intellectually.

The young Ezra was tall, energetic, and intellectually precocious. William Carlos Williams described him as a "physical phenomenon."[3] Pound kept himself in good physical condition by walking, playing tennis, fencing, and doing "odd jobs with knife and tools."[4] He was educated at Hamilton College and the University of Pennsylvania (Ph.B., 1905; A.M., 1906). By the time he entered college Pound thought of himself as a poet, and he was described by one of his Pennsylvania classmates as a lone wolf. According to Williams, Ezra was gregarious but "too proud to try to please people."[5] Williams said he always held it against Ezra "that he'd never let you in on his personal affairs." Even when they were pals, says Williams, he never knew what Pound was up to. "Never explain anything, was his motto."[6]

In his autobiography Williams provides a portrait of the young Hilda Doolittle and of Ezra Pound, who "was wonderfully in love with her." Of H.D. Williams writes:

> There was about her that which is found in wild animals at times, a breathless impatience, almost a silly unwillingness to come to the point. She had a young girl's giggle and shrug which somehow in one so tall and angular seemed a little absurd. She fascinated me, not for her beauty, which was unquestioned if bizarre to my sense, but for a provocative indifference to rule and order which I liked.[7]

Although Williams minimizes her extraordinary beauty, it was this quality that was a determining factor in the course of H.D.'s life and in the direction of her work. H.D. was tall, at least five foot nine, and slender; she was beautifully shaped and well coordinated, although her height often caused her to feel awkward in social situations. There was often a faraway look in her eyes, and she tended to be pensive. When she spoke her voice was rhythmic and musical. Her long, slender neck supported a head of classic proportion and features — when lost in thought she had something of the look of a Greek statue — and she sometimes had a startled look, as if suddenly awakened.

Hilda entered Bryn Mawr in 1904, but her college career was interrupted by her stormy engagement to Ezra Pound. In 1906 she withdrew from college for reasons of health, and for the next five years lived at home, studying and writing. It was primarily Pound who influenced what she read during this period. The books he encouraged her to read are significant in the context of the mutual attraction they felt. In *End to Torment* H.D. recalls:

> It was Ezra who really introduced me to William Morris. He literally shouted "The Gilliflower of Gold" in the orchard. How did it go? *Hah! hah! la belle jaune giroflée.* And there was "Two Red Roses across the Moon" and "The Defence of Guenevere." It was at this time that he brought me the *Séraphita* and a volume of Swedenborg — *Heaven and Hell?* Or is that Blake? He brought me volumes of Ibsen and of Bernard Shaw. He brought me Whistler's *Ten O'Clock* . . . He read me "The Haystack in the Floods" with passionate emotion.
>
> He brought me the Portland, Maine, Thomas Mosher reprint of the Iseult and Tristram story. He called me Is-hilda and wrote a sonnet a day; he bound them in a parchment folder. There was a series of Yogi books, too.[8]

There were also some volumes of Renaissance Italian poets. Hilda diligently studied Latin, Greek, and the classics. She and Pound read Rossetti and the Pre-Raphaelites. There were, of course, other literary influences in these formative years. In *Advent* H.D. lists such works as Blackwood's *The Centaur,* the illustrations in the Doré Bible, and *Grimm's Fairy Tales* as being important early influences in the life of her imagination.

Several of H.D.'s short stories written during this five-year period at home were published in a New York syndicated newspaper and, with the assistance of Ezra Pound's father, Homer, in a local Presbyterian paper.

In 1905 Hilda Doolittle and Ezra Pound became engaged. He gave her a ring and they informed their parents of their plans to marry. In her autobiographical novel about that period of her life in Pennsylvania, "Her," written in 1927, H.D. gives us a startlingly vivid picture of the period of their engagement and sets an emotional context for the Imagist poetry that later launched her literary career. The story H.D. tells in "Her" suggests that Pound and H.D.'s early relationship was one of mutuality and trust. It was the parents, particularly H.D.'s, who were distrustful.

In her Pound memoir, *End to Torment,* H.D. writes: "We were curled up together in an armchair when my father found us. I was 'gone.' I wasn't there. I disentangled myself. I stood up; Ezra stood beside me. It seems we must have swayed, trembling." Professor Doolittle opposed the marriage, and the young Ezra Pound was responsive to authority — almost more responsive to the authority of her parents than Hilda was. After being found curled up with Hilda in the armchair, Ezra was quick to justify himself. Hilda's father replied: "Mr. Pound, I don't say there was anything wrong." But in retrospect (*End to Torment* was written in 1958), H.D. says it was "all wrong":

> Mr. Pound it was all wrong. You turned into a Satyr, a Lynx, and the girl in your arms (Dryad, you called her), for all her fragile, not yet lost virginity, is *Maenad, bassarid.* God keep us from Canto LXXIX, one of the *Pisan Cantos.*
>   Mr. Pound, with your magic, your "strange spells of old diety," why didn't you complete the metamorphosis? Pad, pad, pad, . . . come along, my Lynx. Let's get out of here. You are suffocating and I am hungry. You spoke of grapes somewhere — you were starving.[9]

In *End to Torment* H.D. remembers the fiery moments of their first kisses in the woods, in the winter, which she recalled with even greater intensity in her poem "Winter Love." She writes: "First kisses? In the woods, in the winter — what did one expect? Not this. Electric, magnetic, they do not so much warm, they magnetize, vitalize. We need never go back."[10]

In "Her," in which she characterizes herself as Hermione Gart and Pound as George Lowndes, H.D. recalls these moments of their early engagement with fervor and feeling.

> Underneath her hand was the clear sweet flax-blue shantung, fine nice shoulder beneath the thin shirting. Hermione slipped a long hand into the open space of the wide flung wide collar . . . Never had her hand reached out in darkness and felt the texture of pure marble, never had her forehead bent forward and as against a stone altar, felt safety, I am now saved.[11]

In spite of or perhaps because of the intensity of Hilda's attraction to Ezra, Hilda's parents were adamant in their disapproval of him. They questioned his respectability, his upbringing, his behavior. They felt that he was neither mature enough nor reliable enough to support a wife. An incident in Indiana had created a small scandal among the faculty wives at the University of Pennsylvania. "Why do the faculty ladies concern themselves with such small matters?" asks H.D.[12] Pound had taken in a woman for a night, and the incident had created enough of a stir that he was fired from his newly won position as an instructor in French and Spanish at Wabash College in Crawfordsville, Indiana. Pound maintained that the woman had been hungry and needed a place to stay, but the administration at Wabash College and Hilda's mother's friends at the University of Pennsylvania apparently believed otherwise.

H.D. recalls her mother's reaction to the scandal and the prospect of Ezra Pound as a son-in-law in the following dialogue from "Her."

> "But you can't *marry* George Lowdnes."
> "On what compulsion must I, — I mean mustn't I — tell me that?"
> "Be serious. Do you know what you are saying?"
> "I am saying George has been asking me to marry him —."
> "But you can't, you can't possibly —."
> "Why, just why can't I possibly?"
> "Well there are — there is — why — you can't — there are the university ladies —."
> "What have the university ladies got to do with me, with George Lowdnes?"
> "Why, why — why — Hermione, you know — surely you're only joking — surely you must remember —."
> "What? What exactly Mama?"
> "That horrible — well — fiasco — you remember —."
> "But I thought that was all forgotten and anyhow everyone knew George took the poor creature to his room to feed her."
> "People don't take people to their rooms to feed them. You're out of your mind, Hermione."[13]

H.D.'s name for herself in the novel is Hermione Gart; "Her" is the heroine's nickname. The appellation is sometimes confusing to the reader, but it does very effectively convey the idea of Hermione as an object caught in a tempest of opposing wills, plans, and expectations.

Pound explained the Indiana incident to H.D. in a letter, which she recalled in *End to Torment:* "I found her in the snow, when I went to post a letter. She was stranded from a traveling variety company. She had nowhere to go. I asked her to my room. She slept in my bed. I slept on the floor." [14]

Following his dismissal from Wabash College at midterm of the 1907 school year, Ezra Pound, like the fictional George Lowdnes, had no "respectable" vocation; he was a poet. But Hilda had no doubt that she was madly in love with him. Under the tremendous amount of parental pressure she was receiving, she was becoming somewhat hysterical in the romantic mode. She was beginning to have terrible arguments with her mother, which she re-created in "Her."

> "When I marry George Lowdnes, when I marry George Lowdnes —."
> "And when exactly are you going to marry George Lowdnes?"
> Eugenia [her mother] spoke ironically, she was speaking up nicely, they were making snap and spark between them, George Lowdnes the flint for spark and snap and steel sparks flying . . .
> "Don't you know what marriage *means,* Hermione?"
> "Marriage means me whirling like a water spout, swirling out of everything, whirling over fences, out, out, out of the forest primeval." . . .
> "With what are you going to swirl and how are you going to swirl and where are you swirling to?" [15]

Eugenia, the mother, was of course trying to make Hermione see reason; Eugenia was trying to tell her that she could not live on love. How could this irresponsible "Georgio," with his perverse optimism and childlike rationalizations, hope to take on the responsibilities of a husband?

H.D.'s romantic hysterics are amusingly rendered in the novel in the context of the mother's worldly considerations.

> "You can't live on nothing."
> "I can live on sunlight falling across little bridges. I can live on the Botticelli blue cornflower pattern on the out-billowing garments of the attendant to Aphrodite and the pattern of strawberry blossoms and the little daisies in the robe of Primavera. I can live on the doves flying (he says) in cohorts from the underside of the faded gilt of the balcony of Saint Mark's Cathedral and the long corridors of the Pitti Palace . . ."
> "You can't live on nothing. Your father won't permit it. Do you think your father and I would have such inhumanity as to let you — to *let* you marry a man of George Lowdnes' reputation, and marry a man of George Lowdnes' reputation on simply nothing?"

"You mean if this man George Lowdnes had a heap — had a steam yacht and a million of dollars you would let me?"

"I mean the whole thing is unsuitable and you are mad altogether."[16]

As Pound's biographer Charles Norman tells the story, "Pound went one day to the observatory to ask for [Hilda's] hand, and Professor Doolittle, a tall, gaunt man who spoke with deliberate slowness, said in his slow, deliberate voice: 'Why, you're nothing but a nomad!' "[17]

Whether or not Pound was willing (or able) to commit himself to the traditional masculine role of breadwinner and faithful husband to Hilda while also becoming a responsible citizen in the eyes of this turn-of-the-century Pennsylvania community, in his own way he was undoubtedly as madly in love with her as she was with him. Yet the social institution of the American family was a concrete, experiential reality for Hilda. She came from a strong, closely knit family. She experienced her parents as two granite rocks. It was not easy for her to leave the comforts and security of home.

There was no doubt in H.D.'s mind that it was Ezra who severed her from her friends and family and introduced her to a world that neither she nor he could have foretold from the vantage point of the rolling Pennsylvania countryside surrounding the observatory in Upper Darby. In her *End to Torment,* H.D. says:

> In Ezra's early poem, "The Goodly Fere," a tough Anglo-Saxon peasant fisherman tells the original Galilean story. He is the center of some kind of communal integration — disintegrating toward rebirth, as personally, Ezra severed me (psychically) from friends and family. If having been severed, painfully reintegrated, we want only to forget the whirlwind or forked lightning that destroyed our human, domestic serenity and security, that is natural. It is, in a sense, *sauve qui peut.*[18]

This early attraction was full of ambivalence for both H.D. and Pound, as first love so often is, and in "Her" H.D. manages to capture the flavor of such ambivalence. As Hermione's marriage continues to be so vehemently opposed by her family, her ambivalence becomes acute and painful.

> She wanted for George to make the thing an integral, herself integrally. She wanted George to make one of his drastic statements that would dynamite her world away for her . . . "Why is it that I can't *love* George Lowdnes properly?" . . . George being funny is piglike . . . George, so beautiful, healing her by his presence was a hideous Harlequin being funny on a wood path.[19]

Hilda and Ezra in Pennsylvania § 1 5

The novel quite clearly relates how for H.D. the ambivalence became oppressive; one moment Pound was the all-powerful lover, the next moment he was piglike. Under opposite sorts of pressures from Pound and her family, she was coming apart. She began to experience the ambivalence she felt toward him physically, or, we might say, psychosomatically. One moment she felt too strong; the next moment, weak and broken. "She was stronger than anything. She was too strong. She wished she were not so strong . . . She wished she could love George."[20]

H.D. presents George as not understanding Hermione's mounting hysteria. But perhaps he did. She was trying to maintain the integrity and identity of "Her," but she was breaking down. One moment she felt so strong; she was a tree; she was Aum;* she was sufficient unto herself. The next moment she felt she could not walk; her ankles were "frankly broken" and she was "frightened" and "blubbering" against his shoulder.

> "I didn't mean, Hermione, to hurt you."
> "You didn't — didn't." Her teeth were chattering. George had dragged a shawl from somewhere. How did you find that old carriage rug? We never use it. An old rug she had used to tuck about her feet in the days before the barn was turned into a laboratory, was tucked around her ankles that now were frankly broken.
> "It's funny with me. I'm so strong. I feel so strong, so right. Nothing can ever hurt me — then — " Humiliation choked Her . . . Tears choked and humiliated and George had turned the lamp down a little as the flick and flare of the light had burned against Her . . . Now she said, "I am too strong and I am nothing and I am frightened — " She achieved a very ugly voice that blubbered unbecomingly from somewhere, saying it over and over like a prayer-wheel. "I am frightened. I am the word Aum, I am Her. I am Her." Her blubbered in a child voice against the somewhat London shoulders of George Lowdnes, "I am — so — very — frightened."[21]

Hermione began to lash out at George, attempting to resolve the ambivalence. One moment he was brilliant; the next moment he was a clown, a harlequin. " 'You're nothing, George, I mean precisely nothing.' The branch swayed back of George. He was part of the branches. Why wasn't he part of the branches?"[22]

One can imagine that Pound might have been confused by Hilda's behavior. H.D. leaves us in no doubt that at some level she was trying to break away from Pound and the powerful emo-

---

*"Aum" is a variation of "Om," a mantra used in Hinduism, Sikhism, and Lamaism in mystical contemplation of ultimate reality.

tional relationship that had enveloped them. H.D. characterizes the tensions in her portrait of Hermione and George.

> Her thought, panther-lean cat, strode up ahead of George. Her thought was swifter than George's witty, tricky thought. Thought chased thought like two panthers. Her own thought, swifter than the thought of George, was there beyond him. "You'll never, never catch me . . ." If George would catch her, then George would be, might yet be something.[23]

One can imagine that such a state of mind might be hard to catch hold of both in fiction and in life. One moment George was a beast, the next moment a god. Was this really happening, Hermione wondered, or was he a harlequin with a mask — a demon, a rogue? Was he playing a part in a pantomime? What was the script?

> For a moment he was tawny with his sticking-up hair and his Harlequin features blurred out, cut across by jade green from green eyes. His eyes were green sea-green and wood green but he would never love a tree. I am a tree. TREE is my new name out of the Revelations. He shall have a new name . . . written on his forehead. The mark of the beast. I have the mark of the beast.[24]

While the sense and flavor of Hilda and Ezra's relationship in Pennsylvania is wonderfully re-created in "Her," one wonders whether Pound was in fact subjected to this talk of revelations and beasts and trees. If so, he must have gone a bit mad himself. And there was, of course, all the tension of an unconsummated union.

> George was like a great tawny beast, a sort of sub-lion pawing at her, pawing with great hand at her tousled garments. George had been like a great lion, but if he had simply bared teeth, torn away garments with bared fangs, she would have understood, would have put narrow arms about great shoulders, would have yielded to him.[25]

It would seem that one of them had to break through the ambivalence of first love, one of them had to take command. While Pound was clearly courting her, Hilda apparently did not manifest the predatory behavior that is sometimes exhibited by engaged women. Nor did Pound manifest the sort of commanding behavior that, for instance, Hilda's husband, Richard Aldington, later did. In "Her," H.D. presents herself in her early twenties as more than a little confused, more than just a little bit out of her mind. If she had had the clarity of vision that she had toward Pound when she wrote "Winter Love" in 1958, or if she had been a different sort of person, there might have been a marriage in 1908.

There was also, however, the problem of Pound's ambivalence, and although it was of a very different nature from H.D.'s, it was certainly as real. H.D.'s strong family life and domestic inclinations apparently made Pound nervous. He would have preferred her to be more ornate, more worldly, less matriarchal, more of a companion. Recalling Ezra's uneasiness, she writes:

> "Now it's winter," said Her, sitting on the rug before an open fire-space, "oranges make it winter." She held an orange in her hand not wanting to cut it with the fruit knife and George said, "You are so damned decorative." "I know." She said, "I know" (not having heard George), "oranges are so decorative" and George said "You, you, you, little Miss So-Stupid." And she said, "Have coffee" and she said "But you can't have more than three lumps" and she said "I don't smoke very often but I should so much like to" and he said, "You'll have to smoke when you're my wife, Hermione."
>
> And she said, "Why will I have to?" And he said "Because it's company." And she said, hearing her own laugh peal and break and shake against the roof, against the roof of the room upstairs, against the eaves of the attic and then out and out and out to waiting star-light, "But I won't ever — ever be your wife, my Georgio." And he said, "You're being very funny." And she said, "You just said you didn't want me." And he said, "I always say that in case I never get you." And she said, "Anyhow I love — love Her, only Her, Her, Her." And he said "Narcissus in the reeds." [26]

As Hermione asserts or embodies the matriarchal values of family and the feminine world, George accuses her of being in love with herself rather than with him. The strain in this relationship is clearly related to the difficulty of a man's coming to participate, through his beloved, in a woman's world, and of a woman's seeing more and more clearly into the world of her lover. The strain of those early encounters is re-created brilliantly in "Her."

The central symbol of Hermione's resistance to love is the tree. "I am the word Aum" and "I am a tree" are the primary symbolic motifs of the novel. "Tree on tree on tree. TREE. I am the Tree of Life. Tree. I am a tree planted by the rims of water. I am . . . I am . . . Her exactly."

Pound presents the experience of entering into H.D.'s world in his poem "The Tree":

> I stood still and was a tree amid the wood
> Knowing the truth of things unseen before,
> Of Daphne and the laurel bow

And that god-feasting couple old
That grew elm-oak amid the wold.
'Twas not until the gods had been
Kindly entreated and been brought within
Onto the hearth of their heart's home
That they might do this wonder-thing.
Naethless I have been a tree amid the wood
And many new things understood
That were rank folly to my head before.*

In H.D.'s novel the tree comes to be associated with that great matriarchal festival, Christmas, with its central symbol, the Christmas tree, which was for H.D. a symbol of the family tree. "What was Christmas? A bird had done a trapeze-turn across a window like a bird on a string hung on a Christmas tree and I am the word Aum and I am a Tree. I am Tree exactly. George would never love a tree, she had known from the beginning. If you follow your instinct from the first you will be right. I knew George would never love a tree properly."[27]

The novel ends with Hermione's decision to hold onto "Her"; Hermione's attentions are turned to her girlfriend, Fayne (Frances Gregg).† In this relationship, Hermione transfers some of her idealistic feelings for her mother to her friend. George unsuccessfully attempts to break across Hermione's friendship, but the relationship signifies a need to assert her own reality and integrity as a woman. Hermione identifies with Fayne; as H.D. succinctly states: "I will not have her hurt. I will not have Her hurt. She is Her. I am Her. Her is Fayne. Fayne is Her. I will not let them hurt HER."[28]

Turning to women in times of crisis with men was to become a recurring pattern in H.D.'s life; H.D.'s Hermione decides to "hold on": "Hold on, hold on Her Gart. And don't ask why you are holding on so incandescent. Why don't I go up like a rocket, a sort of decoration that goes off in sizzles?"[29]

---

*Pound first collected "The Tree" in *Hilda's Book,* a handbound book of fifty-seven leaves sewn in vellum which he presented to H.D. in 1907. The poem was later published in *A Lume Spento* (1908) and in *Personae* (1926).
†Frances Gregg (1884–1941) was a writer and girlhood friend of H.D. and Ezra Pound (Pound called her "the Egg"). She married Louis Wilkinson in 1912 and settled in Europe. She contributed poems and short prose pieces to *Poetry, Others, The New Freewoman,* the *Egoist,* the *Dial, Forum, Smart Set,* the *Adelphi,* and other periodicals. In 1941 she was killed in the bombing of Plymouth. *Hilda's Book,* which Pound had given to H.D. in 1907, was discovered among her personal effects and eventually it came into the hands of Peter Russell, who sold it to the Houghton Library of Harvard University.

H.D. did not go off in sizzles, she did not run off with her romantic poet-lover, she says, because she was grounded — grounded in the matriarchal world of women and family tradition.

On February 8, 1908, Pound went off to Europe alone, courtesy of the trustees of Wabash College, who had paid up on his contract when they let him go.

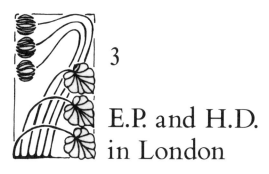

3

E.P. and H.D.
in London

THE IMMEDIATE context of H.D.'s *End to Torment,* her memoir of her years with Ezra Pound in Pennsylvania and London, was the imprisonment of Pound in St. Elizabeth's Hospital for the Criminally Insane in Washington, D. C. The history of Pound's thirteen-year-long sojourn in the "hell hole," as he referred to it, is well known, and there is no need to discuss it here except to point out that the "torment" of H.D.'s title refers to this imprisonment. *End to Torment* was written in 1958, in anticipation of Pound's release from St. Elizabeth's. But its subject is the early years H.D. shared with Pound, and in this context the title comes to have a many-layered meaning; the principal theme of the memoir is the circumstances that led to the final break in Pound and H.D.'s "equivocal" engagement, which marked an end to the particular kind of torment that H.D. suffered in that relationship.

In spite of the fact that H.D. experienced difficulty in breaking from the secure environment of home, all the hysteria she experienced during the years of her engagement to Pound, including the physical breakdown that forced her withdrawal from Bryn Mawr College in 1906, cannot be attributed to her relations with her parents. Her relations with Pound were a contributing factor. While H.D. may have been able to overlook the Indiana incident and rumors about Ezra's involvement with other women in the Philadelphia area, she was undoubtedly more than a little distraught over his second and concurrent engagement, to Mary Moore of Trenton, and to the continuing rumors of still other women in his life. And H.D. was not the sort of woman who would resolve this kind of romantic ambiguity in the culturally prescribed manner; she would not assume a possessive posture, take command of the situation, and lay down the law.

Unlike H.D.'s family, Pound's parents were very supportive of their son's engagement to Hilda: " 'His parents came to see you?' 'Of course.' 'They were pleased?' 'Very — mine weren't, as I say. Mrs. Pound brought me a pearl pendant.' " [1]

When Pound was making plans for his 1908 trip to Europe he asked H.D. to elope with him. Her hesitation to run off with Pound at this time brought an end to the "official" engagement. As she relates in *End to Torment:*

> "You must come away with me, Dryad." "How can I?" His father would scrape up enough for us to live on. I had nothing. "Anyway," an old friend confided, as if to cheer me up, "they say he was engaged to Mary Moore, anyhow. Bessie Elliot could have had him for the asking. There was Louise Skidmore, before that." . . . The engagement, such as it was, was shattered like a Venetian glass goblet, flung on the floor. [2]

If it is the case that the first resistance to the engagement came from H.D. and her family, the second clearly came from Pound. Much later in her life H.D. came to understand how at some level Pound may have experienced their commitment to each other as a kind of confinement.

> Custody? Marriage? . . . Did he want to break away from me? Of course he did. Was I hiding suppressed memories of that infinitely remote equivocal "engagement"? He broke it by subconscious or even conscious intention, the little "scandal," the loss of a job was intentional? Logically, it was all impossible to know that. So long ago, . . . but the two-edged humiliation, from the friends and family, from Ezra, was carefully camouflaged, covered with the weeds and bracken of daily duties and necessities, and a bridge finally crossed the chasm or "canyon," as Norman [Holmes Pearson] called it, a forceful effort toward artistic achievement. [3]

In 1908 Pound left for his extended trip to Europe, from which he was to return in 1910 a changed man. He had fallen in love with Europe and with European ideas, and his enchantment with a European way of life was to have a profound effect on H.D.'s life. It must be stressed that Pound had reservations about marrying H.D. even before he left for Europe, because of her strong matriarchal orientation. He wished that she were more docile, more malleable. In short, in spite of — or perhaps because of — his powerful attraction to H.D., he feared that she was the kind of woman who would limit his freedom as a poet. As Pound stated in notes following a draft of his poem "Shalott," composed in Venice and recorded in the *San Trovaso Notebook* of 1908, "Art and marriage are not incompatible but marriage means art death often because there are so few sufficiently great to avoid the semi-stupor of satisfied passion — whence no art is."[4]

Pound expresses the thought in the poem "Shalott":

> I am the prince of dreams,
> > Lord of Shalott,
> And many other things long since forgot.
> Oer land & sea
> I roam where it pleaseth me
> And whither no man knoweth
> Save the wind that bloweth   free.[5]

In 1909 Pound, who had taken up residence in England, began a series of lectures at the Regent Street Polytechnic in London. The lectures formed the substance of *The Spirit of Romance,* his essay on the troubadour poets, in which he expresses great admiration for (among others) Guillaume, count of Peiteus, grandfather of Richard Coeur de Lion. The count, with whom Pound identifies, was a "man of many energies . . . He was, as the old book says of him, 'one of the greatest counts in the world, and he had his way with women.' He made songs for either them or himself or for his more ribald companions."[6]

Pound was intrigued not only with the lays of the troubadours but with their whole philandering approach to women. By 1910 he was committed both to the troubadour ideal, with all its extra-marital implications, and to the resurrection of this social form in the contemporary world of life and letters. Hilda, on the other hand, who was waiting for Pound to return to America, continued to be devoted to the Moravian — and very American — ideal of marital fidelity. Her orientation in relation to this matter may account for her mixed response to *A Lume Spento* (1908) with its collection of old poems which had been written to her in America and new poems which reflected Pound's European experiences. The book is dedicated to

> . . . *such as love this same*
> *beauty that I love, somewhat*
> *after mine own fashion.*

But by 1910, still in communication with Pound, Hilda had resolved (for herself at least) the fight within her own family, and had decided to marry him against the wishes of her parents. Awaiting Pound's return to the States, she was unaware of his European "engagements" and ignorant of the ways of the troubadours and Pound's newly acquired commitment to European cultural forms.

When Pound returned in the summer of 1910 he asked Hilda to join him in New York, and together they visited William Carlos Williams in New Jersey. It was at this time that Pound persuaded H.D. to make what would turn out to be one of the most momentous decisions of her life: he convinced her to come to London. Their engagement was unofficially — or as she later wrote, "equivocally" — renewed. There was an understanding; they were to be married. After a four-month tour of Europe in 1911 with Frances Gregg, and her mother, H.D. settled in London. She had at last made her final decision to leave home and be with Ezra Pound.

It was shortly after H.D. had taken up residence at 8 Duchess Street in London that she learned of Pound's engagement to Dorothy Shakespear. In "Paint It Today" she implies she heard the news from Richard Aldington, whom she had met through Pound at Brigit Patmore's home (although in *End to Torment* she suggests that she may have heard the news first from an American friend, the composer Walter Morse Rummel, who was in London at the time).

> I asked him [Richard Aldington], pretending I had forgotten the first thing he had said, if he had seen Raymond [Pound] lately.
>
> He said yes. *"Did* you know he was engaged?"
>
> If my companion had been an American youth, I should have inevitably answered, "What again?" As it was, out of respect to his own delicacy and out of loyalty to the ancient Raymond, I answered with a slightly amazed, half interrogatory inflection, "O?"
>
> It seemed to have been an English lady this time. We were all to meet her, though it was very select, at someone or other's mutual friends' studio tea.[7]

H.D. knew immediately that Pound's engagement to Dorothy Shakespear was of a different order from his romantic engagements as a young student of Romance languages at the University of Pennsylvania in Philadelphia. His career as a poet was bound up in this relationship, and Pound wanted to be a poet more than he wanted anything in the world.

Dorothy Shakespear was the daughter of Olivia Shakespear, a novelist and a good friend and former mistress of William Butler Yeats. Dorothy and Olivia, whom Pound had met through a mutual friend, had attended Pound's lectures at the Polytechnic. Dorothy was devoted to Pound. Olivia thought him the perfect husband for her daughter. By late 1909 Pound had been accepted into the Yeats circle following Olivia's introduction of him to Yeats, the poet Pound most admired at this time. Dorothy Shakespear was very much at home in the circle that had welcomed Pound's literary aspirations in England, and she would fit perfectly into his plans for his own literary future. Both Yeats and Olivia Shakespear were actively encouraging him to marry Dorothy, and Ezra Pound was certainly very fond of this lovely Englishwoman.

In *End to Torment* H.D. describes the impact of learning of Pound's engagement to Dorothy Shakespear:

> "What did you feel when this Walter — this Walter told you that?" "Look — it's impossible to say. I felt bleak, a chasm opened —" "But you said that you loved this American girl, this Frances — and you were going around with Richard —." "I don't know what I felt. I had met Walter, years before, in America, in a house the Pounds had for the summer . . .
>
> "Walter said, 'I think I ought to tell you, though I promised Mrs. Shakespear not to . . . there is an understanding. Ezra is to marry Dorothy Shakespear.' "[8]

But having broken from home to follow her fiancé, Hilda would not reverse her decision, and even though her parents came to Europe shortly after she arrived in London to attempt to persuade her to come back with them, she had taken her stand. Now twenty-five years old, she felt that her decision to stay in London was a terrible blow to her mother. She felt like Orestes, with a knife at her mother's throat. It was a terribly difficult time for H.D., and even though she had made her decision she was clearly still pulled toward mother and home.

In "Paint It Today," H.D. describes some of the anguish of this final break. H.D.'s name for herself in this manuscript is Margaret or Midget; Mrs. Defreddie, Midget's mother, is still sheltering her child. In the following paragraph Midget is remembering her childhood and trying to make the break final.

> Do you remember those fruits she used to get you? She redressed that hopeless doll many, many times when any other mother would have flung it on the dust heap. What of that birthday when she put morning glories through the string of every birthday parcel and addressed each of the eight separate parcels with a separate pet-name? What of that wonderful convalescence from scarlet fever when you found on your pillow — "Stop," said the mind of Midget . . . It was then that Midget exploded . . . Midget sat on the floor and cried.[9]

It is certainly not difficult to see how H.D.'s upbringing in a protective family combined with a reasonable amount of enlightened self-interest and Pound's erratic nature and interest in other women were enough to drive her to frantic efforts to escape the force of her attraction to him. Yet after her experience with Pound in Pennsylvania, H.D. realized that to escape this attraction she had to confront it. The power of the relationship had certainly not waned as a result of their separation while Pound was in Europe and she in America. At the same time, H.D. realized that their engagement was impossible. They were drawn to different traditions.

In the tradition in which H.D. was brought up, unmarried men and women lived totally chaste lives. While the sexual symbolism of the Moravian religion is intense, the whole emphasis of the sexual and the spiritual life is on marriage. As in many early American religious communities, illicit passion was forbidden and strongly condemned. For a Moravian girl of the turn of the century, an intimate relationship like that between Hilda and Ezra was a serious affair. Thus, at a time when Ezra was becoming interested in women in general and in having his way with them, Hilda was going through a difficult period in which she was breaking from a sheltered home environment and attaching all hope for future fulfillment to the man to whom she was engaged to be married.

As H.D. began to understand what Pound's involvement in the troubadour tradition meant and what it would mean for their future together, she began to search for a way out. Her poetry, novels, and memoirs make it clear that she did not in fact assimilate the situation at the time; it was too painful. Instead, to use a psychiatric term, she repressed it; and she even attempted to adopt the act of writing poetry as a way of not facing what the direction of Pound's poetic aspirations could mean to her. As she remembers in *End to Torment,* the shock of it all led to "a forceful effort toward artistic achievement." There is, then, a very real sense in which she may have become involved in writing as an intellectual defense against the emotional consequences of Pound's involvement in poetry and the troubadour tradition.

H.D. began to experiment with writing poetry in 1910. Pound had returned from Europe, and for a brief period H.D. was living in New York. Her poems, which she considered akin to translations, were modeled on Theocritus, whose work she knew through a translation that Pound had given her. She also did some translations of Heine, one of which appears in "Paint It Today." The poem is interesting in that it gives us an indication of her early poetic orientation. Speaking about her translation, which is not dated but which was probably completed in 1910, she says, "She had translated it painstakingly from Heine, and she knew that she had brought over a little of the fragrance of the German. She worried about the 'thee' and the 'yourself' but 'thyself' sounded stilted, unnatural." The poem reads:

> I have come again away from the dead,
> Drawn by strange powers to thee,
> Quicken me now nor fear to give,
> Too much of yourself to me.[10]

Although she knew nothing of Pound's relationship with Dorothy Shakespear when she allowed him to persuade her to join him in London, H.D. resolved in late 1911 to make the best of an impossible situation and began seriously to pursue her literary studies. She was studying with the British poet Richard Aldington, a friend of Pound's, and both Aldington and Hilda had rooms across the courtyard from Pound at Church Walk, Kensington. "On 4 December Hilda Doolittle wrote to Isabel Pound [Ezra's mother] to say that Ezra had been most kind to her since her arrival in London. Her cordial reception had been 'due to the efforts of his friends, spurred on by himself.' "[11]

In *End to Torment* H.D. puts the matter in a more dismal light: "Drifting. Drifting. Meeting with him [Pound] alone or with others at the Museum tea room. We all read in the British Museum reading room. Dark walls and statues that looked dingy . . . My father, at 70, had retired from the University. My mother wrote, 'We could meet in Genoa.' I had my own allowance now. Drifting?"[12]

H.D.'s parents still hoped she would return with them to America. They had agreed to permit her to stay in London while they went to Genoa on family business. Then, in the closing months of 1911, Pound said he wanted Hilda again. What about his engagement to Dorothy? What would happen to his literary connections if he broke with Dorothy now? Richard Aldington professed to be in love with H.D. Suddenly Pound, Aldington, and her parents were all fighting for her.

It happened so quickly. Noel Stock guesses that it was probably in April of 1912, and it was probably at their regular convening place, the tea room of the British Museum, that Pound, H.D., and Aldington agreed upon three principles of good writing.

1. Direct treatment of the "thing" whether subjective or objective.
2. To use absolutely no word that does not contribute to the presentation.
3. As regarding rhythm: to compose in the sequence of the musical phrase, not in sequence of a metronome.[13]

It was in August 1912 that Pound read H.D.'s first "Imagist" poems. H.D. recalls the moment in *End to Torment:* " 'But Dryad,' (in the Museum tea room), 'this is poetry.' He slashed with a pencil. 'Cut this out, shorten this line. "Hermes of the Ways" is a good title. I'll send it to Harriet Monroe of *Poetry*. Have you a copy? Yes? Then we can send this, or I'll type it when we get back. Will this do?' And he scrawled H.D. Imagiste at the bottom of the page." [14]

In his letter to Harriet Monroe, the editor of *Poetry* magazine, Pound praised H.D.'s poetry and said, "I've had luck again, and I'm sending you some *modern* stuff by an American, I say modern, for it is in the laconic speech of the Imagistes, even if the subject is classic." H.D.'s poetry was the sort of thing he could show in London and Paris without its being ridiculed: ". . . no excessive use of adjectives, no metaphors that won't permit examination. It's straight talk, straight as the Greek!" [15]

Harriet Monroe's note that accompanied H.D.'s poems in the January 1913 issue of *Poetry* said that these "sketches" from the Greek were neither exact translations nor finalities, but "experiments in delicate and allusive cadences, which attain sometimes a haunting beauty." [16] In a moment of poetic inspiration H.D. had eluded the troubadour's grasp with her elusive and "allusive cadences." Her break into poetry was, at least for that moment, an end to torment.

4

"Priapus" and "Hermes"

WHEN HILDA DOOLITTLE presented Ezra Pound with her newly composed poems, "Priapus" and "Hermes of the Ways," in the tea room of the British Museum in August 1912 she could not have anticipated his response, or for that matter her own.

> I was 21 when Ezra left and it was some years later that he scratched "H.D. Imagiste," in London, in the Museum tea room, at the bottom of a typed sheet, now slashed with his creative pencil, "Cut this out, shorten this line."
> H.D. — Hermes — Hermeticism and all the rest of it.[1]

She had gone to England in 1911 to be with her fiancé and had expected to marry. But instead of marriage, the Pound-H.D. engagement unequivocally ended in the tea room of the British Museum, in Imagism.

As H.D.'s experience reveals, the person with whom we fall in love sometimes puts us in a strange relation to our own lives. Richard Aldington, whose testimony on this matter is not entirely reliable, nevertheless puts the event in the tea shop in an interesting light. According to Aldington, he and H.D. had been studying and writing together at the British Museum. Aldington says: "For some time Ezra had been butting in on our studies and poetic productions, with alternate encouragements and the reverse, according to his mood." Aldington does not recall whether H.D. handed or mailed her poems to Pound, but he reports that "Ezra was so much worked up by these poems of H.D.'s that he removed his pince-nez and informed us that we were Imagists."[2]

Aldington was less than enthusiastic about sharing his afternoons with Pound in tea shops.

> Like other American expatriates, Ezra and H.D. developed an al-
> most insane relish for afternoon tea . . . Moreover, they insisted
> on going to the most fashionable and expensive tea-shops . . . not
> only in London, but in Paris . . . Thus it came about that most of
> our meetings took place in the rather prissy milieu of some infernal
> bun-shop full of English spinsters.
>
> Naturally, then, the Imagist *mouvemong** was born in a tea-
> shop — in the Royal Borough of Kensington.[3]

At the time that H.D. composed "Priapus" and "Hermes of the
Ways," she, Pound, and Aldington had been reading together
from the *Greek Anthology* in the library of the British Museum. In
the *Anthology*, Priapus appears as "he with the beautiful horns."
And no esoteric Freudian understanding is required to grasp the
image presented in the title of this peom; Priapus or *priapos* is the
Greek word for the male genital organ personified as a god. When
H.D.'s poem first appeared in *Poetry* magazine in January 1913, it
was titled "Priapus (Keeper of Orchards)." The poem is not a
translation from the Greek, but it could be described as being inspired by the many epigrams in praise of Priapus that appear in
the *Greek Anthology*. For instance, Crinagoras wrote an epigram
about Priapus which H.D. undoubtedly read.

> Philoxenides offers a modest feast to Pan with the shepherd's
> crook, and Priapus with the beautiful horns. There are grapes ripe
> for wine-making, and fragments of the pomegranate easily split,
> and the yellow marrow of the pine cone, and almonds afraid of
> being cracked, and the bees' ambrosia, and shortcakes of sesame,
> and relishing heads of garlic and pears with shining pips, (?) abun-
> dant little diversions for the stomach of the wine-drinker.[4]

Many of the *Anthology* epigrams on statues of Priapus are meant
to be humorous — for instance, Leonidas's epigram:

> Here on the garden wall did Dinomenes set me up, wakeful Pria-
> pus, to guard his greens. But look, thief, how excited I am. And is
> this, you say, all for the sake of a few greens? For the sake of these
> few.[5]

While H.D.'s "Priapus" attains a beauty that W. R. Paton's English translations in the Loeb Classical Library edition of the *Anthology* do not, its beauty does not preclude the possibility of humor and irony. H.D.'s "Priapus" is, in fact, an ironic comment
upon Pound's phallic/poetic pursuits. There is a section of the *Anthology* titled "Dedicatory Epigrams," in which the Greeks dedi-

---

*The term *mouvemong* presumably stands for "movement." Aldington invented
the term in parody of Pound, who had coined the French-sounding *Imagiste*.

cate the tools of their youthful trade to the gods. In the manner of these epigrams, H.D. assumes the pose of a courtesan grown old and in her "Priapus" dedicates the gifts of her trade, "her womanly charms." She offers "pomegranates already broken,/And shrunken fig,/And quinces untouched," which we immediately recognize as traditional symbols of feminine sexuality.

Thus, when H.D. tells us in the headnote to the poem that "Priapus" is "from the anthology," she is indicating that it at one level derives from epigrams such as those written by Crinagoras and Leonidas and at another brings an offering to the phallic god similar to those of the epigrams — nuts, pomegranates, grapes, and so on.

The stunning clarity of the images presented in H.D.'s early poems was the quality that drew the immediate attention of poets and critics alike. The humorous and ironic quality of "Priapus" was largely unnoticed (except perhaps by Pound). The fundamental irony of H.D.'s poem lies in its relation to the underlying biographical reality as well as in the allusions to the epigrams of the *Anthology,* for the fact of the situation was that H.D. was by temperament and upbringing the very opposite of the courtesan that she felt that Pound was encouraging her to become; she was, as Pound knew, still a virgin at the age of twenty-five.

Like most irony, H.D.'s is of course deadly serious. In the act of writing these poems she was disentangling herself from Pound for good, regardless of how much it hurt either of them. She had had enough, and in a psychic sense chose survival rather than annihilation. Pound could not seem to understand that his romantic plan was a gross insult to H.D. In its January 1913 appearance in *Poetry,* "Priapus" was given the subtitle "Keeper of Orchards" in recognition of the fact that Priapus (Pound) was a keeper of more than one woman — or, shall we say, a keeper of a goodly number of "trees." When the poem appeared in H.D.'s *Collected Poems* in 1925, it was titled simply "Orchard."

"Priapus" is in fact something of a mockery of the troubadour tradition. This makes it all the more amusing that Pound should help publish it as H.D.'s entrance into the world of poetry. The poem calls into question both the troubadour tradition of poetry and the phallic aims of the poet.

> I saw the first pear
> As it fell.
> The honey-seeking, golden-banded,
> The yellow swarm
> Was not more fleet than I,
> (spare us from loveliness!)

And I fell prostrate,
Crying,
Thou hast flayed us with thy blossoms;
Spare us the beauty
Of fruit-trees.

The honey-seeking
Paused not,
The air thundered their song,
And I alone was prostrate.

Oh rough-hewn
God of the orchard,
I bring thee an offering;
Do thou, alone unbeautiful
(Son of the god),
Spare us from loveliness.

The fallen hazel-nuts,
Stripped late of their green sheaths,
The grapes, red-purple,
Their berries
Dripping with wine,
Pomegranates already broken,
And shrunken fig,
And quinces untouched,
I bring thee as offering.[6]

"Hermes of the Ways," the poem that appeared with "Priapus" in *Poetry*, is also closely associated with the *Greek Anthology*. The poem probably takes its title from the dedicatory epigram to Hermes by Phanias, which begins, "To thee, wayside Hermes, I offer this portion of a noble cluster of grapes."[7] (In selecting her title H.D. was of course reading directly from the Greek.)

In H.D.'s early poems the title of the poem often refers to a situation. In Greek mythology, the god Hermes was a "young man on the way up." His duties included making treaties, promoting commerce, and maintaining free rights of way for travelers anywhere in the world. His golden winged sandals carried him about with the swiftness of wind. He foretold the future, summoned the dying, composed the alphabet with the Fates, and invented astronomy, the musical scale, and gymnastics. He hunted with Artemis. He was a well-known thief. All things considered, he was something of a Poundian figure.

The tone of "Hermes" is more solemn than the tone of "Priapus." The poem begins by invoking sea, waves, and shore.

The hard sand breaks,
And the grains of it
Are clear as wine.

Far off over the leagues of it,
The wind,
Playing on the wide shore,
Piles little ridges,
And the great pines
Break over it.

But the poem is really about Hermes, the god of comings and goings, the god of crossroads. And H.D. clearly tells us that this duplicitous or triplicitous god that inhabits the boundaries of social form is a man of infinite patience who is willing to wait for relationships to turn out his way.

But more than the many-foamed waves
Of the sea,
I know him
Of the triple path-ways,
Hermes,
Who awaiteth.

Dubious,
Facing three ways,
Welcoming wayfarers,
He whom the sea-orchard
Shelters from the west,
From the east,
Weathers sea-wind;
Fronts the great dunes.

Wind rushes
Over the dunes,
And the coarse, salt-crusted grass
Answers.

Heu,
It whips round my ankles!

Small is
This white stream,
Flowing below ground
From the poplar-shaded hill,
But the water is sweet.

Apples on the small trees
Are hard,
Too small,
Too late ripened

By a desperate sun
That struggles through sea-mist.

The boughs of the trees
Are twisted
By many bafflings;
Twisted are
The small-leafed boughs.

But the shadow of them
Is not the shadow of the mast head
Nor of the torn sails.

Hermes, Hermes
The great sea foamed,
Gnashed its teeth about me;
But you have waited,
Where sea-grass tangles with
Shore-grass.[8]

In presenting Pound with "Hermes" and "Priapus," H.D. some-what unwittingly made a gesture that was full of ambivalence; so many contradictory stances are expressed in the poetry that it would have been almost impossible for Pound to know what she meant, expected, or wanted on any personal level. There are lines that suggest commitment and trust — "But you have waited," etc. There are lines that express frustration, desperation, and a sense of sexual inadequacy — "Apples on the small trees/Are hard,/Too small," etc. And there are lines, particularly in "Pria-pus," that express disenchantment and bitter amusement. Pound could have responded to these poems in any number of ways. The point is that the way he *did* respond influenced both the Pound-H.D. relationship and the course of modern poetry.

H.D.'s very name as a poet was given to her that August day in the museum tea room by Ezra Pound. The fact that she became a published poet was a decision made by Pound over afternoon tea in August 1912.

While H.D.'s surface response to Pound's reading and accep-tance of her poems was one of liberation and self-satisfaction, her later poetry reveals that at the deep psychic level she experienced his violent editing of her poem and his rechristening her with a pseudonym as traumatic. H.D.'s suppressed sense of trauma, be-trayal, and loss in relation to this event was primarily a result of the way in which Pound appropriated her new poems. It is not immediately obvious why H.D. should feel betrayed by Pound's apparent enthusiasm for her new poems, but if we consider the matter in the light of their early relationship in Pennsylvania, the matter is not so difficult to understand.

From the perspective of 1958, when at the age of seventy-one H.D. wrote her memoir of Pound, it was clear to her that her early poetry was inseparable from her love for Pound. She writes: "The significance of 'first love' cannot be overestimated . . . By what miracle does the marriage *du ciel et de la terre* find consummation? It filled my fantasies and dreams, my prose and my poetry for ten years."[9]

The chasm that had opened when H.D. learned of Pound's engagement to Dorothy Shakespear had led her to a conscious effort toward artistic achievement. In 1912 H.D. realized that her marriage to Pound would never take place, and she was actively attempting to disentangle herself from her emotional relationship with him. At some level she wanted literally to "write him off" and begin her life anew. H.D. and Pound had attended lectures on Bergson given by T. E. Hulme at the home of Mrs. Franz Liebich between November 23 and December 14, 1911, and it was during this time that H.D. became involved in the study and writing of poetry as a process of disentanglement and discovery.

H.D. presented her newly composed poems to Pound in a spirit of triumph; she was frankly pleased with herself. After years of studying Pound and the texts he had recommended to her, she had written her first real poetry, an artistic and intellectual achievement. She gave Pound these first poems to let him know that the pupil had finally understood what poetry is — that she had at last, after ten years' study, mastered the wisdom of her teacher. Her intellectual and aesthetic dependence was over; in a momentary sense, at least, she was free of Pound, liberated by her own artistic effort from this Priapus, this Hermes. Moreover, she had named him and described him accurately, at least from her own perspective.

Pound's immediate response was to edit her, slash her, and put her up on public display as his "discovery." From that day forward he treated the poetry as an invitation to begin a troubadour romance, a public dialogue filled with hidden messages. The impetus of H.D.'s creative efforts had been to establish her life outside of its former emotional context and to put the past behind her, but Pound's actions placed her squarely in the forefront of the public world of poetry as his "lady," and resolved, for Pound at least, the problem of more than one engagement: Dorothy would be his wife; H.D. would be his muse.

Undoubtedly H.D. had not thought in advance how Pound might respond to her efforts, but the way in which he did respond influenced her for the rest of her life. As Freud writes in his *General Introduction to Psychoanalysis,* "An experience which we call traumatic is one which within a very short space of time subjects the mind to such a very high increase of stimulation that assimilation or elaboration of it can no longer be effected by normal means, so that lasting disturbances must result in the distribution of the available energy in the mind." [10]

It was in precisely this sense that this experience with Pound was traumatic for H.D. From her stance, the poems had been written as she came into knowledge; they were written for *her,* for herself. The poems had to do with H.D.'s own relationship to her own experience; they were introspective studies. They were not written for public exhibition, and they were not written for Pound. Pound even acknowledges in his letters that "it was only by persistence that I got to see [these poems] at all." [11] When H.D. presented Pound with them, he behaved as though they were his, as though they had been written to and for him. Then, like Hermes the thief, he stole her poetry; he robbed her of the right to make a decision about the publication of her own work. He took command of it. Later, in *Helen in Egypt,* H.D. alluded to Pound as "The Command."

How to talk about power and the way in which one person goes about achieving it over another? Pound's appropriation of H.D.'s poems was a power play which to some extent worked. In a psychic sense H.D. became, as it were, traumatically bonded to Pound's new poetic culture. Rather than being liberated from her emotional entanglement with Pound, she became involved in a "new cycle of enchantment." Pound accomplished this psychic reversal by treating H.D.'s poetic discoveries in "Priapus" and "Hermes" as discoveries about herself rather than about him. In short, he treated the poetry as though it had been written about her for him, when in reality it had been written about him for her own enlightenment. Quite a coup!

H.D. wrote these first poems in the context of an understanding, and that understanding was violated when Pound rushed the poems into publication. Of course Pound did not intend to betray her, but H.D. experienced the publishing of the poems and the turning of these perceptions into the cornerstone of a literary movement as a betrayal of a trust. The fiery kisses, too, had been exchanged in the context of an understanding. She writes: "Anyway, would she, this — the period Miss of our narrative, have gone on with the fiery kisses that I speak of, in the beginning, unless there had been — had been — at least, an understanding?" [12]

H.D.'s later work reveals her deep sense of violation. In transforming Hilda Doolittle into H.D., Imagiste, and muse, Pound, she felt, was making an object of her. It was a deep insult to her integrity as a woman, and a further rejection of the relationship she had sought in coming to England to join him. But these feelings were not really conscious. At the time she was shocked and traumatized by his action, and it would take her a lifetime to come fully to terms with the nature and effects of this event and its resulting psychic violence. In fact, H.D. never really recovered from that first assault. In *Helen in Egypt,* which H.D. called her Cantos, she alludes to the event as "Apollo's snare":

> Was it Apollo's snare
> so that poets forever,
> should be caught in the maze of the Walls
>
> of a Troy that never fell? [13]

If H.D. had been more aware of her feelings at the time, she might have been less passive. She might have reclaimed her own poems, and the explosion that so changed English and American poetry might never have happened.

"Hermes of the Ways" and "Priapus" were received at the time of their publication as pathbreaking poems. They were widely acclaimed and were collected in several anthologies. Regardless of how Pound may have felt about the implicit characterization of himself in them, he recognized first-rate work. In fact, he built the Imagist movement around these first two poems of H.D.'s.

Later in her life H.D. was to say that the landscape of her early poetry, including "Hermes of the Ways," was not Greek as much as it was the remembered seacoast of her childhood. She often told Norman Holmes Pearson that "her nature imagery, for example, was never really Greek but came from her childhood reminiscences of Watch Hill and the coasts of Rhode Island and Maine, which she used to visit with her friends as a child." [14]

Certainly H.D.'s first experiences with Ezra Pound are present in these poems, even if their use is not fully conscious on the part of the poet. This palimpsest character of the image presented in "Hermes" — that is, a buried level of experience coming through the surface writing — gives the poem its depth. We are reminded of those early outdoor experiences with Pound, described so poignantly in the novel "Her," and in *End to Torment:* "First kisses? In the woods, in the winter — . . . Lie down under the trees. Die there . . . we sway with the wind. There is no wind. We sway with the stars. They are not far." [15]

The shock of learning of Pound's engagement to Dorothy was not unrelated to the act of artistic creation. This was clear to H.D.

in 1958, some forty-six years later. But what a person is conscious of many years afterward may be unconscious, or as H.D. puts it, "suppressed," at the time. H.D.'s psychic make-up was such that she had this sort of delayed realization in relation to many of the traumatic events of her life. Contemporary psychological theory teaches us that such suppressed or delayed consciousness is in part a protection of the integrity of the ego or the self. And there is a sense in which it promotes creative activity, because it allows for a kind of palimpsest quality in a work of art. One level of experience is expressed as the surface layer of the work, but levels of suppressed experience come through, as it were, from beneath the surface. In the act of writing poetry the artist recovers experience that has been buried in the unconscious. The poem is written in a kind of intuitive consciousness and understood later at an analytical level.

If H.D. had been fully aware of how much she cared for Pound, she might have realized how vulnerable this act of self-expression would make her and how susceptible she was rendering herself to being badly hurt. "Priapus" is so full of amusement, and the metaphor is so extraordinarily clever, that one might not expect its author to be vulnerable in relation to it.

Contemporary psychoanalytical critics of H.D. — for instance, Norman N. Holland and Joseph Riddel — maintain that at the deepest psychic level H.D.'s poetry is derived from the universal feminine situation expressed in the technical concept of penis envy, or in lay terms, a wish to obtain the male organ or "priapus." [16] There is no doubt that H.D. presents a sense of loss and loneliness in her early poems, as Holland and Riddel maintain. But it is also quite clear that her project was not to obtain a male organ in the sense of becoming a man, but rather to express unhappiness about the loss of the man she loved. The attachment to Pound had been traumatically broken; H.D.'s poetry emerged as true sublimation in the classical sense.

The classical concept of sublimation is not unrelated to Freud's concept of sublimation. In the process of writing the poem H.D. was vividly aware of her subject (for instance, the boughs of the trees in "Hermes" are vividly presented). While she was acutely aware of her subject, she was not very aware of herself. The poem takes the place of awareness of self; the consciousness of self is sublimated, as it were, into the poem.

> The boughs of the trees
> are twisted
> by many bafflings;

twisted are
the small leafed boughs.

In these early poems H.D. presents self as nature, nature as self. Self and nature correspond; they are one. Repressed emotion breaks out in the disguised form of art. All of the anguish is contained within the poetic expression. Life forces and fears are expressed in what we might understand as sublimated and, to use H.D.'s word, palimpsest form. The result is vivid and intense poetry.

In his essay "On the Sublime," Longinus says, "Sublimity is the echo of a great soul"; that is, sublimity is the echo of great depth of experience.[17] H.D.'s poetry has often been compared to Sappho's, of which Longinus said: "Are you not amazed how at one instant she summons, as though they were all alien from herself and dispersed, soul, body, ears, tongue, eyes, color? Uniting contradictions, she is, at one and the same time, hot and cold, in her senses and out of her mind, for she is either terrified or at the point of death."[18]

Longinus might have been speaking about H.D.'s early poems. In this sense Pound was entirely correct in describing them as "straight as the Greek!" And Plato, too, might have been talking about H.D.'s early poems when he said that all great poets "compose their beautiful poems not by art, but because they are inspired and possessed."[19]

Pound behaved as though H.D. had been possessed by him. When he talked about Imagism as *vers libre* in his many essays on the subject, he was alluding to H.D.'s poems and the poems he had written in response to them. To his credit, he praised H.D.'s poetry with undaunted enthusiasm. In speaking about *vers libre,* he said: "I think one should write *vers libre* only when one 'must,' that is to say, only when the 'thing' builds up a rhythm more beautiful than that of set meters, or more real, more a part of the emotion of the 'thing,' more germane, intimate, interpretive than the measure of regular accentual verse."[20]

H.D. wrote her first poems as a result of inner compulsion; the "thing," as Pound puts it, had built up to a tension that had to be expressed. To the question, "By what miracle does the marriage *du ciel et de la terre* find consummation?" we might answer that in H.D.'s case, it found consummation in the eternal reality of the poem. H.D.'s orientation toward purity of experience, which she had inherited from home and family, became redirected toward the purity of poetry.

5

Rebellious Marriage

IN "PAINT IT TODAY" H.D. tells the story of her relationship with Ezra Pound in England and of her rebellious marriage to Richard Aldington. She tells of how she had been "hurt and baffled" by Pound, whom she describes as a "hectic adolescent" and a "blundering, untried, mischievous and irreverent male youth."

> She had parted with the youth, having gained nothing from him but a feeling that someone had tampered with an oracle, had banged on a temple door, had dragged out small, curious, sacred ornaments, had not understood their inner meaning, yet with a slight sense of their inner value, their perfect tint and carving, had not stolen them, but left them, perhaps worse, exposed by the roadside, reft from their shelter and their holy setting.[1]

H.D. refers to the Pound character as "the fiancé" — not as *her* fiancé, but as *the* fiancé, acknowledging somewhat sardonically that he is engaged to more than one woman. As late as 1958, in *End to Torment,* she clearly had not forgotten the shock of the discovery of Pound's engagement to Dorothy Shakespear. Nor had she forgotten his other engagements. "I remember how he said to me in London, . . . 'Let's be engaged — don't tell . . .' well, whoever it was, not just then Dorothy." "Then you were the third in line?" "No — I was the first — ."[2]

Just what Pound had in mind when in 1910 he asked Hilda to renew their engagement and join him in London is not entirely clear; what is clear is that his intentions in relation to her were not as noble as he had led her to believe. Gradually she began to be interested in Richard Aldington, an aspiring English man of letters six years younger than she, born in Dover and educated at London University. But in a sense H.D.'s interest in Aldington was not entirely separable from her ten-year bondage to Pound. In an un-published novel titled "Asphodel" (1922), she implies that her at-traction to Richard Aldington in 1911 involved an element of re-bellion against Ezra Pound.

> In the light of Darrington's [Aldington's] arrival, she could afford to sting at him, "Don't you think, George [Ezra], it was a little, just a little odd — "
> "Odd, Dryad?"
> "I mean if you were engaged all that time — to — kiss me."
> "The odd thing is not to kiss you, Dryad . . . Listen Dryad, darling —"
> "Oh George, you might — you might have told me —"
> "Dryad developing a Puritan conscience?"
> "No-no that isn't the argument . . . Would you be affable if I were engaged to — to — Darrington?" . . .
> This couldn't conceivably go on forever.[3]

In spite of the fact that H.D. had been deeply hurt by Pound, she blamed not him but herself. She had been naive and gullible enough to be taken in by him. "The fiancé had shown Midget [H.D.] what love might be or become, if one, in desperation, should accept the shadow of an understanding for an understanding itself."[4]

In the springs of 1912 and 1913 Aldington, H.D., and Pound explored Paris and Venice together. In the fall of 1913 H.D. made a rather hasty decision to marry Aldington. According to her, the marriage was based upon a sudden mutual attraction. In his novel *Death of a Hero* (1929), composed ten years after the marriage failed, Aldington suggests with characteristic sarcasm that it was based on a missed menstrual period. In "Paint It Today" H.D. implies that her state of mind in relation to the marriage was one of defiance: "No, I am not engaged. After the Raymond [Pound] fiasco, I couldn't be engaged. I won't be engaged. But I'm going to marry Basil [Aldington]. No, no, no. Just marry him. No one is to come. *No* one. We are going to a registrar's or whatever it is's office. *No* one is to come."[5]

Later H.D. was to conclude that her attraction to Aldington had had more to do with the adventure the three of them had in Paris and Venice than with the man himself; she realized that she had projected her feelings for Pound and for Paris onto Aldington. This realization set the stage for her presentation of Aldington as Paris in her "Iphigeneia" — an appellation that reappears in var-ious poems through *Helen in Egypt*. "Darrington got his job, came over. Paris suddenly became (with the coming of Darrington)

Paris. Space existed as space, Paris as Paris."[6] In her imaginative life, H.D. associated Aldington first with the city of Paris and later with the mythological Paris who had stolen Helen from Menelaus.

In 1913 H.D. was more than a little attracted to the idea of marriage, especially after the cavalier treatment she had received from Pound. Her upbringing had, of course, taught her to have no romantic involvement that would not lead to marriage. For years she had been involved in the idealistic notion of a poetic relationship modeled on the marriage of Robert and Elizabeth Browning. In fact, the Brownings, whom she had learned about from Pound, were a major influence on H.D. as models for future literature and life.

To all outward appearances H.D. and Aldington were a perfect match. In the initial months the marriage seemed to conform to H.D.'s ideal. Aldington was a young poet and like H.D. committed to classical subjects. As Amy Lowell observed, "It is strange to find two young people reading Greek 'for fun.' But this was just what 'H.D.' and Mr. Aldington did."[7] Aldington was handsome, well educated, and talented. "Hilda was good-looking and charming . . . Here were two poets, man and woman, who were happy together and worked together; at this time, at any rate, their relation seemed . . . to be an ideal one."[8]

H.D. and Aldington were married in England in October 1913, with the bride's parents and Ezra Pound as witnesses. In "Winter Love" H.D. recalls Pound's attitude at the ceremony (one of H.D.'s names for Pound in "Winter Love," as in *Helen in Egypt,* is Menelaus):

> and Menelaus by the altar, whispering,
>
> no stinging, honeyed sigh, but
> "it's all right, it's no great matter,
> this will soon be over."[9]

Pound married Dorothy Shakespear about six months after H.D.'s wedding, but his commitment to troubadour romanticism as a poetic and cultural form was as strong as ever. Shortly after his marriage he and Dorothy moved in across the hall from H.D. and Aldington. John Cournos* writes: "H.D. (Hilda Doolittle) and Richard Aldington, newly married, lived in Holland Place

*John Cournos (1882–1966) was a Russian-born American writer whom H.D. met in London through Pound. While not essentially a poet, he was counted among the original Imagists and was an active member of the circle until 1918. His novel *Miranda Masters* (1926) portrays his relationship to H.D. during the war years.

Chambers, not many yards from my lodgings and Ezra Pound, on his marriage, took up his abode with his Dorothy just across the landing from the Aldingtons."[10] In *End to Torment,* H.D. writes,

> Ezra and Dorothy had a slightly larger flat across the narrow hall. I found the door open one day before they were married, and Ezra there. "What — what are you doing?" I asked. He said he was looking for a place where he could fence with Yeats. I was rather taken aback when they actually moved in. It was so near.[11]

Pound consistently refused to take H.D.'s marriage seriously. A quotation from Pound regarding one of his favorite troubadours, Guillaume St. Leider, may give us some sense of his attitude toward it and toward Aldington's capacity as a poet and a lover: "If you wish to make love to women in public, and out loud, you must resort to subterfuge; and Guillaume St. Leider even went so far as to get the husband of his lady to do the seductive singing."[12]

As H.D. relates in her *End to Torment,* the Aldingtons moved out of their flat shortly after the Pounds moved in across the hall: "We went soon after to Hampstead, to a larger flat that a friend had found us."[13]

> Soon after seeing some of these original or early *Canto* variations, in the Pounds' Holland Place apartment in Kensington, opposite our own flat, we moved. [These Cantos contained many allusions to H.D.] Black-out. Just a memory of a shock at the look, the lines, the words on the newly printed pages that Ezra showed us. Mrs. Shakespear's brother said, "Why must he write about things that we all do every day and don't talk about."[14]

Pound's intrusions into H.D.'s privacy at this time were causing grave tensions in her marriage. In spite of the fact that the three poets were friends, Pound's attentions were clearly unwelcome, both by Aldington and by H.D. He would burst without warning into their apartment to read drafts from his poems inspired by Fenollosa — the poems that were later to be collected in *Cathay.*[15]

During this period Pound did a good deal to promote H.D.'s work. He did not simply thrust her into the world and abandon her. One might even maintain that he was in some instances protective of her; he took responsibility for her in the literary world. In a sense Pound's remarks about Imagism are the best description of H.D.'s work that we have. The poet should present, said Pound; poetry must "discover something."[16]

After her marriage H.D.'s poetry presented new qualities of intensity. In "Sitalkas," published in the fall 1913 issue of *The New Freewoman* (the magazine H.D. and Aldington were later to coedit as the *Egoist*), we are presented with an image of quiet fulfillment. The sublime quality developed in the writing of the first poems had become a habit of mind and is still present, but the feeling expressed in "Sitalkas" is no longer of loss but of discovery.

> Thou are come at length
> more beautiful
> than any cool god
> in a chamber under
> Lycia's far coast,
> than any high god
> who touches us not
> here in the seeded grass,
> aye than Argestes
> scattering the broken leaves.[17]

The "broken leaves" of "Sitalkas" can, of course, be read to mean leaves or pages of a book, perhaps a book of poems, just as the "small, curious, sacred ornaments" of "Paint It Today" that the irreverent adolescent tampers with and exposes might refer to the poems appropriated by Pound in the tea room of the British Museum. There is in "Sitalkas" a wry and to-the-point comparison of husband and troubadour, and the husband emerges as the chosen lover. H.D. has begun to tell her story in her poems, and she is now fully conscious of what she is talking about.

Pound rejected H.D. as a wife; H.D. rejected Pound as a troubadour lover; Pound took upon himself the role of literary agent for H.D.'s poetry. Why then should he find cause for complaint when H.D. asked him when her poems were to appear in print? He did, however. We can read his ironic and humorous response in his poem "Tempora."

> The Dryad stands in my courtyard
> with plaintive, querulous crying.
> (Tamuz. Io! Tamuz!)
> Oh, no, she is not crying: 'Tamuz'
> She says, 'May my poems be printed this week?'
> The god Pan is afraid to ask you, may my poems be
> printed this week?[18]

Tamuz is the spirit of annual vegetation and is associated with pagan orgiastic rights. Io is associated with the moon. The call "Io! Tamuz!" usually denotes sexual passion, but Dryad has chosen to sublimate her passion into poetry. Hence Pound's ironic complaint.

In his very insightful and helpful introduction to the *Collected Early Poems of Ezra Pound,* Louis Martz speaks of Pound's poem "The Summons" as being "addressed to a lady who seems to be an image of poetic inspiration (perhaps, literally, H.D.)."[19] Martz is undoubtedly correct, for many of Pound's poems are addressed quite frankly and directly to H.D.

In a poem upon a theme as old as poetry itself, Pound reminds his lady that she will grow old sublimating her passion. The poem is titled "The Tea Shop," an allusion to the tea room of the British Museum. Pound's poem has a note of bitterness in it.

> The girl in the tea shop
>   is not so beautiful as she was.
>   The August has worn against her.
> She does not get up the stairs so easily;
> yes, she also will turn middle aged,
> and the glow of youth that she spread about us
>   as she brought us our muffins
> will be spread about us no longer
>   she also will turn middle aged.[20]

The muffins brought by the girl in the tea shop are analogous to poems. Pastry is a recurring metaphor for poetry in Pound's work; late in his life Pound referred to his early poems as "a collection of stale cream puffs," and also quipped "with a wry gesture of affection, echoing his poem, 'Piccadilly' ":[21]

> Chocolate creams, who hath
> forgotten you?[22]

From H.D.'s point of view, the real problem with Pound's appropriation and acclamation of her poems was that her emergence as a poet would allow Pound to organize his life with her in the troubadour mode. He had won the battle; whether he would win the war (and his lady) would be another matter altogether.

In the October 1912 issue of *Poetry,* Pound published "Middle-Aged (A Study in Emotion)," which speaks to the writing of H.D.'s poems and their emotional impact on him. The key to our understanding of the hidden dimension of this poem is given in a letter which accompanied the poem when it was sent to Harriet Monroe at *Poetry.* In this letter Pound sardonically acknowledges his estrangement from H.D. by describing his "Study in Emotion" as "an over-elaborate post-Browning 'Imagiste' affair."[23] In the poem he writes of his strained relations with H.D. Using the familiar pastry motif, Pound presents an image of a dead Egyptian king — a buried king.

'Tis but a vague, invarious delight
As gold that rains about some buried king.

As the fine flakes,
When tourists frolicking
Stamp on his roof or in the glazing light
Try photographs, wolf down their ale and cakes
And start to inspect some further pyramid;

As the fine dust, in the hid cell beneath
Their transitory step and merriment,
Drifts through the air, and the sarcophagus
Gains yet another crust
Of useless riches for the occupant . . .[24]

The "vague, invarious delight" that has prompted this image is undoubtedly the Imagist poetry written by H.D. — "Hermes" and "Priapus." The poem reveals quite clearly that the content of H.D.'s poems dealt Pound a severe blow. It suggests that Pound felt like a deposed king, as if he had lost his power over H.D. and over the world he had created for them. His reign was over.

So I, the fires that lit once dreams
Now over and spent
Lie dead within four walls
And so now love
Rains down and so enriches some stiff case,
And strews a mind with precious metaphors . . .

The photographs, the ale and cakes, the fine dust, and the crust of useless riches all express how Pound felt about H.D.'s poems. In other words, Pound is saying that while professionally he has to praise the poetry, H.D.'s emergence as a poet and the distance expressed in her poems is hard on him as well as on her.

In attempting to understand why H.D. left Pound for Aldington, we will find it instructive to return to H.D.'s novel "Her" and allow the prose once again to illuminate the life. What H.D. had come at last to understand is that Pound wanted the muse, the poet, not the wife: "He wanted Her, but he wanted a Her that he called decorative. George wanted a Her out of the volumes on the floor."[25]

In imploring Hermione Dart to see him upon his return from Europe, George Lowdnes was saying *"bellisima* and he must see *bellisima."* From abroad he had written: "Hermione, I'm coming back to Gawd's own god-damn country."[26] An enigmatic ultimatum! H.D./Hermione did not know what Ezra/George wanted. "George might have wished there were more coquetry in her, or George might have been relieved there was not."[27]

H.D.'s parents had despised Pound's influence on their daughter; Hermione's parents express their conviction that she is being manipulated by George: "George Lowdnes is teaching you, actually *teaching* you words, telling you what to say."[28] Had H.D.'s parents' rejection of Pound as their daughter's suitor created in him a deep desire to prove himself in the world? It is hard to believe that the attitude of H.D.'s family had no effect on him at all.

In "Her," H.D. characterizes her mother's sarcastic attitude toward Pound's literary achievements thus: "Poor George Lowdnes. I thought you said that he was getting on famously, that all London, Munich, Paris and Berlin were at his feet, that he was chanting his verses to crowded houses, at tea parties." Hermione responds: "I didn't say anything of the sort. I said that Zates [Yeats] had praised him in a review, that Addox Nord [Ford Madox Ford] wanted him to help in a new book he's doing, that —" And Eugenia replies: "Hermione, this will *kill* me."[29]

Although H.D. knew that the attitude of her family, which had torn her apart, was partially to blame for the broken engagement, her final illumination was that her appointed role in Pound's Apollonian scheme to be a poet and create a new Renaissance was muse, not wife. Pound had written that it would be inimical to the spirit of poetry to marry one's muse. As H.D. expressed this matter in "Her":

> It was George back at the beginning, starting where they had left off so long ago, a month ago? A year ago? "How long ago is it, George, since we were here last? I mean since that first day you came back from Venice?" George said, pressing her head down into tufts of soft moss, moss now with moonlight on it, "It's several volumes back if I remember."*[30]

---

*The volumes alluded to are *Hilda's Book* (1907), *A Lume Spento* (1908), *A Quinzaine for This Yule* (1909), *Canzoni* (1909), *Personae* (1909), *Exultations* (1910), and *The Spirit of Romance* (1910).

6

Hawk as Hawk
and Hawk as Persona

EZRA POUND did not coin the word *Imagism* in the first instance
to describe H.D.'s poems. Rather, it seems that in early 1912 he
had conceived of a literary movement that would include H.D.,
Aldington, himself, and perhaps others. The term *Imagism* was
part of the propaganda he was preparing for the movement even
before the poetry that would be called Imagist was written. It was
within this context, Pound later maintained, that he launched the
Imagist movement with the poetry of H.D. and Aldington. But
the poetic principles that came to define Imagism were ideas that
a number of young London poets could ascribe to and were discussing quite independently of Pound.

In the *Egoist* of May 1, 1915, F. S. Flint presented an essay entitled
"The History of Imagism." In it he states that in the course of a
series of lectures on recent books of poetry, he had been advocat-
ing a movement akin in spirit to Japanese poetry, a kind of *vers
libre.* He had become acquainted with the philosopher T. E.
Hulme, who had proposed that they should get together "a few
congenial spirits" and "have weekly meetings in a Soho restaurant."[1] These meetings began in March of 1909. Flint writes:

> I think that what brought the real nucleus of this group together
> was a dissatisfaction with English poetry as it was then (and is still,
> alas!) being written. We proposed at various times to replace it by
> pure *vers libre;* by the Japanese *tanka* and *haikai* . . . In all this
> Hulme was ringleader. He insisted too on absolutely accurate pre-
> sentation and no verbiage . . . There was also a lot of talk and
> practice among us, Storer leading it chiefly, of what we called the
> Image. We were very much influenced by modern symbolist po-
> etry . . .

48

On April 22, 1909, Ezra Pound, whose book, *Personae,* had been published on the previous Friday, joined the group . . . He was very full of his troubadours.[2]

According to Flint, Pound's contribution to the group was little more than an attempt to illustrate (or refute) the theories being discussed by reference to the troubadours. In a January 1915 letter to Aldington, Flint stated emphatically that in 1909 and 1910 "Pound added *nothing* to their meetings — absolutely nothing."[3]

"The group died a lingering death at the end of its second winter. But its discussions had a sequel."[4] In October 1912, at the same time Pound was sending H.D.'s poems off to *Poetry* magazine, he published at the end of his book *Ripostes* five poems — thirty-three lines — called "The Complete Poetical Works of T. E. Hulme." Originally conceived as blackboard exercises, they carried a preface in which these words are written: "As for the future, *Les Imagistes,* the descendants of the forgotten school of 1909 (previously referred to as the 'School of Images') have that in their keeping."[5]

Pound's actual involvement in Hulme's ideas and in modern French poetry coincided with H.D.'s arrival in London in the fall of 1911 and her subsequent involvement with Aldington, who was already writing a kind of *vers libre.* H.D., Aldington, and F. S. Flint, whom H.D. met at Brigit Patmore's at the same time she met Aldington, began to study Henri de Regnier, Rémy de Gourmont, and other contemporary French poets in the context of the poetic theories that Flint and Hulme had been developing since 1909. Pound, who could never be described as a slow learner or one to be left by the wayside, quickly developed an intense interest in Hulme's ideas, and with Hulme's return from the continent in the late fall of 1911 reinvolved himself in the discussions and introduced H.D. to Hulme.

As Pound began to take Hulme's ideas seriously, and about the time H.D. was beginning to conceive her first Imagist poems, we begin to see a transition in Pound's work from what we might call traditional romanticism to a more refined classicism (or Imagism). Undoubtedly Pound's relationship with Hulme, who was an advocate of the new classicism in poetry, added a dimension to his own concept of art.

While H.D. had rejected the direction of Pound's troubadour romanticism, she shared his newfound enthusiasm for Hulme's ideas. Hulme wrote of poetry as a process of discovery and disentanglement. He argued that through a certain tension of mind the great artist is able to discover fresh metaphors of perception. Because of the artist's clarity of vision, readers are convinced of the truth expressed in the poem.

"The object of aesthetic contemplation," says Hulme, "is something framed apart from itself and regarded without memory or expectation, simply as being itself, as an end and not a means, as individual not universal."[6] Hulme believed that the image in poetry is never mere decoration, but the very essence of an intuitive language, a different kind of thinking. He wrote: "A powerfully imaginative mind seizes and combines at the same instant all the important ideas of its poem or picture, and while it works with one of them it is at the same instant working with and modifying all in their relation to it and never losing sight of their bearings on each other."[7] When you read a true poem, says Hulme, you feel at once as though the artist was in an actual physical state in the act of writing it.

It is undoubtedly incorrect to maintain that H.D. was writing from a theoretical perspective. But when she presented Pound with her first Imagist poems, no matter what else he may have thought, he recognized them immediately as a fulfillment of the criteria set out by Hulme. He recognized the authenticity and literary merit of her poetic voice. There is no doubt that on a purely professional level — if we can in this instance separate the professional from the personal — Pound was impressed and moved by what H.D. had accomplished in these first poems written in London. The truth of the matter is that while a number of people were involved in theories that came to be identified with Imagism, H.D. and Pound were the "real" Imagists; they were the creators of something new in poetry. And they had been inspired by each other and by Hulme. Aldington, Fletcher, Flint, and the others who came later to be associated with Imagism were part of a group, an "ism," but the poetical or spiritual connection that gave rise to the actual dynamic poetry was between H.D. and Pound.

A good deal of Pound's critical writing during this period, from 1912 to 1913, is the best we have on this new poetry. Of the meaning of symbols, Pound wrote: "I believe that the proper and perfect symbol is the natural object, that if a man uses 'symbols' he must so use them that their symbolic function does not obtrude; so that a sense, and the poetic quality of the passage, is not lost to those who do not understand the symbol as such, to whom, for instance, a hawk is a hawk."[8] H.D.'s early poetry passed this test. There were many who understood her poetry at the level of the hawk as hawk.

Of the image, Pound wrote:

An image is that which presents an intellectual and emotional complex in an instant of time . . .

It is the presentation of such a "complex" instantaneously which gives that sense of sudden liberation; that sense of freedom from time limits and space limits; that sense of sudden growth, which we experience in the presence of the greatest works of art.

It is better to present one Image in a lifetime than to produce voluminous works.[9]

Pound wrote these words at a time when his enthusiasm for H.D. and her work was at a peak. His comments on language are apropos both for the poems collected in H.D.'s *Sea Garden* and for his own *Cathay:* "Use no superfluous word, no adjective which does not reveal something . . . the natural object is always the adequate symbol."[10]

In her use of the image, H.D. presents "the intellectual and emotional complex in an instant of time." The natural object — reed, weed, rose — is the adequate symbol which both conceals and reveals. The metaphorical layer of meaning in H.D.'s poetry, the layer at which the landscape in nature is a metaphor for the landscape of the mind and body, is one of the most complex in the work. It is interesting because it is deliberately ambiguous; the body referred to metaphorically may be either the physical body or the body of the imagination. There is, in fact, the suggestion that these two dimensions of reality are not only related, but the same.

In *Some Imagist Poets* (1915) H.D. published three poems —"Sea Rose," "Sea Lily," and "Sea Iris" — in which the image of the body of the imagination is presented in three different stances or points of location. In "Sea Lily" the image is of a reed:

> REED,
> slashed and torn
> but doubly rich —
> such great heads as yours
> drift upon temple-steps,
> but you are shattered
> in the wind . . .[11]

In "Sea Iris" the reed is a weed:

> WEED,
> moss-weed,
> root tangled in sand,
> sea-iris, brittle flower,
> one petal like a shell
> is broken, and you print a shadow
> like a thin twig . . .[12]

In the third poem, "Sea Rose," the reed and the weed become a rose:

> ROSE,
> harsh rose,
> marred and with stint of petals,
> meager flower, thin,
> sparse of leaf,
>
> more precious
> than a wet rose
> single on a stem —
> you are caught in the drift . . .[13]

These poems are not merely projections of the physical self onto the natural world, nor are they merely projections of emotions onto the natural world. Nature is not a manifestation of the poet; it would be truer to say that H.D. sees herself as a manifestation of nature.

Is she a weed or a reed or a rose? It depends upon your point of location, and also upon your clarity of vision. But for those to whom a rose is a rose, just as for those to whom a hawk is a hawk, the natural object presented is the adequate symbol. The symbolic function does not obtrude, and the poetic quality of the passage is not lost.

Pound and H.D. were creating a modern metaphysical poetry, but one does not have to be a metaphysician to appreciate and experience the beauty of each poem. Pound conceived of a new literary aristocracy which was to be based not on birth nor on education, not on position nor profession nor class, but on sensibility, one's aesthetic sensitivity to the possibilities and nuances of language. As for twentieth-century poetry, Pound thought we were in for a change: "It will, I think, move against poppycock, it will be harder and saner . . . 'nearer to the bone.' It will be as much like granite as it can be, its force will lie in its truth, its interpretive power." [14]

While they didn't know it at the time, H.D. and Pound were creating a poetry that was conceptually consistent with both the new physics of Einstein and the new psychology of Freud. It is clear that in Pound's concept of poetry he is talking about a world in which the line between subject and object has all but disappeared; emotions are not merely subjective but also objective. A lyric poem, whether his own or H.D.'s is (like a dream) the property of a collective whole. The Imagist vision is of a world in which the most intensely subjective experience becomes the hardest and sanest objective.

Every new idea, said Pound, has its own rhythm, its own form: "I believe in absolute 'rhythm,' a rhythm that is, in poetry, which corresponds exactly to the emotion or shade of emotion to be expressed. A man's rhythm must be interpretive. It will be, therefore, in the end, his own, uncounterfeiting, uncounterfeitable." [15]

H.D.'s poetry fulfilled all of Pound's Imagist criteria. But it added a further dimension as well. H.D.'s poetry is a lyric flow of cadences, full of content; and her ambience is feminine. It is the body of the woman, her own experienced reality, which H.D. recreates in each poem.

In contrast to the Symbolists and the Romantics, the Imagists believed in presentation rather than representation. One thing does not "stand for" another thing in H.D.'s early poems. Rather, all things are emanations, as it were, of life itself. In H.D.'s poetry there is a kind of spiritual etymology, a translation of one set of symbols into another. The poetry enacts a sort of metaphysical intercourse, the translation of the male body into the female body, making these two part of one landscape: the "honey and the bee," "the petal of black poppy and the opiate of the flower." These male and female life energies in union give H.D.'s poetry its dynamic vitality, as in the union of tree and sea in "Oread":

> Whirl up, sea —
> Whirl your pointed pines,
> Splash your great pines
> On our rocks,
> Hurl your green over us,
> Cover us with your pools of fir. [16]

Whether the poet, or for that matter the reader, is consciously aware of the meaning of "the symbol as such," at one level at least the image is always symbolic, because language is itself symbolic. And an image presented phenomenologically is open to varying symbolic interpretations. It is so very difficult to present what one sees, and as Hulme says:

> The great aim [of poetry] is accurate, precise and definite description. The first thing to recognize is how extraordinarily difficult this is. It is no mere matter of carefulness; you have to use language and language is by its very nature a communal thing . . . But each man sees a little differently, and to get out clearly and exactly what he does see, he must have a terrific struggle with the language. [17]

In order to be a true poet, one must create a new way of seeing. One must have "first the particular faculty of mind to see things as they really are, and apart from the conventional ways in which you have been trained to see them. This is itself rare enough in all consciousness. Second, the concentrated state of mind, the grip over oneself which is necessary in the actual expression of what one sees." [18]

On one level H.D.'s work is a perfect expression of the classical tradition (its form is classical in Hulme's sense of the word), and it has been praised as such; on another level it rebels against both the classical and the romantic traditions. In other words, the form of H.D.'s poetry is classical, while the content is a feminine rebellion against romanticism. H.D. had experienced Pound's troubadour romanticism as an imposition. But there is a difference between being imposed upon and being able to write a poem that consciously characterizes and objectifies the nature of the imposition. And both Pound and H.D. became aware in their lives and in their work of a presence against which one must pit oneself for definition.

The freedom from syntax we find in H.D.'s early work (and in Pound's *Cathay*) takes the poems out of time. There is no logic of cause and effect, no timetable for action. The poems take place in the dimension of eternity. The linguistic structure that breaks from the syntactical pressures of cause-and-effect logic creates pressures of its own. No one is taking command. Who, then, is to take command? Or, as H.D. says in *Helen in Egypt,* "Did the Command read backward?" [19]

When a poem does not adhere to the syntactical structure of western analytical thinking, the images presented can in fact be read backward, for all time is present in the present moment. This is the sense in which the Egyptian hieroglyph, to which H.D. compared her poems, is like the Chinese ideogram from which Pound took his inspiration. In *The Walls Do Not Fall* H.D. refers to these hieroglyphs (her poems) and ideograms (his poems) as anagrams and cryptograms. She alludes to them as little boxes with hidden meanings.

> . . . I know, I feel
> the meaning that words hide;
>
> they are anagrams, cryptograms,
> little boxes, conditioned
>
> to hatch butterflies . . .[20]

H.D. is saying that this poetic language functions so well on the "hawk as hawk" level that no one sees the Imagist poems for the perfect metaphors they are; no one, or only "the few," even guesses the inner meaning of the hieroglyphs.

The definitive work on Imagism and the development of modern poetry cannot be written until H.D. is included in it as person and poet. It has been the recent practice of literary critics either to consider Imagism a small and insignificant chapter in literary history and to praise H.D. as the most perfect Imagist, the best writer of a small "ism" (Hughes), or to consider it a real turning point and breakthrough in the history of modern poetry and to minimize almost entirely the role of H.D. (Pratt).[21] The crux of the matter is that while Hulme, Pound, Flint, Ford, and others were discussing literary theory, talking about what a modern poem might be, and even creating images of an impressionistic sort, it was H.D. who actually brought forth the concrete and dynamic Imagist poem that has profoundly influenced modern poetry.

7

A Feminist Stance

"IT IS IMPORTANT," says Norman Holmes Pearson, "to understand the way H.D. uses myth."[1] It is also important to understand the way she uses metaphor. In her very first poems, "Hermes of the Ways" and "Priapus," H.D. was in a sense possessed by the poetic tradition and by Pound. But by the time she published "Sitalkas" in *The New Freewoman* in September 1913 she had become a fully conscious poet. What we have referred to as metaphorical or palimpsest consciousness had become a habit of mind and a way of dealing with and controlling her experience. And from the beginning H.D. was to take a poetic stance that was quite different from anything she had learned from Pound.

In her early poems H.D. expressed a particularly feminine viewpoint in relation to the poetic tradition. As time went on this stance became more and more clearly defined; today we would call it feminist. It is important to understand how H.D.'s particular poetic sensibility, which she expresses in a metaphorical or palimpsest way of thinking and writing, differs from the more masculine poetic thrust.

What we must first come to understand in H.D.'s poetry is what we might call a figural or allegorical interpretation of nature. Every natural occurrence, in all its everyday reality, is correspondingly a part of a spiritual world order, which is also experiential and in which every event is related to every other event. In the western literary tradition, nature has traditionally been understood to be feminine and mute; H.D. makes nature speak. Because her perspective is feminine rather than masculine, she interprets events in terms of the timeless natural world rather than in terms of the historical process. This perspective is immediately recognizable as one of psychological or spiritual realism. Once events occur, they occur for all eternity and persist into the future as a portion of our inherited body of fate. The Greek dramatists, whom H.D. studied, knew full well the tragic personal and political consequences of being unaware of (or forgetting) one's fate. It is important to understand that H.D.'s poems are not poems of desire; neither are they prophecies of historical occurrences or poems of social protest. Rather, they are presentations of a situation.

Pound had presented H.D. with a situation in which she lost either way: she could either go back home to America with her parents or submit to Pound outside of the context of marriage. Both alternatives were unacceptable to her in the sense that they were inconsistent and incompatible with the person she had become. Her response was to *present* the situation as she had experienced it. That presentation turned out to be poetry. In other words, H.D. had been caught by Pound in a double bind. When confronted with two equally unacceptable alternatives it is important to choose a third; that is, it is important to create one's own alternative. This is the feminist basis of H.D.'s poetic stance.

There is a note of hysteria in H.D.'s very first poems. She had become upset in response to perceived threats to her integrity as a woman. Pound's newly acquired European ideas were the primary threat — specifically the idea that she should become his troubadour lady. Pound had been teaching her and had encouraged her to write. But she simply could not and would not accept his new life plan (in reality an old European form), which would keep wife in one abode and mistress in another. Pound apparently expected her both to write and to become his mistress and his muse.

H.D. expresses a good deal of defensiveness and resistance as well as sadness and a sense of loss in her early poetry. The loneliness, vulnerability, and sense of estrangement and uprootedness that come with a decision to defy the masculine impulse and create one's own space is expressed in "Hermonax," published in *Poetry* magazine in February 1914.

> Broken by great waves,
> The wavelets flung it here,
> This sea-gliding creature like a weed,
> Covered with salt foam,
> Torn from the hillocks
> Of rock.[2]

Ironically, H.D.'s act of liberation, her sublimation of her love for Pound into poetry, became the means by which Pound subjugated her to him. They shared a lingering secret about the sexual undercurrents running through these poems. Just imagine the way he must have looked at her, having removed his pince-nez: "But Dryad, this is poetry . . ."

The birth of her early poems was shocking to H.D. In his introduction to the Godine edition of *Tribute to Freud,* Kenneth Fields suggests that writing these poems was an event from which she "was trying to recover" when she sought Freud's help in 1933, and there is certainly truth to this observation. Pound's publicity of the poems — his hailing them and acclaiming her a poet — was hard on her. It was too much for her really to assimilate. It is one thing to write; one writes because one must express oneself. It is quite another thing to publish and put one's inmost thoughts and feelings on public display.

H.D.'s poems had been written according to Hulme's principles as a process of disentanglement. But the manner in which Pound appropriated them and acted as though they were written for him simply shocked her. By his manner he made them his own — his to edit, his to publish, his to interpret. Pound attempted to turn an ending, a process of disentanglement, into a beginning — with partial success. If H.D. had not been in shock, she might have reclaimed her own work, published her poems in her own way, in her own good time, and in her own interpretive context. But once Pound had defined a context for her poetry, it was important for her to redefine that context, so she had to keep writing in order to do so.

It would be charitable to assume that Pound misunderstood what H.D. wanted. Far more likely, he was attempting to transform her to suit his own ends, whether his intentions were romantic or poetical or both. Hermes is, after all, something of a magician.

For H.D., marriage was not a legal but a spiritual issue. The legality of the matter meant little; the spiritual commitment meant everything. She did not want to be another one of the conquests of this latter-day troubadour so that he could celebrate his virility in song. In short, the issue was not marriage per se, but monogamy. Pound wanted H.D. to be sexually and emotionally faithful to him but did not want to be held to the same standard of fidelity. The war between Pound and H.D. was over the double standard, a battle that is far from over. The real issue was betrayal and subterfuge.

In a sense H.D.'s poems came out of the tension of a situation in which two men, Pound and Aldington, were fighting for her. Because Aldington's intentions were noble (he wanted to wed her), H.D. chose him. As she recognized later, this choice was a mistake. Although she was attracted to Aldington, in retrospect she felt she had been seduced or abducted by him; Aldington had taken advantage of the situation. But there is no doubt that at least in the immediate sense, she was saved from the consequences of Pound's motives by her attraction to and love for Aldington, even if that love was not of the same passionate intensity she had felt for Pound.

Another factor to take into account in understanding H.D.'s emergence as a poet is that she certainly did not know what it meant for a woman to publish poetry in the extremely patriarchal world of 1913. In the very act in which H.D. was attempting to recover herself — the act of writing the poem — she was, through the action of men, throwing herself into the center of a man's world as a muse (that is, a woman who is other than a wife; a woman who is considered by men to be in the category of he-taera). Ironically then, the very act by which she is attempting to recover herself as her mother's child can result in a separation from her mother forever.

Following her marriage to Richard Aldington H.D. had a certain security, in the sense that she was a wife; she was, in the cultural sense, still in the mother's world. From 1913 until her separation from Aldington in 1918 she tried hard to keep her marriage together, although in her later work she recognized that she had been "in hiding" in that marriage. How much of the struggle to maintain her marriage was motivated by love of her husband and how much by the fear of living alone in post-Victorian England, in the world of the fathers, is not altogether clear. What is clear is that she did not cross the line from the world dominated by feminine values into the world dominated by masculine ones with no way back. In some sense she crossed that line in her imagination — she had some sense of what it meant to be in the milieu of the masculine wisdom. But instead of being either in the matriarchal or the patriarchal world, she became an artist and created a world of her own — a world in which her mind was in control of her experience.

Although H.D. did try to make her marriage work, she was unwilling to sacrifice emotional honesty for the sake of holding on to her husband. Aldington was not a strong man emotionally. And H.D. refused to protect his need to prove himself. She and Aldington agreed to have a "modern" marriage, but their problems became aggravated when Aldington began to spend a good deal of time with Brigit Patmore. As Patmore writes in her memoirs, *My Friends When Young:* "He said that, although he had married H.D. he had really always been in love with me, but, as I was a married woman with two children, he had felt there was no hope."[3] H.D. makes it clear in *Bid Me to Live* that the problems in the marriage had started with Morgan, as Brigit Patmore was called. As the H.D.–John Cournos correspondence indicates, Aldington was also interested in another woman, Flo Fallas, in southern England, in 1916, and then in Dorothy Yorke in 1917.[4] As it turned out, Aldington too was a man of the double standard. In his mind, the modern marriage meant that he could see other women but not that his wife could see other men. And H.D.'s emotional honesty was hard on him. (The subject of H.D.'s marriage is treated extensively in her prose. Her novel "Hipparchia," included in *Palimpsest,* which we shall consider in a later chapter, gives us an interpretation of some of the problems of that marriage.)

In his novel *Miranda Masters* John Cournos gives us some sense of how deeply committed H.D. was to Richard Aldington in the early years of their marriage and how hard she tried to make it work. H.D.'s letters to Cournos and Amy Lowell, written during this period, substantiate Cournos's perception of her dedication to the marriage. Aldington, however, was aware of the extent to which H.D. was haunted by her relationship with Pound and was not without anxiety about it.

Pound had succeeded in traumatically binding H.D. to him and to his world of poetry at a level from which she could not entirely escape. His actions in relation to those early poems had had an effect of the kind defined by the psychoanalyst Otto Rank as "the second initiation." Rank writes: "This initiation withdraws the child from the influence of maternal training and 'drums' into him (in the true sense of the word) the community ideology represented by the fathers (elders), not *the* father."[5] In other words, the "father" is definitely *not* the father of the home, the blood father, but the symbol of the patriarchy and patriarchal wisdom.

It was this world of the fathers, the world of the poetic tradition — and a very European tradition at that — to which H.D. was traumatically bound by Pound. Pound had been her mentor; he had had a great deal of power over her, intellectually, spiritually, and physically. His appropriation of her poetry bound her to him; but she resisted the sexual implications of that binding and instead was bound, as it were, to the act of writing. And it is against the world of the fathers that the stance and substance of H.D.'s early poetry pits itself for self-definition.

H.D. did not become the happy hetaera that Pound willed her to become. While her entrance into the world of poetry was traumatic, she did not become Pound's mistress in 1913. She could not help but become aware that through the publication of her poetry she had become, as it were, shared property. In several of her prose manuscripts she expresses fear that she is perceived as a "spiritual prostitute," and in "Sea Iris" she speaks directly about how it feels to be characterized by her fellow poets as "on the prow" (in a characteristic Imagist wordplay, the "prow" is contextually related to the "prowl"):

> Do the murex-fishers
> drench you as they pass?
> Do your roots drag up color
> from the sand?
> Have they slipped gold under you —
> rivets of gold?
> Band of iris-flowers
> above the waves,
> You are painted blue,
> painted like a fresh prow
> stained among the salt weeds.[6]

While it does not feel good to be "painted like a fresh prow" by the poets with whom one associates, once the poet has recognized the problems associated with being a woman in the world, it becomes incumbent upon her to speak out, even though she must be "stained among the salt weeds" for the act of speaking as a woman. H.D. came to understand the poem not as an assertion of phallic desire, but as presentation, an act of birth, a means of disentanglement from the burden of the inseminating thought, and a way to recovery of primal integrity.

8

The Secret Doctrine of the Image

In March 1913 Pound published his well-known three principles in *Poetry:* direct treatment of the thing, composition in the sequence of the musical phrase, and no use of words that do not contribute to the presentation. This article, entitled "Imagisme," is signed by F. S. Flint. In it Flint poses as an interviewer of an Imagist (Pound), who says that the Imagists hold, in addition to their three principles, "a certain 'Doctrine of the Image' which they had not committed to writing; they said that it did not concern the public and would provoke useless discussion."[1] In the same issue Pound published an article under his own name, "A Few Don'ts by an Imagiste," which further defined the Imagist credo and by implication permitted others to begin constructing verses that followed the Imagist form.

The secret "doctrine of the image" refers to the hidden dimension of H.D.'s poems. Such "professional" acts on behalf of Imagism as Pound's promotion of this doctrine were, it is true, building interest in the movement in the poetic world, but they were also secretly binding H.D. to Pound, professionally and psychically, for only he and H.D. knew what he meant. The other members of the Imagist circle perceived the doctrine as merely one more piece of meaningless propaganda designed by Pound to interest readers in the new poetry and the movement. To H.D., however, the doctrine was clearly a reference to the hidden personal dimension of the poems. In effect, H.D. and Pound were developing in their poetry a language in which they were writing about one thing under the guise of another.

It is certainly *not* the case that Pound had never hidden his poetic meaning in this way prior to 1912. No doubt H.D. had learned this poetic principle from him. In selecting the title *Personae* for his collection of poems in 1909, he was openly indicating that he should be understood as a poet who wore a mask and assumed various poses. In his pre-Imagist poetry Pound assumes the form of various troubadours, as in "Praise of Ysolt" or "A Villonaud: Ballad of the Gibbet" or "Piere Vidal Old," but this is a traditional poetic stance.

H.D., on the other hand, had broken with traditional forms and created her own metaphorical language. The allusions of H.D.'s poems are not to the tradition but to the context of the relationships and situations in which she is involved. And she creates these allusions through recognizable images rather than traditional symbols. Her vocabulary is not the traditional language of romanticism (which is masculine), nor is it dependent on traditional classical forms. Rather, as Pound said, it is *"modern* stuff by an American, . . . the laconic speech of the Imagistes, even if the subject is classic."[2] H.D.'s poems, with their palimpsest construction, helped to open Pound's mind to a world of overdetermined symbolism. He came to see, in part through H.D., that *anything,* from tea shops to art exhibitions, has metaphorical possibilities. But H.D. had not intended to have this effect on Pound. She had simply found her own voice in the language of nature, and through that event Pound discovered a new world of metaphorical consciousness. In reality, Pound was the first to learn from H.D.'s poems; H.D. herself learned from them later.

In 1914 Pound continued to promote Imagism while at the same time he began to promote his next movement: Vorticism. He edited and prepared for publication *Des Imagistes: An Anthology,* including work by Richard Aldington, H.D., F. S. Flint, Skipwith Cannell, Amy Lowell, William Carlos Williams, James Joyce, John Cournos, Ford Madox Hueffer (Ford), Allen Upward, and himself. Soon afterward Pound began to call himself a Vorticist; but as F. S. Flint says, he was a Vorticist "with a contradiction, . . . for, when addressing the readers of *The New Age* he has made Imagism to mean pictures as Wyndham Lewis understands them; writing later for *T.P.'s Weekly,* he made it pictures as William Morris understands them."[3]

Pound's involvement in Vorticism can be understood as a masculine protest against Imagism, since for Pound the shift involved little change in poetic theory, only a change in name and stance. In a letter to Harriet Monroe dated August 7, 1914, he writes: "My article on Imagism has been stoked into the *Fortnightly Review,* under an altered title ["Vorticism"]."[4] From a certain point of view, Pound's Vorticism represents a movement back toward the very virile aim and stance, if not the style, of troubadour roman-

ticism. Pound the Vorticist is a sort of angry post-Imagist troubadour.

While it is not immediately obvious upon first reading, H.D.'s
poems were in a very real sense a declaration of poetic war on
Pound. The spiritual reality of this fact took concrete, historical
form in 1914, in the quarrel that broke out between Amy Lowell,
H.D., and Aldington on the one hand and Pound on the other.
H.D. understandably wanted to break totally free of Pound's control. Her chance came unexpectedly from Amy Lowell. The quarrel led to a schism and eventually to Pound's total withdrawal
from Imagism and the Imagist circle. In his biography of Amy
Lowell, S. Foster Damon tells us that in 1913,

> Miss Lowell became particularly interested in certain poems ema-
> nating from an active if somewhat mysterious group of poets in
> London who called themselves 'Imagistes.' Their work seemed odd
> at first glance; but the feeling behind them was fresh and direct,
> while the form, though strange, was provocative. Hardly a number
> of *Poetry* appeared without some specimen of their work, or edito-
> rial comment or tantalizing hint. Then, in the issue for January,
> 1913, she read some poems signed 'H.D., *Imagiste';* and suddenly
> it came over her: 'Why, I, too, am an *Imagiste!'* . . . then in the
> March issue, Ezra Pound published some of their principles, . . .
> but annoyingly enough, he said the most important doctrine of all
> was not for the public.[5]

It is true that Amy Lowell never really understood all of the
dimensions of H.D.'s poems (she never understood the secret doctrine of the image), but she admired their form, style, and external
substance. While Pound obviously invited her to contribute to *Des
Imagistes* so as to cultivate her as a potential patron, H.D. and
Aldington were happy to admit her to the Imagist group as a poet
when she came to England in July 1914. And the newly formed
group, which included F. S. Flint and John Gould Fletcher, was
also happy to admit yet another poet suggested by Amy Lowell:
D. H. Lawrence.

Amy Lowell was first introduced to Lawrence through his
poems in *Poetry* and through Pound's favorable review of *Love
Poems,* which appeared in the July 1913 issue. While Pound was
put off by Lawrence's "disagreeable sensations" and "middling-
sensual erotic verses," his overall appraisal was that "there is no
English poet under forty who can get within a shot of him."[6]
Pound never invited Lawrence to join the Imagists, but recognized
qualities in his poetry that were affirmed in the Imagist credo. Of
Lawrence, Pound said: "His prose training stands him in good

stead in these poems. The characters are real. They are not stock figures of 'the poor,' done from the outside and provided with *cliché* emotions . . . Mr. Lawrence has attempted realism and attained it. He has brought contemporary verse up to the level of contemporary prose, and that is no mean achievement."[7] In a letter to Harriet Monroe of the same period, Pound indicated that "he is clever . . . Detestable person but needs watching. I think he learned the proper treatment of modern subjects before I did."[8]

While the inclusion of D. H. Lawrence in the group might well have contributed to Pound's decision to leave it, the "given" reason has to do with the preparation of the Imagist anthology of 1915, which was Amy Lowell's primary motive for coming to England in the summer of 1914.

> Miss Lowell . . . was interested in continuing the *Des Imagistes* anthology, but she had no intention of cooperating unless she were accepted as really one of them. The meager page allotted her [in Pound's first Imagist anthology] had classed her, not with the important *Imagistes,* but as one of the six names used for padding . . .
>
> Her scheme was that each of the poets elect should be allowed equal space in the next anthology. But such a scheme would dispossess Pound, in some measure, of his anonymous editorship. She consulted the Aldingtons, then armed with their approval laid the scheme before Pound, when they were alone together. When she had the others in, there was an excited argument, in which the other *Imagistes* were solidly on the side of Miss Lowell.[9]

By siding with Amy Lowell, H.D. made it clear to Pound that she wanted to be entirely free of his control — professionally and personally. Pound took this very badly.

S. Foster Damon tells of a letter from Pound to Amy Lowell, dated August 1, 1914, which said "it was true he might give his sanction to letting her and the Aldingtons bring out such an anthology, provided it were clearly stated at the front of the book that E. P., etc., dissociated himself . . . He didn't see the use of being saddled with a dam'd contentious, probably incompetent committee; nor could he accept a certain number of people as his critical and creative equals."[10]

A letter from Amy Lowell to Harriet Monroe gives Lowell's account of the break: "You ask about the quarrel between Ezra and the rest of us. It is not a quarrel now, it is a schism."[11] But it was not simply Amy Lowell and H.D. who disagreed with Pound. Richard Aldington and Pound at this point were clearly at war. Aldington's motive in siding with Lowell was to separate Pound and H.D., establish himself as the foremost Imagist, and exclude Pound from the circle. For Lowell and the anthology, Aldington had nothing but praise.

> We were to publish quietly and modestly as a little group of friends with similar tendencies, rather than water-tight dogmatic principles. Each poet was to choose for himself what he considered best in his year's output; and the anthology would appear annually. To preserve democratic equality, names would appear in alphabetical order. Amy undertook to do all the practical work, to get the books published in Boston and London, and to account to us for the royalties. And well and loyally she discharged that task, which involved a good deal of work and correspondence.[12]

It is worth quoting Aldington's account of the battle between Pound on the one hand and Lowell, H.D., and himself on the other, because it gives us a glimpse into his habit of fabricating stories that have no factual basis. In the following quotation from his autobiography, *Life for Life's Sake,* he not only tells a blatant lie but implies that all concerned were the best of friends with no enmity between them. He writes: "On these terms Ezra was invited to contribute, but refused. There is said to have been a row between Amy and Ezra, but I certainly knew nothing about it. I seem to remember that H.D. and I pleaded for Ezra to stay in, but he refused to play ball."[13]

Through the help of Amy Lowell, D. H. Lawrence, and the others, H.D. managed to break with Pound. Liberated from his all-powerful control, his interpretation of her work (editorial and otherwise), she was at last free to live her own life and to speak in her own voice. Pound made one last effort to sabotage the group, but to no avail. Aldington intervened.

> While the last arrangements for publishing *Some Imagist Poets* were being made, trouble loomed again. Pound, who did not know that Macmillan . . . had rejected the anthology, had written an article attacking that publishing house for the *Egoist,* which Aldington stopped only by threatening to resign [Aldington was the editor]. Hueffer (now out of it) thought the best way to prevent future trouble was to drop the name 'Imagist'; Flint agreed; Aldington suggested 'Some Twentieth Century Poets,' and H.D., 'The Six.'[14]

Obviously Aldington in fact knew all about the row between Ezra and Amy, but had his own reasons for lying about it. These reasons will become more apparent as this study proceeds.

Harold Monro, the owner of The Poetry Bookshop in London, had warned Lowell that the withdrawal of Pound would mean collapse of the movement, but she did not agree. Lowell was right. The anthology was a success. "She [Lowell] never suspected the thunder-storms of controversy over the Imagist credo that were to recur and reverberate for several years." [15]

H.D. and her fellow Imagists were well received in America. The 1915 anthology and the subsequent anthologies of 1916 and 1917 sold. Critics were interested, and in some cases hard put to find serious fault with H.D.'s poems. Some of the early criticism of the Imagists was almost silly. Professor William Ellery Leonard's is an example:

1. The Imagists can't see straight.
2. The Imagists can't feel straight.
3. The Imagists can't think straight.
4. The Imagists can't talk straight. [16]

Other critics were more perceptive and articulate in their disapproval — for instance, Mr. O. W. Firkins, who was furious. In the *Nation* on October 14, 1915, he wrote:

> The loneliness in which they dwell is almost polar; they are exiles who have actually accomplished the traditionally impossible feat of fleeing from themselves . . . The solitude above described is not restricted to the observer; the object likewise is a a drifting, homeless, expatriated thing. It is destitute alike of a place in a charted globe and a function in a civilized order. It has no history, no prospects, no causes, no sequels, no association, no cognates, no allies. As the man is abridged into mere vision, the object contracts into pure visibility.
>   The psychology of Imagism . . . contains matter of undoubted interest. Not the least conspicuous of its traits is the supineness or passivity of the attitudes which the faithful assume in relation to the overshadowing or incumbent universe. They have the air of patients, of people under treatment; they *undergo* the things which other men observe or contemplate. [17]

Firkins is clearly distraught about what evils can occur when syntax is broken and traditional symbolic conventions are set aside, but he is nonetheless a more sensitive reader than those who applauded Imagism without understanding it. The breaking down of symbolic and syntactical orders is not, after all, unrelated to the breaking down of "civilized orders," among them the traditional power relations between the sexes.

Conrad Aiken wrote a trite poetic diatribe titled "Ballade of Worshipers of the Image," which appeared in the New York *Sun* on May 9, 1915.

Ezra Pound, Dick Aldington,
    Fletcher and Flint and sweet H.D.,
Whether you chirp in Kensington
    Or Hampstead Heath, or Bloomsbury;
Birds of protean pedigree,
    Vorticist, Cubist, or Imagist,
Where in a score years will you be,
    And the delicate succubae you kissed?

You, of the trivial straining fun,
    Who ape your betters in mirthless glee;
You, whose meticulous clear lines run
    In hideous insipidity;
And you, forsooth, who shinned a tree
    To keep with the gaping moon your tryst,
Where in a score years will you be,
    And the delicate succubae you kissed?

Idols and images, every one,
    Crash down like ancient theory;
Where is the Vortex under the sun
    That spins away emptily?
Cease these jeers at minstrelry,
    You, who perish and are not missed,
For where in a score years will you be,
    And the delicate succubae you kissed?

L'Envoi

Pound, though your henchmen now agree
    To hail the Prince in the Anarchist,
Where in a score years will you be,
    And the pale pink dream blown mouths you kissed? [18]

W. S. Braithwaite, writing in the *New Republic* on June 12, 1915, argued with these critics, saying that "all really great poets have broken the traditional regularities of form handed to them by their predecessors." [19] And Louis Untermeyer, Alfred Kreymborg, Alice Corbin Henderson, Marguerite Wilkinson, and of course Amy Lowell and Harriet Monroe continued to support and promote the Imagists. Soon they had popular support as well, and they were established, at least in America.

The Imagists were, of course, one of the first schools to write in *vers libre*, but that battle was quickly won. Professor John Livingston Lowes of Harvard University published "An Unacknowledged Imagist" in the *Nation* of February 24, 1916, in which he printed some sentences of George Meredith's novels in *vers libre* form to make his point that Imagism was not poetry. Lowell and Hughes argued that the Meredith "poems" were extraordinarily good. But Lowes's is a relatively dated poetic argument. Clearly, the Imagists had made their mark.

As a result of the publication of her poetry in the Imagist anthologies, *Poetry,* and the *Egoist,* H.D. became established as a poet in her own right, apart from Pound. "From the beginning, critics realized in H.D. a phenomenon," wrote Glenn Hughes.[20] "H.D. stands quite alone among the new poets," wrote Herbert S. Gorman in *The New York Times Book Review.* "Even the most conservative reader never doubts the actual poetry that illuminates all of her work."[21] While she had been thrust upon the public somewhat unwillingly, the public had accepted her in a way in which, ironically, they were not to accept Pound until later in his career. It is no wonder that Pound became a bitter man; all his romantic plans had collapsed in his face. His muse had become a recognized poet, independent of his control.

Through the poetry of this period we have a record of Pound and H.D.'s continuing efforts to disentangle from each other; the process took some time and doing. In 1915 Pound's poetry still contained frequent allusions to H.D., even though they were by this time physically separated and emotionally estranged. In his "Exile's Letter," translated from the notes of Fenollosa, Pound is "recollecting former companionship":

> And if you ask me how I regret that parting?
> It is like the flowers falling at spring's end,
>   confused, whirled in a tangle.
> What is the use of talking! And there is no end
>   of talking —
> There is no end of things in the heart . . . .[22]

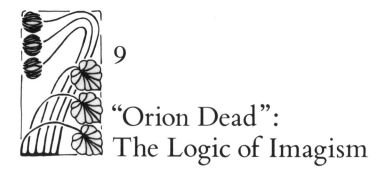

9

"Orion Dead":
The Logic of Imagism

IN A REVIEW of H.D.'s first volume of Imagist poems, *Sea Garden,* her fellow Imagist John Gould Fletcher wrote:

> The great mystics, whether they call themselves Christians or pagans, have all this trait in common — that they describe in terms of ordinary experience some super-normal experience. The unpracticed reader, picking up H.D.'s *Sea-Garden* and reading it casually, might suppose it was all about flowers and rocks and waves and Greek myths, when it is really about the soul . . .[1]

H.D.'s poetry represented something new in the western literary tradition. Pound knew this immediately. Properly understood, it is extraordinarily personal. At the same time, as we have seen, its palimpsest quality offers the reader the potential for perceiving it as impersonal and objective. In fact, most of the critical descriptions of H.D.'s early poetry emphasize this objective quality and ignore or overlook the personal or subjective dimension.

To call H.D.'s poetry (and Imagist poems in general) "objective" is to describe accurately its external or surface dimension. If carefully followed, the litany of "don'ts" recited by Pound in his essay "A Few Don'ts by an Imagiste," in *Poetry* of March 1913, almost requires a poetry devoid of the sentimental qualities usually associated with a subjective poetic orientation. But the quality of objectivity that H.D.'s poems embody is not to be understood in the ordinary western sense, in which their objective existence precludes or diminishes the subject or the subjective meaning.

Each of H.D.'s Imagist poems is a palimpsest, and learning to read its images is like learning to read Egyptian hieroglyphs which have lost their meaning to all but the initiated. If we are properly reading an Imagist poem, it is as though we are, like François

Champollion, deciphering the Rosetta Stone. Only the priests, or in this case the poets, know the hidden meaning. The rules for "direct treatment of the thing" and so forth that Pound announced in *Poetry* magazine permitted others to imitate the surface quality of Imagist poems. But it was the hidden inner language of the poem, what Pound called the doctrine of the image, that permitted this new form to serve as a precise poetic language for H.D., Pound, and later D. H. Lawrence.

In his monumental study *The Pound Era,* Hugh Kenner says that "Pound makes no effort to vanish; he is quite frankly a character in the *Cantos.*"[2] Just as Pound is frankly in his poems, H.D. is frankly in her poems. Art is created by an artist, and the artist is indelibly in the art. "Art does not 'happen', the vision that made it is part of it. The eye of vision sees systems of connectedness; this may not *be* that, but it has the same structure. A bull's form, some drawn lines, are so similar that we 'recognize' a picture of a bull, but part of the picture is the mind that conceived it."[3]

Because of the intensely personal quality of H.D.'s poetry, it is possible to read now from it, as Pound did when it was written, the inner biography of the poet's life. And to understand H.D.'s achievement and her work, we must learn how to read these poems at all the levels of the palimpsest.

The biographical reality within H.D.'s poems is veiled by their mythological or naturalistic presentation. Each poem is a prolonged metaphor, in which actions on the part of deities, nymphs, heroes, or Nature herself are symbolic of the actions and events taking place in the life of H.D.'s circle of poets. Through myth or allegory, H.D. tells the story of her own life. Her story is not expressly stated but implied; the personal pronoun is usually omitted.

In allegory the universal, archetypal events are usually personified; in H.D.'s poetry impersonal events are employed to present particular situations. That is, H.D.'s allegory represents a reversal of the usual form. By denoting specfic people, events, and dramas by their unchanging, impersonal names, H.D. transforms temporal reality — consciousness itself — into an eternal reality, without reduction or distortion. Part of her originality is that she creates her own symbolic system rather than adhering to traditional forms and symbolic conventions.

H.D. and Pound are in their poems, but their presence is merely implied. The person is in the poem in his or her impersonal manifestation, his or her eternal or poetic aspect, his or her "life" or "soul" manifestation. And the person presented becomes a symbol for all persons in the same situation or subject to the same fate.

When H.D. writes of Helen, for instance, Helen is not simply H.D. as a personality, but the Helen situation for all women at all times.

Thus mythology becomes a language of poetic discourse which is more deeply communicative than ordinary discursive speech. H.D. presents the mythological character as a point of location, not as an archetype. In H.D.'s poem "Orion Dead," for instance, we are not looking at Orion as a type; rather, we look to the story of Orion to give us a configuration of character and events in the poet's life.

In an interview with Norman Holmes Pearson in *Contemporary Literature,* L. S. Dembo asked, "Was [H.D.] seeking a myth that would express her own feelings and therefore be really a projection of herself; or was she seeking a universal myth, an archetype, of which she herself was only a manifestation; or one in which she could lose herself?" Pearson replied that both views are correct. "She used art in order to find herself . . . You remember Cummings: 'Why do you write?' 'I write, I dare say, to become myself' . . . Paradoxically, one is swept up into a knowledge of one's identity by the similarities in the patterns of other lives and other races." Pearson continued:

> When you said that she used Greek myth to find her own identity, you hit upon an aspect of H.D.'s poetry which, rather surprisingly, has gone unrecognized. She has been so praised as a kind of Greek publicity girl that people have forgotten that she writes the most intensely personal poems using Greek myth as a metaphor. That is, she can say these things better and more frankly about herself using these other devices than she could if she simply said, "I, I, I." To say "Helen" is really to free oneself.[4]

There is a certain passivity to this poetry of the "objective"; the poetry is a form of passive resistance to the demands of subjective desire. In a sense this is a form that is particularly feminine. It originates from the matrix of existence rather than from the phallic roots of desire. In this respect, the poems are more properly described as presentations than as projections. They are born from the eternal, unchanging, objective principle of the universe rather than from the yearning, desiring, subjective principle. Nothing is sought; nothing is desired.

This poetic conception is based upon an understanding of life that is sometimes associated with primitive or archaic consciousness. Contemporary anthropological and linguistic theory teaches us that the Chinese, Egyptian, archaic Greek, and even Hopi cultures, for instance, manifest a similarity in consciousness which is apparent in the temporal distinctions that emerge in their philosophy and language. H.D.'s "archaic" poetry is objective rather than subjective in the Chinese, Egyptian, Greek, or Hopi understanding of these terms.

In describing the organization of Hopi consciousness, for example, the linguist Benjamin Lee Whorf says: "The objective or manifested comprises all that is or has been accessible to the senses, the historical physical universe, in fact, with no attempt to distinguish between present and past, but excluding everything that we call future." The subjective realm has to do with what is in the heart, what is hoped for and wished for. "It is the realm of expectancy, of desire and purpose."[5]

Western poetry generally is thought to be in this subjective realm of desire and purpose. But H.D.'s poetry is objective in the primitive or archaic sense; it includes the present and the past with no attempt to distinguish between them, but excludes the realm of the future (in both the Hopi and the western sense). So the situation of today is presented in the language — that is, the myth — of the world of the past, or in the timeless world of nature. Orion today is Orion yesterday. The Orion of the present has manifested in the same way as the Orion of the mythological story. A contemporary person and event can be stated in the story of Orion.

It is this kind of "primitive" distinction between objectivity and subjectivity which has led some who have studied H.D.'s poems to compare them to Egyptian hieroglyphs. The hieroglyph is a picture of an objective nature, an image that makes sound-sense as well as sight-sense. H.D.'s poems attempt to reconstruct an experience as it actually occurred or, to use her word, as it "manifested." Because the notion of causality in events is dependent on a notion of linear temporal sequence, this poetry tends to ignore explanations of why events occur or occurred. The emphasis is on presenting *what happened*. The realm of what is in the heart, the realm of wishes and expectations, is consciously excluded from H.D.'s presentation of the manifested reality.

If H.D.'s Imagist poems are akin in temporal organization to at least some prominent forms of archaic or primitive consciousness (many fall into the linguistic genre that anthropologists call animism), their impact on the modern world and their relevance to modern consciousness can be attributed in part to their shared consciousness with the emerging physics of Einstein. In "Murex," the second book of her novel *Palimpsest*, H.D. says: "The present and the actual past and the future were (Einstein was right) one."[6]

It is important to understand that Imagism was born in an Einsteinian world. As we move from Newtonian to Einsteinian physics, we can no longer maintain the notion of a perfect observer independent of the phenomena observed. The observer is no longer separable from the event; what one sees in a relativistic world depends upon one's point of location.

In an Einsteinian world, the act of observing changes the thing observed. This is as true of human relations as it is of the universe. The act of writing a poem cannot be independent of the perception of the artist. Furthermore, what we take to be causal relationships are really projections. The "if . . . then" relationship falls apart. It is possible to observe the same phenomena from different stances and get different answers, and these answers are not inconsistent. Simultaneous perceptions which are not identical with each other are valid.

The idea that what we see depends to a very great extent upon where we are is important to the reading of any Imagist poem. An Imagist poem differs from a Symbolist poem in that the words, symbols, and ideas of the former take their meaning from the context in which they appear. The poet expresses the awareness that the act of observing changes the things observed. The syntax of the Imagist poem is free from causal relationships. The same phenomenon is observed from different stances by different poets, or by the same poet at different times, and all of these stances are valid. Thus the Imagist poem permits simultaneous perceptions of the event presented. Since the meaning of any particular word is not fixed but derives from the context in which it appears, the requirement of Imagism is that the images fit the event. As Pound wrote: "The symbolist *symbols* have a fixed value, like numbers in arithmetic, like 1, 2, and 7. The imagiste's images have a variable significance, like the signs *a, b,* and *x* in algebra."[7]

Being free of the realm of the subjective in the archaic or primitive sense and free of the Newtonian world of causality, in Imagism we are in the world of pure presentation. It ought not be necessary to say that the presentation of beauty is not an invitation for assault, but many of H.D.'s poems have been so misread that it is necessary to state the obvious. The presentation of violence, as, for instance, in "Orion Dead," is not an invitation to be violated; the presentation of terror is not an invitation to be terrorized.

With these general concepts in mind, let us look at a pivotal poem in H.D's career: "Orion Dead," which illustrates many of the Imagist principles and chronicles the poet's life in an objective stance.

One could say that through her relationship with Ezra Pound,

H.D. had acquired literary interests and aspirations. After 1914, as her marriage became increasingly unhappy, her literature became her life. "Orion Dead" was written in the context of the early disappointments that would come to define that marriage. The biographical reality that H.D.'s poem presents is veiled in the mythological story.

Very often in H.D.'s poetry the title tells us a good deal before we begin. "Orion Dead" was originally titled "Incantation." H.D. hoped that the poem could be spoken as a sort of ritual magic, a spell or verbal charm; but as we have seen her metaphysical or poetic stance precludes the illusion of an incantation in relation to the reality expressed. In H.D.'s novel *Hedylus,* the character of that name speaks to this issue: "Metres must be dealt with honestly. I have used mine as a sort of invocation. It's tampering with divinity. I can't be both a poet and a magician."[8] The title "Orion Dead" as opposed to "Incantation" expresses the reality of the situation.

The title invokes a mythological story, which sets a context for the presentation; the story is a counterpart to a concrete situation in the poet's life. The mythologist Robert Graves tells us that "Orion's story consists of three or four unrelated myths strung together. The first, confusedly told, is that of Oenopion. This concerns a sacred king's unwillingness to resign his throne, at the close of his term, even when the new candidate for kingship had been through his ritual combats and married the queen with the usual feasting."[9] H.D. no doubt chose this story because it is analogous to Pound's refusal to quit his pursuit of her after her marriage to Aldington.

Let us look at the mythological story of Orion and read or "translate" it as H.D. might have done. This exercise will enable us to see how the language of Greek myth served H.D.'s poetic purposes.

Orion, we are told by the mythologists, was the handsomest man alive.* He fell in love with Merope. Her father, Oenopion, promised Merope to Orion in marriage if he would free Oenopion's island from the dangerous wild beasts that infested it. Orion performed the deed and brought Merope the pelts, but Oenopion claimed wild animals were still living in the hills — the truth being that he was himself in love with his daughter.

Let us read this myth in the way in which H.D. would have

---

*The primary sources for Orion's story are Homer *Odyssey* xi 310; Apollodorus i.4. 3–4; Parthenius *Love Stories* 20; Lucian *On the Hall* 28; Theon *On Aratus* 638; Hyginus *Poetic Astronomy* ii.34.

read it, not as mythologists but as poets. The myth describes H.D.'s situation: Aldington fell in love with her, but Pound promised H.D. to Aldington in marriage only if he could prove himself as poet and lover — a task that Pound considered to be considerably beyond Aldington's power. Aldington did succeed, or at least H.D. persuaded herself that he had succeeded, but Pound did not want to give her up because he wanted her for himself.

Thus, by using the title "Orion Dead," H.D. presumes that the story of Orion today is very much the story of Orion yesterday — that the truth of her own experience is the same as the truth of everyone's experience in a parallel situation. Once the life situation is expressed in the language of Imagist discourse, it becomes impersonal. That is, the personal is a manifestation of the impersonal. The Orion story or allegory is brought to the poem by the title; there is no reference to Orion in the text of the poem. The title serves only as a determinative, the stage direction for the play of images that follows.

Let us now look at the poem and the images it presents.[10] It begins:

> The cornel-trees
> Uplift from the furroughs.
> The copper roots at their bases
> Strike lower through the barley sprays.
>
> "Arise
> And face me.
> I am poisoned with rage of song.

As in all of H.D's poems the writing has a palimpsest quality, and one level of meaning is superimposed upon another. At a surface layer of meaning "Orion Dead" makes sense in terms of obedience to the pattern of nature. It can be read as a "nature poem" in which the events of the poem follow the laws of the natural world. At another level, it can be read as metaphor, the landscape in nature being equated with the landscape of the body.

There is another layer of the palimpsest, which we might call the symbolic level, in which the action of the natural objects is a symbolic representation of an ontological state. The cornel-trees uplifting from the furroughs and the roots at their bases striking lower through the barley sprays are images of rage. H.D. makes this clear in the next lines: " 'Arise/And face me./I am poisoned with rage of song." The poem continues:

I once tore the flesh
Of the wild deer.
Now I am afraid to touch
The blue
And the gold-veined hyacinths?

I will tear the full flowers
And the little heads of the grape hyacinths.
I will strip the life from the bulb,
Until
The ivory layers lie
Like narcissus petals
On the black earth.

Arise,
Lest I bend my staff
Into a taut bow,
And slay,
And tear all the roots from the earth.

"Orion Dead" is at the primary level an objective statement of a situation; it recognizes a crisis in a relationship.

The cornel-wood blazes
And strikes through the barley sprays
But I have lost heart for this.

I break a staff.
I break the tough branch.
I know no light in the woods.
I have lost pace with the winds.

The winds with which H.D. has lost pace are both a physical and metaphysical reality; they are her own poetic sources. The date of publication of "Orion Dead," February 2, 1914 (just five months after the publication of "Sitalkas"), marks the first serious rupture in the H.D.-Aldington marriage. The emotional honesty H.D. expressed in this poem paved the way for a new beginning in her life and in her work.

II

THE TEMPLE

10

Imagism and Moravianism

IN HER BOOK *Poets and Their Art,* Harriet Monroe writes admiringly and incredulously of H.D.'s poetry: "The astonishing thing about H.D.'s poetry is the wildness of it . . . she is, quite unconsciously, a lithe, hard, bright-winged spirit of nature to whom humanity is but an incident."[1]

Monroe speaks of H.D. as though she came from nowhere: "Her poetry is more akin to that of our aborigines than it is to Elizabethans or Victorians." H.D. emerged, according to Monroe, fully formed. "Reticence had saved her from exposing immature work to the world. Thus there are no juvenilia in her record — she was a finished product when she began."[2]

Monroe continues: "It would be interesting speculation to consider how much H.D. owes to the pioneers whom all Americans descend from more or less."[3] Later in her life H.D. would conclude that she owed a great deal to the American pioneers, and particularly to the early American Moravians of her native community, Bethlehem, Pennsylvania.

On one of her trips to America, H.D.'s friend Winifred Ellerman, who was known as Bryher, drove with Mary Herr through the Pennsylvania countryside. In *The Heart to Artemis,* Bryher writes: "She took me to Bethlehem where H.D. had been born. Hilda was Greek, it is true, but her training and background came through every word she wrote. Her long residence in Europe merely intensified her love for her native country, and to me she has always been the most American of poets."[4]

Those who both understood H.D.'s work and knew something about Moravianism (such as Sigmund Freud and Norman Holmes Pearson) agreed that H.D. was indeed a Moravian. The religious life of the Moravian congregation centered on their hymns. Jacob

John Sessler tells us that "the 'hymn-sermon' was their distinctive invention."

> A knowledge of the hymnal as well as of the Bible was required for inspiration and instruction. Instead of singing all the stanzas of a hymn or several stanzas of the same hymn, they sang selected stanzas from many hymns, successively or interspersed by prayer, testimony or address, according to the nature of the service. The result of these "hymn-sermons" was the composite authorship of many of the hymns, and also the preparation of hymn-books in which verses from many hymns were arranged according to subject-matter. Thus a new and endless combination of verses could be made according to the subject under discussion. "It is supposed that not less than 70,000 hymns are in existence, under the various forms of composition in which they have appeared from time to time."[5]

A study of Moravian hymns reveals that their language, like the language of Imagism, is figurative and symbolic. The Moravians believed that every person contained a world or spiritual light within herself or himself. The almost overly obvious symbolism of the hymns leaves little doubt that love was understood to be the highest and most meaningful form of human expression, containing the potential for the deepest and most profound communication and leading to the deepest knowledge — in a word, communion — between the male and female. Thus, marriage was the most natural condition for the attainment of human joy and fulfillment, and married members of the community formed their own separate choir. The hymns of the Moravians emphasized the hope of human fulfillment, although the church recognized that suffering is involved in the effort required to bridge the gap between the masculine and the feminine; hence the concentration on Christ's suffering, scars, and wounds.

The image of the Moravians saw and celebrated in their liturgy is the same image the Imagists saw. Freud also saw this image and called it "the primal scene." (What H.D. and many of her circle so admired in Freud was his ability to state in rational, or Greek, terms what they had thought could only be apprehended and expressed in religious or poetic language.) Both Imagism and Moravianism begin as meditation upon the primal reality. The Greeks, says H.D., intellectualize it.

According to the structure of Moravian theology, Jesus is symbolically both mother and husband. The Holy Spirit is the mother of the congregation.[6] People of different religious beliefs might understand this as a "feminization"; it is in reality an attempt to downplay the role of the father so as to create a culture based upon the ideal of sexual equality. "When those of the world accept the Father as their God, they lose sight of their Creator and fall into idolatry."[7] Since all souls are female, according to Moravian theology, Christ is the husband of the men as well as of the women.[8] "Physically men are male but spiritually female."[9] Moravianism is not the only religion that has attempted to minimize the power of the father (or king); many religions have a similar structure, and the form is a recurring one in the history of civilization. The idea is to create a culture that is more attuned to love than to power. The Moravians aimed toward a community based upon brotherhood, peace, purity, simplicity, and love. They were pacifists, the opposite of a warrior culture.

Moravianism was a mystical love language as well as a form of religious, social, and familial organization. It was a community of shared experience, of shared symbolism, of a common language about the experience of life. This is the background H.D. brought to Imagism, and this vision perhaps was essential to its formation.

There are some interesting features of Moravianism which explain some of its appeal, especially to women. All members of the faith were permitted to know and use the symbolic language so that it could not be used against them. In most religions, both "primitive" and "modern," only the priests (usually men) are permitted to understand the sexual dimension of the symbolism. The laity (especially the women) are kept in the dark about the real meaning of the religion. Also, Moravianism sanctioned marriage, and no other kind of sexual liaison was permitted — or even conceivable — within the context of its world view.

In the Moravian tradition, Christ is one body, male and female.

> That all souls are married to their one conjugal Lord Jesus was minutely set forth in song and speech. In this married relationship of souls to their God-husband, all aspirations and desires were fully realized. The married state, which is the most intimate connection between two individuals, was the state existing between them and Christ. Souls came forth out of his Side wound.[10]

The reality of Christ is symbolic rather than historical. Christ and Mary Magdalene, God and the Virgin present the varying aspects of love. Christ is experienced physically and sensually. The symbolism has a poetic fluidity. Jesus was celebrated in his various manifestations by the different choirs. He was celebrated as Jesus the hero, Jesus the bridegroom, Jesus the corpse.

As in Imagism, personality is not emphasized but de-emphasized. The truth that is presented is the truth of a particular relation or situation. In her later poetry H.D. moves with a similar great fluidity of symbolism. God and the Virgin, Osiris and Isis, Achilles and Helen: these are not presentations of different persons as much as presentations of the same two persons in different situations or as seen from different points of location. In the same spirit of fluidity of symbolism the same god may manifest himself through different mortals. As H.D. says in "Winter Love":

> Apollo on the Walls, they say
>
> appeared to men as Paris;
> perhaps he manifested as Achilles, too,
> even as Odysseus — who may know? [11]

The most striking, and for our purposes illuminating, structural similarity between Imagism and Moravianism is the level of symbolic consciousness in their modes of perceiving reality. In Moravianism, for instance, the reality of Jesus Christ is understood as presentation; Christ was to become real to the congregation's senses.

Thoughout the long history of the church there was much talk about the secret of Moravianism and the necessity of preserving this secret in the face of persecution. We think of the secret doctrine of the image. There is no doubt that the Moravian secret had a sexual dimension, and that it was an open secret to the faithful. The symbols used to describe it are conventional symbols of sexuality — the chalice, the *Calixenes,* the spear, the wound. In "The Gift" H.D. writes:

> The Cup linked up with the early branch of the church that went back to the 9th century in Europe, that was called the *Calixenes,* which is a Greek word that has something to do with a cup, like calix is the part of a flower that is shaped like a cup. [12]

And the hymns in praise of Christ's wounds leave little doubt that the wound was often represented as both feminine and genital.

> If those dear little wounds I did know,
> Which now with blood's juice overflow,
> What else could satisfy me?
> But Blood, that's good
> Still to wash me, and refresh me;
> In that Ocean,
> I do ever find my potion. [13]

The thoughts of the Moravians were always turned to the sacrificial death of Christ and the Passion. According to Moravian belief, the Passion expresses the mystery of life and death at the heart of every culture. And Christ the Savior is often described in the hymn-sermons in ways that make his sex ambiguous.

> Thy holy testaments,
> Thy sweet nearness,
> Thy embodying in the sacrament,
> Bless us, O dear Lord and God!
>
> My soul feeds on roses sweet,
> When she smells wounds-flavour,
> And reviews her safe retreat
> In thy grave, my Saviour.
>
> Draw us to thee, and we may come
> Into thy wound's deep places,
> Where hidden is the honey-comb
> Of thy sweet love's embraces.[14]

H.D. repeatedly said that Moravianism has Greek origins, and it is likely that her affinity to Greek culture derived in part from her Moravian background. In "The Death of Martin Presser" she writes:

> Was it Greeks of the Orthodox Church who intrigued us away from Rome? Or were we originally heathen, brought into the fold by the Greeks? Whatever we were (and one of our earliest branches was called *Calixenes,* from a Greek word meaning the cult of the cup or chalice) we were driven undergound by the Inquisition; we were reformers, long, long before the Reformation.[15]

Regardless of how we feel about H.D.'s Moravianism, we must acknowledge the deep and lasting influence it had on her creative life; and whatever else it may or may not be, Moravianism is clearly a heretical religious orientation. H.D. herself, after her analysis with Freud, struggled in a scholarly way with the Moravian tradition, and in the end, despite her rejection of several of its doctrines, such as "that horrible doctrine that males perform sexual intercourse in Christ's stead," she understood its contributions to her poetic consciousness.[16]

The church had endured persecution for centuries, and this very fact influenced its ideas. As H.D. writes: "It ran underground. That is what Christian Renatus said, their ideas, the ideas of the few are the same as the ideas of the Hidden Church . . . Things people said about us here, and misrepresentations and scandals invented about Count Zeisberger and the other disciples were the same scandals through the ages."[17]

For instance, Henry Rimius, counselor to the king of Prussia in the 1740s, wrote a treatise entitled *A Candid Narrative of the Rise and Progress of the Herrnhuters, Commonly Called Moravians or Unitas Fratrum, With a Short Account of Their Doctrines, Drawn From Their Own Writings,* in which he maintained that the secret doctrines of the Moravians were immodest. He asserted that Zinzendorf appealed to the imagination and passions rather than to reason. He said that the Moravians were more loyal to Zinzendorf than to the king and suggested that they engaged in indecent behavior, but was unable to give a single instance of it. He objected to their practice of marriage by lots and charged that Zinzendorf's aims were worldly rather than spiritual, that his espoused religious purposes were a cloak for attaining worldly power. He implied that the members of the Moravian brotherhood were deceived into their beliefs by Zinzendorf. He accused Zinzendorf of accommodating his beliefs to other religious faiths to increase his power and the membership of the church, and every time the Moravians were persecuted for their outrageous doctrines, he said, Zinzendorf would plead that they were Lutherans and obedient to the Augsburg Convention. Rimius wrote: "The supreme Bishop or *Papa,* under whose Direction, and by whose Influence all Schemes are carried on, can bend, like a Reed by every Turn of Wind as often as he pleases . . . his Plan is no other than a Worldly one, to which Religion itself only serves as a Cloke or Pretense." [18]

While Rimius is excessive in his critique, from almost any contemporary point of view the Moravian hymns are strange stuff to the uninitiated. The sheer energy devoted to dwelling upon Christ's wounds is most amazing. Both excess and hysteria are expressed in the hymns.

> In a moment stands before us
> The prince with his open side,
> And one feels he's most desirous
> Our poor souls therein to hide.
>
> I wipe my eye from weeping sore,
> That sinful red appears no more;
> Yet the aspect of that God who bled,
> Does keep my eye still wet and red. [19]

In attempting to understand H.D.'s life and her poetry we must remember that H.D. grew up in the late nineteenth century in a prominent Moravian family and in a community that was for the most part Moravian. What might her young mind have made of these words, sung to music, of the confession and absolution?

> All thy smart and sweat-drops bloody,
> All the wounds in thy dear body,

> Thy distress and agony,
> O Lord Jesus, comfort me!
>
> Thy precious sweat when at work, make
> all labour sweet to us![20]

Moravianism stresses the importance of a child's understanding, and certainly all the images of blood and wounds must have made a strong impression with regard to the physical reality of life on any young mind that was exposed to them. Many situations are expressed in the hymns in the *Litany Book* — for instance:

> But he wept, 'cause his dove did stray,
> Decoyed and torn from him away;
> The cruel hawk had her, and die
> Must he or she infallibly.[21]

Does the "cruel hawk" refer to death (this is a hymn for widowers), or is it rather an allusion to a more sinister kind of death, some sort of cruel seduction? There is no doubt that this image, like many in the Imagist poems, has a palimpsest quality and is fully open to multiple interpretations.

It is our purpose here not to decode Moravianism but rather to make it clear that the consciousness of H.D.'s religious heritage was highly symbolic and that its symbolism was very physical and very fluid. Clearly and often, one thing was alluded to under the guise of another. Jesus was in a sense a proxy for something else, or else the something else was a proxy for Jesus. For instance, consider this hymn, in which Christ is invoked to sanctify the married state:

> O God, O Chaste Lamb, Jesus!
> Blow up thy clear flame in us;
> Our marriage stands in need
> of thy blood's overspreading,
> The interim proxy-wedding
> Was done in Jesus' name indeed.[22]

The Virgin was similarly described in terms that invoke specifically sexual connotations. Moravian girls were taught to maintain their virginity but also to obey the will of their elders. In certain circumstances, we might assume, the will of the elders made itself known in unexpected ways, and the symbolism of the hymns was inclusive enough to cover and sanctify varying situations.

> In the Single Sisters' Choir, Jesus was glorified as the "spouse" and "bridegroom" of the virgins. They besought him to become their guest and make their hearts his "bridal palace" . . . The fact that

he was conceived in a virgin's womb made their virgin state especially blessed and made Mary the pattern after which they were to model themselves.[23]

It is certainly not difficult to understand how H.D., reared in this tradition not only by her mother but also by her maternal grandparents, became very conscious of the subtleties of symbolism at a very early age. We must remember, too, that her family was a part of the leadership of the church; the leaders of such a movement must of necessity have a different orientation from the followers. As in the case of the few who understood the doctrine of the image, those who rose to leadership in the Moravian church had the deepest understanding of the symbolic meaning of the language. And perhaps most important, we must remember that H.D.'s father was not a Moravian and took no part in the Moravian church. His own heritage was so close to the opposite end of the Christian theological tradition that H.D. saw herself as being from "two distinct racial or biological entities."

It is certainly true that a misunderstanding of Moravian mysticism can lead to the worst sorts of romanticism and religious fanaticism. At its worst, the sensuality expressed in Moravian hymns is morbid. Freud would surely diagnose hysteria in an individual who manifested these sorts of linguistic symptoms.

During the period known as the Sifting Time, roughly from 1746 to 1750, the Moravians went mad celebrating the wounds of the sacrificial victim, Jesus Christ. From a modern perspective the Sifting Time could be described as a collective nervous breakdown which led to a dissolution of the theocratic society and eventually to the establishment of a civic order independent of the church. In the hymns composed during this period, the victim came to have symbolic overtones that were morbid, not to mention explicitly sexual, in a hysterical kind of way.

> My dearest, most beloved Lamb
> I who in tenderest union am
> To all thy cross-air-birds bound,
> Smell to and kiss each corpse's wound;
> Yet at the Side-hole's part,
> There pants and throbs my heart,
> I see still, how the soldier fierce
> Did thy most lovely Pleura pierce,
> That dearest Side-hole!
> Be praised, O God, for this Spear's slit!
> I thank thee, Soldier, too for it.
> I've licked this Rock's salt round and round
> Where can such relish else be found.[24]

Where indeed! It is as if, in this phase of Moravianism, the sacrifice of the Son of God has been replaced by sacrifice of the daughter. Of this latter-day Moravianism Sessler says:

> This type of sexual pathology is by no means unique. What makes this particular form especially interesting, however, is the extensive use of theological symbols for sexual themes, and the fact that these abnormal traits dominated the whole community. In the Orient such religious eroticism is common and traditional, and Hindu symbolism analogous to Zinzendorf's can be found in the extreme forms of Bhakli and in the Tantric literature; but in the Christian tradition they are comparatively rare.[25]

A dialectical view would maintain that any language of liberation, whether it be that of psychoanalysis or any traditional religious or classical discourse or any expression of political ideology, may become a language of oppression. (This would, of course, be as true of H.D.'s Moravian tradition as it is of psychoanalysis.) A Vichean view would lend the perspective that a language tends to be liberating in the beginning and oppressive at the end of its cycle. This dialectic is further complicated by the fact that a discourse that is moving in the direction of potency for men may at times be moving in the direction of oppression for women.

In the hymns of the Sifting Period we see a virtual outbreak of hysteria. The language of the liturgy and hymns represents both the sexual instinct and antagonism to it. The instinct is manifested in the ardor of expression of sensual delight; the fact that wounds are celebrated in morbid language demonstrates antagonism to the sensual experience.

Most of H.D.'s poetry is allusive and reticent, but one poem reminds us of some of the over-obvious symbolism we find in such Moravian hymns. "Hymen" was written in 1917:

> There with his honey-seeking lips
> The bee clings close and warmly sips,
> And seeks with honey-thighs to sway
> And drink the very flower away.
>
> (Ah, stern the petals drawing back;
> Ah rare, ah virginal her breath!)
> Crimson, with honey-seeking lips,
> The sun lies hot across his back,
> The gold is flashed across his wings.
> Quivering he sways and quivering clings
> (Ah, rare her shoulders drawing back!)
> One moment, then the plunderer slips
> Between the purple flower-lips.[26]

At the time H.D was working with Freud, he was writing *Moses and Monotheism* and the subject of religion was very much on his mind. It was Freud who suggested that H.D. take her religious heritage seriously in her attempt to understand herself. As Freud says in "Analysis Terminable and Interminable," written after his work with H.D.: "What was acquired by our ancestors is certainly an important part of what we inherit . . . Indeed, analytic experience convinces us that particular psychical contents, such as symbolism, have no other source than hereditary transmissions."[27]

We may disagree with Freud about "hereditary" transmissions, but it is difficult to deny that H.D.'s Moravianism influenced her early poetry. What she got from her religious background was a sense of the fluidity of symbols and a sense of the very concrete and immediate physical reality of spiritual experience. Through the mystical discourse of Moravianism she came to understand mystical language as a form of reticence about spiritual (sexual) realities.

When H.D. was a child, the worlds of *Grimm's Fairy Tales*, Greek mythology, and Moravian hymns were all part of a whole for her; the other world was that of political and financial affairs. As an adult H.D. was able to move between the discourse of Christian myth and the discourse of Greek myth with no sense that one was a "true" language and the other merely a myth. She understood God the Father of the Hebrew-Christian tradition and the Greek god Zeus as ways of talking about an individual's spiritual experience, and the differences between them reflected differences between the perceptual and behavioral structures of cultures, not differences between true and false beliefs. Philosophically H.D. was a naturalist, but a person of orthodox religious beliefs might call her a pagan — or a Greek.

11

The Center of the Circle:
H.D. as Poet and Muse

IN MAY 1915 the *Egoist* published a special Imagist number which contained "The History of Imagism" by F. S. Flint, "The Poetry of Ezra Pound" by Richard Aldington, "The Poetry of H.D." by F. S. Flint, "The Poetry of John Gould Fletcher" by Ferris Greenslet, "The Imagists Discussed" by Harold Monro, "The Poetry of F. S. Flint" by Richard Aldington, "The Poetry of D. H. Lawrence" by Olivia Shakespear, "The Poetry of Amy Lowell" by John Gould Fletcher, and poems by Aldington, H.D., Fletcher, Flint, Lawrence, Lowell, Marianne Moore, and May Sinclair.

Aldington wrote, "Mr. Pound has a gift for writing occasional, romantic, intense lyrics; he wants so hard to do more good work that he probably will do so."[1] Of H.D.'s poems, Flint said, "The scene is one that you can place in no country. The thing then will seem to have happened in eternity."[2] John Gould Fletcher contributed a short piece entitled "Chicago," dedicated *"To* Harriet Monroe, *the Editor who discovered Imagism,"* in recognition of the fact that Monroe had given the group its start by publishing its work in *Poetry* magazine.[3]

The *Egoist* had originally been titled *The New Freewoman*, and even after Aldington took editorial control, Dora Marsden, its founder and a Victorian idealist of sorts who had no relation to the rest of the group, continued to publish the lead article. The *Egoist* published prose as well as poetry, notably Wyndham Lewis's *Tarr,* James Joyce's *Portrait of the Artist as a Young Man,* and some Rémy de Gourmont pieces translated by Aldington. But the magazine was primarily a forum for Imagist verse.

It was entirely clear to anyone who had anything to do with Imagism that H.D. was at the center of the group. Although things had not turned out as Pound had wanted, his publication of her poetry had created a literary circle around H.D. — whether she liked the idea or not. In 1930, when Ford Madox Ford wrote his introduction to the *Imagist Anthology* which contained the work of Aldington, H.D., Flectcher, Flint, Joyce, Lawrence, Williams, and himself (Pound refused to contribute), he wrote: "It is my chief pride to be allowed as it were to stand on the platform and say my little piece — and once more to be beside H.D. who was at once our gracious Muse, our cynosure and the peak of our achievement . . . And who still so consummately is all that!"[4]

In his introduction, which was called "Those Were the Days," Ford speaks of "BLASTS, VORTICISMS, CUBISMS, DADA-ISMS, and the rest," implying that all these "isms" were part of the same upheaval against old poetic forms.[5] But these political-poetic groups are not our concern here. Our concern is rather to make it clear that H.D. had been put into the spotlight of a literary scene. As we shall see, she had very mixed feelings about this fate.

On July 30, 1914, shortly after her arrival in England, Amy Lowell "had the Lawrences and the Aldingtons to dinner and read poetry afterwards."[6] This was the first time that H.D. and Richard Aldington had met Lawrence, although as contributors to *Poetry* they were familiar with each other's work. Lawrence recalls the evening, less than three weeks after his marriage to Frieda Weekley, in his letter of July 31, 1914, to Harriet Monroe.

> I was at dinner with Miss Lowell and the Aldingtons last night, and we had some poetry. But, my dear God, when I see all the understanding and suffering and pure intelligence necessary for the simple perceiving of poetry, then I know it is an almost hopeless business to publish the stuff at all . . .
> Mrs. Aldington has a few good poems.[7]

Lawrence liked H.D.'s early poetry. In *Bid Me to Live* H.D. remembers his response on the evening they met. "He liked her flower poems. He had particularly liked the blue iris-poem, that day at the top of the Berkeley, overlooking Green Park. Matrix to jewel, he had flamed around her, he was red-hot lava . . ."[8]

Richard Aldington recalls this evening as the time that World War I began and the British mobilization was announced.* He reports:

> It was the end of a sunny tranquil July day and, if we had been able to see into the future, the end of the tranquility in Europe for

---

*Aldington also confuses the evening with the "Imagist dinner" Amy Lowell hosted at the Dieu-donne Restaurant on July 17, 1914, which included the Aldingtons, Cournos, Fletcher, Flint, Gaudier-Brzeska, the Hueffers, the Pounds, Upward, and Mrs. Russell — but not the Lawrences.

many a long and bitter year. There were several people in Amy's large room . . . At that moment the door opened, and a tall slim young man, with bright red hair and the most brilliant blue eyes, came in with a lithe, springing step. As a rule I don't remember people's eyes, but I shall not forget Lawrence's — they showed such a vivid flame-like spirit.

Before Amy could start the introductions he said quickly:

"I say, I've just been talking to Eddie Marsh,* and he's most depressing. He says we shall be in the war." [9]

A month later, the Lawrences reciprocated Lowell's invitation and invited Lowell and the Aldingtons to visit them at Chesham. "Won't you drive over for the day, with Mrs. Russell or the Aldingtons?" Lawrence wrote. [10] "On Thursday, the twenty-seventh they drove down for the visit." [11] Lawrence was at the pinnacle of his early success. His first three novels, *The White Peacock, The Trespasser,* and *Sons and Lovers,* were all in print, as was his first book of poems, *Love Poems and Others.*

Because of the schism among the Imagists and the importance of the movement to modern poetry, there has been a good deal of talk about who was and who was not in the Imagist group and whether D. H. Lawrence should be considered a member. Insofar as Pound created the Imagist movement to launch H.D., it is only natural to state, as Harold Monro does, that H.D. is the truest Imagist of the group. But as H.D. said, "One writes the kind of poetry one likes. Other people put labels on it." [12] In actuality, Lawrence had as much poetic right to be associated with the group as did Flint, Fletcher, Lowell, or Richard Aldington. Pound, of course, always argued that Lawrence was an "Amygist" rather than an Imagist — he, Pound, had never invited Lawrence to join the group; Amy Lowell had issued the invitation. Pound also made it clear that his decision to exclude Lawrence from "his movement" was not grounded wholly in aesthetics; he had conceded that Lawrence had learned the "proper treatment" of modern subjects. Lawrence, it must be noted, was somewhat amused by the very visible politics of Imagism that were brought into the open by Lowell's proposed anthologies. He did not object to Lowell's insistence that "he too was an Imagist," and he welcomed the opportunity for the greater exposure of his poetry that Lowell's annual anthologies would provide. But he was clearly unwilling to involve himself directly in the 1914 dispute between

*Eddie Marsh (1872–1953) was the editor of the *Georgian Poetry* anthologies and a patron of poets. Aldington identifies Marsh as the private secretary to the prime minister, but Edward Nehls indicates that Aldington is in error here and that in July 1914 Marsh was a secretary in the admiralty under Winston Churchill.

the Aldingtons, Lowell, and Pound; he did not wish to offend Pound, who had given him encouragement and support in 1909 before he had attained his critical success.

In the fall of 1914, Aldington and H.D. moved from Kensington to 7 Christchurch Place, Hampstead. In her memoir of Pound, H.D. suggests that they moved after seeing early drafts of Pound's Cantos. H.D. was expecting her first child in the spring of 1915. Later that year the Lawrences moved to 1 Byron Villas, Hampstead, near the Aldingtons' residence. The Aldingtons and the Lawrences lived in the Vale of Health, a corner of Hampstead Heath surrounded by eight hundred acres of park and woodland.

It was during this period, mid-1914 to mid-1915, that Lawrence became serious about the establishment of a utopian community. "The promised land has many names. Lawrence's name for it was *Rananim* . . . It may have had something to do with the Hebrew root meaning 'rejoice.' "[13]

From the start H.D. was to be a member. Over the years 1914 to 1918, candidates for Lawrence's Rananim changed from month to month. Dr. and Mrs. Eder, Cecil Gray, Hilda Aldington, Dorothy Yorke, S. S. Koteliansky, William Henry Hocking, Catherine Carswell and her husband, Gordon Campbell, his friend Shearman, and Mark Gertler and others were all at times considered. Conspicuously absent from all the known lists of candidates was Richard Aldington.

Lawrence must have discussed the idea of Rananim with H.D. on many occasions. In a letter to Edward Nehls written in 1952, Aldington stressed the spiritual affinities between Lawrence and Hilda Doolittle and commented: "Lawrence's Rananim may have been indebted to New England."[14] Aldington attributes Lawrence's and H.D.'s interest in a utopia to racial heredity. "The New England type," he says, "is your clue to Lawrence, who came from much the same stock":

> Note how proud he was at having been brought up in Oliver Cromwell's sect, the Congregationalists . . . H.D. and L. [Lawrence] had the same passion for flowers and used them as symbols for beauty. Of course, behind both is the ancient Norse-Teuton-Saxon strain, hating big cities, and crazy about ideal little "communities." I was always having to crawfish out of the schemes for them.[15]

Although this statement presents the H.D.–D. H. Lawrence relationship in a distorted light, it gives us some sense of how much the idea of living together in a poetic community was in the two poets' minds during this period. Aldington is undoubtedly correct to see the affinities between Lawrence's Rananim and H.D.'s Moravian background.

In *The Quest for Rananim: D. H. Lawrence's Letters to S. S. Koteliansky*, Daryl Zytaruk says: "The Rananim idea was uppermost in Lawrence's mind in January, 1915." [16] In a letter to W. E. Hopkin * dated January 18, 1915, Lawrence says:

> We will also talk of my pet scheme. I want to gather together about twenty souls and sail away from this world of war and squalor and found a little community where there shall be no money but a sort of communism as far as the necessities of life go, and some real decency. It is to be a colony built up on the real decency which is in each member of the community. A community which is established upon the assumption of goodness in the members, instead of the assumption of badness. [17]

In *Bid Me to Live*, H.D. writes of how Aldington (Rafe) had been upset about her relationship with Lawrence (Rico): "He was worried about Rico . . . It started — I don't know how it started . . . He was the only one who seemed remotely to understand what I felt when I was so ill — well — it was long ago, I know. But he understood that." [18]

The illness to which H.D. is undoubtedly referring is the birth of a stillborn child in the spring of 1915. The child was Aldington's, but Aldington was not involved in her pregnancy and was unsympathetic about her loss of the baby. There is also no doubt that the marriage was all but ended by Aldington's decision to take H.D.'s period of confinement as the occasion for a romantic involvement with Brigit Patmore. Lawrence had comforted her during that very difficult time. Writing about Lawrence in *Bid Me to Live*, H.D. says to Aldington: "He came several times to the flat in Hampstead when you were out. He watched me once peeling apples in one of those Spanish pottery bowls . . ." [19]

During World War II, which brought back memories of World War I, H.D. had a dream in which Lawrence appeared. "Lawrence did not come into War II . . . though once in a dark, bomb–shattered night I had a dream of him. It was a fiery, golden Lawrence, it was nothing but a fleeting presence and the words, 'Hilda, you are the only one of the whole crowd, who can really *write*.' " [20]

Of the Imagist group H.D. was the only one whose work Lawrence admired. During a conversation with Glenn Hughes in May 1929, Lawrence joked a good deal about Imagism "and declared

---

*William Hopkin (1862–1951) was a friend of Lawrence's from Eastwood. As a young man Lawrence discussed socialism with Hopkin and through him met many prominent socialists of the day.

there never had been such a thing as imagism. It was all an illusion of Ezra Pound's, he said, and was nonsense." For the professional Imagists he had little praise. H.D. was an exception. Even after their estrangement Lawrence spoke well of her work. He admired her poems, though he couldn't read many of them at once. "She is like a person walking a tightrope; you wonder if she'll get across."[21]

In 1915 H.D.'s marriage to Aldington was rapidly disintegrating and her involvement with Lawrence was intensifying. It is not entirely clear how much H.D. and Lawrence saw of each other during this period, although the letters from H.D. to Amy Lowell indicate that the Aldingtons and the Lawrences were together a good deal in Hampstead.* We do know that during this time H.D. and Lawrence began to exchange manuscripts and continued to do so for some time. We also know that they were emotionally close during the period from 1915 to 1918, but we have to rely primarily upon their poetry and prose to give us a sense of what form their personal relationship took during these years.

It seems to have been widely known within their circle but only rarely acknowledged publicly that Lawrence's references to Isis in his writing were veiled references to H.D. "The two writers (H.D. and Lawrence) . . . agreed that the world was in pieces and that men should be looking for ways to bring it together . . . After Lawrence died Stephen Guest † gave H.D. a copy of *The Man Who Died,* saying that it was written for her and that she was the priestess of Isis."[22]

The publication of a poem by Lawrence in *Poetry* in December 1914 jarred H.D. into a real recognition of Lawrence's existence as a person and poet in her life. The poem, entitled "Don Juan," has a taunting tone.

> It is Isis the mystery
> Must be in love with me.
>
> Here this round ball of earth,
> Where all the mountains sit

*In a letter of November 27, 1915, to Amy Lowell, written in H.D.'s hand but apparently from Aldington, Aldington says: "We are seeing quite a good deal of Lawrence as he lives just around the corner."

†Stephen Guest (1902–1974) was the son of the Right Honourable Leslie Haden Haden-Guest, M.C., first baron of Saling in the county of Essex, and Edith Low of London. His parents divorced in 1909, and his mother then married Dr. David Eder. Dr. Eder and Dr. Barbara Low, Edith's sister, were leaders in the psychoanalytic movement in England and became close friends of D. H. Lawrence after 1914. During the 1930s Stephen Guest and H.D. were close friends; he was a writer and translator, and became Lord Haden-Guest in 1960 upon his father's death.

Solemn in groups,
And the bright rivers flit
Round them for girth:

Here the trees and troops
Darken the shining grass;
And many bright people pass
Like plunder from heaven:
Many bright people pass
Plundered from heaven.

But what of the mistresses,
What the beloved seven?
— They were but witnesses,
I was just driven.

Where is there peace for me?
It is Isis the mystery
Must be in love with me.[23]

What Lawrence is doing here is "Imagist," even though he wrote the poem in 1913, before he was officially invited to join the Imagist group. Mountains sitting solemn in groups, trees and troops darkening the shining grass — this is an allusion to poems and poets in the language of natural phenomena and is Imagist speech. It came as naturally to Lawrence as it did to H.D. And Amy Lowell was correct in her assessment that Lawrence too was an Imagist. We may assume that Lawrence had been keeping up with developments in England, including the new movement, Imagism, before he actually met the members of the group.

Lawrence published "Don Juan" in the midst of a series of poems that invoke deeply felt emotions over his mother's death. "Grief," "Memories," "Weariness," and "Service of All the Dead" are full of death images: "And black-scarfed faces of women-folk wistfully/Watch at the banner of death, and the mystery."[24] This expression of love in the context of death —particularly his mother's death — is significantly characteristic of Lawrence as a poet. H.D.'s perception of Lawrence as the embodiment of the Achilles archetype, which we will examine in greater depth as this study proceeds, is not unrelated to this early "Don Juan" manifestation in *Poetry* magazine.

In a poem that appeared in the same issue of *Poetry* as Pound's "Exile's Letter" and three months after Lawrence's "Don Juan," H.D. poignantly expressed the sense of separation and estrangement from her husband that she was experiencing during this period in her life. In March 1915 she published "The Wind Sleepers."

> Whiter
> than the crust
> left by the tide,
> we are stung by the hurled sand
> and the broken shells.
>
> We no longer sleep,
> sleep in the wind.
> We awoke and fled
> through the Peiraeic gate.[25]

In subsequent publications of the poem, "Peiraeic gate" was changed to "city gate." In either case, the city to which H.D. refers is a symbol of civilization and, in the classical world she invokes, of marriage. The wind is a traditional classical symbol for inspiration. In the context of the poem, the "wind sleepers" are poets. In the tension of an increasingly impossible marriage, H.D. imagines a state before or beyond marriage, a state of pure communication and communion, a state of poetry and grace. We think of Lawrence's Rananim. Marriage has proven to be a fall from the state of nature.

> Chant in a wail
> that never halts.
> Pace a circle and pay tribute
> with a song.

The poem ends with a lament for a lost time and place. The tone is bleak; there is no hope for another life. The presentation of the situation is stark, and the scene desolate.

> When the roar of a dropped wave
> breaks into it,
> pour meted words
> of sea-hawks and gulls
> and sea-birds that cry
> discords.

12

The Sacrifice
of Iphigeneia

IN THE JUNE 1915 issue of the *Egoist,* an article on Imagism entitled "Two Notes" was published by May Sinclair. It is a remarkable statement which demonstrates an interesting understanding of both H.D. and the movement. Of H.D., Sinclair writes:

> To me H.D. is the most significant of the Imagists . . . I am not sure that I know . . . what Imagism is. But I am pretty certain which of several old things it is *not.* It is not Symbolism . . . the Image is not a substitute; it does not stand for anything but itself. Presentation not Representation is the watchword of the school. The Image, I take it, is Form . . . It is form *and* substance . . . And in no case is the Image a symbol of reality (the object); it is reality (the object) itself.[1]

Of Imagism, Sinclair writes:

> For all poets, old and new, the poetic act is a sacramental act with its rubric and its ritual. The Victorian poets are Protestant. For them the bread and wine are symbols of Reality, the body and the blood. They are given "in remembrance." The sacrament is incomplete. The Imagists are Catholic; they believe in Trans-substantiation. For them the bread and wine are the body and the blood. They are given. The thing is done. *Ita Missa est.*[2]

H.D.'s translation from the *Iphigeneia in Aulis* of Euripides was written in Hampstead and an excerpt was published in the November 1915 issue of the *Egoist* under the title "Choruses from Iphigeneia in Aulis." The text of Euripides was the base upon which H.D. developed her poem, which was not intended to be a literal translation. As Ezra Pound wrote of his translation *Homage to Sextus Propertius,* "There was never any question of translation, let alone literal translation. My job was to bring a dead man to life, to present a living figure."[3]

In her "Iphigeneia" H.D. is presenting in the form of a translation the reality of her situation as it is occurring; the Iphigeneia of Euripides is the discourse through which she does so. The act of presentation is an act of witness to the reality that is being enacted. The historical Iphigeneia is not the issue; the issue is the Iphigeneia being sacrificed at this time, at this place.

But while H.D.'s presentation is not Protestant in Sinclair's sense of the word — it does not confirm historical reality — neither is it precisely Catholic in the sense that Sinclair suggests, for it is an act not of commitment to the perceived reality but rather of witness. In other words, while the consciousness is not, as Sinclair notes, historically oriented Protestantism (such as Calvinism), it is close to the consciousness of the Quakers or Moravians of H.D.'s religious upbringing. It is H.D.'s responsibility to present what is happening, to bear witness. Of the wartime night bombings of London H.D. writes in "The Gift": "If my mind at those moments had one regret, it was that I might not be able to bear witness to this truth, might be annihilated before I had time to bear witness."[4]

In her translation H.D. presents herself as both Iphigeneia and Helen. She is no more condoning the sacrifice of herself than were the early Moravians and Quakers who were persecuted and martyred for what they saw. Rather, she is bearing witness to the event. The reality that she presents is that she, Iphigeneia, is being sacrificed so that the Greeks (the poets) may instead have Helen, the ideal, impersonal presentation of H.D., through her poetry.

> I crossed sand-hills.
> I stand among the sea-drift before Aulis.
> I crossed Euripos' strait —
> Foam hissed after my boat.
>
> I left Chalkis,
> My city and the rock-ledges.
> Arethusa twists among the boulders,
> Increases — cuts into the surf.
>
> I come to see the battle-line
> And the ships rowed here
> By these spirits —
> The Greeks are but half-man.
>
> Golden Menelaos
> And Agamemnon of proud birth
> Direct the thousand ships.

> They have cut pine-trees
> For their oars.
> They have gathered the ships for one purpose:
> Helen shall return.[5]

The situation is that Paris (Richard Aldington) has taken Helen from her first husband, Menelaus (Ezra Pound). "Paris the herdsman passed through them/When he took Helen — Aphrodite's gift." Consequently the Greeks (including Lawrence personified as Achilles) are going to war to reclaim Helen (H.D., the poet) from Paris.

> A flash —
> Achilles passed across the beach.
> (He is the sea-woman's child
> Chiron instructed.)

The association of D. H. Lawrence with light is a central motif of H.D.'s writing. The first reference to Achilles in this translation is to "a flash." He appears later in the poem, "Where light flashed below them on the sand." And again:

> "From Thessaly,
> The great light
>
> Whom Thetis will beget,"
> (He [Chiron] spoke his name),
> "Will come with the Myrmidons
> Spearsman and hosts with shields,
> Golden and metal-wrought,
> To scatter fire
> Over Priam's beautiful land."[6]

The Greeks are making war on the Trojans and the city of Troy, which is H.D.'s symbol for the state of marriage — a walled city, itself a labyrinth, that is always under attack by the lusty Greeks.

H.D. explains how she, Helen, had been possessed by Aldington: "Helen, possessed,/Followed a stranger/From the Greek courtyard./They would avenge this."

Thus, by 1915 H.D. had come to see her marriage to Aldington in the context of the abduction of Helen by Paris. She presents this "image" as her understanding of the reality of her life.

> Paris came to Ida
> He grew to slim height
> Among the silver-hoofed beasts . . .
>
> He came before Helen's house.
> He stood on the ivory steps.

He looked upon Helen and brought
Desire to the eyes
That looked back —

The Greeks have snatched up their spears.
They have pointed the helms of their ships
Toward the bulwarks of Troy.[7]

As we have already seen in "Hermes," "Orion Dead," and other early H.D. poems, H.D. speaks the language of Greek mythology to tell her own story. Landor may have been an influence. What Welby says of Landor in his preface to Landor's *Complete Works* is also true of H.D.'s translation of Euripides: "With some exceptions, he made the people of his conversations and dramatic poems in his own likeness, caring only to secure the minimum of historical colour necessary" for allusion.[8]

The "historical colour" helps to set a context. If the story of Iphigeneia at Aulis were not so well known to H.D.'s audience, it would be necessary for her to do a good deal of explaining to set the context for what she wants to present. The historical story of Helen and Iphigeneia and the Trojan War informs her poem; her translation is a modern interpretation that is not intended to inform the historical story. H.D. chose to translate *Iphigeneia* because what she had to say at this time had been said before, quite well, by Euripides.

In presenting the story of the Trojan War in a new form, H.D. comes to terms with the ironic fact that she (Helen) is being blamed because the poets (the Greeks) are fighting over her. She mentions ironically that it is also Leda's fault, for giving birth to her after being ravished by Zeus. That is to say, the conflict is her fault for being born or the fault of another woman, Leda, for having given birth to her, "if men speak truth" — the implication being, of course, that they do not, that they manage to blame women for all their own misbehavior. In presenting the lament of the Trojan maidens, H.D. is suggesting that all women, Trojan and Greek, are made to suffer for the warrior impulses of men. The implication is that the real war is not between the Trojans and the Greeks, but between men and women.

"Helen has brought this.
They will tarnish our bright hair.
They will take us as captives
For Helen — born of Zeus
When he sought Leda with bird-wing
And touched her with bird-throat —
If men speak truth.[9]

Iphigeneia is H.D.'s symbol for the young woman Hilda. And Iphigeneia as persona includes the girl-child Hilda has just lost; that child was stillborn after some war news was broken to H.D. in a brutal fashion.* H.D. presents Iphigeneia in a way that reinvokes the wild virginal chastity of Pound's "dryad," and gives the scene of her sacrifice a bleak and brutal clarity.

> And like a little beast,
> Dappled and without horns,
> That scampered on the hill-rocks,
> They will leave you
> With stained throat . . .

Iphigeneia, the virgin (that is, Hilda before her marriage), has no sympathy for Helen, who ran off with Paris (that is, H.D. the poet, who ran off with Aldington).

> O wretched, wretched, —
> I know you, Helen, sharp to do hurt.
> I am slaughtered for your deceit.

The "deceit" is a reference to H.D.'s marriage, which she has come to see as a betrayal of herself. In other words, she understands that her rebellion, her marriage, was not only against her parents and against Pound, but also a rebellion against the truest part of herself. She was to explore this theme in fuller detail and depth in the epic poem *Helen in Egypt*. But the curse against the husband, Paris/Aldington, begins here:

> Alas for that Phrygian cleft,
> Beaten by snow,
> The mountain-hill, Ida,
> Where Priam left the young prince,
> Brought far from his mother
> To perish on the rocks:
> Paris who is called
> Idaeos, Idaeos
> In the Phrygian court.

> Would that he had never thrived,
> Would that he had not kept the flocks,
> O that he had not dwelt
> At that white place of the water-gods:

*The war news that so upset H.D. was Aldington's report of the sinking of the *Lusitania* by the Germans on May 7, 1915, with a loss of 1198 lives, including many Americans. Aldington greeted this news with excitement because he felt it would bring the Americans into the war.

In meadows,
Thick with yellow flower-sprays
And flowers, tint of rose,
And the hyacinths we break for gods.

It was in the writing of this poem that H.D. came to the painful realization that Ezra Pound had "sacrificed" her for the spirit of poetry. Through his publication of her poems, she had become the center, the muse, of a circle of poets. And the muse is, to her way of thinking, the sacrifice. "I am sent to death," she writes, "To bring honour to the Greeks."

H.D.'s sense of estrangement from her home and from her mother is sharply expressed in the voice of Iphigeneia, who is about to be separated from her mother forever for the sake of a man's brutal need (Menelaus needs wind in order that his ships may sail; that is, that his career as a poet may flourish). The sacrifice of Iphigeneia will provide him with the wind (inspiration) he needs.

Oh I am miserable:
You cherished me, my mother,
But even you desert me.
I am sent to an empty place.

In H.D.'s translation it is Agamemnon, the representative of the world of the fathers, the patriarchy, who sacrifices her: "My father, as priest awaits me/at the right altar-step." (The original meaning of *altar* is a place of sacrifice, of slaughter.) The right, as opposed to the left, signifies the way of the fathers as opposed to the way of the mothers. From H.D.'s point of view, a woman's birth as a poet is a birth into the world of the fathers and a sacrifice of her maternal heritage and primal integrity. It is therefore appropriate that as Iphigeneia enters the world of the fathers — the world of death — her initiation should take place upon the right altar-step.

The poem builds in drama as it proceeds, and the dramatic irony at its end is certainly in the spirit of Euripides, even though the translation does not pretend to be a literal one. As Iphigeneia is sacrificed she is destroyed. But her sacrifice will bring destruction to Troy; therefore, Helen of Troy is also destroyed. H.D. is saying that the virgin Hilda who was to have wed Pound was destroyed as H.D. was initiated into the world of poetry as the muse of a poetic circle. And she is also recognizing that as she was initiated into the world of poetry she began to lose her marriage (Troy, we will remember, is her symbol for her marriage to Aldington and for the state of marriage in general).

The poem builds quickly to a climax as the actual moment of sacrifice is approached.

> She comes to meet death.
> To stain the altar of the goddess,
> To hold her girl-throat
> Toward the knife-thrust.

There is certainly a sense in which "Iphigeneia," like so many of H.D.'s poems, is a protest against the reality it so starkly presents. While H.D. makes no attempt to cast blame upon the poets by moralizing about their manner, the hope is that the act of bearing witness to this lurid reality will shame the greedy "Greeks" into changing their ways with women. As Bryher writes in her memoir, *The Heart to Artemis,* "We believed that if we stated facts without comment, moral or otherwise, mankind must see its folly and revise its laws."[10]

Traditionally, men have so glorified and exalted the role of the muse in the creative life of the artist that is comes as something of a revelation to hear how it actually feels to be a muse from a woman who happened to find herself in that position. H.D.'s fate, of course, had been decreed by Pound. In *Helen in Egypt,* H.D. uses the sacrifice of Iphigeneia as a central motif of the "Pallinode." Remembering "the lure, the deception, the lie/that brought her to Aulis," she speaks of Ezra Pound's act of luring her to England on the false pretext of marriage.

> "we will pledge, forsooth, our dearest child,
>
> to the greatest hero in Greece;
> bring her here
> to join with hand
>
> in the bridal pledge at the altar";
> but the pledge was a pledge to Death,
> to War and the armies of Greece.[11]

Just as Priapus and Hermes were the subjects of H.D.'s first "translations" from the *Greek Anthology,* so Iphigeneia is in this instance the subject of her translation. In the Greek drama the characters wore masks; in H.D.'s translations Euripides himself is a mask through which H.D. is able to present her situation as it is occurring.

Translation is interpretation. The first meaning of the word *translation* in the dictionary is to bear or change from one place, condition, etc., to another; to transfer. The second meaning is to remove to heaven — originally implying a removal independent of death. Both H.D.'s and Pound's concepts of translation take these primary meanings into account. The third meaning of the word, to turn into one's own or another language, is not as significant in terms of understanding H.D.'s and Pound's translations. These poets knew clearly from the beginning that the line between translation and original work was no line at all for either of them; their translations were simply poems that followed different rules — that is, rules dictated by the original source, which they chose in the same way one chooses one's own words. The original text was simply the foundation from which these Imagist poets worked to get their message across.

H.D.'s *Helen in Egypt* was begun 37 years after she began her translation of Euripides' *Iphigeneia in Aulis* and fifteen years after she published her translation of his *Ion*. While H.D. could not possibly have been aware of the prophetic significance of the "Iphigeneia" translation in 1916, the central cast of characters became relatively fixed in her mind. Pound would continue to be presented as Menelaus and Odysseus; Aldington would always take the form of Paris, and Lawrence would appear as Achilles. H.D. saw her *Helen in Egypt* as a continuation of her Euripides work.

As in the case of the Greek dramatists, H.D.'s aim in her poetry is recognition. As Aristotle writes in his *Poetics*, "Recognition [*ana gnôrisis*], as the name indicates, is a change from ignorance to knowledge."[12] The intent of H.D.'s translation is to move us from ignorance to knowledge, with Euripides, in this instance, as her mask.

13

The War Poems

SUPERIMPOSED, as it were, upon the palimpsest of H.D.'s early experiences with Pound and her marriage with Aldington came the poetry of D. H. Lawrence. Lawrence's poems presented H.D. with an exotic world of chaos against which she pitted herself for definition, but it is also true that she was drawn as by a powerful magnetic force straight to the center of that world.

In a sense Lawrence the poet and Lawrence the novelist were two different people. In a letter of February 12, 1915, E. M. Forster writes: "I like the Lawrence who talks to Hilda and sees birds and is physically restful . . . but I do not like the deaf, impertinent fanatic who has nosed over his own little sexual round until he believes that there is no other path for others to take."[1]

It was Lawrence the poet H.D. came to know during the war; Lawrence the novelist and social critic was to be known to her later. Since our point of location is H.D.'s perception, we will be seeing Lawrence the poet from her perspective, a perspective that is somewhat at variance with what H.D. called the "growing tidewave or gulf-stream of the Lawrence legend."[2] As H.D. understood experience, we all materialize or manifest in different ways at different times, and no point on the spectrum is static.

In a letter to Cecil Gray dated November 7, 1917, Lawrence writes with a note of defensiveness and bitterness of his relationship with H.D.

> You are only half right about the disciples and the alabaster box. If Jesus had paid more attention to Magdalene, and less to his disciples, it would have been better. It was not the ointment-pouring which was so devastating, but the discipleship of the twelve.
>
> As for me and my "women," I know what they are and aren't, and though there is a certain messiness, there is a further reality.

Take away the subservience and feet-washing, and the pure under-standing between the Magdalene and Jesus went deeper than the understanding between the disciples and Jesus, or Jesus and the Bethany women. But Jesus himself was frightened of the knowl-edge which subsisted between the Magdalene and him, a knowl-edge deeper than the knowledge of Christianity and "good," deeper than love, anyhow.

And both you and Frieda need to go one world deeper in knowl-edge. As for spikenard, if I chance to luxuriate in it, it is by the way: not so very Philippically filthy either. Not that it matters.

I don't mind a bit being told where I am wrong — not by you or anybody I respect. Only you don't seem to be going for me in anything where I am really wrong: a bit Pharisaic, both you and Frieda: external.

It seems to me there is a whole world of knowledge to forsake, a new, deeper, lower one to *entamer*. And your hatred of me, like Frieda's hatred of me, is your cleavage to a world of knowledge and being which you ought to forsake, which, by organic law, you must depart from or die. And my "women," Esther Andrews, Hilda Aldington, etc. represent, in an impure and unproud, subser-vient, cringing, bad fashion, I admit — but represent none the less the threshold of a new world, or underworld, of knowledge and being. And the Hebridean songs, which represent you and Frieda in this, are songs of the damned: that is, songs of those who inhabit an underworld which is forever an underworld, never to be made open and whole. And you would like us all to inhabit a suggestive underworld which is never revealed or opened, only intimated, only *felt* between the initiated. — I won't have it. The old world must burst, the underworld must be open and whole, new world. You want an emotional sensuous underworld, like Frieda and the Hebrideans: my "women" want an ecstatic subtly-intellectual un-derworld, like the Greeks — Orphicism — like Magdalene at her feet-washing — and there you are. *[3]

The relationship between H.D. and Lawrence began in London in the opening days of World War I and deepened during the en-suing months, particularly during the time they lived near each

*When this letter was first published in Aldous Huxley's 1932 edition of *The Letters of D. H. Lawrence,* H.D.'s name was deleted. The deletion was continued in several subsequent publications, including Harry T. Moore's two-volume edi-tion of *The Collected Letters of D. H. Lawrence,* published after H.D.'s death. Her name has been deleted from other published Lawrence letters of the period, and other letters that associate her with Lawrence have been destroyed — most no-tably Lawrence's letters to her, which were destroyed by Aldington after the breakup of the Aldington-H.D. marriage. In his recent book, *D. H. Lawrence's Nightmare,* Paul Delaney reinserted H.D.'s name into this letter as it appeared in the original manuscript, and H.D.'s name will presumably reappear in the new six-volume edition of Lawrence's letters now under way under the editorship of J. T. Boulton.

other in Hampstead in 1915. Each had an appreciation of the other's work, and they began to exchange manuscripts during this time. As Richard Aldington remarked, "As anyone can see from his *Collected Poems,* even Lawrence was for a time influenced by H.D."[4] Aldington in typical fashion minimizes the relationship.

The influence of D. H. Lawrence's poetry on H.D.'s poetry was far-reaching and long-lasting. H.D. read the very early poems he had written but not yet published when he met her and was enormously affected by them. She felt Lawrence was the only one who really understood how deeply she felt the loss of her first child in the spring of 1915 (see *Bid Me to Live*). They had both experienced a deep loss — H.D. had lost a child, Lawrence had lost his mother —and H.D. was very moved by the "mother" poems in *Amores.*

If we consider the poetry written during this period seriously, we find that a rare sympathy existed between H.D. and Lawrence. We will not find evidence of this relation in letters, for their letters to each other were destroyed. But the relationship was apparently not part of the social world they and their respective spouses inhabited so much as it was the essence of the intellectual and poetic world in which they lived. Since they lived close to each other in Hampstead and later in southern England, they did, of course, share friends and geographical location. Of the Imagist group, now defined by their regular appearances in *Poetry,* the *Egoist,* and the anthologies published by Amy Lowell, *Some Imagist Poets,* they were the outstanding poets. But if we are really to understand anything of the world of "knowledge and being" in which they lived, we must look to their poetry, for it was largely in the poetry that this "other world" was created and lived.

The exchange of manuscripts between Lawrence and H.D. continued throughout the war years. As the relationship deepened between the two writers, H.D. took Lawrence's poems more and more seriously. As she writes of Lawrence's *New Poems* in an unpublished memoir: "My heart contracted when I opened the book and found the poem he had sent me to Corfe Castle, when I was near Richard — was it in 1917 . . . . There was that other poem, *when you are dead I will bring roses and roses to cover your grave.* It seems I had been dead but the roses were to come later."[5] (The second poem referred to here is easily identifiable as "On That Day," originally written after Lawrence's mother's death in commemoration of her birthday.)

Many of the images presented in Lawrence's *New Poems* became central images in *Helen in Egypt.* One of the most striking of these is from Lawrence's poem "Seven Seals," from which H.D. took her image of "his fingers' remorseless steel." "Seven Seals" may have been the poem H.D. was referring to when she said, "My heart contracted . . ." It is that sort of poem. "The seven arcs," "the seven slats of the ladder," and the "wheel as a seal," all recurring images of H.D.'s visions, poems, and novels, are anticipated in it.

> And there
> Full mid-between the champaign of your breast
> I place a great and burning seal of love
> Like a dark rose, a mystery of rest
> On the slow bubbling of your rhythmic heart.
>
> Nay, I persist, and very faith shall keep
> You integral to me. Each door, each mystic port
> Of egress from you I will seal and steep
> In perfect chrism.
> Now it is done. The mort
> Will sound in heaven before it is undone.
>
> But let me finish what I have begun
> And shirt you now invulnerable in the mail
> Of iron kisses, kisses linked like steel . . .[6]

"Seven Seals" uses mystical language to speak of an erotic experience. D. H. Lawrence, as is suggested in the letter to Gray, was at this time involved in the Greek Orphic mysteries. The Orphic mysteries are, of course, related to the Egyptian mysteries — later Orphic priests wore Egyptian costumes — and the Egyptian mysteries are related to the Moravian liturgy. These mysteries all concern the fate of a sacred king — Orpheus, Osiris, Christ — who is killed and brought back to life. In the Greek case, Orpheus's wife, Eurydice, is killed; Orpheus descends to Hades and is allowed to lead her back to earth on the condition that he must not look to see if she is following him. But he does make the mistake of looking back, and Eurydice vanishes among the shades.

In February 1919 D. H. Lawrence published in *Poetry* magazine a group of poems which included "Pentecostal" as well as other war poems. These were collected later that year into a slim volume, *Bay*. Of them Lawrence writes: *"Bay* appeared in 1919, but the poems were written mostly in 1917 and 1918, after I left Cornwall perforce."[7] Like "Seven Seals," these poems of the war years often use mystical discourse to describe an erotic encounter. The change of title of "Pentecostal" to "Shades" is, as we shall see in chapter 15, related to the vanishing of Eurydice among the shades. It is also indicative of the way Lawrence moved from one world of metaphor to another — in this case, from the mystical Christian to the Orphic Greek. "Pentecostal," or "Shades," invokes a memory of a searing, soul-binding experience.

> Shall I tell you, then, how it is? —
> There came a cloven gleam
> Like a tongue of darkened flame
> To flicker in me.
>
> And so I seem
> To have you still the same
> In one world with me.
>
> In the flicker of a flower,
> In a worm that is blind, yet strives,
> In a mouse that pauses to listen
>
> Glimmers our
> shadow; . . .
>
> In every shaken morsel
> I see our shadow tremble
> As if it rippled from out of us hand in hand.
>
> As if it were part and parcel,
> One shadow, and we need not dissemble
> Our darkness: do you understand?
>
> For I have told you plainly how it is.[8]

A few of the poems of *Bay* rang so true to H.D.'s experience with Lawrence that, as we have noted, the images were indelibly stamped in her mind and appear in *Helen in Egypt,* written some thirty-five years later. H.D. seems to concur that she and Lawrence were shades.

> . . . true, I had met him, the New Mortal,
>
> baffled and lost,
> but I was a phantom Helen
> and he was Achilles' ghost.[9]

But elsewhere in *Helen in Egypt* she argues with herself. The argument has to do with the question of illusion and reality: Which world is real, the world of war, which is also the world of ordinary sensuous consciousness inhabited by Frieda and Cecil Gray which Lawrence had spoken of in his letter to Gray, or the world of poetry? Surely, says H.D., these worlds are not compatible. Her alternative statement on this issue is that Helen and Achilles were "not shadows nor shades,/but entities living a life/unfulfilled in Greece."[10]

In *Helen in Egypt* the world of poetry is set always in opposition to, and often in defiance of, the world of war. As H.D. says in her "Notes on Thought and Vision," "Egypt in the terms of world-consciousness is the act of love. Hellas is a child born."[11] But the world of poetry is also, paradoxically, one of war; it is a different kind of war. Lawrence's "The Attack" is a poem about transfiguration set in the context of London at war, with the air raids and the bombings, the attacks on London. It is an Imagist poem in the sense that we are presented with a double image. The poem is about the external war, World War I, and about the war in Lawrence himself. And it is difficult to deny that a kind of war between the ego and the passions occurs in the experience of transfiguration as Lawrence understands it. Lawrence's poem describes a mystical experience which for all its luminous brilliance he felt as an attack on the substance of his very self. But it led, at the same time, to a rebirth.

When we came out of the wood
Was a great light!
The night uprisen stood
In White.

I wondered, I looked around
It was so fair. The bright
Stubble upon the ground
Shone white . . .

After the terrible rage, the death,
This wonder stood glistening?
All shapes of wonder, with suspended breath,
Arrested listening

In ecstatic reverie;
The whole white Night! —
With wonder, every black tree
Blossomed outright.

I saw the transfiguration
And the present Host.
Transubstantiation
Of the Luminous Ghost.[12]

The kind of image invoked in this poem — the transfiguration of the "present Host" and the transubstantiation of the "Luminous Ghost" — is recognizably Laurentian. We find it recurring, most notably in *The Man Who Died*: "Suddenly it dawned on him: 'I asked them all [women] to serve me with the corpse of their love. And in the end I offered them only the corpse of my love. This is my body — take and eat — my corpse.'"[13]

To believe in transubstantiation — the body being transfigured from death to life, the body coming alive in the Passion — is to believe that such a change actually occurs. To believe in transfiguration in Lawrence's terms is to believe that such supernatural change occurs in the appearance of Jesus and that such a transformation is a recurring reality of human experience. But again we have a palimpsest image, for the host presented in this poem invokes the war dead, as in "Resurrection": "Now all the hosts are marching to the grave . . ."[14] And the white night invokes the "white searchlight rays" of Lawrence's "Zeppelin Nights," a poem about the night raids, the air bombings of London.[15] In many poems of this period, love is presented as the eternal reality and juxtaposed to the historical reality of a world at war.

The image of white night evoked in this poem also suggests a deepening of experience and a movement toward an eternal reality, the threshold of the world "deeper in knowledge" of which Lawrence speaks in his letter to Gray. In this poem it is the night that emerges as the ecstatic reality. The concept of night conveyed here is related to "the frightening knowledge which subsisted between the Magdalene and him." It is the kind of spiritual (and by implication sexual) knowledge that goes beyond or deeper than ordinary sensual experience. It is a knowledge of the more primal sexual bond, the bond that threatens the structure of the adult ego and the autonomy of the individual.

Lawrence's understanding of these religious concepts is close to the Moravian understanding of the same mystery. H.D.'s unpublished Moravian novel, "The Mystery," is thematically related to Lawrence's "The Attack," as is her poem "Hymn (for Count Zinzendorf, 1700–1760)," which presents the same paradox of life and death. Zinzendorf, like Lawrence, had a vision of a utopian community to be based upon fulfillment rather than renunciation. Lawrence, like Zinzendorf, believed that it was possible to live in a state of peace in the world but that such peace depended upon the creation of another world of consciousness (as in Rananim). H.D.'s "Hymn" employs the same language of mystical discourse as Lawrence's "Attack."

> Of unguent in a jar,
> We may ensample myrrh;
>
> So were His fragrance stored,
> Sealed up, compact, secure,
>
> In flawless alabaster,
> But for the spear;
>
> This is the wound of grace,
> This is the nesting-place

Of the white dove,
This is the wound of love;

The spear opened for us
The rose of purple fire,

The rose of iciest breath,
White rose of death;

The spear opened for us
The narrow way

Into the dust,
To the eternal day.[16]

In this poem, as in the Moravian symbolism of H.D.'s child-hood, the dust (symbol of darkness and death) becomes the eternal day. Sexuality (symbolized by the spear) inflicts the wound which opens both "the rose of purple fire" and "the rose of iciest breath." Death is equated with sexuality — the spear enters through the birth canal ("The spear opened for us/The narrow way") — but the sexual act is paradoxically equated with rebirth and "the eternal day."

Lawrence's presentation of "The Attack" inflamed H.D.'s imagination. The attack — whatever it was, however it material-ized — is a central image of *Helen in Egypt*. For H.D. it took place on a stretch of beach.

have you seen a gerfalcon
fall on his prey?
so my throat knew that day,

his fingers' remorseless steel,
when I had strength only to pray
Thetis, *let me go out, let me forget,*

let me be lost . . .[17]

The colophon of *Bay,* a woodcut engraving of a ship, became the eidolon, the "wooden image," of *Helen in Egypt. Helen in Egypt* is in part a meditation upon these early Imagist poems, which H.D. calls the "old pictures." She imagines their images as "hier-oglyphs, 'painted in bright primary colours.' "[18]

It might be objected that H.D. would have had to be a bit mad to take these words written during World War I so seriously so many years later. We must remember that words are spoken or written in a context of events, experiences, and actions, and it is this historical context that gives them their emotional impact. We have every reason not to respond to Lawrence's words with quite the same level of emotional intensity that H.D. did. We were not part of the landscape of the Imagist movement. Nor can we even begin to guess in what depths of being two people of such extraordinary sensitivity and intelligence responded to one another.

In her poem "Hippolytus Temporizes," written during this period, H.D. explains the image of sand as an image of the body: ". . . her bones/under the flesh are white/as sand which along a beach/covers and keeps the print/of the crescent shapes beneath."[19] In H.D.'s poems (as in her novel "Her"), if she writes of a "her," she is referring to herself. For instance, when she writes a poem about Thetis or Lais or Cassandra, she is using these all as personae for herself. She is by turns a mythological character, a vessel, a cup, a bowl, a tree, a stretch of sand, a river.

H.D. begins "She Rebukes Hippolyta" by asking, "Was she so chaste?" She explains that the landscape she describes in her poems has a human dimension. "The broken ridge of the hills," she writes, "was the line of a lover's shoulder."

> was she chaste?
>
> Who can say —
> the broken ridge of the hills
> was the line of a lover's shoulder,
> his arm-turn, the path to the hills,
> the sudden leap and swift thunder
> of mountain boulders, his laugh.[20]

Think about what I am saying, she seems to be telling her readers. Translate if you will. This language is no mere solipsistic projection of human emotions onto a natural landscape. This is a language for communication between poets. As she says of Rico (Lawrence) in *Bid Me to Live*, "There it was, the union, the two minds that yet had the urge, or the cheek you might say, to dare to communicate."[21]

The communication became a kind of communion.

> She was mad —
> as no priest, no lover's cult
> could grant madness;
> the wine that entered her throat
> with the touch of the mountain rocks
> was white, intoxicant:
> she, the chaste,
> was betrayed by the glint
> of light on the hills,
> the granite splinter of rocks,
> the touch of the stone

where heat melts
toward the shadow-side of the rocks.[22]

In July 1919 Harriet Monroe published a few poems from D. H.
Lawrence's manuscript of war poems, "Bits." The manuscript,
now in the University of Chicago Library, contains thirty poems,
twelve of which were published in *Poetry* under the title "War
Films." These poems are set during World War I in England and
were written in 1915–1916. They were not included in Lawrence's
Collected Poems (1928) and remained unpublished until 1964, when
they were included in *The Complete Poems of D. H. Lawrence.* As
the "War Films" description implies, the poems are Imagist; they
are pictures. This poetry describes a love affair in the context of
the war. Many of the poems employ religious language which is
strongly suggestive of Moravian discourse. "Litany of Grey
Nurses," for example, is addressed to a Sister.

> Sister, oh holy Sister
> Thou door to heaven, Sister!
> Thou of the dark, clenched tomb!
> Thou newcomer to the Angels!
> Thou silver beam in the Presence![23]

One poem, "Pieta," is addressed to Mary. (In Lawrence's poetry and prose, the Virgin Mary is equivalent to Mary Magdalene.)

> Thou our Maiden, thou who dwellest in Heaven
> We pray for thee, Mary delightful, that God may bless thee![24]

Other poems of this period reveal Lawrence's developing concept of God and resurrection. In "Resurrection of the Flesh" Lawrence writes of a relationship with a woman which is to be spoken
of to no one.

> Oh then be nameless and be never seen!
> And speak no syllable, and never be
> Even thought of! — but between
> Your nothing and my nothingness, touch me!
>
> They should never have given you names, and never, never
> Have lent you voice, nor spoken of the face
> That shone and darkened. They were all too clever.
> Now let it be finished! leave no trace!
>
> Reveal us nothing! roll the scripts away!
> Destroy at last the heavy books of stone!
> Kill off the Word, that's had so much to say!
> And show us nothing! leave us quite alone!

Go, go away and leave us not a trace
Of any Godhead, leave us in the dark!
And let the dark be soundless, without face
Or voice or any single spark
Of what was God! . . .[25]

In "Maiden's Prayer" Lawrence writes: "I have come to the house of God."[26]

These poems mark a departure from Lawrence's previous poetry. Not only is he employing a religious language to speak of his experience, but he is also, in the Imagist manner, writing quite clearly and deliberately of one thing under the veil of another. To put it another way, he is writing of ordinary experience as extraordinary experience, natural as supernatural. "The Girl in Cairo" is an Imagist poem which speaks of his lover as a friend — a very monastic, Quaker, or Moravian form of speech. The poem also invokes the image of the canopy or tent which the narrator hangs to shelter the lovers. The poem reads in its entirety:

Oh Colonel, you from Embaba
Join me to my well-beloved friend.
  And if this night my love should come to me
  My cashmere shawl I'll hang for a canopy
  And say — Be welcome, dearest friend;
  Oh, how this night has happened perfectly![27]

In "Mourning" Lawrence writes of the shed as another place where the lover and his beloved meet:

Why do you go about looking for me, mother?
I and my betrothed are together in the shed
sitting there together for a little while.[28]

In "Swing Song of a Girl and a Soldier," the girl addresses her lover as brother:

Brother, I like your fragrance.
It smells like the shouting of men
Womanless shouting in anger.
Brother, let me die down again.[29]

These poems are strikingly devout, but the poetic quality is that of a primitive religious sensibility, as in "The Well in Africa."

Thou well of Kilossa, thy well-chords are of silver
And a draught of thee is strength to a soul in hell.
Kilossa, sweet well of my strength, thou corded with silk
Heal me, for body and soul I am not well.[30]

In these poems of "Bits" Lawrence has moved into a world of consciousness that is more purely devotional than the world he explored in his earlier poems. It is the milieu of which he writes to Gray — the world of himself and the Magdalene; and it is one he will reinvoke in moments of *Lady Chatterley's Lover* and *The Man Who Died*. But "Bits" is a definite departure from his other work; it is recognizably his most Imagist poetry. It also reveals in a very real sense an intensely religious phase. God, by which Lawrence means the substance of the union of the lovers, is the eternal reality. And no mere "external" or purely sensual experience of love can take away what God has given. In "Neither Moth nor Rust" Lawrence writes:

> God, only God is eternally.
> God is forever, and only He.
> Where, white maid, are the men you have loved?
> They are dead, so God was between you, you see.[31]

§ § §

Images of the tent, hut, shrine, or little house in the woods recur in H.D.'s poetry. They present a lover's meeting place. They also recur in H.D.'s novels written between 1921 and 1951. The hut or house is presented with unusual clarity in the unpublished auto-biographical novel "Paint It Today." Following is an excerpt of a letter from Midget (H.D.) to her friend Frances Josepha (Frances Gregg).

> I have a lover — not Basil [Basil is the Aldington character].
> I don't see him very often, but I know he is there. He is a distinguished poet.
> I suppose you might say I was a spiritual prostitute, but I don't think so; no, I don't think so, because I have only one lover and he is a great poet.
> You might say that he is one of those evil things you read about in great tomes, who come and seduce women, those ghouls or whatever. You know what I mean, from Anatole France we read on the boat crossing. But he is not a ghoul. He is a spirit. He is a great poet.
> We don't know each other very well yet. We simply meet by accident in the woods, or in the little house in the woods. We usually look and look at each other. Sometimes he says a poem. Sometimes it grows dark and my ecstasy becomes so great that I leave him there alone and come back myself to my room and try to read and try to work. Sometimes I write a poem. Of course, none as beautiful as his poems.[32]

In her "Autobiographical Notes," H.D. relates "Paint It To-day" to *Bid Me to Live (A Madrigal).* The narrative of *Bid Me to Live,* she says, is a continuation of the narrative of the earlier novel.

> We wrote at St. James Court, unpublished novel, *Paint It Today.* At Riant Chateau we wrote two or three short-story sequences, as for the war experience in London and Cornwall; these, we later destroyed. This "novel" was continued through the years; in 1939 it was assembled. But it was not until Christmas, 1948, Hotel de la Paix, Lausanne, that the MSS. was re-read (it had been in Kenwin, during the war years). Two-thirds of the MSS was destroyed, but a new end was assembled and the whole re-typed and now called *MADRIGAL.*[33]

Bid Me to Live (A Madrigal) is H.D.'s novel about her relation-ship with D. H. Lawrence. In her "Notes on Recent Writing," written in 1949, H.D. explains that she has been writing and re-writing the story of the war years and that all of her prose work, from "Paint It Today" to "Madrigal," is related to the early poems. Her biography, she tells us, is in the poems and autobio-graphical novels. Of *Bid Me to Live* she writes on December 12, 1949:

> *Madrigal:* This story of War I was roughed out summer, 1939, in Switzerland . . .
> I had been writing or trying to write this story since 1921. I wrote in various styles, simply or elaborately, stream of conscious-ness or straight narrative. I re-write this story under various titles, in London and in Switzerland. But after I had corrected and typed out *Madrigal,* last winter I was able conscientiously to destroy these earlier versions.† I had expected at first sight of the torn and weath-ered MS., to destroy *Madrigal.* The last sections were carelessly as-sembled. I finished the story after the "Greek" prelude when Julia writes to Rico. On rereading the typed MS., I realize that at last the War I story had "written itself."[34]

"Madrigal," she writes, "is a novel in historical time. It is the eternal story of the search. The mythical or religious love-story continues through all the writing." "Pilate's Wife" (an unpub-

---

Bid Me to Live was the publisher's title for the book H.D. called *Madrigal.* At H.D.'s insistence the book was subtitled *A Madrigal,* but she usually refers to *Bid Me to Live* as *Madrigal.*

†Only a few of the early versions of the story were destroyed; the surviving versions are in the Norman Holmes Pearson collection in the Beinecke Library at Yale University.

lished novel), she writes, "is the same story." She tells us over and over in various ways that most of these stories and novels are about her relationship with D. H. Lawrence. And so is the poetry. She writes: "The Greek or the Greek and Roman scenes and sequences of these prose studies are related to the early poems. The first *Palimpsest* is *Hipparchia, Hedylus,* and *Pilate's Wife.*"[35]

H.D. gives us several more clues; she seems determined to tell us how to read her work. At the time she made her "Notes on Recent Writing," she was working on a novel, "The Mystery." Of this novel she says:

> We have not finished *The Mystery* — that is, we have not yet written it down. But it is in part the same mystery that is presented in the *Advent* section of the Freud *Writing*. It is a mystery not uncommon to folk and fairy tales, the mystery of the appearance of a stranger, or a near-stranger, at a time and in a place where he could not possibly have been. Such things have happened . . . This mystery was experienced by me but I could not record it.[36]

For those of us who will ask the inevitable biographical questions raised by her work, H.D. gives a directive. From a certain point of view it might sound enigmatic and evasive, but we will come closer to understanding the meaning of H.D.'s life and work if we follow it. "When, where and how were these things written? That seems a more adequate autobiographical directive than the when, where and how did the events described happen, or when, where and how was the dream dreamed."[37] My biography is in my work, says H.D. It is no ordinary story.

14

Poetry of Rural England

IN H.D.'S POETRY the perfect fusion of physical and metaphysical reality in the single image creates a mystery. As readers we wonder whether what "happened" on the metaphysical level happened also on the physical level.

It was winter, 1915–1916, when the Aldingtons and the Lawrences left Hampstead for southern England. Lawrence hoped H.D. would settle in Cornwall. In a letter to Dollie Radford* dated January 15, 1916, Lawrence writes: "I am glad you like Mrs. Aldington. Ask her if she doesn't want a cottage in Cornwall."[1] The Aldingtons did not settle there, but in nearby Devonshire.

> During the winter of 1915–16, both the Lawrences and Aldingtons set out for the south of England, Lawrence to Cornwall, where (near Cecil Gray and — briefly — the Middleton Murrys) he remained for twenty-two months . . . H.D. and Richard obtained a cottage in neighboring Devonshire near two friends of John Cournos who was well acquainted with Richard and who intended to join the company later in the spring of 1916. During the Aldingtons' stays in Devon and later in the adjoining county of Dorset, H.D. and Lawrence continued to exchange manuscripts and letters.[2]

In a letter to F. S. Flint of May 17, 1916, H.D. speaks of Aldington's imminent enlistment in the army and the receipt of the galleys of *Sea Garden*. In another letter, of May 10, she thanks Flint for his congratulations and for sending a *Times* article that praised her translation of Euripides, the "Choruses from the Iphigeneia in

---

*Dollie Radford (1864?–1920) was a friend of Lawrence's whom he had met before World War I. She and her husband, Ernest (1857–1919), helped the Lawrences with housing after they were forced out of Cornwall.

Aulis," as an outstanding achievement. The reviewer ranked H.D. above several of her fellow Imagists and "participants in the revival of interest in classical texts," noting that H.D. "has applied to those choral lyrics an interpretative genius which is both provocative and singularly illuminating." The praise she received in these weeks, "Cournos wrote Flint (unpublished, May 16, 1916), was to make H.D. more determined than before to continue her work as a poet."[3] As we shall see, Cournos was unaware of H.D.'s deep involvement with D. H. Lawrence, and his understanding of her career as a poet is accordingly overly simplistic. Nevertheless, it is true that at this time H.D. made a decision to continue that career.

During the war years H.D.'s marriage disintegrated; she lost her husband to the war and to another woman, Dorothy Yorke.* In spite of the fact that the sexual connection between H.D. and Aldington had broken perhaps as early as 1915, H.D. worked strenuously to keep her marriage together, even after Aldington enlisted in the army in the early summer of 1916. A reading of her early poems and her novels, memoirs, and letters makes it clear that D. H. Lawrence was deeply involved in the dissolution of her marriage. After their breakup, Aldington told H.D. he had burned Lawrence's letters to her, so we shall presumably never see them. "I am sorry, Dooley," he said.[4]

H.D.'s poem "After Troy" gives some insight into the relationship that existed between the Lawrences and the Aldingtons during this period; in fact, it gives a rather clear picture of one marriage, a city, a civilization — Troy — pitted against another.

> We flung against their gods,
> invincible, clear hate;
> we fought;
> frantic, we flung the last
> imperious, desperate shaft
>
> and lost:
>
> . . .
>
> we lost yet as we pressed
> our spearsmen on their best,
> we knew their line invincible
> because there fell
> on them no shiverings

*Dorothy "Arabella" Yorke was an American woman from Pennsylvania with whom John Cournos had a long-standing romantic involvement. She arrived in London in 1917 and became involved in an affair with Aldington that lasted until 1928.

of the white enchantress,
radiant Aphrodite's spell:

we hurled our shafts of passion,
noblest hate,
and knew their cause was blest,
and knew their gods were nobler,
better taught in skill,
subtler wit of thought,
yet had it been God's will
that *they* not we should fall,
we know those fields had bled
with roses lesser red.[5]

We think of the poem Lawrence had sent her at Corfe Castle: "On that day/I shall put roses on roses, and cover your grave . . ."[6] In *Bid Me to Live* H.D. provides another account of the impact of Lawrence's poems on her and her relationship with Aldington. Julia (H.D.) says to Rico (Lawrence): "You sent out a flare to me, that time at Dorset before Rafe [Richard] went. Couldn't you at least have waited until he was gone?"[7]

Being true to the spirit of poetry, to Eros, H.D. lost everything in the war. In *Contemporary Literature*'s special number on H.D. in August 1969, Norman Holmes Pearson published three poems from the 1916–1917 period. He titles them "Amaranth," "Eros," and "Envy," and writes:

> The letters from H.D. to F. S. Flint . . . show vividly her personal anguish and loyalty to writers and writing in the early days of World War I . . . "Amaranth," "Eros," and "Envy" are from that period. The manuscripts were bound as a trio and were among the unpublished manuscripts she left at her death. On the introductory blank leaf she wrote simply, "Corfe Castle — Dorset — summer 1917 from poems of *The Island* series . . ."[8]

While she was at Corfe Castle that summer, near Aldington's army station, she continued to write feverishly. In "Fragment Forty-One," which is a previously published version of "Amaranth," she sustains herself by maintaining that although she has lost in love, she has been faithful to the spirit of sexual passion (personified as Eros or Aphrodite). The "Amaranth" version published by Pearson (presumably the first version of the poem) contains a section IV and a section V which are omitted from "Fragment Forty-One," which was collected in H.D.'s *Heliodora* (1924). In the last lines of section V the poet affirms Aphrodite, her symbol for the consummated love that brings the deepest fulfillment and peace: ". . . *you will find/no peace in the end/save in her pres-ence.*" [9]

In "Telesila" H.D. presents the image of a Greek statue: *"In Argos — that statue of her; at her feet the scroll of her/love-poetry, in her hand a helmet."* [10] The vision she is developing in these poems takes account of the relationship of love to war. If she had never written her poetry, she seems to be saying, Lawrence would never have fought to possess her. And had it not been for the upheaval of World War I, none of these events would have occurred.

In "Why Have You Sought" H.D. asks of Eros, "Why have you sought the Greeks . . .?" Why us?

> Love, why have you sought the horde
> of spearsmen, why the tent
> Achilles pitched beside the river-ford? [11]

H.D.'s attitude toward "the god" in this period is ambivalent, as in a poem she published in the Imagist anthology of 1916, "The Shrine ('She Watches Over the Sea')." [12] Within the palimpsest of the poem, the galleys referred to in the second line are both ships and poetry manuscripts or page proofs. H.D. and the Imagists were fond of the pun. In asking, "Have you sent galleys from your beach?" she might be asking her fellow Imagist, D. H. Law-rence, now living on the Cornish coast, whether he has sent more poems. But the deeper subject of the poem is the danger associated with a poetic or actual visit with a lover.

> Are your rocks shelter for ships?
> Have you sent galleys from your beach —
> Are you graded — a safe crescent,
> Where the tide lifts them back to port?
> Are you full and sweet,
> Tempting the quiet
> To depart in their trading ships?
>
> Nay, you are great, fierce, evil —
> You are the land-blight —
> You have tempted men,
> But they perished on your cliffs.
>
> Your lights are but dank shoals,
> Slate and pebble and wet shells
> And sea-weed fastened to the rocks.

And she has been warned about this particular "god" by many.

> Many warned of this.
> Men said:

There are wrecks on the fore-beach.
Wind will beat your ship.
There is no shelter in that headland.
It is useless waste, that edge,
That front of rock.
Sea-gulls clang beyond the breakers —
None venture to that spot.

H.D. had been warned about Lawrence. He was not fully accepted by her circle. He was too reckless, too far out of civilization. Cornwall, Lawrence's home for most of 1916 and 1917, became for H.D. an image of Lawrence's writing. The fierce wind blowing the desolate beach, the windswept house fronting the bleak moors, the sharp, angular rocks, even the "knockers" from the disused mine shafts — all this came to be in her mind a metaphor for the man and the muse, for the terrible fierce power of his vision, for a world without illusion, without comfort, without the trappings and solace of civilization. But in spite of warnings, she begs him to stay.

Stay — stay —
But terror has caught us now.
We passed the men in ships.
We dared deeper than the fisher-folk,
And you strike us with terror,
O bright shaft.

Flame passes under us,
And sparks that unknot the flesh,
Sorrow, splitting bone from bone —
Splendour athwart our eyes,
And rifts in the splendour —
Sparks and scattered light . . .

But hail —
As the tide slackens,
As the wind beats out,
We hail this shore.
We sing to you,
Spirit between the headlands
And the further rocks.

Though oak-beams split,
Though boats and sea-men flounder,
And the strait grind sand with sand
And cut boulders to sand and drift —

Your eyes have pardoned our faults.
Your hands have touched us.

You have leaned forward a little
And the waves can never thrust us back
From the splendour of your ragged coast.

Both H.D. and Lawrence were deeply moved by the terrain of rural England. The rocky coast, the desolate sand beaches, and the moors inflamed H.D.'s imagination. In his January 15, 1916, letter to Dollie Radford, Lawrence wrote:

> Really it is stunning what with the great bruising shocks of the wind, the shuttering of the old house, and the incessant heaviness of the sea, we wonder where we are . . .
> This is a bare, bleak country, but it is not cold. One feels the past very much, always the darkness of the past, violent and rather passionate. Today scarcely exists here.[13]

H.D. was every bit as taken with the secluded countryside. She spent a good deal of time walking the area. On April 28, 1916, she wrote to Flint: "I wish you could have come this week-end as there is such a startling change in the foliage. It is too lovely. One feels almost drugged with it."[14]

Their love of the English countryside is important to note because it enters so emphatically into the poetry that Lawrence and H.D. composed during the Hampstead–southern England period. Because they were exchanging manuscripts, they were able to share the experience and communicate their feelings at a deep level. Both poets, deeply sensitive to nature, were hardly exaggerating their response. The looming menace of the war and the threat of conscription were hanging heavy over England. Not only did these threats create an unbearable tension, but the contrast of the world of war to the world of nature in some sense served to consecrate the place they had found to retreat from the harsh reality.

Both the tension of the times and the sense of having found a sanctuary enter into the haunting but beautiful cadences of H.D.'s poem "The Cliff Temple," published under the title "Temple — The Cliff," in *Some Imagist Poets* (1916).[15] In the first stanzas H.D. creates a lovely image of an outdoor place of worship.

Great, bright portal,
Shelf of rock,
Rocks fitted in long ledges,
Rocks fitted to dark, to silver-granite,
To lighter rock —
Clean cut, white against white.

High — high — and no hill-goat
Tramples — no mountain-sheep
Has set foot on your fine grass.
You lift, you are the world-edge,
Pillar for sky-arch.

The world heaved —
We are next to the sky.
Over us, sea-hawks shout,
Gulls sweep past.
The terrible breakers are silent
From this place.

The next image is Imagist, and the scene becomes anthropo-
morphic.

Below us, on the rock-edge,
Where earth is caught in the fissures
Of the jagged cliff,
A small tree stiffens in the gale,
It bends — but its white flowers
Are fragrant at this height.

And under and under,
The wind booms:
It whistles, it thunders,
It growls — it presses the grass
Beneath its great feet.

She is the tree which "stiffens in the gale." The wind or gale
is both her inspiration and the voice of a fellow poet. The great
feet are the insistent beat of his poetry.

In parts II and III of the poem we have the appearance of an
"I" — the first-person singular speaking to a fellow spirit. Some
intense images emerge.

I said:
Forever and forever, must I follow you
Through the stones?
I catch at you — you lurch:
You are quicker than my hand-grasp . . .

I was splintered and torn.
The hill-path mounted
Swifter than my feet . . .

Shall I hurl myself from here,
Shall I leap and be nearer you?
Shall I drop, beloved, beloved,
Ankle against ankle?
Would you pity me, O white breast? . . .

Have you heard,
Do you know how I climbed this rock?
My breath caught, I lurched forward —
I stumbled in the ground-myrtle.

Have you heard, O god seated on a cliff,
How far toward the ledges of your house,
How far I had to walk?

"The god seated on a cliff" is, we presume, above it all, aloof. Why must the narrator climb the rock? Is the walk toward the ledges of his house a physical or a metaphysical walk — or both?

Perhaps above all else in these 1915–1918 poems, one is aware of H.D.'s total and unequivocal attraction to all that is masculine — the masculine physique of the god, the suggestion of masculinity in the rocks the expression of masculinity in the work of her fellow poets. Given the circumstances of her life at this time, her frenzy is understandable. Her husband is about to go away to fight in the war (as it turned out, the conscription bill passed and Aldington enlisted). The war is in one way or another threatening to deprive her of all her masculine companions — Aldington, Flint, Cournos, Lawrence. H.D. expresses a longing for the masculine presence in these poems, as well as a sense of the threat of the loss of that presence. It was not only loss in a physical sense that threatened her, but loss of the masculine impulse toward woman and nature. The men had their minds on the war; H.D. was attempting to define and maintain the reality of poetry.

In "Pursuit" we have the sense of woman, as nature, cut off from and pitting herself against the world of war, trying to call the poet back to reality. H.D. presents the image of Achilles in the print of his heel on the sand.

What do I care
that the stream is trampled,
the sand on the stream-bank
still holds the print of your foot:
the heel is cut deep.
I see another mark
on the grass ridge of the bank —
it points toward the wood-path
I have lost the third
in the packed earth.[16]

The print on the sand is an Imagist metaphor for a poem. Was a poem somehow lost? Or did H.D. in reality lose track of him? Does this refer to a missed message or a missed encounter, or both? At any rate, she has "lost the third."

In the H.D./Flint correspondence we get some indication of how hard H.D. worked to keep the world of poetry alive during this time of stress and war turmoil. She not only continued to write profusely (most of the poems in H.D.'s *Collected Poems* were written during the Hampstead and southern England period), but also edited the literary columns of *Egoist* and helped her husband get the magazine published. After Aldington enlised she edited the magazine herself. She also continued "to try to administer the sometimes hectic affairs of the Imagist group."[17]

As "Pursuit" continues, we get a sense of "his" sensibility ("his" being a reference to a fellow poet) upon hers. There is in this poem a beautiful contrast between the maculine and the feminine. In the following lines H.D. presents an experience that becomes a poem.

> But here
> a wild-hyacinth stalk is snapped:
> the purple buds — half ripe —
> show deep purple
> where your heel pressed.
>
> A patch of flowering grass,
> low, trailing —
> you brushed this:
> the green stems show yellow-green
> where you lifted — turned the earth-side
> to the light:
> this and a dead leaf-spine
> split across,
> show where you passed.
>
> You were swift, swift!
> here the forest ledge slopes —
> rain has furrowed the roots.
> Your hand caught at this;
> the root snapped under your weight.[18]

In "Pursuit," in contrast to "The Cliff Temple," *"he"* rather than *"she"* is climbing. Presumably they are climbing toward the same place. But instead of reaching the goal, "he" falls.

> And you climbed yet further!
> you stopped by the dwarf-cornel —
> whirled on your heels,
> doubled on your track.
>
> This is clear —
> you fell on the downward slope,
> you dragged a bruised thigh — you limped —
> you clutched this larch . . .

Did you clutch,
stammer with short breath and gasp:
wood-daemons grant life —
give life — I am almost lost.

The dwarf-cornel is an allusion to the cornel-trees of H.D.'s poem "Orion Dead." H.D. seems to be saying that Lawrence pursued her until he realized that his pursuit was endangering her marriage, at which point he backtracked, but "fell."

"The Cliff Temple" and "Pursuit" are remarkable Imagist poems. The nature imagery could stand on its own, in the sense that the landscape is remarkably invoked: we can see the terrain of rural England as we read; we can feel the windswept coast. Although the symbolism is overdetermined, the fact that H.D. speaks of poems and poets through the medium of nature does not detract from the presentation of scene. The human drama and the stage of nature upon which or in which it is enacted fuse into one perceptual whole. We may break the whole into its component pieces or bits for analysis, but the separate logics do not compete with or diminish it; rather, each level of analysis infuses the whole with further depth of meaning. As Pound says of a canzone by Arnaut Daniel, "The form is good art because its complexity is not apparent until one searches for it or presents it . . . dissected."[19]

In "The Gift," originally published in the March 1916 issue of the *Egoist* under the title "The Last Gift," we find the same clarity of image, the same overdetermined symbolism, the same expression of longing. We are in the same place; the same landscape is invoked. There is a poignant sense of rare beauty.

Your garden sloped to the beach —
myrtle overran the paths:
honey and amber flecked each leaf:
the citron-lily head —
one among many —
weighted there, over-sweet.

The myrrh-hyacinth
spread across low slopes:
violets streaked black ridges
through the grass.

The house, too, was like this,
over-painted, over lovely —
the world is like this.[20]

This is not sublimation but testament of fulfillment, or near fulfillment. Fulfillment is the goal and the speech is direct:

This I forgot last night:
you must not be blamed,
it is not your fault,
as a child, a flower, any flower
tore my breast . . .

I reason:
another life holds what this lacks,
a sea, unmoving, quiet —
not forcing our strength
to rise to it, beat on beat —
a stretch of sand . . .

In these poems of *Sea Garden* there is a contrast between inland worship, which takes place within the confines of marriage, and worship in the wind. These images are stated clearly and defiantly in "Sheltered Garden."

I have had enough.
I gasp for breath . . .

I have had enough —
border-pinks, clove-pinks, wax-lilies,
herbs, sweet-cress.

O for some sharp swish of a branch —
there is no scent of resin
in this place,
no taste of bark, of coarse weeds,
aromatic, astringent —
only border on border of scented pinks.

Have you seen fruit under cover
that wanted light —

. . .

O to blot out this garden
to forget, to find a new beauty
in some terrible
wind-tortured place.[21]

The longed-for "wind-tortured place" is the place of "Temple — The Cliff." In *Helen in Egypt* it is called Leuké, the island where, mythologically speaking, Helen met Achilles and a child was conceived. It is a metaphysical reality that was to become a physical reality, an eternal reality that would become a reality in time.

15

In the *Gloire*

H.D.'s NOVEL *Bid Me to Live* is concerned primarily with the time Lawrence and Frieda stayed in the Aldington's London flat in November and December 1917. Although written about a short period in the H.D.–D. H. Lawrence relationship, it is read by many as a narrative about the *whole* of that relationship. But a careful reading of H.D.'s poetry and prose makes it clear that *Bid Me to Live* is about only a period of her relationship with Lawrence, which in actuality began in the fall of 1914.

In 1917 H.D. was living in fact out of a suitcase between Corfe Castle, where Richard Aldington was stationed, and her rooms at 44 Mecklenburgh Square, where she and Richard returned when he had leave. The latter address was the home of their marriage; she and Richard had lived in these rooms since they had left southern England. But nothing was the same; everything had changed. London was being bombed by the Germans; there was broken glass on the floor from the last air raid.

For H.D. there were wars within the world war. There was the war within Imagism, which was at base a conflict between Ezra Pound and H.D. and had led to her meeting with Lawrence and the dissolution of her marriage. And, as foreshadowed in her poem "After Troy" and told in greater detail in *Helen in Egypt,* there was a war between the Aldingtons and Lawrence (and, of course, Frieda). The deeper war was the one within H.D.'s own mind — as the matter is put in *Helen in Egypt,* how to reconcile Trojan and Greek (Paris and Achilles, Aldington and Lawrence)? Not to reconcile them to each other, but to reconcile them in her own mind. In other words, why did things turn out as they did?

In a Christmas charade in 1917, Lawrence identified H.D. as the tree of life. As H.D. tells the story in *Bid Me to Live,* *

> There was Rico, saying "We'll do a charade; You be the tree of life, Julia."
> Adam and Eve were Rafe and Bella [Richard Aldington and Dorothy Yorke] of course, Vane [Cecil Gray] was the angel at the gate. It was the end of madness. It was the beginning. Vane was the angel . . .
> "Dance" said Rico, "you dance," he said to Julia.
> "But I'm the tree," she said, "or what am I?"
> "You are the apple-tree," said Rico, "you dance. Now Adam and Eve, you come along here and Elsa [Frieda], you be the serpent," he said, "you growl and writhe."
> "Serpents don't growl," said Elsa . . .
> "What are you?" said Rafe, "what's left for you? Oh, I see, old Rico is Gawd-a'-mighty."
> Rico took up a Jehovah-like pose by the fireplace . . .[1]

According to H.D.'s version of the story (Frieda and Aldington tell this story too), Lawrence as "Gawd-a'-mighty" quotes from Paul rather than Genesis.† At his worst, Lawrence's attitudes toward women were, from H.D.'s perspective, Pauline: "Woman, I say unto thee . . ." and so on.[2]

During this period the Lawrences were temporarily living at 44 Mecklenburgh Square with H.D. After their eviction from Cornwall late in 1917 Lawrence and Frieda were homeless, and H.D. offered them shelter until they were able to find a new place to live. Lawrence was, understandably, at his very worst. It is a terrible experience to lose the home one loves. And Lawrence had to contend with the added humiliation of having been forced by the authorities to leave because he was a suspected German spy.

But H.D. and Lawrence had had time together before — they had shared a world of poetry in Hampstead and southern England.

Bid Me to Live was begun, as we have noted, in 1921. The first writing on the palimpsest that would become *Bid Me to Live* was

---

*In an interview with H.D. published in *Newsweek* May 2, 1960, Lionel Durand writes: "H.D. had no hesitation in admitting that the book [*Bid Me to Live*] was completely autobiographical." During the course of the interview H.D. told Durand: "I think they [the publishers] like it because I have D. H. Lawrence in it. Half the book is devoted to him . . . It is a *roman à clef*, and the keys are easy enough to find. I even thought there might be some libelous material in it, but some lawyers said no. I am Julia. And all the others are real people."

†Frieda Lawrence tells of the Christmas charade in *Not I, But the Wind* . . . ; Aldington's version appears in *Life for Life's Sake.*

"Paint It Today." Other novels would follow, all variations on a single theme: the dissolution of H.D.'s marriage and the roles of Lawrence, herself, and others in that very painful period of her life. The final "Madrigal" was roughed out in 1939, but it was not finally assembled until 1949. H.D. calls the novel a romance, in contrast to her classical poetry; it is *her* romance: "I left a MS. with books and other papers with Bryher when I returned to England, soon after the outbreak of War II . . . In leafing over the un-corrected papers, I found an unexpected force in energy. I would reassemble the romance."[3]

H.D. compares writing her novel to the process of making wine; she is aware that it is something different from her usual style.

> *Madrigal,* left simmering or fermenting, is run through a vintner's sieve, the dregs are thrown out . . . we began on that vineyard in 1921. It was a story. We grubbed up dead roots, trimmed and pruned. But the grapes were sour. We went on. It was a pity to let that field (1914–1918) lie utterly fallow. We returned to it (from time to time). At last, winter, 1949, we taste the 1939 gathering. Impossible, but true. The War I novel has been fermenting away during War II. This is intoxicating, the red grapes of — War? Love?[4]

Love and war were to become major themes of *Helen in Egypt.* There began to be parallel structures everywhere in H.D.'s writing. World War II brought memories of World War I, and in spite of the pain she endured, the second world war brought a new period of creativity very much related to the earlier one. The Madrigal stories are indeed the bedrock of H.D.'s later poetry.

Because *Bid Me to Live* was twenty-seven years in the writing, it is difficult to know where to place it in a sequential reading of H.D.'s poetry. Several volumes of her poems appeared in the 1920s: in 1921, *Hymen;* in 1924, *Heliodora and Other Poems;* then the *Collected Poems* in 1925. But most of this poetry was actually written prior to 1919. "Paint It Today," written in 1921, was the beginning of a prose phase.

Since we will examine in the succeeding chapters some correspondences between "Paint It Today" and the three drafts of D. H. Lawrence's *Lady Chatterley's Lover,* we might begin with a look at Julia's letter to Rico at the end of *Bid Me to Live,* for in that letter H.D. restates some central thematic elements of her first novel (and of Lawrence's drafts) in an interesting context. In Julia's letter from Cornwall, H.D. writes again of the little house or hut in the forest and of the experience of waiting for her lover.

When I "got out" in Corfe (I was in a fever) I went into a little house, quite a simple little house in the forest. You were out cutting wood, like a woodcutter in a fairy-tale. It was the air. I felt cooped-up in that cottage. I was writing the Orpheus sequence for you. But when I "got out" it was all very simple.

I was waiting for you.

I could sit on the porch-steps . . .[5]

Since the beginning of their relationship H.D. had been afraid of the power of Lawrence's writing, afraid she might become "material" for one of those novels of his about which she had always been ambivalent. She knew, in fact, that he would write the book; by 1939 he had already written it several times. To Rico Julia writes:

There would be no use writing you voluminous letters. I would be thinking, "What will he think," I would be feeling, foolishly, that I might be "material." I know that this is stupid, self-conscious. You can write a book about us, if you want to write a book about us, without my help.[6]

H.D. has begun this letter: "I will never see you again, Rico." She is trying to explain Julia's relationship to Vane (Cecil Gray). "Vane told Mrs. Farrer [the housekeeper] that I was his sister. It is like that."[7]

Julia is trying to tell Rico that she cannot live in two dimensions. "It didn't seem difficult in Corfe, and then he [Rafe/Aldington] went to France."[8] H.D. is trying to explain why she did not go up to Lawrence's room when he and Frieda stayed with her at Mecklenburgh Square. She is trying to say that she wants to be neither his lady nor his wife but a writer. She has had enough of marriage. She wants the *gloire,* the creative light: "The child is the *gloire* before it is born. The circle of the candle on my notebook is the *gloire,* the story isn't born yet. While I live in the unborn story, I am in the *gloire.*"[9] And she realizes that he is a fellow spirit. He too must live in the *gloire,* the sublime vision. "You are driven by your genius. You will express love."[10]

She must explain to him why she left him — why she, like Thetis in *Helen in Egypt,* let him go back to the sea, the creative turmoil: "Why does it drive you mad, that desire to create your mother . . . I could not be your mother. Anyhow, I need a great-mother as much as you do."[11]

To be not yet born is to be in the *gloire.* The vision from which her later poetry will be born is the *gloire.* From Cornwall Julia writes: "You said I was a living spirit, but I wasn't living until you wrote to me, 'We will go away together.' We have gone away together, I realise your genius, in this place. I would like to serve your genius, not only because it is personally, your genius, but because it is part of this place." [12]

"This place" is Cornwall or, in *Helen in Egypt,* Leuké, the white island. From here H.D. can remember the fall of Troy (her marriage) and Lawrence (her inspiration). In Cornwall, away from both Aldington and Lawrence, the experience and the inspiration could come together.

Rafe (Richard Aldington) was associated in H.D.'s mind with Paris and Venice, the settings of her first consummated love affair, a *"season of mists and mellow fruitfulness."* [13] Their marriage was an experiment, a modern marriage: "They might have made a signal success of it, but in the tradition not so much of Robert Browning and Elizabeth Barrett as of Punch and Judy. They both wanted to be free, they both wanted to escape, they both wanted a place where they could browse over their books; they had friends in common." [14]

But Richard did not want to include the Lawrences in their circle of friends; *he* would decide who their friends would be. "Already Frederick was writing, 'Why don't you and Rafe come to Cornwall?' Rafe did not want to go to Cornwall, did not want to get mixed up with the Fredericks." [15]

In the context of Julia's letters from Rico, Rafe became the "hearty, oversexed . . . young officer on leave." [16] What had happened to the young poet she had married? Had he ever been a poet? "Why can't you write your own poetry?" says Julia to Rafe. [17]

H.D. saw Aldington as Roman or Trojan — "a late Roman rather than Greek image." [18] This image is developed in further detail in "Hipparchia," another writing on the palimpsest of the war novels. H.D. associates him with a "picture of a Roman soldier in the Judgment of Solomon." [19] He has made a judgment. He has a mistress, Bella (Dorothy Yorke). He will eventually leave her for Bella. " 'Bella,' he says, 'is a star performer . . .' Why had she not just let it all go? Two years, three years, Paris, the Louvre?" [20]

A candle burns in a jar beside the marriage bed — a constant symbol in *Bid Me to Live,* a recurring image in *Helen in Egypt.* "It was a small room,/yes, a taper was burning/in an onyx jar . . ." [21] H.D. concludes in *Bid Me to Live,* as she does later in *Helen in Egypt,* that "the flame and the brand of this gift that Rafe and Julia had had between them was but a secondary refracted light, the light of a second reflection of the rainbow, not the blaze and the blue flame of the sun-shelf. Rico." [22] Thus the candle is the symbol in both the novel and the poem of the secondary refracted light, a constant contrast to the flame H.D. associates with Lawrence.

Richard Aldington was jealous of H.D.'s relationship with Lawrence, both before and after the breakup of their marriage. In *Helen in Egypt,* H.D. compares her image of Achilles and "the white fire of unnumbered stars" to Rafe's pronouncement that "Bella is a star performer." They (H.D. and Aldington) live in different dimensions. In *Helen in Egypt,* Paris (Aldington) asks:

> why, why would you deny
> the peace, the sanctity
> of this small room,
>
> The lantern there by the door?
> Why must you recall
> the white fire of unnumbered stars,
>
> rather than that single taper
> burning in an onyx jar? [23]

The blaze and the blue flame of the sun-shelf. The white fire of unnumbered stars. Nature. Night. Poetry. "Words had made a pattern, delicate yet firm." [24]

If Aldington's mistress was a star performer, why was he so jealous? He had, after all, *his* star. At the same time that Rafe flaunts his relationship with Bella, he blurts out, "Old Rico . . . what's darn' old Frederico writing?" [25]

"What's darn' old Frederico writing?" Letters. Poetry. H.D. and Lawrence were exchanging manuscripts, reading each other's work.

> "Read it, she said."

> Dear Julia,
> There is no use trying to believe that all this war really exists. It really doesn't matter. We must go on. I know that Rafe will come back. Your frozen altars mean something, but I don't like the second half of the Orpheus sequence as well as the first. Stick to the woman speaking. How can you know what Orpheus feels? It's your part to be the woman, the woman vibration, Eurydice should be enough . . . [26]

Yes, Lawrence *would* tell H.D. to "stick to the woman speaking." Yet in spite of his dogmatism, his sexism, his tyranny, he really understood what poetry was all about. He liked her "frozen altars"; he liked her poems. He really cared what she had to say for and about herself.

But Rafe asks Julia, "What's this Orpheus that you've been writing for old Rico?" [27] She tries to tell him she didn't write it for Rico, at least not in the way that he is insinuating. But she did.

> "I didn't particularly write it for Rico," she repeated, seeing the pale face, the burnt eyes, hearing the words that flamed alive, blue serpents on the page that Rico wrote her, that were just ordinary letters that you could chuck across the breakfast-tray to any husband, but that held the flame and the fire, the burning, the believing. [28]

There was no use trying to explain to Rafe. Rafe was not an artist. He would not, could not understand. How could she expect him to understand when he could not himself write? His pseudo-Imagist verse had proved that. There was no danger of Rafe's mixing dimensions; he thought in only one dimension. She did not write the "Eurydice" for Rico in the dimension in which Bella was a star performer. How explain that? How explain, among other things, that she was trying to end something with Rico, not begin it?

The *Bid Me to Live* version of H.D.'s "Eurydice" presents some rather striking contrasts to her "Eurydice" published in the *Egoist* in May 1917. The *Bid Me to Live* version begs Orpheus not to look back to what had been.

> . . . your rock is burnt-sun in that upper light, the grain glows and the inner heart of rock gives heat . . . Unknot the woody stem of last year's vine, twist garlands of the dead-wood, do not think that present look or nod or word or breath can reach me in this cavern under-earth. Here it is dark . . . Touch not your lyre, nor seek to wake what lies forgotten. [29]

H.D. had asked Lawrence to leave her; he had not. She had asked him not to look back; he had looked back. The second version was written after he had in fact looked back — and in so doing destroyed her marriage, or what was left of it.

> Why did you turn back,
> that hell should be reinhabited
> of myself thus
> swept into nothingness?
>
> Why did you turn?
> why did you glance back? [30]

Lawrence had sent poems to Corfe Castle. The poems rein-volved H.D. in memories of Hampstead and southern England.

Lawrence had jeered at her desire to sublimate, and he had jeered at her marriage; "Kick over your tiresome house of life," Rico had written.[31] Now, from Cornwall in 1918, H.D. writes in Julia's letter to Rico: "You jeered at my making abstractions of people — graven images . . . I wrote that cyclamen poem for him [Aldington] in Dorset, at Corfe Castle, where I wrote your Orpheus . . ."[32]

"What did he really know about her house of life?" H.D. asks in *Bid Me to Live*.[33] What did Lawrence know of her marriage? Why had he wanted to end it? In "Eurydice" H.D. writes of his arrogance and ruthlessness:

> So you have swept me back —
> I who could have walked with the live souls
> above the earth.
> I who could have slept among the live flowers
> at last.
>
> so for your arrogance
> and your ruthlessness
> I am swept back
> where dead lichens drip
> dead cinders among moss of ash.[34]

The glance of Orpheus is also the glance of Achilles; Orpheus is another persona for Achilles. Lawrence is cast as the great warrior because he had, almost from the first day they met, made war upon H.D.'s marriage. Why, she asks in "Eurydice," did he want to break it up?

> What was it that crossed my face
> with the light from yours
> and your glance?
>
> What was it you saw in my face —
> the light of your own face,
> the fire of your own presence?[35]

The marriage had been strained during these war years, before the time of the writing of *Bid Me to Live,* before Dorothy. H.D. had been stifled; she had had to get out: "When I 'got out' in Corfe (I was in a fever) I went into a little house, quite a simple little house in the forest. You were out cutting wood . . ."[36]

As Lawrence writes in *John Thomas and Lady Jane:*

> "Shall yer sit i' th' hut but a while?" he asked.
> "I think I will."
> He went before her, and got the rustic stool he had made, brushed aside the lumber, and set the stool facing the door.

"Should yer like the door shut?" he said.

"Oh no!"

He looked at her sideways, as if he didn't want to look at her really. But he was kindly. He felt for her the sympathy one fugitive feels with another. He went back to the coop he was repairing.

She sat with her back to the timber wall of the hut, and leaned back her head, closing her eyes. She was so tired, so tired! Fugitives from the social world: that's what it was. The man had fled too, and now guarded the wood like a wild-cat, against the encroaching of the mongrel population outside. This was at least a little sanctuary.[37]

As H.D. writes of the little house, "It was the air. I felt cooped-up in that cottage. I was writing the Orpheus sequence for you . . . I was waiting for you . . . I could sit on the porch-steps . . ."[38]

Aldington criticizes her Orpheus poem: "Look not back," he says, is Victorian. " 'You might boil this one down', he said, 'about quarter the length and cut the *clichés*.' "[39] Julia tries to tell him she saved the poem for the paper rather than the poetry (paper was very scarce during the war). " 'What does Frederick want, what does Frederico want with you?' . . . He spoke as if he cared, as if it mattered that Rico was writing her, that she was writing Rico."[40]

Did they matter, the letters H.D. exchanged with Lawrence? "They were burning in her head, blue-fire, the things he wrote and the things that he didn't write, the way the blue-flame licked out of the paper, whatever it was he wrote."[41] In *Helen in Egypt* the blue and the white fire and the lightning associated with Achilles is a constant contrast to the single taper burning in an onyx jar associated with Paris. Lawrence's letters were lightning; Lawrence himself was lightning. "Sheet lightning. Blue lightning. She had been struck by lightning."[42]

Rafe had said Julia's "Eurydice" poem was Victorian. Old-fashioned. The letter from Rico about the Orpheus sequence? "Yes she had locked up that and one or two others in the red-plush lined leather jewel-box that she had got in Florence. Inside the box was the portrait of her mother, with the hair dressed high, 1880 and Victorian."[43]

Victorian mother, Victorian daughter. Old-fashioned . . . pre-war . . . "But Rico's flaming letters had been no ordinary love-letters, they were written to her in 'pure being,' as he said."[44] This out-of-time dimension of pure being is the same dimension Lawrence writes of in *John Thomas and Lady Jane:* "Fugitives from the social world: that's what it was." It reappears in the parallel universe of *Helen in Egypt:* "But this host of Spirits, the Greek heroes? Without the Trojan War, she never would have found them or they never would have found her. Nor, we may presume, would she and Achilles have met in this out-of-time dimension."[45]

In Mecklenburgh Square in 1917 the past with Lawrence was a memory, a memory that impelled H.D. to write. Would she put her marriage back together or not? Long before she met Lawrence, she and Aldington, "homeless," had "found each other." H.D. once again invokes the candle with "its exact circle of light," as well as another symbol: "an exact geometrical definition, as exact as the clock-dial on the clock."[46] The clock symbolizes the relationship "in time" as opposed to the out-of-time dimension of H.D.'s relationship with Lawrence.

Julia tries to tell Rafe how she feels about Rico. " 'What is this about you and old Rico?' 'Oh-nothing — I mean — I told you — but she had not told him.' "[47] " 'Do I love Rico? Do I love Frederico? Do I love old Rico?' 'No, not at this minute. He is part of the cerebral burning, part of the inspiration. He takes but he gives.' "[48]

Or as Julia concludes, yes, she does love Rico, but in another dimension: "As the war crept closer . . . she seemed to tune-in to another dimension . . . a world where she walked alone with an image and that image was Rico."[49] Imagism. The cerebral burning. "Truly, yes, she loved him but loved him in another dimension . . . Rico himself had written, 'You are entangled in your own dream.' But this was reality."[50]

In *Helen in Egypt,* H.D. writes, "I remember a dream that was real."

> the sail, they said,
> was the veil of Aphrodite,
> and I am tired of the memory of battle,
>
> I remember a dream that was real . . .[51]

But she and Aldington, too, had shared a world. "Was, or wasn't it the dream that mattered?" "She had kept the flame alight, this candle on the table."[52] Nothing had been decided. H.D. kept the flame burning on the table next to their bed; she and Aldington were still together, even if he did spend his nights with Dorothy Yorke. "Bella makes me forget. You make me remember," Rafe says.[53]

16

Tracks in the Sand

THE FACT THAT the H.D.–D. H. Lawrence relationship is not widely known should not surprise us; it was covered up. One of the most interesting things about H.D.'s image of Achilles' track in the sand in *Helen in Egypt* is that such a track is easily covered; it is the perfect image for an event that occurs, then disappears from sight. The practice of covering one's tracks in matters of the heart is an old one, dating back perhaps to the beginnings of the custom of marriage.

A good part of the cover-up was accomplished by Richard Aldington, whose motives could be interpreted as noble; perhaps he was trying to protect his wife from scandal. But since he in no way behaved in a protective role in other aspects of their relationship, it is more realistic to interpret his motives as related to his pride; he was attempting to protect *himself* from a scandal. A scandal that implicated his wife would not speak well for his ability to satisfy her in marriage and would thereby put his masculinity in question. That Aldington was sensitive about his sexual relations with H.D. can be inferred from his comments about the sexual potency of the other men she knew; he maintained that Lawrence was unable to function sexually and implied that Ezra Pound had the same problem. In "Nobody's Baby," a satire on Pound which appeared in *Soft Answers* (1931), he implies that no one believed that the poet was capable of fathering a child and surprised everyone when his wife had a baby. Aldington presents Pound very satirically as Charlemagne Cox, a complete charlatan, a total fraud in every respect. In *Portrait of a Genius, But . . . ,* Aldington's bitter biography of Lawrence, he writes of *Lady Chatterley's Lover:* "Clearly, it was a case of 'sex in the head', from every point of view (such as he was always denouncing in others), since there is every reason to suppose that when he wrote the book he was already virtually if not completely impotent."[1]

Aldington had reason to be bitter toward both Pound and Lawrence. Pound had never pretended to have any real respect for his ability to satisfy H.D. in marriage, and Lawrence had a poor opinion of Aldington, consistent with his portrayal of the broken husband, Sir Clifford, in *Lady Chatterley's Lover*. To Aldous Huxley, Lawrence wrote on October 28, 1928:

> Dear Aldous:
>
> I have read *Point Counter Point* with a heart sinking through my boot-soles and a rising admiration. I do think you've shown the truth, perhaps the last truth, about you and your generation, with really fine courage. It seems to me it would take ten times the courage to write *P. Counter P.* than it took me to write *Lady C:* and if the public knew *what* it was reading, it would throw a hundred stones at you, to one at me. I do think that art has to reveal the palpitating moment or the state of man as it is. And I think you do that, terribly. But what a moment! and what a state! if you can only palpitate to murder, suicide, and rape, in their various degrees — and you state plainly that it is so — *caro,* however are we going to live through the days? Preparing still another murder, suicide, and rape? But it becomes of a phantasmal boredom and produces ultimately inertia, inertia and final atrophy of the feelings. Till, I suppose, comes a final super-war, and murder, suicide, rape sweeps away the vast bulk of mankind. It is as you say — intellectual appreciation does not amount to so much, it's what you thrill to. And if murder, suicide, rape is what you thrill to, and nothing else, then it's your destiny — you can't change it *mentally*. You live by what you thrill to, and there's the end of it. Still for all that it's a *perverse* courage which makes the man accept the slow suicide of inertia and sterility: the perverseness of a perverse child. — It's amazing how men are like that. Richard Aldington is exactly the same inside, murder, suicide, rape — with a desire to *be* raped very strong — same thing really — just like you — only he doesn't face it, and gilds his perverseness. It makes me feel ill . . .[2]

Lawrence's association of Aldington with a Sir Clifford type of character is something from which Aldington attempted to extricate himself, and with a good deal of success. There was however no doubt in Lawrence's mind, as he suggests in this letter to Huxley, that Sir Clifford, who suffers from "inertia, inertia, inertia and final atrophy of the feelings" and is paralyzed in a wheelchair to symbolize this state, was related to Aldington.

Lawrence was clearly moved by Huxley's book in which he was characterized as Rampion. In a letter to S. S. Koteliansky on

December 3, 1928, Lawrence said that *"Point Counter Point* was 'the modern sort of melodrama, what *East Lynne* was in its day.' "[3] What Lawrence seemed to object to is that Huxley does not create an alternative to the world of Rampion and Lucy. Lawrence was certainly aware of this world; he had characterized it in the letter of November 7, 1917, to Cecil Gray in which he wrote of an underworld inhabited by Gray and Frieda. But Lawrence continued until the end of his life to believe in the possibility of another world — the world he shared with H.D., the world he tried to create or re-create in his portrait of the relationship that existed between Lady Constance Chatterley and Mellors, a world in which relations between man and woman are based not upon murder, suicide, and rape but upon tenderness. In fact, one of Lawrence's titles for the book that became *Lady Chatterley's Lover* was "Tenderness"; in it, Lawrence argues that the relationships that are part and parcel of the civilized world are based upon not a real love impulse but rather a power impulse.* Since the relationship of Connie and Mellors has no motive outside itself and takes place in a realm of the pure life instinct, it is untainted by the power motives that occur in relationships that are part of a civil or worldly order.

Lawrence's portrait of Sir Clifford as an Aldington-type character would have been unspeakably cruel if Aldington had been physically crippled in the war. Like Aldington, Sir Clifford is a writer. Like Aldington he fought in World War I. It is a well-known fact, admitted by Aldington, that he broke down psychically after the war. But Clifford is of course more than a simple portrait; he is a class type, and his attributes resemble other characters from Lawrence's past. After her husband's death, Frieda identified Clifford with Lawrence. Yet to Richard Aldington the psychic and situational resemblance to himself was all too recognizable.

Lawrence has portrayed the broken man as physically paralyzed to symbolize his impotent spirit. In *The First Lady Chatterley* Lawrence says of Sir Clifford:

> He was as it were cut off from the breathing contact of the living universe . . . He would get real aesthetic pleasure from books and

---

*Lawrence wrote three complete versions of *Lady Chatterley's Lover* between October 1926 and March 1928. The third version, *Lady Chatterley's Lover,* was published by Giuseppe Orioli, in Florence, Italy, in 1928. The first version, *The First Lady Chatterley,* was published by Dial Press in 1944. The second version, *John Thomas and Lady Jane,* was published in Italian in 1954 and in English by Viking Press in 1972. In the first two versions of the novel the Lawrence character is named Parkin; in the last version he is called Mellors.

pictures, something that thrilled his nerves and gave him a feeling of pride of conquest . . .

His terrible accident, his paralysis or whatever it was, was really symbolical in him. He was always paralyzed, in some part of him. That part in a man which can wake a woman's heart once and for all was always dead in him.[4]

In his biographical study of Lawrence, *The Priest of Love,* Harry T. Moore asks: "What made Lawrence, after so many protests that he never wanted to produce another novel, suddenly begin *Lady Chatterley's Lover* a few weeks after his return to the Villa Mirenda [Scandicci, Italy] in that autumn of 1926?"[5] Moore answers his own question with direct reference to Richard Aldington.

Richard Aldington, who kept his promise to visit the Mirenda during the grape harvest, in early October, didn't recall that Lawrence mentioned the projected novel to him at the time, but across the years he guessed that Lawrence's inspiration for the book was his visit to the Midlands in the preceding year — that's the summer of 1925, when the Clarkes [Lawrence's sister Ada and her husband William Clarke] took him motoring through Derby and Notts.[6]

Moore makes it clear that Aldington's conjecture about Lawrence's inspiration for the novel does not completely satisfy him, and points out that Lawrence had also visited England in 1926, immediately before he began writing *Lady Chatterley.* During the 1926 trip Lawrence also saw H.D. again, for the first time since their separation in 1919.

Moore goes on to ask: "But why look for a single 'inspiration' for such a novel?"[7] Richard Aldington was more than a little unhappy about *Lady Chatterley's Lover* and did what he could to disguise its origins and in general divert people from asking questions about it. Aldington would have us think instead of this story about Lawrence and Norman Douglas:

According to Aldington, one day when Lawrence and Frieda were talking with Orioli in his shop, Douglas strode in. After a moment of tight silence, Douglas, in a gesture that for him was one of friendship, stretched out his snuff box and said, 'Have a pinch of snuff, dearie.' Lawrence took it, saying, 'Isn't it curious' — *sniff* — 'only Norman and my father' — *sniff* — 'ever give me snuff?' And, Aldington has reported, the friendship was on again.[8]

Harry T. Moore tells this story in the context of his discussion of the origins of *Lady Chatterley's Lover.* Why? Aldington undoubtedly told the story to Moore exactly as Moore reports it.

But what is the intended message of Aldington's anecdote? Aldington furnished colorful and supposedly off-the-record anecdotes to those interested in Lawrence (including, of course, the biographers) that implied that Lawrence was effeminate, homosexual, impotent, and writing for the pornographic market. After Lawrence's death Middleton Murry elaborated the theme of Lawrence's latent homosexuality in his book *Son of Woman* (1931). When Aldington wrote his biography of Lawrence, *Portrait of A Genius, But . . .* (1950), he maintained that his understanding of Lawrence's "dark abdomen"[9] was derived from Murry's book, but in fact he had been characterizing Lawrence as a latent homosexual privately since at least 1928. According to Harry T. Moore, Aldington was also the source of the rumor that "in the last five years of Lawrence's life (1925–1930) Frieda used to go about complaining that he had become impotent."[10] At the same time Aldington took the public stance that Lawrence was one of the greatest writers of his generation, a devoted husband, and a man of real moral courage. It should be noted that Aldington's double messages continue to be accepted as gospel by many.

For the ten years following the break between H.D. and Lawrence (and the dissolution of the Aldington marriage), Aldington and Lawrence had very little to do with each other and actually held each other in low personal regard. Their infrequent meetings were characterized by mutual hostility. But upon Lawrence's death in 1930, Aldington formed a literary alliance with Frieda and suddenly emerged as a principal guide to the Lawrence literature. He quickly established himself as the expert through his many books, essays, biographies, and introductions to reprint editions of Lawrence's novels, which he edited. In the twenty-five years following Lawrence's death, Aldington published twenty-two separate books or essays on him, including his *Portrait of a Genius, But . . .* , which he hoped would be accepted as the definitive biography. When it became clear that his own biography would be superseded by the books being written by Edward Nehls and Harry T. Moore, Aldington became actively involved in these projects, offering his services as an interpreter of the Lawrence material and always avoiding (and in some cases actually destroying) the H.D.–Lawrence information upon which comprehensive biographies could be built. Aldington's correspondence of the 1950s and early 1960s is filled with venomous remarks about Harry T. Moore, whom he considered a "business man out for a successful academic career."[11] As far as Aldington knew, Moore was unaware that Aldington was using him for his own purposes. Of course, Aldington did steer the biographers and others toward much useful information; there is no doubt that he actually became an expert on Lawrence. But the Lawrence that he presented and led others to see is a Lawrence that had no connection with his former wife.

It is not our intention here to castigate careful and serious scholars, including Moore and Nehls, who were misled by Aldington (and others) or denied access to important information as they went about their work. Suffice it to say, however, that the key actor in the suppression of the H.D.–D. H. Lawrence story is easily and convincingly identified.

In *Lady Chatterley's Lover,* Lawrence gives this portrait of Sir Clifford:

> He had so very nearly lost his life, that what remained was wonderfully precious to him. It was obvious in the anxious brightness of his eyes, how proud he was, after the great shock, of being alive. But he had been so much hurt that something inside him had perished, some of his feelings had gone. There was a blank of insentience.[12]

Lawrence clearly felt this way about Aldington and did not confine his opinion to his novels; he let Aldington know in person what he thought of him. In a letter of May 24, 1927, Lawrence writes: "I never knew a man who seemed more to me to be living from a character not his own, than you. What is it that you are afraid of? *Ultimately?* — is it death? or pain? or just fear of the negative infinitude of all things? What ails thee, lad?"[13]

H.D. writes a good deal about Aldington's lack of sensitivity and fear of death; Aldington himself writes of it. Lawrence's portrait of Sir Clifford is a rather good caricature of the sentiments, attitude, and stance Aldington expressed in his poems written during the war and in his novel *Death of a Hero.* Lawrence writes: "And if he heard a rabbit scream, caught by a weasel or caught in a trap, his heart would stand still for a second, then he would think: 'There's another one gone to death! Another one! And I'm not gone!' And he exalted curiously. He never betrayed his preoccupation with death to Constance, but she divined it, and avoided the subject."[14]

Instead of making a fuss about the way he had been characterized in the *Lady Chatterley* novels, as so many of Lawrence's friends had done following the publication of earlier novels (thus drawing attention to themselves), Aldington helped to circulate *Lady Chatterley* once it had been published, and then proceeded to interpret the book in such a way as to disassociate himself from Sir Clifford. Aldington's actual feelings about *Lady Chatterley's*

Lover were partially revealed in a letter of April 13, 1959, to Harry T. Moore, in which Aldington reveals that "from the beginning I have wondered if DHL were not a little hopeful to cash in on the pornographic market of *Ulysses,* especially as his royalties were declining rapidly. I think the book is one of his least good novels, in spite of brilliant passages."[15]

However, the chief interest of *Lady Chatterley's Lover* is not Sir Clifford but the lovers. Lawrence's vision of the hut in which they meet is strikingly close to H.D.'s description of the house presented in "Paint It Today" in 1921. We have already read of how H.D. describes it: "We simply meet by accident in the woods, or in the little house in the woods." She continues:

> In the house we have in the woods, you could be as well as not. It is a Roman house. It is very small, low, with columns, the ice white stones stand sheer on the floor of the forest. There ought, I suppose, to be a square of grass about the place, but the moss and Virginia Creeper and poison-ivy and little toadstools shove right up against the stones of the floor. They do not break through the floor like the English stone-crop in the old gardens here. It is as if the stones froze them back.
>
> I have hardly looked inside the house, except for the first little entrance hall which is rather dark and has a whortle-berry crimson blanket on the floor. If my lover asks me to come into the room beyond, I run away at once. I do not think I am afraid or shy. It simply does not seem fitting, or it does not seem the time to see him or something. I almost prefer finding the place empty because then I sit in the sunlight in the porch and lean my head against a pillar and sleep. That is queer isn't it, to sleep in one's sleep.[16]

Lawrence's hut in *John Thomas and Lady Jane* has the same primitive, outdoorsy, woodsy quality. But more important, perhaps, than the physical description and location of the little hut in the woods is the quality of restfulness it brings. Lawrence writes of it as a sanctuary, invoking the concept of the temple, a place of refuge, stillness, and rest: "This was at least a little sanctuary. Here she could rest. She closed her eyes, and all her life went still within her, in a true quietness. She heard the soft tapping of the keeper, but that only made her more peaceful. He gave her stillness and rest."[17]

Lawrence writes: "The hut and the clearing were in a hidden place among the oak-trees and the remnants of last year's bracken. It was here the pheasants were raised, when the time came. It seemed one of the secret places of the forest, very still and remote."[18]

Since the cottage or hut represents a reality that is in another world, a world that is quite divorced from preoccupations of power and war, it is presented by both authors in contrast to images of civilization. The lovers' meetings seem to take place in an out-of-time dimension. Lawrence writes: "He seemed to slide through centuries, thousands of years of human culture, in his hour with her."[19]

Both Lawrence and H.D. infuse the scene with light. Lawrence writes: "She went slowly across the park. It was a blowy day, and she felt weak. But the sunshine blew in sometimes, and the world was bright. It seemed strangely bright. She was glad to flee into the wood, like a stricken thing."[20] H.D. writes:

> You might think the light was very shallow in this forest. Shallow — that is quite an idea. The word shallow came of itself just as my lover slides of himself, without being called, without being expected, around a pillar or out the door when I am just going to sleep on the whortle-berry coloured blanket. You might think the light was shallow in this forest. You would think, I think, that it would be a sort of silver, a glorified grey. I would think so if I used my imagination. But the light is very full and rich. The light is very warm. The light has a whole, crumbling feeling about it, you know, like when you crumble out the center of a dog-wood blossom and the pollen dusts your fingers. The light seems to dust your fingers but it does not really.[21]

The theme of the woman sitting on the porch is common to all three versions of *Lady Chatterley's Lover* as well as to H.D.'s "Paint It Today" and *Bid Me to Live*. In *John Thomas and Lady Jane* Lawrence writes: "She must get out. The wood drew her as by some silent magnetic force. In an interval when there was no rain, she put on her old blue water proof and escaped . . . The hut was closed and locked. But there was a little pent-roof over the door . . . She sat on the wooden door-step, gathering her mackintosh round her skirts. Yes, and the place was a sacred place, silent and healing."[22]

There are further similarities in H.D.'s and Lawrence's manuscripts. Both present a scene of the woman standing naked, looking in the glass. H.D. writes:

> Here I look at myself too much in the glass. Sometimes I say to it; "there is *one* person I recognize." Perhaps I look as odd to other people as other people look to me. Well, of course, I know I must. Though the little boys here [in England] never shout at one as they do in America.
> When my lover wrote . . . "Ah, psyche from the regions which," he was thinking of me when I stand with my clothes off and admire myself, turned half sideways in the glass.[23]

Lawrence writes in *Lady Chatterley's Lover:* "When Connie went up to her bedroom she did what she had not done for a long time: took off all her clothes, and looked at herself naked in the huge mirror. She did not know what she was looking for, or at, very definitely, yet she moved the lamp till it shone full on her."[24]

In *John Thomas and Lady Jane* as well as in "Paint It Today" the lovers make love on a blanket. H.D. makes repeated reference to the "whortle-berry coloured blanket." Lawrence writes:

> He held her with one hand, and with the other drew down an old blanket from the shelf.
> "You can lie your head on the blanket," he said.
> And with queer obedience, she lay her head on the old blanket. She felt him slowly, gently but with queer, blind clumsiness fumbling at her clothes, then the quiver of rapture, like a flame . . .[25]

In *Lady Chatterley's Lover* the blanket is a brown soldier's blanket, which presents a vivid contrast between the lovers' use of it and the soldier's use of it in war.

As important as the correspondence of central images in these novels is the presentation of a self divided between two worlds. H.D. writes: "I think it is my body that lives there and my soul here . . . Did my soul get transmuted here by some chance and does my body wait for it there with my lover? Will they come together some day, my soul and my body?"[26] In *John Thomas and Lady Jane* Lawrence speaks of the same division of the self. Of Connie he writes: "She was at the mercy of her two selves. But the self that mostly ruled was the self of her own, critical spirit, that was fiercely independent, and resented his clutches, and his blindness, and even the soft, lapping intimacy of his voice, the *thee* and the *thou* of his dialect."[27]

As in the poems discussed in chapters 13 and 14, the lovers often meet outdoors. In both H.D.'s and Lawrence's works, the sexual experience has a healing effect. In *Helen in Egypt,* H.D. writes, "as if I, Helen, had withdrawn/from the bruised and swollen flesh,/the arrow from its wound."[28] In *John Thomas and Lady Jane* Lawrence writes:

> And somehow she realised that it was the soul of his phallus, the overweening blind male soul in him, that had been wounded all his life, wounded through his mother and his step-father from the beginning of his days and whose wound gaped with the pain and hatred of sex. Because, his phallus was rooted in his soul, and rose erect from the soul's deeps, in naive pride of creation. And it was this queer, sightless, mindless phallic nature that had been hurt in

him all his life, and whose wound only closed now, in sleep, while she lay submissive in the circle of his flesh.[29]

§ § §

"Paint It Today" was written in 1921 and was H.D.'s first novel. The style is impressionistic, as the title suggests, like a series of paintings; it is, in a word, Imagist. The novel covers a longer time span than does *Bid Me to Live*. It begins in Philadelphia with a portrait of H.D. (Midget) as a child. Then comes a portrait of the confused and baffled Midget in love with Raymond, an arrogant and pretentious young poet (Ezra Pound). There is a portrait of Frances Josepha (Frances Gregg), the girl with whom H.D. traveled on the journey that led her to England and to separation from home and country. We also have a portrait of Aldington as Basil, the handsome young British writer — very refined, very articulate, very bourgeois — and a picture of H.D.'s parents, who are called Mr. and Mrs. Defreddie in the novel. And there is a portrait of Midget's lover, who is neither Raymond nor Basil. Nor is he Cecil Gray, for these meetings pre-date H.D.'s acquaintance with Gray and her stay in Cornwall.

"Paint It Today" is the story H.D. "had been writing or trying to write . . . under various titles," the Madrigal story. "I was to have told a story or set a scene of a blue world. I will tell it in my own time, in my own way."[30] She tells it here in a letter written to Frances Josepha some indefinite time after Midget's marriage to Basil. Frances has written to her after a long silence, just as she, Frances, is about to give birth to a son. Midget responds with a letter telling Frances about her lover: "I will not tell you exactly what he looks like nor what he wears for you would laugh and say you thought it very much like a cheap steel engraving of an idealized eighteenth century portrait of Catullus. My description would give you that idea."[31]

Finally H.D. includes in "Paint It Today" a portrait of her friend Bryher, whom she calls White Anthea. It was Bryher who rescued H.D. from the painful experience described in *Bid Me to Live,* the dissolution of her marriage in the context of her relationship with D. H. Lawrence. (In *Lady Chatterley's Lover,* Connie in the end goes off with her sister, Hilda, who is intended by Lawrence as both an H.D. double and a portrait of Bryher.)

Many of the significant facts of H.D.'s life during the World War I years were painful. Her marriage was finally over in 1917, when Aldington began to live with Dorothy Yorke. In 1918 H.D.'s brother Gilbert was killed in action in France. Her father died shortly after the shock of his son's death. In the summer of 1918 H.D. became pregnant, and in March 1919 her daughter, Perdita, was born. The birth of the child, an event about which she was very happy, nevertheless put her under an incredible nervous strain. At the time of the birth she was ill with double pneumonia, and there was a question as to whether she would survive the ordeal of childbirth at all. And she was at this time virtually deserted by the men in her life. Pound appeared the day before the child was born to say, "My only real criticism is that this is not my child."[32] Aldington was hostile and threatened to have H.D. thrown in prison for perjury if she registered the child in his name. Lawrence expressed concern but was ill himself and apparently did nothing to help. Cecil Gray, who some have assumed to be the father of the child, appears not to have acknowledged paternity in any way.

In a letter to Koteliansky dated March 31, 1919, D. H. Lawrence wrote: "Heard from Arabella: Hilda's baby born last week: a girl: 'Gray behaving wretchedly, Richard very fine.' " Lawrence was quoting Dorothy Yorke. He continued: "Hilda and baby doing well." In the next paragraph of the letter he wrote: "Don't say anything about Hilda — except to Sonia," Koteliansky's wife.[33]

Lawrence had also written to Amy Lowell in March that H.D. had pneumonia; everyone was afraid she would lose the baby or that she would die before giving birth. But an April 6, 1919, letter from Lawrence brought the news to Lowell that the baby had been born safely and both mother and daughter were well.

Lawrence was very sick with influenza, complicated no doubt by his worsening tuberculosis. H.D.'s pneumonia had developed from influenza; there was at the time a serious epidemic in London. Lawrence was not in good spirits. His relationship with Frieda was quite strained. He never again regained the health he had enjoyed prior to the events of the war years, and his marriage was never again what it had been during the *Rainbow* years. On March 14, 1919, he wrote to Koteliansky:

> I am not going to be left to Frieda's tender mercies until I am well again. She is a devil — and I feel as if I would part from her for ever — let her go alone to Germany, while I take another road. For it is time, I have been bullied by her long enough. I really could leave her now, without a pang, I believe. The time comes, to make an end, one way or another. If this illness hasn't been a lesson to her, it has to me.[34]

In "Compassionate Friendship" H.D. writes of Lawrence's desertion of her: "I was waiting for Frances Perdita . . . I was so happy. I had double pneumonia. It was late at night or in the middle of the night. Havelock Ellis had been in my thoughts, Lawrence had disappeared. He never wrote me after I told him I was expecting this child." [35]

Deserted by all the men in her life, H.D. was cared for and brought through the ordeal of the birth of the baby and recovery from her illness by Bryher. Bryher helped H.D. to care for the child, and the two women became lifelong friends. In 1920, after the death of her father, H.D. traveled with Bryher to Greece.

> I could say, I did say that I had had a number of severe shocks; the news of the death of my father, following the death in action of my brother in France, came to me when I was alone outside London in the early spring of that bad influenza winter of 1919. I myself was waiting for my second child — I had lost the first in 1915 from shock and repercussions of war news broken to me in a rather brutal fashion.
>
> The second child, for some reason, I knew, must be born. Oh, she would be born, all right, though it was an admitted scientific fact that a waiting mother, stricken with that pneumonia, double pneumonia, would not live. She might live — yes — but then the child would not. They rarely both live, if ever! But there were reasons for us both living, so we did live. At some cost, however! The material and spiritual burden of pulling us out of danger fell upon a young woman whom I had only recently met — anyone who knows me knows who this person is. Her pseudonym is Bryher and we all call her Bryher. If I got well, she would herself see that the baby was protected and cherished and she would take me to a new world, a new life, to the land, spiritually of my predilection, geographically of my dreams. We would go to Greece. [36]

"Paint It Today" was written, as we have previously noted, in 1921. H.D. was with Bryher. She had miraculously survived.

Although D. H. Lawrence spoke only rarely of the birth of H.D.'s child in his letters, the birth to the heroine of a child of uncertain paternity is a topic of many of his major works after 1919. It is certainly a central topic of *The Man Who Died* and figures prominently in all three versions of *Lady Chatterley's Lover*.

Although Aldington had good reason to cover up the H.D.–D. H. Lawrence relationship and he was good at distorting history, it is certainly true that H.D. also went to great lengths to conceal the events of the relationship and was incensed and terribly upset about the possibility that those events would come into the public domain too soon. In "Compassionate Friendship" she writes:

> I saw nothing of the Lawrences after leaving Richard and taking the trip to Greece with Bryher, in 1920. But he came into my dreams, rarely, it is true, but poignantly and his name came up on occasion during my limited time with Professor Freud in Vienna. It was something of a shock to find a letter of his to me, printed in the book [Harry T. Moore's *The Intelligent Heart*]. How did that letter come to be at large — who found it or who stole it, and who sold it and to whom and for how much?[37]

"Compassionate Friendship" is a cryptic piece of writing. It was written after *Bid Me to Live* and *Helen in Egypt*, in 1955, while H.D. was convalescing at the Am Strand sanatorium, "guest of Dr. Brunner," under the care of Dr. Erich Heydt. Heydt had been asking her questions about her relationship with Lawrence, Pound, and others. As we read "Compassionate Friendship" we have the sense that H.D. is torn between concealing and revealing. She evades questions or answers them indirectly. Sometimes she answers a question poetically. The style of the work is not unlike that of her Pound memoir, *End to Torment*, but the manuscript is much less candid. She calls it a "reassessment."

Norman Holmes Pearson, H.D.'s literary executor, collected with the "Compassionate Friendship" manuscript a note written to Bryher which reads: "These memoirs were written to lessen rather than to reveal to the public all the unhappy incidents of my life." It is in this spirit that "Compassionate Friendship" should be read. If we read it in the wrong light, it will throw us far off track.

We must remember that while H.D. had no wish to distort the truth, as did Aldington, her standards for what was and was not a subject for the public were in accordance with her Victorian upbringing. She is frank about any question that relates to her public life and discreet about any question that relates to her private life. The questions asked by Heydt are for the most part not stated in the text but implied by H.D.'s responses. Sometimes she writes in relation to an event rather than a question; for instance, "I just received a book that Norman [Holmes Pearson] sent me on D. H. Lawrence; Norman wants me to confirm or qualify some references to H.D. in the volume. I have not the courage to do this at the moment."[38]

The book in question is Harry T. Moore's *The Intelligent Heart*, in which Moore publishes a previously unpublished letter from Lawrence to H.D., written in 1929. Lawrence writes: "But now it's more than ten years since we met, and what should we have to say? God knows! Nothing, really. It's no use saying anything. That's my last conviction. Least said, soonest mended: which assumes that the breakage has already happened." [39]

H.D. makes it clear that she is upset not only by Moore's publication of the letter, but also by his inaccurate explanation of it. Moore writes: "Actually, Lawrence mistrusted H.D.'s loyalty: although he usually didn't hold grudges, he couldn't forget that in a quarrel with some American friends of theirs a few years before, H.D. had taken the opposite side." [40]

This explanation may have come from Aldington. Aldington wrote to Moore, who was then editing Lawrence's *Collected Letters* (eventually dedicated to Aldington), that Lawrence and H.D. "had a row about something, God knows what." Aldington told Moore that H.D. was too "sensitive about such things." [41] It was, of course, Aldington who was sensitive about Lawrence's relationship with H.D., although he maintained in this letter that he didn't mind the publication of anything about himself in D. H. Lawrence's letters. (In the end, on Aldington's advice, Moore silently edited out of the *Collected Letters of D. H. Lawrence* all but five references to H.D.)

It was painful for H.D. to read such misrepresentations of the truth about her relationship with Lawrence. But by being silent she had participated in the cover-up. What could she expect? In "Compassionate Friendship" she writes: "I glanced at the D. H. Lawrence that Norman had sent me. The result was that I had a wretched night." [42] Moore's explanation hurt her. The notion of questioning her loyalty cut deep.

> I have been deep in the Harry T. Moore book on Lawrence that Norman sent me. I find that Lawrence wrote *The Escaped Cock* or *The Man Who Died* at Gsteig, Switzerland, in the summer of 1928. He also painted a picture of a love-scene. "The naked woman . . . is not, for a change, Frieda." Is this the image that he recreated as Isis, the priestess in *The Man Who Died?* Stephen Guest insisted that H.D. was this Isis. I read myself into the story. I do not think I was disloyal to Lawrence as this Mr. Moore implied. It was a matter of life and death, spiritual as well as physical. [43]

In writing "Compassionate Friendship" H.D. realized that, as she puts it, "I was unconsciously struggling against this growing tide-wave or gulf-stream of the Lawrence legend." [44] She knew Aldington's lies had influenced the public understanding of Lawrence. It was very difficult for her to come to terms with the lie, even though she had silently consented to its emergence in this form. It was a real struggle for her to remain silent in 1955, and it is painful for us to feel her attempting to maintain this silence. If we read between the lines of "Compassionate Friendship," the hidden story emerges just as it does from the poetry and prose. H.D. seems to want to tell us at least that she knew a different Lawrence from Harry T. Moore's portrayal, even if she can say nothing else. It is really very difficult to keep such things to oneself. In her memoir H.D. talks about the appropriation of some of her writing that mentions Lawrence's name directly (rather than in fictional form):

> But especially, I worry from time to time because Stephen Guest and I, at one time, agreed to write memoirs or novels, helping one another with criticism. This was to be experimental work. I received his story, as far as it went, and handed it back. But when it came to getting mine back, he simply refused to hand it over. I have never recovered that rough story — and rough it was, a sort of sub-psychoanalytical dimension. It was a sketch. Unfortunately, I had mentioned Lawrence in this story and Stephen said, "But you wrote of Lawrence. That must be saved." I was rather cut off at that time, living in a little flat in Sloane Street . . . But where and how will those pages turn up, sold where and how and to whom and for how much?
>
> When I spoke to Bryher of this once she said I should not worry, Stephen must have destroyed them. But has he? The pages are not evil, but intimate in a rather crude fashion.[45]

As we read "Compassionate Friendship," we continue to wonder whether H.D. is going to tell us the details of her relationship with Lawrence. She is not. And for those who are sensitive to what she is saying, she provides the reason. Quite simply, she knows that even if she were to speak out quite openly about it, she would be misunderstood, misinterpreted, and possibly ignored. What has happened — the lies, the cover-up — she concludes, is for the best. "Surely I have been guarded, guided, in a miraculous manner and I can analyze for myself my antipathy to the pages that Stephen appropriated."[46]

H.D. addresses the question of the letters she received from Lawrence directly.

> Letters? I had a bundle of letters from Lawrence. I left them in a suit-case in the basement of 44 Mecklenburgh Square with great stacks of Richard's letters. When I saw Richard and Brigit in Paris after the *Port-Cros* episode, I asked Richard what had become of my old letters. He said he had burned them, "I am sorry, Dooley."[47]

It is quite clear that H.D. felt that this treatment of her correspondence from Lawrence was a low and ignoble gesture on the part of Aldington; but it is also clear that she includes it in "Compassionate Friendship" as one of the series of events that helped her to keep her silence about her relationship with Lawrence. And she was well aware that the tension of maintaining that silence had a good deal to do with her ability as a creative artist. So we must again take her at her word. She says she wrote these memoirs "to lessen rather than reveal," and this is precisely what they do. If we want to understand a fuller rather than a diminished or lessened version of the H.D.–D. H. Lawrence relationship, we will find it in the poetry and the prose.

H.D. says in "Compassionate Friendship": "I have been anonymous for so long and have woven myself into my present-self or protected my present with the writing, the re-covery of the past — the near past, still so near to me, the War II years and the final epitome of the novel or the novels in the Helen poem. I am alive in the Helen sequence."[48] The word *re-covery* is crucial. H.D. speaks of art as recovery, which, as she uses the word, means both a recovering of one's experience in the sense of a repossession or reclamation of it and at the same time a covering or re-covering, a covering again.

17

Tenderness

IN *The First Lady Chatterley* D. H. Lawrence writes of Constance as a dryad. The husband says, "You are like a flower: and rather like a dryad."[1] Dryad, we will remember, had been Pound's favorite name for H.D. A dryad is a wood nymph, a free spirit of the forest. Lawrence also calls Constance Parkin's "wife in the wood."[2]

Sometime during H.D.'s pregnancy, she and Lawrence separated. H.D.'s "dryad" nature — her unwillingness to make civilized claims on a man — may have had something to do with the break. Lawrence was more than a little angry about H.D.'s spring 1918 trip to stay with Cecil Gray in Cornwall, and Connie's trip and the subsequent breakup of the lovers is a theme of all three versions of *Lady Chatterley's Lover*. In each Lawrence paints a portrait of Gray, the musician and composer who offered H.D. a room in which to work at Bosigran, his Cornish home. In *The First Lady Chatterley* the portrait is mildly disguised:

> A man who did music came to the villa for a few days. He was not young, not handsome nor famous: a smallish man with an ascetic grey sort of face and a weak digestion, a restless nerve-wracked creature who would have been a nonentity save for some little power of music in him. He made no fight for prestige, didn't care what the crowd thought of him and was thoroughly miserable . . . He played the piano well — but unwillingly: and his own compositions in the dainty Elizabethan style of music were charming if not memorable.[3]

H.D. decided to make the trip at the time the Lawrences were staying with her at 44 Mecklenburgh Square, in December 1917.

As she tells the story in *Bid Me to Live,* Rico (Lawrence) says in a rage:

> "Do you realize . . . what you are doing?"
> "Why — yes, I am going away with Vane [Gray]. Or he is going first. I want to go over the books, pack."
> "But — but — do you *realize?*"
> What did he mean? She simply did not understand him.[4]

H.D. was not being naive. She knew what Lawrence was angry about. When she says, "She simply did not understand him," she means she does not understand why a man thinks he has the right to tell a woman what to do with her life when he has already made the decision not to share his life with her. The experience at 44 Mecklenburgh Square had been the test — H.D. called it "the crucible." She and Lawrence had come to a decision, each for different reasons, to go their separate ways. From H.D.'s point of view, he no longer had any right to object. Anyway, in a sense Lawrence had known that either she or Frieda would go off with Gray. They had all known that. Elsa (Frieda) had said that if Julia (H.D.) went with Rico (Lawrence), it would leave her "free for Vanio."[5] As H.D. writes: "It was Rico who had brought him to the house and it was Rico ironically who had precipitated this . . . 'You and Vane are made for each other,' Rico had jeered."[6]

After Lawrence and H.D. separated finally in 1919, they went their own ways. But as we have seen, their work from 1919 on has distinct parallels. Lawrence began his *Psychoanalysis and the Unconscious* in December 1919 and continued to work on it in 1920. H.D. was at the same time writing her "Notes on Thought and Vision." Lawrence completed *The Lost Girl* in 1920, and H.D. wrote "Paint It Today" in 1921. While H.D. worked on her novel *Palimpsest,* Lawrence completed *Aaron's Rod,* which he had begun at 44 Mecklenburgh Square. Both continued to write Imagist poems. And as Lawrence traveled in Italy and Mexico, pursuing his interests in the primitive Etruscan and Mayan cultures, H.D. traveled to Greece and Egypt, pursuing her interests in the archaic Greek and the early Egyptian cultures; both writers focused on forms that pre-dated European civilization.

Lawrence was not to return to England except for brief visits to London from mid-December 1923 to early March 1924, a few weeks in October 1925, and again from July 30 through September 1926. During these years H.D. lived in London and Switzerland but made extended trips to Greece, Venice, Paris, America, and Egypt. When Lawrence returned to Hampstead in September

1926, he wrote: "I feel, if ever I were going to do an English novel, I'd have to come to England to do it. Perhaps this neighbourhood."[7]

In August 1926 Lawrence spent a weekend with Richard Aldington in Padworth, Berkshire. From October 6 to 11 "the Aldingtons [Richard and Dorothy Yorke] stayed with Lawrence at the Villa Mirenda." By October 26 "Lawrence had reached p. 41 of the first draft of *Lady Chatterley's Lover.*" On October 31, 1926, Frieda Lawrence wrote: " 'Lawrence goes into the woods to write, he is writing a short long story, always breaking new ground, the curious class feeling this time or rather the soul against the body, no I don't explain it well, the *animal* part.' At this point Lawrence interpolated: *'Ooray! Eureka!'* "[8]

In November 1926 "Lawrence continued with and possibly finished *The First Lady Chatterley.*"[9] The novel represents a real breakthrough in Lawrence's career as an artist; the images are astonishingly clear and vivid. At the same time he plunged into painting. On November 24, 1926, Lawrence writes: "I have started painting, quite seriously on my own . . . I've done a nice biggish picture — that is, I like it — a man and woman in a pink room, and a child looking up — modern. Now I'm going to do a long one, about 1½ yards by ¾ yard — of Boccaccio's story of the gardener and the nunnery."[10]

In December 1926 Lawrence began his second version of *Lady Chatterley, John Thomas and Lady Jane.* He describes himself as writing "so differently from the way I have written before!" And he says, in the next line of that same letter in fact, "I spend much more time painting."[11] On January 8, 1927, he writes, "I'm getting on with the novel . . . and am doing a landscape with figures."[12]

Lawrence had nearly died of malaria early in 1925. The new burst of energy he experienced following his return to his native England was a rebirth. "Suddenly I paint away," he wrote on December 6, 1926.[13] And on December 19, "Now it's a lovely sunny day, and I sat out in the wood this morning, working at my novel — which comes out of me slowly, and is good, I think, but a little too deep in bits — sort of bottomless pools . . ."[14]

The painting, the three drafts of *Lady Chatterley,* and *The Man Who Died,* as well as the assembling of his entire body of poetry for his *Collected Poems,* were all part of the same spirit and energy. To Earl Brewster, Lawrence wrote in February 1927:

> I . . . put a phallus . . . in each one of my pictures somewhere. And I paint no picture that won't shock people's castrated social

spirituality. I do this out of positive belief, that the phallus is a great sacred image: it represents a deep, deep life which has been denied in us.[15]

In April 1927 Lawrence wrote "The Escaped Cock," a first draft of the first half of the book known as *The Man Who Died*.* Both *Lady Chatterley* and *The Man Who Died* were close to Lawrence's heart. Of *Lady Chatterley* he wrote on April 12, "To me it is beautiful and tender and frail as the naked self is, and I shrink very much even from having it typed."[16] Lawrence expressed the same sentiments about the finished version of *The Man Who Died*. The two works are very similar in theme. Both are about a relationship between a man and a woman which takes place outside the context of social mores. In both the woman becomes pregnant but the lovers must separate for very real, "worldly" reasons. *Lady Chatterley's Lover* tells the story in the world of everyday reality, the secular world; *The Man Who Died* tells the story in a spiritual or religious context. But for Lawrence, as for H.D., the secular and the spiritual are simply different languages of discourse which address the same reality.

In *The First Lady Chatterley* are religious images which invoke Lawrence's poems of the Hampstead period — images, for instance, of transfiguration: "A transfiguration. A man suffused with the brightness of God."[17] In "Erinnyes" Lawrence had written:

> So many ghosts among us,
> Invisible yet strong,
> Between me and thee, so many ghosts of the slain.[18]

We recall the transubstantiation images of "Shades." In *The First Lady Chatterley* Lawrence writes: "Like a ghost he came, through the drizzling rain. And like a ghost he saw her sitting, waiting in the porch of the hut."[19]

In his poem "Resurrection of the Flesh," a touch had led to the speaker's awakening. In *The First Lady Chatterley* Parkin asks Constance, "Don't you think you've lowered yourself with the likes of me?" and she answers, "Not when I touch you."[20] We must think of this touch when we infer from *Bid Me to Live* that Lawrence repudiated H.D.'s touch at Mecklenburgh Square.

In Lawrence's novel we recognize correspondences to his

*In February 1928 Lawrence published the original short-story version of part I of the novel in *The Forum* magazine. In 1929 the complete novel was published by Harry Crosby's Black Sun Press in Paris under the title *The Escaped Cock*. In 1931 the Knopf (New York) and Secker (London) editions of the complete novel appeared under the title *The Man Who Died*.

poems. On December 6, 1918 he sent a series of poems to Harriet Monroe which were published in *Poetry* in February 1919. One of these was titled "Bread Upon the Waters."

So you are lost to me!

Ah you, you ear of corn strait lying,
What food is this for the darkly flying
Fowls of the Afterwards!

White bread afloat on the waters,
Cast out by the hand that scatters
Food untowards,

Will you come back when the tide turns?
After many days? My heart burns
To know.

Will you return after many days
To say your say as a traveller says
More marvel than woe?

Drift then, for the soundless birds
As fish in shadow-waved herds,
To approach you.

Drift then, bread cast out;
Drift, lest I fall in doubt
And reproach you.

For you are lost to me![21]

In 1926 Lawrence wrote in *The First Lady Chatterley*, "And now the bread that he had cast upon the waters was beginning to return to him."[22] His characters talk of having a child by the Holy Ghost. Many passages contrast the eternal moment with Plato's concept of immortality, and Parkin declares that he would rather be a Plutonist than a Platonist — an allusion to the underground world of Orpheus and Eurydice that had been a subject of Lawrence's and H.D.'s poetry and correspondence.

Lawrence uses many images that invoke the dissolution of the ego, the coming of spring, the unfolding of buds, and the experience of pure communication between lovers. In *Lady Chatterley's Lover* these images are set in contrast to the portrait of Sir Clifford, who is "cut off from the breathing contact of the living universe" and can get "real aesthetic pleasure" only from "books and pictures."

Lawrence describes Sir Clifford as a bully. In an early issue of the *Egoist,* Aldington had been called the "British bully." Lawrence says that Parkin, in contrast to Clifford, would fight Constance openly: "Open warfare, if there must be war . . . She had yielded something to him. That was true. But not to his bullying. Only to his sudden real desire."[23]

Constance is compared to Mary Magdalene; the passion brings the world to life for her. "I'm like this woman who touched Jesus. You touch the living body, and the flow starts in you, the dead dries up."[24] Finally Constance tells Parkin, "I don't ever want anybody to know about us — about you and me . . ." " 'I shan't tell anybody,' he said laconic."[25]

In spite of an effort to save appearances, Lawrence and Frieda were not getting along at all well in 1926. Frieda had recently taken a new lover, but the relationship between Lawrence and his wife had been stormy for years. There were the famous fights, but Lawrence was also bitter about Frieda's gossip concerning his own sexual life: she had accused him of being impotent. He had been particularly irritated about her characterization of his relationship with Esther Andrews.* In *The First Lady Chatterley* Frieda is portrayed, rather monstrously, as the wife of Parkin. Lawrence writes that Parkin's wife accused him of "a curious, almost medieval assortment of sexual extravagances and minor perversities" and calls her "that foul woman, his wife. The truant wife . . . has aired in minute detail every incident in her married life with Parkin that reflects to his discredit."[26]

In "Making Another Lawrence: Frieda and the Lawrence Legend," Emile Delavenay argues that Frieda was in fact very much the "loose, florid," unintelligent sort of person Lawrence portrayed as Parkin's wife in *The First Lady Chatterley*. Delavenay states: "The impression she made on me in 1932 was of not quite knowing what Lawrence was about, and of making hesitant pretense that she did." He goes on to say:

> Stupid is a word that recurs on Huxley's typewriter when discussing Frieda about that same time. It mostly refers to her incompetence in dealing with people or practical affairs. This has its relevance to the commonly held idea that Frieda helped prolong Lawrence's life after his grave illness of 1925, when he should by any medical standards have been given strict and regular treatment for tuberculosis. It is clear from Aldous Huxley's letters that he might have been made amenable to it, had his resistance to friends' persuasion not been reinforced by Frieda's complicity or bungling.[27]

---

*After Lawrence's death this particular piece of gossip emerged as a tale of seduction and impotence in Mabel Dodge Luhan's strange memoir of Lawrence, *Lorenzo in Taos*.

Delavenay argues that Frieda was, in Huxley's words, "worse than useless as regards D.H.L.'s health," and that Lawrence told her days before his death, "Frieda, you have killed me." Delavenay goes on to discuss Frieda's affair with Angelo Ravagli:* "Lawrence, and no doubt his sisters, knew by then [1926] that Frieda was Ravagli's mistress."[28]

Delavenay implies that Frieda's interest in the "Lawrence legend" after her husband's death had to do with the fight for Lawrence's royalties. Lawrence had left no will, and the estate was contested by his family.

> When she came to London in 1932 to fight for Lawrence's royalties before the High Court of Justice, she had begun to build up the legend. She admitted her many quarrels with him, but claimed she always had faith in his greatness as a writer. Her testimony was not wholly convincing . . . My own vivid impression . . . was that everything she said required careful scrutiny. Her mind was totally untrained for any kind of intellectual or even factual consistency. Yet she used her undoubted intelligence with a sort of cunning . . . suggestive of Maupassant peasants.[29]

By 1925 Lawrence was no longer dependent on Frieda; she was in many ways a terrible burden to him. He portrays her both as Parkin's wife in *The First Lady Chatterley* and as the peasant's wife in *The Man Who Died* in very much the same way as others who also knew her at this time portrayed her. By 1925 Lawrence saw her without illusions. Parkin's wife is portrayed as older than Parkin (Frieda was six years older than Lawrence) and of her bizarre behavior Lawrence writes: "She is older than Mr. Parkin, and it may be her time of life has something to do with it."[30]

Delavenay argues convincingly against Martin Green, Frieda's biographer, that Frieda was far from the "very maker of [Lawrence's] genius." He portrays her as immoral, malicious, and slovenly — more of a parasite than a creative source. He writes:

> Frieda's many contradictory utterances are difficult to explain except in the light of her interest of the moment and her general intellectual inconsistency. In July, 1932, a sculptor friend, Lawrence Bradshaw, asked her whether it was true that Lawrence had been sexually impotent as we know that Frieda, possibly in self-justification, told her friends he was after 1926. She protested that this was "an enormous lie spread by J. M. Murry." She also hotly de-

---

* Angelo Ravagli was the Lawrences' landlord at Villa Bernarda, Spotorno, Italy, from November 1925 to April 1926. Frieda's affair with Ravagli continued over the years, and in 1950 he became her third husband.

nied to Bradshaw Catherine Carswell's "insinuations" that she, Frieda, ever had been Murry's mistress. Until the question of Lawrence's estate was settled in her favour, on Murry's sole testimony, it was then better for her that her liaison with Murry be not too widely talked about. Those were the days when she professed to be profoundly affected by Murry's *Son of Woman,* and when she told me (27 St. Peter's Square, Hammersmith, 18 June, 1932) that "Murry had always been jealous of Lawrence!" She could lie brazenly when it suited her, as when she denied Lawrence's first sex experience with Alice Dax. Her comments on Harry Moore's *Intelligent Heart* . . . are part of her build up of the Lawrence legend she had set out to create after Lawrence died.[31]

In *The First Lady Chatterley* Lawrence writes in great disgust of the wife of Parkin, who is going around telling one lie after another about him. In these lines of the novel, Ivy Bolten, the nurse, is speaking to Constance: "My Lady, it makes me feel bad to hear the things she is going about saying about him, awful things, fearful things. Of course nobody believes her altogether, but something's bound to stick."[32]

In her foreword to *The First Lady Chatterley* Frieda makes an astonishing statement which reveals both her barely disguised hostility to Lawrence and her will to outlive him and create the legend of which Delavenay speaks. She writes: "To see him right through to the end makes me forever glad! I am grateful that I could see him back into the earth that he loved. He had made me his wife in the fullest meaning of the word, and more; he had given me his very self to keep. I cannot conceive that I would have died and he be left without me."[33] This is a monstrous statement, but it is not unique; Frieda was not really capable of being altogether decent to Lawrence after he wrote *Lady Chatterley's Lover.* There is considerable evidence, apart from Lawrence's portraits of her, that she was not altogether decent to him before he wrote it.

In our attempt to understand their work, we propose in this study to take the testimony of the artists — H.D. and D. H. Lawrence — more seriously than the testimony of their respective spouses, Frieda Lawrence and Richard Aldington. If we accept the hypothesis that the novel, the work of art, presents the truth of experience in a fictionalized form with names changed and events symbolized, we put ourselves in the artist's relation to reality. From this perspective, we find that Lawrence's and H.D.'s versions of what happened correspond; essentially, they tell the same story. It is as though the authors wrote their novels in part as testimony. In a sense Aldington's and Frieda's realities also correspond.* We are, then, forced to choose. Who is telling the truth — Frieda and Aldington or Lawrence and H.D.?

Let us entertain the hypothesis that D. H. Lawrence is telling the truth of his experience in *The First Lady Chatterley*. The test of any hypothesis is, does it account for the facts? In this case the facts are poems, novels, events, situations, and most important, the psychic reality of what is presented. If the novel is "true," it ought to prevail against the statements that others have furnished to account for (or distort) these facts.

We are in dangerous territory, for the tests of this hypothesis do not yield the kind of evidence that is easily and objectively verified. How can one judge or verify the depth and meaning of another's experience? We can prove that Lawrence and H.D. knew each other, even that they spoke to each other and read each other's poetry, but how can we prove what they meant to each other? Lawrence wrote to Cecil Gray that he and H.D. shared a deeper knowledge. What can we know of this knowledge?

Can we talk about the verifiability of a novel? Can we establish the existence of a "literary fact"? Character identification is a complex issue in the work of the Imagists, for the accent is not on the "I," the ego, the character, but on the deep spiritual reality.

Lawrence has painted a portrait of a Lady Chatterley. She has large blue eyes. She is shy and soft-spoken, sometimes quiet and brooding. She is an outdoors sort of person, "country-looking" with "wondering blue eyes."[34] This doesn't tell us much. We can't identify people with the characters solely on the basis of their physical and superficial characteristics. Insofar as Lady Chatterley is intended to "be" H.D., the character is somewhat disguised. The situation, however, is thinly disguised. As Lawrence tells us, "Trust the tale."

Lawrence's portrait of Lady Chatterley is general enough to describe many women, but by any account it is most certainly not a portrait of Frieda. Frieda was neither shy nor soft-spoken, nor quiet, nor brooding, even when she was young. In Lawrence's novels we do have portraits of Frieda; for instance, the character of Ursula in *Women in Love*. Constance is not like Ursula, but the

---

*Aldington and Frieda corresponded regularly after Lawrence's death, and Aldington's introduction to Lawrence's posthumously published *Apocalypse* (1932) is presented in the form of a letter to Frieda. In a letter to H.D., Aldington indicated that he destroyed Frieda's letters to him after her death in 1956, when he was asked to contribute them to a volume of her letters that was being prepared for publication.

portrait of Bertha Coutts, Parkin's wife, does correspond to many descriptions of Frieda.

On what basis, then, do we determine the real identity on which a character in a novel is based? In the case of Lawrence we would be better informed if we looked at the novel as an expression of the life situation and employed a nonfictional test of truth; that is, what is the underlying reality of the events being presented? What are the actual circumstances that inform the picture? If we think in terms of fidelity to the spiritual reality, in terms of *what happened* essentially or psychically in a given circumstance (always realizing that Lawrence distorts external detail), then we come closer to understanding the biographical reality underlying the novel as a work of art. *Lady Chatterley* is in this sense an Imagist novel. In order to read the book correctly we, as readers, must separate a certain deep spiritual reality from a superficial descriptive reality. While this is not particularly difficult to do if we know the background of the story, it does require certain sensitivity to the special nuances of the situation.

In *The First Lady Chatterley* Lawrence writes of Connie and Clifford's marriage: "But, of course, there was the tragedy that had fallen upon them! He could never be a husband to her. She lived with him like a married nun, a sister of Christ. It was more than that, too. For of course they had had a month of real marriage."[35]

Of the marriage of Rafe and Julia, H.D. writes in *Bid Me to Live:* "They had had that year in Italy, before the war, almost a year of married life in England after. Two years. One married year in England and the time together, before that, in Paris, in Rome. In Capri, Verona, Venice."[36] And, as if in refutation of Lawrence's picture of her marriage to Aldington, H.D. writes of "the Christ child of their battered integrity."

In his *Death of a Hero* Richard Aldington tells essentially the same story about his marriage as did H.D. and Lawrence. His hero's brief marriage to his wife, Elizabeth, is destroyed by what has happened to him in the war. John Cournos relates a similar story in *Miranda Masters,* a novel about H.D. and the dissolution of her marriage, but Cournos's portrait is somewhat misleading because he never understood the basis of the problems in the Aldington marriage and was out of the country, in Russia, at the time the marriage collapsed. The point is that this group of people — Richard Aldington, H.D., D. H. Lawrence, Frieda Lawrence, Ezra Pound, and in a peripheral sense John Cournos and Cecil Gray — knew to whom and about whom they were speaking. The allusions to persons and situations were crystal clear to those involved, but camouflaged to protect them and the artists from the public.

In an attempt to identify Lady Chatterley and knowing that she could not be based on Frieda, some scholars have said she might be based on Lady Cynthia Asquith. In their book *D. H. Lawrence and His World,* Harry T. Moore and Warren Roberts tell us: "Lawrence made barmecide love to her through his stories . . . and when he chose the name of the heroine of his most famous book, he picked one Constance Chatterley — suggesting Cynthia Charteris," Lady Asquith's maiden name.[37] H.D. mentions this identification in "Compassionate Friendship," and was quite content to have Lady Chatterley identified with someone else. It is certainly true that Lawrence had a *social* relationship with Lady Cynthia Asquith and valued her patronage. However, he did not have a deep *spiritual* relationship with her. Lady Cynthia herself was amused that scholars identified her with Lady Chatterley. But the imagination seizes upon the materials of social realities as well as those of experiential realities. The idea of calling Constance by the title of "Lady" might well have been suggested to Lawrence's imagination by his acquaintance with Lady Asquith.

In his book *The Life of D. H. Lawrence,* Keith Sagar suggests that *Lady Chatterley's Lover* was inspired by a story Sir George Sitwell probably told Lawrence in June 1925 about William Arkwright, the previous owner of an eighteenth-century estate, Sutton Scarsdale, which Sitwell's son Osbert was trying to save. It seems that Arkwright was rendered impotent in an accident at the age of twenty. Seven years later he married a beautiful young woman: "The marriage was unhappy and they lived apart for most of their lives."[38] After the publication of *Lady Chatterley,* the Sitwells stated that Lawrence had characterized Osbert Sitwell as Clifford Chatterley, although the first two versions of *Lady Chatterley* had been written before Lawrence ever met him. If it is in fact the case that the Sir Clifford of the third *Lady Chatterley* bears some superficial resemblance to Osbert Sitwell, Lawrence's intention was clearly not to characterize Sitwell but rather further to disguise the true identity of the man on whom he based his Sir Clifford character.

When H.D. read *Lady Chatterley* in 1928 she knew full well — too well, in fact — who and what Lawrence was talking about. Aldington also knew only too well what Lawrence was saying about him. And this knowledge and Aldington's relation to the events discussed in the book led him into a career of misrepresenting Lawrence and his work. While others read the book as a novel, H.D. read it as a continuation of her correspondence with

Lawrence — a correspondence that took place at a deeper spiritual level than everyday social correspondence. H.D. was not as much a part of Lawrence's social world as she was a part of his spiritual world. And as Lawrence says in his November 1917 letter to Cecil Gray, this world was very important to him; it became increasingly so in the last five years of his life. H.D. took it all as seriously as Lawrence knew she would. As she repeatedly acknowledged, she and Lawrence had a life in "another dimension," a dimension that after their separation became increasingly cerebral or sublimated.

In *The First Lady Chatterley* Parkin only refers to himself as "Lady Chatterley's lover" when he is angry at the whole situation: " 'I'm Sir Clifford's servant an' I'm Lady Chatterley's' — he looked her in the face — 'What do you call me, in *your* sort of talk?' 'My lover!' she stammered. 'Lover!' he re-echoed — A queer flash went over his face. 'F — er!' he said, and his eyes darted a flash at her, as if he shot her." [39]

The story that is told in *Lady Chatterley's Lover* is essentially the story of H.D.'s life from 1914 to 1918. The story is, as we have observed, that of a tragic marriage which continues in form but not in substance. The woman becomes involved with a lover, with whom she is able to experience true passion. In the course of this relationship she becomes pregnant. Sometime during her pregnancy she and her lover become separated through events that are somewhat beyond their control. The story contrasts a legal marriage with a spiritual marriage.

Just as Parkin acknowledges in *The First Lady Chatterley* ("Tenderness") that Constance is his "real" wife, his "wife in the wood," H.D. wrote of Rico in *Bid Me to Live:* "She realized in a strange detached way, that he really cared. Tenderness . . . Yes, he was her husband." [40]

18

The Paternity
of the Child

THE MODES OF THOUGHT operative in the Imagist poem carried over into the novels written by those associated with the Imagist movement and the Imagist way of thinking. It might be argued that John Cournos and Richard Aldington were more successful in employing Imagist principles in their novels than in their poetry. As we have seen, H.D. and D. H. Lawrence wrote Imagist novels too; the secret doctrine of the image is applicable to all of H.D.'s novels and much of Lawrence's fiction after he met H.D.

As in an Imagist poem, the writer may present one person under two or more different names in a work of fiction. H.D. develops this principle in the Raymonde and Ray Bart characters of the "Murex" section of her novel *Palimpsest;* the woman is Raymonde; the writer is Ray Bart. Conversely, the same name may refer to four entirely separate characters in different drafts of the same story. In Lawrence's *The First Lady Chatterley,* for instance, Duncan Forbes is clearly a Pound persona. In *Lady Chatterley's Lover,* the third version of that novel, Duncan Forbes just as clearly is based upon Cecil Gray.

How do we know who is who? It is really quite simple; we need to know the biographical situation upon which the imaginative reconstruction is based. The novel is simply a more elaborate presentation of event than the Imagist poem.

The Duncan Forbes that appears in *The First Lady Chatterley* bears a striking resemblance to H.D.'s Fabius Noblier in "Pilate's Wife." Both manuscripts present an Ezra Pound of 1918 — an Ezra Pound still very attentive to all the events of H.D.'s life. If we assume that the character of pages 251 to 310 of *The First Lady Chatterley* is in fact modeled upon Pound's behavior in 1918 (the events described are precisely the same as those described by H.D. and other members of the group), then we must assume that the Connie persona is in this instance based upon H.D.

The situation is as follows: Connie, married to an Englishman of the bourgeois class whom she has come to detest, finds herself pregnant by the gamekeeper. She is not so much afraid to tell Sir Clifford that she is pregnant by another man as she is reluctant to tell him exactly who is responsible. She turns to her long-time friend Duncan Forbes for advice. "And it was to Duncan that Constance confessed her condition. 'Don't tell anybody,' she said, 'I'm going to have a child.' 'Of Clifford's?' The question came like a gunshot. 'No! Another man's.' "[1]

Connie asks Duncan whether he might be willing to come forth as the "missing father." He is upset and reacts with characteristic irony.

> "Would you hate it?" she said.
> "I've no idea at all! I've no idea how I should react. I should have to think for ages before I knew what I should feel in such a complicated issue. — You know you and I *were* once engaged — what a lovely word."[2]

Pound was more than a little upset about the whole situation. In Canto V he may be alluding to it:

> And out of England a knight with slow-lifting eyelids
> *Lei fassa furar a del,* put glamour upon her . . .
> And left her an eight months gone.[3]

Pound and H.D. had continued to be entangled in 1913 and 1914, in spite of their marriages and the schism within Imagism. As H.D.'s marriage to Aldington began to disintegrate, she found herself involved in further complications with Pound. As she tells us in "Pilate's Wife":

> Fabius [Pound] had slid through the curtains, without lifting them, as was his manner, when he was a little anxious about her. Well everyone knew he had been here and how long he had stayed. Why did they all go on pretending? Of course, it would be impossible if they started not to pretend. Life would be so full of explanation, the whole color of the social world about her, would change. And, she said to herself, we are too tired, too lazy. We don't want to change. Fabius comes to me, or Memnonius comes. Pilate's chief concern is, their political affiliation. I don't care to know where Pilate goes nor whom he sees, so long as he is courteous (and he is that, always) to me, before strangers.[4]

In this period, Pound is often full of irony in his poetry. As he translates in one of his most ironic and worldly poems, *Homage to Sextus Propertius:* *

> If she with ivory fingers drive a tune
> through a lyre,
> We look at the process.
> How easy the moving fingers, if hair is
> mussed on her forehead,
> If she goes in a gleam of Cos, in a slither
> of dyed stuff,
> There is a volume to write on the matter; if
> her eyelids sink into sleep,
> There are new jobs for the author;
> And if she plays with me with her shirt off,
> We shall construct many Iliads.
> And whatever she does or says
> We shall spin long yarns out of nothing.[5]

In *The First Lady Chatterley* Lawrence presents Pound in an ironic spirit, but also as a person aware of his irony and of its underlying source. Parkin/Lawrence recognizes Duncan/Pound's negative feelings for him, but he is faithful to Pound's manner and wit in presenting the situation in the novel. The name Op, which the Pound character uses to refer to Oliver Parkin, stands for his initials, O.P.; this was Pound's usual shorthand for a person's name, but also represents an Imagist pun on "Pop." Connie says in answer to Duncan's question regarding her lover:

> "Parkin."
> "Op?"
> "Yes."
> "Hm!"
> He mused for some time. "And how long does this sort of fire last?" he asked.
> "I don't know. I never know."
> "And do you like it or don't you?" he asked impatiently.
> "I don't know that either. It's so strong. It's just him, as if everything in me was on fire, and the fire was him."
> "Hm! — And do you want to be with him?"
> "Terribly."

*In his *Life of Ezra Pound* Noel Stock tells us: "The work [Propertius] was dated by the author 1917 but was probably not finished until the middle of 1918 at the earliest and was not published until the following year. It was not a direct translation but an approximation and a re-arrangement: a personal statement by Pound's Propertius or by Pound, which places the joys and trials of female company and the inspirations derived from love above imperial police-work."

"Do you want to be with him now?"

She sighed. "Yes!" she said.

"Hm! Then I hope the fire will soon die down, for it makes you boring. — How do I throw water on it? — I find people *in love* a bore, but apparently they're a beauty chorus compared to the genuine article. Ha ha!" He laughed a little theatrically and pushed himself into a corner of the big sofa, sulking.[6]

In spite of the worldly tone that comes through in Pound's work and in both H.D.'s and Lawrence's presentation of the Pound persona of this period, both Pound and Lawrence had strong feelings about H.D.; they agreed that she was an entirely remarkable woman. In *The First Lady Chatterley,* Lawrence has Duncan Forbes say to Constance: "I might have been the father of Op's child, instead of Op, if you didn't draw words out of me instead of the seed of man."[7]

Throughout the whole ordeal Connie conducts herself with dignity. And both men have a good deal of respect for her. Lawrence presents this conversation between Parkin and Duncan:

> The car sped on in silence. The two men sat in the unspoken sympathy of men who have suffered from the same woman. Duncan and Parkin liked one another instinctively.*
>
> "Did she tell you she was four months gone then?" said Parkin.
>
> "Oh, we've known one another since we were kids," said Duncan. "My father was the minister where her grandfather was the laird, in the same village. We were engaged to be married once — ten years ago —."[8]

Pound and H.D., we will remember, were engaged ten years before the birth of H.D.'s child. And Pound had continued to be attentive to her.

As the conversation between the two men proceeds, Parkin explains to Duncan that he will not allow himself to be supported by Connie.

> ". . . But I told her I couldn't live in her house and take her money and let her be top dog. That's what set her off."
>
> "It would! Letting a paltry thing like money stand between you!" Duncan smiled slyly and ironically. "I can hear her. Mind you, she'd never begrudge you."
>
> "I know it. I know it. She'd never be mean," said Parkin . . .[9]

The events discussed in these novels are those surrounding H.D.'s pregnancy. She had become pregnant during the summer

---

*In 1909, when Lawrence and Pound first met, they "liked one another instinctively." Both Pound's and Lawrence's letters of that year describe the other with respect and regard; Pound's dislike for Lawrence came later.

of 1918 and, as in the case of Lawrence's Constance in *The First Lady Chatterley,* expected the child in February or March.

While Cecil Gray has been named by some as the father of H.D.'s child, D. H. Lawrence took responsibility in his work for the birth (or, as he put it in *The Escaped Cock,* "He ascended to the Father").

In *Lady Chatterley's Lover,* the third version of the novel, Connie's father, Sir Malcolm, says to Mellors: "Oh, gamekeeper or not, you're a good cock." [10] These words are set in the context of Lawrence's explanation of how Duncan Forbes is asked to take the blame for the paternity of Mellors's child. At this point in the novel Constance is traveling with her sister, Hilda, and her father. Mellors's wife, Bertha Coutts, has come back, and Constance is feeling angry with Mellors for his inability to free himself from Bertha. Connie does not want to name Mellors as the father. "If Mellors were named, then there was an end to *his* divorce." [11]

Sir Malcolm was Lawrence's fictional presentation of Bryher's father, Sir John Ellerman, who took upon himself the financial responsibilities of a father to both Hilda and her child after she and Bryher became friends. "What Sir Malcolm could not bear, was the scandal of his daughter's having an intrigue with the gamekeeper. He did not mind the intrigue: he minded the scandal." [12]

In Lawrence's final version of the story, it is Connie who comes up with the idea of pinning the paternity of the child on someone other than Mellors, and in the third version Duncan begins to take on the characteristics of Cecil Gray.* "Talk is beastly: especially if you live in society. And he wants so much to get his own divorce. I thought we might perhaps say it was another man's child, and not mention Mellors' name at all." [13] Sir Malcolm says:

> "Another man's! What other man's?"
> "Perhaps Duncan Forbes. He has been our friend all his life. And he's a fairly well-known artist. And he's fond of me."
> "Well I'm damned! Poor Duncan. And what's he going to get out of it?"
> "I don't know. But he might rather like it, even."
> "He might, might he? Well, he's a funny man, if he does. Why, you've never had an affair with him, have you?"
> "No! But he doesn't really want it. He only loves me to be near him, but not to touch him."

*Cecil Gray (1895–1951), a Scottish composer and later a music critic, was a neighbor of the Lawrences in Cornwall. The Lawrences' expulsion from Cornwall on October 15, 1917, derived in part from an incident at Gray's home, Bosigran, which led local authorities to suspect that the Lawrences were acting as spies.

"My God, what a generation!"

"He would like me most of all to be a model for him to paint from. Only I never wanted to."[14]

In his novel *Miranda Masters,* John Cournos also presents a Cecil Gray character as an artist who wants Miranda (based on H.D.) to model for him. " 'From the moment I saw you I knew you'd make an ideal figure for my picture . . .' Barely a week had elapsed before Miranda and Wilfred were on their way to his studio cottage among the Welsh hills overlooking the sea."[15]

Cecil Gray was in reality a composer, as Lawrence had first presented him, and not a painter. But Gray had made it clear that he wanted H.D. to be with him in Cornwall so that she might inspire him in his composition. It is, then, totally understandable that any member of the Imagist circle writing about these events would translate the situation into the story of a painter and a model — a somewhat Imagist image.

Sometime between writing the first version of *Lady Chatterley* and the final version, D. H. Lawrence read Cournos's *Miranda Masters,* so there is a possibility that the evolution of his story was influenced by his reading of Cournos's. In his autobiography Cournos writes: "Visiting me in my room he [Lawrence] insisted upon taking with him a copy of my latest novel, *Miranda Masters.* I do not imagine he liked this particular book."[16]

John Cournos was a would-be lover who was rejected by H.D. His testimony on matters related to H.D. has to be taken with a grain of salt as he was clearly wounded by her lack of erotic interest in him (according to his own testimony in *Miranda Masters*).*

---

*As Cournos indicates in *Miranda Masters,* he unsuccessfully pursued a romantic involvement with H.D. during the 1916–1917 period. In 1917 he was apparently aware that H.D. had had some kind of an involvement with Lawrence (Richard Ramsden in *Miranda Masters*), but he was unaware of the depth of the personal involvement. He writes, "Gombarov [Cournos] was aware that he [Lawrence] and Miranda [H.D.] knew one another and had now and then corresponded, but he did not know that their relation was anything more than of two sympathetic acquaintances who admired each other's work." To the extent that Cournos was aware of the relationship he advised H.D. in his fictionalized account, "You must have nothing to do with him! He is a great flame, it is true, but a disintegrating flame. Everything he touches falls to ashes in the contact! Frankly I don't like him as a man!"[17]

Cournos left England for Russia in the fall of 1917 and did not return until the spring of 1918. His relationship with H.D. was over when he returned, and he apparently remained generally uninformed about the 1917–1918 events in H.D.'s life until he read *Bid Me to Live* in 1960. According to Alfred Satterthwaite, Cournos's stepson, Cournos hated H.D. "implacably" from the time he returned from Russia in 1918 until his death in 1966.

After 1918 he was bitter toward H.D. and blamed her for Dorothy Yorke's affair with Aldington; Cournos had been in love with Arabella on and off since at least 1911. His hostility toward H.D. is revealed in a letter written in great bitterness over the minor role he is given in H.D.'s *Bid Me to Live.* In the letter, dated October 5, 1960, Cournos writes:

> Dear H.D.,
>
> It was not without pity that I read your little book, *Bid Me to Live.* I experienced with something like compassion the fact that D. H. Lawrence should have pulled your leg unmercifully and placed you in the position of "a woman scorned," a position which naturally no woman likes. But he, with his peculiar play of the mind, not unmixed with malice, was that kind of a man, and you, had you the sense you were born with, should have exercised discretion, though I realize that a woman who imagines herself loved too often flings discretion to the winds. Odd of him, wasn't it, to prefer fat Frieda to you? Of course one can hardly be blamed for accepting second choice on the rebound. You shouldn't be troubled on this score.[18]

In 1916 H.D. was terrified about her relationship with Lawrence, which she felt she could discuss with no one, and very dependent upon John Cournos; unfortunately Cournos mistook her dependence for a romantic involvement, although H.D.'s letters to Cournos are pleas for help rather than expressions of romantic love. Cournos's bitterness was compounded when he learned that H.D. had gone to Cornwall with Gray. In a letter to Cournos of May 1918, written from Cornwall, H.D. pleads: "Don't feel bitter towards me! What I write to you must be secret — even my *moods* — do not say to anyone I seem sad even. I can't explain about the *others.* I feel loyal to them. I should die if I allowed myself to resent all that has happened."[19]

H.D. felt unhappy and even guilty about not confiding everything to Cournos. In November 1919 she wrote: "You and I are like people in a play. I don't think I suffer any more. I doubt if you do. Someday I must tell you of my life."[20]

To return to *Lady Chatterley's Lover,* the story Lawrence tells in his final version of the novel is that Duncan Forbes is to take the blame for the paternity of the child. Hilda, the sister of Constance, explains the scheme to Mellors:

> "We have a friend who would probably agree to be named as co-respondent, so that your name need not appear," said Hilda . . .
> "Duncan Forbes!" he said at once, . . . "And how would you shift the blame on to him?"

"They could stay together in some hotel, or she could even stay at his apartment."

"Seems to me a lot of fuss for nothing," he said.

"What else do you suggest?" said Hilda. "If your name appears, you will get no divorce from your wife, who is apparently quite an impossible person to be mixed up with."

"All that!" he said grimly.

There was a long silence.

"We could go right away," he said.

"There is no right away for Connie," said Hilda. "Clifford is too well known."

Again the silence of pure frustration.

"The world is what it is. If you want to live together without being persecuted, you will have to marry. To marry, you both have to be divorced. So how are you both going about it?"

He was silent for a long time.

"How are *you* going about it for us?" he said.

"We will see if Duncan will consent to figure as co-respondent. Then we must get Clifford to divorce Connie: and you must go on with your divorce, and you must both keep apart until you are free."[21]

Duncan agrees to pose as father of the child, but only on the condition that Connie will model for him. Mellors offers to model for him as well, but Duncan has no use for "Vulcan."

Connie writes to Clifford asking for a divorce. She tells him she is staying with Duncan in his flat and that she is in love with another man, implying that the man she loves is Duncan. Clifford begins to bully her. "She was frightened. This was bullying of an insidious sort. She had no doubt he meant what he said. He would not divorce her, and the child would be his, unless she could find some means of establishing its illegitimacy."[22]

When Sir Clifford first learns of Connie's pregnancy he wants her to remain his wife. He tells her that the child of Duncan Forbes is welcome under his roof. Because he argues with her that she really loves him better than Duncan, which she must admit is true, she is forced to tell him that it is really Mellors, the game-keeper, she loves. His response to this confession is presented by Lawrence:

If he could have sprung out of his chair, he would have done so. His face went yellow, and his eyes bulged with disaster as he glared at her.

Then he dropped back in the chair, gasping and looking up at the ceiling.

At length he sat up.

"Do you mean to say you're telling me the truth?" he asked, looking gruesome.

"Yes! You know I am."

"And when did you begin with him?"

"In the spring."

He was silent like some beast in a trap.

"And it *was* you, then, in the bedroom at the cottage?"

So he had inwardly known all the time.

"Yes."

He still leaned forward in his chair, gazing at her like a cornered beast.

"My God, you ought to be wiped off the face of the earth!"

"Why?" she ejaculated faintly.

But he seemed not to hear her.

"That scum! That bumptious lout! That miserable cad! . . . My God, my God, is there any limit to the beastly lowness of women!"

He was beside himself with rage, as she knew he would be.

"And you mean to say you want to have a child to a cad like that?"

"Yes! I'm going to . . ."

"You'd wonder," he said at last, "that such beings were ever allowed to be born." [23]

"It was obvious," writes Lawrence, "he couldn't even accept the fact of the existence of Mellors, in any connection with his own life. It was sheer, unspeakable, impotent hate." Connie's confession proved to Clifford that she was "not normal." "You're one of those half-insane, perverted women who must run after depravity, the *nostalgie de la boue*." [24] (Aldington portrayed H.D. in a similar manner in *Death of a Hero* and elsewhere in his writing after their separation.)

Aldington's letters to H.D. from the front in France (her letters to him did not survive) suggest that when he first learned of her pregnancy in early August 1918 he believed her child to be Cecil Gray's. He knew that it could not possibly be his; he had been in France since mid-April. In his letters through the end of August he tells H.D. that he will accept the child as his own. He encourages her to seek medical assistance and to tell Gray of her condition. In a letter of September 1, 1918, he writes, "I will accept the child as mine and give it my name." [25] Between the time he wrote this letter and his postscript to it Aldington received a letter from H.D. which spoke of Lawrence in connection with her pregnancy. Aldington writes in his postscript: "Your letter of 26-8-18 has just come. I am sorry about the Lawrence business for your sake; but people are like that. I suspected the Gray business too. Artists! My God: *quel canaille*." In a letter of September 2 Aldington writes:

"Don't trouble about L. [Lawrence] and G. [Gray]. If I can I will provide for the child." He reaffirmed this stance in a letter of September 8.

Both Aldington and H.D. had had lovers during the course of their marriage. On June 2, 1918, Aldington had written to H.D.: "Of course it makes no difference that we have had other lovers." And on August 12, just nineteen days before the letter that mentions Lawrence in connection with the pregnancy, Aldington had written: "Of course, dear, you will always be my lover, won't you. And we will have each other in spite of your husbands and children and so on." And in another letter of the same date, Aldington had written: "It is not these extraneous love affairs which separate us but the fact that for more than two years we have known each other only in snatches."

Before H.D. wrote her letter of August 26, Aldington urged her repeatedly to tell Gray of her pregnancy, and he could not understand why she had not done so. He had written that in spite of the lovers each had had, their own relationship was the one that mattered, and that he would take responsibility for providing for the child and give the child his name if this was her wish. He had written to H.D. that her pregnancy would never have happened had it not been for his own relationship with Arabella. His letters also make it clear that he never considered Gray a rival. On August 14 he wrote: "I never worried about G. I knew he wasn't human enough for you."

But after Aldington's letter of September 1, in which he calls both Lawrence and Gray scoundrels (in French), his tone toward H.D. changed completely. He became very chivalrous but began to back off from his earlier commitment to care for her and the child. On October 6 he wrote: "You are not a wife but a dryad." As soon as it became clear that H.D. would continue to refuse to name the father of the child and that she had broken off with both Lawrence and Gray, Aldington told her that he would do absolutely nothing to provide for her and the child and that she could perhaps come to a satisfactory arrangement with Gray in this regard or "get work of some sort through your friends." Aldington's letters to H.D. from this point on became increasingly hostile and bitter. In H.D.'s unpublished novel "Asphodel," Darrington (based on Aldington) continues to assure the pregnant Hermione (the H.D. character) of his support until she has precluded the possibility of a further relationship with any other man. In *Hedylus,* when H.D. writes of a betrayal by Clarix, the Aldington character, it is this betrayal she means.

When H.D.'s child was born in March 1919, Aldington refused

to give it his name. As H.D. tells the story in "Asphodel," Aldington threatened to have H.D. thrown in prison if she registered the child in his name (this threat is confirmed in her letters). For years H.D. lived in mortal fear of Aldington because she did do so and could not withdraw the registration without acknowledging perjury.

There is some reason to believe that Gray covered for Lawrence by not denying that he might be the father. In his *Musical Chairs,* Gray writes bitterly that he covered for Lawrence at a very crucial point in Lawrence's life and that all he got for his trouble was to be brutally characterized in Lawrence's novels. Cecil Gray writes: "Let me be perfectly frank. I stood by Lawrence and helped him through a very difficult moment in his life and the only reward I ever had for it was to be pilloried and caricatured in two of his books." [26]

Like Aldington, Sir Clifford would not give his wife a divorce. " 'No! You can go where you like, but I shan't divorce you,' he said idiotically." [27] In "Asphodel," written in 1922, H.D. presents Darrington's reaction to Hermione's pregnancy in virtually identical terms. Aldington did not, in fact, give H.D. a divorce until after Lawrence's death (although he led people to believe it was *she* who would not divorce him).

At the end of *Lady Chatterley's Lover,* Mellors, waiting for his divorce, goes to work on a farm. He expects that Connie will eventually get her divorce and they will someday be together. The letter Mellors writes to Connie is full of philosophical statements about the state of civilization and impressions of the people he encounters; this letter is reminiscent in substance and tone of Lawrence's postwar philosophical writings. Of the child Mellors writes: "There's the baby, but that is a side issue. It's my Pentecoste, the forked flame between me and you . . . But of course what I live for now is for you and me to live together." [28]

Lawrence's book ends in a letter; in a sense the whole book is a letter, the letter Lawrence never wrote. As H.D. says, "He never wrote to me again after I told him I was expecting this child." [29]

19

"Pilate's Wife"

IN *ADVENT* H.D. speaks of one of her Madrigal novels, "Pilate's Wife": "I had told friends of a book that I wanted to write, actually did write. I called it *Pilate's Wife*. It is the story of the wounded but living Christ, waking up in the rock-tomb. I was certain that my friends had told Lawrence that I was at work on this theme. My first sudden reaction was, 'Now he has taken my story.' "[1]

H.D.'s reaction to Lawrence's use of the same theme in *The Man Who Died* is understandable. They both had the same story to tell, but H.D. was perfectly aware of Lawrence's power as a writer. Her fear was that his understanding and presentation of their experiences would annihilate her own — would in fact annihilate her.

H.D. began "Pilate's Wife" in 1924 and finished it in January or February 1929. Certain sections of the story were revised in July and August 1934 after her sessions with Freud. She finished it after the publication of the original short-story version of Lawrence's *The Escaped Cock* in *Forum* magazine in February 1928. "The Escaped Cock" (Lawrence's only title for the story) corresponds closely to part I of *The Man Who Died*, which was published in 1931, and undoubtedly influenced the conclusion of H.D.'s "Pilate's Wife" and the revisions she made in 1934. But the original text in the Beinecke Library at Yale University does not indicate any revisions; it is simply a complete typed manuscript. Whatever the subsequent influence of *The Man Who Died*, H.D. began her novel in 1924 with no knowledge that Lawrence was or would be at work on a thematically similar story.

The protagonist of "Pilate's Wife" is Veronica, "the wife of the Roman Consul-General arch-legate and Vice-governor" of

Rome.[2] An Isis figure, Veronica is a persona of H.D., and Pilate is a persona of Aldington. As the wife of Pilate, Veronica occupies an exalted but totally powerless position, a useless position, in Roman society. And she exhibits character traits associated with women in her position. "She was wise with pertness, and a little ridiculously, like some bird, taught to chatter." It is her duty to make conversation, small talk. "Wisdom, it has already been well recognized, does not become a woman."[3] Veronica chatters.

Pilate's wife has a lover of sorts, "Fabius Noblier who, as was openly whispered, had access to the wife of Pontius."[4] Fabius is recognizably a Pound persona. The whole tenor, tone, and stance of Veronica in relation to Fabius reinvokes the relationship of Hermione to George in H.D.'s novel "Her."* But this Fabius is Pound in England (or Rome) rather than in New England.

Veronica and Noblier's relationship is portrayed as a kind of sensual dalliance in the finest Roman tradition. "Fabius' love-making seemed part of the equipment of the polished Roman. He was courteous to the wife of his superior yet he hinted (with just as obvious political intention) that he would dare further, anything (all this part of the machinery of the moment) for some more intimate encounter."[5]

Fabius is a Roman troubadour. The relationship between Veronica and Fabius also invokes H.D.'s *End to Torment* in its emotional tone and content. At moments it transcends its "courtly" form: "And his kiss when he sought her, was not exactly of Augustan precedent. Kisses may fall un-stylized and freshly exquisite and yet bear the mark of subjugation to rote, to rule, to convention or to bestiality. His bore none of these . . . His kiss was the first he had given, the first she had received."[6] We are reminded of H.D.'s memories in *End to Torment*: "First kisses? In the woods in the winter — what did one expect? Not this."[7]

As H.D. conveys in "Pilate's Wife," Veronica is emotionally and psychically frustrated in her unconsummated relationship with Noblier. "They continue in this manner."[8] Her marriage is merely legal; it has lost substance. The final result of this impossible situation is a new love.

> From the first Memnonius had been specifically different. It was he who suggested these same lilies to shed color and warmth, in the clear water of the basins, sunk for summer-coolness in the tiled space of the court-yard, underneath the window. The lilies were part of his consideration for her, along with other adornment, both

---

*It also corresponds in great detail to the relationship of Hermione and George in "Asphodel," a continuation of "Her" set in London in the war years.

spiritual and frankly physical. His line of demarcation between those two states, was, he said, so indefinite, that any chance rose, flung by Tiberius' least dancing-girl or boy, might hold the same paradisical nectar, as the very golden lotus of the God or Goddess shining in astral or Ka-form . . .[9]

The lilies and the lotus were to become central symbols in Lawrence's *The Escaped Cock.* They are very central in H.D.'s *Helen in Egypt.*

> and long corridors of lotus-bud
> furled on the pillars,
> and the lotus-flower unfurled.[10]

The Egyptian symbolism invoked in "Pilate's Wife" corresponds with that of *Helen in Egypt.* Egypt signifies bondage. As H.D. says in her "Notes on Thought and Vision," "Egypt in terms of world-consciousness is the act of love."[11] H.D.'s symbol in *Helen in Egypt* is "the thousand-petalled lily."

> a hieroglyph, repeated endlessly,
>
> upon the walls, the pillars,
> the thousand-petalled lily,
> they are not many, but one,
>
> enfolded in sleep,
> as the furled lotus-bud,
> or with great wings unfurled,
>
> sailing in ecstasy . . .[12]

But in "Pilate's Wife," H.D.'s tone is less mystical, more worldly.

> Rome offered no spiritual sustenance, Veronica knew, to Memnonius. This, the more surprised her, that he should so signally solicit her companionship. "What," she said, "then do you find in me?"
>
> He had answered, "You have the same eyes. The Nile buds spring from knobs of lustrous fiber, roots of amber, and rise on thin stems toward sunlight. You have not risen."
>
> "You mean you think there is some possibility — you think I might flower differently?"
>
> He said, "No. I think you may wither there where your bud is curled under, where petals are really curling inward."
>
> She had said, "I have all outer circumstances to prove otherwise."
>
> He said, "Maybe Rome and Egypt stumble toward understanding, speaking awkward dialect."[13]

H.D. identifies Lawrence, whom she characterizes as Memnonius, with Egypt. She is in a Roman (or Trojan) marriage. The "awkward dialect" reminds us of the speech of Parkin or Mellors. The talk of flowers corresponds to the flower symbolism in Lawrence's poetry (particularly his postwar poetry) and *The Man Who Died*. H.D. has a vision of Memnonius as a "water-beast."

> Memnonius . . . brushed the tip of the spread feathers with lips that but lately, had uttered such logical and peculiar sentiments. His thighs, Veronica noted as he bent, were slight as some Nile serpent. He was altogether boneless, swaying and stepping aside, moving to her quickened apprehension like some water-beast in water . . . She believed he spoke sincerely when he said, "It behoves me to instruct you." [14]

As in *Helen in Egypt*, Memnonius, like Achilles, is the "love adept."

> "Love," said Memnonius from the first noe of lower Egypt, "takes many forms. If," as he had specially and logically, stated to Veronica, "you know all of them, you will find me an apt pupil. If it seems possibly not unlikely, I am, in some slight particular, your superior, it behoves me, as a very ardent duty, to instruct you." [15]

Veronica and Memnonius meet secretly. As we have previously noted, the secret meeting had been a recurring theme of H.D.'s and D. H. Lawrence's poetry since 1915.

> Their meetings were of necessity secret, yet without trepidation.
> "What must be, must be," he repeatedly asserted. When on occasion she herself (contrary to her manner with the later Fabius) prescribed caution, he replied wryly, "This is written." His "this is written" or "this" somehow forbade further argument . . . his least word fell like clipped stone on marble. [16]

The theme "this is written" reappeared in H.D.'s work in *Bid Me to Live*, where Rico says his love is "written in blood for all eternity," [17] and again in *Helen in Egypt*.

> Few were the words we said
> but the words are graven on stone,
> minted on gold, stamped upon lead . . .
>
> . . .
>
> "I am a woman of pleasure,"
> I spoke ironically into the night,
> for he had built me a fire . . . [18]

H.D. writes of the incredible gamble involved in Veronica's relationship with Memnonius. Veronica's interest in numerology is a practical matter: Lucky days are safe days. "With Memnonius, she was the emotional, social and fantastic gambler. She learned to play at names and numbers and the names of numbers of the stars and dates of shifting calendars . . . On lucky days she would dare unwontedly for 'what must be, must be.' "[19]

On lucky days Veronica is in the habit of walking a good deal, and she begins to visit "outlying shrines." The theme of walking long distances to a temple or shrine had been recurring in H.D.'s poetry since her early 1916 poems "The Shrine" and "The Cliff Temple" (examined in chapter 14). In "Pilate's Wife" these walks are associated with Veronica's involvement in the cult of Isis. "She visited new deities in the fashionable manner, and found refuge for the aesthetic side of her nature, a modernized cult of Isis. The increasing visits of the wife of the Governor to the shrine, caused no apprehension."[20]

Memnonius and Veronica discuss the relationship of Isis to Aphrodite. Memnonius associates Veronica with Isis, and she identifies herself as "the seated Isis."[21] He tells her: "In lower Egypt, the sun, low-lying, sheds beams like a great star. Such sun-light, Isis knew, was the love-soul of her Master, Osiris, rising, dying; dead to be awakened. Each day he rose, each day he died. She knew the body of the god, her earthly consort, waited elsewhere for her. How could she have other lovers?"[22]

Veronica admits that she has been overpowered by the Isis-Osiris reality as Memnonius has presented it to her. But it is a secret passion. Outwardly she is indifferent. "The cult of Isis for all her apparent indifference, save to the mere husk or literal shell of it, had yet flamed her imagination, as no other conventional state-festival of the Roman Venus, or of transplanted, literary Greek parallel, had ever done."[23]

Veronica's adherence to this philosophy is not simply a consequence of her sexual encounters. It is a profound spiritual conviction for her and a kind of spiritual warfare with Rome and her Roman marriage. Even the Greeks, she says, were too Roman — they "had had to split the perfect image."

> Isis was magician and goddess of wisdom. The Greeks, for all their immense pragmatism and logical philosophy, had had to split the perfect image of the perfect Woman, say this is Love, faithless, and here is Wisdom, loveless. Yet even Aphrodite and Athene, re-modeled, flung into some blasting furnace, to return, one perfectly welded figure, would yet lack something — something of the magic that Isis held in Egypt.[24]

Veronica's secret meetings with Memnonius continue for some indeterminate length of time. Her involvement in Isis (which can certainly be equated with H.D.'s involvement in Imagism) is synonymous with these secret meetings. "Veronica had continued to meet him furtively and retained exquisite memory of their converse. 'The Goddess will protect us,' he had asserted when she, as her habit then was, had spoken of possible censor. His 'what must be, must be' and her well recognized habit of visiting outlying, foreign shrines, had fortified and made sufficient excuse for meeting."[25]

Lawrence too wrote of a series of mysterious secret meetings. In 1923 he published *Kangaroo*, a novel in which he discussed at some length the war years and, among other things, his relationship with "John Thomas," who has been identified as William Henry Hocking, a Cornish farmer friend two or three years older than Lawrence. It has been a matter of some speculation why Lawrence gave the phallic name of John Thomas to William Henry. Taking their cue from Aldington, many biographers have suggested that Lawrence's visits with Hocking might have had something to do with a homosexual attraction. In his biography of Lawrence, *Portrait of a Genius, But . . .* , Aldington writes:

> He made friends with a farmer named William Henry, in *Kangaroo* infelicitously given the fictious name 'John Thomas' (Freudians, avaunt!), who helped him to plough and plant a whole field with vegetables . . . Night after night he left Frieda all alone, to be with William Henry, for whom he had evidently developed one of his mystical-sensual *Bludbruderschaft* relations. "In those days," writes Frieda blithely, "Lawrence seemed to turn against me, perhaps on account of the bit of German in me." The bit of German! But of course it wasn't that at all, it was the temporarily superior attraction of William Henry.[26]

In *Kangaroo* Lawrence writes: "Poor Harriet [Frieda] spent many lonely days in the cottage. Richard [Lawrence] was not interested in her now. He was only interested in John Thomas." He goes on to speak of his nights away from Frieda:

> And then the Cornish night would gradually come down upon the dark, shaggy moors, that were like the fur of some beast, and upon the pale-grey granite masses, so ancient and Druidical, suggesting blood-sacrifice. And as Somers [Lawrence] sat there on the sheaves in the under-dark, seeing the light swim above the sea, he felt he was over the border, in another world.

The Druidic symbolism and talk of human sacrifice becomes more intense. "Human sacrifice! He could feel his dark, blood-consciousness tingle to it again, the desire of it, the mystery of it."[27]

It is no wonder that H.D. found *Kangaroo* "pretty heavy going."[28] H.D. knew where Lawrence had spent some of those days and nights, and they had not all been with William Henry Hocking. Lawrence had indeed been with his "John Thomas," the same John Thomas who spent time with Lady Jane, the Constance of *John Thomas and Lady Jane.** In other words, at the poetic level Lawrence uses "John Thomas" in *Kangaroo* as an Imagist expression for his phallus, which spent nights with Lady Jane.

---

*Lawrence presents the explicitly genital meaning of "John Thomas" and "Lady Jane" in his description of the sexual encounter between Mellors and Constance at the end of chapter 15 of *Lady Chatterley's Lover,* pp. 289–92.

20

The Escaped Cock

D. H. LAWRENCE'S cock is a fine cock "which put on brave feathers as spring advanced, and was resplendent with an arched and orange neck by the time the fig-trees were letting out leaves from their end-tips."[1] Lawrence's cock is not only a bird and symbol of his phallus (the pun was too obvious for his English and American publishers), but, as Lawrence makes clear, himself as poet.

> The young cock grew to a certain splendour. By some freak of destiny, he was a dandy rooster, in that dirty little yard with three patchy hens. He learned to crane his neck and give shrill answers to the crowing of other cocks beyond the walls, in a world he knew nothing of. But there was a special fiery colour to his crow, and the distant calling of other cocks roused him to unexpected outbursts.[2]

The peasant in this story represents Lawrence — just plain Lawrence, living in poverty as Lawrence did most of his life. But in Lawrence's story the cock escapes.

In his republication of the early version of *The Escaped Cock*, Gerald Lacy tells of an image that inspired the story. Lawrence and Earl Brewster saw an Easter toy in a little shop window in Volterra. Brewster remembers it as a "toy white rooster escaping from an egg." Lawrence remembers "a little Easter toy of a cock escaping from a man."[3] Lawrence's story undoubtedly had a deeper formative image than an Easter toy, but at a superficial level at least the toy was an inspiration. The cock that escapes from the man in the story is his "John Thomas," as in *John Thomas and Lady Jane*, and it is an Easter image, a resurrection image as well. While Lawrence did have his disagreements with

Freud, his own heretical vision led him to see an erection in the Resurrection (or, conversely, a resurrection in the erection).

The peasant and his wife of course try to control the cock. Lawrence writes of his cock's valiant efforts to escape the confines of the peasant and his wife (perhaps a reference to Lawrence's marriage) until he finally realizes that he is "tied by the leg."

> The young cock, freed, marched with a prancing stride of indignation away from the humans, came to the end of his string, gave a tug and a hitch of his tied leg, fell over for a moment, scuffled frantically on the unclean, earthen floor, to the horror of the shabby hens, then with a sickening lurch, regained his feet, and stood to think. The peasant and the peasant's wife laughed heartily, and the young cock heard them. And he knew, with a gloomy, foreboding kind of knowledge, that he was tied by the leg.[4]

Lawrence is externalizing the poet's predicament in the form of the peasant and the cock. The peasant is a symbol of the domesticated Lawrence and also represents Lawrence's perception of where he fits into the social structure of civilization. Lawrence as mere man is a peasant.

The cock is Lawrence's symbol of himself as poet — "tied by the leg." What's a man to do? The cock "gobbled up the best bits of food" and even "saved an extra-best bit for his favorite hen of the moment." But "his voice, above all, had lost the full gold of its clangour. He was tied by the leg and he knew it. Body, soul, and spirit were tied by that string."[5]

But there is a serious solution to a serious problem. The cock escapes. "Underneath, however, the life in him was grimly unbroken. It was the cord that should break." The breaking of the cord suggests a breaking of a relationship. The first cord, the umbilical cord, binds the child to its mother. The cord in this instance seems to be matrimonial: "One morning, just before the light of dawn, rousing from his slumbers with a sudden wave of strength, he leaped forward on his wings, and the string snapped. He gave a wild strange squawk, rose in one lift to the top of the wall, and there he crowed a loud and splitting crow."[6]

The splitting crow signifies the breaking of the cord. In modern vernacular, the cock splits. And at the same time a man wakes from a long sleep. The cock's escape, then, is equated with the man's awaking; the cock *is* the man. "At the same time, at the same hour before dawn, on the same morning, a man awoke from a long sleep in which he was tied up."[7] The man, like the cock, had been tied up.

"He woke numb and cold, inside a carved hole in a rock."[8]

Both Lawrence and H.D. had a vision of the wounded Christ. Lawrence writes: "Through all the long sleep his body had been full of hurt, and it was still full of hurt. He did not open his eyes. Yet he knew he was awake, and numb, and cold, and rigid, and full of hurt, and tied up. His face was banded with cold bands, his legs were bandaged together. Only his hands were loose."[9]

The man, the Christ figure, is banded like the tied cock. His awakening involves a realization of his condition. But resurrection is not a conscious choice. "He had not wished it. He had wanted to stay outside, in the place where even memory is stone dead. But now something had returned him, like a returned letter."[10]

Consistent with Freud's position in *Beyond the Pleasure Principle,* Lawrence asserts that man is most comfortable being dead. We begin to understand that he is presenting death in *The Escaped Cock* as a symbol of a certain style of life and also that condition toward which we gravitate. The death instinct is as powerful as the life instinct. There is a war between these forces in each individual psyche. To be alive is to be in pain.

> . . . and in the return he lay overcome with a sense of nausea. Yet suddenly his hands moved. They lifted up, cold, heavy and sore. Yet they lifted up, to drag away the cloth from his face, and to push at the shoulder bands. Then they fell again, cold, heavy, numb, and sick with having moved even so much, unspeakably unwilling to move further.
>
> With his face cleared and his shoulders free, he lapsed again and lay dead, resting on the cold nullity of being dead. It was the most desirable.[11]

The unbearable tension of life is the subject of Lawrence's vision. At least the cock — the pure animal — is not burdened by the oppressive structures of civilization. Furthermore, the cock is not conscious; like the poem, he is free. But the man, in his consciousness, is pulled between civilization and freedom, death and life. The deciding factor in the man's resurrection is the light.

> He leaned forward, in that narrow cell of rock, and leaned frail hands on the rock near the chinks of light.
>
> Strength came from somewhere, from revulsion; there was a crash and a wave of light, and the dead man was crouching in his lair, facing the animal onrush of light. Yet it was hardly dawn. And the strange, piercing keenness of daybreak's sharp breath was on him. It meant full awakening.[12]

To understand Christ, says Lawrence, we must wake up. It is a new dawn, a new morning. Resurrection is an awakening, a breaking of the cord, a cry of freedom, a cock escaping from a man. The experience is precipitated by the light. In *Helen in Egypt* H.D. sees it as a white light, "brighter than the sun at noonday,/yet whiter than frost/whiter than snow."[13]

The resurrected Christ is wounded. As in the Moravian symbolism and in *Helen in Egypt* (where the Christ figure is represented as Achilles), the emphasis on the wound is significant. As we have noted, this theme is also present in Lawrence's and H.D.'s Imagist poetry (see chapter 13). The man in *The Escaped Cock* is "bitterly wounded." It is painful to pass from one life into another. The passage is no mere change of circumstance, nor a move from one stage of life to another; the life into which we pass is the other, the unknown.

> Slowly, slowly he crept down from the cell of rock, with the caution of the bitterly wounded. Bandages and linen and perfume fell away, and he crouched on the ground against the wall of rock, to recover oblivion. But he saw his hurt feet touching the earth again, with unspeakable pain, the earth they had meant to touch no more, and he saw his thin legs that had died, and pain unknowable, pain like utter bodily disillusion, filled him so full that he stood up, with one torn hand on the ledge of the tomb.
> To be back! To be back again, after all that![14]

The return. As H.D. asks in *Advent,* after one has crossed the line, how does one return? This is the Ancient Mariner's story. How does one tell it? How does one write it? "He was alone," but "even beyond loneliness." He is disillusioned, "filled with the sickness of unspeakable disillusion." He can no longer relate to his fellow man, symbolized by "the sleeping soldiers." Yet "he felt a certain compassion."[15] The soldiers are alive but asleep. He is dead but awake. As Memnonius says to Veronica of Isis, "It was only the dead held her."[16] Lawrence's man has died from "the natural world of morning and evening, forever undying."[17]

Wandering in "deep nausea of disillusion and a resolution of which he was not aware . . . Advancing in a kind of half-consciousness," the man becomes aware of the cock. "He was roused by the shrill wild crowing of a cock just near him, a sound which made him shiver as if electricity had touched him."[18]

The peasant, of course, wants his cock back. Here is Lawrence crying to the "Master" in himself, "O stop him, Master! . . . My escaped cock!"

The man, the Master, subdues the cock with his death shroud. The Master "opened his great white wings of a shroud in front of the leaping bird. The cock fell back with a squawk and a flutter, the peasant jumped forward, there was a terrific beating of wings, and a whirring of feathers, then the peasant had the escaped cock safely under his arm, its wings shut down, its face crazily craning forward."

The peasant gratefully reclaims his cock: "It's my escaped cock!" he says. But almost instantaneously Lawrence as grateful peasant with reclaimed cock realizes Lawrence as "the man who had died."

> The peasant changed countenance and stood transfixed, as he looked into the dead-white face of the man who had died. That dead white face, so still, with the black beard growing on it as if in death; and those wide-open, black sombre eyes, that had died! and those washed scars on the waxy forehead! The slow-blooded man of the fields let his jaw drop, in childish inability to meet the situation.[19]

In *The Escaped Cock* D. H. Lawrence tells the same story as H.D. tells in "Pilate's Wife" — the story of the crucified Christ who is taken down from the cross too soon and who is thus wounded but not dead. In both Lawrence's and H.D.'s novels the historical period is the time of Christ, but the stories are actually about the persecution of D. H. Lawrence by the British authorities during the war. "The childish inability to meet the situation" is a reference to Lawrence's inability to face the truth about his relationship with H.D., and he hides in the peasant's house, that is, with Frieda. (H.D. alludes to this presentation in *Helen in Egypt,* where Achilles is hiding in the "women's quarters.") The Master also hides in the peasant's house — that is, Lawrence will stay with his peasant wife — until his strength returns. Inside the house "the ass stood within the high walls, safe from being stolen. There the peasant, in great disquietude, tied the cock."[20]

The Master, the peasant, the ass, the cock — safe but stranded in the confines of the house. The peasant and his wife urge the Master to eat, but he has lost his appetite. They regard him as a stranger, someone from another time and place. Lawrence the peasant sees Lawrence the writer as "a dead king from the region of terrors."

> They saw with terror the livid wounds in the thin waxy hands and the thin feet of the stranger, and the small lacerations in his still dead forehead. They smelled with terror the scent of rich perfumes that came from him, from his body. And they looked at the fine, snowy, costly linen. Perhaps he really was a dead king, from the region of terrors. And he was still cold and remote in the region of death, with perfumes coming from his transparent body as if from some strange flower.[21]

As H.D. writes in *Advent,* Lawrence was "buried alive." But he has returned. There is to be a second advent, a second coming. But first he must rest; wounds must heal. The room in which he rests is a tomb — "The sun had risen bright, and in the dark house with the door shut, the man was again as if in the tomb"[22] — and the tomb is a womb image. He will be reborn, he will return — in time.

The woman prepares a place for him to rest in the yard, "and he lay down under the wall in the morning sun." As he lies recovering, the cock "caught and tied by the leg again, cowered in a corner." But as the man heals the cock begins to crow again. "As he came out, the young cock crowed. It was a diminished, pinched cry, but there was that in the voice of the bird stronger than chagrin. It was the necessity to live, and even to cry out the triumph of life."[23]

H.D. asserts in *Helen in Egypt* that the triumph of Achilles is not petty. Through Lawrence's identification with the cock he similarly characterizes his outbursts as "brave" and "effective."

> The man who had died stood, and watched the cock who had escaped and been caught ruffling himself up, rising forward on his toes, throwing out his chest and parting his beak in another challenge to all the world to deny his existence. "Deny my existence if you can!" the brave sounds rang out, and though they were diminished by the cord round the bird's leg, they were effective enough.[24]

Lawrence has been hurt by the suppression of his work. It is one of the minor wounds of life, perhaps, but a wound nonetheless. The world has attempted to deny the existence of his vision, his experience, and he knows the suppression is largely political — a matter of spiritual or cultural warfare. This issue is also a major theme of the second part of "Pilate's Wife."

The man who had died has risen up, but he wants to keep it a secret. When he meets Madeleine (a French form of the Biblical name Magdalene), he tells her that he has been sheltered in a house.

> "Don't be afraid," said the man in the shroud. "I am not dead. They took me down too soon. So I have risen up. Yet if they discover me they will do it all over again . . ."
> He spoke in a voice of old disgust. Humanity! Especially humanity in authority! There was only one thing it could do.[25]

Humanity in authority, says Lawrence, can only crucify. There is only one thing to do to protect oneself: hide.

Lawrence had been expelled from Cornwall; he had been suspect. He had been accused of being a spy. Where are we in biographical time? 1917? Mecklenburgh Square? The scene Lawrence next describes parallels one in *Bid Me to Live*.

> "Madeleine! Do not be afraid. I am alive. They took me down too soon, so I came back to life. Then I was sheltered in a house."
> She did not know what to say, but fell at his feet to kiss them.
> "Don't touch me, Madeleine," he said, "Not yet! I am not yet healed and in touch with men." [26]

The H.D.-Lawrence story is commonly believed to be fully told in H.D.'s *roman à clef Bid Me to Live* (*A Madrigal*). Some read it as a story of love offered and rejected. Rico (the Lawrence character) repudiates the touch of Julia (the H.D. persona).

In *The Escaped Cock* the man repudiates the touch of Madeleine. Understandably, she feels betrayed. "Do you betray us all?" she says. It is not betrayal, he explains. He has died. Judas betrayed him. "Death has betrayed me. I am different. My poor Judas, he handed death to me. He rescued me from my own salvation." Madeleine is reproachful, hurt. "Have you risen for yourself alone?" she asks. "A man would not die the same death twice," he says to her. He asks her for money; he asks if he might come and live with her at her house. "Now?" she asks. "Not now! Later, when I am healed, and I am with my Father." [27]

Madeleine slowly comes to the realization that he has changed forever; she had believed he would be the Messiah again, but he is no longer immortal. "He had lost caste." Like Achilles of *Helen in Egypt*, he has returned as a new mortal, wounded; he will not be young forever. "The enthusiasm and the burning purity were gone, and the rapt youth. His youth was dead. This man was middle-aged and disillusioned, with a certain terrible indifference, and a resoluteness which love would never conquer . . . This risen man was the death of her dream." [28] He is now more comfortable with the peasant woman.

The peasant woman likes the dead man. She calls the dead man Master:

> "Where have you been, Master?" she said shyly. "Why did you go away?"
> "I have been to walk in a garden, and I have seen a friend who gave me a little money. It is for you."
> He held out his thin hand with the small amount of money, all that Madeleine could give him. The peasant's wife's eyes glistened, for money was scarce, and she said:

"Oh Master! And is it truly mine?"
"Take it!" he said. "It is due you." [29]

Lawrence is making an interesting point here — or rather, taking an interesting point of view. Madeleine, the traditional prostitute figure, gives rather than takes the money, which is "due" the peasant woman.* This is a perceptive comment on the structure of civilization. We are asked to look at marriage and ask, who suffers? who benefits? The man now lives a "death in life." "And in the safety of the yard, the young cock was dear to him, as it crowed in the helpless zest of life, then finally finished in the helpless humiliation of being tied by the leg. This day the ass stood swishing her tail under the shed." [31]

Who is this ass? The "peasant" wife who would accuse Lawrence of being impotent?

> But the woman brought wine and water and sweetened cakes, and roused him, so that he ate a little to please her. The day was hot, with a fierceness after a shower of rain, and as she crouched to serve him, he saw her breasts from her humble body sway from her smock. He knew she wished he would desire her . . . But he could not want her . . . Perhaps it was her thoughts, her consciousness, he could not mingle with. He had given her money, and she was pleased, so now she thought he would want this other of her. [32]

Thinking how "the body could live a greater life," the man rises and finds Madeleine again. In total rebellion against "civilized" values, Lawrence implies that the peasant wife rather than Madeleine is the lower form of life. He will be crucified for seeing things this way. We are reminded of Lawrence's letter to Cecil Gray (chapter 13) in which he asserts that the world of H.D. and himself is more significant than that of Frieda and Gray.

Insofar as *The Escaped Cock* refers to the events of the war years (1914–1918), we now approach the sequence of Lawrence's narrative that relates to an event that may have occurred in the summer of 1918. If "a stranger" did appear at a time and in a place where he could not possibly have been, as H.D. writes in "The Mystery," it was probably during the summer of 1918. In *Helen in Egypt,* H.D. relates "the human content of the drama" in part III, "Eidolon." The story she tells is that Achilles, who has been ac-

---

*Horace Gregory reports, "It was [H.D.] who persuaded Amy Lowell to send money to Lawrence — at a time when she herself was in great need of it." [30] H.D.'s letters to Lowell on Lawrence's behalf are collected at the Houghton Library, Harvard University.

cused of spying, returns to the beach after his friend Patroclus takes his place. He is disguised and, as in *The Escaped Cock,* no one recognizes him. Perhaps, as Lawrence relates earlier in the *The Escaped Cock,* "the soldiers" are sleeping. At any rate, both authors tell of a disguised and secret meeting between the Master/Achilles and Madeleine/Helen. This is the way H.D. tells the story in *Helen in Egypt:*

> Achilles sulks in his tent,
> they said, but it was not true,
> Achilles avoids the battle;
>
> we will trick him
> and lure him out,
> Patroclus shall bear his shield
>
> and lead his men;
> so they armed Patroclus
> and Patroclus was slain,
>
> where is Achilles?
> they sought for him everywhere,
> but never thought the unarmed
>
> hostler who tended his steeds,
> was Achilles' self,
> wrapped in a woolen cloak
>
> with the hood drawn over his head;
> he sulks in his tent, they said,
> but he was a far shadow upon the beach;
>
> "a spy, an emissary of Troy?"
> but he answered the sentinel's threat
> with the simple pass-word
>
> of Achilles' Myrmidons,
> *Helena;* so he went to the prow
> of his love, his beloved,
>
> feeling her flanks,
> tearing loose weed from her stern,
> brushing sand from her beams,
>
> not speaking, but praying:
> I will re-join the Greeks
> and the battle before the gate,
>
> if you promise a swift return,
> if you promise new sails for the fleet
> and a wind to bear us home,
>
> I am sick of the Trojan plain,
> I would rise, I would fall again
> In a tempest, a hurricane.[33]

The anger of Achilles, says H.D., was misunderstood, misinterpreted. Harry T. Moore had said that Lawrence exploded in a puritanical rage when H.D. went off to Cornwall with Cecil Gray. It was rather, explains H.D., a jealous rage.

> He was the tempest self
> as he roused the host,
> and they said, see Achilles' anger
>
> his unspeakable grief,
> for his friend is dead;
> he is thundering over the plain,
>
> where is Hector?
> when the heroes meet,
> the very world must crash
>
> in the clash of their arms;
> so they circled the city-wall
> three times, till Hector fell;
>
> was this vengeance?
> was this answer to prayer?
> so the legend starts,
>
> and Patroclus — Achilles are names
> to be conjured together;
> but the warriors never saw
>
> a shadow upon the beach,
> nor knew the power of the tempest
> was roused by another.[34]

H.D. says: "Yes — Helen is awake, she sees the pattern; the 'old pictures' are eternal."[35] The eternal pictures are an allusion not only to their poems, but also to Lawrence's paintings in "bright primary colors" for *The Man Who Died*. The man in the frontispiece painting of the Black Sun Press edition of the novel has been identified as Lawrence. But who is the tall, statuesque, Greek-looking woman? Lacy describes the painting:

> The frontispiece . . . is a sketch of two figures, obviously the priestess of Isis in her yellow robe and the naked man who had died. She is facing him, leaning forward, and both hands appear to be intent upon "the death wound through the belly." He is arched away from her, appearing both to resist and to yield to her efforts to heal him. Between them is a shallow incense burner or "brazier," and up from this leaps a long tongue of flame.[36]

"Was there ever such a brazier?" asks H.D. in *Helen in Egypt*.[37] This is not to be read, "Did such a brazier ever exist?" but rather, "Would you believe the flame of that brazier!" It *is* a remarkable painting. It is no wonder that, in her final version of *Bid Me to Live* (1949), H.D. alludes to Rico (Lawrence) as Van Gogh.

Returning to Lawrence's story, we find that the man takes more money from Madeleine. He tells her, "I must go to my Father." She protests, "There is your mother."[38] *Father* is capitalized; *mother* is not. The concept of Father invoked by Lawrence has a special meaning.

The man's wounds are healing; he wants to be alone. The sun and the spring are helping him heal; people are not. He is realizing the Father. "Now may I stand within the Father . . . I will wander the earth and say nothing; for strange is the phenomenal world, whose essential body is my Father." The phenomenal world is the world of reproduction. "I will go with the Father around me, with my body erect and procreant."[39] The man who has died becomes the Father.

He decides to become a physician, a healer. Having been sorely wounded and having healed, he now possesses the gift of healing, "because the power was still in him to heal whomsoever touched him within the Father."[40]

He must leave the peasant couple "to return to the Father." He asks the peasants: "Give me the cock that is now tied by the leg. For he shall ascend with me." Lawrence connects the cock to the Father through "the phenomenal world, whose inner air is the body of the god of cocks also."[41] The cock, he tells two men he meets on the road, "hath virtue." After an argument about the location of the Father, the man tells the two men that he is a healer and that the "bird is full of life and virtue." They accuse him: "You are not a believer." In the discussion about the whereabouts of the Father they tell the man, "The Father is in Heaven above the cloud and firmament."[42] Lawrence teases them a bit about their underdeveloped consciousness. When the men finally recognize the man they cry in fear: "Master!" Do they think that he is the Father?

At the conclusion of Lawrence's story the cock fights with "a rooster of the inn walking forth to battle." The man's cock wins the battle and is awarded a kingdom. There is a touch of pride here — Lawrence wins the battle in the barnyard. The man says to his cock, "Thou at least hast found thy kingdom and the females to thy body." In the end the man acknowledges the Father, his paternity, and asks the question that H.D. alludes to in *Helen in Egypt* as "the question which has no answer": "From what, and to what, could this infinite whirl be saved?"[43]

21

The Ankh
and the Cross

THE "INFINITE WHIRL" of which Lawrence speaks in the last line
of his story is related to the headpiece of part II of the Black Sun
Press edition of *The Escaped Cock.* Gerald Lacy tells us:

> The headpiece for part II is again circular and again in reds and
> greens. There is a figure of a woman, the priestess of Isis, head
> bowed and holding in her hand an ankh, the ancient Egyptian sym-
> bol of life. Since she is alone, and since there is a certain sadness in
> the muted green of her figure, we can assume that this is a picture
> of "Isis in Search." There are swirling patterns, as in the frontis-
> piece, and they are suggestive perhaps of the infinite flux of life.[1]

In part I of the novel Lawrence described Madeleine as a devotee. "She had been so happy to be saved from her old rapacity and
to devote herself to a pure Messiah . . . she was now greedy to
give her selfless devotion, as before she had been greedy to take
from her lovers."[2] In his painting for the headpiece of part II, the
priestess of Isis holds an ankh in her hand. There are also two
ankhs in the background. In H.D.'s "Pilate's Wife," we will remember, Veronica becomes a devotee of Isis and contemplates the
meaning of the ankh — the T-cross or mystic cross. She associates
it with the staff of Hermes of the Greeks and Thoth of the Egyptians. It is a symbol of the "wisdom of heaven and earth," that is,
poetry.[3]

Before we turn to part II of Lawrence's novel we will look at
the second part of "Pilate's Wife," for H.D. undoubtedly wrote
most of it before she read the conclusion of Lawrence's story. We
re-enter H.D.'s story at the time when Veronica's sexual relationship with Memnonius is over and her interest in the Isis mysteries
is deepening as she becomes involved in the cult. A new character

is introduced — Mnevis, a woman who is an initiate and priestess of Isis.* Memnonius, with whom Veronica is still in touch, is interested in her involvement with Mnevis and the Isis mysteries. " 'What is that cross?' The woman [Mnevis] looked up. Veronica perceived eyes, blotted out with pupils. Did her own look like that? Memnonius had said, 'those blotted-out half-eyes of the psychic-gifted? . . .' It seemed for the first time that she had caught him (to use his own phrase) 'speaking awkward dialect.' "[4]

Mnevis associates the Isis mysteries with a young visionary ("From the first, Mnevis had insisted that this was some sort of paragon who loved women"[5]), a young Jew. Jesus.

> The sky, he says, is a parchment and the message of any bird, flying across it, has more meaning than any craft or priesthood . . . He believed that flowers too, opening, speak in the curl-back of their petals, further of mystery. The Prophet has enjoined on his followers to study flowers, those wild lilies in particular, that (red and blue . . . and kingly purple) open wide to the sun-rays, along the Gallilean foothills. By minute contemplation of the unfolding of a wild-flower, you gain, he claims, hieratic knowledge of the inner mystery. Instead of confining his knowledge to the temple and the somewhat forbidding line of the initiate, the Jew says *all* are initiate. The heaven is open to all who read.[6]

The particular Christ figure described by H.D. more clearly suggests D. H. Lawrence than the Biblical Jesus. H.D. implies that the visionary is a sort of double of Memnonius, a different manifestation of the same presence. " 'Does Memnonius know the Jew then?' That, Mnevis couldn't or she wouldn't answer. Mnevis said, 'The man comes and goes. I told you he had no habitation.' "[7]

At this point in the story Veronica has not yet encountered the prophet. She has heard both Mnevis and Fabius speak of him. But Mnevis seems to be turning against him. For one thing, she wants "no Cross" in her religion. "But where, last time Mnevis had chanted paeons of this paragon, with a lilt and fine flow of prophetic feeling, today her words fell silent, with no upward wing of the inspired utterance, that seemed to flutter with visible light when she last spoke of this same Prophet."[8]

It begins to become clear that "Pilate's Wife" is written about the same events in historical time that at the deepest level inspired *The Escaped Cock*. It is the story of Lawrence's emergence as a writer and the persecution he endured for saying what he believed.

---

*The character Mnevis in "Pilate's Wife" corresponds to Morgan of *Bid Me to Live* and is based on Brigit Patmore.

As Lawrence identifies with the Christ figure of *The Escaped Cock,* so H.D. sees him as a prophet, a Christ figure who is crucified by society. H.D. writes of the soldiers taking her prophet prisoner, a reference (as in *The Escaped Cock*) to Lawrence's troubles of 1917 — the "nightmare" of Lawrence's novel *Kangaroo.* In H.D.'s story we are in A.D. 33, in Rome. A.D. 33 Rome is symbolically England in 1917. "Outside, was a cluster of soldiers, a slight argument. Fortunately, Fabius Noblier stood among them. A prisoner with face turned half toward her, wore a wreath of blossoms. The heavy branch was twined to make a crown. Veronica saw it was not blossoms, it was a branch of the flowering-thorn, but a branch, not yet in blossom or newly stripped of blossom."[9]

Veronica feels implicated in the persecution. "That lady was making her way down, toward them. She had caught up a scarf, was still in her indefinite incognito garments, the ones set aside to be discarded on entry, for these 'secret' visits."[10]

H.D.'s story at this point corresponds so closely to *The Escaped Cock* that it is quite possible that she wrote it (about the last third) after she read the *Forum* edition of Lawrence's story. She writes that the prophet was "arguing as they claimed he did of Light, of Darkness, of an Eternal Father."[11]

Veronica has a moment of recognition, a "shock of recognition."

> Veronica stepped nearer. She saw a young face, bearded in the manner of certain of the Eastern devotees. She realized with a shock of recognition that it was the face of her little sun-god. "Is it true then? Have you been taken falsely?" The man bent his head, whether in affirmation or despair or pride, Veronica couldn't fathom.[12]

Pilate is among the cluster of soldiers, "asking every sort of question with the subtlety of a viper."[13] H.D.'s description of his role is an excellent characterization of Aldington's behavior as Lawrence's "friend" during Lawrence's time of turmoil.

> Pilate said, "You have heard my opinion on these matters, on more than one occasion. But this time, the Jewish Priesthood are trying to persuade me that there *is* a sort of inner brotherhood or circle. The man has spoken openly of prayer in secret . . . of a King or Father in secret. There has always been something secret. He speaks, it is also rumored, to his followers, in a sort of code. He says one thing that obviously, means another. He has openly admitted, on more than one occasion, that his words hold different meanings . . ." Pilate, it appeared, was thinking of his own pride.[14]

The Ankh and the Cross § 201

When he finally began to suspect that Imagist speech held meaning he had not understood, Aldington developed an acute interest in suppressing its meaning. And it was, as H.D. says, a matter of his own pride. If Lawrence was understood, he, H.D.'s husband, would look like a fool in the eyes of the world. "Checkmated, Pontius Pilate was considering not that Jew outside, but his own predicament." [15]

Paralleling the situation in *Bid Me to Live,* Pilate puts questions to Veronica that she manages to evade. " 'I was out this afternoon, came back, veiled as usual. I went to the shrine of Isis.' So far, so good. She was not lying to him." [16]

H.D. implies that Aldington was in some way behind Lawrence's troubles in 1917 and 1918. They were also due, of course, to "war-hysteria." But why was Lawrence suspect in the first place? It has been suggested by David Garnett and reported by Harry T. Moore that Ford Madox Ford might have warned the government in 1915 that Lawrence was pro-German, thus causing all of Lawrence's troubles during the war years. [17] It should also be noted, however, that during the time that Ford is alleged to have taken this action Richard Aldington was serving as his private secretary. H.D.'s story suggests that Aldington was in the middle of things when the cry to crucify rang out in Rome/England. "The 'crucify him' was a cry to war, having nothing to do with any set of voices, or peoples; war-madness, war-hysteria." [18] But it was war-hysteria directed to a particular scapegoat; "We must actually nail him up there . . ." [19]

In "Pilate's Wife" a scene follows which invokes the man's meeting with Madeleine in *The Escaped Cock.* In both stories the man tells the woman that there is nothing she can do. H.D. writes:

> "Memnonius, long ago you loved me. You said often I was a bud unfolded. You said you would give anything to see me ray-out, my buds unfolding. Memnonius, no amount of physical ecstasy has given me what he gave me. Help me to save this Jew of the Etruscans, this Jew of the Greeks, this Jew of the Egyptians."
> Memnonius answered, "You cannot, I tell you, save him." [20]

In H.D.'s story, Memnonius is Lawrence the man, Christ is Lawrence the writer. One is crucified, she says, not for anything one does, but for what one says. Any kind of behavior is tolerable; it is talking about it publicly that is intolerable. The poet is the perpetual victim of society. Like Iphigeneia, Christ is a victim of civilization's need to maintain its fictions, its ordering principles. A new poem is a new fiction, a new ordering principle. And if it is stronger than the old fiction, the new conception will prevail. As Pilate appeals to the masses he says, "How do I know that the kingdom that he preaches is not a sort of direct intimation that they intend setting up fortresses here or in the Islands?"[21]

Pilate maintains that the prophet is innocent, but does so in such a way that he implies his guilt. This characterization applies to the tone and tenor of all of Richard Aldington's duplicitous literary "support" of D. H. Lawrence.

H.D.'s own support of Lawrence as a poet was unwavering. They shared beliefs, precepts, intuitions. Veronica's support of the new prophet, or as H.D. calls him in *The Walls Do Not Fall,* "the authentic Jew," is constant. Like Lawrence's Madeleine, she is devoted.

> *The grain of mustard seed, the seed cast into the ground* was Elusinian precept. He had no new doctrine really. The novelty was the bringing of that precept into line with everyday existence. The man was in that, as great as Osiris, greater than the Hellenic sun-god. Yet for all that, he *was* Osiris, *was* exact Hellenic sun-god . . . What he was and could do, he constantly asserted, all men could do and would do. All men and (this was the oddest thing about it) all women. What Eastern prophet had ever given women a place in the spiritual hierarchy? The Greek certainly, but the Greek, Veronica knew, had sublimated and intellectualized the old set of symbols.[22]

H.D. and D. H. Lawrence both had a vision that linked the Christ story to the Osiris story, the T-cross (the ankh) of the Egyptians to the Christian cross. H.D.'s Moravian upbringing had in some sense preconditioned her to a mystical and poetic understanding of Christian symbols; Lawrence's vision of the mysteries was in some sense so akin to H.D.'s that it is no wonder that he and H.D. should develop a strong spiritual bond.

> This Jew seemed to combine Greek intellectualism and occult wisdom in a curious precise manner. His *consider the lilies* linked up his cult of nature, with the old shrines where lilies always floated before the feet of the blue-robed Isis. The lilies were the flower, notoriously, of Isis. His talk of birds, of doves, noticeably again brought the dove-worship into human consciousness; every tree had its own fruit, he asserted, the fruit of the tree and the vine made him one with the Elusinian Dionysus.[23]

From H.D.'s point of view, Lawrence's affirmation of Isis —the whole woman, rather than the woman split by the patriarchy into wife and hetaera — made him fundamentally sympathetic to women. H.D.'s basic orientation was poetic and religious. She desperately needed the spiritual connection, particularly in the context of her worldly, spiritually barren marriage to Aldington. In "Pilate's Wife" she tells us that Jesus made Veronica realize that her whole marriage had been built upon a falsehood; this realization, she says, was liberating. Veronica was grateful.

> This Jesus dared put forward a new axiom, God was imagination. He insisted that God, though he had the eye of an eagle (that bird of Jupiter) had yet the tenderness of the dove, or even the common domestic fowl who fluffs out her feathers to collect her chicks. He stripped off the outer shell of the soul. She herself was as defenseless as a new-hatched chick; why all this was my egg-shell . . . Her mind swung between grandiose and simple images. He made one see things like that. The whole of her existence had been built upon a falsehood. [24]

He broke down her defenses; she saw the truth about her marriage, and she thanked him for it. And, unlike her husband, he treated her with tenderness. *Tenderness* — Lawrence's original title for *Lady Chatterley's Lover*.

In "Pilate's Wife" as in *The Escaped Cock,* the man is "ordinary" after the crucifixion. "His feet" symbolize his poetry, the pentameters of his words. "The sailors had been warned. It was his feet that mattered. Suddenly the ignominy of it came over me." [25] Christ was taken down from the cross too soon; Lawrence's life as a poet had ended too soon. "The man would be ordinary now, with an ordinary companion. Bread would taste different. Bread would be just bread to him, while to them — Fabius broke a crisp loaf. To us? Has he bequeathed to us his terrible discovery of the unity of all things? Their symbol? Fabius supposed, when his fatigue passed, he would see things in their orderly dimension." [26]

Not only had Lawrence been forced out of his home in Cornwall and not only had his novels been suppressed, but somehow, because of Aldington's influence and Pound's compliance, the Imagist circle had dissolved. As a consequence of the events of this period, Lawrence and H.D. were separated. "He had burnt out, she had burnt out. There was an end to psychic endurance, somewhere. There was a beginning. Spring is too beautiful, wild white narcissus is too beautiful. Jesus had been too beautiful. He knew nothing of the Greek moderation, the Roman pragmatism. He burnt up and out to that impossible divinity . . . O yes — he was impossible." [27]

But, says H.D., between the two of them they had created a new world that would live. "Poetry, he thought with an inner lilt of conviction, is living . . . They had created a new world, because through them, in the eyes of the populus, a poet had been murdered; through them, a poet still lived."[28] Society had demanded a sacrifice; once sacrificed, the poet could be incorporated into the structure of the old. The poet is the sacrificial victim who, at the cost of his or her own life, infuses the culture with new life. The new world emerges like a phoenix from the ashes of the victim.

The cross and the ankh are symbols of life that parallel the sun piercing the closed leaf of the lily: "She had been thinking in her old fervid manner, then realized that something was breaking in her head. It was an actual sensation. She thought, a lily must feel like that at the exact second that the sun pierces its closed leaf."[29] It is not merely sexual connection but the breaking through into another life — the man's life breaking through into the woman's, hers into his. The ankh and the cross, says H.D., symbolize the miracle.

> This is a miracle, yes, this is a miracle. She remembered Memnonius and his earlier remark that she was a flower unfolded . . .
> She wouldn't refer to Pilate, think at all of the matter. Because — there was something, she believed, that she could tell no one.[30]

In the last sentence of *The Escaped Cock* Lawrence asks, "From what, and to what, could this infinite whirl be saved?"[31] In the last sentence of "Pilate's Wife" H.D. says, "She had no answer, had she waited for an answer? Well, she had given him no chance to answer. She had not waited in that cool, empty rock-cavern for an answer."[32]

22

The Priestess of Isis

IN *ADVENT* H.D. tells us: "Lawrence came back with *The Man Who Died*. Whether or not he meant me to be the priestess of Isis in that book does not alter the fact that his last book reconciled him to me. Isis is incomplete without Osiris."[1] Through the help of Freud, H.D. saw herself as that manifestation of Isis which forever searches for and gathers together the lost pieces of the body of her mate, Osiris. H.D. told Freud "about the little statues or images in the house that Lawrence had first spoken of in Cornwall. He asked me what the images were? I said there was a painted Osiris on the shelf; seated on the end was a bronze Isis."[2] In the midst of fragmentation and duality H.D.'s quest was for the integration and unity symbolized by Isis and Osiris. It is Isis who finds the escaped Christ in Lawrence's *The Man Who Died*.

The Man Who Died is not only a continuation of "The Escaped Cock" but also a second version; it concentrates on the woman. The central symbols of part II of *The Man Who Died* are the temple and the cave (the rock-cavern). The woman of the temple serves the goddess Isis. The temple is in Lebanon but faces "south and west, towards Egypt." It is located on a desolate coast with "steep slopes coming down to the sea" and stands in the middle of a forest. The woman is alone, "save for the goddess," Isis.[3]

"She went towards the sun, through the grove of Mediterranean pine-trees and evergreen oaks, in the midst of which the temple stood, on a little, tree-covered tongue of land between two bays."[4] The image recalls the seacoast of southern England, the setting of H.D.'s poem "The Cliff Temple." It reminds us of the woods in which the woman meets her lover in H.D.'s unpublished manuscript "Paint It Today." The temple facing Egypt becomes a central symbol, the Amen temple, of *Helen in Egypt*.

The woman in *The Man Who Died* meets the stranger in January on a small humped peninsula in Lebanon where the temple secretly hid. "The sea was dark, almost indigo, running away from the land."[5] In accordance with the laws of poetry, southern England may appear as Greece, Egypt, Lebanon.

The Man Who Died, part II, begins with an image: "two slaves, half naked . . . crouching in the rocks." The poet or priestess (Isis) watches as the slaves perform a sacrifice: "They pierced the throat of a blue, live bird, and let the drops of blood fall into the heaving sea, with curious concentration. They were performing some sacrifice, or working some incantation."[6]

The woman of Lawrence's story is presented in the image of an escaped pigeon (as the man is presented in part I as the escaped cock): "A black and white pigeon, vividly white, like a ghost escaped over the low dark sea, sped out, caught the wind, tilted, rode, soared and swept over the pine-trees, and wheeled away, a speck, inland. It had escaped." The boy slave, like the peasant in *The Escaped Cock,* protests. "He raised his arms to heaven in anger as the pigeon wheeled away, naked and angry and young he held out his arms. Then he turned and seized the girl in an access of rage, and beat her with his fist that was stained with pigeon's blood."[7]

In the two parts of Lawrence's story we now have many images within images: two peasants, a male and a female; two slaves, a male and a female; a cock and a pigeon, male and female; and the two central figures — the man who died, who is alone, and the priestess of Isis, who is also alone. The image within the image is the act of coitus; within the large spiritual context of the world of poetry is the personal human dimension — the sexual encounter. After he expresses his rage, the slave boy attempts to revive his companion. In this moment the slaves become slaves of their instincts.

> The boy suddenly left off beating the girl. He crouched over her, touching her, trying to make her speak. But she lay quite inert, face down on the smoothed rock. And he put his arms around her and lifted her, but she slipped back to earth, like one dead, yet far too quickly for anything dead. The boy, desperate, caught her by the hips and hugged her to him, turning her over there. There she seemed inert, all her fight was in her shoulders. He twisted her over, intent and unconscious, and pushed his hands between her thighs, to push them apart. And in an instant he was covering her in the blind, frightened frenzy of a boy's first passion. Quick and frenzied his young body quivered naked on hers, blind, for a minute. Then it lay quite still, as if dead.[8]

The two slaves realize they are being watched by a man and the priestess. The boy is in terror. He scuttles "lamely" toward a door in the wall. The girl, too, realizes she has been seen. She becomes sullen, but acts as if she has noticed nothing: "She turned away, as if she had seen nothing, to the four dead pigeons and the knife, which lay there on the rock. And she began to strip the small feathers, so that they rose on the wind like dust."[9]

The priestess could be disinterested. She has the capacity of detachment. "The priestess turned away. Slaves! Let the overseer watch them. She was not interested. She went slowly through the pines again, back to the temple."[10]

The temple of Lawrence's Isis becomes for H.D. the Amen temple in her *Helen in Egypt:*

> The great Amen, Ammon or Amun temple still stands, so we may wander there with Helen. She and we need peace and time to reconstruct the legend. Karnak? Luxor? Thebes, certainly. This is the oldest city in the world. Homer knew it. But we look back, not so far geographically and historically. They had met on the coast in the dark. Achilles has been here with her; no doubt, he will come again. But for the moment, she wants to assess her treasure, realize the transcendental in material terms. For their meeting in eternity was timeless, but in time it was short, and 'few were the words we said.'
>
> > How did we greet each other?
> > Here in this Amen-temple,
> > I have all-time to remember.[11]

In Lawrence's story the temple is associated with "the swollen lotus-bud of Egypt."

> It was a small temple of wood, painted all pink and white and blue, having at the front four wooden pillars rising like stems to the swollen lotus-bud of Egypt at the top, supporting the roof and the open, spiky lotus-flowers of the outer frieze, which went around under the eaves. Two low steps of stone led up to the platform before the pillars, and the chamber behind the pillars was open. There a low stone altar stood, with a few embers in its hollow, and the dark stain of blood in its end groove.[12]

Interestingly, this temple reinvokes the temple motif which had permeated both Lawrence's and H.D.'s poetry (and much of their prose) since 1915. It bears some resemblance, certainly, to "the house we have in the woods" described in "Paint It Today": "It is a Roman house. It is very small, low, with columns, the ice white stones stand sheer on the floor of the forest."[13] In both cases the place is small, and the emphasis is on the pillars or columns and the stones. The altar with "the dark stain of blood in its groove" in Lawrence's description corresponds to the "whortleberry crimson blanket on the floor" in H.D.'s description. Appropriately, the blanket, upon which the lovers engage in the act of coition, is equivalent in Lawrence's rendition to the place of sacrifice.

H.D. tells us in "Compassionate Friendship" that she and Lawrence discussed a vision or picture H.D. had spoken of while the Lawrences were staying at Mecklenburgh Square.

> There was a burnt-brown figure seated in a closed-doorway or against a wall, cross-legged in the traditional manner, wearing the traditional wrap-around half garment. He was static. A girl walks across the flat court-yard or paved way before this house, a temple, possibly, but there is no suggestion of ritualistic glamour. There is nothing pretty or even striking or mysterious. It is a geographical scene, a real picture in real time — where? India, certainly. When? I cannot say. The girl has a water-jar, a large Greek-Indian water-pot. She does not turn her head to look at the familiar figure — beggar or saint? She perceives him and he does not appear to bat an eye-lid, maybe he sees her. He must see her as she crosses his line of vision, though maybe his eyes are closed. The girl makes for a flat-water tank, a square set into the pavement, not a natural pool. She fills her jar. I cannot remember if she places it on her head, I suppose she does. She returns the way she has come across the flagged pavement or outer floor of this gray-stoned massive walled house — there is no feeling that anyone is going *in* to that house, least of all the saint-beggar who seems a fixture on the door-step. It is just one stone-step. I told this to Lawrence. He seemed receptive but we never mentioned this "picture" again and I could almost say that I had "forgotten" it. But it seems in some way to relate to the meaning of the Priestess of Isis and the deposed Prophet in the *Man Who Died,* though there Lawrence has invoked or created a small marble temple on the coast of Lebanon.[14]

We must always keep in mind that the stated purpose of "Compassionate Friendship" is, as H.D. wrote to Bryher, "to lessen rather than to reveal." But even if H.D. tells of this vision to de-emphasize the meaning of the temple as it appears and reappears in her own and Lawrence's writing after 1915, her "picture" is worth taking into consideration in our reading of *The Man Who Died.*

It might be illuminating at this point to think about the meaning of the actual word *temple.* The most common meaning is, of course, "an edifice dedicated to the worship of a deity." Both H.D. and Lawrence use the word in this sense, although their meaning of *deity* might be considered by some to be heretical.

Temple also means, significantly, *tempora* — the space on either side of the forehead.

The next movement in the story is the entrance of the priestess into the temple, "passing through to the dark inner chamber, lighted by a perfumed oil-flame . . . and once more she threw a few grains of incense on the brazier before the goddess, and once more she sat down before her goddess, in the almost-darkness, to muse, to go away into the dream of the goddess."[15] The woman is not the goddess. As in Lawrence's first Isis poem, the goddess is the muse, the poet; the woman is simply a woman. But the woman can enter into "the dream of the goddess"; that is, the goddess is a manifestation of the woman, her divine or other-worldly incarnation.

Lawrence presents a bereaved Isis, Isis in search. This is the figure that Lawrence painted for *The Man Who Died*. (There is, we will remember, a brazier in one of the pictures, and T-crosses in another. The brazier, as we have previously noted, prefigures that of *Helen in Egypt*.) Isis is in search of her lost lover, Osiris.

> The goddess, in painted marble, lifted her face and strode, one thigh forward through the frail fluting of her robe, in the anguish of bereavement and of search. She was looking for the fragments of the dead Osiris, dead and scattered asunder, dead, torn apart, and thrown in fragments over the wide world. And she must find his hands and his feet, his heart, his thighs, his head, his belly, she must gather him together and fold her arms round the re-assembled body till it became warm again, and roused to life, and could embrace her and could fecundate her womb.[16]

The "goddess in painted marble" recalls H.D.'s descriptions of her poetry as "chiseled marble." We think of the marble floor of *Helen in Egypt*, of the thoughts that break through the legend "like fire/through the broken pictures/on the marble-floor."[17] The broken pictures, the broken body, the poems. Lawrence's poetry is scattered to the winds, as was his book of poems *Bits* — "fragments of the dead Osiris, dead and scattered asunder, dead, torn apart, and thrown in fragments over the wide world." The broken body of Osiris symbolizes the state of mind of the separated lovers. Isis is in search of reconciliation. The body must be reassembled before it can be resurrected. Unless Isis is able to reassemble the broken and scattered pieces, there will be no reconciliation, hence no resurrection.

> And the strange rapture and anguish of search went on through the years, as she lifted her throat and her hollowed eyes looked inward, in the tormented ecstasy of seeking, and the delicate navel of her

bud-like belly showed through the frail, girdled robe with the eternal asking, asking, of her search. And through the years she found him bit by bit, heart and head and limbs and body.[18]

H.D. has said that her writing is a search, and she has said in her "Notes on Recent Writing" that "this Isis takes many forms as does Osiris."[19] The scattered body of their writing appears and reappears in many forms: poems, plays, verse dramas, novels, short stories, autobiographical notes, polemics, essays. In *The Man Who Died* Lawrence tells us that Isis had not found "the last reality" — and that, apparently, was her problem. "And yet she had not found the last reality, the final clue to him, the genitals that alone could bring him really back to her and touch her womb. For she was Isis of the subtle lotus, the womb which waits submerged and in bud, waits for the touch of that other, inward sun that streams its rays from the loins of the male Osiris."[20]

In Lawrence's short story "Sun," a woman, Juliet (who reminds us of Julia of *Bid Me to Live*), is "given" to the sun.

> Something deep inside her unfolded and relaxed, and she was given. By some mysterious power inside her, deeper than her known consciousness and will, she was put into connection with the sun, and the stream flowed of itself, from her womb. She herself, her conscious self, was secondary, a secondary person, almost an onlooker. The true Juliet was this dark flow from her body to the sun.[21]

In H.D.'s vision, the sun is the white light of *Helen in Egypt*. In "Pilate's Wife" H.D. says that the condemned man, the man to be crucified, bears the face of her "sun-god." The sun, as well as being a homonym of son, the Christ figure, takes the deeper meaning in *Helen in Egypt* of the most intense kind of heat or relationship between man and woman.

In "Sun" Juliet is both the person who "had always been mistress of herself" and the other, deeper self.[22] This particular reality of the divided self can be presented in a variety of ways; the torn and scattered body of Osiris is but another way — a mythological language, as it were — of addressing the reality of the self torn between conflicting impulses.

The woman of *The Man Who Died* lived as a child in Rome, Ephesus, and Egypt. We note that in *Helen in Egypt* the young Helen was kept in Egypt by Proteus. In H.D.'s set of symbols, Egypt is an image for a certain kind of instinctual bondage. It is also associated, as we have seen, with Moravianism, H.D.'s childhood religion, and with primal sexuality.

The Priestess of Isis § 211

In *The Man Who Died* Lawrence gives a brilliant metaphoric description of H.D.'s relationships with Pound and Aldington. First we have an account of the Pound-H.D. relationship in terms of the woman's first sexual encounter. It occurred, as did H.D.'s relationship with Pound, when the woman was "a girl of nineteen, beautiful but unmarried." Lawrence writes: "When she was young the girl had known Caesar, and had shrunk from his eagle-like rapacity."[23]

The second characterization, that of the woman's relationship with Anthony, corresponds perfectly to H.D.'s account of her relationship with Aldington in the first book of her novel *Palimpsest,* where the woman is the slave or mistress of a Roman, Marcius Decius. Strong parallels also exist between Lawrence's characterizations of Anthony in *The Man Who Died* and of Antony in his *Aaron's Rod* ("Cleopatra But Not Antony"). Lawrence's portrait of the Aldington-H.D. relationship also corresponds to H.D.'s portrait of the Pilate-Veronica relationship in "Pilate's Wife."

> The golden Anthony had sat with her many a half-hour, in the splendour of his great limbs and glowing manhood, and talked with her of the philosophies and the gods. For he was fascinated as a child by the gods, though he mocked at them, and forgot them in his own vanity . . . But it was as he said: the very flower of her womb was cool, was almost cold, like a bud in shadow of frost, for all the flooding of his sunshine. So Anthony, respecting her father, who loved her, had left her.[24]

Aldington had likewise left H.D. Aldington's accusation that H.D. was frigid in her marriage is a recurrent theme of Aldington's and H.D.'s prose and poetry. The heroine's frigidity is the theme of John Cournos's book about H.D., *Miranda Masters.* Aldington's poems express the situation rather succinctly, with their images of marble and the motif of unrequited passion. In "To a Greek Marble" he writes:

> POTNIA, Potnia,
> White grave goddess,
> Pity my sadness
> O silence of Paros.
>
> I am not of these about thy feet,
> These garments and decorum;
> I am thy brother,
> Thy lover of aforetime crying to thee,
> And thou hearest me not

I have whispered thee in thy solitudes
Of our loves in Phrygia,
. . .

I have told thee of the hills
And the lisp of reeds
And the sun upon thy breasts.
And thou hearest me not,
Potnia, Potnia,
Thou hearest me not.[25]

In "Lesbia" Aldington expresses a similar sentiment.

GROW weary if you will, let me be sad.
Use no more speech now;
Let the silence spread gold hair above us,
Fold on delicate fold.
Use no more speech;
You had the ivory of my life to carve . . .

And Picus of Mirandola is dead;
And all the gods they dreamed and fabled of,
Hermes and Thoth and Christ are rotten now,
Rotten and dank . . .
And through it all I see your pale Greek face . . .[26]

The Man Who Died, which is not unrelated to the course of H.D.'s unsatisfying marriage, now returns to the subject of the first part of Lawrence's story — resurrection and rebirth. The woman in Lawrence's story asks, "Are all women born to be given to men?"

To which the old man [a philosopher] answered slowly: Rare women wait for the reborn man. For the lotus, as you know, will not answer to all the bright heat of the sun. But she curves her dark, hidden head in the depths, and stirs not. Till, in the night, one of those rare invisible suns that have been killed and shine no more, rises among the stars in unseen purple, and like the violet, sends its rare, purple rays out into the night. To these the lotus stirs as to a caress, and rises upwards through the flood, and lifts up her bent head, and opens with an expansion such as no other flower knows, and spreads her sharp rays of bliss, and offers her soft, gold depth such as no other flower possesses, to the penetration of the flooding, violet-dark sun that has died and risen and makes no show.[27]

The sun invoked here by Lawrence, the sun that has been killed, is an obvious allusion to the son who has died in part I — the son of God, the Christ figure. Lawrence seems to issue a warning and a command. "But for the golden brief day-suns of show such as

Anthony, and for the hard winter sons of power, such as Caesar, the lotus stirs not, nor will ever stir. Those will only tear open the bud. Ah, I tell you, wait for the reborn and wait for the bud to stir."[28]

In "Pilate's Wife" H.D. tells us that Veronica did not wait in that empty cavern for an answer. At the beginning of Lawrence's story the slave crouches in the rocks, naked, performing a sacrifice. The poet, Isis, detached and alone, watches the slaves. But the slave girl is really the woman in bondage to her instincts. Both slave and woman meet in the temple of Isis, in the poet's vision. In the poet's thought the instinct and the vision come together like the fragments of the body of Osiris gathered by Isis.

As Veronica in H.D.'s "Pilate's Wife" found a direction for her search in the cult of Isis, so the woman in *The Man Who Died* discovers a direction for her search in the temple of Isis.

> So she had waited, but the bud of her womb had never stirred. For all the men were soldiers or politicians in the Roman spell, assertive, manly, splendid apparently, but of an inward meanness, an inadequacy . . . And she was a woman to herself, she would not give herself to a surface glow, nor marry for reasons. She would wait for the lotus to stir.
>
> And then, in Egypt, she had found Isis, in whom she spelled her mystery.[29]

While the woman is performing a "last brief ritual to Isis," a man, a stranger, appears. "A stranger in a dark, broad hat rose from the corner of the temple steps, holding his hat in the wind. He was dark-faced, with a black pointed beard."[30] It is the same man who appeared in "The Escaped Cock."

The man asks the woman for shelter. He is identified with the slaves, of whom he was one; but now he appears in different guise or aspect. He is described as a vagabond, without home. The woman looks like the woman in the pictures Lawrence painted to accompany the story; she looks like H.D. "Her face was rather long and pale, her dusty blond hair was held under a thin gold net. She looked down on the vagabond with indifference. It was the same she had seen watching the slaves.[31]

He says he saw the temple "like a pale flower on the coast." At one level the woman herself is the temple, as in *Helen in Egypt* she herself is the writing. In one dimension the temple is the place from which the poetry is conceived. The scene described by Lawrence at this point of the story corresponds to the scene described by H.D. in *Bid Me to Live*. The man who sought shelter at her flat at Mecklenburgh Square was a stranger who had suffered a good deal, not the man she had known before. Lawrence's man who confronts the woman in her temple is a broken man, the man who had died. "She looked at him still with mistrust. There was a faint remote smile in the dark eyes lifted to her, though the face was hollow with suffering. The vagabond divined her with hesitation, and was mocking her." [32]

Lawrence describes the priestess as "a woman entangled in her own dream." [33] In *Bid Me to Live,* Rico says to Julia, "You are entangled in your own dream." [34]

At this point in Lawrence's story the man is led to the rock cavern, "a little gully in the rock, where, almost in darkness, was a small cave." Surrounding the cave is a forest "of the tall heaths that grew on the waste places of the coast, under the stone-pines." As in H.D.'s "picture" that she described to Lawrence, there is "a little basin of rock." Lawrence presents an erotic image: the "maidenhair fern fringed a dripping mouthful of water." The stranger is now directly equated with the man who had died: "The man who had died climbed out to the tip of the peninsula where the waves thrashed. It was rapidly getting dark, and the stars were coming out." [35]

The stranger, the man who had died, proceeds to eat. Another erotic image: "He took bread from his leather pouch, dipped it in the water of the tiny spring, and slowly ate." [36]

The prose of *The Man Who Died* is at this moment pure poetry. Lawrence seems to be less inhibited in the poetry that he can hide, as it were, in the prose. As in H.D.'s *Helen in Egypt,* when Helen meets Achilles on the edge of a desolate beach, stars are everywhere: "He looked once more at the bright stars in the pure, windy sky . . . Outside was brilliantly starry." There is an image of the bay, which invokes Lawrence's book of poems *Bay.* The breaking of the waves prefigures H.D.'s vision described in *Advent* — the meeting with someone named Peter Van Eck, which occurred in a dream. "I remember a dream that was real," says H.D. in *Helen in Egypt.* In Lawrence's story, "the sea was fair and pale blue, lovely in newness, and at last the wind was still, yet the waves broke white in the many rocks, and tore in the shingle of the little bay. The woman came slowly, towards her dream." [37]

The dream is then interrupted. The slave brings evil news: "The man is an escaped malefactor." "By what sign?" asks the woman. "Behold his hands and feet," says the slave. [38] We are, of course, now close to part I of Lawrence's story, "The Escaped Cock." We are also close to the prominent symbolic motif of H.D.'s childhood religion, with its concentration on Christ's wounds.

The woman sees the scars on the feet of the sleeping man. The scars are important to both parts of *The Man Who Died*. In part I Lawrence writes, "He went on, on scarred feet, neither of this world or the next."[39] The scars are, of course, the result of the crucifixion. But in both "Pilate's Wife" and *The Man Who Died* Christ does not die on the cross. He almost dies, but he is revived. The scars symbolize the transition from this world to the next, but as we have seen in part I, the next or other world is not some-where above the clouds but rather far below them — somewhere in a cave where consciousness passes from one's own world to the world of the other. The "other world" to which one crosses is a human reality. Thus, when the woman sees the man who has died she is moved from her dream, the confines of her own world: "For the first time, she was touched on the quick at the sight of a man, as if the tip of a fine flame of living had touched her. It was the first time. Men had roused all kinds of feelings in her, but never had touched her on the yearning quick of her womb, with the flame-tip of life."[40]

Lawrence's symbolism is overdetermined. The womb is the tomb, the death into which the man dies. The womb, the tomb, is the cave, which represents the primal sacrificial act of coition. Coitus is death. We wake into another life. "The man who had died woke up."[41]

The man is informed by the slave that the lady would like to speak with him "at the house of Isis." When she appears (or rather, reappears), the woman addresses him in Greek. He tells her his Greek is limited and asks if he may speak the common dialect, "vulgar Syrian." There are repeated references in "Pilate's Wife" to Memnonius's "awkward dialect." We recall, too, the dialect of Parkin and Mellors in *The First Lady Chatterley, John Thomas and Lady Jane,* and *Lady Chatterley's Lover.*

The woman again becomes aware of scars; this time she sees the scar on the man's hand. "See! the scar." The recognition of this, the mark of his suffering, seems to rouse her from her dream. She had not wanted to realize his suffering; she is afraid she too will suffer. He thanks her for his sleep; she bids him to look at Isis, whom Lawrence compares to a ship. (This image reappears in *Helen in Egypt,* where the eidolon upon the prow of the ship is an Isis figure.) The woman would have the man praise Isis to divert his attention from her; he does so in a kind of mock tone. We are reminded of Lawrence's "Isis" poem; the woman wants the man to think only of poetry. But she seems to be defending herself against a certain knowledge. In the sequence of events of Law-rence's story, Christ and Osiris are again equated. The woman continues to resist thinking about the scars because she does not want to wake from her dream (her self). But she is troubled. "But the woman was pondering, that this was the lost Osiris. She felt it in the quick of her soul. And her agitation was intense."[42]

It is one thing to seek, quite another to find. One searches within the circumscribed psychic boundaries of one's ego; when one finds, the ego boundaries give way like dams in a flood. One passes from one's own life into the other life, the other world. The woman thus attempts to defend herself from the suffering and the pain of finding her mate, but in spite of her initial resistance she becomes convinced that the stranger is in fact Osiris. "Stay! I am sure you are Osiris!"

"Not yet," he answers. But he promises to "sleep another night in the cave of the goats."[43] The man argues with himself. He too is agitated.

> Shall I give myself to this touch? Men have tortured me to death with their touch. Yet this girl of Isis is a tender flame of healing. I am a physician, yet I have no healing like the flame of this tender girl . . . How could I have been blind to the healing and the bliss in the crocus-like body of a tender woman! Ah tenderness! more terrible and lovely than the death I died . . .[44]

Tenderness again. "Dare I come into touch?" he asks himself. "For this is further than death. I have dared let them lay hands on me and put me to death. But dare I come into this tender touch of life? Oh, this is harder . . ."[45] The woman and the man continue to wonder whether to come together. She meets him on the peninsula by the bay: "She passed intent through the door in the wall, on the bay."[46] She orders her slaves to prepare a bed. There is much commotion about this preparation, and Lawrence writes a good deal of the comings and goings of the slaves — all pure poetry. The overseer, the slaves, the myrtle on the bed, the wine jar, the oil jar, the terra-cotta drinking cup are all part of the scene. The man and the woman are full of desire. "Best of all was her tender desire for him, like sunshine, so soft and still. 'She is like sunshine upon me,' he said to himself, stretching his limbs. 'I have never before stretched my limbs in such sunshine as her desire for me.'"[47]

But the man is "haunted by fear of the outer world," the world of the slaves, of her overseer (which may be a reference to Aldington). "If they can, they will kill us, he said to himself. But there is a law of the sun which protects us." The only law that protects such lovers is the law of poetry. The man says, "I have risen naked and branded. But if I am naked enough for this contact, I have not died in vain."[48] Brave words. Does this son of the sun have the courage of his words? The lady comes.

> So at last he saw the light of her silk lanthorn swinging, coming intermittent between the trees, yet coming swiftly. She was alone, and near, the light softly swishing on her mantle-hem. And he trembled with fear and with joy, saying to himself: "I am almost more afraid of this touch than I was of death. For I am more nakedly exposed to it."[49]

The man and the woman are now in the shrine. "She unlocked the door of the shrine, and he followed her. Then she latched the door shut again."[50] This motif, the lovers inside the shrine and the latching of the door, reappears throughout H.D.'s work, significantly in her poem "Vale-Ave."* In "Vale-Ave" the temple is a hut, and now we recognize this setting as a lover's meeting place. H.D. writes:

> I hardly knew my Lord, true we met
> in a sudden frenzy, parted in the dark,
> and all the rest was mystery and a portent . . .
> but still enchantment rose
> out of the sea, when in the
> centurion's tent
> or by the dunes in a fisher's hut
> following inexorable destiny, we met.[51]

The brazier appears again in *The Man Who Died* ("Was there ever such a brazier?"). The woman flings incense. The man compares her courage of life to his courage of death. They are opposites. She is Greek, and full of Greek rhythms. The woman who serves Isis is a poet.

> So she tipped in her strange forward-swaying rhythm before the goddess. Then she broke into a murmur of Greek, which he could not understand. And, as she murmured, her swaying softly subsided, like a boat on a sea that grows still. And as he watched her, he saw her soul in its aloneness, and its female difference. He said to himself: "How different she is from me, how strangely different! She is afraid of me, and my male difference. She is getting herself naked and clear of her fear. How sensitive and softly alive she is, with a life so different from mine! How beautiful with a soft strange courage, of life, so different from my courage of death!

---

*In "Thorn Thicket," a memoir written in 1960, H.D. identifies "Vale Ave" as the *"Madrigal* poem sequence." It was written between April 15 and May 13, 1957.

What a beautiful thing, like the heart of a rose, like the core of a flame. She is making herself completely penetrable. Ah, how terrible to fail her, or to trespass on her.[52]

He will not fail her, even though she sees the ghost of death in him. She recognizes him as the lost Osiris and as Christ. She must tend to his wounds, actually face the fact of the crucifixion he has endured. He endured it, in a very real sense, for her sake, but he will not tell her so. He remembers "the nails, the holes, the cruelty . . ."[53] But he comes to understand, through her, that in his life as savior of mankind he was out of touch with life. It is the woman who serves Isis, the feminine impulse which embodies the life instinct, who brings him back to life. "There dawned on him the reality of the soft warm love which is in touch."[54]

What sort of wounds are these? What sort of a healing is this? In the rather bad poetry of the Moravian hymns, the first wound is circumcision. "With his 'first wound' which occasioned his first suffering, Christ made a covenant with God:"[55]

> Therefore let all our boys classes,
> In remembrance of dead Jesus;
> And through his boy's — age's merit,
> His first wound's full bliss inherit.
>
> . . .
>
> But to those hearts dear and precious
> Of the choir-boys fellowship,
> Who close to the corpse of Jesus
> And his bitter passion keep,
>
> Shows the first wound's power
> In the Covenant hour,
> How their limbs obtain by this, corpse-likeness,
> And their mind is made like his.[56]

We mention the Moravian mysteries here to make the point that wounds are associated in at least one religious tradition (H.D.'s) with circumcision, and thus symbolically with castration — symbolic castration, or impotence.

The man who died has lost something. As Achilles says to Helen in *Helen in Egypt,* "I thought I had lost that."[57] At a dramatic moment in Lawrence's story, the woman becomes attentive to the man's wound. Lawrence's description reminds us of the Moravian hymn: "She was stooping now, looking at the scar in the soft flesh of the socket of his side, a scar deep and like an eye sore with endless weeping, just in the soft socket above the hip. It was here that his blood had left him, and his water, and his essential seed."[58]

This poet/priestess with her Greek cadences restores the man to life. "The woman was trembling softly and murmuring in Greek. And he in the recurring dismay of having died, and in the anguished perplexity of having tried to force life, felt his wounds crying aloud, and the deep places of his body howling again: I have been murdered, and I lent myself to murder . . . The woman, silent now, but quivering, laid oil in her hand and put her palm over the wound in his right side . . . In silence, she softly rhythmically chafed the scar with oil." [59]

This is a priestess's task; the myrrh or ointment which she bring is on one level poetry, and the motions of her poems are rhythmic. The man begins to gather strength as her power surrounds him. He comes alive: "As she gradually gathered power, and passed in a girdle round him to the opposite scar, gradually warmth began to take the place of the cold terror, and he felt: 'I am going to be warm again, and I am going to be whole! I shall be warm like the morning. I shall be a man. It doesn't need understanding. It needs newness. She brings me newness.' " [60]

In the Moravian tradition scores of hymns are devoted to Christ's wounds and the healing of them. As we have mentioned, the central symbolic motif of D. H. Lawrence's *The Man Who Died* corresponds with this central symbolic motif of the Moravian devotions. It must be said that, from a critical point of view, Lawrence's excesses often parallel those of the Moravian liturgy. For example, Lawrence writes:

> Having chafed all his lower body with oil, his belly, his buttocks, even the slain penis and the sad stones, having worked with her slow intensity of a priestess, so that the sounds of his wounds grew dimmer and dimmer, suddenly she put her breast against the wound in his left side, and her arms round him, folding over the wound in his right side, and she pressed him to her, in a power of living warmth, like in the folds of a river. And the wailing died out altogether. [61]

"The sounds of his wounds" suggests that the man's wounds are symbols of Lawrence's poems. The woman's poems heal; his are wounds. Lawrence in fact compares the woman's poems to flowers. In the temple of Isis, we will remember, "the columns rise to the swollen lotus-bud of Egypt." What does Lawrence see in this poetry? He sees, H.D. tells us in *The Flowering of the Rod,* what the wise man saw.

>   . . . literally as his hand just did-not touch her hand,
>   and as she drew the scarf toward her,

the speck, fleck, grain or seed
opened like a flower.

And the flower, thus contained
in the infinitely tiny grain or seed,

opened petal by petal, a circle,
and each petal was separate

yet still held, as it were,
by some force of attraction

to its dynamic centre;
and the circle went on widening

and would go on opening
he knew, to infinity,

but before he was lost,
out-of-time completely,

he saw the islands of the Blest,
he saw the Hesperides,

he saw the circles and circles of islands
about the lost centre-island, Atlantis;

he saw what the sacrosanct legend
said still existed,

he saw the lands of the blest,
the promised lands, lost;

he, in that half-second saw
the whole scope and plan

of our civilization on this
his and our earth, before Adam.

And he saw it all as if enlarged under a sun-glass;
he saw it in minute detail,

the cliffs, the wharves, the citadel,
he saw the ships and the sea roads crossing

and all the rivers and bridges and dwelling-houses
and the terraces and the built-up inner gardens;

he saw the many pillars and the Hearth-stone
and the very fire on the Great-hearth,

and through it, there was a sound as of many waters,
rivers flowing and fountains and sea-waves washing the
    sea-rocks,

and though it was all on a very grand scale,
yet it was small and intimate,

Paradise
before Eve . . .[62]

Lawrence saw much of this vision in *The Man Who Died,* where he depicts the man's coming to consciousness as a new dawn. "Then slowly, slowly, in the perfect darkness of his inner man, he felt the stir of something coming: A dawn, a new sun. A new sun was coming up in him, in the perfect inner darkness of himself."[63] The opening of the lotus flower corresponds to the resurrection, the dawn. What Lawrence sees is that the resurrection is intimately related to the opening of the flower. In "Pilate's Wife" H.D. writes of the vision of the condemned man in precisely these terms.

As we read H.D.'s *Sea Garden* we find flowers that open on page after page. In the unfolding of the flower is the revelation of the mystery. Each flower (or each flower poem) is a hieroglyph through which we gain knowledge. "The heaven is open to all who read."

H.D. said that *The Man Who Died* reconciled Lawrence to her. In this text she read, rightly, an affirmation of her work and her very being as well as an affirmation of their relationship. In *The Man Who Died* Lawrence is able to affirm the suffering, the passion. "And his death and his passion of sacrifice were all as nothing to him now, he knew only the crouching fulness of the woman there, the soft white rock of life . . . 'On this rock I build my life.' "

> The deep-folded penetrable rock of the living woman! The woman, hiding her face. Himself bending over, powerful and new like dawn.
> He crouched to her, and he felt the blaze of his manhood and his power rise up in his loins, magnificent.
> "I am risen!"[64]

Again Lawrence emphasizes that the opening of the flower is inextricably related to the resurrection. This vision, Lawrence would tell us, is reality: " 'Lo!' he said. 'This is beyond prayer.' It was the deep, interfolded warmth, warmth living and penetrable, the woman, the heart of the rose! 'My mansion is the intricate warm rose, my joy is this blossom!' "[65]

Lawrence's *Aaron's Rod* and H.D.'s *The Flowering of the Rod* come from the same source. "She looked up at him suddenly, her face like a lifted light, wistful, tender, her eyes like many wet flowers."[66] H.D. says the wise man saw "Paradise/before Eve." Lawrence says: "And he drew her to his breast with a passion of tenderness and consuming desire, and a last thought: 'My hour is upon me I am taken unawares — ' So he knew her, and was one with her."[67]

The scars become the man's atonement. Atonement means concord, reconciliation. In Christian terms atonement means the reconciliation of man and God. In the Moravian theology the atonement is the redeeming effect of Christ's incarnation. "They [the scars] are my atonement with you," says Lawrence to the woman.[68]

As Lawrence's story continues, the man and the woman continue to meet in the cave; "the contact was perfected and fulfilled." Lawrence writes: "How full of curves and folds like an invisible rose of dark-petalled openness, that shows where dew touches its darkness!"[69] The image is of blossoming. H.D. writes in her *Tribute to the Angels,* "a half-burnt-out apple-tree/ blossoming."[70] Lawrence writes:

> Plum-blossom blew from the trees, the time of the narcissus was past, anemones lit up the ground and were gone, the perfume of bean-field was in the air. All changed, the blossom of the universe changed its petals and swung round to look another way. The spring was fulfilled, a contact was established, the man and the woman were fulfilled of one another, and departure was in the air.[71]

H.D. writes:

> This is the flowering of the rood,
> this is the flowering of the reed,
>
> where Uriel, we pause to give
> thanks that we rise again from death and live.[72]

Lawrence's man asks the woman, "Hast thou conceived?" He says, "Thou art like a tree whose green leaves follow the blossoms, full of sap." Yes, she tells him, she is with child: "I am with young by thee." They are pleased. But he asks her, "Where wilt thou bear the child, for I am naked of all but life."[73]

They agree to part. He must go. Trouble is coming to him from the slaves (his friends, his public): "But he said: 'Not twice! They shall not twice lay hands on me. They shall not now profane the touch in me. My wits against theirs.' "[74] The resurrected man of part II of Lawrence's story will be discreet. He will no longer preach about love in such a way that the slaves, the populace, can understand him. He will cover his tracks. He knows that if he stays he will become a victim of Roman justice, the justice of the state. He will not be twice crucified.

He bids the woman to live in peace with her child, and promises to return. " 'If I stay,' he said, 'they will betray me to the Romans and to their justice. But I will never be betrayed again. So when

The Priestess of Isis § 223

I am gone, live in peace with the growing child. And I shall come again; all is good between us, near or apart. Ths suns come back in their seasons: and I shall come again.' "[75] Inspired by Lawrence, H.D. wrote in *Helen in Egypt:*

> I only saw him from the ramparts
> and on the desolate beach,
> and we talked apart in the temple;
>
> true, we followed a track in the sand
> though we spoke but little,
> and the absolute final spark,
>
> the ember, the Star, had no personal,
> intimate fervour; was it desire?
> it was Love, it was Death,
>
> but what followed before, what after?
> a thousand-thousand days,
> as many mysterious nights,
>
> and multiplied to infinity,
> the million personal things,
> things remembered, forgotten,
>
> remembered again, assembled
> and re-assembled in different order
> as thoughts and emotions,
>
> the sun and the seasons changed . . .
>
> and if I think of a child of Achilles,
> it is not Pyrrhus, his son,
> they called Neoptolemus,
>
> nor any of the host that claimed as father,
> the Myrmidon's Lord and Leader,
> but the child in Chiron's cave;
>
> and if I remember a child that stared
> at a stranger and the child's name is Hermione
> it is not Hermione
>
> I would stoop and shelter,
> remembering the touch on my shoulder,
> the enchanter's power.[76]

Lawrence had said, "The suns come back in their seasons." H.D. wrote, "The sun and seasons changed." As H.D. says, "the million personal things" would be "remembered again, assembled/and re-assembled in different order." That is, she and Lawrence would continue to write.

At the end of Lawrence's story the man is discovered by the

Roman overseer, the Aldington figure. A symbol of the repressive forces of civilization, the overseer sees the man's "gross and scandalous mysticism" as a threat to the state, not to mention to his own masculine pride. Lawrence's scene corresponds in great detail to the taking of the prisoner under Pilate's order in H.D.'s "Pilate's Wife." The Roman overseer says: "Lead softly to the goat's den. And Lysippus shall throw the net over the malefactor while he sleeps, and we will bring him before justice, and the Lady of Isis shall know nothing of it."[77]

Both Lawrence and H.D. are aware that the religion of Isis affirmed in *The Man Who Died* and in "Pilate's Wife" is a heresy. This kind of thinking is perceived as a threat to the orthodoxy of the Christian church. It is, moreover, the same kind of heresy as that of the Moravians. In "The Mystery," H.D.'s Moravian novel, she addresses this subject directly, writing of the martyrdom of those who follow the heretic religion. She might be speaking of the persecution of D. H. Lawrence.

> I would only say that your Mysticism is naturally repulsive to men, who would at all costs elevate the Father above all, and above all, above the Mother. Your poem to that effect — I will not quote it — was enough to burn you at the stake, like that John Huss whom they bound, outside here by the Cathedral. Your heresy goes deeper than his, but you are an older soul, my Dresden Socrates, and the Dominicans had a part in your instruction. You worshipped the Wounds of Our Lord — the Wounds *in excelsis* in Our Lord's side as the *rosa mystica*. This, my friend, is gross and scandalous mysticism, as the Protestant court decided.[78]

In part II of *The Man Who Died* the emphasis is on the mother, the goddess, rather than on God the Father. Isis corresponds to Mary Magdalene (Madeleine) of part I, but in part II Lawrence stresses the Immaculate Conception and the Virgin Birth (as he interprets these events). The fact of paternity in part I is replaced in part II by the feminine reality, the mystery.

At the end of Lawrence's story we are presented with the return of the slave. "Art thou not that slave who possessed the maiden under the eyes of Isis? Art thou not the youth? Speak!"[79] The slave and the man who died escape together. The former is the double of the latter, the other aspect of man as son of God.

They sail off in a boat, which will reappear in Lawrence's late poetry as "The Ship of Death." It also appears as a central symbol in *Helen in Egypt* — the death ship of Osiris. Thus, *The Man Who Died*, like "Pilate's Wife," ends with the Christ figure's being carried away in a boat. Lawrence writes:

I have sowed the seed of my life and my resurrection, and put my touch forever upon the choice woman of this day, and I carry her perfume in my flesh like essence of roses. She is dear to me in the middle of my being. But the gold and flowing serpent is coiling up again to sleep at the root of my tree . . . So let the boat carry me. Tomorrow is another day.[80]

In the opening sentences of *Lady Chatterley's Lover* D. H. Lawrence wrote, "Ours is essentially a tragic age, so we refuse to take it tragically. The cataclysm has happened, we are among the ruins."[81] *The Man Who Died* does not have a happy ending; the D. H. Lawrence–H.D. relationship did not have a happy ending. The literary output that their relationship ignited, however, was enormous. But the question remains: To what extent did the realities described in these works occur somewhere, somehow, in historical time at a particular place or location, and to what extent was the H.D.–D. H. Lawrence vision conceived and born within the temple of twin minds?

III

CROSSING
THE LINE

23

"Notes on Thought and Vision"

DURING HER PREGNANCY H.D. learned a hard lesson about the men in her life; their possessive instincts were strong, but their nurturing instincts were not. She was left alone. True, Pound was present, briefly, at St. Faith's Nursing Home in London, "pounding, pounding" with his cane: "My only criticism is that this is not my child."[1]

In the spring of 1918, her marriage in shambles and her relationship with Lawrence all but concluded, H.D. sought a place of refuge and seclusion and found some peace at last in Cornwall as a houseguest of Cecil Gray.

This spring and early summer were significant for a number of reasons. H.D. found time and space to write in the attic room provided by Gray. It was here that she began her work on her Euripides translations, *Hippolytus Temporizes,* published in 1927, and *Ion,* finally published in 1937. It was during her stay in Cornwall that she met Winifred Ellerman (Bryher), a person who was to become an important part of the rest of her life. Deeply moved by the poetry of *Sea Garden,* Bryher wrote to H.D. in early July 1918 that she would like to meet her, and H.D. invited her to Cornwall. Following their meeting Bryher became infatuated with H.D. In her novel *Two Selves,* Bryher describes this first encounter:

> The Phoenician path stopped at a grey cottage that faced the south-blue sea. Familiar yellow covers, French books, were piled at an open window. Better not to try to find . . . oh, take a chance on adventure.
> This was the place. She knocked.
> She was too old to be disappointed if an elderly woman in glasses

bustled out. Poets, of course, were not what they wrote about. It was the mind that mattered.

A tall figure opened the door. Young. A spear flower if a spear could bloom. She looked up into eyes that had the sea in them, the fire and the colour and the splendour of it. A voice all wind and gull notes said:

"I was waiting for you to come."[2]

In early summer 1918, H.D. conceived a child in Cornwall. The precise circumstances of the conception are a mystery — a mystery H.D. would bequeath to the world, for she consistently refused to name the father.

The war had been easy on no one, and was harder on some than on others. H.D. did not expect to survive the birth of her child; her deepest fear was that she would survive but the child would not. She could not bear to lose a second baby. But they did survive, both mother and child. Bryher helped her through the ordeal. And Bryher helped her to nurture and rear her daughter, Frances Perdita, in the difficult years ahead.

Winifred Ellerman helped H.D. too in her work. Beginning with "Notes on Thought and Vision," written with Bryher in the Scilly Isles in 1919, and through all the short stories, novellas, and novels published during the twenties and thirties, the presence of Bryher in H.D.'s work is strongly felt. The companionship the two women shared would help H.D. through many of the most serious crises of her life. To underestimate the significance of Bryher's friendship would be seriously to misunderstand H.D.'s life as a writer. After their trip to Greece together in 1920, H.D. spent a good deal of the rest of her life with Bryher and her family and friends. By introducing H.D. to a whole new world of experience, travel, and society, Bryher helped her to create a new life independent of her companions of the Imagist years (1911–1919).

H.D.'s "Notes on Thought and Vision" is her only fully developed essay on poetic principles. In these notes H.D. expresses a poetic doctrine that is compatible with modern poetic theory informed by both Sigmund Freud and Giambattista Vico — that "memory is the mother, begetter of all drama, idea, music, science or song."[3] As Vico, James Joyce's philosopher, expressed it in his *New Science,* "Imagination is nothing but extended or compounded memory."[4]

While modern, H.D.'s poetic theory is not new; her vision is also Platonic. "Socrates' whole doctrine of vision was a doctrine of love," writes H.D. While Lawrence was writing at 44 Mecklenburgh Square, H.D. watched a plane tree in the background (see *Bid Me to Live*). As in Plato's *Phaedrus,* the mysteries of love and vision are apprehended by H.D. in the presence of the tree. "We must be 'in love' before we can understand the mysteries of vision," she says.[5]

H.D.'s "Notes on Thought and Vision" really presents a doctrine of sublimation, but it is a feminist doctrine. The poem, she says, is born. H.D. refers to her writing as a whole as a "matrix." The first meaning of this word is, of course, "womb." A matrix is a place or enveloping element within which something originates, takes form, or develops. It is that within which a form is embedded, and that which gives form or origin to something enclosed or embedded in it. The consciousness that results in a poem is born from the matrix or womb. In "Notes on Thought and Vision" H.D. tells us: "I first realized this state of consciousness in my head. I visualize it just as well now, centered in the love-region of the body or placed like a fetus in the body."[6]

In this essay H.D. describes "the swing from normal consciousness to abnormal consciousness" as she experienced it in her creative life. By "abnormal consciousness" she means the supernormal consciousness of a poet's perception; her word for it is "over-mind." She is, of course, speaking about sublimation. She admits that sublimation is "accompanied by grinding discomfort of mental agony."[7]

The creative act, says H.D., requires an inseminating spirit. "We begin with sympathy of thought . . . the minds of the two lovers merge, interchange in sympathy of thought . . . The love region is excited by the appearance or beauty of the loved one, its energy not dissipated in physical relations, takes on its character of mind."[8]

Having been abandoned by or having broken with the men in her life, H.D. would win her final victory through artistic expression — sublimation. She would later identify with Niké, the Greek symbol of "Winged Victory." This image is not unrelated to the wings described in Plato's *Phaedrus*. The difference is that H.D. is a woman, and it is female sexuality and the act of giving birth that she presents as the matrix or source of creativity. Remembering her experience — "emotion recollected in tranquillity" — her art would become her life. Her friend Bryher would help her to achieve this victory. Through her work she would win back what the men in her life and the social structure itself had denied her: a sense of self-worth and a position of respect in the world.

In a turning of the tables H.D. describes how she will use her experience for the purposes of art. *He* will become *her* muse. She will combine her own experience with the tradition; centuries of literary presences will serve as models. H.D. is saying that there is no biological reason that women cannot be great artists; women, too, have life energies and ought to be free to direct those energies to art and the creation of world consciousness rather than only into sex and birth, if they so choose. H.D. recognizes that women have been excluded from the realm of art only because they have been culturally conditioned to be slaves to men. As Pound had put it some fifteen years earlier, "You are a poem, though your poem's naught." H.D. now understands Pound's judgment as a traditional pronouncement about the proper role of women in the creative process. But the woman artist as well as the man can do as Lo-fu did. "Lo-fu was a poet. To him that apple branch, outside in the orchard, existed as an approach to something else . . . The body of a man is a means of approach."[9]

Of course, the traditional role of the woman is to be the muse, the object of memory which the poet uses as a means of approach to a "higher reality," the more objective realm of experience which is the goal of all true art. In her "Notes on Thought and Vision" H.D. states simply that the prerogatives of thought and vision are not in any way limited to men. The right sort of mind, male or female, receives the artistic image as a message of a definite pattern to be apprehended in and of itself. Art is the end of experience, not the other way around. The expression of beauty in the moment of artistic creation is an end in itself, because to create beauty is to perceive beauty; to create art is to transform one's own consciousness and the world to an objective plane of perception and experience. Of the Delphic charioteer as a work of art, H.D. says:

> This figure has been created by a formula arrived at consciously or unconsciously.
> If we had the right sort of brain, we would receive a definite message from that figure, like dots and lines picked off by one receiving station, received and translated into definite thoughts by another telegraphic centre.[10]

This idea of sending messages like dots and dashes from one center to another will recur in H.D.'s experience — most notably in her Corfu vision and later, as metaphor, in her discussion of the messages exchanged with the fictional Lord Howell in her novel "Magic Ring." "There is no trouble about art," she writes. "It is appreciators we want."[11]

In "Notes on Thought and Vision" man as muse is to be understood in an impersonal dimension — impersonal and transcendental.

The body of the Greek boy, Polycleitus used for his Diuademenos, was as impersonal a thing as a tree. He used the body instead of a tree. That boy's body was, of course, capable of human passions but Polycleitus' approach to that body was not through the human passions.

But of course he was in love with it just as Lo-fu was in love with the pine branch and Leonardo with the boy's face or the Galilean with the field lilies.[12]

According to the cultural norms of her era, H.D. assumed male prerogatives in refusing to play the passive role of the muse and in taking on the creative and imaginative role of the artist. It is of course extraordinarily sexist, and in our day downright silly, to believe that only men are capable of thought and vision, that artistic activity is "wholly phallic." Yet it is not a confusion about their sexuality or an affirmation of transsexuality that has led women writers until very recently to assume pseudonyms; rather, it is a realistic assessment of the masculine politics of power and suppression in the formation of a culture — what Pound called "the tradition."

H.D.'s own experience with thought and vision, the development of what she calls her "over-mind," began sometime during her first pregnancy, in late 1914 and early 1915. She thus associates the birth of artistic consciousness with the physical act of giving birth. The one is not, however, a substitute for the other, although a common set of metaphors can be used to describe all creative acts.

"Is it easier for a woman to attain this state of consciousness than for a man?" asks H.D.[13] In her view, the birth of life is on one level the birth of a human child, on another level the birth of a literary child. But neither experience excludes the other. These separate dimensions may in fact enhance and enrich one another; each may bring the other within the realm of possibility.

It is H.D.'s theory in "Notes on Thought and Vision" that the moment of artistic creativity is one of discovery, not entirely different in kind from scientific discovery. And it is memory that is the source or matrix of artistic birth. Thus the moment of artistic creativity is a moment of knowledge; it is also a moment of recovery of a more primal connection to life. "When we are 'born again' we begin not as a child but as the very first germs that grow into a child."[14] At the instant of creation we are recovering the truth of our own experience, our own soul.

H.D.'s concept of art is informed by Plato but also by a more ancient, feminine wisdom. The male spirit inseminates; the artistic vision is born from the matrix, the feminine center. "The spirit, we realize, is a seed . . . This is the mystery of Demeter, the Earth Mother." And every person, regardless of sex, can write, every person "can till the field, can clear weeds from about the stems of flowers." Every person "can water his own little plot, can strive to quiet down the overwrought tension of his body." [15]

The attainment of this state of consciousness is in some sense something that just happens to us. But once we are in the state of creativity, it is "sheer, hard brainwork" to maintain and record the vision. It is *not* a matter of refusing physical love for art. H.D. makes no such pronouncement. But it *is* a matter of choosing the dimension in which we will live.

> There are two ways of escaping the pain and despair of life, and the rarest, most subtle, danger and ensnaring gift life can bring us, relationship with another person — love.
>
> One way is to kill that love in one's heart. To kill love — to kill life.
>
> The other way is to accept that love, to accept the snare, to accept the pricks, the thistle.
>
> To accept life — but that is dangerous.
>
> It is also dangerous not to accept life. [16]

H.D. had accepted love and life and its consequences. Now she would take upon herself a task of another order; she would devote her life to art. The decision was made with Bryher in the Scilly Isles in 1919. H.D. was thirty-two years old.

Professor and Mrs. Doolittle on the porch of their
home in Upper Darby, Pennsylvania, c. 1910

H. D. at home with her five brothers: Gilbert, Harold,
Alfred (standing), Eric, Charles (seated on floor),
c. 1902

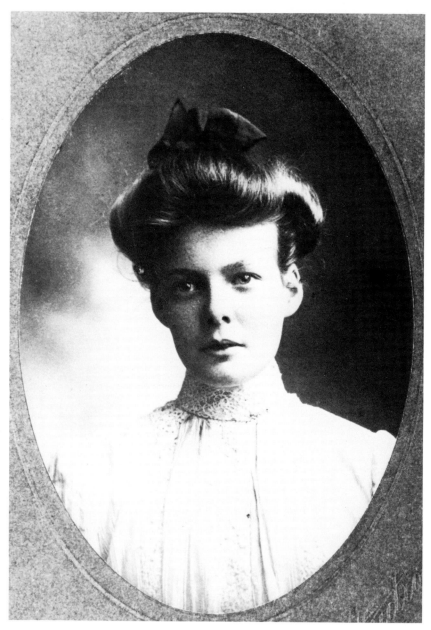

H. D.'s high school graduation picture, 1904

Ezra Weston Pound,   Philadelphia, Pa.
" Ezra "
" Bib's" pride. Leader of the anvil chorus at
the Commons. Oh, how he throws those
legs! Peroxide blonde.

Ezra Pound's senior picture in the
Hamilton College yearbook, 1905

Ezra Pound by Alvin Langdon Coburn, 1913.
Appears as the frontispiece for *Lustra*.

D. H. Lawrence by
W. G. Parker, 1913
"I first met Lawrence in
August 1914 at the time of
the actual outbreak of war;
... It was the only time I saw
this unbearded manifestation
of Lawrence."

Richard Aldington by
Man Ray, c. 1920

H.D., c. 1921. Inscribed to Marianne Moore.

Bryher in Capri, 1922

Bryher in Capri, 1922

H.D. and Perdita, Capri, 1922

Bryher and Perdita, London,
1925

H. D. and Perdita, Switzerland, 1923

H. D. and Perdita, London, 1925

Great-Aunt Laura and Grandmother Doolittle (H. D.'s aunt
and mother) with Perdita, Switzerland, 1923

D. H. Lawrence by Edward Weston, c. 1925
"I had this picture in Vienna. I think the original was on the
Taos volume. I had it on my table in the *Hotel Regina,* during
the time of my sessions with Professor Freud."

D. H. Lawrence's painting of
Dorothy "Arabella" Yorke

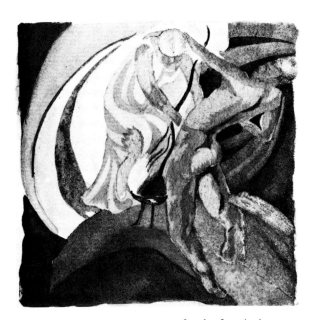

Painting by D. H. Lawrence for the frontispiece
of the Black Sun Press edition of
The Escaped Cock, 1929
"Is this the image that he re-created as Isis, the
priestess in *The Man Who Died*?"

Freud in his study in Vienna
"I think if the chow hadn't liked me I would have left,
I was so scared by Oedipus..."

Sir John Ellerman and young Winifred (Bryher)
in London, c. 1903

Bryher in Switzerland, 1954

Ezra Pound on his release from
St. Elizabeth's Hospital, 1958

to ope-n a tiny bank-account for her here ?

They have them for children,   under" guardian" .

If you could let me know her NAME, I mean for

pass-port purposes- her legal name, nd give me a

little note - or I could arrange through my lawyer .

What do you think ?

I am very proud and happy that the "fleece of gold"

continues.

I will write again. I dash off letters, after my own

bad typing.

I have no good poems by the way.

The youth you sepk of, is I presume L. 3rd ? I had a

note from Merrill Moore saying he might be in Vard or

in Lon-don.   Do you know if he is likel-y to come

here ? There seems very little to offer- but if I know in

time, I might dig up one/or two"contacts" for him.

I presume he will go direct, Elliot.

Do let me hear again.

Love

"Dryad"

Letter from H. D. to Pound,
dated 4/6/38, with
Dryad signature

H. D.'s bookplate

LOVED OF LOVE

HD

H.D. in 1956

24

The Man
on the Boat

IT WAS TO H.D.'s advantage as an artist that her consciousness was delayed in times of severe shock; her sense of irony preceded her rage and in some very real sense mitigated or refocused it. With no focus or outlet, rage is a futile and destructive emotion; but if one can refocus such emotion in artistic presentation, even the most devastating personal blows can have creative and rewarding results. In the creative process the tables are turned at some very deep psychic level; the victim becomes the victor through her or his creative expression.

"Shock can . . . uncover buried treasure," H.D. wrote in "The Gift."[1] In H.D.'s case the shock of the war years, the death of her brother and father, and her own near death of pneumonia in 1919, the birth of her child, and the abrupt termination of her relationships with virtually all the men in her life in 1918–1919 led to a nervous and physical breakdown. As she explains in *Advent,* she had "forgotten" the years of her life between 1910 and 1920. That whole war period, forgotten. Suppressed. Repressed. "It was as if a curtain had dropped . . . between the ten years of my life away from America, and the then (spring 1920) present."[2]

Part of the process of recovery was a trip she took with Bryher to Greece aboard one of Bryher's father's ships, the *Borodino,* in 1920. On this trip H.D. had two visions — hallucinations or waking dreams, if you will — in which she projected directly, in an unmediated form, images of her creative experience. These visions were traumatic experiences in themselves, but they were full of "buried treasure."

In *Advent* H.D. speaks of an encounter with a man on the deck of the *Borodino* as a dream, but in 1920 she did not experience it that way; at the time, the experience was too vivid. "We do not always know when we are dreaming."[3]

Freud's way of helping H.D. to remember her forgotten years so that she could come to terms (in the psychoanalytic sense) with her own experience was to help her to understand these visions. H.D. had apparently held on to the visions until she could deal with them safely. She was so very worn down physically that she was sometimes unable to cope with the life she had lost (she had no one with whom to share these experiences until she began working with Freud), and this inability to confide fully in anyone, including Bryher, added a component of mental fatigue to her physical exhaustion. She tried to write of these visions, but she was unwilling to bring them to the surface in psychoanalytic sessions that she had with Mary Chadwick and Hanns Sachs before her sessions with Sigmund Freud. In *Advent* she tells of how she began to discuss them with Freud:

> I tried to outline several experiences I had had on my first trip to Greece. I have tried to write of these experiences. I [sic] fact, it is the fear of losing them, forgetting them, or just giving them up as neurotic fantasies, residue of the war, confinement and the epidemic, that drives me on to begin again and again a fresh outline of the "novel."[4]

The novel of which H.D. speaks is the one she began in 1921 with "Paint It Today" and which she finally completed in 1949 with *Bid Me to Live*. Why did she have to write and rewrite that novel in so many different settings and styles of presentation? She tells us: "I can decide that my experiences were the logical outcome of illness, separation from my husband, and loss of the friendship with Lawrence; but even so I have no technique with which to deal with the vision."[5]

The psychologist Havelock Ellis and a man named Peter Rodeck were aboard the *Borodino* on the trip to Greece in 1920, invited by Sir John Ellerman; "Dada" (Ellerman) did not believe that women should travel unchaperoned. The powerful dreamvision of an encounter with a man which H.D. experienced on the ship was not unrelated to Peter Rodeck, but it related primarily to events of the World War I period which she had repressed. By the time H.D. wrote *Advent* in 1948, from notes she had made during her psychoanalysis with Freud, she had realized that Peter Rodeck (whom she called Peter Van Eck in *Advent*) was, as she wrote much later to Bryher, a smokescreen. What actually happened is that H.D. met Lawrence in a dream on board the ship.

By the time H.D. had completed her analysis with Freud, she

had come to speak of Peter Van Eck as a conscious persona for D. H. Lawrence. In "The Sword Went Out to Sea," an unpublished novel she completed in 1947, the narrator says: "I did not want to talk about my writing, but I felt frustrated when I looked back and recalled the number of times I had rewritten that novel of myself and Peter Van Eck."[6]

Forgetting — repressing — and not talking about it. This is, of course, what Freud would need to work on with her. How extraordinary that he would be able to help her. Before her first meeting with him she sorted through the rough drafts of the novel, making ready, as she put it, "for a last voyage out." Significantly, she could not bring herself to destroy the early drafts. She writes: "Sorting books, manuscripts, notebooks, I felt as if I were indeed making ready for a last voyage out. But in the general house-cleaning, I did not get on any further with the 'novel,' though I could not bring myself to destroy the last rough copies. There it is hanging over me, that 'novel.' "[7]

In *Advent* she writes about the vision or dream. It concerns a man on board the *Borodino*, about fourteen years older than she was at the time, by the name of Mr. Van Eck. But "the man on the *Borodino,* a certain Mr. Van Eck (we will call him for convenience) was a man on the *Borodino,* but the Man was not Mr. Van Eck."[8]

H.D. describes the *Borodino* as being "more than sea-worthy." She tells us that the ship, which had a double hull, had been used as a mail ship by the navy during the war. Bryher's father, who was a financier and shipping magnate, had personally selected this particular ship from his fleet for the voyage of his daughter and her friend. Nevertheless, traveling to Greece by boat was very dangerous after World War I. "There were still floating mines everywhere."[9]

H.D. tells Freud of how she met the man who was not Mr. Van Eck.

> It is true I thought he was Mr. Van Eck but there was a catch. I knew that from the beginning. Mr. Van Eck had a startling heavy scar above his left eyebrow; it was noted in his passport, under any noticcable marks. The captain I remember spoke of it. The Man on the boat had no scar above his left eyebrow.[10]

Like Mr. Van Eck, H.D.'s father had had a scar. In her beautiful memoir of her family, "The Gift," which is a series of essays or family portraits, H.D. talks about the serious injury that left a scar on her father's head. It had been a terrible trauma for the family; her father's hair had turned white almost overnight, and he never totally recovered from the accident. Surely Mr. Van Eck, at some level of H.D.'s consciousness, invoked memories of her father. (Freud certainly knew this.) She writes of the accident in *Advent:* "The cause of my father's accident always remained a mystery. He might have slipped off the old-fashioned steam tram or the local train engine might have backfired. We were not allowed to see our father for some days. We were afraid he might be dead. When we finally went to his room he was propped up . . . but his hair and beard had turned white. It was another father, wax-pale, a ghost." [11]

H.D. tells of how she repressed the memory of this incident: "My interest in 'numbers' was checked at the time of my father's accident and though I did not remember the accident, I remembered how long-division had blocked me or set a wall between my happy and most unhappy school-days." [12]

H.D. continues to tell Freud the story of Mr. Van Eck. She tells of how she had been "trudging around the deck with Bryher and Dr. Ellis." [13] Havelock Ellis was a friend of H.D.'s; her circle was impressed by his work. H.D. drew a portrait of him in "Secret Name," one of the books in her novel *Palimpsest,* where he appears as Jerry. As the pathbreaking psychologist of sexuality and teacher to a generation that was becoming sexually educated, he also found his way into *Helen in Egypt* as Chiron, the teacher of Achilles.

On the day that the vision appeared to her, H.D. was dressed casually in clothes appropriate to "slipping and sliding" around the deck. But she would of course dress for dinner. When she went to the stateroom to change her clothes, she had the vision. She did not realize that she might have gone to sleep for a few minutes. She tells us: "It was, by clock time, before dinner as I had gone to the stateroom to change as usual . . . Perhaps I had thrown myself down on the bunk for a few minutes' rest before changing . . . Perhaps I was there in the bunk, normally resting, when I climbed the now level flight of steps to the upper deck." [14]

She had begun to dream, although she did not experience this as a dream at the time. In her dream she began to climb the stairs. (As we shall see in the next chapter, these stairs are related to the ones the heroine does not climb in *Bid Me to Live.*) When she reached the deck, everything was quite still. There were no deck chairs, no people. What she experienced on the deck is significant from a Freudian point of view: "We were crossing . . . the line . . . Perhaps it was more than a few minutes, but we were crossing something, 'the line'? What line? We were coasting along in the Bay . . . there was a violet light over the sea." [15]

H.D.'s first thought (remember, she was dreaming) was that she must get Bryher.

> I must get Bryher, I thought; Bryher must not miss this, but as I am about to turn back I see Mr. Van Eck standing by the deck rail, to my *right* . . .
> Well — he sees me. I must at least say good-evening. I notice to my surprise that he is somewhat taller than myself . . . He is taller than I thought him. I must not stare at Mr. Van Eck. I am always afraid he will catch my eyes focused, in some sort of uncontrollable fascination, on that curious deep scar over his left eyebrow. All the same, one cannot in decency *not* meet the eyes of the person one is greeting. His eyes are uncovered; Mr. Van Eck wore thick-rimmed glasses.
> His eyes are more blue than I had thought, it is mist-blue, sea-blue . . .
> He is taller. He is older — no, he must be younger. It is near evening, it is this strange light. But the light is not strange.
> One cannot stare. But it is certain the scar is not there.[16]

H.D. did not, could not, realize in 1920 that this was a dream — it was too vivid, too real. But she was aware that the Van Eck she met on the deck of the boat was different in some ways from the Van Eck (Rodeck) with whom she was traveling on the *Borodino*. The man in the vision did not have glasses; his eyes were "more blue." He did not have a scar. H.D. continues to describe her vision.

> On his right as he stands there, there is an indented coastline. 'Land,' I said. I did not in my thought realize that land, were there land, would be on the other side of the boat. Or had the boat turned round? Or were these some off-lying islands of which I in my ignorance knew nothing? There were dolphins. Yes, there were dolphins.[17]

H.D. continually alludes to the "Bay" in her vision, and like Mr. Van Eck, this Bay has something of another dimension. It becomes symbolic. "There had been rough weather and I was told that the Bay (I had not heard the Bay of Biscay referred to as the Bay before) was always rough anyway."[18]

D. H. Lawrence had published a book of poems, *Bay,* just one year before H.D.'s vision. Significantly, the original cover of the book — the cover of the volume H.D. would have seen — was printed with a regular and recurrent pattern of dolphins. In *Advent* H.D. writes of her vision: "The dolphins are joined by other dolphins; they make a curiously unconvincing pattern, leaping in rhythmic order like crescent moons or half-moons out of the water, a flight or a dance of dolphins. Yet, they are dolphins."[19]

H.D. apparently put none of this together until the completion of her psychoanalysis with Freud. Her vision was a precise description of the cover of Lawrence's book, but she was at the time unaware of the correspondence. She wanted desperately to believe that the man in her vision was simply her fellow traveler Mr. Van Eck. She writes: "I thought, Mr. Van Eck for some reason (perhaps he is a secret agent) 'makes up.' Could he rub in or put on that scar? Well perhaps it wasn't Mr. Van Eck who 'made up' as a secret agent; perhaps the secret agent made up as Mr. Van Eck."[20]

These notes describing her vision of Peter Van Eck and the dolphins were recorded by H.D. on March 11, 1933, in Vienna. She had been keeping notes during her first set of sessions with Freud. In her jottings of March 13 she tells us that the Professor "was curious to see how the story would proceed, now we had the frame," and she admits that she too was curious.[21] H.D. was at last not unwilling to come directly to terms with the events of the World War I years. All during her sessions with Freud she kept a picture of D. H. Lawrence on her table in the hotel. "I had this picture in Vienna," she writes. "I think the original was on the *Taos* volume. I had it on my table in the *Hotel Regina,* during the time of my sessions with Professor Freud."[22]

At the time of her vision H.D. wanted to focus on Mr. Van Eck, or Rodeck, even though she knew in some way that he was not the man she met on the deck. Obviously she would prefer dealing with this living historical man to remembering the "real" man behind her vision. "An asbestos curtain had dropped between me and my past, my not-so-far-past bitter severence from love and friendship."[23] The breaking of her relationship with Lawrence was still too painful to remember. So she would focus on this new acquaintance. Was she at some level hoping to substitute him for what she had lost? She writes: "I was fascinated with Peter Van Eck. He had traveled widely, had lived in Greece for some time, had worked on excavations in Crete, was an architect by profession and he said an artist by choice but he had had little choice in the matter. He had been in Egypt at one time, helping to restore some Caliph's or Khedive's shrine or tomb."[24]

When H.D. and Bryher arrived at their destination in Greece, they went for a walk with Mr. Rodeck "through a cork forest; the ground was starry with February narcissus." H.D. wanted Rodeck or Van Eck to be who he was, the widely traveled, urbane architect; but she wanted him to be something else too, someone else. As she tells us, "This was Mr. Van Eck, it was not the Man on the boat, but I had then neither the wit, the temerity, nor the courage to work this all out. If Mr. Van Eck was the Man on the boat, then I lost something. If Mr. Van Eck was not the Man on the boat, then I lost something."[25]

If Mr. Van Eck was not the man on the deck of the boat, then she lost the man, for her fascinating fellow traveler, interesting as he was, was not the man to whom she was emotionally attached. So if Mr. Van Eck was not the man she met when she climbed the stairs of the *Borodino,* she lost the possibility of a new love relationship. "To answer the question meant loss of one or the other, Mr. Van Eck or the Man on the boat."[26] In other words, she had to give up either her suppressed memory of Lawrence (she had to let him go and relinquish any suppressed hope of reconciliation) or Peter Rodeck, with whom she might share a new relationship. She was drawn to a new relationship, but she had not yet let go of the past.

At the time H.D. had this vision she did not want to give up the possibility of a new relationship. That evening at dinner on the *Borodino,* H.D. turned to Mr. Rodeck and said, "It was beautiful watching the dolphins." Bryher asked, "Where were you anyway?" H.D. answered that she was watching the dolphins with Rodeck.

> I turned to Mr. Van Eck for confirmation.
>
> He smiled at Bryher across the table. He had an engaging manner. The captain said, "Dolphins? The wireless-operator is our dolphin expert. He reported no dolphins." "But there were dolphins." I turned to Mr. Van Eck again for confirmation. "Which way were they swimming?" said the captain. I indicated above the table the direction of the frieze of flying dolphins. "They were swimming this way," I said, indicating a line "forward," past Mr. Van Eck down the table. "That's right," said the captain, "That's how they would be swimming. They swim with the wind . . ."
>
> But now I said to the Professor, "Where was I, if Bryher couldn't find me?"[27]

This question, "Where was I, if Bryher couldn't find me?" was to be answered by H.D. during the course of her analysis. She was, she came to realize, in another dimension — the dimension about which she spoke in *Bid Me to Live,* the dimension in which she walked with an image, and that image was Rico.

By the time H.D. wrote "Magic Ring" (1943–1944), Peter Van Eck had become a conscious persona or a second name for D. H. Lawrence. Van Eck. Van Gogh of *Bid Me to Live.* H.D. had an

Uncle Frederick. Frederico. Her father. It all made sense by the time she finished her sessions with Freud. In "Compassionate Friendship" she writes, "I managed at last, in *Magic Ring,* to present that earlier mystery of Peter Van Eck (as I called *him*) and the phenomenon of that 1920 Greek trip with Bryher, on one of her father's boats."[28]

H.D. elaborated her vision in "Magic Ring." It is not clear whether the "single dolphin that detached itself from the frieze-like vision" in this novel was part of the original vision; probably not. By 1944 H.D. was a conscious visionary, knowingly using many names to speak of one presence.

> There was the hand of Mr. Van Eck; the square-palm was turned flat downward, above the water. It seemed, even as I looked, that the single dolphin that detached itself from the frieze-like formation between the ship-rail and the sky-line was being drawn-up by the magnetic attraction of Mr. Van Eck's firm flat palm. The dolphin leapt above the level of the deck, almost on a level with the deck-rail and fell back into his element.
>
> "That one," said Mr. Van Eck, "nearly landed."[29]

In "Magic Ring" H.D. continues to speak of the dolphins and Mr. Van Eck, explaining that she has had almost twenty-five years to think about it. At the time of the writing of this novel she had not yet finally assembled *Bid Me to Live* (that was to come five years later, in 1949), but she had been working on it since "Paint It Today," 1921. It was, however, almost twenty-five years from the time that D. H. Lawrence published *Bay* to H.D.'s writing of "Magic Ring." Once we have worked our way down through the palimpsest of images presented in "Magic Ring" we can understand that H.D. is saying that she has had almost twenty-five years to think about what Lawrence was saying in *Bay,* which was written during the war years.

> I have had almost 25 years in which to ponder on that cryptic or that Delphic utterance of Mr. Van Eck's, and I am still at a loss to know exactly what he did mean. In moments of depression and of stagnation I am apt to interpret it as a symbol of failure. I am apt to think that Mr. Van Eck meant to say:
>
> "Here is the scene. I show it to you. I have for a moment drawn aside the curtain, the *veil* for you. You see it all there. This is the land of every man's desire, of your desire, this is the land of poetry, of myth, of prophecy. You see those dolphins? They are my prophets. One once carried a poet on his back. Arion. Do you remember?[30]

Surely she remembered her own dolphin poems, the "Thetis" poems.* In the "Thetis" published in *Heliodora*, H.D. writes:

> So I crept, at last,
> a crescent, a curve of a wave,
> (a man would have thought,
> had he watched for his nets
> on the beach)
> a dolphin, a glistening fish,
> that burnt and caught for its light,
> the light of the undercrest
> of the lifting tide,
> a fish with silver for breast,
> with no light but the light
> of the sea it reflects . . .[31]

In this poem H.D. creates the world of Thetis (a persona for herself) and Achilles which she will re-create on a larger scale in *Helen in Egypt.* If we follow the sequence of the poem we see that Thetis becomes the dolphin.

> . . . but one alert, all blue and wet,
> I flung myself, an arrow's flight,
> straight upward
> through the blue of night
> that was my palace wall,
> and crept to where I saw the mark
> of feet, a rare foot-fall:
>
> Achilles' sandal on the beach,
> could one mistake? . . .

H.D.'s poem says that a nymph or goddess might "so mistake/ Achilles' footprint," but not the poet, not Thetis, not herself:

> Not I, the mother, Thetis self,
> I stretched and lay, a river's slim
> dark length,
> a rivulet where it leaves the wood
> and meets the sea,
> I lay along the burning sand,
> a river's blue.

In "Thetis" we are presented with an image that becomes the central eidolon of *Helen in Egypt:* an image of the goddess in "the blue of the painted stuff/it wore for dress."

*H.D. wrote two poems with this title. She was working on the one printed here in 1919; it was first published in *Poetry* on June 23, 1923, and subsequently collected in *Heliodora* (1924).

H.D.'s reference in "Magic Ring" is specifically to her first "Thetis" poem, that published in *Hymen*.*

> On the paved parapet
> you will step carefully
> from amber stones on onyx
> flecked with violet,
> mingled with light,
> half showing the sea-grass
> and sea-sand underneath,
> reflecting your white feet
> and the gay strap crimson
> as lily-buds of Arion,
> and the gold that binds your feet.
>
> You will pass
> beneath the island disk
> (and myrtle-wood,
> the carved support of it)
> and the white stretch
> of its white beach,
> curved as the moon crescent
> or ivory when some fine hand
> chisels it:
> when the sun slips
> through the far edge,
> there is rare amber
> through the sea,
> and flecks of it
> glitter on the dolphin's back
> and jewelled halter
> and harness and bit
> as he sways under it.[32]

There is a remarkable continuity of image in H.D.'s symbolic consciousness from the first Imagist poems through *Helen in Egypt*, in spite of the many personae through which H.D. tells and retells her story.

H.D.'s image of Thetis riding naked upon a harnessed dolphin presents the Freudian primal scene. Were the events surrounding the breakup of her marriage so painful that she repressed the basis of the Van Eck vision, or did something else occur — a kind of suppression as well as repression? In other words, did H.D. manage to will herself to be silent about those events? Was this part of her decision to live a life of poetry? Did she feel that she had no

*This poem was first published in *The Sphere* in August 1920 and subsequently collected in *Hymen* in 1921.

choice? In "Magic Ring" she writes of the Peter Van Eck of her vision rather than her fellow traveler on the boat; in her now very conscious vision, she tells us that when she is depressed she imagines Mr. Van Eck says to her:

> "What do you make of it? We meet here for this moment and you think we will meet again below deck. We will meet again from time to time but not at the captain's table. It is a little over crowded for one thing and for another, I cannot expect you to be altogether discreet, for you do not know that I am not Mr. Van Eck. You might mix the dimensions, before a lot of people, and make a fool of yourself. You have done that before. You might retort, if you knew now what I was saying to you. But you will later remember one or two apparently disconnected incidents, chiefly of your life in London, and you will say . . . *that I have loved thee.*" [33]

Suffice it to say that through her experience with Freud H.D. learned not to mix dimensions. In order to do so one must achieve a certain clarity in relation to one's experience. Through her psychoanalysis, which was a powerful healing experience, H.D. was liberated into a new phase of artistic consciousness. But because of the shock of the events surrounding World War I, she had to struggle for many years to achieve and maintain her clarity. She had been very nearly totally overwhelmed. Niké, which we will examine in further depth in the next chapter, became H.D.'s symbol of her victory.

25

Writing
on the Wall

THE VISION of Peter Van Eck on the deck of the *Borodino* on her 1920 Greek trip with Bryher was startling and confusing to H.D. Nothing quite like this had ever happened to her before. During periods of fatigue she had had visual distortions and in periods of illness she had had fever dreams, but never before had she had any confusion about the reality of her experience.

But the Greek trip yielded for H.D. a second and in some ways more mysterious and mystical vision. In this case, however, there was no possibility that what she experienced might have been merely an extra-vivid dream. H.D.'s second vision — what she and Freud later referred to as "the writing on the wall" — occurred in her bedroom at the Hotel Belle Venise on the Greek island of Corfu in 1920, and Bryher was present when it occurred.* In *Writing on the Wall,* the collection of essays in tribute to Freud which was published in *Life and Letters Today* in 1945–1946 and collected in book form with *Advent* as *Tribute to Freud,* H.D. describes it in vivid detail.

The vision appeared to her on the wall of her hotel room, and was essentially an image of primitive sacrifice, of a woman uniting with Helios, the sun. The woman slowly walked up the slats or the rungs of a ladder to be consumed by the sun's fire. H.D. saw the head and shoulders of a soldier or airman, then a goblet suggesting the mystic chalice — definitely a male symbol and a female symbol. Another picture, the tripod of Delphi, formed next,

---

*Havelock Ellis was quite disturbed when he heard about the vision and brought the story back to London literary circles that H.D. had gone *"right out of her mind."*[1]

in perspective; the tripod is a symbol of prophecy and poetry and is linked with Helios. At the time of her vision H.D. was aware that she was thinking in an unusual way. She saw the ladder of light form; then the angel, Niké; then a series of broken curves in an S-pattern that opened out toward Niké, who was moving toward the sun. H.D. writes, "I thought, 'Helios, the sun . . .' and I shut off, 'cut out' before the final picture, before (you might say) the explosion took place."[2]

In her *Tribute* H.D. writes, "THE PROFESSOR translated the pictures on the wall, or the picture-writing on the wall of a hotel bedroom in Corfu, the Greek Ionian island, that I saw projected there in the spring of 1920, as a desire for union with my mother."[3] Freud called the vision her *only* "dangerous symptom."[4]

At the time of writing *Tribute to Freud* in 1944, H.D. was still shocked by Freud's response to her vision. Not only did he interpret it as a desire for union with her mother — a death wish, no doubt — but as if to add insult to injury, he showed her the figure of the wingless Niké, pointing out to her that it had lost its spear (presumably introducing her to his theory of femininity). In other words, Freud not only told her the vision was a dangerous symptom, implying that it was an instinct run amuck, but he also said, in effect, "You are, after all, a woman, my dear." H.D. was aware that if a man had had a similar experience Freud would recognize the effort of mind involved in the attempt to contain or control instinctual forces.

Freud must have understood, as H.D. came to understand in the years following her work with him, that she was knitting together the pieces of a previous experience into a singularly powerful image. Her angel, Niké, is a perfect symbol of a still-innocent young woman; but Niké is surrounded by ancient symbols of sexuality and knowledge. H.D.'s Corfu vision presents an innocent young woman coming into sexual knowledge.

We don't know the context of Freud's interpretations. He may have been attempting to awaken dormant memories. In the mode of a Zen master or of Socrates, he may have suggested a paradoxical explanation in order to rouse H.D. to consciousness, to force her to face what he saw as the truth of her relationship with Lawrence. Perhaps he was attempting to enrage her to break the force of the trauma. Freud was a practical man, and H.D. was difficult to reach. Her portrait of him as Theseus in *Helen in Egypt* suggests that H.D. finally realized that Freud may have been attempting to force her to see for herself what he saw — that is, that H.D. was only another sacrifice to Lawrence's Oedipus complex. In *Helen in Egypt* H.D. presents Freud's interpretation of her vision as a desire to return to the "shell," which is synonymous with mother, self, and her own integrity.

We see, as Freud must have seen, the relation between H.D.'s Corfu vision and her experience with Lawrence. In *Bid Me to Live* the Helios image is associated with the Druidic sun-circle and with Rico, the Lawrence persona. "There was an actual Druid circle on the hill . . . She sat down on a flat rock and wondered if the asymmetrical set of stones, just as the hill dipped, was the Druid sun-circle Rico wrote of . . . on the slope, just out of sight was the sun-circle."[5]

In *Bid Me to Live* the Druidic sun-circle is also associated with the stairs that lead to Rico's room, which in that "crucible" situation Julia, the H.D. character, chose not to climb. "How could I climb those stairs, not knowing what you wanted? . . . How could I walk up those stairs? . . . I would be drawn, literally, up those stairs."[6] Julia was expected to climb them. In real terms, H.D. resisted Lawrence's will, which was tremendously powerful; it almost pulled her up. In her letter to Rico, Julia writes: "I'm trying to explain to you why I didn't climb those stairs to your room."[7]

The central issue of *Bid Me to Live* is H.D.'s unwillingness to go up the stairs to the room Lawrence occupied during his stay at her flat in the winter of 1917. It had been arranged. If she had gone up to Lawrence's room (Frieda was not sleeping with him), something would have been decided, would have been made final. Richard Aldington would have held off his decision about whether to stay with his mistress, Arabella, until H.D. made her decision about Lawrence. She and Aldington had both had their liaisons and affairs — it had been part of their agreement to have a modern marriage. It was one thing to meet her lover by accident, as it were; it was another thing altogether to walk up those stairs in the presence of her husband and Lawrence's wife. If she had done so, she would have made a decision to stay with Lawrence. *Bid Me to Live* tells the story of her refusal to decide.

In *The First Lady Chatterley*, neither Parkin nor Constance makes a decision. As Lawrence tells the story, the issue is not whether to have a relationship (they already have one); it is whether to dissolve their respective marriages and find some way to live together.

In the last pages of *Bid Me to Live*, Julia attempts to tell Rico in a letter why she was unable to cast her lot with his. As Lawrence suggests in all three versions of *Lady Chatterley,* it was at least partially an issue of class, or rather, as H.D. puts it, of Julia's inability to do without nonessentials. But for H.D. it was really an inability not so much to live a bohemian life as to conceive of herself playing the role of "great mother" to him. Frieda had given up everything for Lawrence's genius. H.D. could not, would not, give up everything. If *he* had claimed *her,* it would have been different; if he had been willing to make the decision, she might have — probably would have — followed. But she could not take all the responsibility for the relationship; she could not be Eve. Frieda was Eve. Lawrence, H.D. decided, needed Eve. She knew she had made a decision by not going up those stairs, but she had been put in an impossible situation. Her response was to do nothing; her response was to flee this madness. "Englishmen, madmen," Julia says.[8]

Cecil Gray was willing to rescue H.D. from the situation. He could at least decide to shelter her at Bosigran. In choosing to go with him, H.D. realized she was choosing neither Aldington nor Lawrence nor Gray, but herself.

But the unresolved choice she had been presented with came back to haunt her in the Corfu vision. At the time she had the vision she was recovering from illness and severe mental strain. Psychically H.D. was still fleeing from the choice she had been expected to make in that "crucible" situation at 44 Mecklenburgh Square in December 1917. As the pictures of her vision began to appear on the wall, she at first thought they were shadows; but they were light on dark rather than dark on light. Fortunately Bryher was with her. Bryher continued the "reading" where H.D. left off. As H.D. "let go, from complete mental and physical exhaustion," Bryher saw the concluding symbol or "determinative" (which H.D. describes as "the picture . . . that is used in the actual hieroglyph . . . that contains the whole series of pictures in itself or helps clarify or explain them"). Bryher said she saw "a circle like the sun-disk and a figure within the disk; a man, she thought was reaching out to draw the image of a woman (my Niké) into the sun beside him."[9]

In her vision H.D. was experiencing or re-experiencing the pull of Lawrence's will. As she says in *Bid Me to Live,* she felt "drawn, literally," up those stairs by his powerful will. It had required all of her strength to resist the force of that attraction. Now she had to go through the whole experience again. As she says over and over in *Advent,* she was haunted by Lawrence. His power was still compelling her.

When she wrote *Helen in Egypt* H.D. associated the ladder with Achilles. She specifically alludes to the Corfu vision when she writes:

> . . . I might have counted seven
>
> and seven, like the bars of light
> that have slowly climbed up the wall.[10]

It is obvious that the stairs H.D. did not climb to Lawrence's room reappear in her Corfu vision as the ladder of light. At least it was obvious to H.D. when she wrote the 1939 draft of *Bid Me to Live* after completing her psychoanalysis with Freud. Just how crucial the decision was is shown by H.D.'s explanation of the situation in the novel, where she describes the pressures she felt in this way: "Already, there was this neat pairing off, Rafe, Bella [Aldington, Dorothy Yorke] . . . Rico, Julia [Lawrence, H.D.], and to show that it was all neat and rounded off . . . there was this vague distant young musician [Gray] who was coming to town to be with them, at Christmas . . . obviously he and Elsa [Frieda] had it all fixed up between them."[11]

As H.D. presents the situation, Elsa acquiesced. " 'This will leave me free,' she muttered in her German guttural, 'for Vanio' [Gray]."[12] Frieda had been having an affair with Cecil Gray in Cornwall during the time Lawrence spent with "John Thomas."

Did Frieda acquiesce, as H.D. puts it, or did she attempt to define the situation? Lawrence was quite unhappy about the whole state of affairs. And all H.D. could see at 44 Mecklenburgh Square was Lawrence's total dependence on Frieda. As she writes in her novel:

> Rico was able to dart out, make his frantic little excursions into any unknown dimension, because there, firm as a rock, was Elsa. He cropped round and round, eating up field-flowers, grass; goat-like, his teeth made furrows in symbolic olive trees. When he had got his full, his genius would demand fresh fields and up would pull the totem-pole, Germania, obligingly plant itself in another meadow.[13]

At any rate, it was H.D.'s confrontation with Lawrence *and* his wife that finally broke her love for him. It was during their stay in H.D.'s flat that Frieda told H.D. that Lawrence cared only for men, that H.D. had no idea what he was *really* like. There were now, in H.D.'s mind, two distinct Lawrence personalities: the Lawrence as a man alone, and the Lawrence with Frieda. (Lawrence portrays himself as two persons in *Aaron's Rod,* which he was writing during his stay at 44 Mecklenburgh Square.)

We all know the way this chapter of the story ended. H.D. and Lawrence separated. Isn't this what Frieda had intended all along? But H.D. suppressed the pressure to climb the stairs — and the desire to climb them — with great effort. The fear and desire would resurface in H.D.'s life in the "hieroglyph" of the Corfu vision. Sigmund Freud evidently had no problem in recognizing the vision as a representation of the sexual act — he had written about this kind of dream and had heard it described by other analysands. In his *General Introduction to Psychoanalysis,* in the chapter titled "Example of Dreams and Analysis of Them," Freud writes of "the act of going up the steps as symbolic of the sexual act." [14]

Freud thought this vision of H.D.'s a dangerous symptom only because it appeared as writing on the wall rather than inside her mind, so to speak. But her Imagist poetry, too, had been projected out, onto the page. Was this such a different mental process? * She was tired — exhausted; her mind was playing tricks on her. But it is interesting that the vision should appear as writing on the wall. It is often the case that when we think we have come to the end of something — when, so to speak, the jig is up — we say, "I see the writing on the wall." It is an old saying, a way of stating that we see clearly that something is finished. When H.D. saw Lawrence and Frieda together in the crucible situation, she saw, but could not consciously accept, the "writing on the wall."

Elements of this "picture" appeared in H.D.'s novels of the 1920s. A particularly vivid re-creation of the central images associated with the Corfu vision appears in *Hedylus,* a 1928 novel that H.D. called in retrospect "hallucinated writing."

On the surface *Hedylus* is about a mother and a son. The child is illegitimate and nearing ten years old; he is understandably curious about his parentage and knows that his mother is uncertain or unwilling to discuss the identity of his father. Hedylus knows only that he is the child of an illicit relationship and that his mother, Hedyle, is sensitive about the circumstances of his birth. H.D.'s story takes place when the child is at an age when we might expect a child born under such circumstances to be curious about his lineage.

As the novel opens Hedylus is living with Hedyle on the Greek island of Samos, where his mother brought him from Athens when she became the mistress of Douris, king of the island. The

*In *Writing on the Wall* H.D. says, "We can read my writing . . . in two ways . . . megalomania . . . or . . . an extension of the artist's mind, a *picture* or an illustrated poem . . . projected from within . . . (though apparently from outside)." [15]

whole novel takes place over the course of one day and evening. It contains some surface mother-son relationship themes which are not well developed. The novel is really about the arrival of a man who in one meeting establishes a kind of long-lost-father posture in relation to the young Hedylus. Hedylus was named after his mother; now it is as though the missing father, whom H.D. calls Demion or Helios, attempts to claim him in the same way that he once attempted to claim Hedyle.*

In H.D.'s "Asphodel" manuscript as well as in *Hedylus,* the heroine originally places the decision to have her child in the hands of the gods. If a sign is given she will give birth. In both manuscripts an omen (a grass snake or a bird) is read as a sign that the child is to be favored by Helios — or by God.

"What did the Virgin Mary do on this occasion?" asks H.D in "Asphodel." And she answers: "Of course, God, her lover, would look after her . . . I mean he came in all that glory . . . and love entered . . . and the beauty of the moment and the joy of her own realization of her acceptability of God, entrapped her." [16]

According to Moravianism, God and the Virgin have their counterparts in Jesus and Mary Magdalene. The Virgin and Mary Magdalene are symbolically one. As H.D. says in "The Gift," "It is terrible to be a virgin because a Virgin has a baby with God." [17] In *Hedylus* she writes: "Weren't women, so importunate as to let God love them, always later tacitly abandoned?" [18]

The parallel situation in H.D.'s life was complicated by the fact that in 1919 she wanted her baby, but "she didn't want the letter of the covenant." [19] And, of course, it was further complicated by H.D.'s unwillingness to acknowledge the identity of the father of her child. In "Asphodel" she writes: "But she must remember Vane. After all, it was his child. If it *was* his child." [20] But the heroine does not really believe that the father is Vane. H.D. writes: "For God having ordained this would not leave one of his prostitutes; no, one of his concubines (a wise virgin anyway) empty, forsaken . . . For she didn't any more think (had she ever thought?) that Vane might be its father." [21]

In Lawrence's story "Sun," Juliet is "given" to the sun. In "Asphodel" H.D. writes, "It might just be the sun-self loving her. Daemon or angel." [22] In *Hedylus* this daemon is Demion, or Helios. She writes: "When my child becomes stern and aloof and secretive, it is his father in him. That is DEMION. DEMION was the sun and the sun and the sun." [23]

---

*The scene in which Demion meets Hedylus was first published in a 1925 anthology edited by Robert McAlmon entitled *Contact Collection of Contemporary Writers;* the complete novel did not appear until three years later.

Invoking the night when Demion appears suddenly, without warning, at the home of Demetrius, H.D. writes as Hedyle: "You waited until I was utterly forsaken. Then came to me, not as a shining apparition but as a mere man. God to attain his immortality does that. He attains humanity. But what use? To whom could I tell this? I have been a blind CASSANDRA smitten with my secret . . . I have lived like the swan hiding his song in secret."[24]

Judging by the textual clues in "Asphodel" and H.D.'s other work, it seems likely that Demion is a persona for Lawrence. At the time H.D. began her novel, when her child was still very young, she and Lawrence had not seen each other since he left England after the war in 1919. But she continued to follow his "image" in his work. As she writes in Hedylus: "You sit stolid there in the daylight, DEMION of OLYMPIA, but I don't altogether, even now, accept you."[25] And she alludes to "Tenderness": "It seemed odd that I should have escaped, in spite of my obvious outward indifference, from tenderness."[26]

Hedyle says to Demion, "You asked me to go to EGYPT."[27] He also asks her to go to India. "You asked me to leave ATHENS, to go to INDIA. I knew I couldn't do that. I was staring into my own fate, knowing I couldn't do that. — why? One does know these things. Perhaps I loved you too much."[28] Hedyle also says: "You have never left me. As a god you never left me. As a mortal, it was obvious, you were the perfect lover . . . You offered everything that I never had been offered, strength with beauty, simply. What man can give it to a high-bred woman?"[29] The idea of the high-bred woman, the lover, and the resulting child are, of course, themes of Lawrence's novels of the period as well as of Hedylus.

Demion arrives on the island, rather mysteriously, by boat. He also leaves by boat. As in H.D.'s vision of Peter Van Eck, Demion is "the man on the boat."

In "Compassionate Friendship" H.D. writes of Lawrence: "He was admittedly a father-image to me."[30] She says this in the context of Frieda's attempt to "break across" her relationship with Lawrence, and she alludes to the "new ideas from Vienna." But it is clear that H.D.'s use of the psychoanalytic term "father image" includes the concrete situation; that is, an actual child was born to her, and biologically that child must have had an actual father.

H.D. states in Hedylus that Hedyle will not reveal the identity of the father to Hedylus: "If his father were a god, you simply, resplendent, making yourself appear to me one day at holy SUNIUM then it were better, if he shouldn't know it."[31]

In The Hedgehog, written in 1925, H.D. tells the story of a little girl named Madge who is very curious about the identity of her father. The little girl, who makes us think of H.D.'s own daughter, is taught that stories have "double sorts of meanings."[32] Madge believes that she has a "Father-which-art-in-Heaven for a father." The mother explains: "There were so many, many children, Bett said, who had that kind of 'Father who art in Heaven' for a father . . . And all . . . these children . . . were all sort of odd little brothers and sisters."[33]

Hedylus, who has many of the same characteristics as Madge, hopes that Demion is his father, but seems to think that Demetrius might be. (Demetrius is based upon Cecil Gray.) "DEMETRIUS? Mother seemed somewhat intent on proving that he wasn't. Was it just because he might be?"[34] This theme is echoed in the *Ion* which H.D. was translating from Euripides at this time and which she refers to in *Hedylus:* "Hadn't she all these years tried to make the affair clear to HEDYLUS? He didn't know his father's name, it's quite true. But neither did ION, really, neither did young ERECHTHEUS. There was nothing for such as HEDYLE and HEDYLUS but to claim blatant kinship with divinity."[35]

It was not, then, only Lawrence who was writing novels in the twenties that addressed the topic of the paternity of an illegitimate child. H.D. was every bit as concerned with the issue. While there was apparently reason to believe that Cecil Gray was the father of H.D.'s child, there was also, at least in H.D.'s mind, reason to believe he wasn't. As H.D. says, "DEMETRIUS simply isn't."[36]

H.D. has already told us that *Hedylus* tells the same story as *Bid Me to Live,* "Paint It Today," "Asphodel," and the other Madrigal manuscripts. And of course we think of the three versions of *Lady Chatterley's Lover* and *The Man Who Died,* all of which take up the same paternity themes as H.D.'s prose and translation work of this period.

In *Hedylus* H.D. identifies Demion with Helios: "HELIOS, architect, leader of the colonists. HELIOS, father of the lost ION, father of the small AESCULAPIUS, lover and ravisher of DAPHNE, slayer (indirectly) of tall HYACINTH. HELIOS, lover, founder of far city, colonizer. Wearing shield, helmet if need be, greaves if necessary."[37] While the tone and style of *Hedylus* is sophisticated and "modern," its whole theme invokes the vision H.D. had of Helios on Corfu with Bryher in 1920. What H.D. "saw" was a vision of Helios trying to claim her. H.D. writes, "DEMION would have gathered me to him as the sun a rain-cloud."[38] Of Hedyle's meeting with Demion at the home of Demetrius she writes: "You might have been god or man. Both claimed me."[39]

"This spring of 1920 held for me many unresolved terrors,"
H.D. wrote in *Tribute to Freud*.[40] She had not recovered in 1920
or even in 1928 when she completed *Hedylus*. Her poetry of the
1920s, like the staccato and sometimes hallucinated writing in her
novels, is breathless, distraught. In "Chorus Sequence (From *Morpheus*)" she writes:

> Achilles stayed a moment and is gone,
> man,
> man,
> and child,
> the warrior,
> all are one;
> I charmed the three
> to unity in my arms . . .
>
> . . .
>
> now you have been a father to yourself,
> let poppies wither
> for this lovelier crown;
> see,
> I would pluck the olive
> from my own
> chaplet
> to name you,
> poet with the rest;
> love and lover,
> man-child and a god . . .[41]

In *Hedylus* H.D. portrays herself in the ordinary human dimension as Hedyle, a courtesan in the court of Douris. "She saw herself as a tired woman, grown ill and worn with waiting." As she says to Demion when he at last returns, "I waited so long for you."[42]

In the years since the war had ended H.D. had drifted into strange circumstances. She could not entirely accept the life she was living, patronized by Bryher and her father. " 'Hetaira' wasn't the right word. You couldn't say HEDYLE was an 'indifferent prostitute.' What was there left but 'goddess'?"[43]

H.D. and Lawrence met again on September 22, 1926, at Dorothy Richardson's home.* When Lawrence returned to London for a brief visit, H.D. was traveling in "higher" circles; Lawrence was now, as he saw it, in about the relation of a mere gamekeeper

---

*In his autobiography, *From Another World*, Louis Untermeyer recalls this meeting between H.D. and Lawrence and a discussion of his forthcoming novel *Moses*, which states a thesis similar to Freud's thesis in *Moses and Monotheism*. Moses, Untermeyer argued, is an Egyptian.

to a great and sophisticated lady. He had lost contact with his friends in England while he was in Ceylon, Australia, Mexico, and New Mexico; he must have been surprised — shocked, in fact — to find H.D. in such changed circumstances. She now traveled in the same social circle as the Sitwells,* whose house at Renishaw is thought to be the physical setting that Lawrence used as his model for Wragby in *Lady Chatterley's Lover*. He began to write that novel in October 1926, one month after seeing H.D. in Hampstead.

*Edith and Osbert Sitwell became and remained close friends of H.D.'s. During World War II Osbert Sitwell arranged a public poetry reading for Queen Elizabeth and the two princesses, Elizabeth and Margaret, at which H.D. and twelve other poets (including T. S. Eliot, Walter de la Mare, Vita Sackville-West, Osbert and Edith Sitwell, and others) read.

26

The Road to Freud

IN ENGLAND H.D. was a transplanted American. When she first met him, D. H. Lawrence appealed to her with all the force of an obsession. In Freudian terms he was her superego, the very incarnation of her family and religious background come to repossess her. Lawrence was in a very real sense the complete Puritan and represented to H.D. what Freud called the "return of the repressed" — the father. But he also represented the brother whose images corresponded with those of the "hidden church," the Moravianism of her childhood. Lawrence at some level invoked H.D.'s fondest memories of her earliest life in the midst of the foreign culture of post-Victorian England.

In this atmosphere H.D. was out of her natural element. Many of her early poems are the sort of pictures of a new milieu that could be recorded only by a foreigner. Her 1916 poem "Evening" reflects an impression richly steeped in Victorian floral design:

> The light passes
> from ridge to ridge,
> from flower to flower —
> the hypaticas, wide-spread
> under the light
> grow faint —
> the petals reach inward,
> the blue tips bend
> toward the bluer heart
> and the flowers are lost.
>
> The cornel-buds are still white,
> but shadows dart
> from the cornel-roots —
> black creeps from root to root,

each leaf
cuts another leaf on the grass,
shadow seeks shadow,
then both leaf
and leaf-shadow are lost.[1]

H.D.'s work has an immediacy which is akin to painting. The contrast of milieu between an ascetic American community and the damp, foggy interiors of London made a vivid impression on the poet. What she experienced she expressed in poetry. What she took in she recorded in a clear impression. The inability to "become" what she experienced led in a real way to the clarity of the expression. H.D.'s character structure was too well formed, too resistant, too resilient to bend and blend into her new milieu. Therefore she did not assimilate but presented what she received. She was like a tourist with a high-technology camera. H.D. often used the photography metaphor to explain the way her creative mind worked, and in the late twenties and thirties she took an active interest in film and film criticism in addition to her involvement in poetry. She continually had the sense of being both in and outside of a situation. The mind that stands outside and takes pictures was always at work.

H.D. experienced the floral patterns of Victorian England in the same way that she experienced the hieroglyphs on the temple tombs in Egypt in 1923. In Victorian designs the flower is exaggerated in size; so, too, are the hieroglyphs of chick, hare, and bee on the Egyptian friezes. This kind of sensual exaggeration was intoxicating; in the midst of a new culture H.D. felt drugged, sometimes oppressed. Occasionally her poetry expresses a feeling of suffocation, a longing for clear air, for wind. In "Garden" she writes:

O wind, rend open the heat,
cut apart the heat,
slit it to tatters.

Fruit cannot drop
through this thick air — . . .

Cut the heat:
plough through it,
turning it on either side
of your path.[2]

The heat to which H.D. refers was coming not only from Victorian floral designs but from Englishmen. Sometimes her experiences overwhelmed her. She wanted to be like a receiving station, receiving impressions and images and transmitting them. In her memoir, *My Friends When Young,* Brigit Patmore says that H.D.'s "obsession for expression was almost like a drug."[3] From the standpoint of health, that which is ingested must be incorporated or expelled. If it is suppressed or repressed, it causes disease. H.D. wanted to express life-energy creatively, in art; the Englishmen with whom she associated preferred a more physical form of expression. But H.D. managed to hold her own in this new environment until she met D. H. Lawrence. The incarnation of her childhood in the guise of a foreigner, he traumatized her.

"Cut the heat," she cried, but the psychic damage had already occurred. Inspiration demands expression. H.D.'s need was to be healthy, to be free, to express the tension, to find release in writing. *Red Roses for Bronze* is a book of poetry published in 1931, after Lawrence's death, but most of the poems were written in the 1920s; H.D. was still haunted by his memory. The poem that gives the book its name gives us a glimpse into the function of art for the artist.

> If I might take weight of bronze
> and sate
> my wretched fingers
> in ecstatic work,
> if I might fashion
> eyes and mouth and chin,
> if I might take dark bronze
> and hammer in
> the line beneath your underlip
> (the slightly mocking,
> slightly cynical smile
> you choose to wear)
> if I might ease my fingers and my brain
> with stroke,
> stroke,
> stroke,
> stroke,
> stroke at — something (stone, marble, intent,
>   stable, materialized)
> peace,
> even magic sleep
> might come again.[4]

The "stroke, stroke, stroke, stroke" is illustrative of H.D.'s writing just prior to her analysis with Freud. This repetition has the character of a hysterical attack. In section II of this poem we find:

> . . . the question that's an answer
> and the thing
> that means that what's said
> isn't answering;
> this,
> this,
> or this,
> or this thing,
> or this other; . . .
>
> the casual sort of homage that you care
> to flick toward this
> or this odd passing whim;
> the one above the second on the marble stair,
> the smaller (or the taller) or those two,
> chattering,
> chattering,
> by the fountain-rim.

The chattering repetition gets on our nerves. In the poetry published in *Red Roses for Bronze,* the nervous nature of H.D.'s poetry reached a high-water mark which makes *Sea Garden* seem calm in comparison. Most of this poetry was written in the late 1920s, the same period in which *Hedylus* was written. The poetic expression of suppressed thoughts helps to relieve the inner tension of the poet's mind. But the poetry is strained, high-pitched, high-strung in tone and content. Too much is suppressed, repressed, as in "Chorus Sequence (From *Morpheus*)."

> Give me your poppies,
> poppies, one by one,
> red poppies,
> white ones,
> red ones set by white;
> I'm through with protestation;
> my delight
> knows nothing of the mind
> or argument;
> let me be done
> with brain's intricacies;
> your insight
> has driven deeper
> than the lordliest tome
> of Attic thought
> or Cyrenian logic;
> O strange, dark Morpheus,
> covering me with wings,
> you give the subtle fruit

> Odysseus scorned
> that left his townsmen fainting on the sands,
> you bring the siren note,
> the lotus-land;
> O let me rest
> at last,
> at last,
> at last,
> your touch is sweeter
> than the touch of Death . . .[5]

The poem, which is a prayer for sleep, is so close to hysteria, so breathless, that the reader cannot easily respond to its cadences. It was in this frame of mind that H.D. sought Freud's help in 1933.

Between the time of the birth of her child and her sessions with Freud, H.D. had retreated from the public eye. The 1920s were the period of the "lost generation," and through Bryher and her first husband, Robert McAlmon, H.D. became associated with this new group of artists. Her involvement in the group was minimal; she was at the periphery, an outsider by choice. Unlike many of her new associates, her roots as a writer were in the prewar and wartime period.

The intellectual avant-garde of the 1920s centered in Paris rather than London. McAlmon, whom Bryher had met and married in New York in 1921, was a central figure in the Paris group. His Contact Publishing Company was founded on and partially subsidized by Bryher's allowance from her father. The venture was "the leading expatriate press of the day, a showcase for the new and experimental writers." In the course of its short life it published many well-known artists. *"The Contact Collection of Contemporary Writers* (1925), included Djuna Barnes, Bryher, Mary Butts, H.D., Norman Douglas, Havelock Ellis, Ford Madox Ford, Wallace Gould, Marsden Hartley, Ernest Hemingway, John Herrmann, James Joyce, Mina Loy, Ezra Pound, Dorothy Richardson, May Sinclair, Edith Sitwell and William Carlos Williams."[6]

Bryher and McAlmon's marriage was pragmatic rather than romantic — it was never consummated. Bryher thought of it as an arranged match which would allow her to gain a measure of independence from her family. McAlmon's gain was monetary.

Bryher came from an extraordinarily wealthy family. Her father, Sir John Ellerman, became a baronet in 1905 after he had made his fortune in shipping.

> Indeed ships meant romance as well as business to him. His idea of
> a holiday . . . was to cast off from a British port for Egypt, Italy

or the south of France, and the more picturesque the port of entry the better. His house overflowed with mosaics, tapestries, carvings, furniture, and a medley of objects, some of them works of art and others without value, which had caught his fancy in the markets and bazaars of Europe and Africa.[7]

It is said of Ellerman that he was at heart an artist; he had been a painter as a young man. During World War I his fleet of ships (which included the Leyland line, the Ellerman line, the Wescott and Lawrence line, the Papayanni group, the City line, the Hall line, the Bucknalls Steamship Company, the Shaw, the Savill and Albion Company, the Wilson line, and other concerns) was of immense value to the country because of its great size and efficient management. Ellerman was a financial wizard with wide-ranging real-estate holdings in the British Isles and on the Continent, including hundreds of acres of London property. He was also deeply involved in newspapers, not only financially but editorially. At one time he held a major interest in *The Times* and Associated Newspapers Limited. Later he took over the "Big Six," which included the *Illustrated London News,* the *Sphere,* the *Tatler,* the *Sketch, Eve,* and the *Illustrated Sporting and Dramatic News.* One of the most striking things about him, from the public point of view, was his intense desire for privacy, a trait that his daughter shared.

During the years H.D. lived on and off with Bryher (and sometimes with the Ellermans), her primary concern was the rearing of her young daughter and the care of her aging and ailing mother, who lived with her for a long period before her death in 1927. With the financial assistance of the Ellermans H.D. was able to travel to Greece in 1920, America in 1920–1921, and Egypt in 1923 (at the time of the Tutankhamen excavation). There were trips to Florence and Vienna and periods of residence in Paris and London. Her apartment at the Riant Chateau in Territet, Switzerland, which she shared with her daughter and her mother, became her home.

Bryher was in love with H.D., but her feelings were complicated from the beginning, for Bryher was a complex person. She was dedicated to H.D.'s career as an artist; prior to Perdita's birth, Bryher wrote to H.D. that she would fight the child for H.D.'s poetry. H.D.'s feeling for Bryher was a simple emotion of immense gratitude. Bryher had saved her life; Bryher in some sense owned her life.

Although H.D. was immensely grateful to Bryher throughout her life, she had entered into the friendship somewhat unwillingly and not at all happily. As she explains over and over, none of the men in her life would help her after she became pregnant. And Bryher, in spite of her financial resources, was not able to give H.D. the emotional support she needed; rather, H.D. thought of Bryher as a "tragic personality" who was "madly in love" with her and "possessed with devils." This was not the kind of attention H.D., alone with her young child, wanted. In spite of the fact that H.D. lived with Bryher after the birth of Perdita, she was desperately unhappy about the whole situation. Of Bryher's "madness" H.D. wrote to John Cournos in 1919:

> I am writing you in strict confidence about her. You must not not speak to Fletcher or anyone. But she is going everyday to a specialist and there is possibility of insanity. The doctor tells me that her sanity for the present depends on me. This sounds like exaggeration but you are used to the exaggerations of life. She likes you but remember she is horribly sensitive and covers it. She is devoted to me. I can do nothing, am only hoping, if I have the strength, to open her mind to possibilities. She is shut in and blind to life and I have never, never met so tragic a personality.
>
> I have again and again told her that I can not stand the strain of living with her and yet I can not leave her. She helps me in many ways but I want freedom and if the tie becomes too much, I must leave her. Yet I know my influence may help her and may help many, many others later. But I am not a philanthropist. I must have my freedom first and if the strain becomes too great, I shall just chuck her and the maddening problem of her life. There may be a doom over her and I may be only hurting myself trying to help her. On the other hand, she may be made for happiness, her own and other peoples and I may be her means of escape, her one means, and it would be base of me not to help her. I am fond of the girl, but I am not strong and if this thing is not soon helped, this madness of hers, a real suicidal madness, I can not stay with her. She is better than she was, but I am certain I can not stand it if the doctors do not help her soon.
>
> Do not let her know I write to you so personally . . . you may be able to help her . . . You will burn this letter and you know it is confidential. The worst thing is, the girl is in love with me, so madly that it is terrible. No man has ever cared for me like that. She seems possessed at times with a daemon or spirit outside herself. One side of her is so childlike that I am moved and must be tender, then this other thing comes. It is awful, like something from without, a possession . . . I have not the strength nor the love to banish this thing . . .
>
> I have been all alone — can you understand — facing all those problems that South Audley Street stands for, quite alone yet not willing to be flung into that maelstrom of capital and social evils. Do you think I wanted to face all those things? I have been quite

alone, moving without my own will, moving, tired to death, like a shell from which the spirit has departed, but moved like a piece in a play, pushed forward.

Do you think anyone would help me? That was the funny thing. No one would really. They were all afraid. I had to take the thing into my hands and the doctors said she would certainly go mad if she stayed another year in that house.

Perhaps I have played my part in this play and it is your clue to enter . . . If you are free, Monday, can you see me here as the girl goes home to dinner and we could talk.[8]

In spite of H.D.'s pleas to her friends for help and her difficulty in coping with Bryher's problems, she soon realized she would receive no aid and she had nowhere to go. H.D. tended to think of her relationship with Bryher during the 1920s as an odd sort of second marriage — a conception that appealed to Bryher, who had never wanted to be a woman and enjoyed being referred to as "He." For a time the relationship took an active physical turn, and Bryher's emotional involvement could be accurately described as an extreme form of possessiveness; but her love was not returned in kind. While the two women were close friends, traveling together and at times residing together, they felt a mutual distrust and a mutual distance. Their nicknames for each other, Fido (Bryher) and Cat (H.D.), accurately represent a recognition that they were not of the same species.*

Because of Bryher's possessiveness H.D. was never fully candid with her about the men in her life. She did not tell Bryher that Aldington was not Perdita's father until she sought Bryher's help in desperation after Aldington threatened to have her imprisoned for falsely registering the baby in his name. Bryher was overjoyed that H.D. had come to her and told H.D. that she hated Aldington, although she had only met him once. In 1927 Bryher made arrangements to adopt Perdita legally. This action removed the possibility of a suit against H.D. by Aldington and clearly established Perdita as Bryher's heir, but it also left H.D. in a kind of legal bondage to Bryher with regard to her daughter.

Through H.D., Pound met Bryher in late 1918, and they quickly developed a mutual hatred. Later in his life Pound reproached H.D. in a letter for taking up with "the murderer's daughter" and indicated that he felt that Bryher had suppressed his work of forging a renaissance in the arts by patronizing and

---

*During the early 1920s one of H.D.'s nicknames was Horse; H.D.'s mother's nickname was Beaver, and Perdita's nickname was Pup. For most of her life, H.D.'s nickname was Cat or Lynx.

promoting a large number of inferior artists and financially supporting the psychoanalytic movement. He himself never received any financial support from Bryher, although he asked for help in the 1930s. Later in her life H.D. managed to establish trust funds for Pound's children out of her own resources.

Although H.D. wrote again and again of Lawrence in her poems and novels, during his lifetime she did her best to hide her involvement with him from Bryher. She told Bryher that she was interested in him only as a writer and that she had never slept with him. Bryher met Lawrence for the first and only time in 1925, and was deeply puzzled by his insistence that she should give Hilda his love. After Lawrence's death H.D.'s relationship with Bryher continued to be complicated by the half-truths and outright lies that she had told. For the rest of her life she felt compelled to apologize to Bryher whenever she wrote about Lawrence because of the discrepancy between her writings and the minimal relationship she had described to Bryher shortly after they met.

H.D. never discussed the paternity of Perdita with anyone. Bryher presumed that Cecil Gray was the father. In 1922, using Brigit Patmore as an emissary, Bryher attempted to establish Perdita's paternity under the guise of recovering her financial investment in H.D.; Patmore was expected to persuade Gray to acknowledge paternity and assume financial responsibility for H.D. and her child. Although Patmore had several meetings with him, Gray did not admit he was the father of the child — and he did not deny it. She told him that H.D. had no means of providing for the child and that the child must be supported; Gray agreed that H.D. and the child were in need, but said he did not know from where the money was to come.[9] Patmore's account of their meetings seemed to satisfy Bryher, and when Perdita's questions with regard to her father received no answer from H.D., Bryher told her that her father was Cecil Gray.*

In 1926 H.D., who had lived for most of the previous seven years in her apartment at the Riant Chateau, returned to England to live; Bryher permitted her to lease an apartment in London. Shortly thereafter she began an affair with Kenneth Macpherson,† whom she met through her childhood friend

---

*Perdita Schaffner, personal interview, July 9, 1980. In response to my question as to whether her mother had ever told her the identity of her father, Perdita indicated that H.D. had not.

†Kenneth Macpherson (1907–1971) was an artist, writer, and filmmaker. He married Bryher in 1927 and with her edited the silent film magazine *Close-Up* from 1927 to 1933. After World War II Macpherson lived in Capri, Italy, where he was host to Norman Douglas.

Frances Gregg. Bryher's retaliatory response to this threat to her relationship with H.D. was to offer Macpherson a marriage contract. His acceptance put an end to his romance with H.D., but H.D., Bryher, and Macpherson remained friends. As with her marriage to McAlmon, Bryher's marriage to Macpherson was never consummated.[10] H.D. wrote to Pound that she, Kenneth, and Bryher had a "classical marriage."

In 1928 H.D. wrote to Pound about Aldington's request for a divorce and about the life she was then living with Bryher and Macpherson. To quote in part:

> I put down a lot of myself after Perdita's birth. I loved Richard very much and you know he threatened to use Perdita to divorce me and to have me locked up if I registered her as legitimate. This you see, was after he had said he would look after us, up to the point at least of seeing me on my feet again. I was "not on my feet" was literally "dying." I mean, anything in the way of a shock brings that back and I literally go to pieces . . .
>
> I seem to remember always the indignity of being unsheltered and then the treachery of the betrayal. It doesn't make any difference to my LOVE and I will always love Richard. But you see it built up a wall . . . and this side and that side of the wall are so very different . . .
>
> But I want there to be NO misunderstanding in this case or in any future decision of Richard. I want him to find out what he wants. I know how you feel about "formalities." I feel the same. But R. [Richard] and A. [Arabella] had told me they didn't want to marry and I suppose their turning on me afterward when I was actually crippled, has put me out of touch with my own integrity. I mean I do not care, only suddenly they were howling at me, screaming illegitimacy and what not, and they started it . . .
>
> I have no feeling at all . . . only here I am, with a very static and "classic" and peaceful relationship with Bryher and Macpherson. I admit, I am at times, very lonely, not that they do not understand, they just ARE not of that cycle and I was made by that pre-war London atmosphere and cycle . . . Br. [Bryher], between ourselves has been in a very difficult way and is going through a trying "analysis." She is a "borderline case," so that sometimes I seemed actuated by weakness in giving in to her, when I alone knew what she was and what terror came into my heart at her peculiar kind of suffering. Then I had nothing anyway . . . and Ezra, you know as well as I, that you might just as well be killed for a sheep as a lamb. Br. looked after Perdita and as that seemed to be the only thing I was hanging on for . . . I looked after Br. Of course, this is all very bald . . . but I am tired of mincing matters and "pretending." It does me more good than you know, just to write things out anyway, not thinking of any censor.[11]

H.D. did a good deal of writing during this period. The series of stories and novellas often referred to as the Dijon novels because of their place of publication include *Kora and Ka, Mira-Mare, Two Americans, The Usual Star, Nights,* and "Narthex." Several of H.D.'s friends of this period appear in these novels, particularly Bryher and Macpherson, and many other memoirs and novels record H.D.'s occasional presence in the literary circles of the twenties and thirties. In the case of those such as William Carlos Williams, whose loyalty was to McAlmon, the portrait is not flattering. Williams blamed H.D. for Bryher's involvement with her and for the failure of the Bryher-McAlmon marriage. H.D.'s loyalty to Bryher and to women writers in general, and her apparent disinterest in seeking another marriage, has led some to see this period of H.D.'s life as a time of "bisexual miseries."[12]

Bryher writes with considerable frankness and sensitivity of her lifelong friendship with H.D., their travels, and their mutual friends in her autobiography, *The Heart to Artemis.* In part because of these memoirs and in part because of H.D.'s Dijon novels, the path of this long friendship is quite accessible and easy to follow. In the late 1920s, as film emerged as a major international art form, H.D. helped Bryher and Kenneth Macpherson found and edit the film magazine *Close-Up.* In 1930 she starred with Paul Robeson in the film *Borderline,* which was written and directed by Macpherson. Bryher played a cigar-smoking innkeeper.

The general picture that emerges from H.D.'s poetry and novels of the twenties and early thirties and from her discussion in *Tribute to Freud* of why she sought out Freud suggests that from her own point of view, this was a period of general distress and unhappiness. In 1919 John Maynard Keynes had written *The Economic Consequences of the Peace,* which foretold the coming war as a result of the "peace" just concluded. One group of her friends talked of nothing but European politics, says H.D.; the other group was, in her mind, in flight from the inevitable.

H.D. went to Freud primarily to free herself "of repetitive thoughts and experiences," but she went too to prepare herself for the imminent war.

> I did not specifically realize just what it was I wanted, but I knew that I, like most of the people I knew, in England, America, and the continent of Europe, was drifting. We were drifting. Where? I did not know but at least I accepted the fact that we *were* drifting. At least, I knew this — I would (before the current of inevitable events swept me right into the main stream and so on to the cataract) stand aside, if I could (if it were not already too late), and take stock of my possessions. You might say that I had — yes, I had

something that I specifically owned. I *owned* myself. I did not really, of course. My family, my friends, and my circumstances owned me. But I *had* something. Say it was a narrow birch-bark canoe . . . With the current gathering force, I could at least pull in to the shallows before it was too late, take stock of my very modest possessions of mind and body, and ask the old Hermit who lived on the edge of this vast domain to talk to me, to tell me, if he would, how best to steer my course.[13]

He would, and he did. Bryher had met Freud in May 1927 with a letter of introduction from Havelock Ellis. It was undoubtedly Bryher's introduction as well as the recommendation of Hanns Sachs that enabled H.D. to have sessions with him in 1933 in Vienna. Freud was seventy-seven years old and was not seeing many analysands.

The purpose of H.D.'s psychoanalysis, she tells us in her *Tribute to Freud,* was to "substantiate something." She writes: "We had come together to substantiate something. I did not know what. There was something that was beating in my brain . . . I wanted it to be let out. I wanted to free myself of repetitive thoughts and experiences — my own and those of many of my contemporaries."[14]

H.D. went to Freud to substantiate her World War I experience, to establish the existence or truth of it. She needed to talk to someone wise enough to understand it. She had not discussed this experience with her new group of friends; she knew that she had avoided coming to terms with the events of the 1911–1919 period. As H.D. explains in *Advent,* "I HAD SAID, in the beginning, that I only wanted to tell the story, it was like the *Ancient Mariner."*[15]

The "repetitive thoughts and experiences" had been the subject of much of her prose and poetry between 1921 and 1933, which went in two entirely separate directions. There were the Dijon novels, which dealt with current situations, and there were the Madrigal novels ("Paint It Today," "Asphodel," "Pilate's Wife," *Palimpsest, Hedylus*), and the poetry, which dealt with the past, the "story." Freud would help her to come to terms with the events of the Imagist years; Freud would help her finally to tell the story, to lay the ghost. As we have seen in previous chapters, H.D. was obsessed by the Peter Van Eck vision, the Corfu vision, and her World War I experience. But she had not talked with anyone about these events; they had been repressed, suppressed.

To be repressed, she tells us, is to be buried alive. Writing of D. H. Lawrence, who is very much the subject of *Advent,* H.D. says: "Yes I was 'Buried Alive.' Is this why my thoughts return to Lawrence? I can only remember that last book he wrote. *The Man Who Died* was buried alive." [16]

Repression is suffocation. We free ourselves from our obsessive dreams and visions if we give them expression. Psychoanalytically speaking, health is a matter of expression rather than repression. Repression is a block in the body and/or mind. What is repressed must somehow find expression. Repression is unexpressed inspiration. The pain of unexpressed inspiration is unbearable. Expression is a letting go. From a psychoanalytic point of view, a poem, like H.D.'s first Imagist poems, arises from a break in the primal integrity. The poem, then, is a symptom, a wound inflicted in the conflict of wills — a primordial scream.

As we have seen in previous chapters, H.D.'s early poems were written under the influence of minds not her own. But H.D. had a mind of her own, and her whole impetus as a poet was to restore her original integrity. From a psychoanalytic point of view, a strain of music or poetry is paradoxically both a wound to be healed and a process of healing. The expression of the image facilitates the healing. Of her creative process, H.D. writes: "The dream escaping consciousness is perceived. In one vivid moment, it may be held, circled in a ring of complete understanding . . . This is madness, or is it inspiration?" [17]

The masculine expression, dream, or vision is her inspiration. In breathing in the essence of the male spirit she has become inspired. As she is able to find expression through art, her vision inspires new forms.

As in H.D.'s Peter Van Eck experience, a vision or dream may be so close to ordinary experience that a person may have difficulty distinguishing one from the other. After World War I it was sometimes hard for H.D. to know whether something *really* happened or she imagined the occurrence so vividly it seemed real. In the case of Peter Van Eck, with time and distance and help from Freud it became clear to H.D. that the vision actually occurred "only" in the realm of the imagination, although it might still have seemed to have a greater reality than the events that occur in everyday life. One of the differences between everyday seeing and what poets and mystics call vision is the clarity of the image presented to consciousness. Did H.D. meet the person she calls Van Eck on the deck of the boat or didn't she?

> Sometimes Mr. Van Eck was the Man on the boat but he was not the Man on the boat I met the first time in the Bay. I should have known. I did know, though I could not yet admit it, that not only were the dolphins unconvincing but the sea itself was impossible.

That is, it was all right at the time but you do not have a quiet sea and a boat moving with no tremor, with no quiver or pulse of engine, on a sea that is level yet broken in a thousand perfectly peaked wavelets like the waves in the background of a Botticelli. No, it was all wrong.[18]

Perhaps H.D.'s Peter Van Eck experience actually occurred in another dimension of time and space. In other words, perhaps H.D.'s vision was a transposed reality. As she has explained, her imagination worked in this way. An event that occurred in one time and place, one dimension, was often transposed by her imaginative processes to another time and place, another dimension. As she explains in her "Notes on Recent Writing": "I do not wish it to be thought that I am dealing with a vague, mystical commonplace when I speak of 're-incarnation.' It is the sense of continuity that inspires me."[19]

In "Compassionate Friendship" H.D. makes the same point on another level. She is speaking about her novel *Palimpsest*.

> I run upstairs and get the only copy that I have of this book. I read, on the title page, "Palimpsest; i.e. a parchment from which one writing has been erased to make room for another . . ." I have been reading in the *Palimpsest,* the first of the three sections of stories, *Hipparchia.* The writing is, as Edith Sitwell said, perceptively, of a later Greek reconstruction, *Hedylus,* "hallucinated." It is hallucinated and I must become hallucinated in order to cope with it.
>
> The writing though un-even in the original script and badly punctuated, has held and astonished me. I do not think I have read this story for 20 or more years.
>
> It is actually the same story as the much later *Madrigal* where I assemble the same set of players in modern dress; it took me 20 years or more to get the Greek characters into time. They are out-of-time in the Greek scene, the only way I could assemble them in the early or mid-twenties.[20]

While it is true that H.D.'s mind presents us with a fascinating glimpse into the creative process, it is in some sense frustrating that we may never know the real story, for all the Madrigal novels present a different perspective on it. What is it that we want to know? Perhaps the concept of the real story is the *real* fiction.

From a Freudian point of view, the important thing is that H.D. somehow managed to remember all the traumatic events. Bringing this material to consciousness and expressing it, either in the analytic session or in art, is essential to the healing process.

Poems are "symptoms"; visions can be "dangerous symptoms." H.D. had a certain control over her inspired poetry;

the visions were another matter. A vision is like a poem out of control, occurring when the overwrought psyche has apprehended something it cannot assimilate. The vision is in a very real sense *other*. The mind must strain to overpower it, capture it in writing, before it has its own way and seduces the mind.

An Imagist poem by H.D. is a less intense vision than the Van Eck (or the Corfu) vision, but these experiences are on a continuum. Like her visions, H.D.'s poetry was inspired by an experience she couldn't assimilate. At the biographical level, it was inspired first by Pound, then by Lawrence. Freud would become another poetic inspiration, though one difference between Pound and Lawrence on the one hand and Freud on the other was that Freud was not romantically involved with H.D. He was attempting to restore her primal integrity. He was attempting to restore H.D. to herself, to help her to create her own legend: "Yes, my own LEGEND. Then, to get well and re-create it."[21]

We could describe H.D.'s Van Eck experience and the way her mind worked in the writing and rewriting of the Madrigal novels in Freudian terms, as displacement. And in a sense all truly creative literature is displacement. As in H.D.'s case, the process is both conscious and unconscious; the full consciousness may be delayed. The artist knows he or she is using a literary technique in the creation, for instance, of a poem, but the artist informs herself or himself as she or he fulfills the form. The displacement opens the gates of the unconscious. The technique, then, allows for a creative process through which one discovers oneself in one's own disguises.

Artistic creativity also involves the psychoanalytically defined concept of projection. In our projections we discover the "other." The other is not necessarily an individual, but that which we have not yet assimilated, that which is still alien — everything, in fact, that we have experienced but not yet recognized as ourselves. From this perspective the autonomous self is an illusion; what we conceive is life itself.

According to Freud, the suppression of emotion is the disease of civilization. With Freud's help and through her creative efforts, H.D. found the courage to open the floodgates and ride the rapids. The vivid moment is the breakthrough in the structure of repression, the character structure. Express, don't repress, H.D. learned from Freud, for in a moment the dream is gone, "running wild in the pastures of the mind's *hinterland*."[22]

"She wanted to forget about that," said Norman Holmes Pearson. "She wanted to forget about Lawrence."[23] But as Freud taught her, sometimes we must remember in order to forget.

D. H. Lawrence was dead. He had died March 2, 1930, at Vence, France. It was better to forget, and to let go of the painful memories. But first it was necessary for H.D. to substantiate her experience, to give it substance, to give it concrete form, to re-create it in vision or poetry and in dialogue with Freud. To remember in order to forget. As Helen says to Theseus in *Helen in Egypt:*

> take my hands in your hands,
> teach me to remember,
> teach me not to remember.[24]

27

The Professor

IN ADDITION to his regular medical practice Freud accepted a limited number of analysands in the capacity of students. H.D. wrote to Bryher and Kenneth Macpherson that she would be studying psychoanalysis. In a letter of December 22, 1932, she writes: "Papa [Freud] speaks of his patients and 'pupils,' and rather seems to convey that H.D. is among the latter."[1]

H.D. was fascinated with Freud's concept of transference because it involves the superimposition of one form upon another, as does Imagism. In the *Writing on the Wall* section of her *Tribute to Freud* H.D. calls Freud Asklepios, the blameless physician, or simply the Professor.

> He (Asklepios) was the son of the sun, Phoebos Apollo, and music and medicine were alike sacred to this source of light . . . Our Professor stood this side of the portal. He did not pretend to bring back the dead who had already crossed the threshold. But he raised from dead hearts and stricken minds and maladjusted bodies a host of living children.[2]

H.D. understood Freud's psychoanalytic paradigm not as the truth of what is, as our generation has come to understand it, but rather as the story of his own enlightenment. The theoretical statement is the equivalent of the poetic statement in that it is one of the acts by which the individual — in this case Freud — comes into recognition and consciousness of himself. A theoretical document such as, for example, *The Interpretation of Dreams* is a recreation of the Greek drama, the Oedipus drama. *"Know thyself,* said the ironic Delphic oracle, and the sage or priest who framed the utterance knew that to know yourself in the full sense of the words was to know everybody."[3]

Although education does play a part in analysis, Freud draws a clear distinction between the two. He writes: "If knowledge about his unconscious were as important for the patient as the inexperienced in psychoanalysis imagine, it would be sufficient to cure him for him to go to lectures or read books."[4] In Freud's theoretical formulation, self-knowledge is acquired in the therapeutic transference relationship, which can be generally defined as the relationship between the patient and the analyst. In psychoanalytic language transference is an "artificial neurosis," and it is sometimes difficult to distinguish in Freud's writings how this relationship differs from a permissive but "aim-inhibited" love. Since the analysis is carried out in genital abstinence, Freud describes the relationship as frustrated and libidinized, though it may be perceived, presumably from the outside, as merely friendly.[5]

The transference is encouraged rather than rebuffed as unrealistic because it is within the transference that therapy takes place. In general, in his analytic writing Freud recommends that the analyst not define the quality of the transference but rather act "as a mirror, reflecting nothing but what is shown to him."[6] He or she is to listen without judging, for making judgments could preclude understanding. "He must bend his own unconscious like a receptive organ towards the emerging unconscious of the patient, be as the receiver of the telephone to the disc."[7] The analyst must also "be in a superior position in some sense if he is to serve as a model for his patient in certain analytic situations and, in others, to act as his teacher."[8]

It is within the transference that the patient remembers and works through repressed infantile memories. Aside from sexual abstinence, the fundamental rule of analysis is that the patient should report whatever comes to his or her mind. With the establishment of positive transference the patient abandons the neurotic compulsion to repeat and develops a compulsion to remember. The reason for this dramatic change appears to be that the repressed infantile ego–object cathexis of childhood becomes symbolically re-established in the form of the transference relationship. The repressed memories related to this ego–object configuration, which is a form of ego organization, are more accessible to consciousness within the context of this infantile reality principle. Freud says: "We admit [the compulsion to repeat] into the transference as to a playground, in which it is allowed to let itself go in almost complete freedom and is required to display before us all the pathogenic impulses hidden in the depths of the patient's mind."[9]

It is precisely the intention of the therapeutic situation to translate neurotic symptoms into mental and verbal constructions so that disguised (and thus meaningless) but repetitive thoughts or actions, which may be terrifying, can become meaningful. And by the process of "working through," the patient synthesizes the symptoms into consciousness.

Both the analyst and the analysand provide interpretations of the material brought to light in the course of the analysis; these are "constructions," meaningful contexts or metaphors for the disguised and thus meaningless memories. The constructions of the patient often indicate resistance to making unconscious ideas conscious. The analyst must be particularly sensitive to such resistance. Since the analysis takes place within transference, any resistance must be seen as a resistance to transference. The form of the resistance is in a very real sense the subject of the analysis.

Since the inability to remember is a manifestation of resistance, the analyst uses a variety of techniques, such as the reporting of dreams and free association, to bring seemingly meaningless material that manifests neurotic or perhaps psychotic symptoms into consciousness. Of her analysis H.D. says in her *Tribute to Freud:*

> My imagination wandered at will; my dreams were revealing, and many of them drew on classical or Biblical symbolism . . . Fragmentary ideas, apparently unrelated, were often found to be part of a special layer or stratum of thought and memory, therefore to belong together; these were sometimes skillfully pieced together like the exquisite Greek tear-jars and iridescent glass bowls and vases that gleamed in the dusk from the shelves of the cabinet that faced me where I stretched, propped up on the couch in the room in Berggasse 19, Wien IX.[10]

What H.D. remembered in her analysis is what she came to express in her poetry: images or pictures. These images are more primary than the theoretical formulations that are advanced to describe them. As her readers, we come to share the images or pictures. "These pictures are so clear. They are like transparencies, set before candles in a dark room."[11]

Through the process of psychoanalysis we find access to the elaborate buildup of past memories. The consequence is not an answer, a categorical formulation of an abstract problem and its solution, but vision. Freud, as well as H.D., knew that what we call madness and what we call inspiration come from the same source.

> He had said, he had dared to say that the dream had its worth and value in translatable terms . . . He had dared to say that the dream came from an unexplored depth in man's consciousness and that

this unexplored depth ran like a great stream or ocean underground, and the vast depth of that ocean was the same vast depth that today, as in Joseph's day, overflowing in man's small consciousness, produced inspiration, madness, creative ideas or the dregs of the dreariest symptoms of mental unrest and disease. He had dared to say that it was the same ocean of universal consciousness . . . he had dared to imply that this consciousness proclaimed all men one; all nations and races met in the universal world of the dream; and he had dared to say that the dream-symbol could be interpreted; its language, its imagery were common to the whole race . . . the picture-writing, the hieroglyph of the dream, was the common property of the whole race; in the dream, man, as at the beginning of time, spoke a universal language.[12]

Freud and H.D. were each concerned with the problem of reality and illusion, the true and the false dream. H.D. says: "There are trivial, confused dreams and there are real dreams. The trivial dream bears the same relationship to the real as a column of gutter-press news-print to a folio page of a play of Shakespeare." And a great many of these real dreams, H.D. believes, "come from the same source as the Script or Scripture, the Holy Writ or Word."[13]

As the patient "remembers" the repressed material, the dream content and symbol, during analysis, the structure of consciousness becomes modified; this is the process of "working through." Psychoanalysis, as Freud knew, as H.D. came to know, is work. As the patient accepts interpretations of dreams and associations in a new structure of consciousness, repressions that "behave like dams in time of flood"[14] give way and "ought to end in the patient's recollection."[15]

Since repressions act as a protection of the ego from unconscious desires and fears, the individual stripped of this protection is vulnerable to being overwhelmed and experiencing a breakdown. The danger is mitigated, Freud writes, by the fact that "the essence of the analytic situation is that the analyst enters into an alliance with the ego of the patient to subdue certain uncontrolled parts of his id., *i.e.,* to include them in the synthesis of the ego."[16]

This relationship (the transference), which is narcissistically satisfying for the patient, also allows the patient emotionally to reexperience the remembered unconscious ideas. Remembering and translating unconscious ideas into the context of an adult reality principle (represented by the constructions) supposedly detaches them from the libido and makes the original repression unnecessary. The patient can now remember formerly unconscious ideas in a conscious language, the language of analysis, which is rational and essentially nonerotic.

But H.D. was a poet, and the poem too is a construction in analysis, although it might be a delusion. Freud says: "The delusions of patients appear to me to be the equivalents of the constructions which we build up in the course of an analytic treatment — attempts at explanations and cure." And he maintains that the delusion "owes its convincing power to the element of historic truth which it inserts in the place of rejected reality." Hence Freud comes to see that people suffering from delusions are suffering from memory; they are "suffering from their own recollections." And just as the individual suffers from delusions, mankind too suffers from delusions.

> If we consider mankind as a whole and substitute it for the single human individual, we discover that it too has developed delusions which are inaccessible to logical criticism and which contradict reality. If, in spite of this, they are able to exert an extraordinary power over men, investigation leads us to the same explanation as in the case of the single individual. They owe their power to the element of historic truth which they have brought up from the repression of the forgotten and primaeval past.[17]

H.D. would agree with Freud that this "truth" is sometimes inaccessible to logical criticism. Of Freud's thought, H.D. says:

> The point was that for all his amazing originality, he was drawing from a source so deep in human consciousness that the outer rock or shale, the accumulation of hundreds or thousands of years of casual, slack, or even wrong or evil thinking, had all but sealed up the original spring or well-head. He called it striking oil, but others — long ago — had dipped into that same spring. They called it "a well of living water" in the old days, or simply the "still waters."[18]

The therapist-patient relationship in psychoanalysis invokes the mental paradigm of childhood. That is, in the transference or "love" relationship that develops in the course of a successful analysis, the patient for the time being denies the adult reality principle or paradigm by which he or she usually lives and re-enters and remembers that of childhood. By invoking a different paradigm, a different relationship of the knowing mind to what is known becomes possible. Suddenly events, thoughts, fears, dreams, and hopes take on a different meaning. A lost reality asserts itself in a new dimension. The world is made new. Cognition becomes recognition, and recognition paves the way for a new mode of seeing, a new vision.

28

To Bryher
from Vienna

IN A DISCUSSION of *Writing on the Wall,* Norman Holmes Pearson correctly observed of H.D.'s account of her encounter with Freud: "You don't learn very much about Freud's particular psychiatry — or rather I mean his theology of psychoanalysis — but you do learn an enormous amount about how Freud proceeded with an analysand."[1] *Advent* gives us further insight into Freud's psychoanalytic method, but a third and in some ways more revealing record of the analysis exists in the letters H.D. wrote to Bryher during its course. Bryher was paying for the analysis and she demanded a firsthand account of the proceedings.

H.D.'s description to Bryher of her first encounter with Freud does not give us the familiar portrait of the detached scientist, aloof and eschewing judgments, but rather an image of a magician-king who has the power to shatter the adult ego defenses and reduce the analysand to the state of a terrified and defenseless child. In a letter of March 1, 1933, following her first session, H.D. writes:

> I think that if the chow hadn't liked me, I would have left, I was so scared by Oedipus . . . A sphinx faces the bed. I did not want to go to bed, the white "napkin for the head" was the only professional touch, there were dim lights, like an opium dive . . .
>
> He said he would prefer me to recline. He has a real fur rug, and I started to tell him how Turtle [Hanns Sachs] had done, he seemed vaguely shocked, then remarked, "I see you are going to be very difficult. Now although it is against the rules, I will tell you something: YOU *WERE* DISAPPOINTED, AND YOU *ARE* DISAPPOINTED, IN ME."
>
> I then let out a howl, and screamed, "but do you not realize you are everything, you are priest, you are magician." He said, "No. It

is you who are poet and magician." I then cried so I could hardly utter and he said that I had looked at the pictures, preferring the mere dead shreds of antiquity to his living presence. I then yelled, "but you see your dog liked me, when your dog came, I knew it was all right, as it would not have liked me if you had not." He said, "ah an English proverb but reversed, like me and you like my dog." I corrected him, "love me, love my dog" and he growled and purred with delight. He then gave me a long speech on how sad it was for a poet to listen to his bad English. I then howled some more and said he was not a person but a voice, and that in looking at antiquity, I was looking at him. He said I had got to the same place as he, we met, he in the childhood of humanity — antiquity — I in my own childhood. I cried some more and the hour was already more than half gone. It was terrible . . . He is not there at all, is simply a ghost and I simply shake all over and cry. He kept asking me if I wanted the lights changed. He sat, not at, but on the pillow and Hammered with his fists to point his remarks and mine. I am terrified of Oedipus Rex.

What am I to do?[2]

Freud read H.D.'s work before he accepted her as a student. He also read the works of Ezra Pound and D. H. Lawrence. Havelock Ellis had written to Freud and sent him his erotic fantasy of H.D., "The Revelation." Moreover, Freud had received Hanns Sachs's diagnosis of H.D.'s "mother fixation" (H.D. had sessions with Sachs in late 1932 in preparation for her work with Freud).

H.D.'s letters to Bryher reveal that Freud applied a variety of different theories as the analysis progressed, and he changed his mind about her several times during the course of her sessions, or "séances" (French for sessions) as she called them. From the beginning of the analysis H.D. called Freud "Papa." She could never swallow his idea that she had a mother fixation to him and joked to Bryher, "this old Mummy of an Oedipus-Rex is right out of my own phantasy world."[3] Nine days into her analysis H.D. wrote to Bryher, "One interpretation of ANY thing with a person like myself was not sufficient"; there must be "two or multiple interpretations."[4] Her response to Freud's inability to pin her down and analyze her with any of the standard formulas is amusing. She continues, "O my god, talk of the two-faced oracle of Delphi . . . Papa has a hundred."

Four weeks into the analysis Freud told H.D. that her particular kind of fixation had not been known until three years before (1930); she had become "stuck" at the early pre-Oedipal stage. "Back to the womb," writes H.D., "seems to be my only solution." Freud related H.D.'s interest in islands, the sea, and Greek primitives to this fixation. Her "triangle," he told her, was "mother-brother-self." Rodeck, says H.D., was the phallic mother.[5] Aldington, Kenneth Macpherson, and Bryher were brothers. H.D. told Bryher that she, Bryher, was very likely the younger brother. "Trust this does not offend your masculinity," she wrote.[6] Bryher was delighted with this identification and pleased that Freud had said she looked like a boy, a northern explorer in fact, in the picture H.D. showed to him.

On March 23, 1933, H.D. wrote that Freud had told her she was a good "life" vibration "as I went on and on, repeating, wanting to give life or save life, never . . . to destroy life." Two days later she told Bryher that she and Freud had "gone over all the historical war and post-war matter" and that Freud had given her his forgiveness. This absolution cannot be overemphasized as a liberating factor in the analysis. As we shall see, Kaspar plays this role in *The Flowering of the Rod*. To Bryher, H.D. wrote: "He . . . gave me his blessing and forgiveness and dispensation for all past 'sins,' said it was not really necessary to dwell on all that, only as an indication of guilt toward mother; that otherwise there was nothing 'wrong.' " On March 27 H.D. wrote that Freud was "the present-day Jesus who wishes to rationalize the miracle."

Eight weeks into the analysis Freud revealed to H.D. his new theory of femininity, the penis-envy theory.* In retrospect we can see it had been present as an underlying structure from the beginning of the analysis, but in her session of May 1, 1933, Freud made his theory explicit. In her letter to Bryher of that date H.D. writes: "Papa has a complete new theory but he says he does not dare write it, because he does not want to make enemies of women. Apparently, we have all stirred him up frightfully."

H.D.'s first response to the theory was to endorse it. In her May 1 letter, written just after Freud told her of it, she wrote to Bryher:

> His idea is that all women are deeply rooted in penis-envy, not only the bi-sexual or homo-sexual woman. The advanced intellectual woman is frank about it. That is all. But that the whole cult and development of normal womanhood is based on the same fact; the envy of the woman for the penis. Now this strikes me as being a clue to everything . . . He just flung out the idea. I screamed at him, "but the supreme compliment to WOMAN would be to trust women with this great secret." I said Br. [Bryher], the Princess and myself would appreciate it, and keep it going.

*Freud's theories of femininity evolved and changed over the course of his career. His last, the penis-envy theory, attempts to explain feminine psychology as a compensation for the absence of a penis. See his chapter titled "Femininity" in *New Introductory Lectures on Psychoanalysis* (1933).

H.D. at first thought that the theory could account for some elements of her psychic make-up and that it would explain a lot of feminine behavior. It seemed to her that in the case of Bryher, who relished masculine roles and dressed like a man, the theory was right on the mark. But Bryher was not complimented by "this great secret" and told H.D. so. H.D. responded that she needn't be so "beastly" about Papa's theory.[7] She said, "It is important as book means penis evidently and as a 'writer,' only am I an equal, in the right way, with men. Most odd. However . . . we will work it all out."[8] Interestingly, however, as the analysis proceeded, Freud did not draw on his penis-envy theory to explain H.D.'s psyche.

Bryher had arranged for H.D.'s sessions and hoped and expected that Freud would help H.D. to become reinvolved in her; the attachment of the first days of their relationship had waned considerably. Early in her analysis H.D. wrote to Bryher:

> I talked all last hour about us at Scilly Isles and Papa was MOST sweet about you. He seems to have some very clear idea of the jelly-fish saga ["Notes on Thought and Vision"], and says you, by a miracle of love and intuition, understood what Dr. Ellis could never have understood . . . So you see, Papa thoroughly approves and you have been "in" the analysis all along, via the first Greek trip and your rescue of the war-time stray-cat [H.D.] with cat-on [Perdita]. The H.D.-Bryher saga is well established.[9]

But H.D.'s letters during the analysis reveal that in spite of the lesbian episode in their relationship, she was not sexually attracted to Bryher. If and when Bryher came into her dreams her presence was experienced as maternal; she was an image not of desire but of safety. H.D. tried, without success, to impress this upon her. While H.D. loved persons of both sexes, her sexual attraction was to men. Freud's final conclusion about H.D. seemed to be that it was psychically possible for her to live with women in a woman's world and that her relationship with Bryher was inextricably bound up with her need to nurture and provide for her daughter. H.D. was filled with gratitude to Bryher for her sessions with Freud: "I can never, never repay you for this marvelous old Greek oracle that I go to daily."[10]

Since she had never been candid with Bryher about Lawrence, reporting on her conversations with Freud about him presented a problem and was a source of a considerable amount of guilt and frustration for H.D. In her letters she told Bryher that Freud found it necessary to talk about Lawrence and asked Bryher to consent to this by sending her a picture of Lawrence. On March

8, 1933, H.D. wrote: "Can you find the Times Book Review of a few weeks past, with a portrait of D. H. Lawrence? It is a full face, there are two in the number, one a small one in an advt. at the back. I was talking to papa about his book (or rather I intended to) *The Man Who Died*."

As the analysis proceeded H.D. discussed her affair with Lawrence, but was still not able to tell Bryher about it directly after keeping it from her for so many years. On May 11 she wrote to Bryher that she and Freud had had a long talk about "that man that Lawrence got in touch with," an independent Baltimore "analyst," Trigant Burrow.

> Freud said it showed the state of the UC-N [unconscious] of D.H.L. that he should have hit on Burrow, of all people . . . I got out the vol. of letters of D.H.L. *The Letters of D. H. Lawrence*, edited by A. Huxley . . . in it, are letters to Grey [sic] and letters from 44 Mecklenburgh Square, with dates and so on and the insinuating letters after Port Cros and the bust-up with R.A. [Aldington] and Bgt. [Brigit Patmore]. These letters . . . put a whole lot on the map for me, and it is as well anyhow, I think to have this printed record (though not explicit/ no mention of my name or anything to give it away, of course) of my stay in Cornwall, the dates and so on.

Throughout her stay in Vienna H.D. worked with a copy of Lawrence's letters edited by Aldous Huxley. She wrote to Bryher, "It's really most illuminating, has, in fact, stirred me up, so I could not sleep at all."

> I was especially surprised to find C.G. [Cecil Gray] of all people, had coughed up his little packet, quite an illuminating side-light on Grey [sic] and Cornwall altogether. Also L. [Lawrence] wrote some very delightful descriptions of Bosigran and so on, from there to other people . . . All this has come up, made a violent purple-patch in my analysis, but I presume it is a good thing, as the past was alive and kicking under the debris.[11]

H.D. and Freud talked a good deal about Lawrence, but Bryher gave no encouragement to this theme. H.D. again responded by minimizing her involvement with Lawrence to Bryher and suggesting that this phase of the analysis would soon be over. She wrote, for instance, "NO one . . . could endure the DHL vibration for long . . . as witness many of the letters."[12] She thanked Bryher ad infinitum for her "séances" with Freud and pleaded with her for her blessing to go over this Lawrence material. She was terribly afraid Bryher would cut off her sessions. She wrote: "I have been soaking in D.H.L. letters, not too good for me, but

Freud seems to agree with me for once. Evidently I blocked the whole of the 'period' and if I can skeleton-in a vol. about it, it will break the clutch."[13]

She asked Bryher to send her Mabel Dodge Luhan's book *Lorenzo at Taos* and told her: "It's pretty sure that Peter Rodeck was a smoke-screen."[14] H.D. wrote that "papa seems to believe explicitly that it would be best for me to make this vol. of mine about 1913–1920 explicit."[15] And to this purpose she asked Bryher for the Murry book *Son of Woman,* explaining that she was "collecting data from the outside" about this period of her life. She writes of her own novel: "It will need a lot of 'guts,' (my word) my end, to get the thing down in a stern manner and not leap goat-like on top of things in a dope-y stream of consciousness like Narthex."

By the time of H.D.'s May 18 letter, the political situation in Austria had become very tense and she was encouraged by Bryher and Kenneth to leave Vienna. She did not want to leave if Freud stayed behind. She pleaded to Bryher for Freud's life; she was terribly worried about his safety. She said that the terror in the streets did not compare to the terror she was still experiencing as a result of her World War I experiences. She wrote: "My heart is here with this old, old Saint at the moment . . . and I would almost rather stay here and risk death . . . I have been so terrorized those war years and after . . . I am so sick of that special sort of terror."

On May 20 she again apologized to Bryher for her concentration on Lawrence: "You must be sick of L. but Freud thinks it good to 'lay' that." On May 24 another apology: "I have been reading too much Lawrence, but it puts everything on the map." And on May 26: "I am sorry to be crippled like this this morning. Its all reading D.H.L. But I think it as well to FACE it." On May 26 she went on to thank Bryher again for her "terrific generosity" to Freud. Bryher had sent him a substantial monetary gift in response to H.D.'s concern for his safety.

At the end of May the Nazis burned copies of Freud's books in Berlin. On June 15, 1933, at Bryher's insistence in relation to the deteriorating political situation, H.D. returned to Kenwin, the house that she and Bryher and Kenneth had built in Switzerland on Lake Geneva, to let the analysis "set." In the last month of the analysis H.D. had written to Bryher of Freud: "I think he is like your father, both of them are Taurus, you see . . . work like an ox."[16] On July 18 came word of Sir John Ellerman's death. H.D. went to pieces.

In spite of the fact that Sir John and Lady Ellerman had not entirely approved of H.D. — they called her "Dolly" — both Bryher's and H.D.'s letters make it clear that H.D. and Sir John had shared a special sort of intimacy. H.D. stayed at Kenwin while Bryher and Kenneth planned the funeral ceremony in London. She wrote to Kenneth August 19: "It's been hell for me — but don't tell Br. It's been Hell." The next day she wrote to Bryher of "a lovely, exquisite, un-ending love, you and your dada and you and me, and so the three of us together." In this rambling and incoherent letter she tells Bryher to be strong and then writes with a shock of recognition: "YOU are SIR JOHN." On September 22, she wrote:

> I think this [Sir John's death] will dissolve or resolve finally P.R. [Peter Rodeck]. I feel that. That fixation was some queer combination of father-mother . . . I feel now the two separate . . . THE FATHER is the great mind, the sweep of sea and sky, my own father, yours and our dear old "papa" . . . Those three men are the three wise men to me . . .

H.D.'s letter prefigures her vision of Kaspar in *The Flowering of the Rod:* "Sir John — bird. His is the great red star. ALDEBARAN, I know — an arab, age-old star. Older influences than Freud would admit."

On October 27, 1933, following her first series of sessions of analysis, Freud wrote to H.D.: "I am deeply satisfied to hear that you are writing, creating. That is why we dived into the depths of your unconscious mind I remember." He was convinced of the fact that she was indeed an artist. In fact, it would not be too far afield to state that he believed that she was *essentially* an artist. In December he wrote: "Very glad to hear you are reading in my new lectures. I imagine you writing, creating at what you had been hinting to me and in due time I am sure you will let me enjoy it too." [17]

In October 1934 H.D. returned to Vienna to resume her work with Freud. Sir John Ellerman had left her eight thousand pounds, enough to make her financially independent of Bryher's allowance. For the second series of sessions she insisted on paying the fees herself, and Freud adjusted them so as to fit her more limited ability to pay.

On October 31 H.D. wrote to Bryher: "I am working harder this time. Papa says we are 'deep down in a tunnel.' I think it is doing me a lot of good. But O — how tired I am after."

H.D. did not write as often to Bryher during the second session of her analysis, and while her letters touched on issues raised with Freud, she clearly no longer felt obligated to keep Bryher fully informed. On November 27 H.D. wrote that "Papa said I had become so independent and clear in my outlines that there was no reason for him to speak at all."

In the same letter she wrote of how she had "lost" both parents at the age of three or four, and built her whole love life on "love and terror" mixed, that is, love of parents and fear of loss. Freud diagnosed her as bisexual; she wrote to Bryher:

> . . . usually a child decides for or against one parent, or identifies himself with one but for me . . . it was simply the loss of *both* parents, and a sort of perfect bi-sexual attitude arises, loss and independence. I have tried to be man, or woman, but I have to be both . . . I may get that in writing, and will become more abstract toward the writing in life, now that I know WHAT I am.

And on November 18, 1934: "You evidently in some way, are food, help, support, mother."

Of one of her many dreams Freud explained she was afraid she would die and leave Perdita alone, and this fear for Perdita was the basis of her bisexuality. Of another dream, she wrote to Bryher, "I got up such a lovely dream of self as Pup [Perdita] in a shell with a sort of mother-goddess-of-the-sea, the last day, it was supposed to be 'birth' . . . I want to get strong and go on pushing out vol.'s, that is 'birth.' "[18]

In a letter of November 23 H.D. pleaded with Bryher not to probe her about her writing because it gave her terrible pain. She asked: "Let me write, then let me FORGET my writing . . . My whole life, literally, is one Pure and Perfect Crucification." She was begging Bryher to allow her to live a separate life and to pursue her life as an artist in an independent domain.

During the course of her analysis with Freud, H.D. realized that she "had a sort of split-infinitive, or split or dual personality."[19] She realized that she had been living two separate lives, the one with Bryher (and Sir John and Kenneth), and the one that had been repressed after the war — her life with Lawrence, Pound, and Aldington, the "novel." Toward the end of her second series of "séances" H.D. finished "Pilate's Wife" and sent it to her publisher, but the manuscript was rejected; she later learned that Bryher had not wanted it published. But through her sessions with Freud H.D. gained clarity of mind, and whether a manuscript was published or not was not so terribly important. She had been split, schizophrenic. As she wrote to Bryher at the conclusion of her analysis: "The only problem is to get the two rails going together."[20]

29

D. H. Lawrence
Everywhere

ADVENT IS the nativity, the birth, of the Christ Child. The celebration of Advent includes the four Sundays before Christmas; the word *advent* conveys the idea that something miraculous is about to occur. It announces a coming. Advent also signifies the coming of Christ as judge on the last day (Second Advent).

H.D. chose her title *Advent* in recognition of the transference relationship that had developed between herself and Freud. In choosing it she was consciously equating the religious concept of the Second Coming with the psychoanalytic concept of transference. In "Thorn Thicket" H.D. equates her concept of advent with D. H. Lawrence's symbol for resurrection, the phoenix, and tells us that the *Advent* manuscript is but a part of the material she wrote about Lawrence during her psychoanalysis with Freud. She writes of how the "Lorenzo letter" at the end of *Bid Me to Live* rose like a phoenix from the ashes of the mass of material that she destroyed after the *Advent* manuscript had been assembled.

> I remember that I assembled the *Advent* notes from a mass of material, most of which I tore up, in that cold, alien room at [Hotel] *La Paix* where I finished *Madrigal*. Perhaps the Lorenzo letter rose like his proverbial Phoenix from the symbolic ashes, as it were, of those of the *Advent* notes that I discarded. For there were in the "ashes," several dreams of Lawrence, that I had jotted down in the familiar blue-lined copy-book, after I had told them to the Professor in Vienna.[1]

Insofar as H.D. transferred her feelings for Lawrence to Freud, the psychoanalysis resulted in a second coming of Lawrence, a second advent or rebirth. "And now that this transference is understood between us, I go on to talk of Lawrence."[2] When H.D. first met Freud he reminded her of Lawrence: "I asked him how he was and he smiled a charming, wrinkled smile that reminded me of D. H. Lawrence."[3]

In 1933 H.D. had not yet recovered from the loss of her relationship with Lawrence at the end of the war. She had attempted to forget about him and to begin a new life. But she had been stunned by Lawrence's death.

At the time of her sessions with Freud, H.D. saw Lawrence everywhere. She was haunted by the memories and the overwhelming images, the literature, she and Lawrence had created in response to each other. When she saw Freud, she saw Lawrence: "Sigmund Freud is like a curator in a museum, surrounded by his priceless collection of Greek, Egyptian, and Chinese treasures; he is 'Lazarus stand forth'; he is like D. H. Lawrence, grown old but matured and with astute perception."[4]

Similarities between Freud and Lawrence account for H.D.'s transference of feelings; ironically, the point at which the transference occurred had to do with Lawrence's repeated outbursts on the matter of feminine submission to phallic power. In *Aaron's Rod*, for instance, Lawrence had asserted: "The woman must submit, but deeply, deeply submit. Not to any foolish fixed authority . . . But to something deep, deeper. To the soul in its dark motion of power and pride . . . The woman must now submit — but deeply, deeply, and richly!"[5]

In illustrating his new theory of femininity, Freud lectured to H.D. on this very subject. On March 4, 1933, she wrote to Bryher that Freud was very "excited and pleased" that she had been born in Bethlehem and gave her a "lecture on the phallic significence [sic] of the lighted candle."[6]

H.D.'s response to all this talk of the importance of phallic power is amusingly recorded in *Advent*. In much the same way as her early poetry emerged as a resistance to male thought forms, so in these notes H.D. presents a counterreality, a symbol of feminine sexuality in the image of a red water lily. In the March 4 entry of *Advent* H.D. refers to the lighted candle lecture, but she focuses upon other primal images, the most striking of which is the water lily. She writes:

> My three-inch strip of tough cactus fiber began to glow, it did not grow, it simply burst into a huge flower. It was like a red water-lily. Its petals were smooth and cold, though they should have been blazing. Well, perhaps they were. I thought the gardener would be so pleased. He said, "I have had my plant for years and not a sign of a blossom."[7]

D. H. Lawrence Everywhere § 287

In the face of Freud's theory of the primacy of the penis, which he felt she must accept in order to achieve a normal adjustment, H.D. invoked a separate reality, a feminine sexual image. Freud finally asked H.D. to stop making her notes in preparation for the analysis; if she was to be properly analyzed, she had to accept the truth of phallic supremacy.

Interestingly, H.D. had the same reaction she had had to Lawrence's insistence on the same point. As she says in *Advent:* "It wasn't fair but I could hardly cope with his enormous novels. They didn't seem to ring true. That is, I was not susceptible to the frenzy in them."[8] Freud's frenzy on the matter of phallic power was so reminiscent of Lawrence's that H.D.'s transference was immediate and deep. It occurred during her first meeting with Freud.

Interestingly, D. H. Lawrence was associated in H.D.'s mind not only with her father but also with her mother. In the memory of Lawrence there seemed to be some kind of integration of father and mother. H.D. confused the date of her father's birthday with the date of Lawrence's death. "I substituted my father's birthday for the death-day of D. H. Lawrence," she writes.[9] But she also associated the death of Lawrence with that of her mother. "I told him again that my mother died in spring, at this very time, and again I remember that Lawrence died too, in March."[10]

H.D.'s inability to remember was not unrelated to her sense of loss. Loss of father. Loss of mother. Loss of Lawrence. She was afraid she would also lose Freud. "I have this constant obsession that the analysis will be broken by death. I cannot discuss this with the Professor. When he first greeted me, he reminded me of Lawrence."[11]

During the course of her analysis, H.D. had a dream of an un-bearded Lawrence (she had only once actually seen him without a beard).

> I dream of a photograph of an unbearded D. H. Lawrence. I had such a photograph of my father, taken when he was sixteen or seventeen before he went with his brother to the war . . .
> I first met Lawrence in August 1914 at the time of the actual outbreak of war; he looked taller in evening-dress. It was the only time I saw this unbearded manifestation of Lawrence.[12]

In H.D.'s dream we can find correspondences to her vision of Peter Van Eck — not the historical Van Eck, Peter Rodeck, but the Van Eck she met on the deck of the *Borodino*. "I notice to my surprise that he is somewhat taller than myself. I had not thought he was quite so tall, though he stood a good military height . . . He is taller than I thought him." [13]

The Peter Van Eck of H.D.'s vision is taller, as Lawrence had looked taller in evening dress. The Peter Van Eck vision represented Lawrence as she first met him, but in another form; Lawrence was superimposed upon the historical person Peter Rodeck. And he was associated with her father and her older brother, both of whom she had lost as a result of the war.

In *Bid Me to Live* H.D. writes about her first meeting with Lawrence. Interestingly, we find a striking contrast between the character Rico and the Lawrence who appeared in her dreams during her analysis with Freud. H.D. writes of Rico:

> The first time she met him was during the first days of the war. In a fabulous suite of rooms overlooking Green Park on Piccadilly. They discussed him before he came in. Someone heard he was tubercular, was that true? He had run away with someone's wife, a baroness, was that true? His novel was already being spoken of as over-sexed (sex-mania), was that true? A damn shame if they suppress it. Then the little man came in, looking slender and frail in evening dress that Rafe said made him look like a private soldier of the already-pre-war days, in mufti. [14]

In *Bid Me to Live* (and this is true of some of the other Madrigal novels as well), Lawrence is somehow minimized. Rico is spoken of by H.D. as "the little man." He looks "slender and frail." But in her dream Lawrence "looked taller in evening-dress." Obviously H.D. attempted at the time of that first meeting with Lawrence, and subsequently in her life and in her novels, to minimize her overpowering attraction to him. At the time she met him she was pregnant with her first child. She and Richard had been married less than a year. The last thing in the world she wanted was to be attracted to Lawrence. So she played it down; in fact, she suppressed (or repressed) what she felt. Because she was unable or unwilling to face the reality of the situation, her attraction came through in dreams and poetry (disguised forms) and later in the disguised Peter Van Eck and Corfu visions. At the time of the analysis she had "forgotten" the Lawrence she had known in Hampstead and southern England and Corfe. (She had tried to dismiss all the wartime liaisons as a result of the strain and stress of World War I.)

She associated Lawrence with her older brother Gilbert, who was killed in 1918 in combat in France. That brother was only a year older; she felt he was almost a twin. In a sense she also saw

Lawrence as her twin. "For one day in the year, H.D. and D. H. Lawrence were twins. But I had not actually realized this until after his death. He was born September 11, 1885: I was born September 10, 1886."[15] Like her brother Gilbert, Lawrence was one year older.

Lawrence as father, Lawrence as brother, Lawrence as twin. At the time of her analysis H.D. was seeing Lawrence everywhere. "When I switch off my bed-light, I realize that I might have seen Lawrence there."[16]

In 1933, with the help of Freud, H.D. was finally beginning to come to terms with her overwhelming attraction to Lawrence. The Peter Van Eck vision recalls the first meeting with Lawrence at the Berkeley in 1914. The taller Lawrence. Unbearded. The attraction to him she had deliberately denied. She had willed herself to experience him as alien, other, "the little man." Any other recognition could pose a threat to her already precarious marriage to Aldington. Even after they began to see more of each other, she tried to minimize the importance of their bond; she attempted to think of it as something that was happening to her, an event over which she had no control, like the bombing of London, like the war itself. And so the suppressed and repressed knowledge of Lawrence returned, as it were, in her dreams, poems, and visions.

At the time of her psychoanalysis, she not only had to come to terms with Lawrence as a living presence in her life, but she had to come to terms with the fact of his death. "I now remember that I will be forty-seven on my next birthday. On my birthday, for that one day, Lawrence would be forty-seven."[17] But Lawrence had died. He was *The Man Who Died*.

H.D. also had to come to terms with his work and with what she knew to be the fact of his powerful attraction to her, the bond that they had both acknowledged in their poetry and denied in the choices they made, or did not make, after Lawrence was expelled from Cornwall. In *Advent* H.D. expresses her ambivalent attitude toward Lawrence's work:

> *The Man Who Died?*
> I don't remember it, I don't think of it. Only it was a restatement of his philosophy, but it came too late.
> I don't mean that.
> I have carefully avoided coming to terms with Lawrence, the Lawrence of *Women in Love* and *Lady Chatterley*.[18]

Was H.D. afraid that she would find too much of herself in *Lady Chatterley*? On July 30, 1928, she wrote to Bryher: "D. H. Lawrence's new book has taken all the shock out of me."[19] She had begun reading the book the day before and her initial reaction was positive. On July 29 she had written that *Lady Chatterly's Lover* "is better than anything (fiction) of his I have read for years." She was almost afraid to read further. "The spite and spit I imagine will come later." She wrote, "I have been reading and writing."[20] Interestingly, she could not even finish reading the book before she began to write herself. There is quite a lot of mention of *Lady Chatterly's Lover* in later correspondence, and it is much along the lines of her first reactions. She always felt protective about the book, but she never quite recovered from the initial shock. How does a woman come to terms with finding herself in *Lady Chatterley?*

> I don't want to think of Lawrence.
> "I hope never to see you again," he wrote in that last letter.
> Then after the death of Lawrence, Stephen Guest brought me the book and said, "Lawrence wrote this for you."
> Lawrence was imprisoned in his tomb; like the print hanging in [Freud's] waiting room, he was "Buried Alive."
> We are all buried alive.
> The story comes back automatically when I switch off the bed-lamp.
> I do not seem to be able to face the story in the daytime.[21]

Lawrence, too, had wanted to forget. Lawrence, too, had sublimated, suppressed, repressed, displaced. He, too, had projected their situation into another dimension — art. Just as he had been in some very real sense her inspiration, she had been in as real a sense his inspiration. Not that H.D. was Lawrence's only muse; he wrote about many people, and inspiration is not one-dimensional; it comes from many levels of the palimpsest of experience. As H.D. realized, Lawrence's muse at the deepest level of experience was the mother. And she had come to realize through Freud that at the deepest level of her own experience was a familial configuration — a pattern still further repressed, a fate, if you will, which D. H. Lawrence re-presented.

30

Crossing the Line

FROM A PSYCHOANALYTIC point of view H.D.'s analysis was successful; as we have seen, H.D. became involved immediately in a transference relationship. Most important, she transferred feelings for Lawrence to Freud.

But Lawrence was a brother as well as a father figure. In H.D.'s life brothers were accessible; fathers were enforcers of prohibitions. H.D. talked about how her father stopped her and her brother when he found them playing with fire: "My older brother and I took our father's magnifying glass, and he showed me how to 'burn paper.' Our father stopped us as he found it dangerous, 'playing with fire.' "[1]

In her cathedral dream, which she had related to Freud, were "two chief companions." H.D. writes: "Richard Aldington and D. H. Lawrence had both seemed to like my writing. But I was unhappily separated from Aldington and it was impossible at that time to continue my friendship with Lawrence."[2]

Lawrence and Aldington were both brother figures.* H.D. did not choose to have sexual relations with father figures. In fact, it might be argued that if a brother figure began to take on the aspect of the father, H.D. became terrified and withdrew from the relationship.

Obviously we are now speaking of the incest taboo.

H.D. has written of poetry as a screen or a veil. In its externalized form a new art form, such as Imagism, excludes those who would relate to it in a certain way and includes those who would

*According to Freud's psychoanalytic equations, Bryher was H.D.'s real baby brother, Charles; Aldington was the younger brother, Harold (Aldington was six years younger than H.D.), and Lawrence was both an older brother, Gilbert, and the "father-mother."

relate to it in another way. The poem is a kind of screening. Lawrence had liked H.D.'s poetry, had read it as a deep communication from the feminine spiritual center to the masculine spiritual center. The poetry, then, included Lawrence in his brother mode in a way in which it excluded many others.

If we look at the matter from H.D.'s point of view, the problem was not with her but with the expectations put upon her by cultural representatives (men) in the father mode. As we have seen, the poem as metaphor presents in miniature a whole world, a world view. The poem is a structuring principle or a language which permits soul-mates, if you will, to participate in a created reality. Insofar as some are excluded from participation through their own lack of proper understanding, the poem is itself a presentation of the incest taboo — the world of the fathers is excluded from H.D.'s presentation (or the fathers are relegated to the status of voyeurs; they are excluded from participation).

The social function of the artist is to give voice to the experience, or soul, of a generation through the presentation of his or her experience. Insofar as the poem performs a screening function it manifests and re-creates the incest taboo. Understood in this sense, art is the structuring principle of the consciousness of a generation, even if it is at one level a retelling of individual experience. The individual experience is presented in such a way so as to circumscribe reality in a particular context; that context then becomes the structuring principle of the experience.

In her "Notes on Thought and Vision" H.D. writes about how great art is always a collective enterprise, always an artistic revolution. Every revolutionary generation of artists re-creates the incest taboo.

The desire of the woman artist, H.D. would argue with Freud, is for self-expression. In *Helen in Egypt* the poem is the veil, the screen, a protection against the risk of deeper self-exposure. H.D.'s stance in 1933 was radically feminist. If they had their own way, women would choose men for their own generative purposes, biological and/or artistic; they have no inherent masochistic need to be bullied or subjugated by men. In terms of mythology, H.D. identified her own stance with that of Artemis and Isis. In her identification with the Isis-Osiris myth, she then was with the brother-lover Osiris, symbol of spiritual equality. The threat was always the totalitarian father. And when the brother began to take on the aspects or attributes of the totalitarian father, her incest taboo was violated.

Freud did not like H.D.'s feminist stance; he argued with her that the brother is only a substitute for the mother. Freud argued that Lawrence was also, like Bryher, a substitute for H.D.'s mother.

H.D. writes of a dream she had during the analysis about her mother, and she remembers Lawrence.

> I dream Joan and Dorothy are arguing. Joan possesses herself of some boxes and jewel-cases of mine: she treats my dream treasures as common property, spreads them out on a table. I am angry at her casual appropriation of my personal belongings. I take up one red-velvet-lined box (actually Bryher had got this for me in Florence) and say passionately, "Can you understand *nothing?*" Joan is a tall girl, we stand level, challenging each other. I say, "Can't you understand? My *mother* gave me this box." I press this red-velvet-lined red-leather Florentine box against my heart. Actually, physically, my heart is surcharged and beating wildly at the vehemence of my passion.
> I recall the Phoenix symbol of D. H. Lawrence.[3]

This same red velvet-lined box appears in *Bid Me to Live;* it is the box in which H.D. kept a few very special letters from Lawrence and a picture of her mother. It is important in considering this image to recognize the depth of the cultural differences between Freud and H.D. Freud implied that Lawrence, like Bryher, was somehow female. H.D. was astonished. Freud also implied that H.D. had not been properly initiated into the world of the fathers.

In *Advent* H.D. tells us that the whole crux of the analysis had to do with the issue of "crossing the line." And in spite of what she took to be really ridiculous prejudices in Freud about the extent to which men ought to subjugate women, she nevertheless was deeply impressed by the discovery of the radical incest taboo in her own psychic make-up. In other words, she believed that Freud was wrong not in what he saw but rather in what he prescribed. Through her analysis H.D. came to realize that any hint of "crossing the line," the incest taboo, filled her with unbearable anxiety, and that this anxiety was not unrelated to her poetry, dreams, and visions. Her Moravian background required and built into its social structure (in the choir arrangements) a strict separation of generations and a very strict taboo against sexual relations that transgressed age barriers. Older men were prohibited from having any contact with young women. H.D. speaks of Algernon Blackwood's novel *The Centaur* in the context of her concept of crossing the line.

> I had read *The Centaur* a number of times, first in America. There was that same theme, that same absolute and exact minute when

everything changed . . . At an exact moment, the boat slipped into enchantment . . . there was a 'crossing the line.' I think in *The Centaur,* the narrator or hero knew the minute, the second that the line was crossed. I, the narrator of this story, did not know I had crossed the line.[4]

H.D. had crossed the line with Lawrence, but as she says, "I, the narrator of the story, did not know I had." She had forgotten: she had repressed it. That is why she had to continue to tell and retell the story; she was obsessed with it in her visions and dreams. When she said that she forgot, she meant not that she forgot the facts about the relationship but that she had forgotten the whole emotional content of the experience. She only remembered meeting Mr. Van Eck (she recognizes that one crosses the line on a boat); but she could not bring her vision of Van Eck together with her experience with Lawrence until her work with Freud. H.D. writes: "When I did realize it, it was too late."[5] D. H. Lawrence was dead. She writes: "I can decide that my experiences were the logical outcome of illness, separation from my husband, and loss of the friendship with Lawrence: but even so I have no technique to deal with the vision."[6]

While H.D. came to accept many psychoanalytical concepts as rich and useful to her life and work — projection, regression, displacement, repression (to name just a few) — she had a fundamental argument with Freud over the issue of spiritual (sexual) equality. While it is possible to call H.D.'s rejections of Freud's prescriptions resistance, we might just as well call Freud's interpretations of her dreams and visions resistance. It is not a matter of objective truth; rather, it is fundamentally a matter of politics (and religion).

Freud felt that H.D. had not had a normal development. "The Professor speaks of the mother-layer of fixation being the same in girls and boys, but the girl usually transfers her affection or (if it happens) her fixation to her father."[7] H.D.'s own analysis was that she had experienced loss, grief, and terror as an objective reality and that it was the circumstances of her adult life rather than of her childhood that caused her to regress to an earlier stage of development.

Psychoanalysis has in general underplayed the component of real fear in the etiology of neuroses. Fear of men's brutality (or lack of sensitivity) may be a more significant factor than desire in the course of a woman's psychosexual development, particularly in the very patriarchal social order of Freud's time. An excerpt from *Advent* tells of a dream:

Then down to Freud . . . I felt a little lost. Perhaps that was partly because of the dream I had last had. I tried desperately to get back to my flat in Sloane Street, London. The flat is at the top of the house. As I enter the downstairs hall, a man and then a rough boy barred my way to the staircase and seemed to threaten me. I did not dare challenge them . . . (I could not tell the Professor that this terror was associated in my mind with news of fresh Nazi atrocities.) As I stood threatened and terrified I call, loudly, "Mother." I am out on the pavement now. I look up at the window of my flat. It has different curtains or a suggestion of Venetian blinds. A figure is standing there, holding a lighted candle. It is my mother.

I was overpowered with happiness and all trace of terror vanished.[8]

H.D. related another dream, of a hotel in which she is kicked out of her room by an irate landlady. Freud identified himself as the landlady. In her dream she finally reached Bryher and her mother who are in another room. "My mother says, 'You are only safe on *this* side of the river.' "[9]

Freud wanted H.D. to cross the line. In order to do so she would have to become fixated to him. Why? For whom is the benefit of the "normal development"? Freud speaks of crossing the line and H.D. thinks of the Nazi menace.

Freud associated many of the men in H.D.'s life (Pound and Lawrence, specifically) with the "mother side." Aldington was the exception, possibly because — and only because — he was her legal husband at the time of the analysis. But H.D. was unhappy with Aldington. Was she unhappy with him because he was on the "father side" or for more complicated reasons?

"It will simplify out," said Freud.[10] But it did not. Freud's concept of masculinity and femininity was too narrow, too rigid, too stereotyped. And his notions of what normal women were expected to put up with from men was from H.D.'s point of view ridiculous. There are, H.D. would remind him, other traditions.

In *Advent,* H.D.'s very subtle suggestion is that perhaps we should all be a little more on the "mother side"; perhaps European civilization is lopsided in the direction of the fathers. H.D. was afraid of the German cult of the father. "It is better to have an unsuccessful or 'delayed' analysis than to bring my actual terror of the lurking Nazi menace into the open."[11]

H.D.'s argument is not for or against any specific sexual or spiritual orientation; rather, it is for a tolerance of a wider range of religious differences. Sexual orientation is basically religious orientation in the sense that the religious drama enacted in a culture mirrors and defines permitted social relations. It would seem that H.D. was determined to live according to the laws of her own culture. Like the early Moravian expatriates in America from whom she was descended, she believed in freedom of religion, which is of course a deviant orientation — possibly, in Freudian terms, a regressive orientation. H.D. had very American ideas about the extent to which women are by nature free from male subjugation. She could experience Freud's ideas about feminine sexuality only as a logic of oppression. She was not about to be bound to male supremacy. "Sigmund Freud said at our next session that he saw 'from signs' that I did not want to be analyzed." [12]

H.D. was admittedly afraid of certain sorts of men. Was such fear purely hysterical, as the Professor would imply? H.D. was afraid of masculine brutality. H.D. was afraid of the male will to power. These fears were not groundless. But as Freud knew, she was also afraid of loss. "The Professor said to me today, when I entered the consulting room, 'I was thinking about what you said, about it's not being worthwhile to love an old man of seventy-seven.' I had said no such thing and told him so . . . I said, 'I did not say it was not worthwhile, I said I was *afraid*.' " [13]

The question of H.D.'s analysis seems to be, did she cross the line? Did she make the "conventional" transference from mother to father? H.D. writes: "We discuss someone — who? Perhaps it was Ezra or it may possibly have been Lawrence, whose fiery diatribes sometimes reminded me of the early Ezra. In my dream, the Professor restores my faith. 'If I had known Ezra, I could have made him all right,' he says." [14]

Freud associated all the artists — Pound, Lawrence, Van Eck — to H.D.'s mother fixation because they were related to art, like her mother, rather than to science, like her father. The clear implication in H.D.'s account of Freud's analysis of her is that, according to Freud, art or poetry is somehow "feminine" while science is "masculine." "The Van Eck episode or fixation was to be referred back to my mother." Why? Freud's answer: " 'The maternal uncle, church, art.' " [15]

Freud was disappointed that H.D. had a mother fixation to him. H.D. did not feel that this was so. She says:

> The Professor's surroundings and interests seem to derive from my mother rather than from my father, and yet to say the "transference" is to Freud as mother does not altogether satisfy me. He had said, "And I must tell you (you were frank with me and I will be frank with you), I do *not* like to be the mother in transference — it

always surprises and shocks me a little. I feel so very masculine."
I asked him if others had what he had called this mother–transference on him. He said ironically and I thought a little wistfully,
"Oh, *very* many." [16]

Because Freud reminded H.D. of her maternal grandfather (Papalie), he was the mother in the transference? If we apply Freud's
most rigorous general concepts regarding the defensive structure
of the ego to his theory of the psychology of women, it might
not be too farfetched to suggest that his anxieties regarding his
own masculinity were determining factors in the formulation of
his special theory about women and in the sorts of things he was
saying to H.D. in analysis.

What, after all, was the Professor helping H.D. to achieve? Liberation or death? To cross the line in the way that Freud suggested
was to break the Moravian incest taboo, since relations of inequality that take a sexual form violate that taboo. And as H.D.
knew from her study of Greek drama, the penalty for breaking
the incest taboo is blindness, madness, or death. From her point
of view, women who are blindly subjugated to men in general do
not have minds of their own. And not to have a mind of one's
own is to be in the realm of blindness, madness, and death.

Perhaps Freud felt that he partially failed with H.D.; she had
not become fixated to him and thus to men in the father mode.
From H.D.'s point of view, however, Freud helped her to recover
from the trauma of both finding and losing Lawrence. Like the
butterfly or moth she speaks about in *Advent,* which managed to
escape the box and land on her father's skull, H.D.'s work with
Freud liberated her so that she was able to re-create herself in new
ways and begin a new life. Like Athena, she was reborn from the
skull of Zeus, from Freud's wisdom.

Norman Holmes Pearson remarked in an interview with L. S.
Dembo: "She did not get from him what we usually refer to as
Freudianism. Fortunately, he hardly got that from himself either.
What she got was what Freud knew that any analysand had to
get — her own cohesion, her own frame of reference, the rounding out of her own personality and psyche." [17]

The truth of the matter is that H.D. was not fixated to men or
to women. She had wanted to marry Ezra Pound, but Pound
chose to marry Dorothy Shakespear. She had been attracted to
Richard Aldington and had married him. The marriage had not
worked because it was an unequal match. Aldington could not
keep up with her and became treacherous and unworthy. She had
loved Lawrence and had crossed that line which Freud had wanted

her to cross; she had become fixated, not through a power relationship but through a passionate and consuming love experience. And in that relationship she had sacrificed everything and lost. It was too late for H.D. to become fixated in Freud's terms; she was a free spirit, or as Pound, Aldington, and Lawrence had called her, a dryad.

§ § §

If we look at the dates of the entries in *Advent,* we discover that almost all of them were written from notes taken in March of 1933, the first month of the analysis. There is an entry on June 12, the day Freud placed a statue of Pallas Athene with a missing spear in H.D.'s hands. The last entry is on June 15, when H.D. asks in her dream, "Are we dead?"

We know that *Advent* was not substantially rewritten for publication but rather was assembled in 1947–1948 directly from the notes H.D. had kept of her sessions with Freud. It is primarily a record of the first month of those sessions and not a statement about the whole content of the work she and Freud did together.

If we follow their acquaintance from its beginning in March 1933 to the time of H.D.'s later accounts of the relationship in *Writing on the Wall, Trilogy,* and *Helen in Egypt,* we become aware that during the course of the analysis Freud changed and mellowed his original perceptions and prescriptions. In the last analysis, Freud was too sensitive a scientist to allow his preconceived theories to interfere with his findings. The Theseus character of *Helen in Egypt,* for instance, *does* seem to understand the reasons and necessity for — perhaps even the wisdom of — Helen's "regression."

H.D.'s outward circumstances did not immediately change as a result of her work with Freud, but in time she began to live a new life. She had been subtly transformed through Freud's affirmation of her, even if she did not accept everything he wrote and said as gospel. The *Advent* title, then, has a further meaning; it is a record of the days that led to H.D.'s own second birth.

H.D. returns again and again in *Advent* to the crossing-the-line motif. The line between mother and father, between safety and fear, is also the line between feminine and masculine consciousness. H.D. crossed the line as she came to understand the true meaning of "the word," as she began to record the image in all of its concreteness, and when words began to invoke biological reality. In *Advent* we get a sense of how it feels to have a poem come and of how it feels to give birth to what has been conceived. H.D. would translate or reinterpret Freud's formulation. Mother-father in Freud's system is symbolic. Attachment transcends duality and separation of mother-father. Sexual or spiritual orientation is no simple matter of choosing sides. "The miracle of the fairy-tale is incontrovertible," says H.D. "Sigmund Freud would apply, rationalize it." [18] The knowledge that her religion, like all religions, was a fairy tale did not challenge H.D.'s faith but rather vitalized it.

Of her family preparing for the ritual of Christmas H.D. writes: "Our perception recognised it, though our minds did not define it. God had made a Child and we children in return now made God; we created Him as He had created us, we created Him as children will . . . we knew our power." [19]

Freud had analyzed H.D.'s positive feelings toward her Moravian grandfather as being on the "mother side." H.D. says that Freud reminded her of this grandfather. But her grandfather *was* a man, even if he was a member of the "maternal" religion.

H.D. told Freud of the Moravian Christmas candle ceremony.

> He said, "There is no more significant symbol than a lighted candle. You say you remember your grandfather's Christmas Eve service? The girls as well as the boys had candles?" It seemed odd that he should ask this . . . Sigmund Freud got up from his chair at the back of the couch, and came and stood beside me. He said, "If every child had a lighted candle given, as you say they were given at your grandfather's Christmas Eve service, by the grace of God, we would have no more problems . . . That is the true heart of all religion." [20]

The lighted candle is, of course, only a symbol of the *real* light, just as the Moravian cross is the symbol of the line crossed.

Some of the issues that H.D. became aware of in her sessions with Freud are addressed in her memoir of her childhood, "The Gift," written in 1941. In "The Dream," a chapter published in *Contemporary Literature,* H.D. speaks of her mother and father. She deeply loved her family and was a deeply loved child. One whole impetus of her life and work was to recapture the joy she had known as a child. She did not think of her father as a "cold man" as Freud had said he must have been. In consonance with her earlier dream of her mother as a symbol of safety, her orientation in the following passages seems to be as positive toward her father as toward her mother. H.D. writes of her father's contribution to the Moravian Christmas celebration. She remembers the time he took her and her two brothers to the big toy store for a gift.

"What was this gift?" H.D. asks. Her father bought twelve large animals for the three children.

We had divided them up, each taking one, then coming round again and each choosing one. Gilbert had first choice and took the elephant but I did not care; for first, I wanted the deer with antlers, and Harold afterwards said, for first, he wanted the polar-bear so we each got our first animal; this was the way we divided things . . .

What was this gift? . . .

Now Papa's hand was in my hand.

He called me *Tocterlein* and I couldn't help it. It made a deep cave, it made a long tunnel inside me with things rushing through . . .

I wondered if Papa remembered how he had bought the box of animals. Papa said, "Well, I must be off, *tempus fugit* . . ." he let go my hand. I looked at him and saw that he was going.[21]

From H.D.'s perspective, our primary experience is the primal scene, and on another level the parental dream. As children we live in the realized dreams of our parents, but we also begin to live in their unrealized and unspoken dreams. This is our fate. Freedom is a matter of realizing our past fully enough and consciously enough to break through the heritage of generations into a new space that involves a transmutation, a translation, or a new interpretation. The parental dream is not negated; the primal scene is not negated. It is rather a matter of transformation and perpetual metamorphosis, constant movement and change within the structure of the given. We move through the ruins of time and tradition to a new melody, a new variation on the original theme. The tradition is not rejected but reinterpreted in a new light — and this is an eternal recurrence, yet paradoxically always new.

Our consciousness is first conceived in the parental romance. The mother and father merge in the mind of the artist. From this merging comes the creative conception, a new perspective. For H.D. the given was "the gift" — not a burden to be repudiated but a buried treasure in which spiritual resources are to be dug up. We dig up treasure or mine the unconscious for new strength to meet the challenges of a new day. The unconscious is not, as Freud said, a labyrinth that leads to a devouring Minotaur but rather a path that leads through the woods to a clearing . . . All this is *given* in the beginning. We are lost in the woods, groping toward a clearing. Where we may see the original vision. And begin again. The unconscious (the primal scene) is not a terrible Minotaur but a presence (present or gift) of perfect peace. From this integrity (union of father-mother) comes the strength to love anew and the will to survive.

"We are all haunted houses," says H.D. "Inside the Cathedral we find regeneration or reintegration . . . The house is home. The house is the Cathedral . . . The house in some indescribable way depends on father–mother. At the point of integration or regeneration, there is no conflict over rival loyalties."[22] Perfect love is possible, for what is given cannot be entirely lost; it is transferred or translated. Displaced, it finds a new form. To find it again in a new context is to begin again.

31

The Walls Do Not Fall

ONE OF THE REASONS H.D. sought Freud was to prepare herself for war. She was living in London when World War II came to England, and she lived there throughout the conflict. In 1942, in the midst of the bombed-out ruins of the city, H.D. wrote the first of three book-length poems which would in time be known as her war trilogy. The first of these is titled *The Walls Do Not Fall*.

In terms of world events, H.D. came to understand her experience in Corfu, "the writing on the wall," as a vision of the coming war — an externalization or projection of a fear that the losses she had suffered in World War I would be re-experienced in an even more catastrophic war. Her Corfu vision had brought together in vivid imaginative pictures her principal memories of the first war and prophecies of the onslaught of the second. The tripod (ancient symbol of prophecy) linked to the profile of a soldier became in retrospect an omen of apocalyptic catastrophe. Niké, the angel, foretold the promise of peace and victory. *The Walls Do Not Fall* was written after World War II had begun, or to use her own word, "materialized."

Since the beginning of the 1920s both she and Bryher had been seriously concerned with the international political climate. Sir John Ellerman, whose ships and financial skill had helped England to win World War I and who was privy to inside information, kept the women informed. As the heiress of his fortune in 1933, Bryher inherited the responsibility of directing funds to appropriate channels. H.D.'s 1933 and 1934 letters to Bryher reveal that a significant portion of her analytical hours with Freud were devoted to discussing the financing of the Jewish emigration, which Freud helped to coordinate and Bryher helped to pay for. As the political situation deteriorated, Bryher became actively involved in helping Jews cross the border from Germany to Switzerland. Following the Nazi invasion of Austria on March 11, 1938, Freud and the members of the Vienna Psychoanalytical Society were permitted to emigrate to London. Marie Bonaparte, Ernest Jones, American ambassador to France W. C. Bullitt, and many others worked out the complicated diplomatic arrangements for this migration, and Bryher assisted with funds for relocation and the payment of the necessary bribes.

When the war came to England, H.D. was living in a small apartment on Sloane Street in London. Freud had died in 1939 in Hampstead. During the last years of his life, he and H.D. had kept in touch. Bryher, still living in Switzerland, was marked by the Nazis and barely managed to escape to England in the fall of 1940. Her journey to reach H.D. in London took her on a long and dangerous detour through Spain.

H.D.'s whole orientation during the thirties had been antifascist, antitotalitarian, and anti-Hitler. Her lifelong friendship with Pound was virtually broken during this period owing to Pound's support of fascism in Italy. Carl Jung, the leading Swiss psychoanalyst, was too politically tainted for H.D., and she and Bryher developed a lasting hostility to his ideas for political as well as intellectual reasons.*

The Walls Do Not Fall, written in the midst of the holocaust, is not only a hope but a plea for peace. It is no accident that H.D.'s *Tribute to Freud* was written in the context of the three poems of the war trilogy. H.D. saw Freud as a peacemaker, in that he had developed a secular language for speaking of matters of the heart which, while cumbersome and prosaic, is potentially free from the old religious connotations that divide peoples into warring camps.

Not only did H.D. see Freud's philosophy as a hope for peace in the world, but it was Freud who had brought peace to her own soul. From the time of her work with him, the wars of the world at large and those of her particular psyche would be woven together in H.D.'s mind. And she would side with the fighters for

---

*There has been some speculation as to why H.D., living in Switzerland and deeply involved with mythology, never showed any positive interest in Jung and his work. As Perdita Schaffner, H.D.'s daughter, remembers, "My mother did not like Jung."[1] Part of the reason was that H.D. was aware that Jung acted as president of the Nazi-controlled International General Medical Society for Psychotherapy from 1933 to 1940 and as editor of *Zentralbatt für Psychotherapie,* the official organ of the society. After the war H.D. lived just down the road from Jung for many years. She never spoke to him, and when asked about his work she dismissed it with the comment: "I like to take my alchemists straight."[2]

freedom against the dictatorship of the totalitarian father, manifested at the time in the person of Adolf Hitler.

The walls that do not fall are the walls of London, the structure of the western world which stands up to the threat of Hitler and fascism. But *The Walls Do Not Fall* has a palimpsest quality; one metaphor is superimposed upon another. And the walls that do not fall are also those of the poet's individual being, the psychic structure which has its foundation in the new strength H.D. found through her work with Freud.

On September 7, 1940, Luftwaffe bombers attacked London en masse. The hits were direct: the Woolwich arsenal, the wharves and warehouses of the London docks area, Victoria and Albert docks, the West India dock, and the Commercial docks. Ships were sunk, bridges collapsed. The bombing of London's East End and other residential areas left hundreds dead and thousands injured and homeless. London's antiaircraft defenses and the Royal Air Force Fighter Command, commanded by Air Chief Marshal Dowding, were humiliated.

Over the next seven days thousands of Londoners were killed, wounded, or entombed in rubble. Ancient edifices crumbled. On Sunday, September 15, "Battle of Britain Day," about four hundred bombers and seven hundred fighters appeared as blips on British radar screens. But on this day the British RAF fought back. The air battles over London continued, but most Londoners went about their business as usual. During the night raids people sought shelter in basements or in subways. Soon pieces of railing began to disappear; they were needed to be melted down for munitions.

The people of London were, as we all know, valiant and courageous in the midst of the Battle of Britain. While the bombs of the German raiders fell all around them, they continued to work and live, not as though nothing had changed but with the certain knowledge that their determination not to fall into fear was a necessary component of the war effort and of their own survival as a people. H.D. lived as a Londoner through this terror.

In 1942 she wrote *The Walls Do Not Fall*, bearing witness to this destruction. The smell of burning was in the streets. The newspapers called the air battles over Britain "incidents." H.D. writes:

> An incident here and there,
> and rails gone (for guns)
> from your (and my) old town square . . .[3]

Londoners did not flee the city; H.D. herself would not leave. Though not so devastating, she had lived through the bombings of World War I. Londoners endured; *The Walls Do Not Fall* is a poem about survival. The Londoners did not know when the next raid would come. A big raid was apt to kill a thousand. Five or six times more would be injured. In Christmas season of 1940, on on December 29, the City of London was bombed; ancient churches and old landmarks were destroyed. The ancient City was in flames. This "ordeal by fire" united Britain against the Nazi terrorists.

<blockquote>

. . . we pass on

to another cellar, to another sliced wall
where poor utensils show
like rare objects in a museum;

Pompeii has nothing to teach us,
we know crack of volcanic fissure,
slow flow of terrible lava,

pressure on heart, lungs, the brain
about to burst its brittle case
(what the skull can endure!):

over us, Apocryphal fire,
under us, the earth sway, dip of a floor,
slope of a pavement

where men roll, drunk
with a new bewilderment,
sorcery, bedevilment:

the bone-frame was made for
no such shock knit within terror,
yet the skeleton stood up to it:

the flesh? it was melted away,
the heart burnt out, dead embers,
tendons, muscles shattered, outer husk dismembered,

yet the frame held:
we passed the flame: we wonder
what saved us? what for?[4]

</blockquote>

The raids continued. Often the whole sky was lit up with fire from burning buildings and explosions. Parliament, Westminster Abbey, the Tower of London were hit; the British Museum, where H.D. and her young companions had studied and written their first Imagist poems, was hit, and its library was demolished.

During one of the World War II blitzes, H.D. had a vision of her own death. She recorded it in a story she wrote in June 1941, "She Is Dead."

Who is this lady? Yes, it is part of myself, I conclude, that had died
. . . now it is projected out . . . She was wise, she was not so
much arrogant in her wisdom, as lost. She had only this peculiar
garment of my own body to live in. It must have been a burden to
her. There were very few occasions when she could express herself,
sometimes I wrote for her, stalactite-shape running verse . . . broken . . . frozen.

I am free of her, she is dead. She died the night of June 20th,
1941, I think after mid-night, yes, surely it must have been just
before dawn.[5]

During the air raids H.D. had many visions and dreams which
informed her writing of *The Walls Do Not Fall* and her unpublished World War II novel, "Magic Ring," including one she had
during the big air raid on Saturday and Sunday, May 9 and 10,
1941, which destroyed the library of the British Museum. "Delia"
is a pen name, taken perhaps from Pound's early poem "Impressions of François-Marie Arouet (De Voltaire)," in which he addresses his lady as such. In the dream it is as if H.D. is attempting
to recall Pound, to dissuade him from his profascist orientation.
This dream also seems to go back to the Quaker church H.D. and
her family attended after they left Bethlehem and their Moravian
church.

Delia is standing in a large empty hall or meeting house . . . Delia
is in a sense the most "American" here, because she is typical of
the American women — or girls, rather, of this part of the world.
I say girls because Delia is dressed in that familiar Edwardian white
summer-frock, she is, as years go, say 17, she is very grown-up,
her skirts are long and she wears that summer-straw [hat] that almost seemed to bring in the season.[6]

It is this American girl in her Edwardian white summer frock
who died in the Battle of Britain. Or rather, the experience of the
battle brought about the final realization that the girl that H.D.
had been was dead. At this time H.D. was going through the
change of life, and her own particular cycle (her "worm cycle" as
she calls it in *The Walls Do Not Fall*) had a psychic parallel in the
destruction of London. The girl who had written the poems in the
library of the British Museum was dead; the library itself was
burned and gutted — destroyed.

H.D.'s description of her dream in "Magic Ring" continues
with the appearance of a masculine figure whom she calls Amen,
which means "hidden one" in Egyptian.

He is dark, he is fair . . . for this is our "Master in modern dress"
. . . There is light everywhere, the room is high, there is a feeling

of a stair-way and a gallery and the elegant "colonial" clarity and classical perfection that we have known, for this is Philadelphia or outside Philadelphia, it is "home," it is the American scene as Delia might have known it. Even as she stands there, though she does not wonder where she is, she might think, "This is a meeting-house, this is not a church, not an assembly room — but a meeting-house, it suggests in its simplicity and sparse elegance a Quaker meeting-house — but no, this is not Quaker — but yes, this is Quaker — in this sense, yes, it is a Quaker meeting-house as it is the *House of Friends*." [7]

These are acutely vivid visions. It is as though the confrontation with death and her survival in the fire storms of London has been cathartic for H.D. — the hurt and the pain have been burnt up. The self-protective, self-conscious girl, burdened with a resolute defense of herself, is dead; a new self sees the old pictures with a new clarity. The dream recorded in "Magic Ring" finds poetic expression in *The Walls Do Not Fall*.

> Ra, Osiris, *Amen* appeared
> in a spacious, bare meeting-house;
>
> he is the world-father,
> father of past aeons,
>
> present and future equally;
> beardless, not at all like Jehovah,
>
> he was upright, slender,
> impressive as the Memnon monolith,
>
> yet he was not out of place
> but perfectly at home
>
> in that eighteenth-century
> simplicity and grace;
>
> then I woke with a start
> of wonder and asked myself,
>
> but whose eyes are those eyes?
> for the eyes (in the cold,
>
> I marvel to remember)
> were all one texture,
>
> as if without pupil
> or all pupil, dark
>
> yet very clear with amber
> shining . . .[8]

As the poem writes itself H.D. remembers that it has been given to her by the dream: "The Dream/deftly stage-managed the bare, clean/early colonial interior."[9] She experienced a kind of re-membering that would lead to regeneration. She had never for-gotten the green, gold, and amber eyes of Ezra Pound. Now those eyes reappeared in a vision. "The eyes were set straight in the face, like a deer or a hawk." H.D. identified the eyes with Christ and the Passion and also with Gautama, the Buddha, and Nirvana.

> You see his eyes were amber — fire and amber. They were light-amber in colour and there was colour. They were globes of fire but yet they were eyes — they looked at me and it would be the nearest I could get to nothing — and — everything, to everything and nothing, to Nirvana in fact — to exactly the phrase of Gautama, the Buddha, *the ending of sorrow.*[10]

In the *Walls Do Not Fall* the eyes belong to "Velásquez' cruci-fied," a Christ image, the "authentic Jew."

> He might even be the authentic Jew
> stepped out from Velásquez
>
> those eye-lids in the Velásquez
> are lowered over eyes
>
> that open, would daze, bewilder
> and stun us with the old sense of guilt
>
> and fear, but the terror of those eyes
> veiled in their agony is over;
>
> I assure you that the eyes of
> Velásquez' crucified
>
> now look straight at you,
> and they are amber and they are fire.[11]

The dream was overpoweringly real. It belonged to that same level of consciousness that had given H.D. the Corfu vision and the vision of Van Eck. In "Magic Ring" she writes: "It seemed to me, that in trying to find some picture that might remotely fit him, that there was Velásquez' *Crucifixion.*"[12]

Consistent with the logic of dream, the "amber-gold eyes" be-came "deep sky-blue or lapis blue," the color of D. H. Lawrence's eyes.[13] Both Pound and Lawrence became, in the dream, manifes-tations of the Passion. As H.D. had looked at a Velásquez exhibit in Geneva just before she returned to London before World War II, she had had a final realization of the actuality of Lawrence's death.

> . . . and suddenly there, in the gallery at Geneva, it came over me, why, he is dead, — I thought — "why, he is dead" . . . *He is dead. He is dead. He is not suffering any more.*[14]

The fires of London rekindled memories of the real fire, the Passion, the fire from which she had fled. H.D.'s vision of Za-ke-nu-to, the Master, which she recorded in "Magic Ring," invokes Lawrence's *The Plumed Serpent* with its vision of Quetzalcoatl. Again in H.D.'s imagination Pound merges with Lawrence as the amber eyes are associated with the Aztec Savior.

> The most memorable thing about Za-ke-nu-to was his eyes — those great burning, amber sun-orbs, amber filling the complete circle of the eye-socket, without white-of-eyes iris or pupils.
> Za-ke-nu-to was given as a red-flame when I was finally given a synonym — if not a translation of his name.
> Za-ke-nu-to was given as Aztec and now I find a calendar given me as an Easter card . . . December 20th is given to "Quetzalcoatl," the feathered serpent. "Aztec form of Savior . . ."[15]

In *The Walls Do Not Fall* Amen becomes the Savior associated with the phoenix; this is affirmation of the Passion.

> *Amen,*
> only just now,
>
> my heart-shell
> breaks open,
>
> though long ago, the phoenix,
> your *bennu* bird
>
> dropped a grain,
> as of scalding wax;
>
> there was fragrance, burnt incense,
> myrtle, aloes, cedar;
>
> the Kingdom is a Tree
> whose roots bind the heart-husk
>
> to earth,
> after the ultimate grain,
>
> lodged in the heart-core,
> has taken its nourishment.[16]

The Passion, the sacrifice, is affirmed. The Passion is the path to resurrection, rebirth. In H.D.'s vision, the flame is associated with light. "The pure white light is broken up and the red light burns on a green jade altar, as a symbol of blood."[17] These visions represent a coming to terms with Lawrence as a person, but also important, they reflect an assimilation of those of his novels with which H.D. had tried without success to come to terms previously.

The Walls Do Not Fall is primarily a poem about the sacred function of the poet, or the scribe. As H.D. wrote in a letter to Norman Holmes Pearson, "Protection for the scribe seems to be the leit-motif. And the feeling of assurance back of it, of the presence of the God of the Scribe, — Thoth, Hermes, Ancient-of-Days, Ancient Wisdom, AMEN."[18] God is Amen, Christ is Amen. As in Moravianism, Amen or Christ is an experience, a presence rather than a particular person, although Amen may manifest in particular persons at particular times. "It is only a child," writes H.D., "who could literally, expect to see God."[19] God manifests as the patriarch, a father figure whose attributes are tenderness and compassion, and H.D. presents him as the alternative to the totalitarian father who rules by brute authority and demands irrational submission to twisted values. In her dream she had a vision of the patriarch, a vision of God.

> His eyes were downcast, he is very tall and as he looks down at me on the bed, I could not say what color his eyes would be. His face though so serene, so benign, was expressionless, like a masque. His countenance was white, but the white of old ivory in contrast to the white of his garment, *exceeding white . . . as no fuller on earth can make them.*[20]

These dreams came from great depths; the threat of death undoubtedly was a factor in bringing them forth. So, too, was the change of life. H.D. was being born into a new state of consciousness. She was getting in touch with her childhood in a way she had never before experienced. She had first encountered this "good" father in her own father. In her dreams she experienced herself as a very young child, "almost a baby, well under 7, anyway."[21] She describes her dream as the "Easter dream." Again she is describing the patriarch.

> The expression actually is *exceeding white as snow,* and I have said that when he drew me to him, I was absorbed back into him like a small drift of snow into the original snow-cloud. But this, though not warm was not actually not cold, the significance, the *translation* of the white was rather the flowering of white, the white of flowers that are conditioned, are perfected by the perfect merging of fire and water, of sun and rain. The Patriarch is a child's vision, he is *the Lord is my Shepherd.*[22]

These visions presented in "Magic Ring" are echoed in *The Walls Do Not Fall.* There is a realization of helplessness as the narrator pleads, "Take me home, Father."[23] There is an exaltation of the protective role of the patriarch — Amen or Sirius — which is at one level a tribute to the men who defended England, at another level a tribute to the men H.D. had loved and the men who had loved and protected her. The Easter dream of the patriarch is presented.

> *Sirius:*
> *what mystery is this?*
>
> you are seed,
> corn near the sand,
> enclosed in black-lead,
> ploughed land.
>
> *Sirius:*
> *what mystery is this?*
>
> you are drowned
> in the river;
> the spring freshets
> push open the water-gates.
>
> *Sirius:*
> *what mystery is this?*
>
> where heat breaks and cracks
> the sand-waste,
> you are a mist
> of snow: white, little flowers.
>
> O, Sire, is this the path?
> over sedge, over dune-grass,
>
> silently
> sledge-runners pass.
>
> O, Sire, is this the waste?
> unbelievably,
>
> sand glistens like ice,
> cold, cold;
>
> drawn to the temple-gate, O, Sire,
> is this union at last? [24]

As H.D. writes earlier in the poem, "We have had too much consecration,/too little affirmation." [25] She might be speaking of her own previous work. She alludes to that work when she writes of "jottings on a margin,/indecipherable palimpsest scribbled over/with too many contradictory emotions." [26] She is hard on her own poetic efforts, but she will no longer listen to critics; this poem is a dedication to poetry.

> so let us search the old highways
>
> for the true-rune, the right-spell,

recover old values;

nor listen if they shout out,
your beauty, Isis, Aset or Astarte,
is a harlot . . .[27]

It is her religious heritage that sustains her. *Blessed are the pure in heart,"* she writes in "Magic Ring," *"for they shall see God."* She continues:

> There is also that final dictum about Heaven; actually it says that unless those grown people *become as little children,* they won't get in. There was the dream about the Master or about a Master. We may speak of a girl who has seen God — as indeed I did, intending to qualify the remark later. Perhaps the girl could see God. Perhaps the girl in the Edwardian white frock and the large summer-hat, did see God. Perhaps the woman going to Greece in the early spring of 1920, did see God. Possibly, the girl and the woman did see projections of the white light that is final illumination. But there was separateness; the girl and the woman were separate people, they were outside looking into, as it happened, amber-gold eyes and deep sky-blue or lapis blue eyes.[28]

Pound's amber-gold eyes, Lawrence's deep sky-blue or lapis blue eyes, the girl with Pound, the woman with Lawrence — both relationships affirmed. Love of one's own father-mother is the first writing on the palimpsest of experience which makes other illuminations possible. Would H.D. have understood her dream and vision sequence of World War II had it not been for her work with Freud? She goes on:

> In the first scene, the Greek scene of 1920 [the Peter Van Eck experience], the age of the woman in the dream or vision on the deck of the ship, was approximately the same age as her ordinary rational or material or physical self. In the second dream or encounter, the physical person is some four decades older than the Edwardian girl. In the last encounter, the woman is no longer recognizable; the child is 2 or 4 or 6.[29]

The World War II experience had brought H.D., along with many others, close to the edge of physical and mental endurance. In the "actual Blitz, there is that last desperate re-valuation or final valuation . . . we do not know if we live to tell the tale, but we still cling to our standards — To this, I mean, our PROFESSION."[30] Pound and Lawrence and H.D.'s profession — poetry. Poetry had been her inheritance, her gift. Poetry is recording the "eternal realities." As a poet it was her responsibility to bear witness to the eternal as well as the historical truth.

"The Walls Do Not Fall" § 313

in the rain of incendiary,
other values were revealed to us,

other standards hallowed us;
strange texture, a wing covered us,

and though there was whirr and roar in the high air,
there was a Voice louder,

though its speech was lower
than a whisper.[31]

In *The Walls Do Not Fall* H.D. identifies Karnak with London. She had tried to escape London (her Egypt), but in World War II she recognized England to be the home of her true birth, or as she called it, her "second birth." "Egypt? London? Mystery, majic — that I have found in London! The mystery of death, first and last."[32] From H.D.'s point of view, *The Walls Do Not Fall* is testament and affirmation of her World War I experiences with Pound and Lawrence. With Freud's help she had come to terms with these experiences. In *The Walls Do Not Fall* H.D. goes beyond acceptance to affirmation of spiritual realities that had been all but forfeited by her avant-garde contemporaries.

The Nazis had debased Christian symbolism to the point that it had become suspect; everything had been debased. "The Christos-image," writes H.D., "is most difficult to disentangle/from its art-craft junk-shop/paint-and-plaster medieval jumble/of pain-worship and death-symbol."[33] The impetus of her poem is toward recognition of religious and poetic realities in the face of twisted values. In her concluding stanzas, H.D. reaffirms her dedication to the task of the poet: to create new modes of communication, to discover new values. It is the poet's task to re-create language. H.D. presents us with a vision of the hoped-for heaven, or haven, the hoped-for peace.

> Still the walls do not fall,
> I do not know why;
>
> there is a zrr-hiss,
> lightning in a not-known,
>
> unregistered dimension;
> we are powerless,
>
> dust and powder fill our lungs
> our bodies blunder
>
> through doors twisted on hinges,
> and the lintels slant
>
> cross-wise;
> we walk continually

on thin air
that thickens to a blind fog,

then step swiftly aside,
for even the air

is independable,
thick where it should be fine

and tenuous
where wings separate and open,

and the ether
is heavier than the floor,

and the floor sags
like a ship floundering;

we know no rule
of procedure,

we are voyagers, discoverers
of the not-known,

the unrecorded;
we have no map;

possibly we will reach haven,
heaven. [34]

32

Tribute
to the Angels

H.D. WROTE *The Walls Do Not Fall* in the context of the bombing of London. As she had written to Norman Holmes Pearson:

> The parallel between ancient Egypt and "ancient" London is obvious. In I [*The Walls Do Not Fall*] the "fallen roof leaves the sealed room open to the air" is of course true of our own house of life — outer violence touching the deepest hidden subconscious terrors, etc. and we see so much of our past "on show," as it were "another sliced wall where poor utensils show like rare objects in a museum." [1]

Osbert Sitwell, who helped arrange for the publication of the poem with the Oxford University Press, also wrote a review of *The Walls Do Not Fall* for the *Observer*. Pearson and Sitwell encouraged H.D. to write more, and in May 1944 she wrote *Tribute to the Angels,* a poem in forty-three sections, the same number as made up *The Walls Do Not Fall*. She called it "a premature peace poem." Her inspiration was the Revelation of St. John. As she wrote in her letter to Pearson in December 1944, "I really DID feel that a new heaven and a new earth were about to materialize." Pearson writes: "The twenty-first chapter of *The Book of Revelation* and its vision of a New Jerusalem blended with a green-white of the may-tree, the charred tree, 'an ordinary tree in an old garden square.' " [2]

So *Tribute to the Angels* is a continuation of *The Walls Do Not Fall,* but in it H.D. brought to light the "deepest hidden subconscious terrors" in herself — in her own "house of life," as she puts it. And *Tribute to the Angels* is both more esoteric in symbolism and more personal in revelation than *The Walls Do Not Fall*.

H.D. was not without benefactors in her lifetime, and as the poem gives thanks we feel the demands of patronage; it is as though she has been asked to speak directly to certain issues. Frustration is expressed in this poem; we sense external influences. It is as if H.D. has been asked to elaborate certain spiritual realities; she is irritated.

> I do not know what it gives,
> a vibration that we cannot name
>
> for there is no name for it;
> my patron said, "name it";
>
> I said, I can not name it,
> there is no name,
>
> he said,
> "invent it".[3]

The poem presents a thematic structure of sevens: "But *I make all things new,*/said He of the seven stars,/he of the seventy-times-seven/passionate, bitter wrongs,/He of the seventy-times-seven/bitter, unending wars."[4] The most obvious group of sevens is the seven angels to whom the poet pays tribute. These angels, traditional enough, are biographical realities in H.D.'s life. In "Compassionate Friendship" she identifies the first angel, Azrael, with Ezra Pound. If we say "Azrael" out loud, it is not so difficult to see how H.D. makes this identification.

In "Compassionate Friendship," another piece written under external pressures and, it is clear, interrogation, H.D. identifies seven "initiators" who seem to conform to the seven angels of *Tribute to the Angels.* She had been looking through a book Norman Holmes Pearson sent her on D. H. Lawrence (Harry T. Moore's *The Intelligent Heart*).

> I tried to work out [Lawrence's] place in the sequence of my initiators. He would come in the middle, if I counted them as seven. Ezra, Richard, John Cournos, as one-time friend and later agent of destruction when he brought Bella (of *Madrigal*) to our house. Then Lawrence in the middle, Cecil Grey [sic], the friend of his and Frieda's (Vane of *Madrigal*), Kenneth Macpherson as a later double, as it were of Grey, then I think Walter Schmideberg with whom I worked two years at psychoanalysis in London, 1936 and 1937.[5]

The second angel listed in H.D.'s poem seems to be the second initiator mentioned in "Compassionate Friendship" — Richard Aldington. In the poem the angel, Raphael, asks a characteristic Aldington question, *"Lovest thou me?"*[6]

Raphael (whose name reminds us of Rafe, of *Bid Me to Live*) is appropriately "chief of the order of virtues"; he is "governor," "overseer," and "guardian of the Tree of Life in the garden of Eden." He has been called "a guide in Hell" — "an ophite diagram represents Raphael as a terrestrial daemon with a beast-like form." He is the "sociable archangel" in Milton's *Paradise Lost.* He is also portrayed (in *Tobias and the Angel*) as a "scoffing and jesting angel." Significantly for H.D., the "magic ring" was brought to the Hebrew king personally by Raphael. The ring, engraved with the pentalpha (five-pointed star), had the power to "subdue all demons."[7]

John Cournos does not seem to appear in H.D.'s list of angels, although it is possible to identify him as the John of Revelations in relation to his revealing novel *Miranda Masters,* which is full of color and light symbolism. The angel at the gate, Gabriel, is undoubtedly a reference to Cecil Gray. We will recall that this is the role that Lawrence assigned to Gray in the Christmas charade of 1917 at 44 Mecklenburgh Square.

The red fire of "Magic Ring" is identified with the fourth angel, Uriel — "those eyes that were globes of fire, sun fire." We recall the vision of Za-ke-nu-to in which the Master is identified with Quetzalcoatl of Lawrence's *The Plumed Serpent:* "And Za-ke-nu-to is given the descriptive title of Red Flame."[8] In *Tribute to the Angels* H.D. writes of Uriel: "Yet he, red-fire is one of seven fires,/judgment and will of God,/God's very breath — Uriel."[9] Uriel is the angel of war.

According to Gustav Davidson's *Dictionary of Angels,* the name Uriel means "fire of God, regent of the sun, flame of God." He is the "dark angel" and is said to have disclosed the mysteries of the heavenly arcana to Ezra. In Milton he is "Regent of the Sun" and the "sharpest sighted spirit of all in Heaven."[10] Uriel is most certainly the Lawrence angel.

We can see what fun H.D. had naming her angels. These are, however, shallow images; they were hardly called up from great depths, and were more likely found, as we find them, in a book of angels.*

The angels in *Tribute to the Angels* are drawn from a variety of sources. Gabriel, for instance, appears in Judeo-Christian and Mohammedan religious lore as well as the apocryphal Book of Tobit. He also appears in the work of Milton and Rembrandt. Mohammed claimed that Gabriel dictated the Koran to him; in Jewish

---

*Davidson's *Dictionary of the Angels* is an appropriate reference book to consult in relation to this poem. As Davidson indicates in his preface, H.D. was a friend and contributed information and rare reference books to his project.

legend Gabriel dealt death and destruction to the sinful cities of Sodom and Gomorrah. It was, of course, Gabriel who announced the birth of the Virgin's God-child.

Coming to *Tribute to the Angels* after the powerful *Walls Do Not Fall* we are likely to be disappointed; the naming of angels strikes us as trivial, superficial. In terms of the content of the entire poem, however, it sets a context for what is to come from the depths. The ritual naming gives way to the deeper presence of Uriel.

> To Uriel, no shrine, no temple
> where the red-death fell,
>
> no image by the city-gate,
> no torch to shine across the water,
>
> no new fane in the market-place:
> the lane is empty but the levelled wall
>
> is purple as with purple spread
> upon the altar,
>
> this is the flowering of the rood,
> this is the flowering of the reed,
>
> where, Uriel, we pause to give
> thanks that we rise again from death and live.[11]

Past begins to link to future. The image of the crucible which H.D. presents next is central to *Bid Me to Live,* and invokes the star Hesperus, central to another Madrigal story, "Hesperia." And these images recall the "impious wrong" done to Venus, who has been linked with venery, "for venery stands for impurity/and Venus as desire/is venereous, lascivious."[12] In the crucible situation at 44 Mecklenburgh Square H.D. had discovered the Oedipal drama, the mother.

> Now polish the crucible
> and in the bowl distill
>
> a word most bitter, *marah,*
> a word bitterer still, *mar,*
>
> sea, brine, breaker, seducer,
> giver of life, giver of tears;
>
> Now polish the crucible
> and set the jet of flame
>
> under, till *marah-mar*
> are melted, fuse and join

and change and alter,
mer, mere, mère, mater, Maia, Mary,

Star of the Sea,
Mother.[13]

Through the alchemy of language — poetry — and the memory of Uriel, Venus becomes "Aphrodite, holy name" and "venerator." In the crucible of the poem Uriel is linked to Venus or Aphrodite and H.D.'s last angel, Annael. As H.D. wrote in "Magic Ring":

> I have read somewhere in some "wisdom" series, that "Thou shalt not commit adultery" does not refer to our rather tiresome and not very important love-affairs, but to the higher teaching. Thou shalt not adulterate claret with vinegar nor sugar with salt. Thou shalt not adulterate poetry with the lingo of the counting-house or love with mercenary matters. Thou shalt not not adulterate inspiration with doubt nor joy with do-nots. Thou shalt not adulterate judgment with wavering nor courage with stipulations. Thou shalt not adulterate *for, lo, the winter is past.*[14]

The poem begins to gain momentum and depth as H.D. discovers her own poetic source. Annael and Uriel linked become "peace of God."

> *Annael* — and I remember the sea-shell
> and I remember the empty lane
>
> and I thought again of people,
> during the blinding rage
>
> of lightning, and I thought,
> there is no shrine, no temple
>
> in the city for that other, *Uriel,*
> and I knew his companion,
>
> companion of the fire-to-endure
> was another fire, another candle,
>
> was another of seven,
> named among the seven Angels,
>
> *Annael,*
> peace of God.[15]

H.D. saw herself as this companion, the angel Annael. She felt she had passed through death twice. A tree blooming in an old garden square among the ruins of London brought memories of World War I, the miraculous birth of her child, and now a precognition of her own rebirth. This was transubstantiation.

We are part of it;
we admit the transubstantiation,

not God merely in bread
but God in the other-half of the tree

that looked dead —
did I bow my head?

did I weep? my eyes saw,
it was not a dream

yet it was vision,
it was a sign,

it was the *Angel which redeemed me,*
it was the Holy Ghost —

a half-burnt-out apple-tree
blossoming,

this is the flowering of the rood,
this is the flowering of the wood

where Annael, we pause to give
thanks that we rise again from death and live.[16]

The realization of herself as Annael announces a verbalization of the vision of "my own lady." Pound had given H.D. visions of his lady, of H.D. from his perspective — the troubadour's lady. "My own lady," H.D. tells us, is thus "the Troubadour's or Poet's lady."[17] Aldington had written of her in his *Death of a Hero* — with invective, to be sure, but it was nonetheless a portrait. During the composition of *Lady Chatterley's Lover,* D. H. Lawrence and Frieda had referred to Lady Chatterley as "Our Lady." H.D.'s own vision of "our lady" in "Magic Ring" came out of séances she had been attending with Bryher. In the novel she writes of the kind of work she and Bryher did with a young Eurasian medium, whom she calls Arthur Bhaduri, in London during the war. He had presented H.D. with images, many of them from her own poetry. The result of the work was strong recollection of the past. Her first recording of the vision is in "Magic Ring."

> Actually I was seeing her slightly foreshortened, as if I were standing below a statue-base, but she was not a statue . . . That is the odd thing. I looked at my lady and she was a white statue, but she was not a statue, she was not a white stone. I thought of snow, of rock, I thought, she is like a snow-queen. She was a queen, she had a high crown, delicate as frost; she was alive, she was not-alive, she certainly was alive, she did not move but she could move. There she stood. She might have been dragged from the Aegean or she

might have stood in a niche in Chartres Cathedral, but she was not Greek; she was not archaic Greek and she was not medieval. She was something quite apart, quite different and if I could compare my feeling of joy with any recognized joy, I should have said that she was familiar to me, I had long, long wanted to contact her, though I did not know how much I wanted to contact her, until I stood slightly below, to the right as she appeared out of nowhere, as I was dropping off to sleep.[18]

"Our Lady," in H.D.'s lexicon of symbolic equations, is also the Virgin Mary, who to Roman Catholics is the Queen of the Angels. And the Virgin Mary is equated, as in Lawrence, with Mary Magdalene. She is, as H.D. says, "the moon."

In *Tribute to the Angels* H.D. describes "Our Lady" as she appeared to her just as she was dropping off to sleep.

> . . . for it was ticking minute by minute
> (the clock at my bed-head,
>
> with its dim, luminous disc)
> when the Lady knocked;
>
> I was talking casually
> with friends in the other room,
>
> when we saw the outer hall
> grow lighter — then we saw where the door was,
>
> there was no door
> (this was a dream of course),
>
> and she was standing there,
> actually, at the turn of the stair.[19]

"Our Lady" appeared in the dream as visions come in séance — through a sort of superconcentration combined with a letting go of ordinary ego-consciousness. H.D. had tried to think of Gabriel (Gray), but "Our Lady" appeared instead. "I had thought/to address him as I had the others,/Uriel, Annael;/how could I imagine/the Lady herself would come instead?"[20]

Before describing her vision, H.D. tells us how "Our Lady" has been depicted by countless other artists, in various civilizations:

> We have seen her
> the world over,
>
> Our Lady of the Goldfinch,
> Our Lady of the Candelabra,
>
> Our Lady of the Pomegranate,
> Our Lady of the Chair;

. . .

we have seen her sleeve
of every imaginable shade

of damask and figured brocade;
it is true,

the painters did very well by her;
it is true, they missed never a line

of the suave turn of the head
or subtle shade of lowered eye-lid

or eye-lids half raised; you find
her everywhere . . .[21]

Then she invokes or recalls her own vision.

But none of these, none of these
suggest her as I saw her,

though we approach possibly
something of her cool beneficence

in the gracious friendliness
of the marble sea-maids in Venice,

who climb the altar-stair
at *Santa Maria dei Miracoli,*

or we acclaim her in the name
of another in Vienna,

Maria von dem Schnee,
Our Lady of the Snow.[22]

H.D.'s vision of "Our Lady" is surely a portrait of herself. She had been named by her fellow artists in so many different ways; she had been portrayed under so many different guises. D. H. Lawrence, Ezra Pound, Richard Aldington, John Cournos, Havelock Ellis, Robert McAlmon, Kenneth Macpherson, and Ford Madox Ford were just a few of those who wrote portraits of H.D. How difficult to center oneself in one's own vision after being defined so variously by so many. But H.D.'s vision also includes Bryher and her own daughter; it is of a woman as seen through a woman's eyes. Her own portrait has a Biblical purity:

For I can say truthfully,
her veils were *white as snow,*

*so as no fuller on earth
can make them;* I can say

she looked beautiful, she looked lovely,
she was *clothed with a garment*

> *down to the foot,* but it was not
> *girt about with a golden girdle,*
>
> there was no gold, no colour
> there was no gleam in the stuff
>
> nor shadow of hem and seam,
> as it fell to the floor; she bore
>
> none of her usual attributes;
> the Child was not with her.[23]

The worldly visions of "Our Lady" had clothed her with worldly attributes. In H.D.'s view she is immaculately pure. This is a vision not so much of woman's physical, material reality as of her spiritual essence. H.D.'s lady carries a book.

> Ah (you say), this is Holy Wisdom,
> *Santa Sophia,* the SS of the *Sanctus Spiritus,*
>
> so by facile reasoning, logically
> the incarnate symbol of the Holy Ghost;
>
> your Holy Ghost was an apple-tree
> smouldering — or rather burgeoning
>
> with flowers, the fruit of the Tree?
> this is the new Eve who comes
>
> clearly to return, retrieve
> what she lost the race,
>
> given over to sin, to death;
> she brings the Book of Life, obviously.[24]

This is affirmation of H.D.'s self and of her work. It is an affirmation of Bryher and Bryher's work. It is also an affirmation of H.D.'s daughter. In her "Autobiographical Notes" (1933), H.D. records a dream of Perdita as Venus on March 1, 1933, in Vienna — the day before she began her analysis with Freud.[25] In a single image H.D. will throw off the castigations of men. Lascivious Venus as well as seductive Eve are projections of men's minds which have nothing to do with the essence of womanhood. H.D. will cast off the "ancient wisdom" and begin a new book, a book to be written about women by women.

> she carries a book but it is not
> the tome of the ancient wisdom,
>
> the pages, I imagine, are the blank pages
> of the unwritten volume of the new;

. . .

> but she is not shut up in a cave
> like a Sybil; she is not
>
> imprisoned in leaden bars
> in a coloured window;
>
> she is Psyche, the butterfly,
> out of the cocoon.[26]

"Our Lady" is the embodiment of the new feminine wisdom, yet to be written; "her book is our book." H.D. invokes the other angels (men), who have helped her to realize her vision: Michael, associated with justice (Kenneth Macpherson), and Zadkiel, associated with righteousness (Walter Schmideberg). She is thankful; she has survived. She has achieved a reconciliation with her own past; she has come to terms with her own illicit passion. No one is to blame. And the birth of the child with "a face like a Christmas rose" brings the final affirmation of the passion which creates life. The god is the jewel; the lady is the crucible; from their union is born a child.

> but when the jewel
> melts in the crucible,
>
> we find not ashes, and ash-of-rose,
> not a tall vase and a staff of lilies,
>
> not *vas spirituale,*
> not *rosa mystica* even,
>
> but a cluster of garden-pinks
> or a face like a Christmas-rose.[27]

It is not necessary for women to repudiate men, asserts H.D., but it is necessary to discover the feminine as opposed to the masculine wisdom. It is necessary for a woman to achieve her own perception of her own nature in order to begin again. "Our Lady" is not shadow but light.

> And the point in the spectrum
> where all lights become one,
>
> is white and white is not no-colour,
> as we were told as children,
>
> but all-colour,
> where the flames mingle
>
> and the wings meet, when we gain
> the arc of perfection,
>
> we are satisfied, we are happy,
> we begin again.[28]

33

The Flowering
of the Rod

IN THE WEEK preceding and that following Christmas 1944, H.D.
wrote the last book of her war trilogy, *The Flowering of the Rod.*
Its central motif is the identification of Mary Magdalene with the
Virgin Mary. This identification held a special meaning for H.D.;
it was given to her by Freud in the context of her psychoanalysis
and was for her no mere academic equation. H.D. had loved out
of wedlock, as had Mary Magdalene, and she had borne a child
out of wedlock, as had the Virgin Mary. She had never responded
to the Bible as history; her whole religious upbringing had focused
her mind on the symbolic and eternal realities contained in the
Biblical stories. Freud, too, had always read the New Testament
mythologically. In *The Flowering of the Rod,* H.D.'s first Mary appears as Mary Magdalene, whose very name means "bitter."

> I am Mary, she said, of a tower-town,
> or once it must have been towered
>
> for Magdala is a tower;
> Magdala stands on the shore;
>
> I am Mary, she said, of Magdala,
> I am Mary, a great tower;
>
> through my will and my power,
> Mary shall be myrrh,
>
> I am Mary — O, there are Marys a plenty,
> (though I am Mara, bitter) I shall be Mary-myrrh;
>
> I am that myrrh-tree of the gentiles,
> the heathen . . .[1]

Mary is then equated with "Attis-Adonis-Tammuz and his
mother who was myrrh"; this is the mother in the story of Myr-

rha and Cinyras, who turned into a myrrh tree as a result of her passion, as told by Ovid in his *Metamorphoses*. H.D. writes:

> she was a stricken woman,
> having borne a son in unhallowed fashion;
>
> she wept bitterly till some heathen god
> changed her to a myrrh-tree;
>
> I am Mary, I will weep bitterly,
> bitterly . . . bitterly.

The bitter, resinous perfume of myrrh was one of the gifts brought by the Wise Men to the Virgin Mary. To become the Virgin is to change one's point of location in relation to perceived realities. It was the Wise Men, the Magi, who helped H.D. to see herself as the Virgin after she had been painted by her contemporaries as the whore. In her poem Kaspar is the patriarch, and in his wisdom we certainly see a reflection of Freud. Mary calls Kaspar "Sir," and we also think of Sir John Ellerman. In the last stanzas of the poem the transformation in consciousness is complete, and Mary has become the Virgin with the Child in her arms. The myrrh which symbolically contains the seed of life has become life itself, the Child.

> But she spoke so he looked at her,
> she was shy and simple and young;
>
> she said, Sir, it is a most beautiful fragrance,
> as of all flowering things together;
>
> but Kaspar knew the seal of the jar was unbroken.
> he did not know whether she knew
>
> the fragrance came from the bundle of myrrh
> she held in her arms.[2]

The Virgin and the Wise Men parallel the symbolic structure in *Tribute to the Angels;* the vision of "Our Lady" links symbolically to the Virgin Mary. A thirteenth-century French folktale, "The Juggler of Notre Dame," tells the story of a poor boy who wants to bring a gift to the Virgin Mother and the Christ Child, but all he knows is juggling and tumbling, dancing and singing. While the Magi bring their gifts to the Virgin, the juggler comes secretly to entertain her. He works so hard that he falls exhausted to the floor. "Our Lady," the Virgin Mary, is so touched by these sincere efforts that she gives herself to the care of him. And just before she resumes her statuesque place in the cathedral she bends to kiss and bless the juggler.

Countless medieval legends mixed the dimensions of the Marys and "Our Lady." H.D. had been deep in the study of mystical and occult lore during the World War II years. The symbolic consciousness or truth contained in folklore and fairy tale helped her to achieve her vision in *The Flowering of the Rod,* and to achieve her vision of "Our Lady." Though it was a real vision from the depth of her own experience, it was suggested no doubt by folktales like "The Juggler of Notre Dame" and by memories of her own religious heritage.

As we mentioned, *The Flowering of the Rod* was written in the closing days of 1944. Peace was imminent. World War II was not to bring about the end of the world; it was necessary to build a new world. This was a task for visionaries and poets (jugglers) as well as for the more material reconstructionists. The opening lines of *The Flowering of the Rod* recall Amen-Christ:

> . . . we have shown
>
> that we could stand;
> we have withstood
>
> the anger, frustration,
> bitter fire of destruction;
>
> leave the smouldering cities below
> (we have done what we could),
>
> we have given until we have no more to give;
> alas, it was pity rather than love, we gave;
>
> now having given all, let us leave all;
> above all, let us leave pity
>
> and mount higher
> to love — resurrection.

We cannot dwell on the destruction of the past, says H.D., speaking about her own personal wars as well as the world war. She had lived too long in her own nightmare: "pitiless, pitiless, let us leave/the place-of-a-skull/to those who have fashioned it."[3]

Love and resurrection are the dominant themes of *The Flowering of the Rod*. The title invokes H.D.'s perception of Freud as Moses with his rod and also D. H. Lawrence's *Aaron's Rod*. The rod, a traditional symbol of masculinity, is affirmed by H.D. in connection, we will remember, with the "half-burnt-out tree . . . blossoming." The half-burnt-out tree is a feminine image, and particularly appropriate for H.D. at this time in her life. Blasted by the war, blasted by years (she is now fifty-eight), the tree flowers again in remembrance of things past — a world of peace and of satisfied love.

So I would rather drown, remembering —
than bask on tropic atolls

in the coral-seas . . .[4]

Her project is to escape, in her own consciousness, the world of war, destruction, and death.

I gave pity to the dead,

O blasphemy, pity is a stone for bread,
only love is holy and love's ecstasy

that turns and turns and turns about one centre,
reckless, regardless, blind to reality,

that knows the Islands of the Blest are there,
for *many waters can not quench love's fire.*

H.D. would reinvoke the spiritual realities. She deplores the consciousness that has separated the spirit from the body. What could the spirit be but the body? They are one; it is war and war's destructive mentality that is "other." She would renounce the wartime values (they are no longer necessary) and remember the spiritual realities, which are always, for H.D., physical and sensual.

I am the first or the last to renounce
iron, steel, metal,

I have gone forward,
I have gone backward,

I have gone onward from bronze and iron,
into the Golden Age.

Spiritual realities, H.D. maintains, are not fantasies but biological truths. The existence of a spiritual connection between a man and a woman does not preclude the possibility of the birth of a child. Again she would implore us to reject the wartime division of body and soul. She knows the kind of consciousness she is up against.

No poetic fantasy
but a biological reality,

a fact: I am an entity
like bird, insect, plant

or sea-plant cell;
I live; I am alive;

take care, do not know me,
deny me, do not recognize me,

shun me; for this reality
is infectious — ecstasy.

H.D. realizes that among poets she has been singularly blessed, cared for, and provided for; it has not been so for her fellows. She writes of Lawrence and invokes the themes of *The Man Who Died,* a work of fiction that was testimony to the reality of the life they had lived in World War I. In *The Man Who Died,* the man met Mary (Madeleine); they had been "out of step."

> So the first — it is written,
> will be the twisted or the tortured individuals,
>
> out of line, out of step with world so-called progress;
> the first to receive the promise was a thief;
>
> the first actually to witness His life-after-death,
> was an unbalanced, neurotic woman,
>
> who was naturally reviled for having left home
> and not caring for house-work.

A Biblical story, certainly. Also Lawrence's and H.D.'s story. In *Flowering of the Rod* the seven angels of *Tribute* become seven daemons: "These very devils or *daemons,*/as Kaspar would have called them,/were now unalterably part of the picture."[5] But H.D. was no longer haunted by them. The angels or daemons had been projected out, through the compassion and understanding of the patriarch; as H.D. states in *The Flowering of the Rod,* "Kaspar remembered."

Kaspar of this book of the war trilogy is a palimpsest character. All the allusions to great wealth make one think of Ellerman, reputed at the time of his death to be the wealthiest man in England. It was to him that H.D. felt she owed her very survival, physical as well as spiritual. Many passages make us think of Sir John, with his valuable collection of jewelry and treasures from all over the world.

> and Kaspar, master of caravans,
> had known splendour such as few have known,
>
> and seen jewels cut and un-cut that altered
> like water at sun-rise and sun-set,
>
> and blood-stones and sapphires;
> we need no detailed statement of Kaspar's specific knowledge
>
> nor inventory of his own possessions.

As we have seen, at the time of Sir John's death H.D. had just completed her first sessions of psychoanalysis with Sigmund

Freud. Sir John's death upset her terribly, and she resumed her analysis the following October, in 1934. During her first set of sessions, Freud helped H.D. to come to terms with the loss of Lawrence; during her second sessions he helped her to recover from the loss of Sir John. Freud, like John Ellerman, was a collector of objects of antiquity; often he would show H.D. a precious object, an image, to make his point. It is altogether fitting that these two protective father figures should merge in H.D.'s mind in 1944 in the fictional Kaspar.

Kaspar also is a presentation of that enlightened understanding H.D. encountered in some men (including Lawrence at his best) who saw that the maligned woman is only a perception projected by the ineffectual and wounded male mind. Kaspar is thus symbolic of all men who are self-confident enough not to need to split the image of woman into the chaste virgin and the seductive whore, two categories or definitions that do not conform to any true feminine reality.

> And Kaspar heard
> an echo of an echo in a shell,
> *in her were forgiven*
> *the sins of the seven*
> *daemons cast out of her.*

The thematic structure of *The Flowering of the Rod* is the poet's movement of mind in relation to Mary; but just as important, H.D.'s Kaspar moves into a clarity of vision. An attentive reading of H.D.'s correspondence about her analysis and of her memoir of Freud suggests that Freud did not apply the theories set forth in his essay on femininity to H.D. Just as H.D. changed some of her views, Freud altered some of his; he at least would not apply those particular ideas to H.D. — not after he had talked with her about "deep matters" and read her work.

Although she achieved freedom from trauma through her work with Freud, H.D. also gained an even deeper recognition, which she expresses in *The Flowering of the Rod.* The legendary patriarch of the trilogy, Kaspar, comes to understand that Mary is an extraordinary person; he comes to see her as the Virgin. That is, Freud began to regard H.D. as a Mary figure. And even more important for H.D., she came to see herself as Mary, the Virgin.

At the beginning of the analysis Freud had said that H.D. had come to him to find her mother.

> Why had I come to Vienna? The Professor had said in the very beginning that I had come to Vienna hoping to find my mother. Mother? Mamma. But my mother was dead. I was dead; that is,

the child in me that had called her Mamma was dead. Anyhow, he was a terribly frightening old man, too old and too detached, too wise and too famous altogether, to beat that way with his fist, like a child hammering a porridge-spoon on the table.[6]

Freud was beating his fist like a child with his porridge-spoon on the table. It raises the question, who was the mother in the analysis, and who was the child? H.D. suggests that somehow during the course of her sessions with Freud she found the mother by becoming the mother, by finding the mother in herself. A kind of countertransference occurred in which she became the mother for Freud.

Exactly what happened to change the course of the analysis is in some sense left to our imagination; the record of the transformation is in the poetry. H.D. tells us she and Freud had come together to "substantiate something"; yet what occurred in the end was really closer to transubstantiation or consubstantiation — that is, for a moment in time they become united in substance or vision. Very much reminiscent of H.D.'s experience with D. H. Lawrence, they not only learned from each other but *saw* something together. And part of what they came to see is recorded poetically in *The Flowering of the Rod,* as "our earth before Adam . . . Paradise before Eve" in the opening of the flower.[7]

In *Tribute to Freud* H.D.'s self-understanding is reached through a process of interpretation and translation. For instance, Freud would "interpret" a psychoanalytic "finding," speaking of "striking oil." Slightly jarred by his use of psychoanalytical language, H.D. would translate it into Biblical or poetic language, speaking of, for instance, the "still waters."

Out of this confrontation and exchange, this process of translation and interpretation, came H.D.'s vision of Freud as Moses and her idea of Egypt as a recurring form in human history. Out of their sessions together came her understanding of the concept of the return of the repressed in the history of civilization, and a vision of the Magi, foreshadowed in her vision of the patriarch. And from these translations came a breakthrough for H.D. In *The Flowering of the Rod* she speaks of the transfiguration or metamorphosis:

> And the snow fell on Hermon,
> the place of the Transfiguration,
>
> And the snow fell on Hebron,
> where, last spring, the anemones grew,
>
> whose scarlet and rose and red and blue,
> He compared to a King's robes,

but *even Solomon,* He said,
was not arrayed like one of these;

and the snow fell on the almond trees
and the mulberries were domed over

like a forester's hut or a shepherd's hut
on the slopes of Lebanon.

and the snow fell
silently . . . silently . . .

And as the snow fell on Hebron
the desert blossomed as it had always done;

over-night, a million-million tiny plants
broke from the sand,

and a million-million little grass-stalks
each put out a tiny flower,

they were so small, you could hardly
visualize them separately,

so it came to be said,
snow falls on the desert;

it had happened before,
it would happen again.[8]

H.D. thought of Freud, like Kaspar, the "treasure-master" of *The Flowering of the Rod,* in terms of "unearthing buried treasure." Like Freud, Kaspar brought or invoked the gift of the fragrant but bitter myrrh. Like Freud, "Kaspar remembered."

In his *Moses and Monotheism* Freud writes, "It is important to notice that his name, Moses, was Egyptian. It is simply the Egyptian word 'mose' meaning 'child.' "[9] This observation is interesting in the light of H.D.'s thought patterns. He had named her Mary, mother; she had named him Moses, child.

Moses is the child H.D.'s Princess finds in the bulrushes during her sessions with Freud. Speaking of her dream of finding the child, H.D. says of Freud, "Obviously it was he, who was that light out of Egypt."[10] One meaning of the word *child* is "descendant." Freud is a descendant of Moses; H.D. is a descendant of Mary. They are together in the recognition of the meaning of their religious heritage.

> "You were born in Bethlehem? It is inevitable that the Christian myth — " He paused. "This does not offend you?" "Offend me?" "My speaking of your religion in terms of myth," he said. I said, "How could I be offended?" "Bethlehem is the town of Mary," he said.[11]

The Flowering of the Rod is a testimony to the miracle of transcendence. To transcend is to go beyond what is given or prescribed in experience. A miracle is an event in the world that deviates from what is known; it is something wonderful. The gift of myrrh consecrates the Child; the patriarch affirms the Child, and thus the child (and poet) in Mary.

And because the patriarch had seen what the "legend said still existed," because it had happened to him, he knew it would happen again. Toward the end of the analysis Freud reread H.D.'s poetry. It was his understanding of those early poems in light of her early experiences — *"even Solomon, He said,/was not arrayed like one of these"* — that led to her recovery. The desert blossomed again because he saw "the promised lands lost." "It had happened before,/it would happen again." Kaspar, the wise man, remembered. In his apprehension of H.D.'s work, Freud restored her. Freud, H.D. tells us in *The Flowering of the Rod* (her *real* tribute to Freud), understood more than any of us can imagine; as friend and teacher, he was in touch with the whole secret of the mystery.

IV

HELEN

34

Coming Out

FOLLOWING WORLD WAR II a number of new developments related to old traumas had a profound effect on H.D.'s life and work.

Early in 1946 Richard Aldington wrote to her suggesting a meeting. H.D. and Aldington had not parted amicably after World War I. He had promised to accept Perdita as his child until H.D. had made it clear to both Lawrence and Gray that she wanted to remain married to him; then he had abandoned her. Furthermore, he had threatened to have her imprisoned if she registered the child in his name. When H.D. and Aldington first got back in touch in 1928, after neither hearing from nor seeing one another for ten years, Aldington was obsessed with the subject of Lawrence. Having just seen Lawrence and Frieda on the island of Port-Cros, he proclaimed that Lawrence was "an omelette made of bad eggs." [1] Later he told H.D. that "Lawrence is really malevolent and evil. I hope I never see him again. He is merely a Cournos of genius." [2] He had also formed the opinion that "Lawrence is a homosexual who won't admit it, and that makes the vindictive bitterness. In Cournos it is the Jew." [3]

Aldington renewed his contact with H.D. because he was beginning to consider divorcing her. He talked with everyone but H.D. about this, implying that she refused to divorce him, which was not true. H.D. recognized that as long as she and Aldington continued to be legally married, she continued to be legally vulnerable in relation to him. As she wrote to Brigit Patmore in 1928: "What I can never get over is the fact that even now SHOULD I care for any one or want a little freedom, *HE* can come down on me." [4] In another letter she spoke of Aldington's "possessiveness" and "hypocrisy."

Aldington's interest in obtaining a divorce coincided with the end of his twelve-year liaison with Dorothy "Arabella" Yorke and the beginning of his affair with Brigit Patmore. In early 1929 Pound wrote to H.D. to inquire as to her willingness to divorce her husband. She replied on February 20, 1929:

> I know about Richard. He can get a divorse [sic] anytime if he will do it in the right way. I don't know what I do mean. I mean he could have had it ten years ago if it hadn't been for Perdita. I was quite unprepared for the experience, I mean the terror of feeling that that wadge of bird-feathers and petticoats HAD to be protected. The freedom of my spirit . . . went . . . I want Richard to be happy. Perhaps I could approach things from the Swiss side.

In reality H.D. was still afraid of Aldington. Her fear was undoubtedly out of proportion to the reality of the situation. After she had written to Pound, Aldington wrote to her: "When in Paris in December I was amazed and startled to learn that you had been dreading all these years that I would do, or might be induced to do, something (unspecified) to harm or annoy you."[5] He had succeeded in frightening her with his threats, even if he had had no intention of carrying them out.

On March 20, 1929, he wrote to her:

> First let me deal with this divorce business. There is no hurry as far as I am concerned. I do feel though, that since we have not lived together for so long, it would be more dignified to make the legal separation . . . But I cannot agree to your being the "guilty" party or defendant. If anyone was in the wrong it is I, and it is you who should bring the action against me.

When Brigit Patmore did not insist on marrying Aldington, the discussion of a possible divorce was dropped, but in 1937 Aldington's affair with Patmore came to an abrupt end when he took up with her daughter-in-law, Netta Patmore. Shortly thereafter he decided to marry Netta, and H.D. quickly agreed to set him free. Grounds for divorce were concocted so as to conform with British law, and though Aldington insisted upon paying, it was H.D. who ended up bearing all of the expense of both her own and Netta Patmore's divorces. In 1938 H.D. wrote to Pound, who needed money, that she was unable to help at the moment because of a

> set-back financially due to fact that I had to advance moneys — this is PRIVATE, do not mention — to settle up the divorce proceedings. R.A. was liable but he and his publisher who had guaranteed backing, both stated that they could not meet the costs. This is presumed to be a loan, as to my lawyers. But I don't really pre-

sume that R. will pay it over . . . would have liked it, if R. could have met the costs (not too slight either) simply on principle.[6]

H.D. had financial problems for most of her life. She had been practically destitute when Perdita was born, and her earnings as a writer were very important to her. Sir John Ellerman left her eight thousand pounds in 1933, which gave her the first financial freedom she had ever known, but the high costs of the divorce absorbed the major part of this inheritance. In 1945, after the composition of the war trilogy and the "Good-Friend" section of *By Avon River,* which was dedicated to Bryher along with *The Walls Do Not Fall,* Bryher gave her a gift in excess of twenty thousand pounds, and this sum was enough to make her financially independent for the rest of her life. In gratitude H.D. wrote to Bryher on September 23, 1945: "I have not even tried to cope with the huge sum, the 5; I can not write the 0-s after it, I should pass out. Then here is the 20 with an absolutely astronomical, unbelievable 000 after it."

Walter Schmideberg, an Austrian psychoanalyst who helped H.D. through her difficult divorce case, had become a close friend of Bryher's. During the forties their relationship became serious, which gave H.D. another kind of freedom. As she wrote to Aldington on October 18, 1953, of Bryher and Schmideberg:

> It has been going on for *almost eight years* and I have never spoken of it to my oldest friends in London; this has made me feel at times, cut off psychically, not being able to "confide" in old friends. Of course, my seven years were free, as I felt Bryher had her own interests, though I saw her, of course, in Lausanne and went over to the Villa for lunch, occasionally. But I did my "novels" to my satisfaction and I would not have been able to concentrate on them, if I had not been more or less, alone. So I am grateful to the Bear [Schmideberg] for all that, too.

The distance between H.D. and Bryher had been widening since H.D.'s psychoanalysis with Freud, partly because of H.D.'s writing. In 1939 H.D., then living in London, asked Bryher to send some things from a locked cupboard in Kenwin. Bryher found the Madrigal manuscript that H.D. had written just before she left for London and phoned H.D., very upset. H.D.'s letter of explanation and apology was written June 3, 1939.

> I had started some sheets out in Kenwin during the worst crisis time there — and I got them out, and felt that if I didn't put down the old war theme, finally, I would rot with it . . . What I really want is damn well to FINISH that war-theme which I started many times, and accumulated: the war-talk has sort of crystallized it out.

Another letter to Bryher of the same day explains: "I am so damn sick of the whole thing, all that war-theme, that it seems it really will do me good, D.V., to get it shaped and destroy about a half doz. MSS of the same theme." But Bryher's objection to the Madrigal manuscript had its effect on H.D.; she felt compelled to set it aside and was not able to work on it during the World War II years.

As the war drew to a close H.D. decided that the time had come for her and Bryher to go their separate ways, though they remained friends until the end of H.D.'s life. In January 1946 H.D. was making plans to go to America to teach at Bryn Mawr College. Mary Herr, a longtime friend, was helping her with administrative and lodging arrangements. But H.D. never made the trip. In May 1946 she was hospitalized forcibly, at Bryher's direction, for a "nervous breakdown." Bryher and the Bear (Schmideberg) actually kidnapped her and imprisoned her at Seehof, a private hospital, where she remained until September, when she wrote to Bryher that the breakdown had been due to anxiety about Bryher's welfare, bomb repercussions, superimposition of the last war illness, and anxiety about the birth and future of Perdita.[7] She told Bryher that her problems had been exacerbated by injections the hospital had given her. She also told Bryher: "I was never really afraid, until that 'shock treatment,' then I was so damned *mad,* I sort of got well."[8] After H.D. wrote some very angry and cogent letters that also expressed great gratitude to Bryher, Bryher saw to it that she was released.*

H.D.'s breakdown, which she later referred to as her "coming out," was linked to her break with Bryher.[9] But it was also linked, as she says, to "superimposition of the last war illness." In other words, living through World War II in London had reinvoked memories of World War I. Part of the problem was also, as she tells us in "Magic Mirror," an unpublished novel, her sudden break with Hugh Dowding, with whom she had been working on psychic experiments.

During the second war H.D., along with many others who lived in London, had a great admiration for Lord Dowding, chief air marshal and commander of the Royal Air Force fighter pilots during most of the Battle of Britain. In their minds he was the man who saved Britain, although when the air battle had been

---

*"The Guest" section of *By Avon River,* which was also dedicated to Bryher, was composed at Seehof during the most traumatic period of H.D.'s confinement. An essay in praise of the Elizabethan poets and dramatists, it shows no sign of mental confusion or anger.

virtually won he had been stripped of his command. Thus, throughout the remainder of the war this hero was an outcast. Plagued with guilt and sorrow about the casualties of so many of his pilots, Dowding turned to writing and psychic research. The effort of this research was to contact RAF pilots who had been lost in battle.

H.D. first came into contact with Dowding through a series of lectures that he gave in 1943 in connection with his first book on spiritualism, *Many Mansions*. She exchanged letters with him for two years, and in 1945 they met.

H.D. was clearly intrigued with Dowding and with the spiritualist idiom as a literary form. The "Yogi books" that Pound had given her in Pennsylvania in 1905 had been her first exposure to the Eastern religious ideas that formed the basis of British spiritualism in the 1940s. Like many members of her generation H.D. had also dabbled in theosophy and in a variety of systems of occult discipline such as the tarot, numerology, and astrology, often in the form of party games. While Freud's psychoanalytic method had helped her to recover her own past, she knew that psychoanalysis was but one form of psychical research and that its findings, at least at the poetic level, were not incompatible with other major currents of psychic investigation. Yeats had certainly been productive as an artist as he followed his own version of the Rosicrucian tradition.

H.D.'s novel "Magic Ring," which was written in 1943 after hearing Dowding speak on spiritualism, begins with a series of letters written to Lord Howell, a fictional character modeled after Lord Dowding. The letters contain talk about séances the heroine has been attending with a friend (presumably Bryher). Because of the immediacy of the presentation of this novel, one is tempted to read it as an almost literal rendering of the events of H.D.'s life during the early phase of World War II in London. But in fact it is not clear whether H.D. and Bryher actually attended spiritualist séances or whether the word *séance* is employed to describe a meeting or discussion of some sort.* At any rate, the heroine's

---

*A letter from H.D. to Norman Holmes Pearson dated August 14, 1948, suggests that her involvement in psychic research was literary, in contrast to Dowding's involvement, which apparently was not. She writes: "I think Dowding is sincere in his psychic-research work, but it occurs that it is just possible, that he let himself in on the racket, as sort of espionage — this is of course, so very discreetly *entre nous.*" Perdita Schaffner, H.D.'s daughter, who lived in London during World War II and saw her mother regularly, responded to my question as to whether there was any factual basis to the séances by telling me that she had no knowledge of her mother's attending séances and that it sounded "literary" to her. Bryher has also denied that she attended spiritualist séances.[10]

letters to Howell speak basically of their findings. Images presented by Manesi, the medium who conducts the séances in the novel, are interpreted. Manesi presents Delia (the H.D. character) with images, some of them from H.D.'s own poetry, and Delia weaves a story drawn from present and past associations. In her letters to Howell, she elaborates the meaning of an image mythologically, cross-culturally, and symbolically. But if Dowding was attending séances to contact his lost RAF pilots, Delia (who also appears in "The Sword Went Out to Sea," 1947) was attending to prepare for a new version of "the novel" that she had been trying to write to her satisfaction since the end of World War I. As Delia tells Manesi in "The Sword Went Out to Sea," " 'Yes,' I explained, 'five years ago or ten years ago I might have come for help about some person. In fact, it is because I have given up the thought of that person, or persons, in a personal sense, that I felt free to come at all. It is my writing that matters.' "[11]

In 1945 H.D. had a series of discussions with Dowding about spiritualism. The break that was a precipitating cause of her breakdown or "coming out" occurred during the fourth meeting. As she describes it in "The Sword Went Out to Sea":

> The big chair was empty. It was very empty indeed. Sir John Howell had gone away. A complete stranger was pacing up and down the length of my carpet, from the couch to the window again and back again. He went on talking. He talked about the danger of these things. He talked about the danger of beings of a lower order getting hold of notions of that sort and how their control of some such problematic communicating system, could upset the balance of the world.

As if to apologize, he then remarked: "I don't mean that *you* are a being of a lower order." As far as Delia was concerned, "This made matters worse . . . It only seemed to underline the fact that *they* might be . . . So not only did he repudiate the messages themselves and me, as the bearer of the messages, but he repudiated the fact of the messages and their whole content, as not being 'of any importance.' "[12]

The traumatic event that H.D. describes in her novel was the repudiation of the importance of her own experience, her own mind; this had happened before. But she did not want to believe it had happened again. Delia wrote to Howell. He wrote back: "I cannot be expected to receive messages of this sort . . . it is none of my business but it would be better if you gave up this work."[13]

It is one thing to keep a secret; it is another to have one's experience repudiated and denied. H.D. had, in fact, kept her past secret for so long that when she began to talk about it, she met with hostility from every corner. The break with Dowding and the break with Bryher were related. Both attempted to stop her work; it was not important, they said, to write " the novel."

The encounter with Lord Dowding fictionalized by H.D. in "The Sword Went Out to Sea" was a shock. The break invoked and provided a context for long-suppressed memories. As H.D. puts it: "Lord Howell's well directed blow . . . had by the very force and character of its delivery, awakened the memory of that first shock."[14] Suddenly, traumatically, H.D. began to remember. As she tells the story in "Compassionate Friendship," Achilles of her Helen sequence and the *héros fatale* of the novels that she wrote on her release from Seehof are all related to the awakened memories that resulted from her confrontation with Dowding.[15] As she explains it: "The final father-image . . . came miraculously into my life in the person of the Air-Chief Marshall Lord Howell."[16]

When H.D. left Seehof in September 1946, she returned to Switzerland, but she lived in a series of hotels in Lausanne and Lugano rather than at Kenwin with Bryher. The war experiences in London and the vivid recollection of places and events of World War I led to a whole new period of artistic creativity. Between 1946 and 1951 H.D. wrote three novels, "The Sword Went Out to Sea" (1946–1947), "The White Rose and the Red" (1948), and "The Mystery" (1949–1951). She conceived of these as a prose trilogy.

All of these novels tell H.D.'s story, but as in the case of the Palimpsest novels that she wrote after World War I, each is set in a different time and place. The first is a spiritualist novel set in contemporary time in London, and contains a series of stories that retell as spiritualist messages significant events in H.D.'s life. "The Sword Went Out to Sea" is a continuation of or a sequel to "Magic Ring," which was written in 1943. The central character in both novels is the fictional Lord Howell. The second novel of the trilogy, "The White Rose and the Red," is set in the time of the Pre-Raphaelites, a generation before H.D.'s own in English literary history. The third, "The Mystery," is set in Prague at the time of the first Moravian settlement on Count Zinzendorf's estate. It tells the same story as, or rather relates a parallel set of events to, "The Sword" and "The Rose," but in the context of Moravian history.

Dowding's hostility to and rejection of H.D. contributed to the intense literary effort represented in these novels by jarring buried memories loose. But H.D.'s renewed relationship with Richard Aldington also significantly influenced her writing during this period. Aldington re-established contact with H.D. when he wrote to her out of the blue in early 1946. His letter began a correspondence that lasted until H.D.'s death. Their dialogue, stormy as it was, helped her to remember. Almost as soon as they re-established contact with each other they began to argue; it was as if they finally managed to have the conversation they might have had at the time of the breakup of their marriage in 1919. On April 29, 1948, Aldington wrote to tell H.D. he was working on a short biography of D. H. Lawrence and asked her, "What do you think about the wisdom of doing a Lawrence book at this date?" At first she did not know what to think. She responded: "So much to say about D.H.L. I am glad I never said it, in public — or private for the matter of all that." [17] Her own recently completed novel, "The Sword Went Out to Sea," had been based on Lawrence, Aldington, and others from the Imagist period, as well as her World War II friends — "the few," as she called them. But the whole subject had been so disguised it was hardly recognizable. And now Aldington was going to write directly about Lawrence — what would he say?

H.D. had also recently completed her most direct rendering of the story of her relationship with Lawrence, "Madrigal." She offered it to Aldington but he refused to read it, so she wrote to him of the first book of her trilogy: "You mentioned my writing a 'straight' novel — this is anything but 'straight' but it follows certain very fascinating lines of direction. The dame, Delia, stuck in bombed London, has various imaginative adventures, these are projected or suggested by a little table that was given her." [18]

The metaphor of messages coming from a table, she tells Aldington, had occurred to her after she inherited a writing table, which had originally belonged to William Morris and had been given to her by Dorothy Cole; it had been one of Violet Hunt's treasures. She wrote that it "was a little round table that William Morris kept always near him, and he used it for his paints and brushes." This idea suggested the theme of a table from which pictures come; the pictures, of course, are images, memories. The dots and dashes which she says she received from the table were the sounds of her pen on paper recording the messages. H.D. explained to Aldington:

> Our friend Delia, goes back of course, in retrospect to the last war — she collects or culls her gems! I grieve to say — but I guess you won't mind — that she relives her "honeymoon in Italy," among other things — and to get "John Geoffrey Alton" [Richard Aldington] into the picture, she has to have him "go" into the last

war. He returns in a series of "pictures" along with Allen Flint, the American traitor [Ezra Pound] and others.[19]

H.D. explained that her psychic experiments had unlocked closed doors in her mind, and this process led to the writing of "The Sword Went Out to Sea." In the same letter she wrote to Aldington: "This novel is the outcome of more than 20 years of not so much experimental as explorational prose." On October 10, 1948, she wrote: "I trust you will not mind my quoting from your first letters re Synthesis [i.e., "The Sword Went Out to Sea: Synthesis of a Dream"]."[20] In her "Notes on Recent Writing" in 1949, H.D. wrote: "*The Sword* traces my intellectual and emotional life to its conclusion or rather to its fulfillment. *The Sword* is the crown of all my effort, the final version or rather the new version of the Greek novel that I had written, revised, discarded and re-written, ever since the time of the actual experience in the spring of 1920."[21]

The experience she refers to is the same one described in *Advent* — the meeting of the man on the boat. H.D. wrote: "As I actually assemble the final version of *Madrigal* more than a year after I finished *The Sword,* I feel that the War I novel should be a companion or an introduction to the War II novel. So I sign *Madrigal,* Delia Alton."[22]

On July 11, 1948, H.D. wrote to Pearson: *"Poetry* wrote and asked me for a sort of auto-b. article on poets I have known . . . don't feel at moment, that I can put down 'impressions' other than my own romances" — "Madrigal," "The Sword Went Out to Sea," and her new "romance," "The White Rose and the Red." In H.D.'s mind, the Pre-Raphaelite group of which she wrote in the latter novel is "a parallel to their group of *Madrigal.*"[23] In her "Notes on Recent Writing" H.D. pointed out that she had so identified herself with Elizabeth Siddell Rossetti that she could not "let her die."[24]

In 1949 Aldington agreed to read "Sword." On February 23 H.D. wrote him: "There is a very concise sample of MADRIGAL in the Synthesis of a Dream, which you read. In fact, except for the names being different, the theme is the same, only it ends before the war ends and 'Rafe' (this time) is still in France."[25]

The next day, February 24, 1949, H.D. offered "Madrigal" to Aldington again. She wrote:

> I can post MADRIGAL before I leave or sooner . . . I did this book so many times . . . I left the MS here and was about to destroy it with some other old things, but I could not; so I boiled

it down and tightened up the last chapters, the hail and farewell, and "presented" the Rosigran [sic] scene as semi-Platonic, which in fact it was — but there is only that one last chapter from Rosigran, summing it all up, "a nice novel, eh Rico?" and leaving the episode as a friendship.[26]

But Aldington still refused to read it.

Beneath the surface cordiality of the H.D.-Aldington correspondence was a growing tension. Aldington was planning to write his biography of Lawrence and to tell the Lawrence story *his* way. Unlike H.D., who prominently featured Aldington in her novels, Aldington was planning to ignore H.D. in his rendition of the story.

In response to one of Aldington's queries about Lawrence and Pound, H.D. wrote on October 21, 1948:

> I am interested in your work on Lawrence . . . There is, in some way, an interesting parallel between him and Ezra. They both rushed along, mountain-torrents. E. is the more rugged, a sort of poet 49-er, blasting up rocks, giving up his gold-field in a mad rush on; sifting stones and pebbles for a gleam of gold (and the gleam is there), not properly "panning" the gold-sand when sifted, dangerous, undecorous, no dulce et decorum, potentially magnifico, disguised in harlequin rags. Or harelquin [sic] disguised as Magnifico . . . Lawrence a more native torrent, also rushing, but in valley and predicted channel, if rugged, yet still with European precedent; not so rugged; beautiful tender approach to cyclamen, narcissus, anemone; cottage, rural, village Miracle Play, tempestuous "adultery" — what is adultery? Concern for some sort of Puritan formula, what is sin? . . . I think the parallel in time and space of the two, is a help. They were (are) almost of an age, there is only about six weeks between Lawrence, Sept. 11 and Ezra, October 30, both born 1885 — if the "stars" have anything to do with it.[27]

On May 4, 1949, H.D. wrote to Aldington in relation to his biography of Lawrence, now in progress: "I am very anxious to know more of the DHL memoirs. When does it come out? I hope you let me see the final version, as soon as may be . . . I am keenly interested in the actual story as you knew it and lived it."

In his last letter Aldington had asked her if she had any correspondence, and she replied: "I have only one letter that I can find . . . I think the only one I have left from Lawrence."[28] And H.D. sent Aldington the letter.

Having turned this over and having trusted his sincerity in his project, H.D. could hardly believe Aldington's letter of May 23, 1950. He wrote:

I had a letter from Frieda yesterday, in which she wrote: "Hilda; how is she? I shall always be grateful to her." I kept your name and person out of my book as I thought that was what you want, except for a passing reference so that they couldn't remark on a complete absence. For what it is worth to you, what you did for Lorenzo in 1917 is remembered with gratitude by many who think he is the one great writer in English of this century.

So this was his game; Aldington was going to attempt to erase her from Lawrence's life. H.D. had hoped for the best when she and Aldington re-established contact, but he proved to be as treacherous with her as ever. He assured her that his purpose was protective; "I was a little apprehensive that *private* and *personal* matters might have been revealed." Frieda had been grateful to her for keeping the secret, Aldington assured her. And he, Aldington, would now help her to keep the secret forever.

There was not a thing H.D. could do about his distortions of history. But she was confident that they would not prevail, and she repeatedly reminded Aldington of her "New Haven Professor, who is . . . keeping a shelf for books of and around the pre-first war or first-war group of Imagists and their affiliations or associates."[29] In 1951 she completed her Moravian novel, "The Mystery." On June 17, 1951, she wrote to Pearson promising a "proper-sized old-time *Gone With the Wind* production." And on July 25 she wrote to Aldington that she had "re-read *The Man Who Died,* though nothing else except for occasional pages or paragraphs."[30]

In late summer 1952 H.D. began to write *Helen in Egypt*. She tells us:

> *Helen in Egypt* was begun at the Hotel Lugano . . . I wrote in little notebooks, scribbling for preference on the top of a small round table in the portico or in another tea-room. It was my first summer of freedom from the overwhelming drive that had forced me through, yet sustained me, in the writing of the three novels. The prose phase was finished, you might say, the story was recorded. But there was still the poetry, I discovered to my surprise.[31]

On August 8, 1952, she wrote to Pearson, "I was driven, compelled to get that 'novel' right . . . I began really, after War I as I said in those notes." On September 30 she wrote to him of her plan for *Helen,* suggesting the inclusion of the Euripides myth. On October 2 Pearson replied, congratulating H.D. on the arrival of the first "Canto," that is, book I, "Palinode," and exclaiming that the "birth of Helen is so exciting." On December 28 H.D.

wrote to him that "it is a miracle that [*Helen in Egypt*] came clear like that. And a miracle that it waited until the end of the 'lustre' to manifest from the unconscious to the conscious." The "lustre" is, of course, the novels.

On December 27, 1952, H.D. wrote to tell Aldington that his Lawrence biography had just come: "I am afraid I read a bit backwards, but have the middle–first half left and will write of that." In the same letter she told him she was anxious to have him read her Lawrence book, "Madrigal": "I kept the 1939 version, only scrapped the last chapters; they did not ring quite true and brought in 'others,' if you know what I mean."[32]

The "others" to whom she refers are Perdita, Bryher, and the other persons involved in the breakup of her marriage. She wrote to Aldington that in her final version of "Madrigal," "Julia (this time) somehow knows that she will live in the *gloire,* as she calls it, will, will, will sometime write, as she wants to write, not just slim volumes of Greek Chorus quality, but something else."[33]

On December 31 Aldington agreed to read the book; he wrote, "Yes . . . send me your novel Madrigal." The tension between them had developed into a feud. On January 2, 1953, H.D. wrote to compliment Aldington on his achievement in his Lawrence biography, *Portrait of a Genius, But . . .,* and to tell him: "It reminds me of Ezra, not personally — but the Ezra I knew when I was 15 and he 16."[34] Aldington had been writing letters to her full of insidious comments about Pound. Thus, H.D.'s comment was her way of telling him that his project of writing her out of Lawrence's life was adolescent or childish. She told him she had condensed much into "Madrigal" and that he needn't "worry or hurry" about it.

Aldington was about as happy with "Madrigal" as H.D. was with his Lawrence biography. On January 7 he wrote that he had read 120 pages, complimented her on her achievement, and told her: "I thought of sending you a collection of rough sketches called *Roads to Glory,* not that they have any merit as writing but simply for the curiosity of seeing how simultaneously in Time there may be such utter contrast of experience in Space." Aldington probably was sarcastically reminding H.D. that while she was off with Lawrence, he was doing his duty as a soldier. On January 17, 1953, he wrote to tell her that he had finished reading "Madrigal" and was ill: "I finished reading Madrigal with temp of about 101°, which probably accounts for the fact that towards the end I found myself rather exhausted, by the intensity of all these self-absorbed emotionalists." Characteristically, he reacted with sarcasm, saying that "Madrigal" might be material for a three-act play. "It seems to me, thinking it over, that if you could hit the right structure and tone, you have the material for a good 3-act play. Of course, for the stage, it would have to have some violent ending — tragical or farcical." He told her that although the book was excellent he didn't know who would publish it, and asked if he might show it to a publisher.

Over the course of the next two months Aldington wrote to tell H.D. that he feared there was not a big enough market for "Madrigal," but that he would take responsibility for placing it. Later he wrote that he was "getting opinions on *Madrigal* from two or three people who are supposed to have taste," but was very discouraged.[35] Needless to say, Aldington's "efforts" soured all of the potential British publishers on the book, and *Bid Me to Live* was not published in England until after its American publication in 1960.

On January 14, 1953, H.D. wrote to Aldington:

> I am happy that the *Madrigal* got across to you. You must not think that I minimize your output and your years of hard work. I just had to do my own stuff and was from the first, even with Ezra, in danger of being negated by other people's work. I speak of this, in regard to DHL in the book. I would like to have given my gift to someone but it was just not possible, no one could "take it," in several senses of the phrase. And I went on and on. *Madrigal* literally was on the hob for 30 years. I added and subtracted and worked and destroyed till I got the "perfect formula." It is true, I may have seemed to dash off the long Howell sequence and the two books that followed, on the same theme, in different periods (circa 1850 and circa, no exactly, 1788) but I had the subject, and the years and years of hard work behind me. Now, I am happy with all this and in time, the things will be placed. It must be just the right moment and the right publisher.*[36]

---

*Just before writing this letter H.D. received from Aldington a bibliography of his writings on D. H. Lawrence. The list contained four book-length essays, including his recently completed *Portrait of a Genius, But . . .*, as well as eighteen other books of Lawrence's poems, essays, letters, or novels that he had edited and supplied with introductions. In several of his editions of Lawrence's work Aldington made silent editorial changes to the original text. Most of the volumes of Lawrence's work now in print have been altered by Aldington. The full extent of these adjustments will not be known until a scholarly edition of Lawrence's work is produced.

Until H.D. received the bibliography of Aldington's work on Lawrence, she was completely unaware of the extent of his involvement in creating the Lawrence legend that excluded her. Of course, she never became aware of the hundreds of letters Aldington wrote explaining and interpreting Lawrence's work and supplying character identifications and biographical information to a large number of correspondents. Much of this information was useful, but there was also a con-

She was warning him that it would not be so easy to write her out of the picture. And she was not about to be intimidated. "Madrigal" was finished and she was working hard on her Helen sequence. She had begun book I of *Helen in Egypt* with an argument which she substantiated with a quotation from Stesichorus, a Greek lyric poet (ca. 640–555 B.C.). According to Horace Gregory, Stesichorus "probably inspired Euripides to write his *Helen* which, as the first scene shows us, states that 'Helen was never in Troy. She had been transposed or translated into Egypt.' "[37] Instead of going to Troy with Paris, Helen had spent the war years in Egypt with Achilles.

On January 9, 1953, H.D. asked Pearson if he would write "a few lines, giving the legend, as I have given it to you, of Helen, the phantom — and the meeting, after his death, with Achilles." This is an allusion to *The Man Who Died*. As H.D. had written: "Lawrence came back with *The Man Who Died*."[38] On March 28 she wrote to Pearson, "Could we call Part I of the *Helen,* just *Egypt?* . . . the *Eidolon* concerns the whole sequence." On May 3 she wrote: "The *Helen* sequence has given me a get-away, almost a new body."

She had worked not only with the Stesichorus fragment and the Euripides *Helen* but with many sources, both ancient and modern. The meeting of Achilles and Helen after the death of Achilles had been originally recorded by Pausanias and Philostratus, but Goethe's *Faust,* book II, gave another version of this meeting. E. M. Butler's *Fortunes of Faust,* she wrote, "struck the spark that started my *Helen.*"[39] Even André Gide's *Theseus* contributed to her conception of the poem, as did Pound's Cantos.

Although H.D. consulted many sources, *Helen in Egypt* is essentially original — or as Bryher put it, the story of Hilda as a young woman, and as H.D. told Pearson, the story of Hilda during the World War I Imagist years. She had finally written her own story.

On April 5, 1953, she wrote to Pearson:

> I seem to have put my happiest effort into the *Helen* script, writing the captions, when first here, Oct.-Nov., getting them typed, sending to you, then the return to go over again — so really, I don't suppose I was too lazy — well, you know — it is in the script, "meditation and dream and infinite passionate questioning." I am posting you magazine with some new D.H.L. letters — really I wonder how and why these things are sold — but a fascinating cache, this last.

---

siderable amount of invention and misleading advice which has become enshrined as fact over the years.

On April 19 Pearson wrote to H.D. that he had the final Canto or section of *Helen*. He told her he was full of "intense excitement." H.D., too, was temporarily satisfied. On May 21 she wrote: "I have read and re-read the *Helen,* and much I know by heart — which never happened with other poems of mine. I wanted to forget them and GO ON. Well — I think that I did get what I was looking for from life and art."

But on September 9 she wrote to Pearson that she had begun a second *Helen* series: "It is supposed to be the Trojan side of the story; she gets to Leuké and meets *Paris* not Achilles . . . The Paris image never appealed to me, but I see him, the early shepherd, the defender (as he was called), the Wolf-Slayer." On November 25, 1953, she had completed half the book. She wrote to Pearson: "I have been so happy with this and would like to follow your suggestion, eventually, and have three 'books' of the *Helen.*"

H.D. also gave Aldington occasional progress reports on *Helen in Egypt*. On September 13, 1953, she wrote: "I am trying to work over some scrappy Euripides notes . . . If I do any 'Greek,' it is my old Euripides, as inspiration, as background." She continues:

> I don't mean I translate. I am just keeping my hand in, on the *Helen in Egypt* saga, then, thought we might have a post-mortem, Leuké, the white island, where the myth had it that she had met Achilles after his death. I have her skip Achilles the second time (she meets him in Egypt, in my story) and she finds Paris instead. I never had much feeling for the Paris image or eidolon, but as a contrast to the Achilles, I find the idea stimulating.

When H.D. began to write again on the new section of *Helen* in 1953, the "Leuké" section, she was recovering from abdominal surgery under the care of Dr. Brunner and Dr. Erich Heydt. Heydt was a psychoanalyst, but he was also interested in poetry and in obtaining information about H.D. and her associates from the Imagist years. She quickly developed a close relationship with him, and in "Compassionate Friendship" she writes of having "made this double or triple transference, after all these years, again to Erich."[40] Erich, she said, reminded her of Aldington. Even though she met him after she had completed much of *Helen in Egypt,* she indicated that "Erich did very well as my model for Paris, in the second part of my Helen sequence."[41] He brought her books, "various articles and newspaper-cuttings that had some reference to Ezra or Lawrence or Richard Aldington."[42] Thus Erich Heydt acted as "a dynamic liberator or inspiration" for her Greek epic.[43] On October 6, 1953, H.D. wrote to Aldington: "It is just seven years since I came out in 1946 . . . I am still playing with my Greek *Helen* sequence and am swamped by erudite German books that Dr. Heydt brings me to read."

H.D. spent most of the last eight years of her life residing in a lakeside clinic in Küsnacht, Switzerland, near Zurich, recovering first from abdominal surgery and later from a broken hip complicated by a bone illness. On June 11, 1954, Aldington wrote and offered to answer any letters of inquiry about her relations to Lawrence and Pound. He wrote: "If you will send on any of these letters asking for 'personal recollections' of people we knew, I will answer them for you. No sense in your being bothered by them." Aldington informed her that the British Broadcasting Company had asked him to do a speech for ten minutes on D. H. Lawrence: "In speaking of that 1917 time when the L's were at Mecklenburgh, I said they had 'my apartment.' I did not wish to snatch your gloire, but thought you'd rather be left out." He also left H.D. out of his discussion of the Mecklenburgh Square events in his biography. But she was not about to be bullied by Aldington's assurances that he had the power to reconstruct history. She reminded him that she had the help of both Heydt and Pearson.

On October 1, 1954, H.D. wrote to Pearson that she had "found" the final page of *Helen in Egypt*: "I found this last page in my note-book, un-typed, it seems that if we put it in ITALICS, all of it and just call it EIDOLON, as the very last page of the whole of EIDOLON, that is Book III, it gives the clue, the final — that the figure-head OR the ship is this 'dream' or mother-symbol OR Helen or what you will."

On October 10, Pearson wrote to tell H.D. that book VI of the last part of *Helen* had arrived. The poem was finished. But H.D. wanted to finish the prose captions that introduce each section and each poem of each book. On November 26 she wrote to Pearson that *Helen in Egypt* was "strictly INNER and esoteric and personal" as well as "all war-problems." By January 17, 1955, she had finished writing all the captions. She wrote to Pearson: "I find myself shouting the captions to myself as well as the poems."

On March 16 H.D. wrote to Aldington that she had had a shock when she discovered that one of her letters from Lawrence was printed in Harry T. Moore's new biography of D. H. Lawrence, *The Intelligent Heart*. Aldington apologized and wrote: "I'm sorry about that letter. If I'd known I could have got Frieda to stop publication. It doubtless formed part of a whole lot of my stuff, including my father's gold watch, which the P.'s [Patmores] stole."

H.D. did not like Moore's biography. To Pearson she wrote, "The minute I pick up this enchanting 'story of D. H. Lawrence'

I will begin to scream again."[44] Part of the problem was that she knew from reading it that Aldington had influenced Moore's version of the Lawrence story. She did not know in 1955 how directly Aldington served as a source for and confidant to Moore, but later she learned that Aldington was deeply involved with both Moore and Edward Nehls. Just as she had her Professor Pearson at Yale, to whom she was feeding information about the Imagist years, Aldington had his professors: Moore at Southern Illinois University and Nehls at the University of Illinois.

To H.D., Aldington at first professed great disdain for Moore's work. He called him "the worst kind of unscrupulous self-seeking academic careerist," and told H.D. to beware of him. He advised her: "Don't take notice of him. Don't answer libels in American books, particularly of the sexual sort."[45] Later he explained that Moore was a literary competitor of his who "wants among other things to push me out as the definitive biographer of DHL and to establish himself — in spite of the fact that Frieda reviewed his book very unfavorably."[46] But eventually it became clear that Aldington was "helping" Moore in his Lawrence work. As he put it, "I think it best to keep on amiable terms with him, as I can sometimes influence him. At my request he has cut out two paragraphs very offensive to you, which we shouldn't have known of otherwise."[47]

Aldington's involvement in Edward Nehls's massive three-volume study *D. H. Lawrence: A Composite Biography* was also extensive. But H.D. was unaware of Nehls's work or Aldington's assistance to and influence on Nehls until Aldington mentioned it in a letter: "I am — strange to say — at this very moment writing the introduction to vol. 3, and for once in my life have to be a bit cagey."[48]

Aldington was of course serious in his wish to be the definitive Lawrence biographer, but when he realized there was no way he could stop the production of Moore's and Nehls's books, he assisted them in their projects. He also furnished anecdotal information and recommended deletions so as to assure that H.D. would be excluded from the Lawrence story as told by Moore and Nehls. To the extent that this strategy was visible to Moore, he understood it as protectiveness on Aldington's part. As he later explained: "Richard was always sensitive on the score of his former wife, and continually felt protective toward her." He also explained that he had omitted material about H.D. from his edition of Lawrence's *Collected Letters* at Aldington's request, and in 1965 indicated that "although both Richard Aldington and H.D. are now dead and beyond harm from [the omitted material's] being quoted, I still feel too confidentially bound in about the matter to include the passage just now."[49]

On July 4, 1956, H.D. wrote to Aldington of *Helen:* "I have only one copy of the complet [sic] poem, three books, seven sections in first two, six in the third. This sounds alarming, as I say, but it finally finished for me the 'war' complex or compulsion — and got Helen and Achilles off my chest."[50] A month earlier she had written to Bryher: "I am re-reading *Palimpsest* and living it all over again; it links up with *Helen in Egypt.*"[51]

Erich Heydt had recorded H.D. reading aloud from her manuscript, and the recording pleased her immensely. After listening to it she wrote:

> This is myself, Helen out of the body, in another world, the *eidolon* of the legend. But she is not alone. There she meets the legendary Achilles, a phantom but a reality. There I, there Helen lives out her war — her wars. There in the second long-playing disc is Helen and Achilles on the one side, on the other Helen with Paris. There is the conflict solved — as *The Woman Within* asks, "Is it true, I wonder, that the only way to escape a war is to be in it?"[52]

In H.D.'s mind *Helen in Egypt* and "Madrigal" were inexorably bound together. To Pearson she wrote: "To me *Madrigal* and the *Helen in Egypt* are sacrosanct!"[53] In 1959 Norman Pearson placed "Madrigal" with Grove Press in New York. H.D. wrote to him on September 14:

> I have two copies of *Madrigal* — do you want another . . . I worked off and on at M. for many years, rough sketch was really begun *in situ,* Cornwall, 1918. Just before I made plans to return to London for War II, summer, 1939, at Kenwin, this version "wrote itself." Of course, all earlier versions were destroyed. They were "forced" and without the center — I did write the last part, the letter to Rico, in Lausanne, about 1947 or 1948 — as the end as was, trailed away — and I pointedly made the *book,* the *Child.*

When Aldington learned that the book was to be published he was very distraught and began to give H.D. advice which, if taken, would have had the effect of limiting the publicity the book received and thus its impact. On February 15, 1960, he wrote to advise H.D. not to give interviews. He warned her that "the journalists are very malicious toward genuine artists, and will publish any kind of lies as 'an interview' if they are not intimidated."

On February 26 he wrote: "Tell the publisher NOT to put in 'sent for review notice' . . . but a typed note 'sent by H.D. at the request of R.A.' " Aldington wanted to make sure the book would be read and reviewed the way he wanted it read and that any potential reviewers would get in touch with *him,* not her. On March 3 he wrote to tell her that Moore was "now certainly sorry for his past errors." He would, says Aldington, "have 'Madrigal Booster' stuck on the back window of his car, and will doubtless review." On March 17 he wrote that "in spite of 'not for review' Moore may do the Saturday Review notice."

On March 21 Aldington urged H.D. not to allow herself to be interviewed by *Newsweek,* and on March 22 he wrote to tell her he had spent a terrible night worrying about her and the *Newsweek* affair. H.D. gave the interview and ignored Aldington's attempts to suppress the book and limit the reviews.

In spite of their quarrel, a good deal of H.D.'s late work came out of her renewed relationship with Aldington following World War II. In a very real sense he brought back the past and helped her to get the story off her chest at last. In 1947 she began the letter to Rico which ends "Madrigal" — "I will never see you again, Rico." As she tells us in "Thorn Thicket," written in 1960, it is obvious (at least to her) where "Madrigal" stopped in 1939.

> Somewhere about the middle of Chapter 10, "it" stopped. I could not say what "it" was but the last third or even half of the MS wavered, trembled and wandered, indeed to quote my daughter again, it simply didn't "jell."
> It was easy to see where "it" stopped. ("It" stopped exactly where Julia thought, "I'll get some fresh flowers for that jug.") It was almost as if "it" were a sort of "control" and had gone away. I bundled up the last third or it might have been half of the MS, and put it aside. I would destroy it later. It was easy to see where "it" stopped. The room grew colder as "it" compelled my pencil. It was a letter that I (Julia) was writing to Lorenzo, Rico or Frederico.[54]

H.D. wrote the final letter to Rico after the re-establishment of her relationship with Aldington, after her rebuff by Dowding, after her break with Bryher, and after her nervous breakdown or "coming out" in 1946. In pages 166 to 184 of "Madrigal" she explains in fictional terms why she did not go off with Lawrence, pointing out that she had not wanted to lose her relationship with Aldington, that Lawrence had sent out a flare to her, that she had had to "get out," that she had met him in "a little house, quite a simple little house in the forest," and that — an important point — "there was Elsa." Yes, she admits in the letter, the class differences did matter. And Elsa (Frieda) "could do without non-essentials."

In "Thorn Thicket" H.D. explains the connection between seemingly unrelated work. "The letter to Rico then, must have been finished late autumn or early winter, 1947, before I moved to the more comfortable [Hotel] *La Paix* room where I began *Red Rose and the White.* I have dated the *Rose* 1948, and the *The Sword Went Out to Sea* that preceded it, 1947."[55] Thus the letter to Rico, which she had been trying to write since 1918, was finally written in the same year she wrote her novel featuring Lord Dowding. In H.D.'s writing the story of World War II is superimposed, as in a palimpsest, upon the story of World War I. As she writes in "Magic Mirror": "That war, this war, they were exactly super-imposed on one another."[56] In "Thorn Thicket" she tells us that Dowding was a double of Lawrence:

> Talk of war, waiting for the inevitable, summer 1939, ignites the mines, the chain of association. *Madrigal* is the answer. I leave the script in Switzerland and re-enter the old scene, the same scene, different people, the same people. The meeting with the *double* in War II is super-imposed on the *corps* of the marriage or love-affair of War I.[57]

In the same sense, Heydt is a double of Aldington. Of the coming publication of "Madrigal" H.D. writes:

> The theme is departure, desertion, death. The people are the same. Heydt is Ashton, Julia's or Hilda's husband in *Madrigal.* Rafe Ashton's or Richard Aldington's *Madrigal* loves or mistresses appear; Romana, Joan, Belinda, Gonzales are exact prototypes.* Well, not exact but they catch or reflect a quality or contour of the Bellas and Morgans of the *Madrigal.*[58]

The similarity was reinforced when Richard Aldington came to the Küsnacht clinic in November 1959 for a checkup. He was suffering from nerves and depression. H.D. writes: "The end of November, Richard Aldington came from Sury-en-Vaux, France, to consult a specialist here. I had not seen him for 21 years. He might have stepped out of the pages of *Madrigal.*"[59]

Just as the connection between Dowding and Lawrence had helped H.D. in her work, so that between her doctor and ex-husband proved helpful. As a patient she was attentive to the life of her doctor. When Heydt announced his forthcoming marriage his patients were shattered. H.D. too was upset, because this "desertion" emotionally paralleled Richard's desertion of her. She did

---

*Romana, Joan, Belinda, and Gonzales were analysands of Dr. Heydt at the clinic in which H.D. was living. Bella and Morgan were the names H.D. gave to Dorothy Yorke and Brigit Patmore, Aldington's mistresses.

not immediately see this, but she later realized that she did not want to give up Heydt, her psychoanalyst, just as she had not wanted to give up Aldington. "Is he the coin-side?" she asks of Heydt. "With his fantastic charm, insouciance, indifference, he matched Rafe Ashton of *Madrigal*." [60]

Through reliving the Madrigal experience with Erich Heydt and writing *Helen in Egypt* H.D. realized that she had totally accepted and embraced western civilization: "I had accepted the Establishment. That is, I had accepted the whole cosmic, bloody show. *The war was my husband*." [61]

In "Thorn Thicket" H.D. succinctly summarizes the roles of Dowding and Heydt in her creative process: "The feelings that I should have had in 1917 were awakened or invoked some forty years later, *through other people*." As she saw Heydt's patients at the clinic fall apart at the news of his departure, she re-experienced Aldington's betrayal. "Rafe-Bella of *Madrigal,* the 'primal scene' of classic analysis repeats itself . . . No, I did not have to *see* any more of this. I saw him and the *Madrigal* Bella in bed together and that was enough." [62]

At the time of the writing of "Thorn Thicket" H.D. was anticipating the publication of "Madrigal" and was delighted and incredulous when Norman Holmes Pearson told her the book jacket was a "double-page photograph of an empty beach with the incoming tide." Her relationship with Aldington had occurred indoors; her relationship with Lawrence had occurred outdoors. H.D. writes: "The sea draws Julia out, out, out to Cornwall and beyond. Norman said that he immensely admired the double-page photograph but he did not 'quite get the symbolism.' To me, it is inspiring, a miracle in choice of decor." [63]

The cover reminded her of her relationship with Lawrence, whom she identifies in "Thorn Thicket" as the "magician lover." Lying in bed at the age of seventy-four, H.D. wished Lawrence could see what had become of the world they created. " 'Kick over your tiresome House of Life,' " Frederico says to Julia in "Madrigal." "What would he say, could he see it now? Truly, it is 3 grandchildren and another to arrive soon, and that mother-father . . ." [64]

H.D. had kicked over her marriage for Lawrence. But there was another dimension: "There is another House of Life. Could he see it now, he would recognize it. It is a school copy-book or exercise book with lines, a blue cover, a loose blotter at the back." This is the world of poetry; the book is that in which she had written poems to Lawrence. Of this notebook she writes: "This is my House of Life, but it is not tiresome." [65]

Miraculously, someone had understood "Madrigal"; someone had designed the right cover. She writes: "After my years of exile and wandering, I greet the Sea. The Sea encompasses me, encompasses my Book. The Sea envelopes me. The Sea is a 'jacket,' a folder around me, around my Book."[66] She connects The Book with the Child, "the Child of War I and of that marriage . . . I have the *Madrigal,* the Child of Rafe, Rico and the Cyril Vane of that period, 'for all eternity.' "[67]

In "Thorn Thicket" H.D. writes of how she had attempted, in some of her early prose, to draw a composite figure of the men in her life to achieve a kind of palimpsest. "In Captain Rafton of *Hesperia,* there is a superimposition of the *Madrigal* soldier-husband and the *Madrigal* magician-lover."[68] In "Secret Name" she had tried to combine Lawrence and Aldington into one character, and in "Hipparchia" she had tried to combine Lawrence and Cecil Gray. In "Asphodel" she had tried to write Gray into Lawrence's place and omit Lawrence altogether.

On October 14, 1959, H.D. wrote to Pearson:

> I drag out two rather long MSS. *Her* and *Asphodel.* If carbons ever turn up, please destroy them. These were written in London, 1926–1927. It is the old *Madrigal* and *Gift* material without the daemonic drive or the *daemon* [Lawrence] that (or who) was released by p s - a [psychoanalysis], I suppose, and the second War . . . *Madrigal* only "came true" on the verge of War II, though no doubt, it phoenix-ed out of *Asphodel* that was put away and deliberately "forgotten." The Asphodel "nest" should in the traditional manner, be burnt. Untraditionally, I am picking it apart to see how it was put together.

H.D. was sometimes irritated about Aldington's obsession with the project of negating the existence of her relation to Lawrence but there was nothing she could do about it except to write her own books and occasionally remind him that all of her unpublished manuscripts and notes on her writing were being kept by Norman Holmes Pearson at Yale. H.D. called Pearson a "medium" because he was helping her to realize or materialize the story even though he was not fully aware of the role he was playing. Lord Dowding, she said, was a medium too. She wrote of Aldington and Lawrence: "This soldier-husband, magician-lover theme runs through all this writing. I dream of Lord D., its last physical and psychic manifestation, last night. Was he an instrument or medium of the 'Secret' . . . 'the secret Christ'? I called the first story in my book, *Palimpsest,* published 1926 in Paris, *Secret Name.*"[69]

It is important to understand that H.D. saw all her work (with the exception of the Dijon novels which were blessed by Bryher), from the time of the breakup of her marriage through *Helen in Egypt,* as part of the same book, every work a variation on "the novel" or "the story" as she lived it in World War I. In "Thorn Thicket" she writes: "It was not until December 1948 that I had the courage at the *Hotel de la Paix,* Lausanne, to return to the scene and again to finish a half-written letter, this time as from Assuan, to a magician-lover."[70] After she finally finished "Madrigal" in that cold room, she tore up most of *Advent;* we have the record of what she saved. She asks, quixotically, "Does the *Circle* dictate the material as well as the spiritual aspects of life? . . . The H.D. of D. H. Lawrence almost does the trick, D.H.-H.D. but not quite."[71]

The H.D.-D.H. "circle" is, as H.D. observes, a striking coincidence. In *Helen in Egypt* she calls this literary circle the "iron-ring" and writes: "We were an iron-ring/whom Death made stronger."[72] But the literal coincidence of their initials was not as interesting to her as the events that had occurred in her life. Her encounter with Lawrence was the interesting "coincidence." Her own spiritualist equations were real; the *gloire* is the unborn child, in this case, a grandchild.* She writes:

> Timothy, my fourth grand-child, arrived to-day about noon . . . On March 18, the first copy arrived, air-mail from Norman, and the special edition came yesterday. The Child and the Book are adequately synchronized. Julia writes to Rico that the un-born child or the about-to-be-born Book is the *gloire.* She refers to a rose, *Gloire de Dijon* that he [Lawrence] wrote of, in a poem. Yes the beautiful edition of *Madrigal* is in my hands now, the vibration, the message, *Bid Me to Live,* will go on.[73]

In "Compassionate Friendship" H.D. had written: "Within the circumference of my circle, the legendary duality of the Typhon-Osiris, Mephisto-Christ, is stressed by the *Madrigal* memory of the Frederico, old Rico of my own story. And that story conditioned me to deception, loss, destruction. The later Lord Howell was the perfected image."[74] Dowding had been the cathartic presence in her life that had allowed her to bring the story together. Her contact with him had liberated emotions that she had buried for years and years. Her relationship with Erich Heydt had been cathartic in a different way. As she writes: "He draws the stings out of me (these reconstructed memories) as a magnet draws out

---

*H.D.'s grandchildren, Perdita Schaffner's children, are Valentine, Nicholas, Elizabeth Bryher, and Timothy.

nails — those thorns."[75] Norman Holmes Pearson had been important too: "I knew how tired he was but he kept up this tremendous protective role, this subtle identification and understanding, my poetry, all my scattered 'novels' of which he has copies."[76]

As a patient at the clinic H.D. had achieved a kind of emotional detachment; she had watched her story work itself out in the part of the mind that was not emotionally involved, the part that had become an impartial observer. Dowding and Heydt had played a helpful role in her creative life. Each had provided a shock — not enough to be traumatic, but just the right amount to release the buried and repressed material. As H.D. writes, "Obviously Heydt meant a great deal in filling out the picture, and relating my life here now, with the old scene in London."[77] In the same way the cathartic experience with Dowding had allowed her finally to write the letter beginning, "I will never see you again, Rico." As she writes: "Another story began but in the end it came back to *Madrigal*, the Book, the baby, Timothy lumped against my shoulder on Elizabeth Bryher's 4th birthday."[78]

§ § §

Layers of the palimpsest are assembled and reassembled. H.D. knew that her Achilles character of *Helen in Egypt* transcended the personal characteristics of D. H. Lawrence. In the same way she knew that her Helen character transcended her own personal characteristics. While it is true that one cannot write what one has not known, it is also true that character, culture, and events are recurring realities. In writing *Helen in Egypt* H.D. believed that she had achieved something in the way of artistic conception that went beyond personal idiosyncrasies and private tragedy. Achilles and Paris were figural realities of all time. H.D. believed that the concrete experience of a fully conscious life is in fact the drama of life writ large — it is really the enactment of the whole drama of nature. So even though a specific character may be based on a real person, as Paris was based on Richard Aldington, the character assumes a reality that in an artistic sense subsumes his "character identification." Once Paris was established in this way in H.D.'s poetic structure, Erich Heydt or someone else may have manifested as Paris or served as a model for him in certain parts of the poetic sequence.

In *Helen* the principal characters exist in eternity as well as in time. Within H.D.'s set of symbols, Clytaemnestra, for instance, is a persona for woman as wife, specifically in any situation that involves "the other woman." In H.D.'s own life there had been a number of Clytaemnestra manifestations. She was a Clytaemnestra when Aldington brought home his mistress, Dorothy Yorke. Later Bryher became a Clytaemnestra in her marriage to Kenneth Macpherson. H.D. had certainly seen the Clytaemnestra side of Dorothy Pound and Frieda Lawrence.

Similarly, we can think of Achilles as representative of a particular manifestation of masculine consciousness, or as a specific kind of masculine thrust toward a feminine center. He is, as H.D. says, the "eternal lover." In this sense the work of art is impersonal rather than personal, not only because the same events happen to all of us but because we are more than what happens to us; the work of art is our experience (or soul) stripped of our ego or personal identity.

The specific characters in *Helen in Egypt*, then, may be understood both biographically and figuratively. The sequence of events from the natural and historical world has been transposed by an act of the living imagination, the eternal "I AM" of thought and vision. For the poet, the process of rewriting the same story over and over led at last, in the writing of *Helen*, to a personal liberation. H.D. had finally found the appropriate form in which to tell the story. The reader is gripped by the reality of the presentation and either enriched or overwhelmed, according to his or her own disposition.

H.D.'s images may become her readers' images, for these configurations are recurring realities. Coming to understand the concrete biographical realities from which the images are conceived ought not to diminish the matrix, or mind, from which they are born.

35

Helen and
Achilles in Egypt

HELEN IN EGYPT is an epic poem of great depth and beauty; it is H.D.'s finest achievement. In the *Journal of Women's Studies in Literature* L. M. Freibert wrote that H.D. was "the first American woman to publish a major epic poem and the first American to create a female epic protagonist."[1] *Helen in Egypt* is, as Linda Wagner observed, a "culmination."[2] H.D. conceived of the poem in 1918 in Cornwall (and we still have her 1918 notes); on January 20, 1936, she wrote to Bryher that she had begun working on the "Helen of Euripides."[3]

On February 2, 1960, H.D. wrote: *"Thalassa, Thalassa* or *Thalatta, Thalatta* — this should be written in Greek. Like the soldiers in the Anabasis, after my years of exile and wandering, I greet the Sea. The Sea encompasses me, encompasses my Book."[4] She was speaking of the cover of *Bid Me to Live,* but she might have been speaking of *Helen in Egypt.* Just a few months earlier, on July 13, 1959, she had written to Pearson, "I find re-reading *Helen* comforting . . . — so much real *Sea* in the background."[5] *Thalassa* refers to the work of the psychoanalyst Sandor Ferenczi; H.D. was invoking his *Thalassa, A Theory of Genitality,* in which the author maintains that in the act of coitus we regress toward the sea from which all life originates. As for Ferenczi, so for H.D. the sea is the primal creative source.

Helen in Egypt is divided into three parts: "Pallinode," "Leuké," and "Eidolon." The first two parts contain seven books and the third part contains six books. Each book contains eight sections, each introduced by a paragraph of prose that explains and illuminates the poetry. The work thus is composed of 160 separate poems, including the concluding "Eidolon," which together form one of literature's most extraordinary unities.

Part I, "Pallinode," is a meditation upon the transcendental Helen — the Helen who had visions, "saw things," wrote poetry. Most of its images are from the early poetry revisited. "Pallinode" takes us back through long corridors of time to the pictures of the World War I Imagist period. Part II, "Leuké," is the meditation on the Greek Helen, as opposed to the Egyptian Helen of "Pallinode." "Leuké" concerns the intellectual Helen who attempts to record, analyze, and formulate her poetic experience in intellectual concepts. The third part of *Helen in Egypt*, "Eidolon," is concerned with the human content of the drama and focuses upon the question, what happened and why did it occur?

In *End to Torment* H.D. speaks of the beginning of the process of imagination which led eventually to the creation of *Helen in Egypt*: "It all began with the Greek fragments."[6] Some of these are her "Notes on Euripides, Pausanias, and the Greek Lyric Poets," which she began in Cornwall in 1918. In early issues of the *Egoist* and *Poetry* magazine, and in his early Cantos, Pound had written of the entanglements of the Imagists, poetic and personal, in the context of the Trojan War. It was Pound who named H.D. Helen, identifying her beauty with that of the legendary Helen of Homer's *Iliad*. Pound thought of himself as Homer, recording from a decent literary perspective the fall of Troy (which H.D. understood as a symbol for her marriage). Within this poetic context, H.D. identified Pound as Menelaus, the first husband of Helen, whom Paris (Aldington) snatched away. This story is presented by H.D. in her translation of Euripides' *Choruses from the Iphigeneia in Aulis,* published in 1916. Pound thought of himself too as Odysseus, as he left London (and H.D.) and set off on the poetic and personal journey recorded in the Cantos.

H.D. began to work with the Helen theme as early as 1918, when she conceptualized the first draft of a presentation in Cornwall. She visualized the "Temple tomb of Proteus, King of Egypt . . . She [Helen] is spirit; she who was hatched from an egg by Leda, the mistress of God." As in her later epic, Helen "is no mere dream, wandering in a dream-country, she is a woman, an intellect, a Greek." The metaphor of Greece, at this time of H.D.'s life, is an all-powerful idea. "Greece is indeed the tree-of-life, the ever-present stream, the spring of living-water." H.D.'s 1918 prevision is of a landscape: ". . . a free, large, clear, vibrant, limitless realm, sky and sea and distant islands, and the shore-line such as that in Egypt"; but it is also conceptual: "She tells her story . . .

the whole story of the human spirit is there." And the character Achilles, who will be central to *Helen in Egypt,* is already a part of her imagination: "A stranger drags across the sand. He is swift to recognize her."[7]

This theme of the encounter of Helen and Achilles is of course familiar to readers of *Helen in Egypt.* When Helen and Achilles meet, Helen is "alone, bereft," and Achilles is "shipwrecked." In H.D.'s "Notes on Euripides," as in *Helen in Egypt,* "The new mortal/shedding his glory/limped slowly across the sand." And as in her 1918 vision, he is "swift to recognize her."

> I drew out a blackened stick,
> to darken my arms,
> to disguise my features
>
> but I could not hide my eyes.[8]

It was H.D.'s opinion as early as 1918 that Helen was not beautiful in any conventional sense. She was not "sweet," "soft," or "luxurious," wrote H.D. in "Notes on Euripides"; she was rather intelligent.[*9]

Again we wonder — was H.D. invoking a physical or a metaphysical reality? For the desolate coast is surely, on one level of meaning, Imagism; *Helen in Egypt* is in this dimension a reconstruction of the Imagist scene in one powerfully imaginative landscape. And many of the images presented in "Pallinode" recall the early Imagist poetry, the hieroglyphs. Alone on this desolate beach, H.D. first encountered D. H. Lawrence through his Isis poem that appeared in *Poetry* under the title "Don Juan" and reappeared in *Amores,* surrounded by poems about his mother's death. She answered it with her "Thetis" poem, and both Lawrence's call and H.D.'s answer are recalled in *Helen in Egypt* in the context of the "attack" on the beach, with a full recognition of the earlier experiences as well as the underlying Oedipal motif of the poetry.

> "Isis," he said, "or Thetis," I said,
> recalling remembering, invoking
> his sea-mother . . .[10]

Reflecting upon *Helen in Egypt* in 1958, H.D. inserted a note in "Notes on Euripides." On August 16 she wrote in this manuscript: "Re-reading *Helen,* some quarter century later, or more, gave me an entirely new idea of this enigmatic drama. This play

*In a letter to Norman Holmes Pearson of January 31, 1956, H.D. wrote: "They always make H. of T. [Helen of Troy] a cutie — is it the Male Conception? She was a Spartan, a goddess etc. etc. Well — I suppose mere-men can not swallow that."

in the light of history, the ill-fated Sicilian expedition, is one of the most poignant and devout of the series of the "lost oracle," making a trilogy with *Ion* and *Iphigeneia*."[11]

In some sense, then, "Pallinode" of *Helen in Egypt* was inspired by H.D.'s translations of Euripides (she had translated both *Iphigeneia* and *Ion*), but the physical beauty of Cornwall was also a primary source of inspiration. In her "Notes on Euripides" H.D. writes:

> I visualize the opening scene of the *Helen* of Euripides not with stage-property and ceremonial of the religious drama, but as taking place out of doors upon some exquisite sea-shelf. I do not hear music but a blending of waters . . . the sea is at very low tide almost at rest, yet breaking in the small back-drawn waves, waves that seem, if you can understand how exactly I imagine it, to break backwards, those waves at very low-tide that run out swiftly, spend their strength in that, and creep tentatively back.
>
> The tide is very low. But there is this slight rush of water . . . And I know what it is; though I do not see the river, I can imagine the sand-shelf it cuts over and the edge of that fresh moving tide, where it lies clear and across the white sand it has scooped out and the backs of the shells it has washed so clean of salt.
>
> There are two sounds of water. The sea at the lowest tide and the Nile flowing over the sand.[12]

It is most interesting to see how H.D.'s imagination combined the landscapes of Greece, Egypt, and Cornwall. This picture never left her mind. As she writes: "Perhaps in this opening study of *Helen,* I have been carried away too much by my own imagination, been unbalanced, intoxicated a little with my own idea." But what she discovered through her study of Euripides is that "the lines of the Greek poet . . . are today as vivid and fresh as they ever were . . . as portals . . . that look out from our ship, our world, our restricted lives, on to a sea that moves and changes and bears us up . . . These words are to me portals, gates." H.D.'s own relation to Euripides serves as a guide to readers of *Helen in Egypt.* She writes: "I know that we need scholars to decipher and interpret the Greek, but we also need poets and mystics and children to rediscover this Hellenic world, to see *through* the words; the word being the outline, the architectural structure of that door or window, through which we are all free, scholar and unlettered alike, to pass."[13]

The experience of the Greek language can restructure our minds so that we can see through to a whole new dimension of being. This is what *Helen in Egypt* can do for the reader. While its landscape is an imagined reality and we can read it as a metaphysical reality (that is, the landscape of Imagism), we feel that something more is going on here; we remember that in H.D.'s lexicon, Egypt represents the sexual act. In *Helen in Egypt* Helen and Achilles meet outdoors. Achilles is "piling brushwood." He is angry. She is "under his cloak" when she prays:

> O *Thetis, O sea-mother,* I prayed under his cloak,
> *let me remember, let me remember,*
> *forever, this star in the night.* [14]

D. H. Lawrence presents a corresponding scene in *John Thomas and Lady Jane.* The brushwood of *Helen in Egypt* is fir boughs; the cloak is a coat. Parkin is angry.

> "Was you coming to the hut?"
> "No! No! I was going home — "
> He looked down at her in a flare of anger. [15]

In both *Helen in Egypt* and *John Thomas and Lady Jane* the spark or flare of anger leads to a sexual encounter.

> And his arms tightened instinctively, against his will, around her, and his body pressed strangely upon her. Her instinct was to fight him. He held her so hard. — Yet why fight? . . . Her will seemed to leave her . . . Then he half-carried her through the dense trees, to a place where there was a heap of dead boughs. He threw out one or two fir boughs, and folded his coat. She stood by mute and helpless, without volition. Then he took her and laid her down, wasting no time, breaking her underclothing in his urgency. And her will seemed to have left her entirely. [16]

In *Helen in Egypt* Achilles calls Helen "Hecate — a witch — a vulture, and finally, as if he had run out of common invective, he taunts her — a *hieroglyph.*" H.D. asks:

> How could I hide my eyes?
> how could I veil my face?
> with ash or charcoal from the embers?
>
> I drew out a blackened stick,
> but he snatched it,
> he flung it back,
>
> "what sort of enchantment is this?
> what art will you wield with a fagot?
> are you Hecate? are you a witch?
>
> a vulture, or hieroglyph,
> the sign or the name of a goddess?
> what sort of goddess is this?

where are we? who are you?
where is this desolate coast?
who am I? am I a ghost?"[17]

At about the same time that H.D. began to study hieroglyphs, after her 1923 trip to Egypt at the time of the excavation of King Tutankhamen's tomb, Lawrence began to be interested in early Etruscan images. Both cultures painted heraldic animals on tombs. The chick, the hare, and the bee on the temple walls of Egypt have a parallel in the dolphin, duck, fish, bird, lion, and deer of Etruscan tombs. Hieroglyphs are images; in *Helen in Egypt* they represent Imagist poems. As H.D. says in *Helen in Egypt:* "I have 'read' the lily,/I can not 'read' the hare, the chick, the bee."[18]

The hieroglyphs are "writ large." Both H.D. and Lawrence had come to realize that we are part of something larger than ourselves. We are part of the continuity of life that arises from chaos and ends in the tomb, the underworld. In *The Escaped Cock* Lawrence writes that his public life (the life of his ego) is over. In *Helen in Egypt* H.D. describes Achilles as *"no more immortal."*[19] And Helen, too, had ceased to exist in her ordinary human dimension.

H.D. writes: "The 'old pictures' are eternal . . . painted in bright primary colors."[20] We think of Lawrence's paintings, in bright primary colors. The one at the end of part II of *The Escaped Cock* is a picture of three red acorns — the seeds of a new life — and a green leaf. We will recall the last paragraph of *The Man Who Died:* "I sowed the seed of my life and my resurrection, and put my touch forever upon the choice woman of this day." The tailpiece for part I is of a vivid red flower, a lily. We remember the image of the red water lily H.D. presented in *Advent* in response to Freud's theories of male supremacy. The headpiece for part II of the story is again in primary colors — reds and greens. It is an image of a woman, the priestess of Isis; in her hand she holds an ankh, the Egyptian symbol of life.

In her 1923 trip to Egypt H.D. found the images of her personal life "substantiated" on the tombs of Egypt. The life symbols of Egypt corresponded to her most intense personal experience. The little birth house she discovered in the underground tomb reinvoked the little hut. The bee, the chick, and the hare were exaggerated presentations of primal forms, stone-pictures that evoked the same realities as the word-pictures that Lawrence painted in his *Birds, Beasts, and Flowers* (1923).

The substance of H.D.'s discovery was that her most deeply felt personal experiences were recurring realities of human experience. Everything that had happened to her had happened before, in other cultures, in other times. This substantiation — the objective existence of the hieroglyphs — brought her personal experience within the domain of the impersonal. She found the subjects of her own and Lawrence's poems (which are images) externalized as hieroglyphs on a temple wall. These life energies, translated by the mind into visual images, exist outside the individual self; they are collective images of a culture. Moreover, she and Lawrence were in touch with something very primal.

Just as an experience gives rise to a hieroglyph, one's own experience can become externalized and exist in eternity through the process of artistic presentation. The poem, like the hieroglyph, presents an image that is larger than life; the experience is, as it were, writ large. The hieroglyph appealed to H.D.'s imagination because the sensation experienced and recorded sensually is disproportionate in size to the object through which that sensation is received. The experience presents itself to the imagination writ large. We can think of H.D.'s early poems — for instance, "Sea Rose," "Sea Lily," and "Sea Iris" — as hieroglyphs.

The hieroglyph of the poem presents the primal scene. In *Helen in Egypt* "the thousand petalled lily" and the "unfurled lotus" are presentations of female and male sexuality. We do not know whether H.D. is speaking of a particular sexual act or of a poem that presents the primal scene, because H.D. is attentive to communication in whatever dimension it may occur. And from her own point of view (and as it turned out, in her own life history), the poem and the sexual act were connected and inseparable realities.

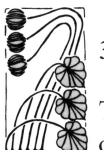

36

The Argument
of "Pallinode"

As AN IMPERSONAL POEM *Helen in Egypt* is a meditation upon the cause of war. War takes place, says H.D., because someone (or some group or culture) will not bend to the will of someone else (or some other group or culture).

H.D. sees the war between the sexes as primal and believes all wars follow the same logic. A person or culture attempts to enforce his will on another person or another culture. Who, then, is to be blamed? The one who attempts to force his will on another or the one who refuses to submit? In H.D.'s experience men had attempted to force their will upon her; resistance leads to strife. Do we then blame the woman for resisting? Or do we blame her for provoking the attack? Or, suggests H.D., is it not the case that men ought to take responsibility for war? They are, after all, the aggressors. Why should women be blamed for simply existing? These are some of the larger questions that prompt the strophes of *Helen in Egypt*.

H.D. had suffered much in her life from World War I and World War II. She had suffered too from the relentless pursuit of men. And because she was so attractive to men, she had been blamed for men's desire and aggressiveness. Forty years after the publication of her first Imagist poems she was still full of amazement that she had been blamed for the tangle of events of the Imagist years.

H.D. was sixty-five years old when she began writing *Helen in Egypt*. She had forgiven everyone in her life any wrong they had done her by the time she wrote the trilogy of war poems. Certainly she had forgiven the poets in her life, the troubadours. In "The Guest," her essay on the Elizabethen poets, she writes: "The love of the troubadour was love of the Spiritual. This love could not be satisfied on earth . . . Reason, as I have said, was well within the intellectual range of each one of them. But love was stronger."[1]

Having forgiven Pound and Lawrence as persons, she was liberated; she was free to tangle with the tradition itself. Yes, certainly she knew Pound would read *Helen in Egypt*. And certainly to quarrel with Homer was to quarrel with Pound. But she never expected to see Pound again.

When she had translated the *Ion* of Euripides she had written:

> There is one law,
> one judgment;
> he who plans ill
> for another,
> must himself
> suffer it.[2]

H.D. felt a very real kinship with Euripides, for she shared his sense of the relevant questions. His play *The Trojan Women* is an invective against Helen. But Euripides reinstated Helen in both *Helen* and *Electra*. According to the story he tells in his *Helen,* which is the same as that told by Stesichorus of Sicily in his *Pallinode,* Helen was carried to Egypt and kept there by King Proteus until Menelaus came to claim her after the war. As H.D. writes:

> Stesichorus was said to have been struck blind because of his invective against Helen, but later was restored to sight, when he reinstated her in his *Pallinode*. Euripides, notably in *The Trojan Women,* reviles her, but he is also "restored to sight." The later, little understood *Helen in Egypt* [Euripides' *Helen*], is again a *Pallinode*, a defense, explanation or apology.
>
> According to the *Pallinode,* Helen was never in Troy. She had been transposed or translated from Greece into Egypt. Helen of Troy was a phantom, substituted for the real Helen, by jealous deities. The Greeks and the Trojans alike fought for an illusion.[3]

The philosophical issue is simply whom to blame for war, specifically for the war between the sexes, the primal war.

In the opening scenes of *Helen in Egypt* Helen is attacked for appearing, presumably in a poem. But the Helen whom Achilles sees upon the ramparts is a phantom, a fiction, a work of poetry. She is, then, as passive as the hieroglyph on the temple wall. H.D.'s Imagist poem is of course open to interpretation. And from Achilles' point of view, her language pays no allegiance to the prevailing reality principle; it is a discourse from which the law of contradiction is excluded, a language of unity rather than distinction. To whom, then, is she speaking?

Because Helen appears, the hero is incited to battle. Freud explains the epic hero's actions in the context of the Oedipus complex. Because Achilles cannot face his own desires, he manages to blame Helen. As Freud writes of the birth of poetry and the epic poet:

> It was then, perhaps, that some individual, in the exigency of his longing, may have been moved to free himself from the group and take over the father's part. He who did this was the first epic poet; and the advance was achieved in his imagination. This poet disguised the truth with lies in accordance with his longing. He invented the heroic myth. The hero was a man who by himself had slain the father — the father who still appeared in the myth as a totemic monster. Just as the father has been the boy's first ideal, so in the hero who aspires to the father's place the poet now created the first ego ideal. The transition to the hero was probably afforded by the youngest son, the mother's favorite, whom she had protected from paternal jealousy, and who, in the era of the primal horde, had been the father's successor. In the lying poetic fancies of prehistoric times the woman, who had been the prize of battle and the temptation to murder, was probably turned into the active seducer and instigator to the crime.[4]

Who is to blame? The issue is the origins of war — war between the sexes to be sure, but also war as a recurring pattern in history. Since the story of Helen and Achilles is not simply a personal story but one with a very long lineage, it must include a genealogy, a consideration of descent or genesis. Just as Achilles is the son of a goddess, Thetis, so Helen is the daughter of a god, Zeus. Helen and her half-sister, Clytaemnestra, are both daughters of Leda, but Clytaemnestra's father is Tyndareus, a mortal.

As the child of a god, Helen reflects upon the contrast between herself and her mortal or earthly sister. She sees Clytaemnestra as the mother of the unfortunate Orestes and as murderer of her husband, Agamemnon. Helen's concern about the fate of Clytaemnestra is not only for her sister but for herself as well.

> why should Helen be given
> peace through eternity,
> and Clytaemnestra doomed,
>
> and slain by her son, Orestes?
> or is it a story told,
> a shadow of a shadow,
>
> has it ever happened,
> or is it yet to come?
> do I myself invent
>
> this tale of my sister's fate?[5]

The Argument of "Pallinode" § 371

Human culture is human sacrifice. The sacrifice of Clytaemnestra's daughter, Iphigeneia, leads at last to the murder of Agamemnon and the matricide. A woman is sacrificed because a man is unable to come to terms with his passion. Love and war, murder and incest; it is an old, old story. The bloody parallel to Achilles' attack on Helen on the beach is Agamemnon's sacrifice of Iphigeneia; hence the identification in H.D.'s thought of Helen and Iphigeneia. In order to follow the strophes of *Helen in Egypt* we must think mythologically. We must follow a logic of event. " 'God does not weave a loose web,' no." For it was Achilles to whom Iphigeneia was promised as a bride.

> You will not understand
> what I have taken years
> or centuries to experience;
>
> you may have a thousand loves
> and not one Lover;
> you may win a thousand wars
>
> and not one Victory,
> so I see further into the past,
> into the future;
>
> Achilles was the false bridegroom,
> Achilles was the hero promised
> to my sister's child,
>
> promised to her,
> promised to me,
> promised to Iphigeneia;
>
> It was Achilles who stood by the altar
> and did not interfere
> with the treacherous plan,
>
> the plot, they said, of Odysseus;
> it was Agamemnon who commanded
> her mother to bring her to Aulis,
>
> But it was Achilles, Achilles
> who sanctioned the sacrifice,
> the gift of his bride to Death.[6]

But Helen has been favored or spared to "decipher/the indecipherable Amen-script,"[7] the "tradition." And just as she and Clytaemnestra are ultimately twins — "Clytaemnestra gathered the red rose,/Helen, the white,/but they grew on one stem"[8] — so also we must see the identity of Achilles with man in general. Achilles is Everyman, one with all the war lords of Greece.

Agamemnon has sacrificed his daughter for winds, for inspiration, to sail to Troy. As projected upon the ramparts, Helen too has been sacrificed, metaphorically and ritually immolated, and subsequently idealized. H.D. is ever mindful of the war years and her own apotheosis. Clytaemnestra, Iphigeneia, and Helen are all victims of the war. H.D.'s vision is that all women are one and all men are one. But men and women are opposites and thus at war, for they have opposite perspectives on the primal realities.

A kind of hermeticism or alchemy of language takes place in *Helen in Egypt,* in which characters transform themselves through correspondence of images. In this context, the setting of "Palli-node" in Egypt is significant because the Egyptian language is one of twins or double identity. "In Egyptian words could . . . *reverse their sound as well as their sense.* Let us suppose the word good was Egyptian; then it could mean 'bad' as well as 'good' and be pronounced *doog* as well as good."[9] The language embodies the paradox of the poem, like a dream, where any symbol may mean its opposite. In the Egyptian language we find an explicit recognition of the primal scene — the union of opposites. From H.D.'s perspective a man and a woman become one through love. In the absence of love they resolve back to their opposite male and female natures.

In his attempt to understand Egypt, Freud asked how we could reconcile the fact of its high level of civilization with such a "strangely contradictory language," the fact "that they used to entrust two most inimical thoughts to be borne by one and the same sound, and used to combine in a sort of insoluble union what was mutually most intensely opposed." In the language of hieroglyph, that is, in H.D.'s poetry as in the language of Egypt, "every experience must have two sides; and either every name must have a double meaning, or else for every meaning there must be two names."[10] In this sense the earthly city and the heavenly city, the world of Battle and the world of Eros, and the world of man and the world of woman are juxtaposed and united at the same time (or in the same image). Such dualism is related to the recognition of the existence of a distinctly feminine consciousness. H.D.'s perspective is that monism recognizes the existence only of masculine consciousness. In *Helen in Egypt* the image that reconciles the masculine and the feminine is the primal scene.

The tale of Troy is certainly a tale of an earthly city, a city in time. And it has been decreed, it would seem, that Achilles will live in eternal time with Helen in another dimension, another dynasty.

> half, part of the tale of Troy,
> half, bound to the Dioscuri;
> twin-sisters of twin-brothers,

half of our life was given
to another hierarchy;
our children were children

of the Lords of the world and Troy,
but our birthright bound us to another dynasty,
other than Trojan and Greek.[11]

The drama seems to come full cycle around to the beginning.
"A simple spiral-shell may tell/a tale more ancient/than these mysteries."[12] Helen identifies herself with the first mother, the sea
mother, Thetis. H.D. comes to realize that "Helen is the Greek
drama. Again, *she herself is the writing.*"[13] But is it her fault?

There is no simple answer to her questions. Helen knows this.
There is only the symbol, the phoenix: the moment of awakening,
resurrection. And the revelation of the final mystery, the gift of
Egypt: "Phoenix/has vanquished/that ancient enemy, Sphinx."[14]

The poem is born of Egypt. H.D. invokes the myth of Isis and
Osiris — the remembering of the body of Osiris and the resurrection of the body of the god, the restoration of the lost and the
conception of the child. The virgin birth is the poem. This is the
heart of the mystery of Egypt; the masculine and the feminine are
united in the child.

> She raised up the prostrate form of him whose heart was still, she
> took from him of his essence, she conceived and brought forth a
> child, she suckled it in secret (?) and none knew the place thereof;
> and the arm of the child hath waxed strong in the great house of
> Seb.[15]

H.D. tells us again of how Achilles and Helen found one another in that out-of-time dimension, in the great Amen, Ammon,
or Amun temple — eternal moments of life's longing to be reborn
of itself. D. H. Lawrence had written of resurrection, and his essay had been collected in the volume of essays published after his
death, *Phoenix.* In *Helen in Egypt,* H.D. writes: "Phoenix, the
symbol of resurrection, has vanquished indecision and doubt, the
eternal why of the Sphinx," and illuminated the mystery of the
Achilles heel, the symbol of phallic desire.[16]

the body honoured
by the Grecian host
was but an iron casement,

it was God's plan
to melt the icy fortress of the soul,
and free the man;

God's plan is other than the priests disclose;
I did not know why
(in dream or in trance)

God had summoned me hither,
until I saw the dim outline
grown clearer,

as the new Mortal,
shedding his glory,
limped slowly across the sand.[17]

Through the telling and retelling of his story, Achilles has created Helen, just as her "hieroglyph, repeated endlessly," re-establishes "the Egyptian mysteries in Greece."[18]

In "Pallinode," having remembered all, Helen would forget the invectives of his writing, "his finger's remorseless steel," and remember the experience, the *"Star in the night."* She does not need to understand the whole of the indecipherable script, and she reminds us again that it was he, Amen, the masculine consciousness, "dreamed of all this phantasmagoria of Troy," that "He is One, yet the many."[19]

You may ask why I speak of Thoth-Amen,
or Amen-Zeus or Zeus separately,
you may think I invoke or recall

a series of multiple gods,
a Lion, a Hawk, or an Ibis,
as we were taught to think

of the child-like fantasy
of this ancient Child, Egypt;
how can you understand

what few may acknowledge and live,
what many acknowledge and die?
He is One, yet the many

manifest separately; He may manifest
as a jackal and hound you to death?
or is He changeable like air,

and like air, invisible?
God is beyond the manifest?
He is ether and limitless space?

you may ask forever, you may penetrate
every shrine, an initiate,
and remain unenlightened at last.[20]

In his insightful book *Violence and the Sacred,* René Girard exposes in rational terms a concept of culture which is close to the vision that H.D. glimpsed through her study of the Greeks. Interestingly enough, Girard also came to his views through the study of ancient Greek myths and drama. He argues that the function of religion or ritual is to keep a culture stable by projecting the violence within its members onto a surrogate victim. The victim is then sacrificed, usually upon an altar, with the whole community present as participants in the act. The community is thus purged or cleansed of its internal violence. The ritual enables the community effectively to forget or repress the origin of the violence that derives from the fact of the primal scene. The fact is not faced; it is rather projected onto the person of the surrogate victim, or to use Girard's word, "scapegoat." A difference between Girard and H.D. is that Girard does not regard woman as the sacrificial victim, while H.D. sees her as the perpetual object of man's violence.

Girard argues that in Greek drama the tragic hero fulfills the need for a sacrificial victim. H.D.'s vision in *Helen in Egypt* is that Iphigeneia fullfills this need in Greek culture as tragic heroine. She comes to see that the sacrifice of Iphigeneia is the means by which the Greeks expel the truth about their own incestuous (Oedipal) desires from their consciousness. Furthermore, she sees that the crimes attributed to Helen are the hidden desires of all men. Helen is accused of incestuous passion; Iphigeneia is the surrogate victim.* In sacrificing Iphigeneia (the victim must be a virgin; she must be pure), the Greek warriors are able to identify with purity and are thereby able, through the mechanism of repression, to maintain that they are going to war to save Helen from *her* incestuous desires. What they succeed in keeping from themselves is that these desires are not Helen's but their own. Helen, like Iphigeneia, is but a victim.

What H.D. acknowledges and understands is that the person (the poet) who presents the primal scene (in the poem) becomes a cult object. The poet who recognizes the primal truth of experience takes upon himself or herself the burden of the collective guilt. Just as man projects his guilt onto woman, he also projects

*The incest concept employed here is defined broadly to include its archaic Latin meaning, as defined by the *Oxford English Dictionary* and *Webster's Third New International Dictionary*. The word means "impure, unchaste." The word as employed here also includes the concept of spiritual incest: marriage or sexual connection between persons related by spiritual affinity or with a person under a vow of chastity, and so on.

his guilt onto the poet who presents the truth. Being both a woman and a poet, H.D. finds that she is doubly cursed.

H.D. recognizes the irony of this situation: the act of writing the poem liberates the material from her consciousness; but in reading the liberated material her readers experience a sense of recognition. Or rather, they do and they don't. Instead of recognizing the truth of the primal scene and the violence in themselves, they project the blame for the whole human condition onto her. It is as though she has created the fact of incest, when in reality she has borne witness to the existence of violence so that men may see their folly and change their ways. Her fate, then, is that of the martyr or saint. She is publicly persecuted for her recognition.

H.D. has come to understand that the same principles that Girard sees at work in the formation of culture at large are at work in the formation of a small culture (the Imagist circle of poets). Furthermore, she sees that the priest who sacrifices the victim at the altar plays the same role as the shaman in primitive culture. In *The Origin and Function of Culture,* Geza Roheim suggests that the shaman has the mastery of the situation and the power in the culture either to accept the burden of the collective anxiety and guilt of the community himself or to project that burden upon the person he chooses to carry it for him. H.D.'s vision in *Helen in Egypt* suggests that Pound had the shaman's power in the cultural community to which they both belonged. In publishing her work, Pound projected the cultural burden of guilt upon her. The effect of his action was to make her the victim and the scapegoat — that is, the muse, Helen. What Roheim and H.D. both understand is that the scapegoat is the cultural embodiment of the forgotten violence and the repressed incest wish of each individual. What is always repeated in the sacrifice of the victim is the primal incest.

To see something is not to advocate it. H.D. is not masochistic; she does not advocate her own murder when she speaks through the voice of Iphigeneia. Rather, she contributes to the tradition that hopes to bring to light the hidden sources of madness in civilization. She has become aware that the woman poet who presents a vision is accused of being in a state of desire in relation to what she presents. This knowledge is the source of her ironic tone; she is aware of the insidious sexism of a cultural orientation in which the underlying premise is that women are creatures of desire, that they do not think and act rationally, as men do. She is aware that women are "read" differently from men.

At the end of *Violence and the Sacred,* Girard invites us "for the very first time, to violate the taboo that neither Heraclitus nor

Euripides could ever quite manage to violate, and to expose to the light of reason the role played by violence in human society."[21] Once H.D. had seen what she had seen about the origin of human culture and the burden of guilt that women must carry to maintain those civilizations that are organized in certain ways (such as the Greek culture), her choice to continue writing was an act of true courage. It was also an obsession, one that eventually led her to Sigmund Freud. When she did find Freud, he recognized in her a kindred spirit. His letter to her of February 26, 1937, regarding her translation of Euripides' *Ion,* is relevant to her translation of *Iphigeneia* as well as to *Helen in Egypt.*

> I have just finished your *Ion.* Deeply moved by the play (which I had not known before) and no less by your comments, especially those referring to the end, where you extol the victory of reason over passions, I send you the expression of my admiration and kindest regards.[22]

It is somewhat ironic to quote Freud in such a context, for he came so close to understanding the whole matter of repressed violence but never understood the role played by the woman. In *Totem and Taboo,* for example, he explored the violence inflicted upon the primal father, but not that inflicted upon the primal mother. Also, he saw the sacrifice of the father as having occurred once, a long time ago, whereas H.D. saw it (as does Girard) as an act that must be perpetually repeated in order to hold the culture together.

It certainly might be objected that the appropriation and publication of a few poems and the formation of a poetic circle around H.D. was hardly cause for her development of an elaborate vision of the origin and function of culture. Yet in raising this objection, we should also realize that when men transform psychic trauma in such a way it is called genius; when women do so it is called hysteria. The reality of the situation is that Imagism, a new poetic movement, was the result of H.D.'s poetry. In order to be free of one reality context, one must create another. It is necessary to have one's own vision. *Helen in Egypt* is a context for apprehending a woman's reality context, as opposed to a man's.

While it is true that H.D.'s vision was informed by far more than Aldington, Pound, and Lawrence, she was always deeply aware that the particular traumatic events involving them had precipitated her coming to consciousness. Her work with Freud enabled H.D. to bring these events into consciousness on an epic scale and to understand the transpersonal nature of her experience.

The Helen-Iphigeneia realization is not a mere metaphor for a personal event; rather, the event was the efficient cause, the precipitating occurrence from which the conception was realized. But the efficient cause is not the sufficient cause. The conception was informed by the entire body of circumstances of the poet's life and mind.

37

Helen and Paris

OF THE SECOND SECTION of *Helen in Egypt* H.D. said, *"Leuké*
means reality to me."*[1]* The story told in "Leuké" is one of past
and present, a story in time and history. In her Greek frame of
mind, which is her stance in this section of the poem, Helen puts
a series of questions to herself; in reality, many of these questions
emerged as a result of H.D.'s renewed correspondence with Richard Aldington. She is "back with the old dilemma — who caused
the war?" — which is a central theme of "Pallinode."[2]

Paris is the central subject of "Leuké." He appears to speak of
the fall of Troy, his own death, and his protective love for Helen.
He admits that he was mortally wounded. He saw the ramparts
upon which Helen had walked destroyed, and he insists that Helen
was destroyed with Troy.

But Paris finds Helen again on the island of Leuké and pleads
with her to accept him once more as confidant, even husband.
(This plea corresponds to the tone of Aldington's letters after he
re-established contact with H.D. in 1946.) He tells Helen he has
not been able to forget her, even though he lost Oenone, his mistress, because of this inability. He implies that his project is to re-
establish himself as her protector, and he insists that she must forget Achilles.

After long arguments about Achilles, Helen at last finds her way
to her "god-father," Theseus. She and Theseus talk about Paris
and Achilles in the context of H.D.'s psychoanalytic understanding of love and death. Although Helen does not altogether accept
his counsel, she finds answers to her questions; she makes sense of
her own story and accepts the consequences of her love for Paris
and her love for Achilles. Although she cannot reconcile these
men to each other, she is able to reconcile her love for both of

them in her own mind. H.D. has confronted her past, partly through her correspondence with Aldington and partly through her work with Freud and her relationships with Dowding, Pearson, and Heydt. And she has understood, to her own intellectual satisfaction, why events worked themselves out the way they did.

In the "Leuké" section of *Helen of Egypt* we find Paris and Helen engaged in the dialogue Aldington and H.D. never had at the time of the breakup of their marriage, but many of the scenes in this section are influenced by the correspondence Aldington and H.D. were carrying on during the late forties and throughout the fifties about the events of the World War I years. H.D. translates her discourse with Aldington into Greek myth and sets her story in the world of ancient Greece, just as she did in her early poetry and prose. Often Helen and Paris are discussing events that occurred long ago; just as Aldington and H.D. argue in their correspondence about Lawrence, so Paris and Helen argue in "Leuké" about Achilles.

In order to follow the logic of the events of this section of the poem, we must move with H.D. into a mythological language of discourse. At the beginning of this section we are in Leuké, *L'isle blanche,* where legend has it that Helen was married to Achilles and their child was conceived. And we begin by awakening from a dream.

> Helen in Egypt did not taste of Lethe, forgetfulness, on the other hand; she was in an ecstatic or semi-trance state. Though she says, "I am awake, no trance," yet she confesses, "I move as one in a dream." Now, it is as if momentarily, at any rate, the dream is over. Remembrance is taking its place.[3]

"I remember a dream that was real."[4] If H.D.'s Helen of "Pallinode" was living in a dream (that is, poetry), her Helen of "Leuké" has awakened from that dream. However, the Helen of book I was awake; that is, she saw through her own eyes, and what she saw was the real world, the world that to ordinary mortals looks like "torment and insanity." From the point of view of ordinary reality, the world of H.D.'s "Pallinode," the world of poetry, is one of insanity, a world of delusion or illusion. H.D.'s Helen of "Leuké" is in this sense without illusion, or disillusioned. She has, as it were, fallen into another reality; and from this Greek or analytical, as opposed to poetic, perspective, it becomes possible for H.D. to tell us just how it is that "Helen, half of earth/outlived the goddess Helen/and Helen's epiphany in Egypt."[5]

Helen had said, "I am not nor mean to be/the Daemon they made of me."[6] They made her a daemon because she sees or says something, because she possesses or is possessed by a truth that passes ordinary human understanding. But it is a capacity for another kind of consciousness, an analytical kind of understanding, that allows her to outlive her epiphany or death in Egypt. And H.D. tells us that it is not Helen but Thetis, or Amen-Zeus — at any rate, the gods — who are to be held responsible for the war: "And now she (Helen) is back with the old dilemma — who caused the war? She has been blamed, Paris has been blamed, but, fundamentally, it was the fault of Thetis, the mother of Achilles." [7]

Thetis is Penelope, weaving words, a web of dreams, to ward off her false suitors. The name Penelope translates as "with a web over her face." [8] This image is parallel to Helen's veil. The web is the veil, the poem. Poetry is weaving. In her defense of herself (that is, in her weaving) the goddess caused the war. Her veil is her shield, parallel to the shield of Achilles, which legend says has the design of history written upon it.

Another important part of the story is the circumstances of the marriage. Thetis, a goddess, married Peleus, a mortal — a marriage arranged by Zeus so that their son, Achilles, would not be immortal and threaten him. Genealogy is significant. If "a goddess marries a mortal, some social discord is sure to arise. The traditional uninvited guest introduces the fatal apple of discord." And the uninvited guest is Eris, strife or envy, the root of all evil. "So the immortals woke to petty strife/over the challenge *to the fairest.*" [9] H.D. associates this "fatal apple of discord" with the apple Paris awarded to Aphrodite in the beauty contest among the goddesses, associating Helen in this instance with Aphrodite and the remembrance of Paris.

> but I would remember only
> how I awoke to familiar fragrance,
> late roses, bruised apples;
>
> reality had opened before me,
> I had come back;
> I retraced the thorny path
>
> but the thorns of rancour and hatred
> were gone — Troy? Greece?
> they were one and I was one,
>
> I was laughing with Paris;
> so we had cheated the past,
> I had escaped — Achilles. [10]

Helen is running away with Paris. Insofar as *Helen in Egypt* is veiled autobiography, we know that Paris represents H.D.'s husband, Richard Aldington. Thus H.D., as Helen, is running away to be with her husband: *"We will hide . . . we will hide among the apple trees."* [11]

This strikes us as an unorthodox interpretation of the legendary Helen of Troy. What H.D. means becomes clear when she tells us that "Paris lures her from Sparta or from her dedication to the Spartan ideal." [12] Helen is abandoning the "Spartan ideal," her dedication to poetry, for Paris. She is relinquishing her dedication to the hard and arduous path, the quest for the eternal truths, for the life of the temporal and sensual. Once again we see that in *Helen in Egypt* ordinary or traditional values are reversed, or rather versed in a different way.

Helen's infidelity, then, is an unfaithfulness to her calling as a poet. As Helen hides with Paris, who exhibits for her the sensuality of "late roses" and "bruised apples" (a somewhat rotten image), she is being unfaithful to her more ascetic nature, her life as an artist and "her overwhelming experience in Egypt."

Helen and Paris are in hiding:

> we will hide,
>
> a hooded cloak was thrown over me,
> now it is dark upon Leuké;
> the same whisper had lured me from Sparta,
>
> we will hide among the apple trees. [13]

In *Helen in Egypt,* as in Greek mythology, a place is a state of mind or being, and to be is to be in a place and in relation to another. H.D. often expresses transitions in place (and also in time) by saying that a character was transposed or translated. To move from Egypt to Greece is really to move from one state of mind to another, and by implication from one language to another. In "Leuké" we move from the language of Egyptian hieroglyph to the language of Greek drama. Thus we come to the story of Helen and Paris, the tragic drama of Troy.

This is the story not only of the Trojan War but also of World War I. As we have seen, H.D. was in fact obsessed with the theme and saw every war in history as a variation on the One War. In *Palimpsest,* written after her break with Aldington, she sets the story in Rome and projects herself into the character of Hipparchia, a captured Greek. Hipparchia's keeper, Marius Decius, is a cultivated Roman. The relationship between them is portrayed with the same heavy sensuality and the same lack of spiritual reality as is suggested by the Paris-Helen relationship in *Helen in Egypt.*

H.D. contrasts the stark Greek stature of Hipparchia with the overly sensual Roman coarseness of Marius Decius. "She sat, half propped aloft, a second darker cushion framed her now set face, features carved, honey-marble after the archaic unfashionable manner of the early Hellenes . . . He sat now the low incurved backless lion-footed foot-stool like Marius Decius, all that he was of Roman, at the head of his charging and blood thirsting legions . . . young, defiant, enough aristocratic, too much a Roman."[14]

Aldington's most relevant account of his active participation in World War I and his relationship with his wife during those years is perhaps to be found in his *Death of a Hero,* a long novel that reflects his life (and death) as a soldier. As Aldington tells the story, the death of the hero leaves both his wife, Elizabeth (H.D.), and his mistress, Fanny (Dorothy Yorke), unmoved.

The story of Oenone in *Helen in Egypt* is that of Aldington's Fanny in *Death of a Hero,* cast in a different setting. The perspectives of the two authors are of course different, but the story is essentially the same. One significant element of the drama that H.D. focuses upon in *Helen in Egypt* is Oenone's refusal to heal her lover because of her envy of Helen. Paris, we will remember, was called to Troy "after years of banishment and obscurity" and was shot by Philoctetes in the last year of the war. "The wounded Paris managed to crawl back to his old home on Mount Ida, and to Oenone, his 'long-deserted companion' . . . Oenone has the magic power of healing but she refuses to help her old lover." Oenone is "one of the many/thousand-thousand lost," living a life of illusion in a war-shattered city that reminds us of London.[15]

In *Palimpsest* Marius Decius says of Hipparchia, "I slept not with a woman but a phantom"; this declaration is a kind of summation of H.D. and Aldington's relationship as related by both authors.[16] Aldington emerges as a kind of phantom in H.D.'s life, and this is the crux of her concern in *Helen in Egypt* with the problem of reality and illusion. Conversely, she is a phantom in his life.

Poetry, for Aldington, was simply one of the styles or kinds of writing. For H.D., on the other hand, poetry was never simply a technique or style; it was rather a way of life. Aldington was a professional writer, who wrote first and foremost for his public. Of poetry Marius Decius says, "Hipparchia. Witchcraft. Illusion. Poetry."[17]

The tension between Aldington's essentially Roman (or Trojan) view of the world and H.D.'s decidedly Greek vision of the real was the tension that finally led to "the fall of Troy," the end of their marriage. But Troy is in H.D.'s cosmology a synonym for the modern world as well as for her marriage. It stands for legal fictions as opposed to spiritual realities. Troy is in every sense a transpersonal symbol. Troy represents the war-torn Europe of World War I, the prelude to contemporary culture.

Just as Helen was to find a soul-mate in her poetic relationship with Achilles, so Paris found a playmate in his friendship with Oenone. After the war, Oenone is bent on revenge. Oenone is insistent. She will relent in her anger only upon one condition. Paris must forget Helen: "Oenone's eyes are wild,/flecked like a wildcat." [18]

Paris as well is filled with bitter rage; he wants to kill Helen, or at any rate see her dead. H.D. had recognized the hatred directed toward her in her early poem, "Helen":

> All Greece hates
> the still eyes in the white face,
> the lustre of olives
> where she stands,
> and the white hands.
>
> All Greece reviles
> the wan face when she smiles,
> hating it deeper still
> when it grows wan and white,
> remembering past enchantments
> and past ills.
>
> Greece sees unmoved,
> God's daughter, born of love,
> the beauty of cool feet
> and slenderest knees,
> could love indeed the maid,
> only if she were laid,
> white ash amid funeral cypresses. [19]

It would seem that as long as Helen remains alive, even as a living memory, Paris must be in bondage or slavery to her. And Paris, wanting to be free of this bondage, must convince us, and himself, that she has died — "that is all there is about it." He says:

> I am the first in all history
> to say, she died, died, died
> when the Walls fell;
>
> what mystery is more subtle than this?
> what spell more potent?
> I saw the pomegranate,

blighted by winter,
I saw the flowering pomegranate
and the cleft fruit on the summer branch;

I wait for a miracle as simple,
as inevitable as this . . .
now it is dark upon Leuké. [20]

There is no doubt that Aldington was deeply hurt by H.D.'s
rejection of him during the war. As he writes in *Death of a Hero,*
"He had tried to tell Elizabeth some of his war experiences. Just
as he was describing the gas bombardments and the awful look on
the faces of men gassed, he noticed her delicate mouth was wried
by a suppressed yawn." [21] H.D. too had suffered terribly during
the war. She was not bored. She felt that Aldington was being
false to himself, and realized that in her marriage to him she had
been false to herself. In "Paint It Today" she writes of this period:

> There was a war. A cloud. Five years. Already a few months before
> the actual panic, old Professor Defreddie [Professor Doolittle] and
> Midget's mother had returned to America. Midget had married
> Basil [Aldington], as she threatened, quietly in a registrar's office
> . . . Time had them by the throat, evil and vicious . . . Who was
> there in the world that mattered? What mattered? The present was
> dead. They were all dead . . .
> When loyalty and sentiment were stowed away, who was this
> person that came back to her, with the smell of gas in his breath,
> with the stench of death in his clothes? "How the war has im-
> proved Basil," she heard on all sides. True, there had been plenty
> of room for improvement in Basil as there always is in any of us.
> But was this improvement?
> Midget felt that Basil was not playing true to himself, that was
> all. He did not believe in the comradeship he spoke of. He did not
> believe in the dastardly enemy he spoke of . . . Even if it were not
> hers, she could have accepted his standards for himself, if he had
> accepted them himself. [22]

What finally broke the H.D.-Aldington marriage was not only
marital infidelity but H.D.'s realization of Aldington's hypocrisy.
In the end she lost respect for him. He knew it, and he could not
forgive her for it. And in spite of his protective pose, which H.D.
recognized as hypocritical, Aldington was bitter about the H.D.–
D. H. Lawrence relationship for the rest of his life.

38

The Spiral Shell
and the Spiral Stair

IN TRANSLATING Egyptian symbols into Greek symbols, which is
H.D.'s task in the "Leuké" section of *Helen in Egypt,* the Amen
temple of "Pallinode" becomes a simple spiral shell. "Surely, her
former state was perfect, but now the temple or the tomb, the
infinite, is reduced to a finite image, a 'delicate sea-shell.' " It is
Thetis, the poet, who has given this image to Helen: "A simple
spiral-shell may tell a tale more ancient than these mysteries."[1]
Why a simple spiral shell, a seashell? We are reminded of Blake's
"world in a grain of sand."[2] The location of the infinite in the
finite — the elimination of the distinction between the physical
and the metaphysical, the embodiment of the form of beauty and
meaning in the single symbol — is a specifically Greek mode. The
seashell resounds with the sound of the sea, and the sea is the
central symbol of this poem. The seashell is the distinctly feminine
symbol of the Greek language or idiom which H.D. discovers or
uncovers.

> O the tomb, delicate sea-shell
> rock-cut but frail
> the thousand, thousand Greeks
>
> fallen before the Walls,
> were as one soul, one pearl;
> I was asleep,
>
> part of the infinite,
> but there is another,
> resilient as fire — Paris? Achilles?[3]

If the seashell is the central feminine symbol of *Helen in Egypt*
as a whole, the fire is the central male symbol. The fire image
H.D. invokes to recall Paris is in constant contrast to the fire im-

age she invokes to recall Achilles. Of Achilles she had said, "the flash in the heavens at noon that blinds the sun"; and of Paris, "it was a small room,/yes, a taper was burning/in an onyx jar."[4]

Paris, as wolf-slayer or would-be Romulus (who killed his brother, Remus), tried to convince Helen that Achilles was never really her lover. From H.D.'s point of view Aldington's obsession to convince her, himself, and the world that Lawrence had never loved her was the underlying motivation of his work on Lawrence. As she characterizes Aldington's posture in her poem, Paris insists:

> he was father, brother,
> he was deserted husband,
> he was never your lover.[5]

In judicial Roman style, Paris would make such distinctions. "Such love, 'lightning out of a clear sky,' argues Paris, destroys not only the love-object but itself as well." Helen, he says, is under the spell of "Egyptian incense wafted through infinite corridors." She is, as it were, drugged or addicted. And, Paris argues, she is not really Helen in Egypt but rather Helen in Rhodes. Helen in Rhodes, he tells us, is *Dentritis,* "Helena of the trees."[6]

Paris says to Helen, "You died in Troy on the stairs." This is an allusion to the stairs H.D. ran down when she found Aldington in their bed with his mistress; they were the same stairs she would not climb to the small room at the top where Lawrence was staying. Paris tells Helen that the sensual experience of "waiting for the sap to rise" is preferable to "lightning out of the clear skies."

> why, why would you deny
> the peace, the sanctity
> of this small room,
>
> the lantern there by the door?
> why must you recall
> the white fire of unnumbered stars,
>
> rather than that single taper
> burning in an onyx jar,
> where you swore
>
> never, never to return,
> (*"return the wanton to Greece"*),
> where we swore together
>
> defiance of Achilles
> and the thousand spears,
> we alone would compel the Fates,

we chosen of Cytheraea,
can you forget the pact?
why would you recall another?

O Helena, tangled in thought,
be Rhodes' Helena, *Dendritis,*
why remember Achilles? [7]

Helen of the Trees is the same as Artemis, the goddess of childbirth. "In Greece the great goddess Artemis herself appears to
have been annually hanged in effigy in her sacred grove . . . and
there accordingly she went by the name of the Hanged One."
Later, figurines of the moon goddess dangled from the boughs of
the orchard trees as fertility charms. In Rhodes, Helen was wor-
shipped "under the title of Helen of the Tree, because the queen
of the island had caused her handmaids, disguised as Furies, to
string her up to a bough." [8] We recall Pound's early poem, "To
Καλόν": "Even in my dreams you have denied yourself to
me,/And sent me only your handmaids," i.e., poems (handmades). [9]

Paris would have Helen think of the poetry as the figurines, the
fertility charms, that hang from the trees in Rhodes; he would
have her think of poetry as ornament (or the veil of Aphrodite).
In other words, he refuses to take poetry seriously. He sees only
the moon aspect, the beauty, and is blind to the sun aspect, the
brilliance. Defensively, he wants to see the poems as mere orna-
mentation, talismans to insure fertility, amulets to ward off evil
spirits.

In other words, Paris is asking Helen to say that her relationship
with him is real, that the Egyptian Helen is the phantom. She
must say that nothing happened with Achilles. Paris tries to convince her that she is spiritually dead. But the poet's (or harper's)
story is that Helen was "rapt away by Hermes, at Zeus' command" (H.D. was, as we know, rescued). And at last even Paris
admits: "Zeus had rapt you away," but he adds emphatically that
Helena died.

> And Helen? The story the harpers tell
> reached us, even here upon Leuké;
> how she was rapt away
>
> by Hermes, at Zeus' command,
> how she returned to Sparta,
> how in Rhodes she was hanged
>
> and the cord turned to a rainbow,
> how she met Achilles — she met Achilles?
> bereft? left? a ghost or a phantom

The Spiral Shell and the Spiral Stair § 389

in Egypt? (you have told me the story) . . .

. . .

but the harpers
never touch their strings
to name Helena and Death.[10]

In H.D.'s set of symbols, the veil is always the poem. There are many veils: "It is true that the 'woven veil by the portal' that Helen clutched to break her fall, was at the beginning of the drama. The shout 'from the banquet-hall, "return the wanton to Greece" was answered by the defiance of Paris and the Trojan War.'" H.D. presents the scene of the abduction, the seduction. This is Paris speaking:

> do you remember how you tore
>
> from my arms and ran?
> but a sentry stood by the door;
> as you dived under his spear,
>
> barring the way; what hand
> stayed your death?
> what hand smothered your cry
>
> and dragged you back?
> what arm, stronger than Hercules,
> sustained you?
>
> it was a small room
> yes, a taper was burning
> in an onyx jar;
>
> so you raged . . .[11]

"The veil caught on a fallen pilaster," in contrast to "the woven veil by the portal," marks the end of the drama, when Helen turns "at the stair-head." "It's only a winding stair,/a spiral, like a snail-shell." [12] Set in juxtaposition to the spiral shell, this spiral stair — the same stair Julia ran down when she found her husband in bed with his mistress — becomes the final symbol for the end of Julia's marriage. Paris, an adumbration of Rafe, would try to convince Helen, another Julia, that she died on this stair. Yet Helen knows that ironically, it was this event that led to her final meeting with Achilles. Paris reiterates his obsessive theme:

> You say you did not die on the stairs,
> that the love of Achilles sustained you;
> I say he never loved you. [13]

Helen asks of Paris, "Did he hate Hecuba?"[14] Did he hate his mother? Hecuba had dreamed before his birth that she bore "a fiery hundred-handed Fury, who with his stern strength hurled all Illium to the ground; and she told the marvel of her slumber."[15] Aesacus, the seer, then advised Priam, the father of Paris, to do away with his son. A familiar hero motif of Greek mythology, the son is sent away by his father at birth to die. His project, then, like that of Oedipus, understandably becomes the killing of the father.

It was the hostility of Paris, an Oedipal problem at heart, that led to the turn of events that brought Helen and Paris together again in Leuké. According to H.D.'s psychoanalytic reasoning in the poem, Helen's relationship with Achilles symbolically placed Paris in the position of their son; it became his project, according to a Freudian logic, to kill both Achilles and Helen. Helen asks Theseus, "Why did he hate Achilles?" And Theseus answers with the question "How could it be other/if he was your first Lover?"[16] This is how H.D. explains Aldington's lifelong project of suppressing one of the most meaningful aspects of Lawrence's work, and his relentless "protection" of her.

> Paris was cursed like Helen;
> his mother dreamed of a fire-brand
> and the Towers a-flame
>
> and War came; Hecuba like Jocasta
> was overthrown (by Paris, by Oedipus
> the son); O the web is sure
>
> and Fate shall net her own,
> And Fate will play another trick
> like Hermes, the jester;
>
> he of the House of the Enemy,
> Troy's last king (this is no easy thing
> to explain, this subtle genealogy)
>
> is Achilles' son, he is incarnate
> Helen-Achilles; he, my first lover,
> was created by my last;
>
> can you understand this?
> it was not Pyrrhus, at the end,
> it was not some waif of Achilles' Chryseis
>
> or Briseis begetting, nor a ghost-child
> or Polyxena; no, it was not the legitimate
> Pyrrhus who slew Priam, the father of Paris,
>
> but Paris himself, Paris whose swift arrow
> (O Wolf-slayer) pierced the Achilles-heel.[17]

The Spiral Shell and the Spiral Stair § 391

In the Leuké section of *Helen in Egypt* H.D. once again tells the story of Aldington's treachery to D. H. Lawrence and to her. In desperation Paris accuses Helen of being a seductress. "Again, the veil motif, Paris calls it the scarf." And we know that the veil or the scarf is the poem. Paris asks: "Was it Thetis/who lured you from Egypt?/or was it Aphrodite?" And Paris answers his own question:

> no matter, there is one law;
> as the tides are drawn to the shore,
> the lover draws the beloved,
>
> as a magnet, a lode-stone, a lode-star;
> a path is made on the water
> for the caravel,
>
> (they called his bark, you said, a caravel),
> you drew Achilles to Egypt;
> I watched you upon the ramparts,
>
> I saw your scarf flutter
> out toward the tents;
> the wind? the will of Helena?
>
> the will of Aphrodite?
> no matter — there was no pulse in the air,
> yet your scarf flew,
>
> a visible sign,
> to enchant him,
> to draw him nearer.[18]

Is this, we wonder, a projection on Paris's part, a projection of the abductor? Did Helen mean really to enchant Achilles? Paris, it would seem, does not understand the process of poetry. He confuses Thetis with Helen. But Thetis, the goddess, is not to be confused with Helen, the mortal, for the goddess is immortal, disregarding and disrespecting mortality. Helen's attitude toward Thetis is always one of anxiety.

> And Thetis? she of the many forms
> had manifested as Choragus,
> Thetis, lure-of-the-sea;
>
> will she champion?
> will she reject me?[19]

When the primal unity is broken there is a coming into speech — a speech that would restore and mend and set the world aright again. The poem attempts to bridge the schism, the split in consciousness, and it inevitably comes into being when the mind has been fragmented and divided against itself. The poem appears like the dream. It would attempt to fuse the disparate parts, mend the pieces together into a whole (even if bizarre) design. The poem is a tapestry woven by the hand of fate; it is Clotho, the Spinner, who spins the thread of life, and it may also be Atropos, who cuts it off. In this mode of understanding neither Thetis nor Amen is to blame for the war. "Even the gods' plans/are shaped by another — /Eros? Eris?"[20]

The image of the simple spiral shell invoked at the beginning of the drama now becomes the "blasted shell" of the city. "I lived/on my slice of the Wall," says Paris, "while the Towers fell."[21] After the war Troy is destroyed — "a blasted shell," says Paris, "my city, my Wall."[22]

39

Theseus and Helen

THE STORY OF Theseus in *Helen in Egypt* is the story of the analyst-analysand relationship in H.D.'s life. Helen (H.D.) eventually encounters the legendary Theseus of Greek mythology (Freud): "So Helen finds her way to another lover, whose story is not so familiar to us as that of Paris and the early suitors. For Helen, we gather, was a child when Theseus, the legendary king and hero, stole her from Sparta."[1]

Theseus, like Oedipus and Paris, was abandoned at birth by his father. In *Helen in Egypt* H.D. identifies his quest with the Argo, thereby identifying him with Jason. Moreover, Jason is remarkably similar to Paris and Oedipus in regard to the circumstances of his birth, since he is reputed to have been "exposed on a mountain, reared by horseherds, and set seemingly impossible tasks by the king of a neighboring city."[2] The task Aegeus set for Theseus, the removal of a hidden sword and sandals from beneath a rock, is similar to the tasks imposed upon Jason. Theseus, Jason, Paris, and Oedipus fall into a pattern which is characteristic of a certain kind of patriarchal hero.

> The hero is the child of most distinguished parents, usually the son of a king. His origin is preceded by difficulties . . . During or before the pregnancy, there is a prophecy, in the form of a dream or oracle, cautioning against his birth, and usually threatening danger to the father (or his representative) . . . He is saved by animals, or by lowly people (shepherds), and is suckled by a female animal or by an humble woman. After he has grown up, he finds his distinguished parents . . . He takes his revenge on his father, on the one hand, and is acknowledged, on the other. Finally he achieves rank and honors.[3]

394

When the young Theseus leaves on his journey to Athens (to find his father) he is advised to take the sea road, a symbol of the mother, but he chooses the dangerous land route. He has many adventures along the way before his encounter with the Minotaur. One of the "hero-gods," Theseus seeks out war and goes willingly into battle. Of him H.D. says, "The love-stories, he tells us, have grown dim and distant, but the memory of the heroes, the Quest and the Argo, is still vivid and inspiring."[4]

Achilles, unlike Theseus and Paris, was raised by his mother, Thetis, a goddess. It was fated that Thetis should have a son more powerful than his father. The "man-hero," Achilles, has no appetite for war, even though he is a great warrior. He is not anxious to go into battle (at the beginning of the war, we will remember, he is hiding in the women's quarters, where he is sought out and found by Odysseus). Although Achilles has fought for the Greeks, he goes into heroic battle only after his friend has been slain and he has lost his armor.

H.D. suggests that it is Freud's nature as Theseus, "because of the Argo and the Quest, to sympathize with the Trojan rather than with the Greek cause."[5] Being similar in genealogy to Paris, he would of course be more sympathetic to Paris than to Achilles.

Sympathizing with the Trojan side and sensing "the danger of Helen's recapitulation to her own apotheosis,"[6] Theseus tells her to return to Paris and to forget Achilles, to find life again with Paris, but Helen answers:

> no god-father
> Paris will never find me;
> I reflect, I re-act, I re-live;
>
> true, he renewed my youth,
> but now, only the memory of the molten ember
> of the Dark Absolute claims me
>
> who have met Death,
> who have found Dis,
> who embraced Hades.

Helen, says H.D., was taken not by any mortal but by Hades, Achilles.

> I was taken, not by Menelaus
> in Sparta, not by Paris
> in Troy or after,
>
> but by Achilles.

She asks:

> can spring defeat winter? never;
> spring may come after,
>
> but the crystal, the center, the ice-star
> dissembles, reflects the past
> but waits faithful . . .[7]

Theseus would convince Helen that it is important for "reality" to recall us from the dream, to bring us back to life. H.D.'s symbol for the Freudian primal scene is in this instance the Minotaur, and the labyrinth is an image of the meandering maze we must go through, in Freud's thought, to get to this primal image. Of his Minotaur Theseus says:

> . . . was he myth or fiction,
>
> an invention of Daedalus,
> even as the Labyrinth?
> or was it true
>
> that I dealt him his death-blow?
> and was it true, as I argued afterwards,
> that I slew Egypt?[8]

Theseus maintains that Helen, too, must slay Egypt: Freud had told H.D. that she must come to terms with her relationship with Lawrence and cease to be haunted by it.

Helen experienced enlightenment in darkness with Achilles, says H.D., and now illumination with Theseus. H.D. was trying to maintain her "Greek state of mind" when she sought Freud's help.

> Helen appears "blown by the wind, the snow" and her garments cling to her, Theseus says, "like the carven folds of the Pallas, but frayed." Though driven by the wind and snow, Helen seems to have taken something of the attributes of the Athenian goddess, and of her "olive-wood statue that directed the Quest." Perhaps she also reminds Theseus of his former encounter with Hippolyta, the devotee of Artemis, in her "huntsman's boots."[9]

Theseus speaks; he is both teasing and comforting.

> are you the Palladium,
>
> the olive-wood statue
> that directed the Quest?
> you are older, your garments cling to you,
>
> (now you have dropped your mantle),
> like the carved folds of the Pallas,
> but frayed, and your delicate feet

wear huntsman's boots;
where have you been? what brought you here?
what kept you there in the cold? [10]

Theseus is helping Helen to realize her state of mind. Always for Theseus the thrust must be toward consciousness; we must become conscious. He reminds Helen that the magic of Crete was inherited from Egypt. And he asserts that "Parnassus, or Greek creative thought, must not be entangled in the Labyrinth or dissolved or washed away by 'the ancient Nile.' "[11] H.D., as we know, identifies herself as a Greek, a Spartan, and the Spartan ideal to which she refers repeatedly is a poetic ideal. As a poet, H.D. is striving for consciousness, or control. Helen, the Spartan, and Theseus, the Athenian, in spite of their differences have certain Greek tendencies in common. Of the Greek temperament H. D. F. Kitto says: "The Greek had little need to simulate passion. He sought control and balance . . . the thought of the tuned string was never very far from his mind. The Mean did not imply the absence of tension and lack of passion, but the correct tension which gives out the true and clear note."[12]

One of H.D.'s images for her poetic consciousness is "let my mind flash with blades."[13] As Helen listens to Theseus, she realizes that he is right when he tells her that her emotional experience has been "too great a suspense to endure."[14] Theseus provides a place, or space, for time to reintegrate. "Theseus unclasps the 'heavy thongs' and finds that Helen's 'feet are wounded.' "[15] This is H.D.'s symbol for the state of her writing. Helen is wearing "huntsman's boots." They are awkward. Her feet — that is to say, the lines of the poetry — are cold. "She is baffled and buffeted and very tired."[16] Her writing is frozen; the tension is inside her and not in her work. She is coming to Theseus for help. He comforts her, telling her that "all myth, the one reality dwells here."[17] He says that she can relate her story in the language of mythology if she feels more comfortable confiding in him in this discourse; Freud, too, explained some of his central concepts in this mode. The flavor of Freud's compassionate manner with H.D. is suggested in the following lines:

why do you weep, Helen?

what cruel path have you trod?
these heavy thongs,
let me unclasp them;

did you too seek Persephone's
drear icy way to Death?
your feet are wounded

with this huntsman's gear;
who wore these clumsy boots?
there — there — let the fire cheer you;

will you choose from the cedar-chest there,
your own fleece-lined shoes?
or shall I choose for you? [18]

Wearing these unwieldy boots and cloak, which don't fit, Helen is Hippolyta or Artemis, Diana of the Woods, a huntress protecting her woods from beasts. Artemis is a prepatriarchal goddess, and her sympathies are with the mother. Her attitude toward the masculine is one of defiance and defensiveness — she is protecting her woods, her turf, her virginity. We recall that when Actaeon happens to come upon Artemis while she is bathing with her maidens, she throws water into his face. H.D.'s poetry prior to her psychoanalysis was defiant, aggressive, full of bravado. She was defensive, throwing water imagery, the feminine element.

One of the aspects of H.D.'s Helen is Artemis. That Helen should become Artemis is in some sense inevitable, for we will remember that Helen as Iphigeneia was sacrificed at Aulis. No matter which version of the story we accept — that she was sacrificed or that she was snatched away at the last moment by Artemis — by the immutable laws of mythology she would become a mouthpiece for the goddess. Freud understood that H.D. had been deeply wronged by men. Through the compassionate, secure relationship with Freud she was able to break down some of her defenses and rid herself of obsessional thoughts. Insofar as her psychoanalysis was a rebirth, she was reborn, like Athena, from her father's head — that is to say, from Freud's wisdom. And through this rebirth she became more open, more sympathetic, more receptive to the father's side, the patriarchal order.

For H.D. psychoanalysis was in a very real sense the beginning of a process of coming into the fullness of her poetic expression, from the self-indulgent, self-righteous, self-sufficient consciousness of a woman in a maternal world to a more compassionate, holistic understanding that was to culminate finally in the *Helen* work. In her *Tribute to Freud* H.D. says: "Niké, Victory, seemed to be the clue, seemed to be my own especial sign or part of my hieroglyph. We had visited in Athens, only a short time ago, the tiny Temple of Victory that stands on the rock of the Acropolis . . . I must hold on to this one word. I thought, 'Niké, Victory.' " [19]

This transformation expressed in the *Tribute to Freud* is comparable to the *Pallinode* of Stesichorus. Just as Stesichorus was restored to sight, H.D. came to realize that the matriarchal state in her own mind had to be put to an end. She had to forgive in order to forget. And insofar as she had embodied this matriarchal principle in her poetry, she was transformed in psychoanalysis through the "Herculean power of Eros."[20]

But for Freud the abolition of matriarchy was equivalent to the assertion of patriarchy. Freud's impulse was to suggest to H.D. that she had to come to see herself as a deformed person, a sort of stunted creature that had lost its phallus.

> "*This* is my favorite," [Freud] said. He held the object toward me. I took it in my hand. It was a little bronze statue, helmeted, clothed to the foot in carved robe with the upper incised chiton or peplum. One hand was extended as if holding a staff or rod. "She is perfect," he said, "*only she has lost her spear.*" I did not say anything. He knew that I loved Greece. He knew that I loved Hellas. I stood looking at Pallas Athené, she whose winged attribute was Niké, Victory, or she stood wingless, Niké A-pteros in the old days . . . She has lost her spear.[21]

In remembering the day Freud presented her with his theory of femininity, H.D. remembered that her reactions had been a continual surprise to him; during the course of the analysis she had not exhibited the neurotic symptoms Freud believed to be characteristic of femininity. He was not able to help her until he realized that her problems were related not to envy but to the reality of loss and trauma. In "Leuké" H.D. re-creates the psychoanalytic understandings she achieved in Greek images such as the Golden Fleece. "Now Helen asks the question, 'must youth and maturity quarrel?' The heroic Spartan Helen had, like the hero-king Theseus, 'passed the frontier, the very threshold.' Theseus had been successful in his Quest of the symbolic Golden Fleece, Helen in her Quest of Love. But in both cases there was an enemy to be conquered, 'they called it Death . . .' "[22]

In their discussion of "the enemy to be conquered," Theseus is on the side of European civilization and patriarchal values; he tries to persuade Helen to compromise. Helen attempts to explain why it is impossible for her to live a lie. Achilles had made her see that her relationship with Paris was a lie. Why maintain such a relationship? (H.D. was still legally married to Richard Aldington at the time of her analysis.) Helen says:

> Paris was my youth — don't you see?
> must youth and maturity quarrel?
> but how reconcile

Theseus and Helen § 399

the magnetic, steel–clad Achilles
with the flowering pomegranate?
in Rhodes (Paris said) they called me

Dendritis, Helena of the trees;
can spring forget winter?
there was no winter in Egypt?

but I passed the frontier,
the very threshold you crossed
when you sought out the Minotaur;

was Achilles my Minotaur?
a dream? a dream within a dream?
a dream beyond Lethe

Crete? magic, you say,
and Crete inherited the Labyrinth,
and Crete-Egypt must be slain,

conquered or overthrown — and then?
the way out, the way back,
the way home.[23]

Theseus has given Helen comfort, given her a place and a space
to reintegrate, but still there is no reconciliation of Trojan and
Greek. Helen cannot or will not fully accept the perception and
advice of Theseus. He is sympathetic to the Trojan side. Freud
would attempt to adjust H.D. to the prevailing reality principle.
But the prevailing reality principle is in actuality Freud himself.
Theseus reminds Helen that after all, he was her first lover. "For
Helen, we gather, was a child when Theseus, the legendary king
and hero, stole her from Sparta." Theseus speaks, encouraging the
transference.

. . . and you? look — yes — you are here —
did you love me in Aphidnae,
where I left you with Aethra, my mother?

you must have loved me a little,
frail maiden that you still were,
when your brothers found you.[24]

Helen has tried to tell Theseus, "I lost the Lover, Paris,/but to
find the Son."[25] But Theseus wants to convince Helen that the
son of whom she speaks is not a living reality. Freud saw H.D.'s
dedication to her art and to Lawrence as a dedication to a death
cult. Theseus thus equates Helen with Persephone, and the quest
becomes the voyage to the underworld to reclaim Persephone, to
bring Helen back to life. Theseus says:

It is one thing, Helen, to slay Death,
it is another to come back
through the intricate windings of the Labyrinth;

the heart? ember, ash or a flower,
you are Persephone's sister;
wait — wait — you must wait in the winter-dark;

you say it is not dark here?
you say the embers make happy pictures
and he reminded you of Troy;

there was a fight on the stairs?
that is all you remember,
it was all a dream until Achilles came;

and this Achilles?
in a dream, he woke you,
you were awake in a dream;

you say this waking dream
was enough, until his mother came,
Thetis or another — it was his mother

who summoned you here;
is it her island, Leuké,
or is it Aphrodite's? no matter,

beloved Child, we are together,
weary of War,
only the Quest remains.[26]

Theseus would "recall, re-vitalize and reawaken Helen." Of her image of Achilles — "brighter than the sun at noon-day,/yet whiter than frost,/whiter than show,/whiter than the white drift of sand/that lies like ground shells,/dust of shells" — Freud retorts,

— dust of skulls, I say;
what beauty, what rapture, what danger,
too great a suspense to endure,

too high the arrow, too taut the bow,
even a Spirit loves laughter,
did you laugh with Achilles? No.[27]

It is difficult to equate this response with the opinions of the master who wrote so brilliantly in *Jokes and Their Relation to the Unconscious* of laughter as a symptom of repression. But paradoxically, Theseus attempts to convince Helen that "the memory of breath-taking encounters with those half-seen must balance and compensate for the too intense primary experience."[28] Theseus seems to be denying the reality of sublimation and deep spiritual connection; he seems to deny that, for instance, as Paul Ricoeur points out in his discussion of the Oedipus drama, "the core [of the tragedy] . . . is not the problem of sex, but the problem of light."[29]

Of the desire that is not in the end wholly carnal, Theseus counsels that Helen's "soul must return wholly to her body."[30] Theseus is, of course, well known for his many love affairs — Ariadne, Phaedra, Hippolyta — and this is the life he would affirm:

> remember these small reliques,
> as on a beach, you search
> for a pearl, a bead,
>
> a comb, a cup, a bowl
> half-filled with sand,
> after a wreck.[31]

And Thesus reminds Helen of the many loves of Achilles. He asks her if she knows of the sacrifice of Polyxena, the daughter of Priam and Hecuba. After the fall of Troy Achilles' ghost claimed her and she was slain on his tomb. Theseus is reminding Helen that she is but a sacrifice to the insatiable appetite of Achilles. He reminds her of the others: Chryseis, Deidamia, and Briseis, all of whom were sacrificed in one way or another to Achilles. He advises her to "leave him with the asphodels," thereby equating Achilles with the narcissus (as the asphodel of Greek poets is supposed to be a narcissus).[32]

But Helen of Sparta speaks to Theseus, saying that Achilles' loves and Helen of Troy's life are unimportant beside their mutual "passionate devotion" to the sea.

> Theseus, god-father, what of that other
> and that other, you speak of,
> the loves of Achilles?
>
> do I care? I am past caring
> and he was past caring
> when he found me;
>
> O, the surge of the sea,
> O, the billows,
> O, the mighty urge
>
> of the oak-prow
> the creak of the oak-beams,
> the sway of the mast,
>
> it was only a small ship, the last,
> (yes, we called it a caravel),
> yet it was a Ship to hold all;

did the Spirits travel with him?
or did they come before?
but listen — it is no matter,

they, Achilles and I
were past caring;
O, the rage of the sea.[33]

In the language of psychoanalysis, H.D. was manifesting resistance to the transference. Theseus, as we all know, is the lawgiver of Athens; Helen apparently cannot understand all of the laws. H.D. speaks of this manifestation more directly in her *Tribute to Freud*.

> For myself, I veer round, uncanonically seated stark upright with my feet on the floor. The Professor himself is uncanonical enough; he is beating with his hand, with his fist, on the head-piece of the old-fashioned horsehair sofa that had heard more secrets than the confession box of any popular Roman Catholic father-confessor in his heyday. This was the homely historical instrument of the original scheme of psychotherapy, of psychoanalysis, the science of the unraveling of the tangled skeins of the unconscious mind and the healing implicit in the process. *Consciously,* I was not aware of having said anything that might account for the Professor's outburst. And even as I veered around, facing him, my mind was detached enough to wonder if this was some idea of *his* for speeding up the analytic content or redirecting the flow of associated images. The Professor said, "The trouble is — I am an old man — *you do not think it is worth your while to love me.*"[34]

The problem was that H.D. was too conscious of the reality of the situation to be properly analyzed. But she cherished a faith, an "illusion" as Freud would maintain, that Freud did not share. H.D. says in her *Tribute:* "One day, I was deeply distressed when the Professor spoke to me about his grandchildren — what would become of them? He asked me that, as if the future of his immediate family were the only future to be considered. There was, of course, the perfectly secured future of his own work, his books. But there was a more imminent, a more immediate future to consider."[35]

If Freud himself was in some sense the reality principle, it is only fair to point out that H.D. herself was in some sense the "more imminent, more immediate future" with which Freud was apparently not enough concerned.

Obviously, a transference as well as a countertransference developed between Freud, the professor, and H.D., the student. But H.D. was as centered in her own thought as Freud was in his. In his review of her *Tribute to Freud* Leslie Fiedler writes:

It is hard to imagine two minds more different than H.D.'s and Freud's. Female and male, gentile and Jew, theosophist and sceptic, American and European, poet and scientist — they come together improbably out of worlds of value and metaphor that seem scarcely compatible . . . they confront each other in Vienna at the moment when Hitler is about to take power and all of the Europe at whose center they sit tilts downward toward darkness and self-destruction . . . For a few months intensely and for five years thereafter, they achieved a kind of intimacy, at once desperate and delicate, a mutual knowledge and respect — a love affair, one must call it finally, though its point was not the meeting of flesh and flesh but the confrontation of self and self . . .

It is the full sense of the intricate human responses called for on either side, from doctor as well as patient, that Miss Doolittle most aptly illustrates. For Freud also adjusts and shifts, learns, advances, capitulates, becomes engaged as a person as the exploration proceeds — an exploration of so terrifying an intimacy that without love it would become blasphemous or comic . . .

The newest name of such understanding may be psychoanalysis, but the oldest is love.[36]

The Theseus story of *Helen in Egypt* is a portrait of Freud, the man; it is also, as is H.D.'s *Tribute to Freud,* a remembrance of the psychoanalysis. And the Theseus-Helen story is as well the tale of a love relationship, or as Fiedler concludes, "a love song — which is to say, the translation of one soul's secret into the language of another."[37]

40

The Moon

AT THE END of book II, "Leuké," as at the end of H.D.'s sessions with Freud, "Helen is at peace, she has found the answer, she will rest."[1] The moon, associated with Thetis and Artemis, is H.D.'s image for feminine consciousness. Leuké is the white moon in the black night and the white isle in the Black Sea; it is white light; it is the eggshell, the mind of Thetis, the moon goddess. Specifically, Leuké is an island; symbolically it includes the moments of light that occurred in H.D.'s life in England.

H.D. is aware that Leuké, her image of the moon, is traditionally associated with lunacy or madness. "Nervous and mental diseases which grow worse and then better at more or less regular intervals were thought to be caused by changes in the moon, and we still speak of a mentally insane person as a 'lunatic' or one who is affected by the moon."[2] The images presented by H.D. suggest a clarity of thought which is perceived by some as visionary and by some as madness; her perception of primal realities is stark and direct. In "Leuké" of *Helen in Egypt* Helen "will encompass infinity by intense concentration on the moment."[3]

> Time with its moon-shape here,
> time with its widening star-circles,
> time small as a pebble,
>
> . . .
>
> if I am small enough,
> held in this smallest sphere,
> this moon-crystal, this shell,
>
> if I dare renounce spring-love,
> Adonis and Cytheraea, and a small room,
> a taper burning in an onyx jar,

(Paris said, *why must you recall*
the white fire of unnumbered stars,
rather than that single taper

burning in an onyx jar),
it is for another (you are right,
god-father) and another;

but the Vision is not Protean,
it is actual, unwavering,
each station separate, each line drawn,

each pillar erect,
each porch level with the rocks,
and rock-steps leading to a throne

or down to a pool, a mirror
and a reflection . . .[4]

The woman is the reflection, a reflection of the sun. In her moon aspect she reflects the light and the "white fire of unnumbered stars." The moon "sheds much less light on the earth than the sun does, and therefore was admired less for its brilliance than for its beauty and its whiteness, which gave it its poetic name, *le bānāh,* 'the white one.' "[5]

From a male point of view the logic of *Helen in Egypt* is lunacy, madness, psychosis; from a woman's point of view it is feminine consciousness. He projects; she reflects. *Helen in Egypt* is a reflection. H.D. would maintain that the woman (Thetis, Helen) is the creative source of the world, not the creator of the world. The man (Achilles, Theseus) is the creator, but his creative energy comes from his connection to the muse — the daemon is the muse, the passional feeling, the inspiration.

Helen is not to be understood as a projection of H.D.'s personality; rather, H.D.'s identification with the figure of Helen is her womanhood, her nonneurotic or poetic manifestation, which she shares with all women. She is, as it were, a mirror in which is reflected the design and pattern of history. And in love she reflects the man's dream. Thus she becomes his dream; she comes to embody it.

In her *Tribute to Freud* H.D. tells of a dream she had during her psychoanalytic relationship with Freud, the dream of the princess.

She was a dark lady. She wore a clear-coloured robe, yellow or faint-orange. It was wrapped round her as in one piece, like a sari worn as only a high-caste Indian lady could wear it. But she is not an Indian, she is Egyptian. She appears at the top of a long staircase; marble steps lead down to a river. She wears no ornament, no circlet or sceptre shows her rank, but anyone would know *this is a*

Princess. Down, down the steps she comes. She will not turn back, she will not stop, she will not alter the slow rhythm of her pace. She has nothing in her arms, there is no one with her; there is no extraneous object with her or about her or about the carved steps to denote any symbolic detail or side issue involved. There is no detail. The steps are geometrical, symmetrical and she is as abstract as a lady could be, yet she is a real entity, a real person. I, the dreamer, wait at the foot of the steps. I have no idea who I am or how I got there. There is no before or after, it is a perfect moment in time or out of time. I am concerned about something, however. I wait below the lowest step. There, in the water beside me, is a shallow basket or ark or box or boat. There is, of course, a baby nested in it. The Princess must find the baby. I know that she will find this child. I know that the baby will be protected and sheltered by her and that is all that matters.[6]

H.D. and Freud both recognized this picture as *Moses in the Bulrushes* from the illustrated Doré Bible. H.D. had seen it often as a child. The Professor discussed the image, the dream. What does it mean? Freud remembers that in the picture a child, Miriam, is half-hidden in the rushes. Is H.D. Miriam? he asks. Perhaps, says H.D. Is H.D. the baby Moses? suggests Freud. H.D. then asks, "Do I wish myself, in the deepest unconscious or subconscious layers of my being, to be the founder of a new religion?"[7] No, she does not believe she has any such aspirations. Does H.D. know that she is reflecting Freud's dream? Does Freud realize this? In 1939 Freud published *Moses and Monotheism*. In her dream H.D. is the princess who will give birth to or adopt a son; Freud is Moses; the new religion is psychoanalysis.

About her dream, H.D. says, "Is it possible that I (leaping over every sort of intellectual impediment and obstacle) not wished only, but *knew,* the Professor would be born again?" She writes of the princess: "She is 'our Princess' — that is, she is specifically the Professor's Princess and mine, 'our' personal guardian or inspiration. She is peculiarly 'his' Princess for this is a life-wish, apparently, that I have projected into or onto an image of the Professor's racial, ancestral background."[8]

Of course, H.D. was not Freud's particular princess; there was a real princess in his life at this time, Marie Bonaparte, Princess George of Greece, who had translated Freud's work from German into French. H.D. says,

> I no doubt, unconsciously covet her worldly position, her intellectual endowments, her power of translating the difficult, scholarly, beautiful German of Sigmund Freud into no doubt equally distinguished and beautiful French. I can not compete with her. Con-

sciously, I do not feel any desire to do so. But unconsciously, I probably wish to be another equal factor or have equal power of benefiting and protecting the Professor.[9]

At this time in her analysis (1933–1934), as H.D. relates, "the Professor had been working on a continuation of his 'Moses, the Egyptian' theme, though we had not actually discussed this when I had my 'real' dream of the Egyptian Princess."[10]

Freud suggested to H.D. that she was the child, Miriam, in her dream, not the real princess, but in H.D.'s vision, she is the real princess, just as Freud is the real hero in *his* vision. In H.D.'s mind, the dream symbolism reflected her relationship with Freud. *Tribute to Freud* is H.D.'s vision of Freud as the new Moses, and she is the princess, the mother or creator of her vision. "The Professor asked me then, if I were the child Miriam who in the Doré picture had stood, half-hidden in the river-reeds, watching over the new-born child who was to become leader of a captive people and founder of a new religion."[11] And in a way Freud was right: H.D. did come to see herself in the child Miriam. She had been given this vision unknowingly; she had been possessed by his dream. She is both the mother and child of his dream.

In the end Theseus tells Helen to "return to the Shell, your mother," whom he has identified with Leda, Thetis, or Cytheraea. It is always reunion with the mother we are seeking, since in love we are always seeking to re-establish the primal narcissism. At the end of the analysis Theseus tells Helen to return to the shell from which she was born. This eggshell, Theseus seems to say, is the same as the poem. He says to Helen:

> beyond Trojan and Greek,
>
> is the cloud, the wind, the Lover
> you sought in the snow;
> I am half-way to that Lover[12]

the last lover being, in Freud's cosmology, death (see Freud, "The Theme of Three Caskets").

But for Helen the way home is the same as the way to Achilles. "Helen seems to ask, how can I compromise? My soul or my spirit was snatched from its body . . . by this 'gerfalcon.' "

> have you seen a gerfalcon
> fall on its prey?
> so my throat knew that day,
>
> his finger's remorseless steel.[13]

Helen symbolizes her knowing mind as her "crystal." In her crystal she sees the future by recalling the past. The crystal, she says, "will reflect the past."

> so I would read here
> in my crystal, the Writing,
> I would measure the star-space
>
> even as Achilles
> measured the stars
> with the sway of a ship's mast.[14]

And "by a miracle of re-adjustment," Helen tells us, through the power and tenderness of Theseus, "the Wheel is still."[15] The wheel is the zodiac, the star-space, the Amen-script. Helen measures the star-space

> even as Achilles counted,
> picture by picture,
> the outline of hero and beast.[16]

The zodiac or star-space is H.D.'s symbol for the twelve labors — the labors of Hercules but also the twelve labors of Achilles, of Helen, of Theseus. It is her symbol for the work to be done. In *Tribute to Freud*, H.D. said of the Professor, "Until we have completed our twelve labours, he seemed to reiterate, we (mankind) have no right to rest on cloud-cushion fantasies and dreams of an after-life."[17] H.D.'s perspective is of continuity, of timelessness, of eternity.

> *Achilles waits,* aye,
> stepping from sphere to sphere,
> aye, the long way;
>
> he will finish his task,
> Hercules' twelve labours,
> in twelve aeons, in twelve years,
>
> in twelve days,
> aye! Hades — Hercules,
> the long way;
>
> to me, the Wheel is still,
> (hold me here),
> The Wheel is as small
>
> as the gold shoulder-clasp,
> I wore as a girl;
> the Wheel is a jewel,

> set in silver; to me
> the Wheel is a seal . . .
> the Wheel is still.[18]

Star-stime is eternal time. And Helen's personal time, her "time-in-time," is at an end. H.D. has concluded, at the end of book II, that Helen has "finished her cycle in time." But there is still labor to be done. She will not yet "attempt to escape" through physical death. "She will bring the moment and infinity together . . . in the crystal . . . in my thought here," that is to say in this poem, *Helen in Egypt*.[19]

"Though herself free from time-restrictions and the Wheel," her karma, "she would endure or share the 'labours' of Achilles." And to Theseus she says:

> what was Helen's task?
> do we know?
> only that it was finished
>
> when she stumbled out of the snow,
> across the threshold
> and found you here.[20]

The deeply psychoanalytical conception of myth and history that informs *Helen in Egypt* would not have been possible had H.D. not been able to work with Freud. It was Freud who enabled her to finish her task — to tell "the story."

41

"Eidolon"

AT THE END of the first book of *Helen in Egypt,* "Pallinode," Thetis calls Helen out of Egypt. After her sessions with Theseus, "Helen is called back to Egypt. It is Achilles who calls her — or it is the image or eidolon of Achilles."[1] H.D. was called back to the memory of her early life as a poet by Lawrence's work, his phallic or life energy, translated as it were into the creative drive of his last novels and stories — his literary output. At the literary level of meaning "Eidolon" is an allusion to Lawrence's phallic images, his escaped cock and his John Thomas. In *Helen in Egypt* the image is the eidolon. As H.D. writes: "I say there is one image/one picture, though the swords flash;/I say there is one treasure."[2] But the image was more than the literature, H.D. tells us in "Eidolon"; it was the experience. "It was a treasure beyond a treasure/he gave her."[3]

In "Thorn Thicket" H.D. had called Rico/Lawrence the "magician-lover"; in *Helen in Egypt* Achilles is correspondingly "dedicated to a new Command, that of the 'Royal sacred High Priest of love rites.' "[4]*

And as we return to Egypt in "Eidolon" we are again faced with double or multiple identity of character. "Eidolon" is the story of Helena or Hilda the person. H.D. refers to Helen's Greek and Egyptian manifestations as her double identity. Twins or double identity served a protective purpose in both Lawrence's and H.D.'s work. He felt himself to be two people, as in *Aaron's Rod;* she often portrayed herself as two people. Each was one person with his or her spouse and a different person with the other. Thus they were "twins" in life as well as in literature.

*As D. H. Lawrence wrote in a letter of December 25, 1912, "I shall always be a priest of love . . . and I'll preach my heart out."[5]

In *Helen in Egypt* H.D. attempts to bring the Helens together: "Pallinode" invokes Helen the poet; "Leuké" is the story of Helen the thinker (H.D.'s argument with Aldington and her work with Freud); and "Eidolon" is the story of Helena, the "human content of the drama."[6] In Egypt, says H.D., "Helen is Persephone,/ Achilles is Dis,/(the Greek Isis-Osiris)." It is Theseus who has brought Helen to Egypt again because it is Freud who helped H.D. to come to terms with her experience, her struggle "to understand Leuké, the light."[7]

There is a spark of light, of communication, says H.D. The exact form its direction takes is various and interesting and can be symbolized and imagined in an infinite number of ways, but H.D.'s focus after her work with Freud was on the original spark of life, the light. It reminds us of the brazier:

> Why do I call him my son and Achilles'?
> because of an ember, because of a Star?
> (was there ever such a brazier?)[8]

The light is always a symbol of Lawrence's work, a specific allusion to the spirit of the man H.D. knew.

The eidolon is a more concrete image. In *Helen in Egypt,* Achilles' eidolon becomes identified with Helen; they are one. What he had lost can be symbolized by his images or hers. They had both lost. In "Eidolon" H.D. symbolizes the unity of Helen and Achilles in the image of a ship. It is "his own ship," says H.D., "and the figurehead, an idol or eidolon . . . a mermaid, Thetis upon the prow."

> did her eyes slant in the old way
> was she Greek or Egyptian?
> had some Phoenician sailor wrought her?
>
> was she oak-wood or cedar?
> had she been cut from an awkward block
> of ship-wood at the ship builders,
>
> and afterwards riveted there,
> or had the prow itself been shaped
> to her mermaid body,
>
> curved to her mermaid hair?
> was there a dash of paint
> in the beginning, in the garment fold,
>
> did the blue afterwards wear away?
> did they re-touch her arms, her shoulders?
> did anyone touch her ever?

had she other zealot and lover,
or did he alone worship her?
did she wear a girdle of sea-weed

or a painted crown? how often
did her high breasts meet the spray,
how often dive down?[9]

While it alludes specifically to all the ship and boat imagery in
Lawrence's and H.D.'s prose and poetry, and at some level to the
ship of Odysseus, the eidolon concept that informs book III of
Helen in Egypt comes from H.D.'s psychoanalytic understanding
of the muse as a substitute for the mother and at the same time a
partial substitute for the phallus. Post-Freudian psychoanalysis,
following the British psychoanalyst D. W. Winnicott, defines the
eidolon as a "transitional object." It is both a substitute for the
mother and an object with which the child identifies himself.
Achilles' first transitional object, says H.D., was "a wooden doll."

O mysterious treasure,
O idol, O eidolon,
with wings folded about her,

her hands are clasped as in prayer . . .

he set her upon a plinth
like the curved prow of a ship,
and perhaps the tree is a ship.[10]

In the meeting of Helen and Achilles, immortality dissolved
into vulnerability — love. It was really Lawrence's mother's fault;
H.D. was not the first woman he had ever loved. In the context
of *Helen in Egypt,* Achilles' heel is also an image of the phallus.
Again the concept is inspired by H.D.'s study of Freud and psychoanalysis.

She had promised him immortality
but she had forgotten to dip the heel
of the infant Achilles

into the bitter water,
Styx, was it?
O careless, unspeakable mother . . .[11]

Here, "careless, unspeakable mother" is ironic; if it was in fact
the Oedipus complex that brought Helen this love, she must affirm the Oedipal reality. "The memory is really that of Achilles
but she lives it with him."

It was only, when I felt
with him, lying there,
the bitterness of his loss,

That I knew he loved, that I knew
the ecstasy of desire had smitten him,
burnt him; touched with the Phoenix-fire,

the invincible armour
melted him quite away,
till he knew his mother.[12]

H.D. recalls her early poetry and her first meetings with Lawrence. She had "met" him in the context of *Amores,* the poems he
had written that speak so deeply of the loss of his mother. She too
had lost in love. They had both written poetry that spoke of loss,
of remembrance of things past. The night they had met at the
Berkeley Hotel they had felt a spark of recognition; loss had conditioned their encounter. They had continued to meet during the
war years, under the shadow of death. They were, as in Lawrence's early poem, shades. As H.D. writes in *Helen:*

true, I had met him, the New Mortal,

baffled and lost,
but I was a phantom Helen
and he was Achilles' ghost.[13]

The Helen of "Eidolon" does not particularly want to analyze
the whys and wherefores of her relationship with Achilles. H.D.
has accepted, with Freud's help, the fact that she is a victim of the
Oedipus complex. Aren't we all? Helen of "Eidolon" is "numb
with a memory"; H.D. wants only to remember all the poems
and experiences that followed the unrecorded dimension of her
first meeting with Lawrence. She records this dimension in a series
of beautiful images:

                    . . . I remember
the crackle of salt-weed,
and the sting of salt as I crept nearer

over shale and the white shells;
O, I remember, I remember,
here with the embers glowing,

but fainter, growing dimmer
as light begins — but far, far
to show outline through the curtain,

as of a ladder — an old shutter
with a broken slat? — but the ladder is even,
seven slats and seven —

what do I remember?
we met on a desolate coast, . . .

I only remember the shells, whiter than bone,
on the ledge of a desolate beach.[14]

Lawrence had remembered when he wrote *Lady Chatterley's Lover* and *The Man Who Died*. In *Helen in Egypt,* H.D. asks: "What did he remember last, what first?"[15] She did not see the whole picture until she wrote *Helen in Egypt.* But even after each had named the other, their story remained a secret. And as both H.D. and Lawrence tell it, they were bound to each other from the time of their first meeting; they both tried to go back to the life they had known before, but failed. Again H.D. tells us that it was not her fault; it was not his fault. There was the light of their first meeting and then a "series or circle of the ever-recurring 'eternal moment.' "[16] She seems to be speaking both of the experiences and of the recording of the experiences in the prose and poetry when she speaks of "thoughts too deep to remember."[17] But in *Helen in Egypt* she expresses certainty: "This is Love, this is Death/this is my last Lover."[18] And just as Lawrence had been the end of her marriage, she had changed his marriage unalterably. There is an ultimate experience, says H.D., but one pays a price.

"The numberless tender kisses, the soft caresses" have no part in the epic, says H.D. "But there is a miraculous birth."[19] The union of Achilles and Helen results in the birth of Euphorion. The name, which signifies something like "graceful bearing," is borrowed from a late Greek legend in which Euphorion was the offspring of Helen and Achilles during their ghostly posthumous life on the island of Leuce (Leuké) in the Black Sea. As H.D. tells us, "The promised *Euphorion* is not one child, but two. It is the 'child in Chiron's cave' and 'the frail maiden.' "[20] The former represents Achilles, the latter Helen. The union of the two gives birth to romanticism, says H.D. — specifically to Lawrence's late novels and her Madrigal novels.

H.D. said repeatedly that E. M. Butler's *Fortunes of Faust,* a genre study of the various Faust legends, sparked her writing of *Helen in Egypt.* Goethe's *Faust* was of course a more primary source. H.D.'s eidolon concept was undoubtedly taken directly from part II, act 3:

PHORKYAS: Yet people say that you appeared in double form
  And were seen both in Ilium and Egypt too.
HELEN: Do not disrange completely sense already wild.
  Not even now do I know fully who I am.

PHORKYAS: They also tell that from the hollow realm of shades
  Achilles also in his ardor rose to join
  You, whom he loved despite the will of destiny.
HELEN: I, as eidolon, joined with him, eidolon also.
  It was a dream, as the reports themselves maintain.
  I fade away, and to myself am an eidolon.[21]

In Goethe's version of the story, Helen meets Faust after she has managed to escape Menelaus's plans for her execution, designed as punishment for her infidelity. Phorkyas helps her to escape to the medieval fortress of Faust. Helen and Faust fall in love and conceive Euphorion.

In "Eidolon," H.D. merges the Achilles-Faust figure. She presents an older, wiser Achilles whom she has imbued with some of the attributes of Kaspar of *The Flowering of the Rod*. The eidolon, then, becomes a transpersonal image of both his awakened desire, the erect phallus, and the woman to whom his desire is directed. H.D.'s marvelous sense of humor, which permeates the entire poem, comes through in the bawdy pun, "Is she carved of red-cedar [seeder]?" The eidolon is always an image.

O mysterious treasure,
O idol, O eidolon,
with wings folded about her,

her hands are clasped in prayer,
in the garment-fold,
is she carved of red-cedar?[22]

Of Goethe's Euphorion, Charles E. Passage writes: "We are to understand that Euphorion signified the generalized spirit of Romanticism, whereas Byron was the particularized incarnation of the Spirit."[23] In the same sense, H.D.'s Achilles signifies the generalized spirit of the Greek warrior, which H.D. understands as embodying a strong Oedipal motif, and D. H. Lawrence is to be understood as a particularized incarnation of that spirit.

The Oedipal motif is certainly central to "Eidolon." Helen is associated with Persephone, Achilles with Pluto. Is Helen simply another sacrifice in the Oedipal drama of the life of Achilles? Speaking for Paris, H.D. writes:

It was not only Iphigeneia,
(you told me the story),
there was always another and another,

(I read all your thoughts, the words
of you and Theseus together),
remember Polyxena, golden by the altar,

remember Pyrrhus, his son slew her;
where did she wander?
O golden sister,

are you still subjugated? enchanted?
are all the slain
bound to this Master? [24]

But for H.D. the spiritual bond is stronger than attachments based strictly on physical love. And the more spiritual as opposed to the more exogamous and culturally preferred form of relationship does not preclude the possibility of a child, even if it has no place in the epic drama. And there is the child Euphorion, the symbol of the writing, the poetry. Of Achilles H.D. writes:

the sun and the seasons changed,
and as the flower-leaves that drift
from a tree were the numberless

tender kisses, the soft caresses,
given and received; none of these
came into the story,

it was epic, heroic and it was far
from a basket a child upset
and the spools that rolled to the floor. [25]

The impossibility of a reconciliation between Paris and Achilles is an important theme of "Eidolon." Aldington had never stopped fighting Lawrence. He had done everything possible to suppress the H.D.–D. H. Lawrence story. He had attempted, with a good deal of success, to dissuade H.D. from writing and from publishing anything that alluded to her relationship with Lawrence.

In 1950, just before H.D. wrote *Helen in Egypt,* Aldington published his biography of Lawrence, *Portrait of a Genius, But . . . ,* which presents Lawrence as both effeminate and impotent. It was his vindictive judgment of Lawrence in this portrait that helped to liberate H.D. from her unspoken agreement with Aldington never to tell the whole story. In *Helen in Egypt* she writes, "But Paris would reduce the valour of the hero to 'woman's robe and ornament.' " [26]

In writing her poem H.D. finally rebelled. She apparently felt some need to apologize for the rebellious spirit of the lines that follow; she writes: "In this last phase or mood, it seems inevitable and perhaps wholly human for Helen to turn on her Trojan lover."

What can Paris know of the sea,
except for the lure and delight
of the sheltered harbours and bays?

what can Paris know of the sea?
he crossed to Sparta, you say,
but the Paphian lightened his craft

and stilled the waves;
what can Paris know of the sea
that Thetis should champion him?

how dared he say to me,
"call on Thetis, the sea-mother"?
I tremble, I feel the same

anger and sudden terror,
that I sensed Achilles felt,
when I named his mother,

true, the world knows her name,
the world may bring her
marble to build her walls,

and ships for her harbours;
but her wings are folded about her
and her wings only unfurl

at the cry of the New Mortal,
or the child's pitiful call;
what had Paris to give her? [27]

Aldington had done his best to convince H.D. that Lawrence had never loved her. His protectiveness, concluded H.D., was related not to his love for her but to his pride. He had argued with her, as had Freud, that she was but another victim of the Oedipal drama. In theory, perhaps, it was possible to reconcile Lawrence and Aldington, but never in life. Aldington had no spiritual resources with which to understand the life she had shared with Lawrence. The final lines of "Eidolon" present an unequivocal affirmation of Lawrence and his work.

But what could Paris know of the sea,
its beat and long reverberation,
its booming and delicate echo,

its ripple that spells a charm
on the sand, the rock-lichen,
the sea-moss, the sand,

and again and again, the sand;
what does Paris know of the hill and hollow
of billows, the sea-road?

what could he know of the ships
from his Ideaen home,
the crash and spray of the foam,

the wind, the shoal, the broken shale,
the infinite loneliness
when one is never alone?

only Achilles could break his heart
and the world for a token,
a memory forgotten. [28]

H.D.'s vision of the sea as the creative source is related to Freud's vision of primal narcissism — the "oceanic" feeling. The creative life springs from that first, intense bond. In *Civilization and Its Discontents* Freud writes: "Originally the ego includes everything, later it separates off an external world from itself. Our present ego-feeling is, therefore, only a shrunken residue of a much more inclusive — indeed, an all-embracing — feeling which corresponds to a more intimate bond between the ego and the world around it." [29]

This oceanic feeling is rediscovered; the recognition results in the Oedipal drama. The search ends in the realization of the primal scene. Of the passion is born the child. The poet is reborn into the world of his own childhood, his own desire.

Finding one's true mate is a matter of fate, says H.D. If Aldington had understood, he would not have continued to fight. On the level of the epic drama, the stage upon which the game of poetry is played, there was no contest, she says.

42

Helen and Odysseus

IN "EIDOLON" H.D. asks: " 'Who set the scene? who lured the players?' The players have no choice in the matter of the already-written drama or script."

> Was it Apollo's snare
> so that poets forever,
> should be caught in the maze of the Walls
>
> of a Troy that never fell?[1]

Who wrote the script? Ezra Pound, answers H.D. "Indeed it was 'Apollo's snare.' None other."[2] Pound appears and reappears in *Helen in Egypt* under a great many names. His first incarnation is as Stesichorus of Sicily in the first lines of "Pallinode." Stesichorus is the choir-setter, the director of ceremonies. H.D. writes: "We all know the story of Helen of Troy but few of us have followed her to Egypt. How did she get there? Stesichorus of Sicily in his *Pallinode* was the first to tell us."[3]

Pound had been the first to write of H.D.'s life; he had begun with *Hilda's Book* in 1905. In *End to Torment* H.D. tells of how she and Aldington had moved after seeing the first Canto variations. "Three Cantos" appeared in *Poetry* magazine in June, July, and August, 1917. Pound had written of H.D. in these *Ur*-Cantos:

> Your "palace step"?
> My stone seat was the Dogana's curb,
> And there were not "those girls," there was one flare,
>   one face.
> 'Twas all I ever saw, but it was real . . .
> And I can no more say what shape it was . . .
> But she was young , too young.
>   True, it was Venice,

420

And at Florian's and under the north arcade
I have seen other faces, and had my rolls for breakfast,
    for that matter.[4]

We recognize the "rolls for breakfast" as a recurrent pastry pun, this one a bit on the bawdy side. These three Cantos allude often to H.D. and name Helen: *"Muy linda,* a woman, Helen, a star,/Lights the king's features."[5]

The tale of Teiresias and the Trojan War is introduced. "I told her news of Troy, and thrice her shadow/Faded in my embrace."[6] Blind Teiresias, the seer, is linked to blind Homer, the alleged author of *The Iliad*. As Pound writes in the final version of "Canto II":

"Eleanor, ἐλέναυς and ἐλέπτολις!"
    And poor old Homer, blind, blind as a bat,
Ear, ear for the sea-surge, murmur of old men's voices:
    "Let her go back to the ships,
Back among Grecian faces, lest evil come on our own,
Evil and further evil, and a curse cursed on our children,
Moves, yes she moves like a goddess
And has the face of a god
    and the voice of Schoeney's daughters,
And doom goes with her in walking,
Let her go back to the ships,
    back among Grecian voices."[7]

In *Helen in Egypt* H.D. alludes to this invective against her, first under the persona of Stesichorus. Like Teiresias and Homer, Stesichorus is blind. H.D. writes: "Stesichorus was said to have been struck blind because of his invective against Helen."[8] The second persona for Pound is "the helmsman," whose "bitter oath" is a reference to yet another invective. H.D. writes:

. . . the helmsman's bitter oath
to see the goal receding

in the night; everlasting, everlasting
nothingness and lethargy of waiting;
O Helen, Helen, Daemon that thou art,

we will be done forever
with this charm, this evil philtre,
This curse of Aphrodite.[9]

In an early recognition that Pound's decision to marry Dorothy Shakespear had launched her into her career as a poet, H.D. had written in "The Helmsman":

But now, our boat climbs — hesitates —
    drops —
climbs — hesitates — crawls back —
climbs — hesitates —
O be swift —
We have always known you wanted us.[10]

"The Helmsman" was published in the *Egoist* in April 1916.
H.D. wrote of her attempt to escape Pound: "We wor-
shipped inland — /we stepped past wood-flowers,/we forgot your
tang,/we brushed wood-grass."[11]

In a sense, H.D. wrote *Helen in Egypt* with Pound very much
on her mind. They were still intermittently corresponding. There
were many things H.D. would like to communicate to him.
Could the ambitious Pound ever understand that she had not originally had any desire to become a separate force in the world? As
H.D. writes in *Helen in Egypt,* "I do not care for separate/might
and grandeur."[12]

As a young woman H.D. had wanted to be Pound's wife. After
the bitter loss of her first child in 1915 she could not help but
think of the tragic consequences of her botched relationship with
Pound. Her translation of Euripides' *Iphigeneia* was a bringing to
consciousness of the disastrous consequences of Pound's actions,
and she blamed herself as well as him. But she did not forget. The
Iphigeneia theme is central to the "Pallinode" of *Helen in Egypt*.
"She again recalls the Greek scene. For it is through her Greek
identity that she understands." H.D. identifies Pound as Odysseus
and cannot help but feel that she, Helen, was the victim of the
"treacherous plan,/the plot, they said, of Odysseus."[13] Pound had
lured her to England under the false pretext of marriage.

Finally, H.D. had "left" Pound for Lawrence. It was after this
happened that he began his Cantos, translating from Divus's Latin
version of book XI of the *Odyssey,* the "Book of the Dead," and
assuming the persona of Homer's hero: "And then went down to
the ship,/Set keel to breakers, forth on the godly sea."[14]

Late in their lives H.D. and Pound were still writing to each
other; even more remarkable, they were still arguing with each
other. Many of Pound's letters to H.D. were written in the form
of poems. In February of 1953 he wrote:

    to Καλλος
    Hang on and come up with the spring,
        of course you did wrong to
    go reading other languages when you
    had a start on a good one.[15]

In her *End to Torment* H.D. writes of Pound and Lawrence:

> The two men, diametrically opposed, set off each other, the London "opposite number" of my life-long Isis search, and the Odysseus-Pound descended into the land of the shades in the *Pisan Cantos*. No. There is no resemblence. But I completed my own *cantos* as Norman [Holmes Pearson] called them, again in the Greek setting; mine is *Helen and Achilles* [*Helen in Egypt*]. There is resemblance in this, the two men meet in war, the Trojan War, the Achilles of my fantasy and imagination and the Odysseus of Ezra's. They do not meet, they never can meet in life.[16]

Lawrence and Pound could not meet in life because Lawrence was dead. But H.D. and Pound could, and did, continue to write.

H.D.'s "Winter Love" addresses the events of her relationship with Ezra Pound directly. Norman Holmes Pearson wanted her to publish it as a part of *Helen in Egypt:* "I myself wanted to publish as a fourth part of *Helen* a . . . section called 'Winter Love.' This was a personal poem . . . At the last minute she withdrew her permission to use 'Winter Love' as the last part."[17]

H.D.'s decision was wise. "Winter Love" is very different structurally from the Helen sequence. Yet Pearson had good reasons for his suggestion. As he writes: "Had this appeared I think one could have seen what lay behind the early parts of *Helen*. It would in that sense have been even closer to the *Cantos* as we read them once the Pisan section is present."[18] Pearson knew that H.D.'s nickname during the late twenties and thirties had been Lynx, and knew that Pound was remembering H.D. when he wrote the *Pisan Cantos*.

Pound, too, was a lynx. In her *End to Torment* H.D. refers specifically to the "Lynx Hymn," Canto LXXIX: "There is a stir of dust from old leaves/Will you trade roses for acorns?"[19] Pound's Canto continues: "Will lynxes eat thorn leaves?/What have you in that wine jar?/ἰχώρ [juice, blood], for lynxes?"[20]

In H.D.'s sessions with him in 1933, Freud had said, "If I had known Ezra, I could have made him all right."[21] His implication is that Pound had a severe Oedipal problem. Was that the problem?

In the cell in Pisa, where Pound was imprisoned at the end of World War II, he remembered "Priapus" and "Hermes," H.D.'s first Imagist poems.

> And now Priapus with Faunus
> The Graces have brought Ἀφροδίτην
> Her cell is drawn by ten leopards

O lynx, guard my vineyard
As the grape swells under vine leaf
   "Ἤλιος is come to our mountain
   there is a red glow in the carpet of pine spikes

   O lynx, guard my vineyard
   As the grape swells under the vine leaf

   This Goddess was born of sea-foam
   She is lighter than air under Hesperus
     δεινὰ εἶ, Κύθηρα
Terrible in resistance
     Κόρη καὶ Δήλια καὶ Μαῖα
trine as praeludio
     Κύπρις ’Αφρόδιτη
a petal lighter than sea-foam
     Κύθηρα
       aram
       nemus
       vult
O puma, sacred to Hermes, Cimbica servant of Helios.[22]

Pound uses recurring names for H.D.: Persephone, Artemis, Delia, Dryad, Mara, mother of Hermes; then Aphrodite, Cytheraea. Mythologically, Aphrodite is from the island of Cythera, but Pound in the Pisan Cantos and H.D. in *Helen in Egypt* call the goddess herself Cytheraea. They also call her Cypris, the Cyprian Aphrodite. "Ἤλιος," the sun, "is come to our mountain." And "aram/nemus/vult," the grove needs an altar. Pound invokes Pomona, the old Italian goddess of fruit trees. He remembers H.S.'s "Hermes" and a poem he had read to her in the apple orchard in Wyncote, Pennsylvania — "Pomona" by William Morris:

I am the Ancient Apple-Queen,
As once I was so am I now.
For ever more a hope unseen,
Betwixt the blossom and the bough.

Ah, where's the river's hidden Gold!
And where the windy grave of Troy?
Yet come I as I came of old,
From out the heart of Summer's joy.[23]

"I was hiding," says H.D. in *End to Torment*. "I was hiding myself and Ezra, standing before my father, caught 'in the very act' you might say. For no 'act' afterwards, though biologically fulfilled, had had the significance of the first *demi-vierge* embraces."[24] Had they both been "in hiding" — in hiding from what Freud had called the "too intense primary experience"? Pound had written in *Hilda's Book* a poem entitled "Shadow":

> I saw her yesterday
> And lo, there is no time
> Each second being eternity.
> Peace! trouble me no more.
> Yes, I know your eyes clear pools
> Holding the summer sky within their depth
> But trouble me not
> I saw HER yesterday.[25]

In reading Canto 90, H.D. says in *End to Torment,* "I could at last accept the intoxication of 'Kuthera sempiterna' and the healing of 'myrrh and olibanum on the altar stone/giving perfume.' "[26] Pound had written:

> Pardus, leopardi, Bagheera
>   drawn hither from woodland,
> woodland ἐπὶ χθονί
>   the trees rise
>   and there is a wide sward between them
> οἱ χθόνιοι myrrh and olibanum on the altar stone
> giving perfume.[27]

Why was it they never married? Did they love one another not enough or too much? At the beginning of their courtship Pound had given H.D. a copy of *Tristan and Iseult,* the story of two lovers doomed to be separated but never to forget one another. The legend holds that aboard ship the lovers are tricked into drinking a potion. In *Hilda's Book* Pound had written the poem "Li Bel Chasteus" about Tristan and Iseult. In a direct allusion to the legend and Pound's early poetry H.D. writes in *Helen in Egypt:*

> The potion is not poison,
> it is not Lethe and forgetfulness
> but everlasting memory,
>
> the glory and the beauty of the ships,
> the wave that bore them onward
> and the shock of hidden shoal,
>
> the peril of the rocks,
> the weary fall of sail,
> the rope drawn taut,

Helen and Odysseus § 425

the breathing and breath-taking
climb and fall, mountain and valley
challenging the coast

drawn near, drawn far.[28]

The potion is poetry, says H.D. Why poetry? Why do these poets talk to each other like this? Why do they use the language of myth rather than everyday language? Pound gives an answer of sorts in his essay "Affirmations," published in 1915 in *The New Age*.

> The first myth arose when a man walked sheer into "nonsense," that is to say, when some very vivid and undeniable adventure befell him, and he told someone else who called him a liar. Thereupon, after bitter experience, when he said that he "turned into a deer," he made a myth — a work of art that is — an impersonal or objective story woven out of his emotions, as the nearest equation that he was capable of putting into words. That story, perhaps, then gave rise to a weakened copy of his emotions in others, until there arose a cult, a company of people who could understand each other's nonsense about the gods.[29]

H.D. and Pound could understand "each other's nonsense about the gods." They follow a logic of event in their speech, but their poetry is no more confessional than great music. Life manifests through us; we are its various forms. Helen, Iseult, Persephone, and Circe are the same girl — the one in Pound's poem "A Girl."

> The tree has entered my hands,
> The sap has ascended my arms,
> The tree has grown in my breast —
> Downward,
> The branches grow out of me, like arms
>
> Tree you are,
> Moss you are,
> You are violets with wind above them.
> A child — *so* high — you are,
> And all this is folly to the world.[30]

In "Rendez-vous" Pound had written: "She hath some tree-born spirit of the wood/About her, and the wind is in her hair."[31] These images of trees, orchards, and nymphs are allusions to Pound's "dryad." "Why," asks H.D. in *End to Torment*, "had I ever come down out of that tree?"[32] Guy Davenport writes: "In 1958 . . . Ezra Pound, a free man, went first to the sea . . . and secondly to a particular apple tree in Wyncote, Penn. . . . there is little in Pound that is far away from Persephone and her trees."[33]

Reading *Hilda's Book,* we see Pound and H.D. as young lovers who lived in innocence and hope. The first poem in *Hilda's Book* reads:

> Child of the grass
> The years pass Above us
> Shadows of air All these shall Love us
> Winds for our fellows
> The browns and the yellows
>   Of autumn our colors
> Now at our life's morn. Be we well sworn
> Ne'er to grow older
> Our spirits be bolder At meeting
> Than e'er before All the old lore
> Of the forests & woodways
> Shall aid us: Keep we the bond & seal
> Ne'er shall we feel
>   Aught of sorrow . . .[34]

But the world Pound and H.D. knew was to be objectified, written in images; an eternal text of poetry was to be created from what was once a living, experienced reality. It would be a world in which all ages are contemporaneous and superimposed upon one another as a palimpsest. As H.D. writes in *End to Torment:*

> I am frozen in this moment . . . Perhaps I held it all my life, it is what they called my "imagery"; even now, they speak of "verse so chiselled as to seem lapidary," and they say, "She crystallizes — that is the right word . . ." This moment must wait 50 years for the right word. Perhaps he had said it; perhaps in the frost of our mingled breath the word was written.[35]

If it begins like this, suggests H.D., it does not really end. As she saw it, Pound lit the fire; Lawrence was another writing on the palimpsest of experience, another flame: white fire. Olga Rudge was another flame in Pound's life; H.D. had been the first.* In the end it is one flame; it is life. "There is no argument, pro or con," says H.D. "You catch fire or you don't catch fire."[36]

Why didn't Pound want to marry H.D.? Why did he continue to pursue her? In "Her," H.D. has George, her Pound character, say, "I think Hermione that you are going to be a tyrant."[39] In *Hilda's Book* Pound had written:

---

*Olga Rudge was an American violinist whom Pound met in Paris in 1923. She was the mother of Pound's daughter, Mary de Rachewiltz.

ONE WHOSE SOUL WAS
SO FULL OF ROSE
LEAVES STEEPED IN
GOLDEN WINE THAT THERE
WAS NO ROOM THEREIN
FOR ANY VILLEINY . . .[40]

Freud had asked H.D. why she had loved two men whom he thought had very difficult Oedipal problems. Why couldn't she love a man who had his head and his heart together? To Pound H.D. was a saint, too high for earthly pleasures.

> Out of thy purity
> Saint Hilda pray for me.
> Lay on my forehead
> The hands of thy blessing.
> Saint Hilda pray for me
> Lay on my forehead
> Cool hand of thy blessing.
> Out of thy purity
> Lay on my forehead
> White hand of thy blessing.
> *Virgo caelicola*
> *Ora pro nobis.*[41]

In *End to Torment* H.D. fantasizes about the child she and Pound might have had: "I would have the Child. But the thought, the wish, the will was cosmogonic."[42] H.D. wrote *End to Torment* in 1958. In 1959 she wrote "Winter Love," which is in some sense a realization of the wish. In response to her own question of why the relationship worked itself out in the way it did, her final answer seems to be a philosophical one: things tend to continue in the form in which they begin. The moment of birth prefigures the moment of death; the first birth had been the poem, and the last birth would be the poem. The poem is in and of itself a resolution of tensions, an expression of life.

In "Winter Love" the hoped-for child is called Esperance, Hope. This poetic child is not unrelated to a wish to be reborn into the child in herself. If she and Pound could re-create the eternal moments in their work, that imagined child would outlive their moments in time. H.D. was ever aware that her love for Pound had led to her love for Lawrence and a life in poetry. In *End to Torment* she writes: "To recall Ezra is to recall my father . . . To recall my father is to recall the cold, blazing intelligence of my 'last attachment' of the war years in London . . . This is not easy . . . Or it is easy enough in terms of *Helen and Achilles,*

my 1952, 1953, 1954 'cantos,' as Norman called them."[43] As
H.D. describes the sequence of events in "Winter Love":

> O Helen, most blest,
> O, *Virgo*, unravaged,
> but knowing the thirst
> of the moment un-mated;
> the insatiable thirst
> will lead to Achilles,
> the forest of masts,
> that moment unsatisfied,
> will brighten the earth
> with the myth and the legend,
> the exquisite breath
> of almond and apple, quince-flower,
> the pomegranate flower-cup . . .
> O, Helen, most blest,
> recall first love and last.[44]

We are reminded of Pound's early poem "Per Saecula": "I met
thee mid the roses of the past/where you gave your first kiss in the
last."[45]

Very many of the images of "Winter Love" invoke Pound's
poetry. As H.D. tells her story we see the images of the *Pisan
Cantos:*

> Comfort me, then, Odysseus, King of Men,
> But do not turn, the cold seeps through
> the fleeces and the furs, the pelts lie heavy on me
>
> but I dare not move; this is reality;
> I chose the spell, or enchantment,
> stronger than my poor will, bore Helen far,
>
> and then Achilles' eyes turned to the Sea,
> and then I felt that Paris yearned
> for his first love, Oenone,
>
> and I was left to vanish like a ghost,
> or seek the stony path, return,
> the thorns, reality;
>
> a wish, a whim, and Menelaus came;
> Theseus had long since found the gods.[46]

The pelts, furs, and later wild panther images of "Winter Love"
remind us of those lynxes of the *Pisan Cantos*. The images come
from the early days of courtship in Pennsylvania. It was cold in the
winter up in the "crow's nest" of a tree. Indoors it was not quite
so cold.

Samos? Samian? it is not so cold,
and Odysseus tears the thick furs from the couch
to make mats and a rug to the fire-place,

and light dances on the walls,
hung with rich tapestries, it seems,
though they are only bear-pelts and wild-panther,

and the fire sings, and "there are more candles,
hidden in this oat-bin," he says;
who had ridden here?

who had prepared the lodge for future visits?
who had hidden candles,
and sealed the precious Samos

in an unpainted jar
to hide it from the others?
what Love, what Lovers' tryst?[47]

Hugh Kenner writes: "He had called her 'Dryad' since Pennsylvania days, when a crow's nest high in the Doolittle's maple tree had been one of their adolescent trysting-places, and the little apple orchard in the Pounds' back garden at Wyncote another."[48] Pound had told H.D. way back then that her poetic efforts were not worthwhile. " 'You are a poem though your poem's naught,' quoted Ezra. From what?" asks H.D. "I did not ask him. We had climbed up into the big maple tree in our garden, outside Philadelphia."[49]

If Hilda was not a poet in Pennsylvania, it must be admitted she learned quickly. During her lifetime many admired her accomplishment. Had she not retreated from the public eye, the meaning of her work would not have become so obscured.

§ § §

In the fall of 1956 H.D. was severely injured. In his introduction to published portions of her Moravian novel, "The Mystery," Eric W. White,* a friend of H.D.'s, writes:

She broke her hip through slipping on a polished floor; and she never made a complete recovery from this fall. Even when she was mobile again, she could get about only with the aid of sticks. I remember a tea-party in the dining-room of the Villa Verena one afternoon, with Bryher and myself sitting down cautiously at opposite ends of the table, while H.D. stomped to her chair and then

---

*Eric W. White met H.D. in Berlin in 1931, and their friendship continued until her death. In 1976 he published in England a selection from "The Mystery" and a remembrance titled *Images of H.D.*

hurled her aluminum crutches over her shoulder with a gesture worthy of Long John Silver.[50]

On November 29 Pound wrote to H.D.: "I am sorry you bust yr/ bone and thankful you bust it in a more moderate place than is fashionable for those seeking affliction . . . I trust the mending will proceed and that you will keep off SOAP and other treacherous substances."[51]

On December 8 H.D. replied: "I don't understand what happened. I was *standing* on a small rug on a new-laid, highly waxed floor — no *faux-pas,* the whole thing puzzles me — why? There must be a *reason* for this 'retreat.' "

H.D. was understandably frustrated about her confinement. A poem written in 1957, "Sagesse," was inspired by a picture of a caged bird published in *The Listener* on May 9 of that year. The circumstances of the long hours abed (she was now seventy-one) caused her to think of the inevitability of her own death. As she writes:

> . . . "I was salt,
>
> a substance, concentrated, self-contained,
> am I to be dissolved and lost?"
>
> "it is fearful, I was a mirror, an individual,"
> cries the shallow rock-pool, "now infinity
>
> claims me; I am everything? but nothing";
> peace, salt, you were never as useful as all that,
>
> peace, flower, you are one of a thousand-thousand others,
> peace, shallow pool, be lost.[52]

This is not self-deprecation but courage in the face of the inevitable. As H.D. sensed her life drawing to a close, she felt a certain urgency about communicating with Pound.

The *Selected Poems of H.D.* was published in 1957, and on April 11 Pound wrote to H.D.:

> Am indebted to the ever industrious NHP for SElected H.D.
> And it is a good thing to have "Pallas" and "Helen" whaar they can be seen by their az etc.*

On April 3, 1958, H.D. wrote to Pearson about the *Pisan Cantos:* "Only now, after 12 years, have I been able to face the Pisan legend — I have made a few *very simple* notes on my reactions. It is Erich's interest and concern that are responsible. He always said,

---

*"az" is Pound's abbreviation for Azrael, the name H.D. gave Pound in her *Tribute to the Angels.*

'You are hiding something.' It seems, yes, my deepest depth did hide the real Ezra relationship." On July 23 she wrote to Pound: "Now, I am desperately trying to get some 'notes' in order that NHP asked me to do, on my general reactions to the Pound getaway." On November 22 Pound wrote to H.D. that he planned to visit her:

> Have had idea of looking in at Kusnacht ever since arrival.
> WANTED to do it when passes were open and transit fairly easy by car.
> Spose that is too late for this year, but some sort of rail transit is possible.

In spite of their attempts to see one another, it never happened. On November 18, 1958, H.D. sent *Helen in Egypt* to Pound. The postscript of her letter read: "Don't worry or hurry with the Helen — don't read it all — don't read it yet — don't bother to write of it." She had asked Pound if he would like to read *End to Torment,* and late in 1958 he wrote: "Yes, glad to satisfy curiosity as to how the hell you cd/ have covered 51 pages (typescript I hope) with my glories."

On October 15, 1959, H.D. wrote to Pound: "I did a sort of *Coda* ["Winter Love"] to my long, long *Helen* sequences, bringing in Odysseus, who did not feature in the original *Cantos* (as N.H.P. calls them). I felt I should send to you to see — just the *Coda.* But fear your reactions to my *altmodisch* manner." She wrote again on November 4 that she had sent the coda and added: "It might be a little *divertissement* to you to slash it to pieces and return — or not." She had not forgotten that first slash in the tea room of the British Museum.

On November 6 Pound replied: "Are you serious about slashing? . . . I have read 'Winter' twice. I think it is written better than you have done . . . and I now go back to End of Torment." Understandably, Pound was not as enthusiastic about *Helen.* He wrote in this letter: "Can't find the long Helen or the Helen Achilles that was upstairs last autumn." He assured her that "Winter" is not "divertissement." And he wrote: "Did I say driving from D.C. to boat, tried to find old Flower Obs. [Observatory], and Bird Orph, but D. H. [T. D. Horton] missed it."

During the 1950s H.D. traveled occasionally to America. "Hermetic Definition" was written in 1960, in relation to her trip to New York to receive the Gold Medal for Poetry from the American Academy of Arts and Letters.* In it she affirms her life as a poet

*The American Academy of Arts and Letters presented H.D. with the award on May 25, 1960. The award is given only once every five years. H.D. was the first

and pays a tribute to her fellow writers, specifically to the poets of the younger generation. The occasion of the award and the contact with younger voices renewed her sense of dedication to her art.

We feel a sense of sadness as we read "Hermetic Definition"; H.D. is once again reaching for life, and life is about to be lost to her forever: "But I went on, I had to go on,/the writing was the unborn,/the conception."[53] In 1959 she had written "Winter Love," and she would never again write poetry to equal its intensity. There is not much to say about H.D.'s "death" poetry; it hardly exists. Her feeling for life, even at the end, was insatiable. In "Winter Love" she writes:

> they said there was a Child in *Leuké,*
> they said it was the Child, Euphorion,
>
> Achilles' Child, grandam,
> or fantasy of Paris and a Child
> or a wild moment that begot a Child,
>
> when long ago, the *Virgo* breasts swelled
> under the savage kiss of ravening Odysseus;
> yes, yes, grandam, but actually and in reality,
>
> small fists unclosed, small hands fondled me,
> and in the inmost dark,
> small feet searched foot-hold,
>
> Hermione lived her life and lives in history;
> Euphorion, *Espérance,* the infinite bliss,
> lives in the hope of something that will be,
>
> the past made perfect;
> this is the tangible
> this is reality.[54]

Life is the reality. Poetry will live on; other poets will continue to write. H.D. has always been a poet loved by poets. It was poets who first discovered and worshiped her work; it has been poets who have kept her work before the public. "The experience of passionate life in its old age, facing death, finds glorious voice, a primary testament of poetry," wrote Robert Duncan upon the publication of *Hermetic Definition.*[55] "Winged words make their own spiral," said H.D. when she received the Gold Medal for Poetry. "Caught up in them we are lost, or found."

H.D. suffered a stroke on June 6, 1961. She regained consciousness but was not able to communicate to her satisfaction, for the

woman to win it; W. H. Auden, St. John Perse, and Jorge Guillén had preceded her.

part of the brain that controls speech had been injured. Pearson reports that she would strike her breast in "passionate frustration" when no words would come.[56]

H.D. died on September 28, 1961, at the age of seventy-five. On September 29 Bryher wrote to Aldington to inform him. She reported that on Wednesday night at about nine-thirty the doctor had phoned to say that Hilda had just died. H.D.'s doctor had seen her in the afternoon; an advance copy of *Helen in Egypt* had arrived that day and she seemed particularly happy. H.D.'s ashes were flown home to be placed beside the remains of her parents and other relatives in Bethlehem, Pennsylvania.

§ § §

H.D. ended her volume of *Selected Poems* with "Epitaph."

> So I may say,
> "I died of living,
> having lived one hour";
>
> so they may say,
> "she died soliciting
> illicit fervour,"
>
> so you may say,
> "Greek flower; Greek ecstasy
> reclaims forever
>
> one who died
> following
> intricate song's lost measure."[57]

H.D. had experienced an "illicit fervour" and had transgressed the mores of society — a slight offense by today's standards, and no offense at all according to the higher standards of love and courage by which she lived most of her life. But she had come from an American middle-class home; she had been reared according to strict Victorian values. The subject of her transgression was the one recurring theme of her work. She had forgiven everyone who had wronged her; did she ever forgive herself?

In 1975 Perdita Schaffner, H.D.'s daughter, published in *Paideuma* a beautiful account of her 1962 meeting with Ezra Pound. She speaks of the death of her mother and writes: "Among my condolence letters was one from 'E.P.' He began with a simple reference to sixty years of devotion; he ended with the line, 'algae of long past sea currents are moved.'"[58]

Ezra Pound had stayed in close touch with H.D.'s work throughout his life. He had been deeply moved by "Winter

Love," and she was satisfied that she and Pound had reached some kind of understanding. Remembering the experiences they had shared in Pennsylvania, Pound had written to H.D. on June 10, 1960: "Wonder if anything left @ Bethlehem, Wolle, etc." As H.D. had written in "Winter Love": "There was a Helen before there was a War,/Odysseus remembered her . . ."[59]

 Notes

PREFACE

1. L. S. Dembo, ed., "Norman Holmes Pearson on H.D.: An Interview," *Contemporary Literature* 10 (Autumn 1969): 439.
2. Robert Duncan, jacket note to H.D., *Hermetic Definition* (New York: New Directions, 1972).
3. Lionel Durand, "Life in a Hothouse." *Newsweek* 55 (May 2, 1960): 92, 93.

I

1. H.D., "The Gift," Hilda Doolittle-Norman Holmes Pearson Collection of American Literature, Beinecke Rare Book and Manuscript Library, Yale University, New Haven, Conn.; ch. I, p. 10. Hereafter this collection will be referred to simply as Beinecke Library, Yale.
2. H.D., *Tribute to Freud, Writing on the Wall, Advent* (Boston: David R. Godine, 1974), p. 34.
3. Ibid., p. 31.
4. H.D., "The Dream," *Contemporary Literature* 10 (Autumn 1969): 619.
5. Ibid., p. 617.
6. H.D., *Tribute to Freud*, p. 115.
7. H.D., *End to Torment* (New York: New Directions, 1979), p. 41.
8. Ibid.
9. H.D., *Tribute to Freud*, p. 31.
10. H.D., "The Gift," ch. I, p. 4.
11. H.D., "The Dream," p. 618.
12. H.D., "The Death of Martin Presser," *Quarterly Review of Literature* 13, nos. 3, 4 (1965): 241–42.
13. Jacob John Sessler, *Communal Pietism Among Early American Moravians* (New York: Holt, 1933), p. 8.
14. Norman Holmes Pearson, "Foreword," in H.D., *Hermetic Definition* (New York: New Directions, 1972), p. v.
15. H.D., "The Dream," p. 610.
16. Ibid.
17. Ibid., pp. 610–11.
18. Ibid., pp. 611–12.

19. Ibid., p. 615.
20. Ibid., p. 617.
21. Ibid., p. 618.
22. Ibid., pp. 618–19, 621.
23. H.D., "Paint It Today," Beinecke Library, Yale; ch. II, p. 12.
24. William Carlos Williams, "A Letter from William Carlos Williams to Norman Holmes Pearson Concerning Hilda Doolittle and Her Mother and Father," *William Carlos Williams Newsletter* 2, no. 2: 2.
25. Emily Wallace, "Afterword: The House of the Father's Science and the Mother's Art," *William Carlos Williams Newsletter* 2, no. 2: 4.
26. Ibid.
27. William Carlos Williams, *The Autobiography of William Carlos Williams* (New York: Random House, 1951), pp. 68–69.
28. Williams, "A Letter," pp. 2–3.

2

1. William Carlos Williams, *The Autobiography of William Carlos Williams* (New York: Random House, 1951), p. 67.
2. Charles Norman, *Ezra Pound* (New York: Macmillan, 1960), p. 5.
3. Ibid., p. 3.
4. Noel Stock, *The Life of Ezra Pound* (New York: Avon, 1970), pp. 42–43.
5. Quoted in Stock, *Life of Ezra Pound*, p. 41.
6. Quoted in Norman, *Ezra Pound*, p. 6.
7. Williams, *Autobiography*, pp. 67–68.
8. H.D., *End to Torment* (New York: New Directions, 1979), pp. 22–23.
9. Ibid., p. 17.
10. Ibid., pp. 3–4.
11. H.D., "Her," Beinecke Library, Yale; pp. 87–88.
12. H.D., *End to Torment*, p. 14.
13. H.D., "Her," p. 114.
14. H.D., *End to Torment*, p. 14.
15. H.D., "Her," pp. 118–19.
16. Ibid., pp. 119–20.
17. Norman, *Ezra Pound*, p. 5.
18. H.D., *End to Torment*, p. 48.
19. H.D., "Her," pp. 70, 73–74.
20. Ibid., p. 79.
21. Ibid., pp. 217–18.
22. Ibid., p. 80.
23. Ibid., pp. 80–81.
24. Ibid., p. 98.
25. Ibid., p. 101.
26. Ibid., p. 209.
27. Ibid., pp. 241–42.
28. Ibid., pp. 223–24.
29. Ibid., p. 252.

3

1. H.D., *End to Torment* (New York: New Directions, 1979), p. 15.
2. Ibid.
3. Ibid., pp. 47–48.

4. Ezra Pound, *Collected Early Poems of Ezra Pound,* ed. Michael J. King (New York: New Directions, 1976), p. 322.
5. Ibid., p. 252.
6. Ezra Pound, "Troubadours — Their Sorts and Conditions," in *Literary Essays of Ezra Pound* (New York: New Directions, 1968), p. 94.
7. H.D., "Paint It Today," Beinecke Library, Yale; ch. IV, pp. 7–8.
8. H.D., *End to Torment,* pp. 17–18.
9. H.D., "Paint It Today," ch. IV, pp. 16–17.
10. Ibid., ch. I, p. 13.
11. Noel Stock, *The Life of Ezra Pound* (New York: Avon, 1970), p. 152.
12. H.D., *End to Torment,* p. 18.
13. F. S. Flint quoting Ezra Pound, "Imagisme," *Poetry* (March 1913), p. 199.
14. H.D., *End to Torment,* p. 18.
15. Ezra Pound, *The Letters of Ezra Pound, 1907–41,* ed. D. D. Paige (New York: Harcourt, Brace, 1950), p. 11.
16. Harriet Monroe, "Notes," *Poetry* (January 1913), p. 135.

4

1. H.D., *End to Torment* (New York: New Directions, 1979), p. 40.
2. Richard Aldington, *Life for Life's Sake* (1941; reprint ed., London: Cassell, 1968), p. 122.
3. Ibid.
4. W. R. Paton, trans., *The Greek Anthology* (Cambridge: Harvard University Press, 1916), vol. 1, bk. VI, no. 232.
5. Ibid., vol. 5, bk. XVI, no. 236.
6. H.D., "Priapus," *Poetry* (January 1913): 122–23, published with minor changes as "Orchard" in *Collected Poems of H.D.* (New York: Boni and Liveright, 1925), pp. 40–41.
7. Paton, *Greek Anthology,* vol. 1, bk. VI, no. 299.
8. H.D., "Hermes of the Ways," *Poetry* (January 1913): 118–20, published with minor changes in *Collected Poems,* pp. 55–57.
9. H.D., *End to Torment,* p. 19.
10. Sigmund Freud, *A General Introduction to Psychoanalysis,* trans. J. Riviere (1924; reprint ed., New York: Washington Square Press, 1960), p. 286.
11. Ezra Pound, *The Letters of Ezra Pound, 1907–41,* ed. D. D. Paige (New York: Harcourt, Brace, 1950), p. 11.
12. H.D., *End to Torment,* p. 15.
13. H.D., *Helen in Egypt* (1961; reprint ed., New York: New Directions, 1974), p. 232.
14. L. S. Dembo, ed., "Norman Holmes Pearson on H.D.: An Interview," *Contemporary Literature* 10 (Autumn 1969): 437.
15. H.D., *End to Torment,* pp. 3–4, 12.
16. See Norman N. Holland, "H.D. and the 'Blameless Physician,' " *Contemporary Literature* 10 (Autumn 1969): 474–506; and Holland, *Poems in Persons: An Introduction to the Psychoanalysis of Literature* (New York: W. W. Norton, 1975). See also Joseph N. Riddel, "H.D. and the Poetics of 'Spiritual Realism,' " *Contemporary Literature* 10 (Autumn 1969): 447–73; and Susan Friedman, "Who Buried H.D.? A Poet, Her Critics, and Her Place in the Literary Tradition," *College English* 36, no. 7 (1975): 801–14.
17. W. Rhys Roberts, trans., in *Criticism,* ed. Mark Schorer, Josephine Miles, and Gordon McKenzie (New York: Harcourt, Brace & World, 1958), p. 14.
18. Ibid., p. 16.

19. Plato, *The Dialogues of Plato,* trans. Benjamin Jowett, ed. William Chase Green (New York: Boni and Liveright, 1927), p. 127.
20. Ezra Pound, "A Retrospect," in *Literary Essays of Ezra Pound* (New York: New Directions, 1968), p. 12.

5

1. H.D., "Paint It Today," Beinecke Library, Yale; ch. I, p. 7.
2. H.D., *End to Torment* (New York: New Directions, 1979), p. 30.
3. H.D., "Asphodel," Beinecke Library, Yale; bk. I, pp. 179–80.
4. H.D., "Paint It Today," ch. III, p. 1.
5. Ibid., ch. IV, p. 18.
6. H.D., "Asphodel," bk. II, p. 179.
7. Amy Lowell, *Tendencies in Modern American Poetry* (New York: Macmillan, 1919), p. 253.
8. John Cournos, *Miranda Masters* (New York: Knopf, 1926), p. 269.
9. H.D., *Hermetic Definition* (New York: New Directions, 1972), p. 110.
10. Cournos, *Miranda Masters,* p. 268.
11. H.D., *End to Torment,* p. 5.
12. Ezra Pound, "Troubadours — Their Sorts and Conditions," in *Literary Essays of Ezra Pound* (New York: New Directions, 1968), p. 94.
13. H.D., *End to Torment,* p. 5.
14. Ibid., p. 26.
15. H.D. to Amy Lowell, November 23, 1914, Houghton Library, Harvard University, Cambridge, Mass.
16. Ezra Pound, "A Retrospect," in *Literary Essays,* p. 6.
17. H.D., *Collected Poems of H.D.* (New York: Boni and Liveright, 1925), p. 88.
18. Ezra Pound, *Personae: The Collected Poems of Ezra Pound* (New York: New Directions, 1926, 1952), p. 110.
19. Louis L. Martz, "Introduction," in *Collected Early Poems of Ezra Pound,* ed. Michael J. King (New York: New Directions, 1976), p. viii.
20. Pound, *Personae,* p. 116.
21. Martz, "Introduction," p. vii.
22. Ezra Pound, "Foreword" (1964), in *A Lume Spento* (1908; reprint ed., New York: New Directions, 1965), p. 7.
23. Pound to Harriet Monroe, August 18, 1912, in *The Letters of Ezra Pound, 1907–41,* ed. D. D. Paige (New York: Harcourt, Brace, 1950), p. 9.
24. Ezra Pound, "Middle-Aged (A Study in Emotion)," *Poetry* (October 1912), p. 8.
25. H.D., "Her," Beinecke Library, Yale; p. 213.
26. Ibid., pp. 43–44, 29.
27. Ibid., p. 78.
28. Ibid., p. 115.
29. Ibid.
30. Ibid., p. 144.

6

1. F. S. Flint, "The History of Imagism," *Egoist* (May 1, 1915), p. 70.
2. Ibid., p. 71.
3. Flint to Richard Aldington, January 12, 1915; quoted in S. Foster Damon, *Amy Lowell: A Chronicle* (Boston and New York: Houghton Mifflin, 1935), p. 203.

4. Flint, "History of Imagism," p. 71.
5. Ibid.
6. T. E. Hulme, *Speculations,* ed. Herbert Read (London: Kegan Paul, Trench Trubner, 1936), p. 136. Hulme is citing Plato in this quotation.
7. Ibid., pp. 139–40.
8. Ezra Pound, "A Retrospect," in *Literary Essays of Ezra Pound* (New York: New Directions, 1968), p. 9.
9. Ibid., p. 4.
10. Ibid., pp. 4–5.
11. *Some Imagist Poets* (1915, 1916, 1917; reprint ed., New York: Kraus Reprint, 1969), p. 24.
12. Ibid., p. 25.
13. Ibid., p. 27.
14. Pound, "A Retrospect," p. 12.
15. Ibid., p. 9.
16. H.D., "Oread," published with minor changes in *Collected Poems of H.D.* (New York: Boni and Liveright, 1925), p. 81.
17. Hulme, *Speculations,* p. 132.
18. Ibid., p. 133.
19. H.D., *Helen in Egypt* (1961; reprint ed., New York: New Directions, 1974), p. 54.
20. H.D., *Trilogy* (New York: New Directions, 1973), p. 53.
21. See Glenn Hughes, *Imagism and the Imagists* (1931; reprint ed., New York: Humanities Press, 1960); also William Pratt, ed., *The Imagist Poem* (New York; Dutton, 1963), and Pratt, "Ezra Pound and the Image," in *Ezra Pound: The London Years, 1908–1920,* ed. Philip Grover (New York: AMS Press, 1978).

7

1. Norman Holmes Pearson, personal interview, January 7, 1970.
2. H.D., "Hermonax," published with minor changes in *Collected Poems of H.D.* (New York: Boni and Liveright, 1925), pp. 86–87.
3. Brigit Patmore, *My Friends When Young* (London: Heinemann, 1968), p. 103.
4. H.D. to John Cournos, Houghton Library, Harvard University, Cambridge, Mass.
5. Otto Rank, *The Myth of the Birth of the Hero* (New York: Vintage, 1964), p. 246.
6. *Some Imagist Poets* (1915, 1916, 1917; reprint ed., New York: Kraus Reprint, 1969), pp. 25–26.

8

1. F. S. Flint, "Imagisme," *Poetry* (March 1913), p. 128.
2. Pound to Harriet Monroe, October 1912, in *The Letters of Ezra Pound, 1907–41,* ed. D. D. Paige (New York: Harcourt, Brace, 1950), p. 11.
3. F. S. Flint, "The History of Imagism," *Egoist* (May 1, 1915), p. 71.
4. Quoted in K. K. Ruthven, *A Guide to Ezra Pound's Personae (1926)* (Berkeley: University of California Press, 1969), p. 16 n.
5. S. Foster Damon, *Amy Lowell: A Chronicle* (Boston and New York: Houghton Mifflin, 1935), p. 196.
6. Ezra Pound, *"Love Poems and Others,* by D. H. Lawrence," *Poetry* (July 1913), p. 149.

7. Ibid., pp. 150–51.
8. Pound to Harriet Monroe, March 1913, in *The Letters of Ezra Pound*, p. 17.
9. Damon, *Amy Lowell*, pp. 236–37.
10. Ibid., p. 244.
11. Lowell to Harriet Monroe, September 15, 1914; quoted in Damon, *Amy Lowell*, p. 237.
12. Richard Aldington, *Life for Life's Sake* (1941; reprint ed., London: Cassell, 1968), p. 127.
13. Ibid.
14. Damon, *Amy Lowell*, p. 281.
15. Ibid., p. 304.
16. William Ellery Leonard, "The New Poetry — A Critique," quoted in Glenn Hughes, *Imagism and the Imagists* (1931; reprint ed., New York: Humanities Press, 1960), p. 56.
17. O. W. Firkins, "The New Movement in Poetry," quoted in Hughes, *Imagism and the Imagists*, pp. 60–61.
18. Quoted in Hughes, *Imagism and the Imagists*, pp. 50–51.
19. "Imagism: Another View," quoted in Hughes, *Imagism and the Imagists*, p. 52.
20. Hughes, *Imagism and the Imagists*, p. 112.
21. Herbert S. Gorman, "A Poet Who Drinks at the Pierian Spring," *New York Times Book Review* (August 31, 1924), p. 5.
22. Ezra Pound, "Exile's Letter,' *Poetry* (March 1915), p. 261; published with minor changes in *Personae: The Collected Poems of Ezra Pound* (New York: New Directions, 1926), p. 136.

9

1. John Gould Fletcher, "H.D.'s Vision," *Poetry* (February 1917), pp. 266–67.
2. Hugh Kenner, *The Pound Era* (Berkeley: University of California Press, 1971), p. 33.
3. Ibid.
4. L. S. Dembo, ed., "Norman Holmes Pearson on H.D.: An Interview," *Contemporary Literature* 10 (Autumn 1969): 441.
5. Benjamin Lee Whorf, *Language, Thought, and Reality*, ed. J. B. Carroll (Cambridge, Mass.: MIT Press, 1964), pp. 59–60.
6. H.D., *Palimpsest* (1926; reprint ed., Carbondale: University of Southern Illinois Press, 1968), p. 166.
7. Ezra Pound, *Gaudier-Brzeska: A Memoir* (1916; reprint ed., New York: New Directions, 1970), p. 84.
8. H.D., *Hedylus* (Stratford: Basil Blackwell and Houghton Mifflin, 1928), p. 66.
9. Robert Graves, *The Greek Myths*, vol. I (Baltimore: Penguin, 1955), p. 153.
10. H.D., "Incantation," *Egoist* (February 2, 1914), p. 55; published with changes as "Orion Dead" in *Collected Poems of H.D.* (New York: Boni and Liveright, 1925), p. 84.

10

1. Harriet Monroe, *Poets and Their Art* (Freeport, New York: Books for Libraries Press, 1967), p. 92.
2. Ibid., pp. 93, 98.
3. Ibid., p. 93.

4. Bryher [pseud.], *The Heart to Artemis: A Writer's Memoirs* (New York: Harcourt, Brace & World, 1962), p. 271.

5. Jacob John Sessler, *Communal Pietism Among Early American Moravians* (New York: Holt, 1933), pp. 108–109.

6. Ibid., pp. 150, 148.

7. Ibid., p. 146.

8. Ibid., p. 117.

9. *Homily of Wounds*, p. 83 ff.; quoted in Sessler, *Communal Pietism*, p. 151.

10. Sessler, *Communal Pietism*, p. 151.

11. H.D., *Hermetic Definition* (New York: New Directions, 1972), p. 105.

12. H.D., "The Gift," Beinecke Library, Yale; ch. V, p. 23.

13. *Collection of Hymns* (1754), pt. II, no. 99; quoted in Sessler, *Communal Pietism*, p. 140.

14. Sessler, *Communal Pietism*, p. 128.

15. H.D., "The Death of Martin Presser," *Quarterly Review of Literature* 13, nos. 3, 4 (1965): 241–42.

16. H.D., "Zinzendorf Notes," Beinecke Library, Yale.

17. H.D., "The Gift," ch. V, p. 19.

18. Henry Rimius, *A Candid Narrative of the Rise and Progress of the Herrnhuters, Commonly Called Moravians . . .* (London: A. Linde, 1752), p. 121.

19. Sessler, *Communal Pietism*, p. 127.

20. Ibid.

21. Ibid., p. 120.

22. *The Litany Book* (London, 1759), p. 196; quoted in Sessler, *Communal Pietism*, p. 118.

23. Sessler, *Communal Pietism*, p. 116.

24. *Zugabe III*, no. 2, 305, translation, *Collection of Hymns* (1749), pt. III; quoted in Sessler, *Communal Pietism*, p. 164.

25. Sessler, *Communal Pietism*, p. 176.

26. H.D., "Hymen," *Poetry* (December 1919), p. 127; published with minor changes in *Collected Poems of H.D.* (New York: Boni and Liveright, 1925), pp. 157–58.

27. Sigmund Freud, "Analysis Terminable and Interminable," in *Therapy and Technique,* ed. Philip Rieff (New York: Collier Books, 1963), pp. 258–59.

I I

1. Richard Aldington, "The Poetry of Ezra Pound," *Egoist* (May 1, 1915), p. 72.

2. F. S. Flint, "The Poetry of H.D.," *Egoist* (May 1, 1915), p. 72.

3. John Gould Fletcher, "Chicago," *Egoist* (May 1, 1915), p. 74.

4. Ford Madox Ford, "Those Were the Days," in *Imagist Anthology* (London: Chatto and Windus, 1930), pp. xv–xvi.

5. Ibid., p. xiv.

6. S. Foster Damon, *Amy Lowell: A Chronicle* (Boston and New York: Houghton Mifflin, 1935), p. 240.

7. D. H. Lawrence, *The Letters of D. H. Lawrence,* ed. Aldous Huxley (London: Heinemann, 1932), p. 207.

8. H.D., *Bid Me to Live* (New York: Grove, 1960), p. 141.

9. Richard Aldington, *Life for Life's Sake* (1941; reprint ed., London: Cassell, 1968), pp. 127–28.

10. Lawrence to Amy Lowell, August 22, 1914; quoted in Damon, *Amy Lowell,* p. 248.

11. Damon, *Amy Lowell*, p. 249.
12. Quoted by Horace Gregory in "Introduction," in H.D., *Helen in Egypt* (1961; reprint ed., New York: New Directions, 1974), p. ix.
13. K. W. Gransden, *"Rananim:* D. H. Lawrence's Letters to S. S. Koteliansky," quoted in *The Quest for Rananim: D. H. Lawrence's Letters to S. S. Koteliansky,* ed. George J. Zytaruk (Montreal: McGill-Queen's University Press, 1970), p. xxxiv.
14. Emile Delavenay, *D. H. Lawrence: The Man and His Work,* trans. Katherine M. Delavenay (London: Heinemann, 1972), p. 262.
15. Aldington to Edward Nehls, January 18, 1952; quoted in *D. H. Lawrence: A Composite Biography,* ed. Edward Nehls, vol. I (Madison: University of Wisconsin Press, 1957), pp. 569–70.
16. Lawrence, *The Quest for Rananim,* p. 22.
17. Lawrence, *Letters,* p. 215.
18. H.D., *Bid Me to Live,* p. 65.
19. Ibid.
20. H.D., "Compassionate Friendship," Beinecke Library, Yale; p. 54.
21. Glenn Hughes, *Imagism and the Imagists* (1931; reprint ed., New York: Humanities Press, 1960), p. 170.
22. In his introduction to the Godine edition of H.D.'s *Tribute to Freud,* Professor Kenneth Fields writes, "Lawrence had described his character [in *The Man Who Died*] in terms that apply very clearly to H.D." Fields also states that Professor Irwin Swerdlow informed him that Stephen Guest's report "is very likely true."
23. D. H. Lawrence, "Don Juan," *Poetry* (December 1914), p. 105.
24. D. H. Lawrence, "Service of All the Dead," *Poetry* (December 1914), p. 104.
25. H.D., "The Wind Sleepers," *Poetry* (March 1915), pp. 265–66.

12

1. May Sinclair, "Two Notes," *Egoist* (June 1, 1915), p. 88.
2. Ibid., p. 89.
3. Pound to A. R. Orage, April 1919, in *The Letters of Ezra Pound, 1907–41,* ed. D. D. Paige (New York: Harcourt, Brace, 1950), pp. 148–49.
4. H.D., "The Gift," Beinecke Library, Yale; ch. IV, pp. 4–5.
5. H.D., trans., "Choruses from Iphigeneia in Aulis," *Egoist* (November 1, 1915), pp. 171–72.
6. H.D., trans., *Choruses from the Iphigeneia in Aulis and the Hippolytus of Euripides* (London: Egoist, 1919), p. 16.
7. H.D., "Choruses from Iphigeneia in Aulis," p. 172.
8. T. Earle Welby, "Preface," in *The Complete Works of Walter Savage Landor,* ed. T. Earle Welby, vol. I (1927–36; reprint ed., London: Methuen, 1969), p. viii.
9. H.D., trans., *Choruses from the Iphigeneia in Aulis and the Hippolytus of Euripides,* p. 13ff.
10. Bryher [pseud.], *The Heart to Artemis: A Writer's Memoirs* (New York: Harcourt, Brace & World, 1962), p. 204.
11. H.D., *Helen in Egypt* (1961; reprint ed., New York: New Directions, 1974), p. 73.
12. S. H. Butcher, trans., in *Criticism,* ed. Mark Schorer, Josephine Miles, and Gordon McKenzie (New York: Harcourt, Brace & World, 1958), p. 205.

13

1. Forster to D. H. Lawrence, February 12, 1915; quoted in Paul Delaney, *D. H. Lawrence's Nightmare* (New York: Basic Books, 1978), p. 54.
2. H.D., "Compassionate Friendship," Beinecke Library, Yale; p. 50.
3. Lawrence to Cecil Gray, November 7, 1917, in *The Collected Letters of D. H. Lawrence,* ed. Harry T. Moore, vol. I (New York: Viking, 1962), p. 532.
4. Richard Aldington, *Life for Life's Sake* (1941; reprint ed., London: Cassell, 1968), p. 127.
5. H.D., "Compassionate Friendship," p. 51.
6. D. H. Lawrence, *New Poems* (London: Martin Secker, 1919), p. 49.
7. D. H. Lawrence, "Note," in *The Collected Poems of D. H. Lawrence* (1928; reprint ed., London: Martin Secker, 1932), p. vi.
8. D. H. Lawrence, *Bay* (Westminster, England: Beaumont Press, 1919), p. 32.
9. H.D., *Helen in Egypt* (1961; reprint ed., New York: New Directions, 1974), p. 263.
10. Ibid., pp. 89–90.
11. H.D., "Notes on Thought and Vision," Beinecke Library, Yale; p. 18.
12. Lawrence, *Bay,* pp. 27–28.
13. D. H. Lawrence, *St. Mawr* and *The Man Who Died* (1925, 1929; reprint ed., New York: Vintage, 1953), pp. 204–205.
14. D. H. Lawrence, "Resurrection," *Poetry* (June 1917), p. 139.
15. D. H. Lawrence, *The Complete Poems of D. H. Lawrence,* ed. V. Pinto and F. W. Roberts (New York: Viking, 1964), p. 755.
16. H.D., *Selected Poems* (New York: Grove, 1957), p. 69.
17. H.D., *Helen in Egypt,* p. 199.
18. Ibid., p. 264.
19. H.D., *Collected Poems of H.D.* (New York: Boni and Liveright, 1925), p. 176.
20. Ibid., p. 205.
21. H.D., *Bid Me to Live* (New York: Grove, 1960), p. 57.
22. H.D., "She Rebukes Hippolyta," in *Collected Poems,* pp. 205–206.
23. Lawrence, *Complete Poems,* p. 753.
24. Ibid.
25. Ibid., pp. 737–38.
26. Ibid., p. 751.
27. Ibid., p. 754.
28. Ibid., p. 756.
29. Ibid., p. 759.
30. Ibid.
31. Ibid.
32. H.D., "Paint It Today," Beinecke Library, Yale; ch. V, p. 13.
33. H.D., "Autobiographical Notes," Beinecke Library, Yale; p. 11.
34. H.D., "Notes on Recent Writing," Beinecke Library, Yale; p. 1.
35. Ibid., pp. 2, 5, 9–10.
36. Ibid., pp. 44–45.
37. Ibid., p. 59.

14

1. Lawrence to Dollie Radford, January 15, 1916; quoted in *D. H. Lawrence: A Composite Biography,* ed. Edward Nehls, vol. I (Madison: University of Wisconsin Press, 1957), p. 355.

2. Cyrena N. Pondrom, "Selected Letters from H.D. to F. S. Flint: A Commentary on the Imagist Period," *Contemporary Literature* 10 (Autumn 1969): 564–65.

3. Ibid., p. 570.

4. H.D., "Compassionate Friendship," Beinecke Library, Yale; p. 61.

5. H.D., *Collected Poems of H.D.* (New York: Boni and Liveright, 1925), pp. 248–49.

6. D. H. Lawrence, "On That Day," in *New Poems* (London: Martin Secker, 1919), p. 64.

7. H.D., *Bid Me to Live* (New York: Grove, 1960), p. 165.

8. Norman Holmes Pearson, "A Selection of Poetry and Prose Introduction," *Contemporary Literature* 10 (Autumn 1969): 587.

9. H.D., "Amaranth," *Contemporary Literature* 10 (Autumn 1969): 594.

10. H.D., *Collected Poems*, p. 272.

11. Ibid., pp. 195–96.

12. H.D., *Some Imagist Poets* (1916; reprint ed., New York: Kraus Reprint, 1969), pp. 21–25.

13. Lawrence to Radford, p. 355.

14. Pondrom, "Selected Letters," p. 568.

15. H.D., *Some Imagist Poets* 1916, pp. 26–28.

16. H.D., *Collected Poems*, p. 12.

17. Pondrom, "Selected Letters," p. 565.

18. H.D., *Collected Poems*, pp. 12–15.

19. Ezra Pound, "I Gather the Limbs of Osiris," *The New Age* (January 18, 1912), p. 251.

20. H.D., "The Last Gift," *Egoist* (March 1, 1916), p. 35.

21. H.D., *Collected Poems*, pp. 25, 27.

15

1. H.D., *Bid Me to Live* (New York: Grove, 1960), pp. 111–12.

2. Ibid.

3. H.D., "Notes on Recent Writing," Beinecke Library, Yale; p. 1.

4. Ibid., p. 60.

5. H.D., *Bid Me to Live*, p. 173.

6. Ibid.

7. Ibid., p. 171.

8. Ibid., p. 175.

9. Ibid., p. 177.

10. Ibid., p. 181.

11. Ibid., pp. 181–82.

12. Ibid., p. 183.

13. Ibid., p. 35.

14. Ibid., p. 11.

15. Ibid., pp. 10–11.

16. Ibid., p. 46.

17. Ibid., p. 35.

18. Ibid., p. 47.

19. Ibid.

20. Ibid., p. 50.

21. H.D., *Helen in Egypt* (1961; reprint ed., New York: New Directions, 1974), p. 126.

22. H.D., *Bid Me to Live*, p. 52.

23. H.D., *Helen in Egypt*, p. 142.
24. H.D., *Bid Me to Live*, p. 50.
25. Ibid., p. 51.
26. Ibid.
27. Ibid.
28. Ibid., p. 52.
29. Ibid., pp. 55–56.
30. H.D., "Eurydice," *Egoist* (May 1917), p. 54.
31. H.D., *Bid Me to Live*, p. 61.
32. Ibid., p. 164.
33. Ibid., p. 61.
34. H.D., "Eurydice," p. 54.
35. Ibid.
36. H.D., *Bid Me to Live*, p. 173.
37. D. H. Lawrence, *John Thomas and Lady Jane* (New York: Viking, 1972), pp. 85–86.
38. H.D., *Bid Me to Live*, p. 173.
39. Ibid., p. 56.
40. Ibid., p. 54.
41. Ibid., pp. 54–55.
42. Ibid.
43. Ibid., pp. 57–58.
44. Ibid.
45. H.D., *Helen in Egypt*, p. 20.
46. H.D., *Bid Me to Live*, p. 62.
47. Ibid., p. 63.
48. Ibid., p. 67.
49. Ibid., p. 68.
50. Ibid., pp. 68–69.
51. H.D., *Helen in Egypt*, p. 110.
52. H.D., *Bid Me to Live*, p. 73, 71.
53. Ibid., p. 71.

16

1. Richard Aldington, *Portrait of a Genius, But . . .* (London: Heinemann, 1950), p. 335.
2. D. H. Lawrence, *The Collected Letters of D. H. Lawrence,* ed. Harry T. Moore, vol. II (New York: Viking, 1962), p. 1096.
3. D. H. Lawrence, *The Quest for Rananim: D. H. Lawrence's Letters to S. S. Koteliansky,* ed. George J. Zytaruk (Montreal: McGill-Queen's University Press, 1970), p. 366.
4. D. H. Lawrence, *The First Lady Chatterley* (New York: Dial, 1944), pp. 55, 99.
5. Harry T. Moore, *The Priest of Love* (New York: Farrar, Straus, Giroux, 1974), p. 422.
6. Ibid.
7. Ibid.
8. Ibid., p. 427.
9. Aldington to H.D., April 29, 1948; Beinecke Library, Yale.
10. Harry T. Moore, "Richard Aldington in His Last Years," in *Richard Aldington: An Intimate Portrait*, ed. A. Kershaw and F. J. Temple (Carbondale: Southern Illinois University Press, 1965), p. 85.

11. Aldington to H.D., June 8, 1961; Beinecke Library, Yale.
12. D. H. Lawrence, *Lady Chatterley's Lover* (1928; reprint ed., New York: Grove, 1962), p. 38.
13. Lawrence, *Collected Letters,* vol. II, p. 978.
14. D. H. Lawrence, *John Thomas and Lady Jane* (New York: Viking, 1972), p. 6.
15. Quoted in Moore, "Aldington in His Last Years," p. 98.
16. H.D., "Paint It Today," Beinecke Library, Yale; ch. V, pp. 13–14.
17. Lawrence, *John Thomas,* p. 86.
18. Ibid., p. 85.
19. Ibid., p. 169.
20. Ibid., p. 83.
21. H.D., "Paint It Today," ch. V, p. 14.
22. Lawrence, *John Thomas,* p. 94.
23. H.D., "Paint It Today," ch. V, p. 15.
24. Lawrence, *Lady Chatterley's Lover,* p. 110.
25. Lawrence, *John Thomas,* p. 114.
26. H.D., "Paint It Today," ch. V, p. 15.
27. Lawrence, *John Thomas,* p. 168.
28. H.D., *Helen in Egypt* (1961; reprint ed., New York: New Directions, 1974), p. 8.
29. Lawrence, *John Thomas,* p. 232.
30. H.D., "Paint It Today," ch. III, p. 6.
31. Ibid., ch. V, p. 14.
32. H.D., *End to Torment* (New York: New Directions, 1979), p. 8.
33. D. H. Lawrence, *The Quest for Rananim,* pp. 170–71.
34. Ibid., p. 165.
35. H.D., "Compassionate Friendship," Beinecke Library, Yale; pp. 51–52.
36. H.D., *Tribute to Freud, Writing on the Wall, Advent* (Boston: David R. Godine, 1974), pp. 40–41.
37. H.D., "Compassionate Friendship," p. 35.
38. Ibid., p. 34.
39. Lawrence to H.D., August 10, 1929; quoted in Harry T. Moore, *The Intelligent Heart — The Story of D. H. Lawrence* (New York: Farrar, Straus, and Young, 1954), p. 415.
40. Ibid.
41. Aldington to Moore, October 23, 1959; quoted in Moore, "Aldington in His Last Years," p. 88.
42. H.D., "Compassionate Friendship," p. 35.
43. Ibid., p. 44.
44. Ibid., p. 50.
45. Ibid., p. 42.
46. Ibid., p. 61.
47. Ibid.
48. Ibid., p. 65.

17

1. D. H. Lawrence, *The First Lady Chatterley* (New York: Dial, 1944), p. 113.
2. Ibid., p. 127.
3. Ibid., p. 173.
4. H.D., *Bid Me to Live* (New York: Grove, 1960), p. 138.

5. Ibid., p. 139.
6. Ibid., p. 121.
7. Lawrence to Martin Secker, September 2, 1926; quoted in Keith Sagar, *D. H. Lawrence: A Calendar of His Works* (Austin: University of Texas Press, 1979), p. 153.
8. Sagar, *D. H. Lawrence,* pp. 154–55.
9. Ibid.
10. Ibid.
11. Lawrence to Else Jaffe-Richthofen, January 10, 1927; quoted in Frieda Lawrence, *Not I, But the Wind . . .* (New York: Viking, 1934), p. 220.
12. Lawrence to Secker, January 8, 1927; quoted in Sagar, *D. H. Lawrence,* p. 157.
13. Lawrence to Dorothy Brett, December 6, 1926; quoted in Sagar, *D. H. Lawrence,* p. 156.
14. Lawrence to Brett, December 19, 1926; quoted in Sagar, *D. H. Lawrence,* p. 156.
15. Ibid., p. 157.
16. D. H. Lawrence, *The Letters of D. H. Lawrence,* ed. Aldous Huxley (London: Heinemann, 1932), p. 683.
17. Lawrence, *First Lady Chatterley,* p. 88.
18. D. H. Lawrence, "Erinnyes," in *Some Imagist Poets* (1916; reprint ed., New York: Kraus Reprint, 1969), p. 67.
19. Lawrence, *First Lady Chatterley,* p. 49.
20. Ibid., pp. 49–50.
21. D. H. Lawrence, "Bread Upon the Waters," *Poetry* (February 1919), pp. 261–62.
22. Lawrence, *First Lady Chatterley,* p. 57.
23. Ibid., p. 76.
24. Ibid., p. 96.
25. Ibid., p. 108.
26. Ibid., p. 185.
27. Emile Delavenay, "Making Another Lawrence: Frieda and the Lawrence Legend," *The D. H. Lawrence Review* (1975), pp. 81–82.
28. Ibid., p. 83.
29. Ibid., p. 84.
30. Lawrence, *First Lady Chatterley,* p. 181.
31. Delavenay, "Making Another Lawrence," p. 85.
32. Lawrence, *First Lady Chatterley,* p. 182.
33. Frieda Lawrence, "A Foreword," in Lawrence, *First Lady Chatterley,* p. xiii.
34. Lawrence, *First Lady Chatterley,* p. 3.
35. Ibid., p. 6.
36. H.D., *Bid Me to Live,* p. 24.
37. Harry T. Moore and Warren Roberts, *D. H. Lawrence and His World* (New York: Viking, 1966), p. 42. Confusion on the subject of character identification abounds in the Lawrence scholarship. For instance, F. B. Pinion writes, "Only a spiteful anti-bourgeois humour can explain the naming of his famed *déclassée* heroine after Constance Chatterley (daughter of the secretary and estate agent for Barber, Walker & Co.), who lived at the Hollies, Eastwood, and travelled daily to school in Nottingham on the same train as Lawrence." Pinion, *A D. H. Lawrence Companion* (London: Macmillan, 1978), p. 289.
38. Keith Sagar, *The Life of D. H. Lawrence* (New York: Pantheon, 1980), p. 211.

39. Lawrence, *First Lady Chatterley*, p. 151.
40. H.D., *Bid Me to Live*, pp. 140–41.

18

1. D. H. Lawrence, *The First Lady Chatterley* (New York: Dial, 1944), p. 257.
2. Ibid., p. 261.
3. Ezra Pound, *The Cantos of Ezra Pound* (New York: New Directions, 1970), p. 18.
4. H.D., "Pilate's Wife," Beinecke Library, Yale; p. 62.
5. Ezra Pound, *Homage to Sextus Propertius* (London: Faber and Faber, 1934), p. 19.
6. Lawrence, *First Lady Chatterley*, pp. 267–68.
7. Ibid., p. 265.
8. Ibid., p. 287.
9. Ibid., p. 289.
10. D. H. Lawrence, *Lady Chatterley's Lover* (1928: reprint ed., New York: Grove, 1962), p. 353.
11. Ibid., p. 350.
12. Ibid., p. 351.
13. Ibid.
14. Ibid.
15. John Cournos, *Miranda Masters* (New York: Knopf, 1926), p. 231.
16. John Cournos, *Autobiography* (New York: G. P. Putnam's Sons, 1935), p. 284.
17. Cournos, *Miranda Masters*, pp. 175–76.
18. Alfred Satterthwaite, "John Cournos and 'H.D.,' " *Twentieth Century Literature* 22, no. 4 (1976): 407.
19. H.D. to Cournos, May 2, 1918, personal collection of Alfred Satterthwaite.
20. H.D. to Cournos, November 1919, personal collection of Alfred Satterthwaite.
21. Lawrence, *Lady Chatterley's Lover*, pp. 354–55.
22. Ibid., p. 364.
23. Ibid., pp. 367–68.
24. Ibid.
25. Aldington to H.D., September 1, 1918; Beinecke Library, Yale. All subsequent letters cited in this chapter are in the Beinecke collection as well.
26. Cecil Gray, *Musical Chairs* (London: Home & Van Thal, 1948), p. 136.
27. Lawrence, *Lady Chatterley's Lover*, p. 368.
28. Ibid., p. 373.
29. H.D., "Compassionate Friendship," Beinecke Library, Yale; p. 52.

19

1. H.D., *Tribute to Freud, Writing on the Wall, Advent* (Boston: David R. Godine, 1974), p. 142.
2. H.D., "Pilate's Wife," Beinecke Library, Yale; p. 1.
3. Ibid., p. 3.
4. Ibid., p. 8.
5. Ibid., pp. 12–13.
6. Ibid.
7. H.D., *End to Torment* (New York: New Directions, 1979), pp. 3–4.
8. H.D., "Pilate's Wife," p. 13.

9. Ibid., p. 15.
10. H.D., *Helen in Egypt* (1961; reprint ed., New York: New Directions, 1974), p. 2.
11. H.D., "Notes on Thought and Vision," Beinecke Library, Yale; p. 18.
12. H.D., *Helen in Egypt,* pp. 20–21.
13. H.D., "Pilate's Wife," p. 17.
14. Ibid., p. 16.
15. Ibid., p. 15.
16. Ibid., p. 18.
17. H.D., *Bid Me to Live* (New York: Grove, 1960), p. 181.
18. H.D., *Helen in Egypt,* pp. 11–12.
19. H.D., "Pilate's Wife," pp. 18–19.
20. Ibid.
21. Ibid., p. 35.
22. Ibid., p. 22.
23. Ibid., p. 24.
24. Ibid., p. 25.
25. Ibid., p. 26.
26. Richard Aldington, *Portrait of a Genius, But . . .* (London: Heinemann, 1950), pp. 195–96.
27. D. H. Lawrence, *Kangaroo* (1923; reprint ed., New York: Viking, 1963), pp. 242–43.
28. H.D., "Compassionate Friendship," Beinecke Library, Yale; p. 50.

20

1. D. H. Lawrence, *St. Mawr* and *The Man Who Died* (1925, 1929; reprint ed., New York: Vintage, 1953), p. 163.
2. Ibid.
3. Quoted in D. H. Lawrence, *The Escaped Cock,* ed. Gerald M. Lacy (Los Angeles: Black Sparrow Press, 1973), p. 136.
4. Lawrence, *St. Mawr* and *The Man Who Died,* p. 164.
5. Ibid.
6. Ibid., pp. 164–65.
7. Ibid.
8. Ibid.
9. Ibid.
10. Ibid.
11. Ibid.
12. Ibid.
13. H.D., *Helen in Egypt* (1961; reprint ed., New York: New Directions, 1974), p. 160.
14. Lawrence, *St. Mawr* and *The Man Who Died,* p. 166.
15. Ibid.
16. H.D., "Pilate's Wife," Beinecke Library, Yale; p. 21.
17. Lawrence, *St. Mawr* and *The Man Who Died,* p. 167.
18. Ibid.
19. Ibid., pp. 167–68.
20. Ibid.
21. Ibid., p. 169.
22. Ibid., p. 170.
23. Ibid., pp. 170–71.
24. Lawrence, *Escaped Cock,* p. 109.

25. Lawrence, *St. Mawr* and *The Man Who Died*, p. 168.
26. Ibid., p. 173.
27. Lawrence, *Escaped Cock*, pp. 112–13.
28. Lawrence, *St. Mawr* and *The Man Who Died*, p. 176.
29. Lawrence, *Escaped Cock*, p. 114.
30. Horace Gregory, "Speaking of Books," *New York Times Book Review*, October 26, 1961, p. 2.
31. Lawrence, *St. Mawr* and *The Man Who Died*, p. 177.
32. Lawrence, *Escaped Cock*, p. 114.
33. H.D., *Helen in Egypt*, pp. 247–48.
34. Ibid., pp. 249–50.
35. Ibid., p. 264.
36. Lawrence, *Escaped Cock*, p. 151.
37. H.D., *Helen in Egypt*, p. 13.
38. Lawrence, *St. Mawr* and *The Man Who Died*, p. 179.
39. Lawrence, *Escaped Cock*, p. 117.
40. Ibid.
41. Ibid., pp. 117–18.
42. Lawrence, *St. Mawr* and *The Man Who Died*, pp. 182–83.
43. Ibid.

21

1. D. H. Lawrence, *The Escaped Cock*, ed. Gerald M. Lacy (Los Angeles: Black Sparrow Press, 1973), p. 151.
2. Ibid., p. 112.
3. H.D., "Pilate's Wife," Beinecke Library, Yale; p. 41.
4. Ibid., p. 39.
5. Ibid., p. 71.
6. Ibid., pp. 77–78.
7. Ibid., p. 91.
8. Ibid.
9. Ibid., p. 104.
10. Ibid., p. 105.
11. Ibid., pp. 107–108.
12. Ibid.
13. Ibid.
14. Ibid., pp. 112–13.
15. Ibid.
16. Ibid., p. 110.
17. Harry T. Moore, "Richard Aldington in His Last Years," in *Richard Aldington: An Intimate Portrait*, ed. A. Kershaw and F. J. Temple (Carbondale: Southern Illinois University Press, 1965), p. 91.
18. H.D., "Pilate's Wife," p. 114.
19. Ibid., p. 117.
20. Ibid., pp. 121–22.
21. Ibid., p. 112.
22. Ibid., p. 129.
23. Ibid., pp. 129–30.
24. Ibid., p. 156.
25. Ibid., p. 161.
26. Ibid., p. 163.
27. Ibid., p. 165.

28. Ibid., p. 166.
29. Ibid., p. 167.
30. Ibid., pp. 153, 167.
31. Lawrence, *Escaped Cock,* p. 120.
32. H.D., "Pilate's Wife," p. 154.

22

1. H.D., *Tribute to Freud, Writing on the Wall, Advent* (Boston: David R. Godine, 1974), pp. 149–50.
2. Ibid., p. 172.
3. D. H. Lawrence, *St. Mawr* and *The Man Who Died* (1925, 1929; reprint ed., New York: Vintage, 1953), p. 185.
4. Ibid.
5. Ibid.
6. Ibid., p. 186.
7. Ibid.
8. Ibid., pp. 186–87.
9. Ibid.
10. Ibid.
11. H.D., *Helen in Egypt* (1961; reprint ed., New York: New Directions, 1974), p. 11.
12. Lawrence, *St. Mawr* and *The Man Who Died,* p. 187.
13. H.D., "Paint It Today," Beinecke Library, Yale; ch. V, p. 13.
14. H.D., "Compassionate Friendship," Beinecke Library, Yale; pp. 48–49.
15. Lawrence, *St. Mawr* and *The Man Who Died,* pp. 187–88.
16. Ibid.
17. H.D., *Helen in Egypt,* p. 259.
18. Lawrence, *St. Mawr* and *The Man Who Died,* p. 188.
19. H.D., "Notes on Recent Writing," Beinecke Library, Yale; p. 76.
20. D. H. Lawrence, *The Escaped Cock,* ed. Gerald M. Lacy (Los Angeles: Black Sparrow Press, 1973), p. 38.
21. D. H. Lawrence, "Sun," in *The Complete Short Stories of D. H. Lawrence,* vol. II (New York: Viking, 1961), p. 535.
22. Ibid.
23. Lawrence, *St. Mawr* and *The Man Who Died,* p. 189.
24. Ibid.
25. Richard Aldington, *The Complete Poems of Richard Aldington* (London: Allan Wingate, 1948), p. 24.
26. Ibid., p. 28.
27. Lawrence, *St. Mawr* and *The Man Who Died,* p. 189.
28. Ibid., pp. 189–90.
29. Lawrence, *Escaped Cock,* p. 40.
30. Lawrence, *St. Mawr* and *The Man Who Died,* p. 190.
31. Ibid.
32. Ibid., pp. 190–91.
33. Ibid.
34. H.D., *Bid Me to Live* (New York: Grove, 1960), p. 69.
35. Lawrence, *St. Mawr* and *The Man Who Died,* p. 191.
36. Ibid.
37. Ibid., pp. 191–92.
38. Ibid.
39. Ibid., p. 167.

40. Lawrence, *Escaped Cock,* p. 43.
41. Lawrence, *St. Mawr* and *The Man Who Died,* p. 193.
42. Ibid., p. 195.
43. Ibid., p. 196.
44. Ibid.
45. Ibid.
46. Ibid., p. 198.
47. Ibid., pp. 201–202.
48. Ibid.
49. Ibid.
50. Ibid.
51. H.D., "Vale Ave," Beinecke Library, Yale.
52. Lawrence, *St. Mawr* and *The Man Who Died,* p. 203.
53. Ibid., p. 204.
54. Ibid., p. 205.
55. Jacob John Sessler, *Communal Pietism Among Early American Moravians* (New York: Holt, 1933), p. 114.
56. *The Litany Book* (1759), pp. 180, 183; quoted in Sessler, *Communal Pietism,* pp. 114–15.
57. H.D., *Helen in Egypt,* p. 12.
58. Lawrence, *St. Mawr* and *The Man Who Died,* p. 205.
59. Ibid.
60. Ibid., p. 206.
61. Lawrence, *Escaped Cock,* p. 56.
62. H.D., *Trilogy* (New York: New Directions, 1973), pp. 152–155.
63. Lawrence, *St. Mawr* and *The Man Who Died,* p. 206.
64. Ibid., p. 207.
65. Ibid.
66. Ibid.
67. Ibid.
68. Ibid.
69. Ibid., p. 208.
70. H.D., *Trilogy,* p. 87.
71. Lawrence, *St. Mawr* and *The Man Who Died,* p. 209.
72. H.D., *Trilogy,* p. 70.
73. Lawrence, *St. Mawr* and *The Man Who Died,* p. 209.
74. Lawrence, *Escaped Cock,* p. 60.
75. Lawrence, *St. Mawr* and *The Man Who Died,* p. 210.
76. H.D., *Helen in Egypt,* pp. 288, 290.
77. Lawrence, *St. Mawr* and *The Man Who Died,* p. 210.
78. H.D. and Eric W. White, *Images of H.D./From the Mystery* (London: Enitharmon Press, 1976), p. 57.
79. Lawrence, *St. Mawr* and *The Man Who Died,* p. 211.
80. Ibid.
81. D. H. Lawrence, *Lady Chatterley's Lover* (1928; reprint ed., New York: Grove, 1962), p. 37.

23

1. H.D., *End to Torment* (New York: New Directions, 1979), p. 8.
2. Bryher [pseud.], *Two Selves* (Paris: Contact, 1923), pp. 125–26.
3. H.D., "Notes on Thought and Vision," Beinecke Library, Yale; p. 7.

4. Giambattista Vico, *The New Science of Giambattista Vico*, trans. T. G. Bergin and M. A. Fisch (Ithaca, N. Y.: Cornell University Press, 1968), p. 75.
5. H.D., "Notes on Thought and Vision," p. 6.
6. Ibid., p. 4.
7. Ibid., p. 3.
8. Ibid., p. 6.
9. Ibid., pp. 25, 27.
10. Ibid., p. 8.
11. Ibid.
12. Ibid., p. 27.
13. Ibid., p. 4.
14. Ibid., p. 30.
15. Ibid., p. 31.
16. Ibid., p. 20.

24

1. H.D., "The Gift," Beinecke Library, Yale; p. 30.
2. H.D., *Tribute to Freud, Writing on the Wall, Advent* (Boston: David R. Godine, 1974), p. 153.
3. Ibid.
4. Ibid.
5. Ibid.
6. H.D., "The Sword Went Out to Sea," Beinecke Library, Yale; p. 5.
7. H.D., *Tribute to Freud*, p. 154.
8. Ibid.
9. Ibid.
10. Ibid.
11. Ibid., pp. 138–39.
12. Ibid., pp. 143–44.
13. Ibid., p. 155.
14. Ibid.
15. Ibid., p. 156.
16. Ibid., p. 157.
17. Ibid.
18. Ibid., p. 155.
19. Ibid., p. 158.
20. Ibid.
21. Ibid.
22. H.D., "Compassionate Friendship," Beinecke Library, Yale; p. 64.
23. H.D., *Tribute to Freud*, p. 159.
24. Ibid.
25. Ibid., pp. 159–60.
26. Ibid.
27. Ibid., pp. 160–61.
28. H.D., "Compassionate Friendship," p. 33.
29. H.D., "Magic Ring," Beinecke Library, Yale; p. 159.
30. Ibid.
31. H.D., *Heliodora* (London: Jonathan Cape, 1924), pp. 33–34.
32. H.D., *Collected Poems of H.D.* (New York: Boni and Liveright, 1925), pp. 169–70.
33. H.D., "Magic Ring," pp. 160–61.

1. Phyllis Grosskurth, *Havelock Ellis: A Biography* (New York: Knopf, 1980), p. 297.
2. H.D., *Tribute to Freud, Writing on the Wall, Advent* (Boston: David R. Godine, 1974), p. 56.
3. Ibid., p. 44.
4. Ibid., p. 41.
5. H.D., *Bid Me to Live* (New York: Grove, 1960), pp. 143–44, 162.
6. Ibid., pp. 163, 167.
7. Ibid., p. 167.
8. Ibid., p. 164.
9. H.D., *Tribute to Freud*, p. 56.
10. H.D., *Helen in Egypt* (1961; reprint ed., New York: New Directions, 1974), p. 272.
11. H.D., *Bid Me to Live*, p. 78.
12. Ibid.
13. Ibid., p. 89.
14. Sigmund Freud, *A General Introduction to Psychoanalysis,* trans. J. Riviere (New York: Washington Square Press, 1960), p. 203.
15. H.D., *Tribute to Freud*, p. 51.
16. H.D., "Asphodel," Beinecke Library, Yale; bk. II, p. 98.
17. H.D., "The Gift," Beinecke Library, Yale; ch. IV, p. 14.
18. H.D., *Hedylus* (Stratford: Basil Blackwell and Houghton Mifflin, 1928), p. 175.
19. H.D., "Asphodel," bk. II, p. 100.
20. Ibid., p. 93.
21. Ibid., bk. I, p. 98.
22. Ibid., bk. II, p. 93.
23. H.D., *Hedylus,* pp. 184–85.
24. Ibid., p. 180.
25. Ibid., p. 178.
26. Ibid., p. 176.
27. Ibid., p. 177.
28. Ibid., p. 183.
29. Ibid., p. 175.
30. H.D., "Compassionate Friendship," Beinecke Library, Yale; p. 59.
31. H.D., *Hedylus,* p. 174.
32. H.D., *The Hedgehog* (London: Brendin, 1936), p. 20.
33. Ibid., p. 27.
34. H.D., *Hedylus,* p. 72.
35. Ibid., p. 14.
36. Ibid., p. 15.
37. Ibid., p. 113.
38. Ibid., p. 184.
39. Ibid., p. 170.
40. H.D., *Tribute to Freud*, p. 41.
41. H.D., *Red Roses for Bronze* (1931; reprint ed., New York: AMS Press, 1970), pp. 86, 88.
42. H.D., *Hedylus,* p. 178.
43. Ibid., p. 21.

26

1. H.D., *Collected Poems of H.D.* (New York: Boni and Liveright, 1925), p. 24.
2. H.D., "The Garden," *Poetry* (March 1915), pp. 267–68.
3. Brigit Patmore, *My Friends When Young* (London: Heinemann, 1968), p. 66.
4. H.D., *Red Roses for Bronze* (1931; reprint ed., New York: AMS Press, 1970), p. 1.
5. Ibid., pp. 66–67.
6. Robert McAlmon, *McAlmon and the Lost Generation: A Self-Portrait,* ed. Robert E. Knoll (Lincoln: University of Nebraska Press, 1962), p. 4.
7. Louise Morgan, "Ellerman, Sir John Reeves," in *The Dictionary of National Biography: 1931–1940,* ed. L. G. Wickham Legg (London: Oxford University Press, 1949), p. 256.
8. H.D. to Cournos, November 1919, personal collection of Alfred Satterthwaite.
9. Patmore to Bryher, February 25, August 29, September 6, and September 12, 1922, Beinecke Library, Yale.
10. Perdita Schaffner, personal interview, July 9, 1980.
11. H.D. to Ezra Pound, Friday 1929, Beinecke Library, Yale.
12. Hugh Kenner, *The Pound Era* (Berkeley: University of California Press, 1971), p. 176.
13. H.D., *Tribute to Freud, Writing on the Wall, Advent* (Boston: David R. Godine, 1974), p. 13.
14. Ibid.
15. Ibid., p. 132.
16. Ibid., p. 139.
17. H.D., "The Dream," *Contemporary Literature* 10 (Autumn 1969): 605.
18. H.D., *Tribute to Freud,* p. 160.
19. H.D., "Notes on Recent Writing," Beinecke Library, Yale; p. 30.
20. H.D., "Compassionate Friendship," Beinecke Library, Yale; pp. 28–29.
21. H.D. to Norman Holmes Pearson, June 17, 1951, Beinecke Library, Yale.
22. H.D., "The Dream," p. 605.
23. Norman Holmes Pearson, personal interview, January 7, 1970.
24. H.D., *Helen in Egypt* (1961; reprint ed., New York: New Directions, 1974), p. 186.

27

1. H.D. to Bryher, December 22, 1932, Beinecke Library, Yale.
2. H.D., *Tribute to Freud, Writing on the Wall, Advent* (Boston: David R. Godine, 1974), p. 101.
3. Ibid., pp. 72–73.
4. Sigmund Freud, "Observations on 'Wild' Psychoanalysis," in *Therapy and Technique,* ed. Philip Rieff (New York: Collier Books, 1963), p. 93.
5. Freud, "The Dynamics of Transference," in *Therapy and Technique,* p. 112. See also *Group Psychology and the Analysis of the Ego,* trans. James Strachey (New York: Bantam, 1965), p. 91, where Freud discusses friendship as a variant of aim-inhibited love.
6. Freud, "Recommendations for Physicians on the Psychoanalytic Method of Treatment," in *Therapy and Technique,* p. 124.
7. Ibid., p. 122.
8. Freud, "Analysis Terminable and Interminable," in *Therapy and Technique,* p. 266.

9. Freud, "Further Recommendations in the Technique of Psychoanalysis: Recollection, Repetition and Working Through," in *Therapy and Technique,* p. 164.
10. H.D., *Tribute to Freud,* p. 14.
11. Ibid., p. 29.
12. Ibid., pp. 70–71.
13. Ibid., pp. 35–36.
14. Freud, "Analysis Terminable and Interminable," p. 244.
15. Freud, "Constructions in Analysis," in *Therapy and Technique,* p. 282.
16. Freud, "Analysis Terminable and Interminable," pp. 252–53.
17. Freud, "Constructions in Analysis," pp. 285–86.
18. H.D., *Tribute to Freud,* p. 82.

28

1. L. S. Dembo, ed., "Norman Holmes Pearson on H.D.: An Interview," *Contemporary Literature* 10 (Autumn 1969): 444.
2. H.D. to Bryher, March 1, 1933, Beinecke Library, Yale. All subsequent letters cited in this chapter are in the Beinecke collection as well.
3. March 5, 1933.
4. March 9, 1933.
5. March 23, 1933.
6. March 14, 1933.
7. May 12, 1933.
8. May 15, 1933.
9. March 5, 1933.
10. March 19, 1933.
11. May 11, 1933.
12. Ibid.
13. May 15, 1933.
14. Ibid.
15. May 18, 1933.
16. May 21, 1933.
17. December 20, 1933.
18. December 15, 1934.
19. H.D. to Bryher, December 7, 1934.
20. Ibid.

29

1. H.D., "Thorn Thicket," Beinecke Library, Yale; p. 38.
2. H.D., *Tribute to Freud, Writing on the Wall, Advent* (Boston: David R. Godine, 1974), p. 144.
3. Ibid., p. 128.
4. Ibid., p. 116.
5. D. H. Lawrence, *Aaron's Rod* (1922; reprint ed., New York: Viking, 1961), p. 288.
6. H.D. to Bryher, March 4, 1933, Beinecke Library, Yale.
7. H.D., *Tribute to Freud,* p. 126.
8. Ibid., p. 133.
9. Ibid., p. 131.
10. Ibid., p. 176.
11. Ibid., p. 141.

12. Ibid., p. 140.
13. Ibid., p. 156.
14. H.D., *Bid Me to Live* (New York: Grove Press, 1960), p. 137.
15. H.D., *Tribute to Freud*, p. 141.
16. Ibid., p. 138.
17. Ibid., p. 141.
18. Ibid., p. 134.
19. H.D. to Bryher, July 30, 1928, Beinecke Library, Yale.
20. H.D. to Bryher, July 29, 1928, Beinecke Library, Yale.
21. H.D., *Tribute to Freud*, p. 134.

30

1. H.D., *Tribute to Freud, Writing on the Wall, Advent* (Boston: David R. Godine, 1974), p. 116.
2. Ibid., p. 149.
3. Ibid., p. 135.
4. Ibid., p. 161.
5. Ibid.
6. Ibid., p. 153.
7. Ibid., p. 175.
8. Ibid., pp. 174–75.
9. Ibid., p. 163.
10. Ibid., p. 176.
11. Ibid., p. 139.
12. Ibid.
13. Ibid., p. 141.
14. Ibid., p. 152.
15. Ibid., p. 184.
16. Ibid., pp. 146–47.
17. L. S. Dembo, ed., "Norman Holmes Pearson on H.D.: An Interview," *Contermporary Literature* 10 (Autumn 1969): 444.
18. H.D., *Tribute to Freud*, p. 187.
19. H.D., "The Dream," *Contemporary Literature* 10 (Autumn 1969): 611.
20. H.D., *Tribute to Freud*, p. 124.
21. H.D., "The Dream," pp. 618, 620, 624, 626.
22. H.D., *Tribute to Freud*, p. 146.

31

1. Perdita Schaffner, personal interview, July 9, 1980.
2. H.D., "Compassionate Friendship," Beinecke Library, Yale; p. 10.
3. H.D., *Trilogy* (New York: New Directions, 1973), p. 3.
4. Ibid., p. 4.
5. H.D., "She Is Dead," in "Twelve Short Stories," Beinecke Library, Yale; pp. 2–3.
6. H.D., "Magic Ring," Beinecke Library, Yale; p. 40.
7. Ibid., pp. 40–41.
8. H.D., *Trilogy*, p. 25.
9. Ibid., p. 27.
10. H.D., "Magic Ring," pp. 57–58.
11. H.D., *Trilogy*, p. 28.
12. H.D., "Magic Ring," p. 63.

13. Ibid., p. 310.
14. Ibid., p. 64.
15. Ibid., pp. 304–305.
16. H.D., *Trilogy*, p. 35.
17. H.D., "Magic Ring," p. 305.
18. H.D., *Trilogy*, p. viii.
19. H.D., "Magic Ring," p. 309.
20. Ibid., p. 308.
21. Ibid.
22. Ibid.
23. H.D., *Trilogy*, p. 31.
24. Ibid., pp. 56–57.
25. Ibid., p. 53.
26. Ibid., p. 42.
27. Ibid., p. 5.
28. H.D., "Magic Ring," pp. 309–10.
29. Ibid.
30. H.D., *Trilogy*, p. vi.
31. Ibid., p. 19.
32. Ibid., p. vii.
33. H.D., *Trilogy*, p. 27.
34. Ibid., pp. 58–59.

32

1. H.D., *Trilogy* (New York: New Directions, 1973), p. vii.
2. Ibid., p. x.
3. Ibid., p. 76.
4. Ibid., p. 65.
5. H.D., "Compassionate Friendship," Beinecke Library, Yale; p. 35.
6. H.D., *Trilogy*, p. 67.
7. Gustav Davidson, *A Dictionary of Angels* (New York: Free Press, 1967), pp. 240, 242.
8. H.D., "Magic Ring," Beinecke Library, Yale; p. 305.
9. H.D., *Trilogy*, p. 67.
10. Davidson, *Dictionary*, p. 298.
11. H.D., *Trilogy*, p. 70.
12. Ibid.
13. Ibid., p. 71.
14. H.D., "Magic Ring," p. 97.
15. H.D., *Trilogy*, p. 79.
16. Ibid., p. 87.
17. Ibid., p. ix.
18. H.D., "Magic Ring," p. 99.
19. H.D., *Trilogy*, p. 89.
20. Ibid., p. 92.
21. Ibid., pp. 92, 94.
22. Ibid., p. 96.
23. Ibid., p. 97.
24. Ibid., p. 101.
25. H.D., "Autobiographical Notes," Beinecke Library, Yale; p. 48.
26. H.D., *Trilogy*, p. 103.

27. Ibid., pp. 109–10.
28. Ibid., p. 109.

33

1. H.D., *Trilogy* (New York: New Directions, 1973), p. 135.
2. Ibid., p. 172.
3. Ibid., pp. 113–15.
4. Ibid., pp. 121–29 passim.
5. Ibid., pp. 146, 149.
6. H.D., *Tribute to Freud, Writing on the Wall, Advent* (Boston: David R. Godine, 1974), p. 17.
7. H.D., *Trilogy,* pp. 154–55.
8. Ibid., pp. 160–61.
9. Sigmund Freud, *Moses and Monotheism,* trans. Katherine Jones (New York: Vintage, 1967), p. 5.
10. H.D., *Tribute to Freud,* p. 119.
11. Ibid., p. 123.

34

1. H.D., "Compassionate Friendship," Beinecke Library, Yale; p. 61.
2. Aldington to H.D., March 20, 1929, Beinecke Library, Yale. Unless otherwise indicated subsequent letters cited in this chapter are in the Beinecke collection as well.
3. Aldington to H.D., March 30, 1929.
4. H.D. to Brigit Patmore, 1928.
5. Aldington to H.D., March 14, 1929.
6. H.D. to Ezra Pound, July 9, 1938.
7. H.D. to Bryher, September 26, 1939.
8. H.D. to Bryher, September 21, 1939.
9. H.D. to Aldington, October 6, 1953.
10. Perdita Schaffner, personal interview, July 9, 1980; Susan Stanford Friedman, "Mythology, Psychoanalysis, and the Occult in the Late Poetry of H.D.," (Ph.D. diss., University of Wisconsin, 1973), p. 343 n.
11. H.D., "The Sword Went Out to Sea," Beinecke Library, Yale; p. 5.
12. Ibid., pp. 65, 67.
13. Ibid., p. 74.
14. Ibid., p. 215.
15. H.D., "Compassionate Friendship," p. 30.
16. Ibid., p. 72.
17. H.D. to Aldington, May 14, 1948, Richard Aldington Papers, Special Collections, Morris Library, Southern Illinois University, Carbondale, Illinois. Hereafter this collection will be referred to as Morris Library, SIU-Carbondale.
18. H.D. to Aldington, May 20, 1948, Morris Library, SIU-Carbondale.
19. Ibid.
20. H.D. to Aldington, October 10, 1948, Morris Library, SIU-Carbondale.
21. H.D., "Notes on Recent Writing," Beinecke Library, Yale; p. 22.
22. Ibid.
23. Ibid., p. 30.
24. Ibid., p. 40.

25. H.D. to Aldington, February 23, 1949, Morris Library, SIU-Carbondale.
26. H.D. to Aldington, February 24, 1949, Morris Library, SIU-Carbondale.
27. H.D. to Aldington, October 21, 1948, Morris Library, SIU-Carbondale.
28. H.D. to Aldington, May 4, 1949, Morris Library, SIU-Carbondale.
29. H.D. to Aldington, April 28, 1947, Morris Library, SIU-Carbondale.
30. H.D. to Aldington, July 25, 1951, Morris Library, SIU-Carbondale.
31. H.D., "Compassionate Friendship," p. 94.
32. H.D. to Aldington, December 27, 1952, Morris Library, SIU-Carbondale.
33. Ibid.
34. H.D. to Aldington, January 2, 1953, Morris Library, SIU-Carbondale.
35. Aldington to H.D., February 28, 1953.
36. H.D. to Aldington, January 14, 1953, Morris Library, SIU-Carbondale.
37. Horace Gregory, "Introduction," in H.D., *Helen in Egypt* (1961; reprint ed., New York: New Directions, 1974), p. vii.
38. H.D., *Tribute to Freud, Writing on the Wall, Advent* (Boston: David R. Godine, 1974), p. 149.
39. H.D., "Compassionate Friendship," p. 21.
40. Ibid., p. 86.
41. Ibid., p. 78.
42. Ibid., p. 114.
43. Ibid., p. 79.
44. H.D. to Norman Holmes Pearson, March 15, 1955.
45. Aldington to H.D., February 7, 1955.
46. Aldington to H.D., June 30, 1958.
47. Aldington to H.D., June 8, 1961.
48. Aldington to H.D., June 30, 1958.
49. Harry T. Moore, "Richard Aldington in His Last Years," in *Richard Aldington: An Intimate Portrait,* ed. A. Kershaw and F. J. Temple (Carbondale: University of Southern Illinois Press, 1965), p. 88.
50. H.D. to Aldington, July 4, 1956, Morris Library, SIU-Carbondale.
51. H.D. to Bryher, May 26, 1956.
52. H.D., "Compassionate Friendship," p. 17.
53. H.D. to Pearson, November 19, 1960.
54. H.D., "Thorn Thicket," Beinecke Library, Yale; pp. 27–28.
55. Ibid., p. 28.
56. H.D., "Magic Mirror," Beinecke Library, Yale; p. 7.
57. H.D., "Thorn Thicket," p. 26.
58. Ibid., pp. 6–7.
59. Ibid.
60. Ibid., p. 12.
61. Ibid., p. 13.
62. Ibid., p. 15.
63. Ibid., p. 23.
64. Ibid.
65. Ibid.
66. Ibid., p. 24.
67. Ibid., p. 34.
68. Ibid., p. 36.
69. Ibid.
70. Ibid., p. 37.
71. Ibid., p. 39.
72. H.D., *Helen in Egypt,* p. 55.
73. H.D., "Thorn Thicket," p. 41.

74. H.D., "Compassionate Friendship," p. 35.
75. H.D., "Thorn Thicket," p. 43.
76. Ibid., p. 45.
77. Ibid., p. 53.
78. Ibid., p. 50.

35

1. L. M. Freibert, "Conflict and Creativity in the World of H.D.," *Journal of Women's Studies in Literature* 1, no. 3 (Summer 1979): 270.
2. Linda Welshimer Wagner, "Helen in Egypt: A Culmination," *Contemporary Literature* 10 (Autumn 1969): pp. 523–36.
3. H.D. to Bryher, January 20, 1936, Beinecke Library, Yale.
4. H.D., "Thorn Thicket," Beinecke Library, Yale; p. 24.
5. H.D. to Norman Holmes Pearson, July 13, 1959, Beinecke Library, Yale.
6. H.D., *End to Torment* (New York: New Directions, 1979), p. 41.
7. H.D., "Notes on Euripides, Pausanias and Greek Lyric Poets," Beinecke Library, Yale; pp. 2–8 passim.
8. H.D., *Helen in Egypt* (1961; reprint ed., New York: New Directions, 1974), pp. 7, 15, 10, 38.
9. H.D., "Notes on Euripides," p. 2.
10. H.D., *Helen in Egypt*, p. 14.
11. H.D., "Notes on Euripides," p. 15.
12. Ibid., p. 1.
13. Ibid., p. 10.
14. H.D., *Helen in Egypt*, pp. 12, 17.
15. D. H. Lawrence, *John Thomas and Lady Jane* (New York: Viking, 1972), p. 126.
16. Ibid., pp. 126–27.
17. H.D., *Helen in Egypt*, pp. 15, 16.
18. Ibid., p. 21.
19. Ibid., p. 9.
20. Ibid., p. 264.

36

1. H.D., "The Guest," in *By Avon River* (New York: Macmillan, 1949), pp. 82–83.
2. H.D., *Euripides' Ion* (Boston: Houghton Mifflin, 1937), p. 95.
3. H.D., *Helen in Egypt* (1961; reprint ed., New York: New Directions, 1974), p. 1.
4. Sigmund Freud, *Civilization and Its Discontents,* trans. James Strachey (New York: Norton, 1962), pp. 87–88.
5. H.D., *Helen in Egypt*, p. 69.
6. Ibid., pp. 80–82.
7. Ibid., p. 21.
8. Ibid., p. 85.
9. Karl Abel, "Über den Gegensinn der Urworte, 1894," quoted in Sigmund Freud, "The Antithetical Sense of Primal Words," in *Character and Culture,* ed. Philip Rieff (New York: Collier Books, 1963), p. 49.
10. Ibid., p. 46.
11. H.D., *Helen in Egypt*, p. 71.

12. Ibid., p. 107.
13. Ibid., p. 91.
14. Ibid., p. 94.
15. "Hymn to Osiris," in *The Egyptian Book of the Dead,* trans. E. A. Wallis Budge (New York: Dover, 1967), pp. lii–liii.
16. H.D., *Helen in Egypt,* p. 93.
17. Ibid., pp. 9–10.
18. Ibid., pp. 20, 89.
19. Ibid., p. 17.
20. Ibid., pp. 78–79.
21. René Girard, *Violence and the Sacred,* trans. Patrick Gregory (Baltimore: Johns Hopkins University Press, 1977), p. 318.
22. Quoted in H.D., *Tribute to Freud, Writing on the Wall, Advent* (Boston: David R. Godine, 1974), p. 194.

37

1. H.D. to Norman Holmes Pearson, September 9, 1953, Beinecke Library, Yale.
2. H.D., *Helen in Egypt* (1961; reprint ed., New York: New Directions, 1974), p. 111.
3. Ibid., p. 109.
4. Ibid., p. 110.
5. Ibid., p. 111.
6. Ibid., p. 109.
7. Ibid., p. 111.
8. Robert Graves, *The Greek Myths,* vol. II (Baltimore: Penguin, 1955), p. 404.
9. H.D., *Helen in Egypt,* p. 111.
10. Ibid., p. 116.
11. Ibid., p. 117.
12. Ibid.
13. Ibid.
14. H.D., *Palimpsest* (1926; reprint ed., Carbondale: Southern Illinois University Press, 1968), pp. 12, 6–7.
15. H.D., *Helen in Egypt,* pp. 118–19, 122.
16. H.D., *Palimpsest,* p. 11.
17. Ibid., p. 6.
18. H.D., *Helen in Egypt,* p. 124.
19. H.D., *Heliodora* (London: Jonathan Cape, 1924), p. 24.
20. H.D., *Helen in Egypt,* p. 131.
21. Aldington, *Death of a Hero,* p. 371.
22. H.D., "Paint It Today," Beinecke Library, Yale; ch. V, pp. 1–4.

38

1. H.D., *Helen in Egypt* (1961; reprint ed., New York: New Directions, 1974), p. 114.
2. William Blake, "Auguries of Innocence," in *Selected Poetry and Prose of William Blake,* ed. Northrop Frye (New York: Random House, 1953), p. 90.
3. H.D., *Helen in Egypt,* p. 114.
4. Ibid., pp. 99, 126.
5. Ibid., p. 139.
6. Ibid., pp. 140–41.

7. Ibid., pp. 141–42.
8. Sir J. G. Frazer, *The Golden Bough,* abr. ed. (New York: Macmillan, 1963), p. 413.
9. Ezra Pound, *Personae: The Collected Poems of Ezra Pound* (New York: New Directions, 1926, 1952), p. 96.
10. H.D., *Helen in Egypt,* pp. 129–30.
11. Ibid., pp. 125–26.
12. Ibid., pp. 127–28.
13. Ibid., p. 144.
14. Ibid., p. 156.
15. "Fragment of Paean 8," in *Pindar,* trans. Sir John Sandys (London: Loeb Classical Library, 1915), p. 547.
16. H.D., *Helen in Egypt,* p. 159.
17. Ibid., pp. 184–85.
18. Ibid., pp. 138–39.
19. Ibid., p. 117.
20. Ibid., p. 115.
21. Ibid., p. 128.
22. Ibid., p. 133.

39

1. H.D., *Helen in Egypt* (1961; reprint ed., New York: New Directions, 1974), p. 147.
2. Robert Graves, *The Greek Myths,* vol. II (Baltimore: Penguin, 1955), p. 219.
3. Otto Rank, *The Myth of the Birth of the Hero* (New York: Vintage, 1964), p. 65.
4. H.D., *Helen in Egypt,* p. 149.
5. Ibid., p. 159.
6. Ibid., p. 160.
7. Ibid., p. 196.
8. Ibid., p. 169.
9. Ibid., p. 149.
10. Ibid., p. 150.
11. Ibid., p. 169.
12. H. D. F. Kitto, *The Greeks* (Baltimore: Penguin, 1951), p. 252.
13. H.D., "Winter Love," in *Hermetic Definition* (New York: New Directions, 1972), p. 103.
14. H.D., *Helen in Egypt,* p. 162.
15. Ibid., p. 153.
16. Ibid., p. 151.
17. Ibid., p. 155.
18. Ibid., pp. 151–52.
19. H.D., *Tribute to Freud, Writing on the Wall, Advent* (Boston: David R. Godine, 1974), p. 56.
20. Ibid., p. 103.
21. Ibid., pp. 68–69.
22. H.D., *Helen in Egypt,* p. 181.
23. Ibid., pp. 181–82.
24. Ibid., p. 148.
25. Ibid., p. 155.
26. Ibid., pp. 157–58.
27. Ibid., pp. 160–61.

28. Ibid., p. 162.
29. Paul Ricoeur, *Freud and Philosophy: An Essay on Interpretation*, trans. Denis Savage (New Haven, Conn.: Yale University Press, 1970), p. 517.
30. H.D., *Helen in Egypt*, p. 162.
31. Ibid., p. 164.
32. Ibid., p. 173.
33. Ibid., pp. 176–77.
34. H.D., *Tribute to Freud*, p. 16.
35. Ibid., p. 43.
36. Leslie Fiedler, "Memoir and Parable," *Poetry* (February 1957), pp. 326–29.
37. Ibid., p. 329.

40

1. H.D., *Helen in Egypt* (1961; reprint ed., New York: New Directions, 1974), p. 193.
2. A. van den Born, *Bijbels Woordenboek: Encyclopedic Dictionary of the Bible*, trans. Louis F. Hartman (New York: McGraw-Hill, 1963), p. 1555.
3. H.D., *Helen in Egypt*, p. 200.
4. Ibid., pp. 200–201.
5. Van den Born, *Bijbels Woordenboek*, p. 1554.
6. H.D., *Tribute to Freud, Writing on the Wall, Advent* (Boston: David R. Godine, 1974), pp. 36–37.
7. Ibid.
8. Ibid., pp. 39, 42.
9. Ibid., pp. 42–43.
10. Ibid., p. 108.
11. Ibid.
12. H.D., *Helen in Egypt*, p. 165.
13. Ibid., pp. 198–99.
14. Ibid., pp. 204–205.
15. Ibid., p. 202.
16. Ibid., p. 205.
17. H.D., *Tribute to Freud*, p. 103.
18. H.D., *Helen in Egypt*, pp. 202–203.
19. Ibid., p. 200.
20. Ibid., p. 206.

41

1. H.D., *Helen in Egypt* (1961; reprint ed., New York: New Directions, 1974), p. 208.
2. Ibid., p. 243.
3. Ibid., p. 282.
4. Ibid., p. 210.
5. Lawrence to Mrs. S. A. Hopkin, December 25, 1912, in *The Letters of D. H. Lawrence*, ed. Aldous Huxley (London: Heinemann, 1932), p. 88.
6. H.D., *Helen in Egypt*, p. 255.
7. Ibid., pp. 209–10.
8. Ibid., p. 222.
9. Ibid., pp. 245–46.
10. Ibid., pp. 291–92.
11. Ibid., p. 253.

12. Ibid., pp. 260–61.
13. Ibid., p. 263.
14. Ibid., pp. 223–24.
15. Ibid., p. 239.
16. Ibid., p. 277.
17. Ibid., p. 258.
18. Ibid., p. 268.
19. Ibid., p. 288.
20. H.D., *Helen in Egypt*, p. 288.
21. Johann Wolfgang von Goethe, *Faust, Part One and Part Two*, trans. Charles E. Passage (Indianapolis: Bobbs-Merrill, 1965), pp. 303–304.
22. H.D., *Helen in Egypt*, p. 291.
23. Goethe, *Faust*, p. 337 n.
24. H.D., *Helen in Egypt*, p. 218.
25. Ibid., p. 289.
26. Ibid., p. 213.
27. Ibid., pp. 299–300.
28. Ibid., p. 304.
29. Sigmund Freud, *Civilization and Its Discontents*, trans. James Strachey (New York: Norton, 1962), p. 15.

42

1. H.D., *Helen in Egypt* (1961; reprint ed., New York: New Directions, 1974), pp. 230, 232.
2. Ibid.
3. Ibid., p. 1.
4. Ezra Pound, "Three Cantos: I," *Poetry* (June 1917), pp. 116–17.
5. Ezra Pound, "Three Cantos: II," *Poetry* (July 1917), p. 186.
6. Ezra Pound, "Three Cantos: III," *Poetry* (August 1917), p. 253.
7. Ezra Pound, "Canto II," in *The Cantos of Ezra Pound* (New York: New Directions, 1970), p. 6.
8. H.D., *Helen in Egypt*, p. 1.
9. Ibid., pp. 3–4.
10. H.D., "The Helmsman," *Egoist* (April 1, 1916), p. 52.
11. Ibid.
12. H.D., *Helen in Egypt*, p. 18.
13. Ibid., pp. 80–81.
14. Ezra Pound, "Canto I," in *The Cantos*, p. 3.
15. Pound to H.D., February 1953, Beinecke Library, Yale.
16. H.D., *End to Torment* (New York: New Directions, 1979), p. 32.
17. L. S. Dembo, ed., "Norman Holmes Pearson on H.D.: An Interview," *Contemporary Literature* 10 (Autumn 1969): 442.
18. Ibid.
19. H.D., *End to Torment*, p. 19.
20. Ezra Pound, "Canto LXXIX," in *The Cantos*, p. 491.
21. H.D., *Tribute to Freud, Writing on the Wall, Advent* (Boston: David R. Godine, 1974), p. 152.
22. Pound, "Canto LXXIX," pp. 491–92.
23. William Morris, "Pomona," in *The Collected Works of William Morris*, vol. IX (New York: Russell & Russell, 1966), p. 193.
24. H.D., *End to Torment*, pp. 18–19.
25. Quoted in H.D., *End to Torment*, p. 76.

26. Quoted in ibid., p. 30.
27. Ezra Pound, "Canto 90," in *The Cantos*, p. 608.
28. H.D., *Helen in Egypt*, p. 3.
29. Quoted in Sister M. Bernetta Quinn, "The Metamorphoses of Ezra Pound," in *Motive and Method in the Cantos of Ezra Pound*, ed. Lewis Leary (New York: Columbia University Press, 1961), p. 90.
30. Ezra Pound, *Personae: The Collected Poems of Ezra Pound* (New York: New Directions, 1926, 1952), p. 62.
31. Quoted in H.D., *End to Torment*, p. 84.
32. Ibid., p. 12.
33. Guy Davenport, "Persephone's Ezra," in *New Approaches to Ezra Pound*, ed. Eva Hesse (Berkeley: University of California Press, 1969), pp. 160, 149.
34. Quoted in H.D., *End to Torment*, pp. 68–69.
35. Ibid., p. 3.
36. Ibid., p. 34.
37. Ibid., p. 27.
38. Quinn, "The Metamorphoses," p. 83.
39. H.D., "Her," Beinecke Library, Yale; p. 208.
40. Quoted in H.D., *End to Torment*, p. 76.
41. Ezra Pound, *"Sancta Patrona Domina Caelae,"* quoted in H.D., *End to Torment*, pp. 83–84.
42. Ibid., p. 51.
43. Ibid., p. 48.
44. H.D., *Hermetic Definition* (New York: New Directions, 1972), p. 96.
45. Quoted in H.D., *End to Torment*, p. 75.
46. H.D., *Hermetic Definition*, p. 100.
47. Ibid., p. 101.
48. Hugh Kenner, *The Pound Era* (Berkeley: University of California Press, 1971), p. 174.
49. H.D., *End to Torment*, p. 12.
50. Eric W. White and H.D., *Images of H.D./From the Mystery* (London: Enitharmon Press, 1976), p. 24.
51. Pound to H.D., November 29, 1956, Beinecke Library, Yale. All subsequent letters cited in this chapter are in the Beinecke collection as well.
52. H.D., *Hermetic Definition*, p. 67.
53. Ibid., p. 54.
54. Ibid., p. 112.
55. Robert Duncan, jacket note to H.D., *Hermetic Definition*.
56. Pearson to Robert Duncan, June 8, 1961, quoted in Robert Duncan, *Roots and Branches* (New York: New Directions, 1964), p. 86.
57. H.D., *Selected Poems* (New York: Grove, 1957), p. 128.
58. Perdita Schaffner, "Merano, 1962," *Paideuma* 4, nos. 2, 3 (1975): 514.
59. H.D., *Hermetic Definition*, p. 114.

Selected Bibliography

H.D.'s PUBLICATIONS

"Amaranth." *Contemporary Literature* 10 (Autumn 1969): 589–94.
"Apollo at Delphi." *Poetry* 41 (March 1933): 320–25.
Bid Me to live. New York: Grove Press, 1960.
By Avon River. New York: Macmillan, 1949.
Choruses from the Iphigeneia in Aulis and the Hippolytus of Euripides. Translated by H.D. London: Egoist Ltd., 1919.
"The Cinema and the Classics." *Close-Up* 1 (July, August, and November 1927).
Collected Poems of H.D. New York: Boni and Liveright, 1925.
"Confessions Questionnaire — H.D." *The Little Review* 13, no. 2 (1929): 38–40.
"The Death of Martin Presser." *Quarterly Review of Literature* 13, nos. 3, 4 (1965): 241–61.
"Do You Remember?" *Atlantic Monthly* 201 (April 1958): 42.
"The Dream." *Contemporary Literature* 10 (Autumn 1969): 605–26.
End to Torment. New York: New Directions, 1979.
"Envy." *Contemporary Literature* 10 (Autumn 1969): 599–601.
"Eros." *Contemporary Literature* 10 (Autumn 1969): 595–98.
Euripides' Ion. Boston: Houghton Mifflin, 1937.
The Flowering of the Rod. London: Oxford University Press, 1946.
"Gift." *Transition,* no. 4 (July 1927): 106–107.
The Hedgehog. London: Brendin, 1936.
Hedylus. Stratford: Basil Blackwell and Houghton Mifflin, 1928.
Helen in Egypt. 1961. Reprint. New York: New Directions, 1974.
Heliodora. London: Jonathan Cape, 1924.
Hermetic Definition. New York: New Directions, 1972.
Hippolytus Temporizes. Boston: Houghton Mifflin, 1927.
"In Time of Gold." *Poetry* 91 (December 1957): 149–50.
Kora and Ka. (Includes *Kora and Ka* and *Mira-Mare.*) Dijon: Imprimerie Darantière, 1934.
"Last Winter." *Poetry* 87 (December 1950): 125–34.
"Nails for Petals." *Poetry* 91 (December 1957): 150.
"Narthex." *The Second American Caravan*. Edited by Alfred Kreymborg, Lewis Mumford, and Paul Rosenfeld. New York: Macaulay, 1928.
[John Helforth]. *Nights*. Dijon: Imprimerie Darantière, 1935.

"No." *Transition,* no. 4 (July 1927): 111–12.

Palimpsest. 1926. Reprint. Carbondale: Southern Illinois University Press, 1968.

"People of Sparta." *The Bookman* 60 (December 1924): 417–20.

The Poet and the Dancer. San Francisco: Five Trees Press, 1975.

[Peter Rhoda]. "Pontikonisi (Mouse Island)." *Pagany* 3, no. 3 (1932): 1–9.

"Projector." *Close-Up* 1 (July 1927): 46–51.

"Psyche." *Transition,* no. 4 (July 1927): 107–108.

Red Roses for Bronze. 1931. Reprint. New York: AMS Press, 1970.

"The Revelation." *The Nation* 85 (August 31, 1957): 94.

Selected Poems. New York: Grove Press, 1957.

"Sigel XV." *Poetry* 52 (June 1938): 139–40.

"A Small Grain of Worship." *The Nation* 193 (September 9, 1961): 143.

"Socratic." *Transition,* no. 4 (July 1927): 113–14.

"Sometimes, and After." *Poetry* 91 (December 1957): 151.

"Tatter." *The European Caravan — An Anthology of the New Spirit in European Literature.* Edited by Samuel Putnam, Maida Castelhum Darnton, George Reavey, and J. Bronowski. New York: Brewer, Warren and Putnam, 1931.

"Temple of the Sun." *Life and Letters Today* 21, no. 21 (May 1939): 51–56.

Tribute to Freud. New York: Pantheon, 1956.

Tribute to Freud, Writing on the Wall, Advent. Boston: David R. Godine, 1974.

Tribute to the Angels. London: Oxford University Press, 1945.

Trilogy. Reprint of *The Walls Do Not Fall, Tribute to the Angels,* and *The Flowering of the Rod* (1944, 1945, 1946) (3 vols. in 1). New York: New Directions, 1973.

The Usual Star. (Includes *The Usual Star* and *Two Americans.*) Dijon: Imprimerie Darantière, 1934.

The Walls Do Not Fall. London: Oxford University Press, 1944.

What Do I Love? London: Brendin Publishing Co., 1944.

H.D. and White, Eric. W. *Images of H.D./From the Mystery.* London: Enitharmon Press, 1976.

Unpublished Manuscripts and Correspondence

Letters from H.D. to the following people are held in the Collection of American Literature, Beinecke Rare Book and Manuscript Library, Yale University: Richard Aldington, Gretchen Baker, Sylvia Beach, Bryher, Mary Herr, Mr. and Mrs. Hermann Hesse, Brigit Patmore, Norman Holmes Pearson, Ezra Pound, Walter Schmideberg, and Elsie Volkart.

Letters to H.D. from the following people are also in this collection: Richard Aldington, Sylvia Beach, Bryher, Robert Duncan, Havelock Ellis, Sigmund Freud, Horace Gregory, Robert Herring, Hermann Hesse, Denise Levertov, Robert McAlmon, Kenneth Macpherson, Walter de la Mare, Sheri Martinelli, Marianne Moore, Brigit Patmore, Norman Holmes Pearson, Ezra Pound, Dorothy Richardson, Vita Sackville-West, Walter Schmideberg, Edith Sitwell, Osbert Sitwell, Jean Starr Untermeyer.

Unless otherwise noted, the following materials are, likewise, located in the Collection of American Literature at the Beinecke Library, Yale University.

Doolittle, Hilda [H.D.]. "Asphodel" (1921–1922). Typescript.
———. "Autobiographical Notes" (1933). Typescript.
———. "Classical Fragments." Typescript.

_____. "Compassionate Friendship" (1955). Typescript.

_____. Diary, Paris 1912. Original manuscript.

_____. "Ear-Ring." Typescript.

_____. "Early Short Stories" (ca. 1906–1911). Includes "The Greek Boy"; "Sydney's Triumph"; "John Aimes' Christmas Wish"; "The Strange Experience"; "The Gift of Agatha Ware"; "Monsieur's Princess"; "The Suffragette"; "The Pretend Child"; "Uncle David." Typescript.

_____. "The Gift" (1941–1943). Typescript.

_____. "Her" (1927). Typescript.

_____. "Hirslanden-Zurich." (1957–1959). Manuscript.

_____. Letters to Amy Lowell. Houghton Library, Harvard University, Cambridge, Mass.

_____. Letters to F. S. Flint. The Academic Center Library, University of Texas, Austin.

_____. Letters to John Cournos. Houghton Library, Harvard University, Cambridge, Mass.

_____. Letters to John Cournos. Personal collection of Professor Emeritus Alfred Satterthwaite, Haverford College, Haverford, Pennsylvania.

_____. Letters to Richard Aldington. Richard Aldington Papers, Special Collections, Morris Library, Southern Illinois University, Carbondale.

_____. "Magic Mirror" (1957). Typescript.

_____. "Magic Ring" (1943–1944). Typescript.

_____. "The Mystery" (1949–1951). Typescript.

_____. "Notes on Dorothy and Odle Richardson." Manuscript.

_____. "Notes on Euripides, Pausanias and Greek Lyric Poets" (1918). Typescript.

_____. "Notes on Pre-Raphaelite Brotherhood" (1947?). Manuscript.

_____. "Notes on Recent Writing" (1949). Typescript.

_____. "Notes on Thought and Vision" (1919). Typescript.

_____. "Paint It Today" (1921). Typescript.

_____. "Pilate's Wife" (1924–1929, 1934). Typescript.

_____. "Prose Corybantic" (1929?). Typescript.

_____. "Seven Stories." Includes "Aegina" (1933); "Hesperia" (1924); "The Death of Martin Presser" (1943); "The Moment" (1926); "Jubilee" (1935); "The Last Time" (1936); "The Guardians" (1945). Typescript.

_____. "The Sword Went Out to Sea" (1946–1947). Typescript.

_____. "Thorn Thicket" (1960). Typescript.

_____. "Twelve Short Stories" (1940–1941). Includes "Before the Battle"; "Dream of a Book"; "Bunny"; "Pattern"; "Blue Lights"; "Escape"; "Tide Line"; "Warehouse"; "The Last Day"; "Neftert"; "She Is Dead"; "The Ghost." Typescript.

_____. "Vale-Ave" (1957). Typescript.

_____. "The White Rose and the Red" (1948). Typescript.

_____. "Zinzendorf Notes" (1951). Manuscript.

Lawrence, D. H. Letter of August 10, 1929, to H.D. Lockwood Memorial Library, State University of New York at Buffalo.

Patmore, Brigit. Letters to Bryher (uncatalogued).

OTHER SOURCES

Some previously unpublished works by H.D. and a collection of articles on her were published in *Contemporary Literature* (vol. 10, Autumn 1969). The "Special Number on H.D." is entitled *H.D.: A Reconsideration* and edited, with an introduction, by L. S. Dembo. Included in the issue: L. S. Dembo, ed., "Norman Holmes Pearson on H.D.: An Interview"; Joseph N. Riddel, "H.D. and the Politics of 'Spiritual Realism' "; Norman N. Holland, "H.D. and the 'Blameless Physician' "; Bernard F. Engel, "H.D.: Poems that Matter and Dilutions"; Linda Welshimer Wagner, "*Helen in Egypt:* A Culmination"; A. Kingsley Weatherhead, "Style in H.D.'s Novels"; Cyrena N. Pondrom, "Selected Letters from H.D. to F. S. Flint: A Commentary on the Imagist Period"; H.D., "Amaranth," "Eros," "Envy," "Winter Love" (fragments), "The Dream"; Jackson R. Bryer, "H.D.: A Note on Her Critical Reputation"; Jackson R. Bryer and Pamela Roblyer, "H.D.: A Preliminary Checklist."

Aldington, Richard. *The Colonel's Daughter.* Garden City: Doubleday, Doran and Co., 1931.
———. *The Complete Poems of Richard Aldington.* London: Allan Wingate, 1948.
———. "Confessions Questionnaire — Richard Aldington." *The Little Review* 12, no. 2 (1929): 11.
———. *D. H. Lawrence: An Indiscretion.* Seattle: University of Washington Book Store, 1927.
———. *Death of a Hero.* New York: Garden City, 1929.
———. *Life for Life's Sake.* 1941. Reprint. London: Cassell, 1968.
———. *A Passionate Prodigality: Letters to Alan Bird from Richard Aldington.* 1949–1962. Edited by Miriam J. Benkovitz. New York: New York Public Library, 1975.
———. *Portrait of a Genius, But . . .* London: William Heinemann, 1950.
———. *Roads to Glory.* London: Chatto and Windus, 1930.
———. *Soft Answers.* 1931. Reprint. Carbondale: Southern Illinois University Press, 1967.
———. *Very Heaven.* Garden City, N.Y.: Doubleday, Doran and Co., 1937.
Baumann, Walter. *The Rose in the Steel Dust.* Coral Gables: University of Miami Press, 1970.
Belloc, Hilaire, and Rosenfeld, Paul, trans. *The Romance of Tristan and Iseult.* As retold by Joseph Bedier. New York: Pantheon Books, 1945.
Boyd, Ernest L. "Ezra Pound at Wabash College." *Journal of Modern Literature* 4, no. 1 (1974): 43–54.
Braithwaite, William Stanley. "Imagism: Another View." *New Republic,* June 12, 1915.
Brett, Dorothy. *Lawrence and Brett: A Friendship.* Philadelphia: Lippincott, 1933.
Budge, E. A. Wallis. *Egyptian Language.* London: Routledge & Kegan Paul, 1963.
Bush, Ronald. *The Genesis of Ezra Pound's Cantos.* Princeton: Princeton University Press, 1976.
Butler, E. M. *The Fortunes of Faust.* Cambridge: Cambridge University Press, 1952.
Carswell, Catherine. *The Savage Pilgrimage.* London: Martin Secker, 1932.
Coffman, Stanley K. Jr. *Imagism: A Chapter for the History of Modern Poetry.* Norman: University of Oklahoma Press, 1951.
Collin, G. L. *Moravians in Two Worlds.* New York: Columbia University Press, 1967.
Cournos, John. *Autobiography.* New York: G. P. Putnam's Sons, 1935.
———. *Miranda Masters.* New York: Alfred A. Knopf, 1926.
Damon, S. Foster. *Amy Lowell: A Chronicle.* Boston and New York: Houghton Mifflin, 1935.
Davidson, Gustav. *A Dictionary of Angels.* New York: Free Press, 1967.
Davie, Donald. *Ezra Pound.* New York: Penguin Books, 1975.

_____. *Ezra Pound: Poet As Sculptor.* New York: Oxford University Press, 1964.

de Chasca, Edmund S. *John Gould Fletcher and Imagism.* Columbia: University of Missouri Press, 1978.

Delany, Paul. *D. H. Lawrence's Nightmare.* New York: Basic Books, 1978.

Delavenay, Emile. *D. H. Lawrence: The Man and His Work.* Translated by Katherine M. Delavenay. London: Heinemann, 1972.

_____. "Making Another Lawrence: Frieda and the Lawrence Legend. *The D. H. Lawrence Review* 8, no. 1 (1975): 80–98.

Dembo, L. S. *Conceptions of Reality in Modern American Poetry.* Berkeley: University of California Press, 1966.

_____. *The Confucian Odes of Ezra Pound.* Berkeley: University of California Press, 1963.

_____. ed. *H. D.: A Reconsideration* (Special Number on H.D.), *Contemporary Literature* 10 (Autumn 1969): 433–34.

de Nagy, N. Christoph. *The Poetry of Ezra Pound: The Pre-Imagist Stage.* 2nd rev. ed. Basel: Francke Verlag Bern, 1968.

de Rachewiltz, Mary. *Ezra Pound, Father and Teacher: Discretions.* 1971. Reprint. New York: New Directions, 1975.

de Rougement, Denis. *Love in the Western World.* Garden City, N.Y.: Doubleday Anchor, 1957.

Dowding, Hugh Caswell. *Many Mansions.* 1943. Reprint. Bath, England: Cedric Chivers, 1976.

Duncan, Robert. "The H.D. Book." Published in sections in *Coyote's Journal* 5–6 & 8 (Part I: Chapters 1 & 2); *TriQuarterly* Spring 1968 (Part I: Chapters 3 & 4); *Stony Brook* 1 & 2 (Part I: Chapter 5); *Caterpillar* 1 & 2 (Part I: Chapter 6); *Origin* 10, second series, (excerpts from "The Day Book"); *Sumac,* fall 1968 (Part II: Chapter 1); *Caterpillar* 6 (Part II: Chapter 2); *Caterpillar* 7 (Part II: Chapter 4); *Stony Brook* 3–4 (Part II: Chapter 5); *Chicago Review,* Winter 1979 (Part II: Chapter 9).

_____. "In the Sight of a Lyre, a Little Spear, a Chair." *Poetry* 91 (January 1958): 256–60.

_____. *Roots and Branches.* New York: New Directions, 1964.

DuPlessis, Rachel Blau. "Family, Sexes, Psyche: An Essay on H.D. and the Muse of the Woman Writer." *Montemora* 6 (1979): 137–56.

_____. "Romantic Thralldom in H.D." *Contemporary Literature* 20, no. 2 (1979): 178–203.

Durand, Lionel. "Life in a Hothouse." *Newsweek* 55 (May 2, 1960): 92–93.

Edwards, John Hamilton, and Vasse, William W. *Annotated Index to the Cantos of Ezra Pound.* Berkeley: University of California Press, 1957.

The Egoist: An Individualist Review. London: Egoist Publishing Co., 1914–1917. Reprint (3 vols). New York: Kraus Reprint, 1967.

The Egyptian Book of the Dead. Translated by E. A. Wallis Budge. New York: Dover, 1967.

Ellerman, Winifred [Bryher]. *Development.* New York: Macmillan, 1920.

_____. *The Heart to Artemis: A Writer's Memoirs.* New York: Harcourt, Brace & World, 1962.

_____. *Two Selves.* Paris: Contact, 1923.

Emery, Clark. *Ideas into Action: A Study of Ezra Pound's Cantos.* Coral Gables: University of Miami Press, 1958.

Espey, John J. *Ezra Pound's Mauberley.* Berkeley: University of California Press, 1955.

Fenollosa, Ernest. *The Chinese Written Character as a Medium for Poetry.* Edited by Ezra Pound. San Francisco: City Light Books, 1969.

Ferenczi, Sandor. *Thalassa: A Theory of Genitality*. Translated by H. A. Bunker. New York: Norton, 1968.

Ferrier, Carole. "D. H. Lawrence's Poetry, 1920–1928: A Descriptive Bibliography of Manuscripts, Typescripts, and Proofs." *D. H. Lawrence Review* 12, no. 3 (1979): 289–304.

———. "D. H. Lawrence's Pre-1920 Poetry: A Descriptive Bibliography of Manuscripts, Typescripts, and Proofs. *D. H. Lawrence Review* 6, no. 3 (1973): 333–59.

Fiedler, Leslie. "Memoir and Parable." *Poetry* 89 (February 1957): 326–29.

Firkins, O. W. "The New Movement in Poetry." *The Nation* 101 (October 14, 1915): 458–61.

Fletcher, John Gould. "H.D.'s Vision." *Poetry* 9 (1917): 266–69.

———. *Life Is My Song*. New York: Farrar and Rinehart, 1937.

Flory, Wendy Stallard. *Ezra Pound and the Cantos: A Record of Struggle*. New Haven: Yale University Press, 1980.

Ford, Ford Madox. *It Was the Nightingale*. London: William Heinemann, 1934.

———. *Mightier Than the Sword*. London: Allen & Unwin, 1938.

———. *Return to Yesterday*. New York: Horace Liveright, 1932.

———. *Thus to Revisit*. 1921. Reprint. New York: Octagon Books, 1966.

Frazer, Sir J. G. *The Golden Bough*. Abridged ed. New York: Macmillan, 1963.

Freibert, L. M. "Conflict and Creativity in the World of H.D." *Journal of Women's Studies in Literature* 1, no. 3 (Summer 1979): 258–71.

Freud, Sigmund. *The Ego and the Id*. Translated by J. Riviere; edited by J. Strachey. New York: Norton, 1960.

———. *Beyond the Pleasure Principle*. Translated by James Strachey. New York: Bantam Books, 1967.

———. *Character and Culture*. Edited by Philip Rieff. New York: Collier Books, 1963.

———. *Civilization and Its Discontents*. Translated by James Strachey. New York: Norton, 1962.

———. *The Future of an Illusion*. Translated by W. D. Robson-Scott. Garden City, N.Y.: Doubleday Anchor, n.d.

———. *A General Introduction to Psychoanalysis*. Translated by J. Riviere. New York: Washington Square Press, 1960.

———. *Group Psychology and the Analysis of the Ego*. Translated by James Strachey. New York: Bantam, 1965.

———. *The Interpretation of Dreams*. Translated by James Strachey. New York: Avon Books, 1965.

———. *Moses and Monotheism*. Translated by Katherine Jones. New York: Vintage Books, 1967.

———. *New Introductory Lectures on Psychoanalysis*. Translated by J. Strachey. New York: Norton, 1965.

———. *Sexuality and the Psychology of Love*. Edited by Philip Rieff. New York: Collier Books, 1963.

———. *The Standard Edition of the Complete Psychological Works of Sigmund Freud*. 23 vols. Translated by J. Strachey. London: Hogarth Press, 1964.

———. *Therapy and Technique*. Edited by Philip Rieff. New York: Collier Books, 1963.

———. *Three Contributions to the Theory of Sex*. Translated by A. A. Brill. New York: E. P. Dutton, 1962.

———. *Totem and Taboo*. Translated by A. A. Brill. New York: Vintage, 1960.

Friedman, Susan. "Creating a Women's Mythology: H.D.'s *Helen in Egypt.*" *Women's Studies* 5 (1977): 163–97.

———. "Who Buried H.D.? A Poet, Her Critics, and Her Place in the Literary Tradition." *College English* 36, no. 7 (1975): 801–14.

Gallup, Donald. *A Bibliography of Ezra Pound.* London: Rupert Hart-Davis, 1963.

Gates, Norman T. *The Poetry of Richard Aldington.* University Park: Pennsylvania State University Press, 1974.

Gilbert, Sandra M. *Acts of Attention: The Poems of D. H. Lawrence.* Ithaca, N.Y.: Cornell University Press, 1972.

Girard, René. *Violence and the Sacred.* Translated by Patrick Gregory. Baltimore: Johns Hopkins University Press, 1977.

von Goethe, Johann Wolfgang. *Faust, Part One and Part Two.* Translated by Charles E. Passage. Indianapolis: Bobbs-Merrill, 1965.

Graves, Robert. *The Greek Myths.* 2 vols. Baltimore: Penguin, 1955.

———. *The White Goddess.* 1948. Reprint. New York: Noonday, 1966.

The Greek Anthology. Translated by W. R. Paton. 5 vols. Cambridge, Mass.: Harvard University Press, 1916.

Gray, Cecil. *Musical Chairs.* London: Home & Van Thal, 1948.

Green, Martin. *The von Richthofen Sisters: The Triumphant and the Tragic Modes of Love, Elsa and Frieda von Richthofen, Otto Gross, Max Weber and D. H. Lawrence in the Years 1870–1970.* New York: Basic Books, 1974.

Gregory, Horace. *Amy Lowell — Portrait of the Poet in Her Time.* New York: Thomas Nelson and Son, 1958.

———. "Love in Counterpoint." *Saturday Review* 43 (May 28, 1960): 31–32.

———. "Speaking of Books," *New York Times Book Review,* October 22, 1961, p. 2.

Grosskurth, Phyllis. *Havelock Ellis: A Biography.* New York: Alfred A. Knopf, 1980.

Grover, Philip, ed. *Ezra Pound: The London Years, 1908–1920.* New York: AMS Press, 1978.

Gubar, Susan. "The Echoing Spell of H.D.'s Trilogy." *Contemporary Literature* 19, no. 2 (1978): 196–218.

Ernest Hemingway; Ford Madox Ford; T. S. Eliot; Hugh Walpole; Archibald Macleish; James Joyce; H.D.; and others. *The Cantos of Ezra Pound: Some Testimonies.* New York: Farrar and Rinehart, 1933.

Hesse, Eva, ed. *New Approaches to Ezra Pound.* Berkeley: University of California Press, 1969.

Heymann, David C. *Ezra Pound: The Last Rower.* New York: Viking Press, 1976.

Holland, Norman N. *Poems in Persons: An Introduction to the Psychoanalysis of Literature.* New York: W. W. Norton, 1975.

Hughes, Glenn. *Imagism and the Imagists.* 1931. Reprint. New York: Humanities Press, 1960.

Hulme, T. E. *Further Speculations.* Edited by Sam Hynes. Minneapolis: University of Minnesota Press, 1955.

———. "Notes on Bergson." *The New Age,* volumes 9 and 10 (1911, 1912), London.

———. *Notes on Language and Style.* Edited by Herbert Read. Seattle: University of Washington Book Store, 1924.

———. *Speculations.* Edited by Herbert Read. London: Kegan Paul, Trench, Trubner, 1936.

Hutchins, Patricia. *Ezra Pound's Kensington*. Chicago: Henry Regnery, 1961.

Imagist Anthology 1930. London: Chatto and Windus, 1930.

Jackson, Thomas H. *The Early Poetry of Ezra Pound*. Cambridge, Mass.: Harvard University Press, 1968.

Jacobson, Josephine. "H.D. in Greece and Egypt," *Poetry* 100 (June 1962), 186–89.

Jones, A. R. *The Life and Opinions of T. E. Hulme*. Boston: Beacon Press, 1960.

———. "Notes Toward a History of Imagism." *South Atlantic Quarterly* (Summer 1961), pp. 262–85.

Jones, Ernest. *The Life and Work of Sigmund Freud*. 3 vols. New York: Basic Books, 1957.

———. "Tribute to Freud." *The International Journal of Psycho-Analysis* 38 (March–April 1957): 126.

Kearns, George. *Guide to Ezra Pound's Selected Cantos*. New Brunswick, N.J.: Rutgers University Press, 1980.

Kenner, Hugh. *The Poetry of Ezra Pound*. London: Faber and Faber, 1951.

———. *The Pound Era*. Berkeley: University of California Press, 1971.

Kershaw, A., and Temple, F. J., eds. *Richard Aldington: An Intimate Portrait*. Carbondale: Southern Illinois University Press, 1965.

Kitto H. D. F. *The Greeks*. Baltimore: Penguin, 1951.

Lacy, Gerald Morris. "An Analytical Calendar of the Letters of D. H. Lawrence. Ph.D. Dissertation, University of Texas, 1971. Reprint. Ann Arbor: University Microfilms, 1979.

Landor, Walter Savage. *The Complete Works of Walter Savage Landor*. Edited by T. Earle Welby. 14 vols. 1927–1936. Reprint. London: Methuen, 1969.

Langton, E. *The History of the Moravian Church*. London: Allen and Unwin, 1956.

Lawrence, D. H. *Aaron's Rod*. 1922. Reprint. New York: Viking, 1961.

———. *Amores*. London: Duckworth, 1916.

———. *Apocalypse*. 1931. Reprint. New York: Viking, 1971.

———. *Bay*. Westminster: Beaumont Press, 1919.

———. *The Collected Letters of D. H. Lawrence*. Edited by Harry T. Moore. 2 vols. New York: Viking, 1962.

———. *The Collected Poems of D. H. Lawrence*. 2 vols. 1928. Reprint (2 vols. in 1). London: Martin Secker, 1932.

———. *The Complete Short Stories of D. H. Lawrence*. 3 vols. New York: Viking, 1961.

———. *The Complete Poems of D. H. Lawrence*. Edited by V. Pinto and F. W. Roberts. New York: Viking, 1964.

———. *The Escaped Cock*. Edited by Gerald M. Lacy. Los Angeles: Black Sparrow Press, 1973.

———. *The First Lady Chatterley*. New York: Dial Press, 1944.

———. *John Thomas and Lady Jane*. New York: Viking, 1972.

———. *Kangaroo*. 1923. Reprint. New York: Viking, 1963.

———. *Lady Chatterley's Lover*. 1928. Reprint. New York: Grove, 1962.

———. *Last Poems*. New York: Viking, 1933.

———. *The Letters of D. H. Lawrence*. Edited by Aldous Huxley. London: Heinemann, 1932.

———. *The Letters of D. H. Lawrence*. Vol. 1. Edited by James T. Boulton. New York: Cambridge University Press, 1979.

———. *Look! We Have Come Through!* New York: B. W. Huebsch, 1918.

———. *Love Poems and Others*. New York: Kinnerly, 1915.

———. *Nettles*. London: Faber and Faber, 1930.

———. *New Poems*. London: Martin Secker, 1919.

_____. *Pansies*. London: Martin Secker, 1929.

_____. *Phoenix*. Edited by E. D. McDonald. London: Heinemann, 1936.

_____. *Phoenix II*. Edited by Warren Roberts and Harry T. Moore. New York: Viking, 1968.

_____. *The Plumed Serpent*. New York: Alfred A. Knopf, 1926.

_____. *Psychoanalysis and the Unconscious and Fantasia of the Unconscious*. 1921 and 1922. Reprint. New York: Viking, 1960.

_____. *The Quest for Rananim: D. H. Lawrence's Letters to S. S. Koteliansky*. Edited by George J. Zytaruk. Montreal: McGill-Queen's University Press, 1970.

_____. *The Rainbow*. 1915. Reprint. New York: Viking, 1961.

_____. *Sons and Lovers*. 1913. Reprint. New York: Viking, 1958.

_____. *St. Mawr* and *The Man Who Died*. 1925 and 1929. Reprint (1 vol.). New York: Vintage, 1953.

_____. *Studies in Classic American Literature*. 1923. Reprint. New York: Viking, 1964.

_____. *Women in Love*. 1920. Reprint. New York: Viking, 1960.

Lawrence, Frieda. *The Memoirs and Correspondence*. Edited by E. W. Tedlock, Jr. New York: Alfred A. Knopf, 1964.

_____. *Not I, But the Wind . . .* New York: Viking, 1934.

Leary, Lewis, ed. *Motive and Method in the Cantos of Ezra Pound*. New York: Columbia University Press, 1961.

Leonard, William Ellery. "The New Poetry — A Critique." *Chicago Evening Post,* September 18 and 25, October 2 and 9, 1915.

Levertov, Denise. "H.D.: An Appreciation." *Poetry* 100 (June 1962): 182–86.

Lowell, Amy. *Tendencies in Modern America Poetry*. New York: Macmillan, 1919.

Lowes, John Livingston. "An Unacknowledged Imagist." *Nation,* February 24, 1916.

Luhan, Mabel Dodge. *Lorenzo in Taos*. New York: Alfred A. Knopf, 1932.

McAlmon, Robert. *McAlmon and the Lost Generation: A Self-Portrait*. Edited by Robert E. Knoll. Lincoln: University of Nebraska Press, 1962.

_____. *Being Geniuses Together*. Rev. ed. with supplementary chapters by Kay Boyle. Garden City, N.Y.: Doubleday, 1968.

Macpherson, Kenneth. *Rome 12 Noon*. New York: Coward-McCann, 1964.

Middleton, Christopher. "Documents on Imagism from the Papers of F. S. Flint." *The Review* 15 (1965): 35–51.

Monroe, Harriet. *A Poet's Life*. New York: Macmillan, 1938.

_____. *Poets and Their Art*. Freeport, N.Y.: Books for Libraries Press, 1967.

Moore, Harry T. *D. H. Lawrence: His Life and Works*. New York: Twayne, 1964.

_____. "The Faces Are Familiar." *New York Times Book Review,* May 1, 1960, p. 4.

_____. *The Intelligent Heart — The Story of D. H. Lawrence*. New York: Farrar, Straus and Young, 1954.

_____. *The Life and Works of D. H. Lawrence*. New York: Twayne, 1951.

_____. *The Priest of Love*. New York: Farrar, Straus and Giroux, 1974.

Moore, Harry T., and Warren Roberts. *D. H. Lawrence and His World*. New York: Viking, 1966.

Morris, William. *The Collected Works of William Morris*. 24 vols. New York: Russell & Russell, 1966.

Murry, John Middleton. *Son of Woman*. London: Jonathan Cape, 1931.

Nehls, Edward, ed. *D. H. Lawrence: A Composite Biography*. 3 vols. Madison: University of Wisconsin Press, 1957, 1958, 1959.

Norman, Charles. *Ezra Pound*. New York: Macmillan, 1960.

O'Conner, William Van. "Poetry Quarterly — The Recent Contours of the Muse." *Saturday Review* 45 (January 6, 1962): 68–71.

Patmore, Brigit. *My Friends When Young.* London: Heinemann, 1968.

Peck, John. "Passio Perpetuae H.D." *Parnassus: Poetry in Review* 3, no. 2 (1975): 49–74.

Pinion, F. B. *A D. H. Lawrence Companion.* London: Macmillan, 1978.

Pound, Ezra. *A B C of Reading.* New York: New Directions, 1960.

——. *A Lume Spento.* 1908. Reprint. New York: New Directions, 1965.

——. *The Cantos of Ezra Pound.* New York: New Directions, 1970.

——. *Cathay.* London: Elkin Mathews, 1915.

——, trans. *The Classic Anthology Defined by Confucius.* Cambridge, Mass.: Harvard University Press, 1954.

——. *Collected Early Poems of Ezra Pound.* Edited by Michael J. King. New York: New Directions, 1976.

——. *Gaudier-Brzeska: A Memoir.* 1916. Reprint. New York: New Directions, 1970.

——. *Guide to Kulchur.* 1938. Reprint. New York: New Directions, 1968.

——. *Hilda's Book* in H.D., *End to Torment.* New York: New Directions, 1979.

——. *Homage to Sextus Propertius.* London: Faber and Faber, 1934.

——. "I Gather the Limbs of Osiris." *The New Age,* 1911, 1912.

——. *The Letters of Ezra Pound, 1907–41.* Edited by D. D. Paige. New York: Harcourt, Brace, 1950.

——. *Literary Essays of Ezra Pound.* New York: New Directions, 1968.

——. *Make It New.* London: Faber and Faber, 1934.

——. *Noh, or Accomplishment.* London: Macmillan, 1916.

——. *Pavannes and Divagations.* New York: New Directions, 1958.

——. *Personae: The Collected Poems of Ezra Pound.* New York: New Directions, 1926, 1952.

——. *Selected Prose 1909–1965.* Edited by William Cookson. New York: New Directions, 1973.

——. *The Spirit of Romance.* 1910. Rev. and enlarged ed. New York: New Directions, 1968.

——. "Three Cantos." *Poetry* 10 (June, July, August 1917).

——. *The Translations of Ezra Pound.* New York: New Directions, n.d.

Pound, Ezra, and Stock, Noel. *Love Poems of Ancient Egypt.* New York: New Directions, 1962.

Pratt, William, ed. *The Imagist Poem.* New York: Dutton, 1963.

Quinn, Sister Bernetta. *Ezra Pound: An Introduction to the Poetry.* New York: Columbia University Press, 1972.

Quinn, Vincent. "H.D.'s 'Hermetic Definition': The Poet as Archetypal Mother." *Contemporary Literature* 18, no. 1 (1977): 51–61.

——. *Hilda Doolittle (H.D.).* New York: Twayne, 1967.

Rank, Otto. *The Myth of the Birth of the Hero.* New York: Vintage, 1964.

Rattray, David. "Weekend with Ezra Pound." *The Nation,* November 16, 1957, pp. 343–49.

Ricoeur, Paul. *Freud and Philosophy: An Essay on Interpretation.* Translated by Denis Savage. New Haven: Yale University Press, 1970.

Rimius, Henry. *A Candid Narrative of the Rise and Progress of the Herrnhuters, Commonly Called Moravians or Unitas Fratrum, With a Short Account of Their Doctrines, Drawn From Their Own Writings, To Which Are Added Observations on Their Politics in General, and Particularly on Their Conduct While in the Country of Budingen in the Circle of the Upper-Rhine in Germany.* London: A. Linde, 1752.

478 § SELECTED BIBLIOGRAPHY

Roberts, Warren. *A Bibliography of D. H. Lawrence*. London: Rupert Hart-Davis, 1963.

Roheim, Geza. *The Origin and Function of Culture*. Garden City, N.Y.: Anchor Books, 1971.

Ruthven, K. K. *A Guide to Ezra Pound's Personae (1926)*. Berkeley: University of California Press, 1969.

Sagar, Keith. *D. H. Lawrence: A Calendar of His Works*. Austin: University of Texas Press, 1979.

———. *The Life of D. H. Lawrence*. New York: Pantheon Books, 1980.

Satterthwaite, Alfred. "John Cournos and 'H.D.' " *Twentieth Century Literature* 22, no. 4 (1976): 394–410.

Schaffner, Perdita. "Discretions." *Paideuma* 3, no. 3 (1975): 407–408.

———. "Merano, 1962." *Paideuma* 4, nos. 2, 3 (1975): 513–18.

———. "A Sketch of H.D.: The Egyptian Cat." *Hedylus*. Rev. ed. Redding Ridge, Conn.: Black Swan Books, 1980.

Senior, John. *The Way Down and Out: The Occult in Symbolist Literature*. 1959. Reprint. New York: Greenwood, 1968.

Sessler, Jacob John. *Communal Pietism Among Early American Moravians*. New York: Holt, 1933.

Simpson, Louis. *Three on the Tower*. New York: William Morrow, 1975.

Slaten, Myles. "A History of Pound's Cantos I–XVI, 1915–1925." *American Literature* 35, no. 2 (1963): 182–95.

Smith, Anne, ed. *Lawrence and Women*. London: Vision Press, 1968.

Smith, Richard Eugene. *Richard Aldington*. Boston: Twayne, 1977.

Some Imagist Poets, 1915, 1916, 1917. Reprint (3 vols. in 1). New York: Kraus Reprint, 1969.

Stock, Noel. *The Life of Ezra Pound*. New York: Avon Books, 1970.

Sullivan, J. P., ed. *Ezra Pound: A Critical Anthology*. Baltimore: Penguin Books, 1970.

Swann, Thomas Burnett. *The Classical World of H.D.* Lincoln: University of Nebraska Press, 1962.

Taupin, René. *L'Influence du symbolisme français sur la poésie Américaine (de 1910 à 1920)*. Paris: Librairie Ancienne Honoré Champion, 1929.

Untermeyer, Louis. *American Poetry Since 1900*. New York: Henry Holt, 1923.

———. *From Another World: The Autobiography of Louis Untermeyer*. New York: Harcourt, 1939.

———. *The New Era in American Poetry*. New York: Henry Holt, 1919.

Vico, Giambattista. *The New Science of Giambattista Vico*. Translated by T. G. Bergin and M. A. Fisch. Ithaca, N.Y.: Cornell University Press, 1968.

Wallace, Emily. "Afterword: The House of the Father's Science and the Mother's Art." *William Carlos Williams Newsletter* 2, no. 2, pp. 4–5.

Warner, Rex. "Meditation That Means What It Says," *New York Times Book Review,* December 24, 1961, p. 4.

Watts, H. H. "H.D. and the Age of Myth." *The Swanee Review* 56 (Spring 1948): 287–303.

White, Eric W., and H.D. *Images of H.D./ From the Mystery*. London: Enitharmon Press, 1976.

Whorf, Benjamin Lee. *Language, Thought, and Reality*. Edited by J. B. Carroll. Cambridge: MIT Press, 1964.

Williams, William Carlos. *The Autobiography of William Carlos Williams*. New York: Random House, 1951.

———. "A Letter from William Carlos Williams to Norman Holmes Pearson Concerning Hilda Doolittle and Her Mother and Father." *William Carlos*

Williams Newsletter 2, no. 2, pp. 2–3.

――. *Selected Essays of William Carlos Williams.* New York: Random House, 1954.

Winnecott, D. W. *Playing and Reality.* London: Tavistock Publications, 1971.

Index

"Li Bel Chasteus," 425; "Shadow," 425;
"Affirmations," 426; "Girl, A," 426; "Ren-
dezvous," 426; "Child of the Grass," 427;
"Sancta Patrona Domina Caelae," 428; "Per
Saecula," 429
Pound, Homer, 11, 22
Pound, Isabel, 8, 22, 27
Pratt, William, 55
Priest of Love, The (Moore), 145
Priestess of Isis, 96, 155, 197, 199–200,
206–10, 220, 367
primal scene, 82, 244, 301, 368, 373, 376–77,
396, 419
Princess dream, 406–8
projection, 52, 72, 74, 115, 271, 295, 303,
324, 392, 406
psychoanalysis, 74, 85, 89, 236, 241, 245,
250, 259, 266, 268, 273–86, 288–90, 292,
294–99, 317, 324, 326, 330–332, 334, 339,
341, 358, 398–99, 403–4, 407–8, 413
psychoanalytic concept of femininity, 247,
280–281, 287–88, 296–98, 331, 399
psychoanalytic session, 236, 240, 261, 268,
270, 278–82, 284–85, 287–88, 297, 299–300,
330–333, 405, 411, 423
pun, 124, 172, 188, 416, 421

Quaker, 100, 117, 307–8
Quetzalcoatl, 310, 318

Radford, Dollie, 121, 126
Rafe, 95, 123, 133, 136–38, 140–141, 167,
250, 289, 317, 356–58, 390
Rananim, 94–95, 98, 113
Rank, Otto, 60
Ravagli, Angelo, 164
Regent Street Polytechnic, 23–24
regression, 295, 299
repression, 26, 236–38, 244, 257, 259–60,
268–69, 271, 274, 276–77, 285, 289–91, 295,
332, 360, 376–78, 401
"Revelation, The" (Ellis), 279
Riant Chateau (Territet, Switzerland), 119,
262, 265
Richardson, Dorothy, 255, 261
Rico, 95, 115, 119, 123, 133–41, 159, 169,
184, 194, 198, 215, 241–42, 248, 250, 289,
346, 354–60, 411
Ricoeur, Paul, 402
Riddel, Joseph, 38
Rimius, Henry, 85–86
Roberts, Warren, 168
Robeson, Paul, 267
Rodeck, Peter, 236, 239–41, 280, 283–84,
288–89
Roheim, Geza, 377
Rosetta Stone, 71
Rossetti, Dante Gabriel, 11

Rossetti, Elizabeth Siddell, 345
Royal Air Force, 305, 340–341
Rudge, Olga, 427
Rummel, Walter Morse, 24
Russell, Mrs. Harold, 92–93

Sachs Hanns, 236, 268, 278–79
Sackville-West, Vita, 256n
Sagar, Keith, 168
St. Faith's Nursing Home, 229
St. Leider, Guillaume, 43
Sappho, 39
Satterthwaite, Alfred, 175n
scapegoat, 376–77
Schaffner, Elizabeth Bryher (grandchild),
357, 359n, 360
Schaffner, Nicholas (grandchild), 357, 359n
Schaffner, Perdita, 152–53, 230, 262, 264–66,
281, 285, 304n, 323–24, 337–41n, 348, 359n,
434
Schaffner, Timothy (grandchild), 359–60
Schaffner, Valentine (grandchild), 357, 359n
Schmideberg, Walter (the Bear), 317, 325,
339–40
Scilly Islands, 230, 234, 281
séance, 279, 282, 285, 321–22, 341–42
Secker, Martin, 161n
Seehof, 340, 343
Séraphita (Balzac), 11
Sessler, Jacob John, 82, 89
Shakespear, Dorothy. See Pound, Dorothy
Shakespear, Olivia, 24–25, 91
Shakespeare, William, 276
Shaw, Bernard, 11
Shearman, Sir Montague, 94
Sinclair, May, 91, 99–100, 261
Sitwell, Edith, 256n, 261, 270
Sitwell, Osbert, 168, 256, 316
Sitwell, Sir George, 168
Sloane Street, London, 156, 296, 304
Some Imagist Poets, 51, 65–67, 69, 109, 126
Son of Woman (Murry), 146, 165, 283
spiritualism, 321, 341–42
Stesichorus, 350, 370, 398, 420–421
Stock, Noel, 27, 172n
Storer, Edward, 48
sublimation, 38–39, 44–45, 57, 130, 139, 169,
231, 291, 401
Swedenborg, 11
Switzerland, 119, 159, 262, 265, 283, 304,
309, 343, 352, 356
Symbolist poetry, 48, 53, 74, 99

taboo, 293–94, 298, 377
Tarr (Lewis), 91
Tenderness, 144, 169, 204, 217, 253
Territet, Switzerland, 262; see also Riant
Chateau